PETERSON'S

SSAT*/ISEE**
SUCCESS

2001

Reading: Elaine Bender, Jeffrey E. Levitsky
Mathematics: Christi Heuer, Mark Weinfeld
Verbal Analysis: Dominic Marullo, Patricia Burgess
Writing: Jo Norris Palmore

Australia • Canada • Denmark • Japan • Mexico • New Zealand • Philippines
Puerto Rico • Singapore • Spain • United Kingdom • United States

About Peterson's

Founded in 1966, Peterson's, a division of Thomson Learning, is the nation's largest and most respected provider of lifelong learning online resources, software, reference guides, and books. The Education Supersite[SM] at petersons.com—the Web's most heavily traveled education resource—has searchable databases and interactive tools for contacting U.S.-accredited institutions and programs. CollegeQuest[SM] (CollegeQuest.com) offers a complete solution for every step of the college decision-making process. GradAdvantage[TM] (GradAdvantage.org), developed with Educational Testing Service, is the only electronic admissions service capable of sending official graduate test score reports with a candidate's online application. Peterson's serves over 55 million education consumers annually.

Thomson Learning is among the world's largest providers of lifelong learning information. Headquartered in Stamford, CT, with multiple offices worldwide, Thomson Learning is a division of The Thomson Corporation (TTC), one of the world's leading information companies. TTC operates mainly in the U.S., Canada, and the UK and has annual revenues of over US$6 billion. The Corporation's common shares are traded on the Toronto, Montreal, and London stock exchanges. For more information, visit TTC's Internet address at www.thomcorp.com.

Editorial Development: American BookWorks Corporation

Special thanks to Joan Marie Rosebush and Amy Kierce

Visit Peterson's Education Center on the Internet (World Wide Web) at www.petersons.com

Copyright © 1999 Peterson's, a division of Thomson Learning. Thomson Learning is a trademark used herein under license.

All rights reserved. No part of this work may be reproduced, transcribed, or used in any form or by any means—graphic, electronic, or mechanical, including photocopying, recording, taping, Web distribution, or information storage and retrieval systems—without the prior written permission of the publisher.

For permission to use material from this text or product, contact us by

- Web: www.thomsonrights.com
- Phone: 1-800-730-2214
- Fax: 1-800-730-2215

Library of Congress Cataloging-in-Publication Data

Peterson's SSAT/ISEE success / Elaine Bender . . . [et al.].
   p. cm.
  ISBN 0-7689-0414-5
  1. Secondary School Admission Test Study guides. 2. Independent School Entrance Examination Study guides.
  I. Bender, Elaine. II. Title: SSAT/ISEE success
  LB3060.33.S42 P48 1999
373.126'2—dc21   99-35405
                                                                                  CIP

Printed in the United States of America

10 9 8 7 6 5 4 3 2 1

CONTENTS

Introduction 1
   About This Book 1
   About The Tests 2
   Peterson's Private School Resources 5

SSAT DIAGNOSTIC TEST 49
Part I: Writing Sample 50
   Writing the Essay 50
Part II: Multiple Choice 53
   Verbal 53
   Quantitative Mathematics 56
   Reading Comprehension 60
Explanatory Answers to the SSAT Diagnostic Test 64
   Verbal 64
   Quantitative Mathematics 67
   Reading Comprehension 71

ISEE DIAGNOSTIC TEST 73
   Verbal Reasoning 74
   Quantitative Reasoning 76
   Reading Comprehension 78
   Mathematics Achievement 82
   Writing the Essay 85
Explanatory Answers to the ISEE Diagnostic Test 88
   Verbal Reasoning 88
   Quantitative Reasoning 90
   Reading Comprehension 93
   Mathematics Achievement 95

SUBJECT REVIEWS 101
Red Alert: Verbal Analysis/Reasoning 103
   Verbal Analysis/Reasoning Review 105
Red Alert: Mathematics 115
   Mathematics Review 135
Red Alert: Reading Comprehension 287
   Sample Passage and Questions 291
   Answers and Explanations 296
Red Alert: Writing Strategies and Grammar Review 299
   English Grammar Review 310

SSAT PRACTICE TEST 1 .... **351**
Part I: Writing Sample 352
Writing the Essay.................................... 352
Part II: Multiple Choice 355
Verbal.................................... 355
Quantitative Mathematics 1 361
Reading Comprehension 364
Quantitative Mathematics 2 372
Explanatory Answers to the SSAT Practice Test 1 376
Verbal.................................... 376
Quantitative Mathematics 1 380
Reading Comprehension 384
Quantitative Mathematics 2 389

SSAT PRACTICE TEST 2 .... **395**
Part I: Writing Sample 396
Writing the Essay.................................... 396
Part II: Multiple Choice 399
Verbal.................................... 399
Quantitative Mathematics 1 405
Reading Comprehension 409
Quantitative Mathematics 2 418
Explanatory Answers to the SSAT Practice Test 2 422
Verbal.................................... 422
Quantitative Mathematics 1 428
Reading Comprehension 433
Quantitative Mathematics 2 437

ISEE PRACTICE TEST 1 .... **443**
Verbal Reasoning.................................... 444
Quantitative Reasoning.................................... 448
Reading Comprehension.................................... 452
Mathematics Achievement 462
Writing the Essay.................................... 468
Explanatory Answers to the ISEE Practice Test 1 471
Verbal Reasoning.................................... 471
Quantitative Reasoning.................................... 476
Reading Comprehension 482
Mathematics Achievement 487

CONTENTS

ISEE PRACTICE TEST 2 .... **497**
    Verbal Reasoning 498
    Quantitative Reasoning 502
    Reading Comprehension 506
    Mathematics Achievement 515
    Writing the Essay 521
  Explanatory Answers to the ISEE Practice Test 2 524
    Verbal Reasoning 524
    Quantitative Reasoning 528
    Reading Comprehension 534
    Mathematics Achievement 538

INTRODUCTION

ABOUT THIS BOOK

If you're reading this book now, it's likely you're planning to take a very important test—either the Secondary School Admission Test (SSAT) or the Independent School Entrance Examination (ISEE). The results of these tests can well determine where you go to school. This book is part of our popular "Success" series and is designed to help you prepare for these tests. It is an accepted fact that the more you practice, the better you will do on the test. Therefore, we have provided plenty of practice material for you.

The book is set up to take you step-by-step through each test. The first part of the book contains two diagnostic tests, one for the SSAT and one for the ISEE—of course, you should only take that test that is appropriate for you. Use the results of these diagnostics to evaluate your strengths and weaknesses. While it is important to study and review everything that will appear on the test, the diagnostic test will help you focus on those subjects that need additional work.

Section two of the book contains review material for the four major areas covered on both exams: Verbal Analysis, Mathematics, Reading Comprehension, and Writing an Essay. Read through and study these chapters, answer the practice questions, and take notes on anything you don't understand. You should then ask one of your teachers to help you.

The third section of the book presents two full-length sample tests for both the SSAT and ISEE tests. Take the tests under conditions that are similar to the actual exam. For example, the actual SSAT consists of five sections, and you are given 25 minutes to complete each section. However, one section is experimental and does not count on your final score. Therefore, you will have only four sections on the SSAT tests in this book, so allocate about 2 hours for each test. The actual ISEE contains five sections and takes almost 3 hours, so give yourself enough time to take the sample tests at the end of this book.

We suggest that you take each test, and after a break, check your answers. If you don't understand why you got something wrong, go back and look at the questions again. Then look in the review sections for clarification, and if you still don't understand the answer, go to one of your teachers for help.

ABOUT THE TESTS

THE SSAT

Let's look closely at each exam, starting with the SSAT. As we said, the actual exam consists of five sections. The questions are multiple-choice, with five choices each. (The ISEE questions have only four choices.) The questions cover the following topics:

> Writing an Essay
> Verbal
> Mathematics
> Reading Comprehension

The following chart will give you an idea of what to expect.

Writing an Essay	1 topic	25 minutes
Verbal	30 synonyms 30 analogies	25 minutes
Quantitative Mathematics	2 sections 25 questions each	25 minutes
Reading Comprehension	7 reading passages 40 questions	25 minutes

All questions are equal in value, and there is no penalty for unanswered questions. However, you will lose ¼ point for incorrect answers. It is therefore suggested that if you have a pretty good idea of the answer, perhaps narrowed down to two choices out of five, you should take a chance and guess. If you're truly in the dark, leave that question unanswered.

THE ISEE

The Upper Level ISEE (candidates for grades 9–12) consists of five sections. Except for the essay portion, all questions are multiple-choice. The five sections are:

> Verbal Reasoning
> Quantitative Reasoning
> Reading Comprehension
> Mathematics Achievement
> Essay

Did you notice that there are two math sections? However, the Quantitative Reasoning section is somewhat different than the Mathematics Achievement questions. One half of the questions are regular mathematics, and the other half are called "quantitative comparisons." You are asked to compare two unknowns and make a determination between these as to which is the greater, if they are equal, or if the answer cannot be determined from the given information. You can find greater detail later in this book.

INTRODUCTION

Here is how the sections appear:

Verbal Reasoning	20 synonyms 20 sentence completions	20 minutes
Quantitative Reasoning	35 questions	35 minutes
Reading Comprehension	9 reading passages 40 questions	40 minutes
Mathematics Achievement	45 mathematical ability	40 minutes
Essay	1 topic	30 minutes

The scoring for the ISEE is different than that of the SSAT, since you are not penalized for incorrect answers. It's important to try to make educated guesses using the process of elimination, but NEVER leave an unanswered question on this examination. Since there are only four choices, you have at least a 25 percent chance of getting the answer right—and even if you get it wrong, there's no penalty.

ABOUT YOUR SCORES

Both tests are scored on a scale, and you are ranked against other students. Both the SSAT and ISEE scores are sent to you (or your parents), and you will receive diagnostic information. This report also goes out to the schools (at your request) to which you are applying, and they can use those scores to develop an instructional plan for you.

ADDITIONAL INFORMATION

To get an application booklet and additional information, you can call or write to the following:

SSAT
Secondary School Admission Test
862 Route 518
Skillman, NJ 08558
Telephone: 609-683-4440
Fax: 800-442-7728 (toll-free)
E-mail: mail@ssat.org
World Wide Web: http://www.ssat.org

ISEE

ISEE Operations Office   or   Educational Records Bureau
423 Morris Street   220 East 42nd Street
Durham, North Carolina 27701   New York, New York 10017
Telephone: 800-446-0320   Telephone: 800-989-3721
         (toll-free)   (toll-free)
E-mail: isee@erbtest.com
World Wide Web:
   http://www.erbtest.org

INTRODUCTION

One final reminder: Although these tests are important, they are not the entire picture that will be looked at by the school to which you apply. They will take into account your academic performance, extracurricular activities, and so on. Keep in mind that these tests do not measure how smart you are. Like most standardized tests, they measure your ability to take these types of tests. And to do well, you must practice, practice, practice.

Good Luck!

PETERSON'S PRIVATE SCHOOL RESOURCES

Private School Snapshots

In the following pages you will find valuable data on private secondary schools from *Peterson's Guide to Private Secondary Schools 2000-2001*. These snapshots will guide your search, whether you're focused on a specific geographic region or across the country. We've provided quick answers to key questions about each school, such as:

- Are its students boarding, day, or both?
- Is it coeducational?
- What grades are offered at the school?
- Are SSAT or ISEE scores required?
- How many students are enrolled?
- How large is the faculty?

The chart also provides information about regular and Advanced Placement subjects, and sports.

Peterson's Guide to Private Secondary Schools 2000–2001

Once you've used this chart to help you identify prospective schools, be sure to check out *Peterson's Guide to Private Secondary Schools 2000-2001*, the only comprehensive private school guide available. You'll find detailed profiles on 1,500 accredited private schools worldwide, as well as valuable advice on planning your search and financing a private school education.

Peterson's Private Schools Channel

You can also continue your search on the Internet, by heading to Peterson's Private Schools Channel at http://privateschools.petersons.com. There you can browse private schools by name, location or type, and take a tour of each institution's VirtualCampus. And the Instant Inquiry feature allows you to request more information, or even an application, directly from the school.

	STUDENTS ACCEPTED				GRADES			STUDENT/FACULTY			SCHOOL OFFERINGS (number)		SSAT or ISEE REQUIRED	
	Boarding		Day											
	Boys	Girls	Boys	Girls	Lower	Middle	Upper	Total	Upper	Student/ Faculty Ratio	Advanced Placement Subject Areas	Sports	SSAT	ISEE
Alabama														
The Altamont School, Birmingham			X	X	5-8		9-12	363	190		14	3		X
American Christian Academy, Northport			X	X	K-6	7-9	10-12	448	90	12:1	2	13		
Bayside Academy, Daphne			X	X	PK-4	5-8	9-12	529	183	8:1	8	8		
Briarwood Christian High School, Birmingham			X	X	K-6	7-8	9-12	1,707	442	20:1	5		X	
Indian Springs School, Indian Springs	X	X	X	X			8-PG	254	254	9:1	11	11	X	
Lee-Scott Academy, Auburn			X	X	PK-6		7-12	567	225	12:1	2	10		
Lyman Ward Military Academy, Camp Hill	X				6-8		9-12	240				7		
Madison Academy, Madison			X	X	PS-5		6-12	750	425	18:1		5		
Marion Military Institute, Marion	X	X	X	X			7-12	160	160	8:1		36		
Mars Hill Bible School, Florence			X	X	K-4	5-8	9-12	626	211	10:1	5	2		
The Montgomery Academy, Montgomery			X	X	K-4	5-8	9-12	886	281	7:1	17	12		X
Randolph School, Huntsville			X	X	K-6	7-8	9-12	748	235	12:1	13	15		
Saint James School, Montgomery			X	X	PK-5	6-8	9-12	1,297	370	24:1	9	18		
St. Paul's Episcopal School, Mobile			X	X	PK-5	6-8	9-12	1,568	554	16:1	6	16		
Three Springs, Huntsville	X	X										10		
Tuscaloosa Academy, Tuscaloosa			X	X	PK-4	5-8	9-12	513	158	16:1	5	11		
Westminster Christian Academy, Huntsville			X	X	K-6	7-8	9-12	610	152	10:1	5	8		
Alaska														
Grace Christian School, Anchorage			X	X	K-6	7-8	9-12	611	198	20:1	4	4		
Arizona														
The Abbie Loveland Tuller School, Tucson		X	X	X	K-6	7-8	9-12	191	56	6:1	1	3		
Brophy College Preparatory, Phoenix			X				9-12	1,186	1,186		14	18		
The Fenster School of Southern Arizona, Tucson	X	X	X	X						8:1	1	17		
Oak Creek Ranch School, Cornville	X	X				6-8	9-12	65	57	8:1		18		
The Orme School, Mayer	X	X	X	X		7-8	9-12	185	161	6:1	7	45		
Phoenix Country Day School, Paradise Valley			X	X	PK-4	5-8	9-12	711	241	10:1	14	12		X
St. Gregory College Preparatory School, Tucson			X	X		6-8	9-PG	416	226	18:1	7	16		
St. Paul's Preparatory Academy, Phoenix	X		X				9-12	75	75	7:1		5		
Spring Ridge Academy, Spring Valley		X					9-12	46	46	10:1		28		
Verde Valley School, Sedona	X	X	X	X			9-PG	87	87	5:1	7	41		
Xavier College Preparatory, Phoenix				X			9-12	1,093	1,093	22:1	18	11		

More information on these schools can be found in
Peterson's Guide to Private Secondary Schools 2000-2001

PRIVATE SCHOOL SNAPSHOTS

	STUDENTS ACCEPTED							STUDENT/FACULTY			SCHOOL OFFERINGS (number)		SSAT or ISEE REQUIRED	
	Boarding		Day		GRADES									
	Boys	Girls	Boys	Girls	Lower	Middle	Upper	Total	Upper	Student/Faculty Ratio	Advanced Placement Subject Areas	Sports	SSAT	ISEE
Arkansas														
Pulaski Academy, Little Rock			X	X						16:1	16	10		
Subiaco Academy, Subiaco	X		X				9-12	210	210	9:1	10	49		
California														
Academy of Our Lady of Peace, San Diego				X			9-12	734	734	16:1	6	9		
Armenian Mesrobian School, Pico Rivera			X	X	1-5	6-8	9-12	300	90	7:1	8	2		
Army and Navy Academy, Carlsbad	X		X			7-8	9-12	332	270	15:1	6	33		
Arrowhead Christian Academy, Redlands			X	X		6-8	9-12	553	345	23:1		11		
The Athenian School, Danville	X	X	X	X		6-8	9-12	406	282	9:1	11	13	X	X
Bakersfield Christian High School, Bakersfield			X	X			9-12	153	153	17:1	5	8		
Beverly Hills Preparatory School, Beverly Hills			X	X										
Bishop Amat Memorial High School, La Puente			X	X			9-12	1,586	1,586	20:1	12	7		
Bishop Garcia Diego High School, Santa Barbara			X	X						12:1	8	24		
Bishop O'Dowd High School, Oakland			X	X			9-12	1,127	1,127	13:1	11	18		
The Bishop's School, La Jolla			X	X		7-8	9-12	617	431	9:1	20	15		X
The Branson School, Ross			X	X			9-12	320			13	15	X	
Brentwood School, Los Angeles			X	X						10:1	19	10		X
The Buckley School, Sherman Oaks			X	X	N-5	6-8	9-12	741	248	13:1	14	12		X
Calvin Christian High School, Escondido			X	X	K-5	6-8	9-12	623	213	15:1	4	7		
Campbell Hall (Episcopal), North Hollywood			X	X	K-6	7-8	9-12	900	350	15:1	13	14		X
Capistrano Valley Christian Schools, San Juan Capistrano			X	X	JK-6	7-8	9-12	759	277	13:1	7	9		
Cardinal Newman High School, Santa Rosa			X				9-12	441	441	16:1	6	15		
Cascade School, Whitmore	X	X								3:1	3	36		
Castilleja School, Palo Alto				X		6-8	9-12	392	236	7:1	19	9	X	X
Cate School, Carpinteria	X	X	X	X						5:1	11	25	X	
CEDU Schools, Running Springs	X	X							61	12:1		12		
Christian Junior-Senior High School, El Cajon			X	X		7-8	9-12	614	420	11:1	5	12		
Christian School of the Desert, Bermuda Dunes			X	X						18:1	3	5		
The College Preparatory School, Oakland			X	X						8:1	11	12		X
Convent of the Sacred Heart High School, San Francisco			X	X	K-5	6-8	9-12	867	204	14:1	16	8	X	
Cornelia Connelly School, Anaheim				X			9-12	212	212	16:1		2		

Visit Peterson's Private Schools channel at www.petersons.com

PETERSON'S PRIVATE SCHOOL RESOURCES

	STUDENTS ACCEPTED				GRADES			STUDENT/FACULTY			SCHOOL OFFERINGS (number)		SSAT or ISEE REQUIRED	
	Boarding		Day											
	Boys	Girls	Boys	Girls	Lower	Middle	Upper	Total	Upper	Student/Faculty Ratio	Advanced Placement Subject Areas	Sports	SSAT	ISEE
California—_continued_														
Crossroads School for Arts & Sciences, Santa Monica			X	X	K-5	6-8	9-12	1,123	488	20:1	14	9		X
Crystal Springs Uplands School, Hillsborough			X	X		6-8	9-12	351	248	10:1	15	9	X	
Delphi Academy of Los Angeles, La Canada			X	X	K-6	7-8	9-12	250	75	15:1		13		
Don Bosco High School, Rosemead			X				9-12	900	900	30:1		18		
Drew College Preparatory School, San Francisco			X	X			9-12	185	185	11:1	8	13	X	
Dunn School, Los Olivos	X	X	X	X		6-8	9-12	202	155	5:1	4	13	X	
Escondido Adventist Academy, Escondido			X	X							2	5		
Fairbanks Country Day, Rancho Santa Fe			X	X	PK-5	6-8	9-12	250	42	6:1		4		
Fairmont Private Schools and Preparatory Academy, Anaheim			X	X		7-8	9-12	2,040	260		15	12	X	
Flintridge Preparatory School, La Canada-Flintridge			X	X							8	14		X
Flintridge Sacred Heart Academy, La Canada-Flintridge		X		X						10:1	10	12	X	
Francis Parker School, San Diego			X	X	PK-5	6-8	9-12	1,139	398		15	5		X
Fresno Adventist Academy, Fresno			X	X	K-5	6-8	9-12	290	100	19:1		16		
Fresno Christian Schools, Fresno			X	X						24:1	4	9		
Grace Brethren School, Simi Valley			X	X	K-6	7-8	9-12	842	173	14:1	6	7		
Happy Valley School, Ojai	X	X	X	X			9-12	93	93	7:1	3	27		
The Harker School, San Jose	X	X	X	X	K-5	6-8	9-10	1,217	212	16:1		6	X	X
Harvard-Westlake School, North Hollywood			X	X		7-9	10-12	1,551	810	8:1	18	18		X
The Head-Royce School, Oakland			X	X	K-5	6-8	9-12	760	330	10:1	18	6		X
Idyllwild Arts Academy, Idyllwild	X	X	X	X		8-8	9-PG	227	218	15:1	4	13	X	
International High School of FAIS, San Francisco			X	X			9-12	285	285	6:1	14	18	X	X
Junipero Serra High School, San Mateo			X						965	27:1	4	21		
Justin-Siena High School, Napa			X	X			9-12	636	636	18:1	5	13		
Kings Christian School, Lemoore			X	X	PK-6	7-8	9-12	297	80	10:1	1	9		
Laguna Blanca School, Santa Barbara			X	X	K-6	7-8	9-12	330	138	5:1	19	7		X
La Jolla Country Day School, La Jolla			X	X	N-4	5-8	9-12	996	330	10:1	15	21		X
Le Lycee Francais de Los Angeles, Los Angeles			X	X	K-4	5-8	9-12	1,281	264	15:1	10	2		
Lick-Wilmerding High School, San Francisco			X	X			9-12	377	377	9:1	17	17	X	X
Linfield School, Temecula			X	X	K-5	6-8	9-12	603	181	17:1	5	12		
Loretto High School, Sacramento				X			9-12	450	450	12:1	8	11		
Louisville High School, Woodland Hills				X			9-12	495	495	15:1	14	10		

More information on these schools can be found in
Peterson's Guide to Private Secondary Schools 2000–2001

PRIVATE SCHOOL SNAPSHOTS

	STUDENTS ACCEPTED				GRADES			STUDENT/FACULTY			SCHOOL OFFERINGS (number)		SSAT or ISEE REQUIRED	
	Boarding		Day											
	Boys	Girls	Boys	Girls	Lower	Middle	Upper	Total	Upper	Student/ Faculty Ratio	Advanced Placement Subject Areas	Sports	SSAT	ISEE
California—*continued*														
Loyola High School, Jesuit College Preparatory, Los Angeles.......			X				9–12	1,170	1,170		16	13		
Lutheran High School of Orange County, Orange...............			X	X			9–12	751	751	18:1	5	12		
Lycee International de Los Angeles, Los Angeles..................			X	X						8:1	3	8		
Maranatha High School, Sierra Madre.....................			X	X			9–12	486	486	14:1	9	10		
Marin Academy, San Rafael.......			X	X			9–12	385	385	10:1	15	22	X	X
Marin Catholic High School College Preparatory, Kentfield.........			X	X			9–12	754		12:1	8	21		
Marlborough School, Los Angeles..				X		7–9	10–12	526	242	6:1	20	14		X
Marymount High School, Los Angeles.....................				X			9–12	379	379		10	15		X
Mayfield Senior School, Pasadena...				X							10	10		X
Menlo School, Atherton..........			X	X						12:1	19	16		
Mercy High School College Preparatory, San Francisco.....				X			9–12	573	573	14:1	8	5		
Midland School, Los Olivos.......	X	X					9–12	100	100				X	
Milken Community High School of Stephen Wise Temple, Los Angeles.....................			X	X		7–8	9–12	727	476	7:1	17	17		X
Modesto Christian School, Modesto.			X	X	K–4	5–8	9–12	672	261		3	11		
Montclair College Preparatory School, Van Nuys.............	X	X	X	X	6–8		9–12	430	310		14	4		X
Monterey Bay Academy, La Selva Beach.....................	X	X	X	X			9–12	258	258	15:1		5		
Monte Vista Christian School, Watsonville.................	X	X	X	X		6–8	9–12	1,036	731	16:1	5	18	X	
Moreau Catholic High School, Hayward...................			X	X			9–12	1,184	1,184	19:1	14	21		
Newbridge School, Los Angeles....			X	X	K–4	5–8	9–12	121	41	10:1		13		
North Bay Orinda School, Orinda...			X	X		7–8	9–12	99	86	9:1		1		
Notre Dame Academy, Los Angeles.				X			9–12	485	485	12:1	8	8		
Notre Dame High School, Belmont.				X			9–12	735	735	18:1	10	18		
Notre Dame High School, San Jose.				X			9–12	546	546	11:1	5	10		
Oak Grove School, Ojai..........	X	X	X	X	PK–6	7–8	9–12	187	47	5:1	3	12	X	X
Oakwood School, North Hollywood...................			X	X	K–6	7–8	9–12	743	300	7:1	15	44		X
Ojai Valley School, Ojai..........	X	X	X	X	PK–5	6–8	9–12	340	118	5:1	8	23		
Oxford School, Rowland Heights...			X	X				128	128	14:1	1	2		
Palma High School, Salinas.......			X			7–8	9–12	664	505	17:1	9	5		
The Palm Valley School, Rancho Mirage.....................			X	X	PK–5	6–8	9–12	292	71	8:1	8	15		
Paraclete High School, Lancaster...			X	X						17:1	4	11	X	
Pinewood School of Los Altos, Los Altos Hills..................			X	X	K–2	X–6	7–12	622	310	7:1	13	8		
Presentation High School, San Jose.				X			9–12	715	715	12:1		13		
Providence High School, Burbank..			X	X			9–12	559	559	15:1	6	7		

Visit Peterson's Private Schools channel at www.petersons.com

Peterson's: www.petersons.com

PETERSON'S PRIVATE SCHOOL RESOURCES

	STUDENTS ACCEPTED									SCHOOL OFFERINGS (number)		SSAT or ISEE REQUIRED	
	Boarding		Day		GRADES			STUDENT/FACULTY						
	Boys	Girls	Boys	Girls	Lower	Middle	Upper	Total	Upper	Student/ Faculty Ratio	Advanced Placement Subject Areas	Sports	SSAT	ISEE
California—*continued*														
Ramona Convent Secondary School, Alhambra				X		7–8	9–12	560	489	22:1	12	7		
Redwood Christian Schools, Castro Valley			X	X							1	8		
Remi Vista Ranch School, Corning	X	X												
Rio Hondo Preparatory School, Arcadia			X	X		6–8	9–12	179	79	4:1	7	6		
Ripon Christian Schools, Ripon			X	X	K–6	7–8	9–12	757	282	22:1	1	9		
Robert Louis Stevenson School, Pebble Beach	X	X	X	X	PK–5	6–8	9–12	742	530	10:1	14	20	X	
Rolling Hills Preparatory School, Palos Verdes Estates			X	X		6–8	9–12	224	127	9:1	8	9		X
Sacramento Adventist Academy, Carmichael			X	X	K–6	7–8	9–12	402	147	11:1		6		
Sacramento Country Day School, Sacramento			X	X	PK–5	6–8	9–12	536	127	9:1	11	5		X
Sacred Heart Preparatory, Atherton			X	X			9–12	435	435	7:1	11	14		
Saint Anthony High School, Long Beach			X	X			9–12	350	350	15:1	6	23		
Saint Bernard High School, Eureka			X	X						9:1	5	12		
Saint Francis High School, La Canada Flintridge			X				9–12	610	610	15:1	12	5		
Saint John Bosco High School, Bellflower			X				9–12	1,108	1,108	17:1	9	14		
Saint Joseph Notre Dame High School, Alameda			X	X			9–12	567	567	15:1	8	12		
Saint Lawrence Academy, Santa Clara			X	X				347		15:1	2	8		
Saint Lucy's Priory High School, Glendora				X			9–12	889	889	24:1	10	11		
St. Margaret's Episcopal School, San Juan Capistrano			X	X	N–5	6–8		787		12:1	15	12		X
St. Michael's College Preparatory High School of the Norbertine Fathers, Silverado	X						9–12	67	67	2:1	6	8		
Saint Patrick - Saint Vincent High School, Vallejo			X	X							3	13		
Salesian High School, Richmond			X	X			9–12	524	524	23:1	6	4		
San Domenico School, San Anselmo		X	X	X	PK–5	6–8	9–12	533	140	9:1	8	30	X	
San Francisco University High School, San Francisco			X	X			9–12	389	389	8:1	14	25	X	
Santa Catalina School, Monterey		X	X	X	PK–5	6–8	9–12	575	311	7:1	12	7	X	
Santa Fe Christian Schools, Solana Beach			X	X	K–5	6–8	9–12	730	238	12:1	5	10		
Servite High School, Anaheim			X				9–12	790	790	19:1	8	7		
Southwestern Academy, San Marino	X	X	X	X		6–8	9–12	197	155	4:1	6	11		
Squaw Valley Academy, Olympic Valley	X	X	X	X		6–8	9–12	95	75	5:1	8	12		

More information on these schools can be found in
Peterson's Guide to Private Secondary Schools 2000–2001

PRIVATE SCHOOL SNAPSHOTS

	Students Accepted — Boarding		Students Accepted — Day		Grades			Student/Faculty			School Offerings (number)		SSAT or ISEE Required	
	Boys	Girls	Boys	Girls	Lower	Middle	Upper	Total	Upper	Student/Faculty Ratio	Advanced Placement Subject Areas	Sports	SSAT	ISEE
California—continued														
Stanbridge Academy, San Mateo			X	X					37	8:1				
Sterne School, San Francisco			X	X						12:1		1		
The Thacher School, Ojai	X	X	X	X						6:1	17	30	X	
The Urban School of San Francisco, San Francisco			X	X			9–12	252	252	9:1	5	19	X	
Ursuline High School, Santa Rosa				X			9–12	401	401	12:1	4	4		
Valley Christian High School, Dublin			X	X	K–6	7–8	9–12	1,194	291	11:1	17	7	X	
Viewpoint School, Calabasas			X	X	K–4	5–8	9–12	680	245	16:1	18	17		X
Village Christian Schools, Sun Valley			X	X	K–5	6–8	9–12	1,934	589	16:1	8	8		
Villanova Preparatory School, Ojai	X	X	X	X			9–12	242	242	9:1	6	12	X	
The Webb Schools, Claremont	X	X	X	X			9–12	342	342	7:1	18	28	X	
Westmark School, Encino			X	X	2–5	6–8	9–12	250	100	3:1		9		
Westridge School, Pasadena				X	4–6	7–8	9–12	475	241	9:1	14	11		X
Westview School, Los Angeles			X	X		6–8	9–12	85	65	8:1		2		
Windward School, Los Angeles			X	X		7–8	9–12	420	270		7	10		X
Woodside Priory School, Portola Valley	X		X	X		6–8	9–12	309	211	10:1	16	19	X	
Colorado														
Accelerated Schools, Denver	X	X	X	X	K–5	6–8	9–PG	200	140		4	3		
Alexander Dawson School, Lafayette			X	X	K–4	5–8	9–12	420	168	9:1	20	19		X
Colorado Academy, Denver			X	X	PK–5	6–8	9–12	793	274	9:1	14	13	X	X
The Colorado Rocky Mountain School, Carbondale	X	X	X	X			9–12	165	165	6:1	3	41	X	
The Colorado Springs School, Colorado Springs			X	X	PS–5	6–8	9–12	458	124	16:1	8	17		
Colorado Timberline Academy, Durango	X	X	X	X			9–12	29	29	2:1		19		
Crested Butte Academy, Crested Butte	X	X	X	X			9–12	56	56	7:1	4	1		
Denver Academy, Denver			X	X	1–6	7–8	9–12	340	203	6:1		33		
Forest Heights Lodge, Evergreen	X				K–5	6–8	9–12	24	5	5:1		35		
Fountain Valley School of Colorado, Colorado Springs	X	X	X	X			9–12	220	220	5:1	11	27	X	
Kent Denver School, Englewood			X	X		6–8	9–12	619	400	9:1	12	17	X	X
The Lowell Whiteman School, Steamboat Springs	X	X	X	X				97	97	7:1	4	29		
Lutheran High School, Denver			X	X						13:1	3	2		
Regis Jesuit High School, Aurora			X							16:1	7	17		
St. Mary's Academy, Englewood			X	X	PK–5	6–8	9–12	774	292	11:1	7	12		
St. Scholastica Academy, Canon City		X		X		7–8	9–12	97	60	7:1	5			
Vail Mountain School, Vail			X	X	K–5	6–8	9–12	243	78	10:1	6	6		

Visit Peterson's Private Schools channel at www.petersons.com

PETERSON'S PRIVATE SCHOOL RESOURCES

	STUDENTS ACCEPTED				GRADES			STUDENT/FACULTY			SCHOOL OFFERINGS (number)		SSAT or ISEE REQUIRED	
	Boarding		Day											
	Boys	Girls	Boys	Girls	Lower	Middle	Upper	Total	Upper	Student/ Faculty Ratio	Advanced Placement Subject Areas	Sports	SSAT	ISEE
Connecticut														
Academy of Our Lady of Mercy, Milford				X			9–12	450	450	15:1		11		
Avon Old Farms School, Avon	X		X				9–PG	373	373	7:1	12	45	X	
Brunswick School, Greenwich			X		PK–5	6–8	9–12	704	241	7:1	20	6	X	X
Canterbury School, New Milford	X	X	X	X						6:1	15	21	X	
Chapel Haven, New Haven	X	X								4:1		9		
Cheshire Academy, Cheshire	X	X	X	X						7:1	12	18	X	X
Choate Rosemary Hall, Wallingford	X	X	X	X			9–12	858	858	7:1	20	60	X	X
Convent of the Sacred Heart, Greenwich				X	PS–4	5–8	9–12	573	167	6:1	10	10	X	X
Eagle Hill School, Greenwich	X	X	X	X					102	4:1		4		
Eagle Hill-Southport, Southport			X	X					85	4:1		4		
East Catholic High School, Manchester			X	X			9–12	555	555			15		
The Ethel Walker School, Simsbury		X		X						7:1	9	12	X	
Fairfield College Preparatory School, Fairfield			X				9–12	802	802	17:1	11	19		
The Forman School, Litchfield	X	X	X	X			9–12	170	170	3:1	2	19		
The Glenholme School, Washington	X	X	X	X						10:1		7		
Greenwich Academy, Greenwich				X	N–4	5–8	9–12	729	232	13:1	20	34	X	X
Grove School, Madison	X	X	X	X		7–8	9–12	91	79			69		
The Gunnery, Washington	X	X	X	X			9–PG	255	255		12	2	X	
Hamden Hall Country Day School, Hamden			X	X	PK–6	7–8	9–12	585	245	8:1		15	X	X
Hopkins School, New Haven			X	X		7–8	9–12	630	475		13	33		X
The Hotchkiss School, Lakeville	X	X	X	X			9–PG	541	541	5:1	18	22	X	
Indian Mountain School, Lakeville	X	X	X	X	5–6		7–9	185	143	3:1		12		
Kent School, Kent	X	X	X	X			9–PG	550	550	7:1	19	36	X	
King & Low-Heywood Thomas School, Stamford			X	X	PK–5	6–8	9–12	603	176	10:1	10	16	X	X
Kingswood-Oxford School, West Hartford			X	X		6–8	9–12	582	391	7:1	19	19	X	
The Loomis Chaffee School, Windsor	X	X	X	X			9–PG	716	716	5:1	13	37	X	X
Marianapolis Preparatory School, Thompson	X	X	X	X			9–PG	224	224	9:1	4	19	X	
The Marvelwood School, Kent	X	X	X	X			9–12	165	165	4:1		31	X	
The Master's School, West Simsbury			X	X	1–6	7–8	9–12	309	162	10:1	5	10		
Mercy High School, Middletown				X			9–12	614	614	11:1	8	18		
Miss Porter's School, Farmington		X		X			9–12	300	300	8:1	18	31	X	X
The Oxford Academy, Westbrook	X						9–13	35		2:1	5	2		
Pomfret School, Pomfret	X	X	X	X					311	5:1	13	16	X	
The Rectory School, Pomfret	X		X	X		5–8	9	190	62	3:1		41		
Rumsey Hall School, Washington Depot	X	X	X	X	K–5	6–9		280	173	12:1		26	X	X

More information on these schools can be found in
Peterson's Guide to Private Secondary Schools 2000–2001

PRIVATE SCHOOL SNAPSHOTS

	STUDENTS ACCEPTED				GRADES			STUDENT/FACULTY			SCHOOL OFFERINGS (number)		SSAT or ISEE REQUIRED	
	Boarding		Day											
	Boys	Girls	Boys	Girls	Lower	Middle	Upper	Total	Upper	Student/Faculty Ratio	Advanced Placement Subject Areas	Sports	SSAT	ISEE
Connecticut—*continued*														
Sacred Heart Academy, Stamford...				X			9–12	101	101		5	1		
St. Luke's School, New Canaan.....			X	X		5–8	9–12	417	186	10:1	5	14	X	X
Saint Margaret's-McTernan School, Waterbury....................			X	X	PK–3	4–8	9–12	452	148	6:1	9	17	X	X
Saint Thomas More School, Oakdale......................	X					8	9–PG	186	174	9:1		18		
Salisbury School, Salisbury.........	X		X				9–PG	255	255		8		X	
South Kent School, South Kent	X		X				9–PG	100	100	4:1	8	14	X	
Suffield Academy, Suffield.........	X	X	X	X						4:1	11	22	X	
The Taft School, Watertown........	X	X	X	X			9–PG	554	554	6:1	19	23	X	
Watkinson School, Hartford			X	X		6–8	9–PG	241	157	5:1		25	X	X
Westminster School, Simsbury	X	X	X	X			9–PG	355	355	5:1	15	20	X	X
Westover School, Middlebury......		X		X			9–12	188	188	7:1	17	22	X	
The Williams School, New London.			X	X		7–8	9–12	296	194	5:1	7	14	X	
The Woodhall School, Bethlehem ..	X		X				9–PG	43	43	2:1		41		
Wooster School, Danbury			X	X	K–5	6–8	9–12	406	132	14:1	9	10		X
Delaware														
Archmere Academy, Claymont.....			X	X			9–12	480	480	9:1	17	18		
The Cedars Academy, Bridgeville...	X	X												
St. Andrew's School, Middletown ..	X	X					9–12	271	271	6:1	12	17	X	
St. Mark's High School, Wilmington.................			X	X			9–12	1,563	1,563	15:1	18	16		
Sanford School, Hockessin			X	X	PK–3	4–8	9–12	663	215	12:1	13	11		
The Tatnall School, Wilmington....			X	X	N–4	5–8	9–12	683	208	8:1	15	13		X
Tower Hill School, Wilmington			X	X	PK–4	5–8	9–12	722	221	8:1	16	23	X	X
Ursuline Academy, Wilmington			X	X	PK–6	7–8	9–12	744	205	8:1	11	16		
Wilmington Friends School, Wilmington....................			X	X	PK–5	6–8	9–12	708	197	7:1	7	12		X
District of Columbia														
Edmund Burke School, Washington.			X	X		6–8	9–12	300	225	7:1	11	11	X	X
The Field School, Washington			X	X		7–8	9–12	212	164	6:1	5	10	X	
Georgetown Day School, Washington....................			X	X	PK–5	6–8	9–12	1,041	466	7:1	18	18	X	X
Georgetown Visitation Preparatory School, Washington				X			9–12	430	430	10:1	10	10		
Gonzaga College High School, Washington....................			X				9–12	875			14	21		
National Cathedral School, Washington....................				X	4–6	7–8	9–12	570	291	7:1	17	15	X	
St. Albans School, Washington	X		X			4–8	9–12	559	304	7:1	13	18	X	
St. Anselm's Abbey School, Washington....................			X			6–8	9–12	245	134	8:1	11	3		
Sidwell Friends School, Washington....................			X	X	PK–4	5–8	9–12	1,087	461	9:1	11	19	X	X
Washington Ethical High School, Washington....................			X	X						4:1		24		

Visit Peterson's Private Schools channel at www.petersons.com

Peterson's: www.petersons.com

PETERSON'S PRIVATE SCHOOL RESOURCES

	STUDENTS ACCEPTED				GRADES			STUDENT/FACULTY			SCHOOL OFFERINGS (number)		SSAT or ISEE REQUIRED	
	Boarding		Day											
	Boys	Girls	Boys	Girls	Lower	Middle	Upper	Total	Upper	Student/ Faculty Ratio	Advanced Placement Subject Areas	Sports	SSAT	ISEE
Florida														
Admiral Farragut Academy, St. Petersburg	X	X	X	X	K-2	5-8	9-12	335	210	9:1		22		
Allison Academy, North Miami Beach			X	X		6-8	9-12	120	85			6		
American Academy, Plantation			X	X	1-6	7-8	9-12	366	151	12:1		18	X	
American Heritage School, Plantation			X	X	PK-6		7-12	1,696	927	17:1	5	6		
Atlantis Academy, Miami			X	X	K-4	5-7	8-12	151	83	8:1		7		
Belen Jesuit Preparatory School, Miami			X			6-8	9-12	1,004	554	12:1	13	13		
The Benjamin School, North Palm Beach			X	X	PK-5	6-8	9-12	1,179	328	16:1	11	13		X
Berkeley Preparatory School, Tampa			X	X	PK-5	6-8	9-12	1,172	481	8:1	16	16	X	
The Bolles School, Jacksonville	X	X	X	X	K-5	6-8	9-12	1,673	772	10:1	19	19	X	X
Canterbury School, Fort Myers			X	X	PK-5	6-8	9-12	604	181	8:1	12	10	X	X
The Canterbury School of Florida, St. Petersburg			X	X	PK-5	6-8	9-12	443	112	9:1	12	9		
Cardinal Mooney High School, Sarasota			X	X			9-12	618	618		7	5		
Cardinal Newman High School, West Palm Beach			X	X			9-12	939	939	25:1	5	16		
Carrollton School of the Sacred Heart, Coconut Grove				X	PK-3	4-6	7-12	640	330	15:1	6	9		
Chaminade-Madonna College Preparatory, Hollywood			X	X			9-12	880	880	16:1	10	19		
The Community School of Naples, Naples			X	X	PK-5	6-8	9-12	610	170	7:1	10	10		X
Eckerd Youth Alternatives, Clearwater	X	X			4-5	6-8	9-12	782	319			5		
Episcopal High School of Jacksonville, Jacksonville			X	X		6-8	9-12	849	532	17:1	13	15		
The First Academy, Orlando			X	X	K-5	6-8	9-12	1,035	301	22:1	7	13		
Florida Air Academy, Melbourne	X		X				7-PG	400	400	16:1	9	56		
Gulliver Preparatory School, Miami			X	X	PK-4	5-8	9-12	1,945	799		19	20	X	
Jesuit High School of Tampa, Tampa			X							13:1	5	15	X	
Lake Highland Preparatory School, Orlando			X	X	PK-6	7-8	9-12	1,667	506	21:1	19	21	X	
La Salle High School, Miami			X	X			9-12	624	624		8	13		
Miami Country Day School, Miami			X	X	PK-5	6-8	9-12	920	295	12:1	19	16	X	X
Montverde Academy, Montverde	X	X	X	X		7-8	9-PG	175	150	18:1	3	23	X	
Northside Christian School, St. Petersburg			X	X	PS-5	6-8	9-12	978	235	11:1	4	12		
Oak Hall School, Gainesville			X	X		6-8	9-12	400	231	11:1	12	9		
Palmer Trinity School, Miami			X	X		6-8	9-12	530	322	10:1	16	27	X	X
Pine Crest School, Fort Lauderdale	X	X	X	X	PK-6	7-8	9-12	1,617	752	11:1	20	18	X	

More information on these schools can be found in
Peterson's Guide to Private Secondary Schools 2000-2001

PRIVATE SCHOOL SNAPSHOTS

| | STUDENTS ACCEPTED |||| GRADES ||| STUDENT/FACULTY ||| SCHOOL OFFERINGS (number) || SSAT or ISEE REQUIRED ||
| | Boarding || Day || | | | | | | | | | |
	Boys	Girls	Boys	Girls	Lower	Middle	Upper	Total	Upper	Student/ Faculty Ratio	Advanced Placement Subject Areas	Sports	SSAT	ISEE
Florida—continued														
Rabbi Alexander S. Gross Hebrew Academy of Greater Miami, Miami Beach			X	X	N-5	6-8	9-12	482	123	15:1	6	3	X	
Ransom Everglades School, Miami			X	X		6-8	9-12	877	521	14:1	20	18	X	
Saint Andrew's School, Boca Raton	X	X	X	X		6-8	9-12	738	496	7:1	20	14	X	X
Saint Edward's School, Vero Beach			X	X	PK-5	6-8	9-12	885	314	15:1	14			X
St. Johns Country Day School, Orange Park			X	X	PK-5	6-8	9-12	724	231	10:1	12	16		
Saint Stephen's Episcopal School, Bradenton			X	X	PK-5	6-8	9-12	645	224	10:1	13	18		
Shorecrest Preparatory School, St. Petersburg			X	X	PK-6	7-8	9-12	837	224	6:1	16	13	X	X
Tampa Preparatory School, Tampa			X	X		6-8	9-12	509	356	10:1	17	17	X	X
Trinity Preparatory School, Winter Park			X	X		6-8	9-12	780	469	10:1	16	14	X	X
University School of Nova Southeastern University, Fort Lauderdale			X	X	PK-5	6-8	9-12	1,941	491	15:1	11	10		
The Vanguard School, Lake Wales	X	X	X	X		5-8	9-PG	129	105	10:1		12		
Georgia														
Aquinas High School, Augusta			X	X						12:1	7	12		
Arlington Christian School, Fairburn			X	X	K-5	6-8	9-12	422	128		4	10		
Athens Academy, Athens			X	X	N-4	5-8	9-12	793	297		8	10		
Atlanta International School, Atlanta			X	X	PK-5	6-8	9-12	789	217	8:1		8		X
Benedictine Military School, Savannah			X				9-12	447	447		4	2		
Brandon Hall School, Atlanta	X		X	X	4-5	6-8	9-PG	110	73		4	4		
Brenau Academy, Gainesville		X		X			9-PG	80	80	8:1		8		
Brentwood School, Sandersville			X	X	PK-6	7-8	9-12	395	138	6:1	1	8		
Brookstone School, Columbus			X	X	K4-4	5-8	9-12	886	261	14:1	16	10		
Brookwood School, Thomasville			X	X						10:1	7	13		
Darlington School, Rome	X	X	X	X	PK-5	6-8	9-PG	876	439	6:1	16	21	X	
Flint River Academy, Woodbury			X	X	N-5	6-8	9-12	272	94	13:1	2	13		
Frederica Academy, St. Simons Island			X	X	PK-5	6-8	9-12	329	99	6:1	4	8		
Gables Academy, Stone Mountain	X	X	X	X	4-5	6-8	9-12	27	21	4:1		1		
The Galloway School, Atlanta			X	X	PK-4	5-8	9-12	728	224		10	10	X	
Greater Atlanta Christian Schools, Norcross			X	X	P3-5	6-8	9-12	1,430	517	19:1	10	14		
The Heritage School, Newnan			X	X	PK-4	5-8	9-12	341	66	7:1	8	7		
Hidden Lake Academy, Dahlonega	X	X					7-PG	130	130	7:1	2	28		
Holy Innocents' Episcopal School, Atlanta			X	X	PS-5	6-8	9-12	1,267	525	11:1	10		X	
Horizons School, Atlanta	X	X	X	X	PK-5	6-7	8-PG	125	80	10:1		2		
The Howard School, Atlanta			X	X					84	6:1		4		
The Lovett School, Atlanta			X	X	K-5	6-8	9-12	1,482	585	9:1	16	17	X	

Visit Peterson's Private Schools channel at www.petersons.com

PETERSON'S PRIVATE SCHOOL RESOURCES

	STUDENTS ACCEPTED				GRADES			STUDENT/FACULTY			SCHOOL OFFERINGS (number)		SSAT or ISEE REQUIRED	
	Boarding		Day							Student/ Faculty Ratio	Advanced Placement Subject Areas	Sports		
	Boys	Girls	Boys	Girls	Lower	Middle	Upper	Total	Upper				SSAT	ISEE
Georgia—*continued*														
Marist School, Atlanta			X	X			7–12	1,028	1,028	19:1	19	16	X	
Pace Academy, Atlanta			X	X				519		10:1	14	15	X	
Pacelli Catholic High School, Columbus			X	X			9–12	234	234	20:1	7	10		
The Paideia School, Atlanta			X	X	N–6	7–8	9–12	838	359	7:1	10	13		
Rabun Gap-Nacoochee School, Rabun Gap	X	X	X	X		6–8	9–12	268	185	12:1	7	11	X	X
Riverside Military Academy, Gainesville	X						9–12	261	229	14:1	6	29		
Saint Andrew's School, Savannah			X	X	PK–5	6–8	9–12	407	110	9:1	5	10	X	X
St. Pius X Catholic High School, Atlanta			X	X			9–12	1,050	1,050	18:1	12	13	X	
Savannah Christian Preparatory School, Savannah			X	X	PK–5	6–8	9–12	1,378	425	20:1	5	10		
The Savannah Country Day School, Savannah			X	X	PK–5	6–8	9–12	983	303	10:1	16	12		X
Stratford Academy, Macon			X	X	PK–5	6–8	9–12	901	287	13:1	16	18		X
Tallulah Falls School, Tallulah Falls	X	X				6–8	9–12	160	120	10:1	4	49		
The Walker School, Marietta			X	X	PK–5	6–8	9–12	875	324	14:1	19	12	X	
The Westfield Schools, Perry			X	X	PK–6		7–12	589	259	10:1	5	13		
The Westminster Schools, Atlanta			X	X	K–5	6–8	9–12	1,739	767	8:1	17	19	X	
Westminster Schools of Augusta, Augusta			X	X	PK–6	7–8	9–12	563	163	10:1	10	11		X
Whitefield Academy, Atlanta			X	X		6–8	9–12	169	83	5:1	4	10	X	
Woodward Academy, College Park			X	X	N–6	7–8	9–12	2,835	1,020		19	9	X	
Hawaii														
Academy of the Pacific, Honolulu			X	X		6–8	9–12	130	111	10:1	2	16		
ASSETS School, Honolulu			X	X	K–6	7–8	9–12	377	72	6:1	2	17		
Hawaii Baptist Academy, Honolulu			X	X	K–6		7–12	1,019	617	12:1	6	19	X	
Hawaii Preparatory Academy, Kamuela	X	X	X	X	K–5	6–8	9–12	579	338	7:1	14	33	X	X
Iolani School, Honolulu			X	X	K–6	7–8	9–12	1,795	926		16	24	X	
La Pietra–Hawaii School for Girls, Honolulu				X		6–8	9–12	235	147	10:1	5	18	X	
Maryknoll School, Honolulu			X	X	PK–5	6–8	9–12	1,385	574	11:1	12	25	X	
Mid-Pacific Institute, Honolulu	X	X	X	X		6–8	9–12	1,068	774	12:1	7	29	X	
The Parker School, Kamuela			X	X		6–8	9–12	129	100	6:1		11		
Punahou School, Honolulu			X	X	K–8		9–12	3,745	1,725		13	27	X	
St. Andrew's Priory School, Honolulu				X	K–5	6–8	9–12	450	175	5:1	8	19	X	
Saint Francis School, Honolulu		X		X		6–8	9–12	410	310			12	X	
Saint Joseph Junior-Senior High School, Hilo			X	X		7–8	9–12	211	146	12:1	5	12		
Varsity International School, Honolulu			X	X		6–8	9–12	81	75	10:1		26		

More information on these schools can be found in
Peterson's Guide to Private Secondary Schools 2000–2001

PRIVATE SCHOOL SNAPSHOTS

| | STUDENTS ACCEPTED | | | | GRADES | | | STUDENT/FACULTY | | | SCHOOL OFFERINGS (number) | | SSAT or ISEE REQUIRED | |
| | Boarding | | Day | | | | | | | | | | | |
	Boys	Girls	Boys	Girls	Lower	Middle	Upper	Total	Upper	Student/Faculty Ratio	Advanced Placement Subject Areas	Sports	SSAT	ISEE
Idaho														
Boulder Creek Academy, Bonners Ferry	X	X						98		12:1		11		
Cole Valley Christian High School, Boise			X	X	K-6	7-8	9-12	630	113	18:1		7		
The Community School, Sun Valley			X	X	PK-5	6-8	9-12	305	97	8:1		24	X	
Gem State Adventist Academy, Caldwell	X	X	X	X			9-12	158	158	13:1	1	6		
Northwest Academy, Naples	X	X							75	12:1		11		
Rocky Mountain Academy, Bonners Ferry	X	X							163	12:1		12		
Illinois														
Brehm Preparatory School, Carbondale	X	X	X	X		6-8	9-12	80	55	4:1		1		
The Chicago Academy for the Arts, Chicago			X	X			9-12	140	140	16:1	3			
Chicago Junior School, Elgin	X	X	X	X	PK-3	4-5	6-8	235	43	9:1		8		
Francis W. Parker School, Chicago			X	X	PK-5	6-8	9-12	876	302	8:1		9		X
Governor French Academy, Belleville	X	X	X	X	1-8		7-12	205	95	6:1	5	18		
Illiana Christian High School, Lansing			X	X			9-12	730	730	18:1	3	4		
Josephinum High School, Chicago				X			9-12	198	198	11:1				
Lake Forest Academy, Lake Forest	X	X	X	X			9-12	275	275	7:1	14	22	X	
The Latin School of Chicago, Chicago			X	X	JK-5	6-8	9-12	1,042	384	8:1	13	11		X
Loyola Academy, Wilmette			X	X			9-12	2,000	2,000	15:1	18	27		
Luther High School North, Chicago			X	X			9-12	406	406	18:1	3	13		
Marmion Academy, Aurora	X		X				9-12	480	480	11:1	6	21		
The North Shore Country Day School, Winnetka			X	X	PK-5	6-8	9-12	412	164	7:1	8	10		
Regina Dominican High School, Wilmette				X			9-12	461	461	14:1	15	21		
Rosary High School, Aurora				X					434	14:1	1	10		
Roycemore School, Evanston			X	X	PK-4	5-8	9-12	228	83	7:1	10	5		
Saint Patrick High School, Chicago			X				9-12	1,009	1,009	22:1	7	12		
St. Scholastica Academy, Chicago				X			9-12	323	323	11:1	5	9		
University of Chicago Laboratory Schools, Chicago			X	X						10:1	11	9		X
Wheaton Academy, West Chicago			X	X			9-12	446	446	21:1	10	14		
The Willows Academy, Des Plaines				X		6-8	9-12	194	110	9:1	7	2		
Indiana														
Brebeuf Jesuit Preparatory School, Indianapolis			X	X			9-12	744	744	15:1	11	19		
Cathedral High School, Indianapolis			X	X			9-12	1,064	1,064	14:1	4	17		

Visit Peterson's Private Schools channel at www.petersons.com

Peterson's: www.petersons.com

	STUDENTS ACCEPTED				GRADES			STUDENT/FACULTY			SCHOOL OFFERINGS (number)		SSAT or ISEE REQUIRED	
	Boarding		Day											
	Boys	Girls	Boys	Girls	Lower	Middle	Upper	Total	Upper	Student/ Faculty Ratio	Advanced Placement Subject Areas	Sports	SSAT	ISEE
Indiana—*continued*														
Concordia Lutheran High School, Fort Wayne			X	X			9–12	812	812	16:1	4	13		
Culver Military Academy/Culver Girls Academy, Culver	X	X	X	X			9–PG	702	702	7:1	14	22	X	
Evansville Day School, Evansville			X	X	PK–4	5–8	9–12	340	99	11:1	8	8		X
Howe Military School, Howe	X	X				5–8	9–12	180	126	9:1		22		
La Lumiere School, La Porte	X	X	X	X			9–PG	115	115	6:1	5	17		
Le Mans Academy, Rolling Prairie	X		X			5–9		105	97	12:1		35		
Marian Heights Academy, Ferdinand		X		X			9–12	116	116	3:1	6	6	X	
Park Tudor School, Indianapolis			X	X	PK–5	6–8	9–12	915	351	9:1	14	16		X
Iowa														
St. Katharine's St. Mark's College Preparatory School, Bettendorf			X	X						5:1	7	8		
Scattergood Friends School, West Branch	X	X	X	X			9–12	51	51	4:1		15		
Kansas														
Hyman Brand Hebrew Academy of Greater Kansas City, Overland Park			X	X	K–5	6–8	9–12	350	81	3:1	3	4		
Maur Hill Prep School, Atchison	X		X				9–12	195	195			19		
Mount St. Scholastica Academy, Atchison		X		X			9–12	110	110	8:1		12		
St. John's Military School, Salina	X					7–8	9–12	185	150	12:1		17		
Thomas More Prep-Marian School, Hays	X	X	X	X			9–12	300	300	12:1	2	14		
Wichita Collegiate School, Wichita			X	X	PK–4	5–8	9–12	900	260		17	9		
Kentucky														
Assumption High School, Louisville				X			9–12	930	930	17:1	11	15		
Louisville Collegiate School, Louisville			X	X	K–5	6–8	9–12	614	170	7:1	14	11	X	
Millersburg Military Academy, Millersburg	X		X	X		6–8	9–PG	131	86	9:1		12		
Oneida Baptist Institute, Oneida	X	X	X	X		6–8	9–12	400	300	12:1	4	16		
St. Francis High School, Louisville			X	X			9–12	135	135	8:1	11	16		
Sayre School, Lexington			X	X	PK–5	6–8	9–12	580	168	14:1	11	7		
Shedd Academy, Mayfield	X	X	X	X					18	4:1		5		
Louisiana														
Academy of the Sacred Heart, Grand Coteau		X		X	PK–4	5–8	9–12	347	130	7:1	5	8		
Episcopal High School, Baton Rouge			X	X	K–5	6–8	9–12	1,015	383	10:1	17	16		X
The Episcopal School of Acadiana, Cade			X	X						8:1	10	13		X

More information on these schools can be found in
Peterson's Guide to Private Secondary Schools 2000–2001

PRIVATE SCHOOL SNAPSHOTS

	STUDENTS ACCEPTED				GRADES			STUDENT/FACULTY			SCHOOL OFFERINGS (number)		SSAT or ISEE REQUIRED	
	Boarding		Day							Student/ Faculty Ratio	Advanced Placement Subject Areas	Sports		
	Boys	Girls	Boys	Girls	Lower	Middle	Upper	Total	Upper				SSAT	ISEE
Louisiana—*continued*														
Isidore Newman School, New Orleans			X	X	PK-5	6-8	9-12	1,146	444	8:1	14	11		
Jesuit High School of New Orleans, New Orleans			X			8-8	9-12	1,396	1,122	14:1	12	20		
The Louise S. McGehee School, New Orleans				X	PK-4	5-8	9-12	369	106	8:1	6	18		X
Loyola College Prep, Shreveport			X	X			9-12	375	375	11:1	13	11		
Metairie Park Country Day School, Metairie			X	X	K-5	6-8	9-12	736	231	7:1	10	12		
St. Martin's Episcopal School, Metairie			X	X	PK-5	6-8	9-12	812	268	10:1	10	7	X	X
Saint Thomas More Catholic High School, Lafayette			X	X			9-12	980	980	21:1	5	15		
Westminster Christian Academy, Opelousas			X	X	PK-6	7-8	9-12	1,056	285		4	11	X	
Maine														
Berwick Academy, South Berwick			X	X	K-4	5-8	9-12	545	223	12:1	9	8	X	X
Bridgton Academy, North Bridgton	X		X				PG	175	175	9:1		23		
Carrabassett Valley Academy, Carrabassett Valley	X	X	X	X		8-9	10-PG	92	66	6:1	2	16		
Catherine McAuley High School, Portland				X				310	310	18:1	4	19		
Cheverus High School, Portland			X	X			9-12	396	396	14:1	8	20		
Elan School, Poland	X	X								10:1		16		
Fryeburg Academy, Fryeburg	X	X	X	X						14:1	4	47		
Gould Academy, Bethel	X	X	X	X			9-PG	233	233	7:1	4	26	X	
Hebron Academy, Hebron	X	X	X	X	K-5	6-8	9-PG	332	222	8:1	9	18		
Hyde School, Bath	X	X	X	X			9-PG	235	235	7:1		11		
Kents Hill School, Kents Hill	X	X	X	X						7:1	6	21	X	
Maine Central Institute, Pittsfield	X	X	X	X						12:1	4	23	X	
North Yarmouth Academy, Yarmouth			X	X		6-8	9-12	267	163	8:1	13	21	X	
Maryland														
Academy of the Holy Cross, Kensington				X			9-12	454	454	13:1	7	10		
Archbishop Spalding High School, Severn			X	X			9-12	908	908		9	22		
Baltimore Lutheran Middle and Upper School, Towson			X	X		6-8	9-12	413	255	13:1		9		
The Barrie School, Silver Spring			X	X	N-5	6-8	9-12	508	110	8:1	5	16	X	
The Boys' Latin School of Maryland, Baltimore			X		K-5	6-8	9-12	595	234	8:1	7	4		X
The Bryn Mawr School, Baltimore			X	X	PK-5	6-8	9-12	931	321	7:1	19	40		X
The Bullis School, Potomac			X	X	3-5	6-8	9-12	585	327	10:1	14	20	X	X
Calvert Hall College High School, Towson			X				9-12	1,108	1,108	16:1		24		

Visit Peterson's Private Schools channel at www.petersons.com

PETERSON'S PRIVATE SCHOOL RESOURCES

	STUDENTS ACCEPTED				GRADES			STUDENT/FACULTY			SCHOOL OFFERINGS (number)		SSAT or ISEE REQUIRED	
	Boarding		Day											
	Boys	Girls	Boys	Girls	Lower	Middle	Upper	Total	Upper	Student/Faculty Ratio	Advanced Placement Subject Areas	Sports	SSAT	ISEE
Maryland—continued														
The Calverton School, Huntingtown			X	X	PK-5	6-8	9-12	352	92	8:1	13	8		
The Canterbury School, Accokeek			X	X		6-8	9-12	50	25	7:1	3	20		
The Catholic High School of Baltimore, Baltimore				X			9-12	440	440	12:1	6	10		
Charles E. Smith Jewish Day School, Rockville			X	X	K-6		7-12	1,275	556		2	8		
Connelly School of the Holy Child, Potomac				X		6-8	9-12	416	285	15:1	8	15		
Elizabeth Seton High School, Bladensburg				X			9-12	490	490	11:1	10	11		
Friends School of Baltimore, Baltimore			X	X	PK-5	6-8	9-12	1,001	341	15:1	14	13	X	X
Garrison Forest School, Owings Mills		X	X	X	N-5	6-8	9-12	624	213	8:1	9	15	X	X
Georgetown Preparatory School, North Bethesda	X		X				9-12	420	420	8:1	20	47	X	
Gilman School, Baltimore			X		1-5	6-8	9-12	963	425	15:1	14	9	X	X
Glenelg Country School, Glenelg			X	X	PK-5	6-8	9-12	580	152	7:1	10	5		X
Gunston Day School, Centreville			X	X						10:1	7		X	X
The Heights School, Potomac			X		3-5	6-8	9-12	425	181	19:1	11	9		
The Holton-Arms School, Bethesda				X	3-6	7-8	9-12	661	308		10	18	X	X
Home Study International, Silver Spring			X	X	PK-6	7-8	9-12	1,463	606	21:1				
Institute of Notre Dame, Baltimore				X			9-12	428	428	14:1	6	13		
The Key School, Annapolis			X	X	N-4	5-8	9-12	662	166	10:1	12	24		X
Landon School, Bethesda			X		3-6	7-8	9-12	646	291	10:1	10	19		X
Loyola-Blakefield, Baltimore			X			6-8	9-12	968	726		14	20		
Maryvale Preparatory School, Brooklandville				X		6-8	9-12	310	211	10:1	5	6		
McDonogh School, Owings Mills	X	X	X	X	K-4	5-8	9-12	1,240	530	9:1	16	17		X
New Dominion School, Oldtown	X								72			6		
The Newport School, Kensington			X	X	N-4	5-8	9-12	397	148	15:1	8	5		
Notre Dame Preparatory School, Towson				X		6-8	9-12	685	525	9:1	7	12		X
Oldfields School, Glencoe		X		X			8-12	180	180	4:1	8	12	X	X
Our Lady of Good Counsel High School, Wheaton			X	X			9-12	1,000	1,000		11	1		
The Park School, Brooklandville			X	X	PK-5	6-8	9-12	885	304	8:1	5	10		X
Queen Anne School, Upper Marlboro			X	X		6-8	9-12	234	114		7	10		X
Roland Park Country School, Baltimore				X	K-5	6-8	9-12	698	279	7:1	19	12		X
St. Andrew's Episcopal School, Potomac			X	X		6-8	9-12	450	278	8:1	8	11	X	
Saint James School, St. James	X	X	X	X		7-8	9-12	211	165	7:1	11	17	X	
St. Paul's School, Brooklandville			X	X	P1-4	5-8	9-12	843	298	9:1	12	18		X
St. Paul's School for Girls, Brooklandville				X		5-8	9-12	351	193	9:1	11	11		X

More information on these schools can be found in
Peterson's Guide to Private Secondary Schools 2000–2001

Peterson's SSAT/ISEE Success

PRIVATE SCHOOL SNAPSHOTS

| | STUDENTS ACCEPTED | | | | GRADES | | | STUDENT/FACULTY | | | SCHOOL OFFERINGS (number) | | SSAT or ISEE REQUIRED | |
| | Boarding | | Day | | | | | | | | | | | |
	Boys	Girls	Boys	Girls	Lower	Middle	Upper	Total	Upper	Student/Faculty Ratio	Advanced Placement Subject Areas	Sports	SSAT	ISEE
Maryland—*continued*														
St. Timothy's School, Stevenson		X		X			9–12	120	120	5:1	9	20	X	X
Sandy Spring Friends School, Sandy Spring	X	X	X	X						15:1	4	12	X	
Severn School, Severna Park			X	X		6–8	9–12	547	354	10:1	11	12		X
Stone Ridge School of the Sacred Heart, Bethesda				X	N–4	5–8	9–12	795	330		16	16	X	X
Thornton Friends School, Silver Spring			X	X		6–8	9–12	91	54	6:1		8		
Washington Waldorf School, Bethesda			X	X	1–3	4–8	9–12	273	79	8:1	1	6		
West Nottingham Academy, Colora	X	X	X	X				145				13		
Worcester Preparatory School, Berlin			X	X	PK–6	7–8	9–12	470	112	10:1	8	7		
Massachusetts														
The Academy at Charlemont, Charlemont	X	X	X	X		7–8	9–PG	79	44	7:1		6		
Academy at Swift River, Cummington	X	X					9–12	95	95	7:1		30		
Bancroft School, Worcester			X	X	K–5	6–8	9–12	591	232	7:1	14	12	X	
Beaver Country Day School, Chestnut Hill			X	X		6–8	9–12	353	234	8:1	10	15	X	X
Belmont Hill School, Belmont	X		X			7–9	10–12	428	229	8:1	10	20	X	X
The Bement School, Deerfield	X	X	X	X	K–5		6–9	241	113	5:1		31	X	
Berkshire School, Sheffield	X	X	X	X			9–PG	385	385	6:1	18	35	X	X
Bishop Connolly High School, Fall River			X	X			9–12	420	420	11:1	6	16		
Bishop Stang High School, North Dartmouth			X	X					645	12:1	14	24		
Boston College High School, Boston			X				9–12	1,206	1,206	13:1	19	19	X	
Boston University Academy, Boston			X	X		8	9–12	98	84	10:1		25	X	
Brimmer and May School, Chestnut Hill			X	X	N–5	6–8	9–12	377	102	6:1	5	7	X	X
Brooks School, North Andover	X	X	X	X			9–12	337	337		13	18	X	
Buckingham Browne & Nichols School, Cambridge			X	X	PK–6	7–8	9–12	949	455	7:1	19	21	X	X
Buxton School, Williamstown	X	X						94	94	5:1		20		
The Cambridge School of Weston, Weston	X	X	X	X			9–PG	300	300	7:1	12	16	X	X
The Carroll School, Lincoln			X	X	1–5	6–8	9–12	235	60	6:1		10		
Cathedral High School, Springfield			X	X			9–12	900	900		4	15		
Chapel Hill-Chauncy Hall School, Waltham	X	X	X	X			9–12	162	162	5:1		13	X	
Commonwealth School, Boston			X	X			9–12	134	134	5:1	13	10	X	X
Concord Academy, Concord	X	X	X	X			9–12	327	327	7:1	14	30	X	X
Cushing Academy, Ashburnham	X	X	X	X			9–PG	410	410	8:1	14	12	X	
Dana Hall School, Wellesley		X		X		6–8	9–12	396	267	8:1	12	19	X	X
Deerfield Academy, Deerfield	X	X	X	X			9–PG	599	599	5:1	19	27	X	

Visit Peterson's Private Schools channel at www.petersons.com

Peterson's: www.petersons.com

| | STUDENTS ACCEPTED | | | | GRADES | | | STUDENT/FACULTY | | | SCHOOL OFFERINGS (number) | | SSAT or ISEE REQUIRED | |
| | Boarding | | Day | | | | | | | | | | | |
	Boys	Girls	Boys	Girls	Lower	Middle	Upper	Total	Upper	Student/Faculty Ratio	Advanced Placement Subject Areas	Sports	SSAT	ISEE
Massachusetts—continued														
The DeSisto School, Stockbridge...	X	X							100	10:1		41		
Eaglebrook School, Deerfield......	X		X			6-9		247	221	5:1		43		
Eagle Hill School, Hardwick......	X	X	X	X					120	4:1		30		
Falmouth Academy, Falmouth......			X	X		7-8	9-12	189	107	6:1	4	4	X	
Fay School, Southborough.........	X	X	X	X						11:1		19		
The Fessenden School, West Newton..........................	X		X							7:1		18	X	X
F. L. Chamberlain School, Middleborough................	X	X	X	X		7-8	9-12	70	38			14		
Fontbonne Academy, Milton.......				X			9-12	520	520	13:1	5	7		
Governor Dummer Academy, Byfield.....................	X	X	X	X			9-12	367	367	6:1	14	17	X	
Groton School, Groton.........	X	X	X	X		8-8	9-12	340	315	5:1	15	15	X	
Hillside School, Marlborough......	X		X							6:1		25		
The John Dewey Academy, Great Barrington...................	X	X					10-PG	28	28	3:1				
Landmark School, Prides Crossing...	X	X	X	X					273	3:1		20		
Lawrence Academy, Groton.......	X	X	X	X			9-12	365	365	8:1	8	18	X	X
Lexington Christian Academy, Lexington....................			X	X		6-8	9-12	310	207	10:1	7	18	X	X
Linden Hill School, Northfield.....	X									3:1		11		
The MacDuffie School, Springfield..	X	X	X	X		6-8	9-PG	209	132	7:1	6	9	X	
Matignon High School, Cambridge...			X	X						22:1	6	11	X	
Middlesex School, Concord........	X	X	X	X			9-12	318	318	6:1	18	22	X	X
Milton Academy, Milton...........	X	X	X	X	K-6	7-8	9-12	981	658	5:1	11	22	X	X
Miss Hall's School, Pittsfield.......		X		X			9-PG	118	118	5:1	7	15	X	
Montrose School, Natick..........				X		6-8	9-12	108	49	16:1	2	4		
Newman Preparatory School, Boston......................			X	X			9-PG	250	250	12:1	4	7		
Newton Country Day School of the Sacred Heart, Newton.........				X		5-8	9-12	280	152	7:1	20	27	X	X
Noble and Greenough School, Dedham.....................	X	X	X	X		7-8	9-12	518	401	7:1	16	14	X	X
Northfield Mount Hermon School, Northfield...................	X	X	X	X			9-PG	1,153	1,153	7:1	19	30	X	X
Notre Dame Academy, Hingham...				X			9-12	556	556	11:1	9	16		
Notre Dame Academy, Worcester..				X			9-12	310	310	11:1	12	12		
Phillips Academy (Andover), Andover.....................	X	X	X	X			9-PG	1,077	1,077	6:1	14	28	X	X
The Pingree School, South Hamilton....................			X	X						7:1	10	18	X	X
The Rivers School, Weston........			X	X		7-8	9-12	346	269	8:1	5	14	X	X
The Roxbury Latin School, West Roxbury.....................			X				7-12	285	285	9:1	10	7	X	X
Saint Mark's School, Southborough.	X	X	X	X			9-12	325	325		14	16	X	
St. Sebastian's School, Needham....			X			7-8	9-12	337	253	7:1	9	9	X	
Shackleton School, Ashby.........	X	X							29	4:1				
Stoneleigh-Burnham School, Greenfield...................		X		X			9-12	189	189	6:1	9	10	X	

More information on these schools can be found in *Peterson's Guide to Private Secondary Schools 2000–2001*

PRIVATE SCHOOL SNAPSHOTS

| | STUDENTS ACCEPTED | | | | GRADES | | | STUDENT/FACULTY | | | SCHOOL OFFERINGS (number) | | SSAT or ISEE REQUIRED | |
| | Boarding | | Day | | | | | | | | | | | |
	Boys	Girls	Boys	Girls	Lower	Middle	Upper	Total	Upper	Student/Faculty Ratio	Advanced Placement Subject Areas	Sports	SSAT	ISEE
Massachusetts—*continued*														
The Sudbury Valley School, Framingham.............			X	X				200	200	18:1				
Tabor Academy, Marion..........	X	X	X	X	X-X	X-X	9–12	467	467		19	18	X	X
Thayer Academy, Braintree.......			X	X		6–8	9–12	657	447	7:1	9	14	X	
Valley View School, North Brookfield................	X					5–8	9–12	48	30	5:1		26		
Walnut Hill School, Natick.......	X	X	X	X			9–12	227	227	6:1		6		
Waring School, Beverly..........			X	X		6–8	9–12	128	83	7:1	2	7		
Wilbraham & Monson Academy, Wilbraham...............	X	X	X	X		6–8	9–12	357	277	7:1	6	23	X	
The Williston Northampton School, Easthampton...........	X	X	X	X		7–8	9–PG	534	442	8:1	12	17	X	
Willow Hill School, Sudbury......			X	X		6–8	9–PG	50	30			7		
The Winchendon School, Winchendon.............	X	X	X							6:1	4	27		
The Winsor School, Boston.......				X		5–8	9–12	421	234	7:1	9	11	X	X
Worcester Academy, Worcester....	X	X	X	X		6–8	9–PG	460	330	8:1	12	16	X	
Xaverian Brothers High School, Westwood................			X						861	13:1	11	22		
Michigan														
Academy of the Sacred Heart, Bloomfield Hills...........			X	X	N-5	6–8	9–12	471	126	7:1		6		
Cranbrook Schools, Bloomfield Hills..................	X	X	X	X	PK-5	6–8	9–12	1,575	745	10:1	13	25	X	
Detroit Country Day School, Beverly Hills.............	X	X	X	X	PK-5	6–8	9–12	1,504	604	8:1	19	23		
Eton Academy, Birmingham......			X	X	1-5	6–8	9–12	178	56	8:1		7		
Grand Rapids Christian Schools, Grand Rapids.............			X	X	PK-5	6–8	9–12	3,333	1,171	17:1		21		
Greenhills School, Ann Arbor......			X	X		6–8	9–12	507	296	10:1	8	11	X	X
Interlochen Arts Academy, Interlochen..............	X	X	X	X					435	6:1		3	X	
The Leelanau School, Glen Arbor...	X	X	X	X			9–12	70	70	7:1	2	9	X	
Lutheran High School Northwest, Rochester Hills............			X	X			9–12	286	286	16:1	3	12		
The Roeper School, Bloomfield Hills..................			X	X	PK-5	6–8	9–12	649	189	13:1	7	10		
St. Mary's Preparatory School, Orchard Lake.............	X		X				9–12	375	375	11:1	2	15		
University Liggett School, Grosse Pointe Woods............			X	X	PK-5	6–8	9–12	791	269	9:1	14	16	X	X
Valley Lutheran High School, Saginaw................			X	X			9–12	388	388	20:1	2	10		
The Valley School, Flint..........			X	X	K-4	5–8	9–12	154	54	14:1	1	4		
Minnesota														
Benilde-St. Margaret's School, St. Louis Park..............			X	X		7–8	9–12	1,051	788	14:1	7	14		

Visit Peterson's Private Schools channel at www.petersons.com

Peterson's: www.petersons.com

PETERSON'S PRIVATE SCHOOL RESOURCES

	STUDENTS ACCEPTED				GRADES			STUDENT/FACULTY			SCHOOL OFFERINGS (number)		SSAT or ISEE REQUIRED	
	Boarding		Day											
	Boys	Girls	Boys	Girls	Lower	Middle	Upper	Total	Upper	Student/Faculty Ratio	Advanced Placement Subject Areas	Sports	SSAT	ISEE
Minnesota—*continued*														
The Blake School, Minneapolis			X	X	PK-5	6-8	9-12	1,248	434	8:1	11	15		X
Breck School, Minneapolis			X	X	PK-4	5-8	9-12	1,162	362	8:1	7	16		
Calvin Academy, Mounds View			X	X				36						
Concordia Academy, St. Paul			X	X	1-1	4-4	9-12	399	399	14:1	4	15		
Cretin-Derham Hall, Saint Paul			X	X			9-12	1,286	1,286	16:1	5	20		
International School of Minnesota, Eden Prairie			X	X	PS-5	6-8	9-12	640	95	14:1	15	15		X
Marshall School, Duluth			X	X		5-8	9-12	554	299	10:1	5	14		X
Minnehaha Academy, Minneapolis			X	X	PK-5	6-8	9-12	1,140	483	14:1	16	21		
Minnesota Conservatory for the Arts, Winona	X	X	X	X					10	5:1		21		
Mounds Park Academy, St. Paul			X	X	K-4	5-8	9-12	673	236	9:1	3	11		
St. Croix Lutheran High School, West St. Paul	X	X	X	X			9-12	366	366	15:1	2	13		
Saint John's Preparatory School, Collegeville	X	X	X	X		7-8	9-PG	262	220	11:1	8	20		
St. Paul Academy and Summit School, St. Paul			X	X	K-6	7-8	9-12	878	390	10:1	9			X
St. Thomas Academy, St. Paul			X			7-8	9-12	698	542	12:1	7	1		
Shattuck-St. Mary's School, Faribault	X	X	X	X		6-8	9-PG	295	253	7:1	13	22	X	
Mississippi														
All Saints' Episcopal School, Vicksburg	X	X	X	X			8-PG	105	105	4:1		83		
Brookhaven Academy, Brookhaven			X	X	PK-6	7-8	9-12	579	162		1	2		
Jackson Academy, Jackson			X	X	PK-6	7-9	10-12	1,471	332	15:1	10	8		
Jackson Preparatory School, Jackson			X	X		7-9	10-12	914	425	12:1	9	10		
St. Andrew's Episcopal School, Ridgeland			X	X	PK-5	5-9	9-12	1,105	299	7:1	15	17		
St. Stanislaus College Prep, Bay St. Louis	X		X							14:1	3	3		
Washington County Day School, Greenville			X	X	PK-5	6-8	9-12	930	315	20:1		10		
Missouri														
The Barstow School, Kansas City			X	X	PK-4	5-8	9-12	553	174	8:1	12	10		X
Chaminade College Preparatory School, St. Louis	X		X			7-8	9-12	840	590	11:1	17	15		X
Crossroads School, St. Louis			X	X		7-8	9-12	179	118	9:1	5	19		X
Logos School, St. Louis			X	X		7-8	9-12	130	110	6:1		2		
Lutheran High School North, St. Louis			X	X						12:1		11		
Lutheran High School South, St. Louis			X	X			9-12	699	699	14:1	5	18		
Mary Institute and St. Louis Country Day School (MICDS), St. Louis			X	X	JK-4	5-8	9-12	1,218	559	8:1	18	19		X
Missouri Military Academy, Mexico	X				4-8		9-12	292	208	12:1	5	31		

More information on these schools can be found in
Peterson's Guide to Private Secondary Schools 2000-2001

PRIVATE SCHOOL SNAPSHOTS

	STUDENTS ACCEPTED				GRADES			STUDENT/FACULTY			SCHOOL OFFERINGS (number)		SSAT or ISEE REQUIRED	
	Boarding		Day								Advanced Placement Subject Areas	Sports	SSAT	ISEE
	Boys	Girls	Boys	Girls	Lower	Middle	Upper	Total	Upper	Student/Faculty Ratio				
Missouri—*continued*														
The Pembroke Hill School, Kansas City			X	X	PS-5	6-8	9-12	1,126	388	12:1	13	4		
Saint Louis Priory School, St. Louis			X			7-8	9-12	380	232	8:1	14	13		X
Saint Paul Lutheran High School, Concordia	X	X	X	X			9-12	148	148	13:1		15		
Thomas Jefferson School, St. Louis	X	X	X	X			7-PG	77	77	6:1	12	7	X	X
Visitation Academy of St. Louis County, St. Louis			X	X						12:1	11	1		
Wentworth Military Academy and Junior College, Lexington	X	X	X	X		6-8	9-12	117	100	7:1		6		
Whitfield School, St. Louis			X	X			6-12	446	446	8:1	6	13		
Montana														
Butte Central High School, Butte			X	X			9-12	190	190	13:1		3		
Headwaters Academy, Bozeman			X	X		6-8	9-12	35	20	5:1	1	13		
Lustre Christian High School, Lustre	X	X	X	X						5:1		5		
Montana Academy, Marion	X	X					8-12	40	40	2:1		17		
Nebraska														
Brownell-Talbot School, Omaha			X	X	PK-4	5-8	9-12	430	103	11:1	11	12		
Creighton Preparatory School, Omaha			X				9-12	945	945	14:1	11	18		
Mount Michael Benedictine High School, Elkhorn	X						9-12	138	138	6:1	7	4		
Platte Valley Academy, Shelton	X	X	X	X	1-8		9-12	89	82	10:1		3		
Nevada														
Bishop Gorman High School, Las Vegas			X	X			9-12	1,012	1,012	19:1	13	8		
Faith Lutheran High School, Las Vegas			X	X		6-8	9-12	627	300	15:1	4	11		
The Meadows School, Las Vegas			X	X		6-8	9-12	816	223	7:1	7	16	X	X
New Hampshire														
Bishop Guertin High School, Nashua			X	X			9-12	793	793	21:1	12	17		
Brewster Academy, Wolfeboro	X	X	X	X			9-PG	350	350	6:1	4	27	X	
Cardigan Mountain School, Canaan	X		X			6-9		199	188	5:1		23		
The Derryfield School, Manchester			X	X		6-8	9-12	353	233	8:1	9	17	X	
Dublin Christian Academy, Dublin	X	X	X	X	K-6		7-12	143	100	6:1		13		
Dublin School, Dublin	X	X	X	X			9-12	114	114	5:1	4	18		
Hampshire Country School, Rindge	X				3-6		7-12	25	17	2:1		18		
High Mowing School, Wilton	X	X	X	X			9-12	103	103	5:1		25		
Holderness School, Plymouth	X	X	X	X			9-12	268	268	7:1	11	39	X	
Kimball Union Academy, Meriden	X	X	X	X			9-PG	291	291	6:1	15	32	X	
The Meeting School, Rindge	X	X	X	X			9-12	34	34					

Visit Peterson's Private Schools channel at www.petersons.com

Peterson's: www.petersons.com

PETERSON'S PRIVATE SCHOOL RESOURCES

	STUDENTS ACCEPTED				GRADES			STUDENT/FACULTY			SCHOOL OFFERINGS (number)		SSAT or ISEE REQUIRED	
	Boarding		Day											
	Boys	Girls	Boys	Girls	Lower	Middle	Upper	Total	Upper	Student/Faculty Ratio	Advanced Placement Subject Areas	Sports	SSAT	ISEE
New Hampshire—*continued*														
New Hampton School, New Hampton	X	X	X	X			9–PG	325	325	5:1	5	34	X	
Phillips Exeter Academy, Exeter	X	X	X	X			9–PG	1,002	1,002	5:1	20	33	X	
Proctor Academy, Andover	X	X	X	X			9–PG	324	324	5:1	5	38	X	
St. Paul's School, Concord	X	X					9–12	503	503	5:1		25	X	
Tilton School, Tilton	X	X	X	X			9–PG	208	208	5:1	5	24	X	
Trinity High School, Manchester			X	X			9–12	475	475	17:1	5	15		
Wediko School Program, Windsor	X		X						10	2:1		11		
The White Mountain School, Bethlehem	X	X	X	X						14:1	7	34		
New Jersey														
Academy of Saint Elizabeth, Convent Station				X			9–12	225	225	9:1	9	14		
Academy of the Holy Angels, Demarest				X						10:1	9	12		
The American Boychoir School, Princeton	X		X			6–8		82		10:1		7		
Bishop Eustace Preparatory School, Pennsauken			X	X				782	782	14:1	8	20		
Blair Academy, Blairstown	X	X	X	X			9–PG	412	412	8:1	17	26	X	
Christian Brothers Academy, Lincroft			X						875		7	13		
Collegiate School, Passaic Park			X	X	PK–6		7–12	154	64	9:1				
Delbarton School, Morristown			X			7–8	9–12	540	461		12	16		
Dwight-Englewood School, Englewood			X	X	PK–5	6–8	9–12	998	471	8:1		5		X
Eastern Christian High School, North Haledon			X	X	PK–4	5–8	9–12	973	312	12:1	6	19		
The Frisch School, Paramus			X	X			9–12	500	500		10	13		
Gill St. Bernard's School, Gladstone			X	X	PS–4	5–8	9–12	543	149	14:1	6	10	X	X
The Hudson School, Hoboken			X	X		5–8	9–12	178	60	10:1		7	X	X
The Hun School of Princeton, Princeton	X	X	X	X		6–8	9–PG	570	470	8:1	14	23	X	
Kent Place School, Summit			X	X	N–5	6–8	9–12	608	214	7:1	19	9	X	X
The Lawrenceville School, Lawrenceville	X	X	X	X					782	5:1	11	43	X	X
Montclair Kimberley Academy, Montclair			X	X	PK–3	4–8	9–12	1,035	421	7:1	14	17		X
Moorestown Friends School, Moorestown			X	X	PS–4	5–8	9–12	626	196		12	15		X
Morristown-Beard School, Morristown			X	X		6–8	9–12	432	318	8:1	9	16	X	X
Mount Saint Mary Academy, Watchung				X			9–12	335	335	8:1	5	6		X
Newark Academy, Livingston			X	X		6–8	9–12	547	414		20	26	X	X
The Newgrange School, Trenton			X	X				85	30	3:1		3		
Oak Knoll School of the Holy Child, Summit			X	X		7–8	9–12	282		8:1	7	11	X	X

More information on these schools can be found in
Peterson's Guide to Private Secondary Schools 2000–2001

PRIVATE SCHOOL SNAPSHOTS

	STUDENTS ACCEPTED				GRADES			STUDENT/FACULTY			SCHOOL OFFERINGS (number)		SSAT or ISEE REQUIRED	
	Boarding		Day											
	Boys	Girls	Boys	Girls	Lower	Middle	Upper	Total	Upper	Student/Faculty Ratio	Advanced Placement Subject Areas	Sports	SSAT	ISEE
New Jersey—*continued*														
Oratory Prep School, Summit			X			7–8	9–12	205	170	10:1	10	15		
The Peddie School, Hightstown	X	X	X	X						6:1	10	20	X	X
The Pennington School, Pennington	X	X	X	X		6–8	9–12	405	334	9:1	10	18	X	
The Pingry School, Martinsville			X	X	K–6	7–8	9–12	1,008	507	8:1	16	2	X	X
Princeton Day School, Princeton			X	X				875			13	16	X	
Purnell School, Pottersville		X		X			9–12	94	94	4:1		12		
Ranney School, Tinton Falls			X	X	N–5	6–8	9–12	558	137		15	11		X
Rutgers Preparatory School, Somerset			X	X	PK–4	5–8	9–12	672	275	6:1	20	13	X	
Saddle River Day School, Saddle River			X	X	K–5	6–8	9–12	312	146	8:1	12	2		X
St. Benedict's Preparatory School, Newark			X			7–8	9–12	535	455	11:1		22		
Saint Dominic Academy, Jersey City				X			9–12	477	477	12:1	8	9		
Saint Joseph's High School, Metuchen			X				9–12	760	760	13:1	10	11		
St. Mary's Hall, Burlington			X	X	K–6	7–8	9–12	110	31	8:1	8	4		
St. Peter's Preparatory School, Jersey City			X				9–12	791	791	10:1	8	26		
Seton Hall Preparatory School, West Orange			X				9–12	838	838	11:1	10	19		
Stuart Country Day School of the Sacred Heart, Princeton			X	X	N–5	6–8	9–12	528	130	15:1	12	9	X	
Villa Victoria Academy, Ewing			X	X	PK–6		7–12	266	124	7:1	6	2	X	
Villa Walsh Academy, Morristown				X		7–8	9–12	218	185	8:1	11	10		
The Wardlaw-Hartridge School, Edison			X	X	PK–5	6–8	9–12	460	163	9:1	16	4	X	X
Woodcliff Academy, Wall			X	X					20	3:1		8		
New Mexico														
Albuquerque Academy, Albuquerque			X	X		6–8	9–12	1,037	611	8:1	13	12	X	
The Armand Hammer United World College of the American West, Montezuma	X	X					11–12	200	200	8:1		40		
Brush Ranch School, Santa Fe	X	X								2:1		13		
McCurdy School, Espanola			X	X	K–6	7–8	9–12	401	181		3	5		
Menaul School, Albuquerque	X	X	X	X		6–8	9–12	465	275	14:1	5	15	X	X
New Mexico Military Institute, Roswell	X	X					9–12	500	500	18:1		35		
St. Michael's High School, Santa Fe			X	X		7–8	9–12	741	464	17:1	3	15		
Sandia Preparatory School, Albuquerque			X	X								9		
Santa Fe Preparatory School, Santa Fe			X	X		7–8	9–12	311	202	8:1	8	13		X

Visit Peterson's Private Schools channel at www.petersons.com

PETERSON'S PRIVATE SCHOOL RESOURCES

	STUDENTS ACCEPTED				GRADES			STUDENT/FACULTY			SCHOOL OFFERINGS (number)		SSAT or ISEE REQUIRED	
	Boarding		Day											
	Boys	Girls	Boys	Girls	Lower	Middle	Upper	Total	Upper	Student/Faculty Ratio	Advanced Placement Subject Areas	Sports	SSAT	ISEE
New York														
Adelphi Academy, Brooklyn			X	X	K-4	5-8	9-12	169	75	6:1	3	7		
The Albany Academy, Albany			X	X	PK-4	5-8	9-PG	503	239	15:1	15	16	X	X
Albany Academy for Girls, Albany				X	PK-4	5-8	9-12	363	140	10:1	16	9		X
All Hallows High School, Bronx			X				9-12	446	446	12:1	3			
The Beekman School, New York			X	X						8:1				
Berkeley Carroll School, Brooklyn			X	X	N-4	5-8	9-12	788	196	8:1	9	7		X
The Birch Wathen Lenox School, New York			X	X	K-5	6-8	9-12	400	130		10	19	X	X
Buffalo Academy of the Sacred Heart, Buffalo				X			9-12	389	389		6	10		
The Calhoun School, New York			X	X	N-4	5-8	9-12	545	120	5:1		9		X
Cascadilla School, Ithaca	X	X	X	X						5:1	4	8		
The Chapin School, New York				X	K-3	4-7	8-12	644	216	4:1	17	47		
Christian Central Academy, Williamsville			X	X	K-6	7-8	9-12	256	77	5:1	3	2		
Columbia Grammar and Preparatory School, New York			X	X	PK-6		7-12	757	366	7:1	14	13		X
Convent of the Sacred Heart, New York				X	PK-4	5-7	8-12	605	224	9:1	10	20		X
The Dalton School, New York			X	X	K-3	4-8	9-12	440	440	7:1	11	10	X	X
Darrow School, New Lebanon	X	X	X	X			9-PG	86	86	3:1		8		
Doane Stuart School, Albany			X	X	N-4	5-8	9-12	241	76	7:1	12	7		
The Dominican Academy of the City of New York, New York				X			9-12	232	232	10:1	11	4		
The Dwight School, New York			X	X	K-4	5-8	9-12	400	237	7:1	6	28		X
Emma Willard School, Troy		X		X					286	8:1	13	20	X	
The Ethical Culture Fieldston School, Bronx			X	X	PK-6	7-8	9-12	1,585	520	14:1	14	48		X
Fordham Preparatory School, Bronx			X				9-12	882	882	11:1	9	16	X	X
Friends Academy, Locust Valley			X	X	N-5	6-8	9-12	715	327	6:1	14	15	X	
Friends Seminary, New York			X	X	K-4	5-8	9-12	615	223	8:1	13	9		X
Garden School, Jackson Heights			X	X	PK-6		7-12	401			5	6		
The Gow School, South Wales	X									3:1		26		
Hackley School, Tarrytown	X	X	X	X	K-5	6-8	9-12	784	372	4:1	14	18		X
The Harley School, Rochester			X	X	N-4	5-8	9-12	485	132	8:1	14	2		X
The Harvey School, Katonah	X	X	X	X			6-8	230	150	7:1	10	15		
The Hewitt School, New York				X	K-4	5-7	9-12	384			8	11		X
The Hewlett School of East Islip, East Islip	X	X	X	X	PK-5	6-8	9-12	170	23	15:1	4	5		
Holy Angels Academy, Buffalo				X			9-12	280	280	13:1	1	17		
Hoosac School, Hoosick	X	X	X	X			8-PG	88	88	5:1	3	19		
The Horace Mann School, Riverdale			X	X	N-5	6-8	9-12	1,659	659	9:1	17	22	X	X
Houghton Academy, Houghton	X	X	X	X	K-6	7-8	9-12	225	128	10:1		15		
Immaculata Academy, Hamburg				X			9-12	143	143	6:1	1	10		

More information on these schools can be found in
Peterson's Guide to Private Secondary Schools 2000–2001

PRIVATE SCHOOL SNAPSHOTS

	STUDENTS ACCEPTED				GRADES			STUDENT/FACULTY		SCHOOL OFFERINGS (number)		SSAT or ISEE REQUIRED	
	Boarding		Day										
	Boys	Girls	Boys	Girls	Lower	Middle	Upper	Total	Upper	Student/Faculty Ratio	Advanced Placement Subject Areas	Sports	SSAT	ISEE
New York—continued														
Keio Academy of New York, Purchase	X	X	X	X			9–12	367	367		4	20		X
The Kew-Forest School, Forest Hills			X	X	1–5	6–8	9–12	380	160	10:1		5	X	X
Kildonan School, Amenia	X	X	X	X	2–6	7–9	10–PG	139	74	6:1		9	X	
The Knox School, St. James	X	X	X	X		7–8	9–12	165	140	4:1	5	11		
La Salle, Oakdale	X	X	X	X	K–6	7–8	9–12			17:1		15		
La Salle Institute, Troy			X			6–8	9–12	602	385	10:1	7	7		
Lawrence Woodmere Academy, Woodmere			X	X	N–4	5–8	9–12	385	170	15:1	14	8	X	
Little Red School House and Elisabeth Irwin High School, New York			X	X	N–4	5–8	9–12	440	96		5			X
Long Island Lutheran Middle and High School, Brookville			X	X		6–8	9–12	507	340	12:1	7	13		
Loyola School, New York			X	X			9–12	199	199	10:1	6	2		
Lycee Français de New York, New York			X	X	N–5	6–8	9–12	970	223	15:1		9		
Manlius Pebble Hill School, DeWitt	X	X	X	X	PK–5	6–8	9–12	547	242	8:1	14	14		X
Maplebrook School, Amenia	X	X	X	X					31	8:1		19		
The Mary Louis Academy, Jamaica Estates				X			9–12	957	957	14:1	6	11		
Marymount School, New York				X	N–3	4–7	8–12	446	190	6:1	11	12	X	X
The Masters School, Dobbs Ferry	X	X	X	X		5–8	9–12	394	296	6:1	14	12	X	X
McQuaid Jesuit High School, Rochester			X			7–8	9–12	843	666	16:1	11	26		
Millbrook School, Millbrook	X	X	X	X			9–12	230	230		11	11	X	X
Nardin Academy, Buffalo			X	X	PK–8		9–12	932	453	10:1	9	20		
National Sports Academy at Lake Placid, Lake Placid	X	X	X	X			9–PG	103	100	8:1	3	17		
New York Military Academy, Cornwall-on-Hudson	X	X	X	X		7–8	9–12	268	221	10:1	3	23	X	
The Nichols School, Buffalo			X	X		5–8	9–12	561	390	9:1	17	17		
The Nightingale-Bamford School, New York				X	K–4	5–8	9–12	551	171	6:1	12	14		X
Norman Howard School, Rochester			X	X		5–8	9–12	151	91	12:1		8		
North Country School, Lake Placid	X	X	X	X		4–9		52		3:1		3		
Northwood School, Lake Placid	X	X	X	X			9–12	150	150	8:1	2	22	X	
Oakwood Friends School, Poughkeepsie	X	X	X	X		6–8	9–12	129	99	8:1	8	3		
Our Lady of Mercy High School, Rochester				X		7–8	9–12	580	456	12:1	7	12		
Our Saviour Lutheran School, Bronx			X	X	PK–3	4–6	7–12	448	205	12:1	3	6		
The Packer Collegiate Institute, Brooklyn Heights			X	X	PK–4	5–8	9–12	871	250	7:1	16	12	X	X
Polytechnic Preparatory Country Day School, Brooklyn			X	X	K–4	5–8	9–12	820	416	9:1	13	10	X	X
Portledge School, Locust Valley			X	X	N–5	6–8	9–12	393	124	6:1	10	9	X	

Visit Peterson's Private Schools channel at www.petersons.com

	STUDENTS ACCEPTED				GRADES			STUDENT/FACULTY			SCHOOL OFFERINGS (number)		SSAT or ISEE REQUIRED	
	Boarding		Day											
	Boys	Girls	Boys	Girls	Lower	Middle	Upper	Total	Upper	Student/ Faculty Ratio	Advanced Placement Subject Areas	Sports	SSAT	ISEE
New York—*continued*														
Poughkeepsie Day School, Poughkeepsie			X	X	PK–4	5–8	9–12	325	98	8:1	3	19		
Professional Children's School, New York			X	X		4–8	9–12	172	140					X
Redemption Christian Academy, Troy	X	X	X	X	K–6	7–8	9–PG	77	31	10:1	3			
Riverdale Country School, Riverdale			X	X	PK–6		7–12	1,040	630	8:1	8	15	X	X
Robert Louis Stevenson School, New York			X	X					63	6:1		21		
The Rockland Country Day School, Congers			X	X	K–4	5–8	9–12	179	39	4:1	14	11		X
Rudolf Steiner School, New York			X	X	PK–6	7–8	9–12	288	60	3:1	5	9		X
Rye Country Day School, Rye			X	X	PK–4	5–8	9–12	793	329	8:1	20	12	X	X
St. Thomas Choir School, New York	X					5–8		41	20			3		
Smith School, New York			X	X		7–8	9–12	45	35	3:1	20	3		
The Spence School, New York				X	K–5	6–8	9–12	594	185	7:1	8	27		X
Staten Island Academy, Staten Island			X	X	PK–6	7–8	9–12	469	132	5:1	12	11		X
The Stony Brook School, Stony Brook	X	X	X	X		7–8	9–12	347	279	7:1	16	17	X	
Storm King School, Cornwall-on-Hudson	X	X	X	X			9–12	118	118	6:1	9	44		
Trevor Day School, New York			X	X	PK–5	6–8	9–12	718	209	6:1	6	9	X	X
Trinity-Pawling School, Pawling	X		X			7–8	9–PG	324	295	7:1	14	13	X	
Trinity School, New York			X	X	K–4	5–8	9–12	985	451	7:1	11	14	X	X
Union Springs Academy, Union Springs	X	X	X	X			9–12	79	79			8		
United Nations International School, New York			X	X	K–4	5–8	9–12	1,486	407	9:1		14		X
Waldorf School of Garden City, Garden City			X	X						5:1		6	X	
The Windsor School, Flushing			X	X		6–8	9–13	127	109	13:1	7	11		
Windward School, White Plains			X	X	1–5	6–8	9–12	300	67	5:1		4		
Winston Preparatory School, New York			X	X		6–8	9–12	100	63	3:1		5		
York Preparatory School, New York			X	X		6–8	9–12	240	176	8:1	3	15	X	X
North Carolina														
The Asheville School, Asheville	X	X	X	X			9–12	216	216	4:1	14	16	X	X
Cannon School, Concord			X	X	PK–4	5–8	9–10	508	42	12:1	2	8		
Cape Fear Academy, Wilmington			X	X	PK–5	6–8	9–12	520	161	8:1	9	11		X
Carolina Day School, Asheville			X	X	PK–5	6–8	9–12	543	154	10:1	17	5		X
Charlotte Christian School, Charlotte			X	X	PK–5	6–8	9–12	989	304		12			
Charlotte Country Day School, Charlotte			X	X	PK–4	5–8	9–12	1,589	458	12:1	14	17		X

More information on these schools can be found in
Peterson's Guide to Private Secondary Schools 2000–2001

PRIVATE SCHOOL SNAPSHOTS

	STUDENTS ACCEPTED				GRADES			STUDENT/FACULTY			SCHOOL OFFERINGS (number)		SSAT or ISEE REQUIRED	
	Boarding		Day											
	Boys	Girls	Boys	Girls	Lower	Middle	Upper	Total	Upper	Student/Faculty Ratio	Advanced Placement Subject Areas	Sports	SSAT	ISEE
North Carolina—*continued*														
Charlotte Latin School, Charlotte...			X	X	PK-5	6-8	9-12	1,318	432	9:1	14	15		X
Christ School, Arden.............	X		X				9-12	174	163	6:1	5		X	
Cresset Christian Academy, Durham.................			X	X	K4-5	6-8	9-12	346	82	10:1	5	6		
Durham Academy, Durham........			X	X	PK-4	5-8	9-12	1,025	351	11:1	15	15	X	X
Fayetteville Academy, Fayetteville..			X	X	PK-5	6-8	9-12	456	174	6:1	6	12	X	X
Forsyth Country Day School, Lewisville...................			X	X	PK-4	5-8	9-12	720	215	7:1	8	15		X
Gaston Day School, Gastonia......			X	X	PK-4	5-8	9-12	400	84	4:1	8	13		
Greensboro Day School, Greensboro................			X	X	K-5	6-8	9-12	863	304	10:1	17	17		
Heavenly Mountain Ideal Girls School, Boone...............		X		X			9-12	25	25	2:1	2	12		
The Hill Center, Durham Academy, Durham...................			X	X	K-4	5-8	9-12	144	56	4:1				
Kerr-Vance Academy, Henderson...			X	X	PK-4	5-8	9-12	540	115	10:1	5	10		
Oak Ridge Military Academy, Oak Ridge....................	X	X	X	X						8:1	12	4		
The Patterson School, Patterson....	X	X	X	X		7-8	9-12	46	41	9:1		48		
Providence Day School, Charlotte..			X	X	PK-5	6-8	9-12	1,377	387	10:1	20	22		X
Rocky Mount Academy, Rocky Mount.....................			X	X	PK-5	6-8	9-12	318	78	9:1	4	2		
Saint Mary's School, Raleigh.......		X		X			9-12	275	275	15:1	4	9	X	X
St. Timothy's - Hale School, Raleigh.			X	X		5-8	9-12	455	162	10:1	13	4		
Salem Academy, Winston-Salem....		X		X			9-12	213	213	9:1	9	10	X	
Stone Mountain School, Black Mountain.................	X					6-8	9-12	25	15	4:1		30		
Wayne Country Day School, Goldsboro.................			X	X	PK-6		7-12	278	125	8:1	2	9		X
Westchester Academy, High Point..			X	X	K-5	6-8	9-12	507	125	9:1	12	9		X
Ohio														
The Andrews School, Willoughby..		X		X		6-8	9-12	179	126	8:1	7	24	X	X
Beaumont School, Cleveland Heights...................				X			9-12	449	449	11:1	6	3		
Cincinnati Country Day School, Cincinnati..................			X	X	PK-5	6-8	9-12	856	290	9:1	12	9		X
The Columbus Academy, Gahanna..			X	X	PK-4	5-8	9-12	912	308	8:1	20	13		X
Columbus School for Girls, Columbus..................				X	PK-5	6-8	9-12	654	230	7:1	13	6		X
Gilmour Academy, Gates Mills.....	X	X	X	X	PK-6	7-8	9-12	645	321	9:1	14	33	X	X
The Grand River Academy, Austinburg..................	X		X				9-12	105	105	5:1	3	22		
Hathaway Brown School, Shaker Heights...................			X	X	PS-4	5-8	9-12	719	230	7:1	11	11		X
Hawken School, Gates Mills.......			X	X						9:1	15	7		X
Lake Ridge Academy, North Ridgeville..................			X	X	K-5	6-8	9-12	435	140	8:1	12	5		
Laurel School, Shaker Heights......			X	X	PS-4	5-8	9-12	625	199	9:1	12	9		X

Visit Peterson's Private Schools channel at www.petersons.com

Peterson's: www.petersons.com

PETERSON'S PRIVATE SCHOOL RESOURCES

	STUDENTS ACCEPTED							STUDENT/FACULTY			SCHOOL OFFERINGS (number)		SSAT or ISEE REQUIRED	
	Boarding		Day		GRADES									
	Boys	Girls	Boys	Girls	Lower	Middle	Upper	Total	Upper	Student/ Faculty Ratio	Advanced Placement Subject Areas	Sports	SSAT	ISEE
Ohio—*continued*														
Lutheran East High School, Cleveland Heights............			X	X			9–12	201	201	11:1	4	8		
Maumee Valley Country Day School, Toledo			X	X	N–6	7–8	9–12	474	165	10:1	6	11		
The Miami Valley School, Dayton...			X	X	PK–5	6–8	9–12	502	174	6:1	10	10		
Notre Dame-Cathedral Latin School, Chardon.....................			X	X						15:1	5	15		
Olney Friends School, Barnesville ..	X	X	X	X			9–12	23	23	3:1	2	13		
St. Francis de Sales High School, Toledo			X				9–12	677	677	16:1	11	14		
St. John's Jesuit High School, Toledo			X				9–12	820	820	14:1	7	18		
Saint Xavier High School, Cincinnati			X				9–12	1,400	1,400	15:1	18	14		
The Seven Hills School, Cincinnati..			X	X	PK–5	6–8	9–12	999	260	9:1	10	5		X
Stephen T. Badin High School, Hamilton			X	X			9–12	740	740		2	2		
The Summit Country Day School, Cincinnati			X	X	PK–3	4–8	9–12	1,150	308	9:1	14	17		
University School, Hunting Valley ..			X			K–8	9–12	854	395		13	13		
The Wellington School, Columbus..			X	X	PK–4	5–8	9–12	601	205	15:1	13	10		
Western Reserve Academy, Hudson.	X	X	X	X			9–12	402	402	12:1	14	20	X	X
Oklahoma														
Casady School, Oklahoma City			X	X	PK–4	5–8	9–12	916	330	14:1	16	17		
Cascia Hall Preparatory School, Tulsa......................			X	X		6–8	9–12	565	362	12:1	11	5		
Heritage Hall, Oklahoma City			X	X	N–4	5–8	9–12	836	303	16:1		14		X
Holland Hall School, Tulsa			X	X	PK–3	4–8	9–12	1,026	339	8:1	18	19		X
Oregon														
The Catlin Gabel School, Portland ..			X	X	1–5	6–8	9–12	623	250	11:1	4	11		
Crater Lake School, Sprague River ..	X	X				8–8	9–12	20	17	10:1		34		
The Delphian School, Sheridan.....	X	X	X	X					178			5		
Jesuit High School, Portland			X	X			9–12	1,084	1,084	18:1	4	4	X	
Milo Adventist Academy, Days Creek	X	X	X	X			9–12	155	155	9:1	6	9		
Mount Bachelor Academy, Prineville	X	X							90	4:1				
Oregon Episcopal School, Portland .	X	X	X	X	PK–5	6–8	9–12	724	242	7:1	8	10	X	X
Santiam Christian School, Corvallis .			X	X								12		
Sunriver Preparatory, Bend			X	X	PK–6	7–8	9–12	190	44	6:1		7		X
Valley Catholic High School, Beaverton...................			X	X	K–6	7–8	9–12	780	320		5	10		
Wellsprings Friends School, Eugene			X	X			9–12	43	43	7:1		4		
Western Mennonite School, Salem..	X	X	X	X		7–8	9–12	152	129	11:1	1	10		

More information on these schools can be found in
Peterson's Guide to Private Secondary Schools 2000–2001

PRIVATE SCHOOL SNAPSHOTS

	STUDENTS ACCEPTED				GRADES			STUDENT/FACULTY			SCHOOL OFFERINGS (number)		SSAT or ISEE REQUIRED	
	Boarding		Day											
	Boys	Girls	Boys	Girls	Lower	Middle	Upper	Total	Upper	Student/Faculty Ratio	Advanced Placement Subject Areas	Sports	SSAT	ISEE
Pennsylvania														
Abington Friends School, Jenkintown			X	X	PK-5	6-8	9-12	653	262	10:1		9	X	X
The Agnes Irwin School, Rosemont				X	K-4	5-8	9-12	608	203	8:1	12	3	X	X
Akiba Hebrew Academy, Merion Station			X	X		7-8	9-12	369	260		4	8		
The Baldwin School, Bryn Mawr				X	PK-5	6-8	9-12	619	179	8:1	4	12	X	X
Carson Long Military Institute, New Bloomfield	X								183	11:1		11		
CFS-The School at Church Farm, Paoli	X		X			7-8	9-12	172	132	6:1	1	13	X	
Chestnut Hill Academy, Philadelphia			X		K-5	6-8	9-12	546	198	8:1	14	8	X	X
Christopher Dock Mennonite High School, Lansdale			X	X			9-12	415	415	14:1	1	10		
The Concept School, Westtown			X	X		5-8	9-12	60	30	8:1		12		
Delaware County Christian School, Newtown Square			X	X	K-5	6-8	9-12	1,021	356		10	10		X
Devon Preparatory School, Devon			X			6-8	9-12	250	180	10:1	10	9		
The Ellis School, Pittsburgh				X	K-4	5-8	9-12	459	160	7:1	12	9		X
The Episcopal Academy, Merion			X	X						7:1	12	19	X	X
Friends Select School, Philadelphia			X	X	PK-4	5-8	9-12	496	189		8	9	X	X
George School, Newtown	X	X	X	X			9-12	540	540	7:1	9	25	X	
Germantown Academy, Fort Washington			X	X	PK-5	6-8	9-12	1,105	481	14:1	15	18	X	X
Germantown Friends School, Philadelphia			X	X	K-5	6-8	9-12	900	347	8:1		12	X	X
Girard College, Philadelphia	X	X			1-5	6-8	9-12	550	170	9:1		22	X	
The Grier School, Tyrone		X		X		7-8	9-PG	169	143	6:1	1	23		
The Harrisburg Academy, Wormleysburg			X	X						5:1	11	9		X
The Haverford School, Haverford			X		PK-5	6-8	9-12	893	316	8:1	15	22	X	X
The Hill School, Pottstown	X	X	X	X			9-12	461	461	6:1	14	23	X	
Holy Ghost Preparatory School, Bensalem			X				9-12	478	478	11:1	7	19		
Keystone National High School, Bloomsburg			X	X										
Kimberton Waldorf School, Kimberton			X	X				371				5		
The Kiski School, Saltsburg	X						9-12	215	215	5:1	14	12	X	X
La Salle College High School, Wyndmoor			X				9-12	990	990	11:1	14	12		
Linden Hall, Lititz		X		X		6-8	9-PG	104	77	4:1	4	7		
Malvern Preparatory School, Malvern			X			6-8	9-12	421	265	9:1	14	14	X	
The Mercersburg Academy, Mercersburg	X	X	X	X			9-PG	422	422	6:1	16	22	X	
Mercyhurst Preparatory School, Erie			X	X			9-12	818	818	17:1		13		

Visit Peterson's Private Schools channel at www.petersons.com

Peterson's: www.petersons.com

PETERSON'S PRIVATE SCHOOL RESOURCES

	STUDENTS ACCEPTED				GRADES			STUDENT/FACULTY			SCHOOL OFFERINGS (number)		SSAT or ISEE REQUIRED	
	Boarding		Day											
	Boys	Girls	Boys	Girls	Lower	Middle	Upper	Total	Upper	Student/ Faculty Ratio	Advanced Placement Subject Areas	Sports	SSAT	ISEE
Pennsylvania—*continued*														
Merion Mercy Academy, Merion Station				X			9–12	426	426	10:1	8	9		
Milton Hershey School, Hershey	X	X			K–5	6–8	9–12	1,083	479	9:1	5	11		
MMI Preparatory School, Freeland			X	X		6–8	9–12	228	143	12:1	10	9		
Moravian Academy, Bethlehem			X	X	PK–5	6–8	9–12	787	267	9:1	9	4		X
Mount Saint Joseph Academy, Flourtown				X				549		18:1	10	14		
Nazareth Academy High School for Girls, Philadelphia				X			9–12	468	468	9:1	6	11		
The Oakland School, Pittsburgh			X	X			8–12	66	66	6:1	5	20		
The Pathway School, Jeffersonville	X	X	X	X								6		
Perkiomen School, Pennsburg	X	X	X	X		5–8	9–PG	250	203	7:1	14	16		
The Phelps School, Malvern	X		X		7–8		9–12	146	119	8:1		24		
Philadelphia-Montgomery Christian Academy, Erdenheim			X	X	PK–5	6–8	9–12	630	208	18:1		8		
Pine Forge Academy, Pine Forge	X	X	X	X			9–12	166	166	11:1		8		
Saint Basil Academy, Fox Chase Manor				X					336	9:1	5	11		
Saint Gregory's Academy, Moscow	X						9–12	60	60	5:1		10		
St. Joseph's Preparatory School, Philadelphia			X				9–12	930	930	23:1	14	14		
Sewickley Academy, Sewickley			X	X	PK–5	6–8	9–12	797	299	7:1	14	14		X
Shady Side Academy, Pittsburgh	X	X	X	X	K–5	6–8	9–12	944	501	8:1	6	20	X	X
The Shipley School, Bryn Mawr			X	X	PK–5	6–8	9–12	817	319	8:1	14	19	X	X
Solebury School, New Hope	X	X	X	X		7–8	9–PG	195	169	5:1	3	21	X	
Springside School, Philadelphia				X	PK–4	5–8	9–12	563	167	8:1	11	8	X	X
Valley Forge Military Academy and College, Wayne	X									12:1				
Westtown School, Westtown	X	X	X	X	PK–5	6–8	9–12	647	380	8:1	10	34	X	X
William Penn Charter School, Philadelphia			X	X	K–5	6–8	9–12	839	374	15:1	9	14	X	X
Winchester Thurston School, Pittsburgh			X	X	PK–5	6–8	9–12	595	177	10:1	10	21		X
Wyoming Seminary, Kingston	X	X	X	X	PK–8		9–PG	424	410	9:1	18	3	X	
York Country Day School, York			X	X	PK–5	6–8	9–12	229	90	9:1	5	7		
Rhode Island														
Lincoln School, Providence				X	N–5	6–8	9–12	370	143			26	X	X
Moses Brown School, Providence			X	X	N–5	6–8	9–12	773	387	8:1	10	16	X	X
Mt. St. Charles Academy, Woonsocket			X	X			7–12	930	930	14:1	8	17		
Portsmouth Abbey School, Portsmouth	X	X	X	X						6:1	13	17	X	X
Providence Country Day School, East Providence			X	X		5–8	9–12	278	190	8:1	11	12	X	X
St. Andrew's School, Barrington	X	X	X	X		6–8	9–12	159	128			11	X	
St. George's School, Middletown	X	X	X	X			9–12	334	334	6:1	18	15	X	
The Wheeler School, Providence			X	X	N–5	6–8	9–12	756	282	13:1	11	11	X	X

More information on these schools can be found in
Peterson's Guide to Private Secondary Schools 2000–2001

PRIVATE SCHOOL SNAPSHOTS

	STUDENTS ACCEPTED				GRADES			STUDENT/FACULTY			SCHOOL OFFERINGS (number)		SSAT or ISEE REQUIRED	
	Boarding		Day											
	Boys	Girls	Boys	Girls	Lower	Middle	Upper	Total	Upper	Student/Faculty Ratio	Advanced Placement Subject Areas	Sports	SSAT	ISEE
South Carolina														
Aiken Preparatory School, Aiken			X	X	PK-5	6-8	9-12	162		5:1		11	X	
Ashley Hall, Charleston			X	X	PK-5	6-8	9-12	621	182	9:1	10	26		X
Beaufort Academy, Beaufort			X	X	PK-4	5-8	9-12	385	105	11:1	5	9		
Ben Lippen Schools, Columbia	X	X	X	X						18:1	8	5		
Camden Military Academy, Camden	X					7-8	9-12	228						
Christ Church Episcopal School, Greenville			X	X	K-4	5-8	9-12	875	270	10:1	18	12		X
Hammond School, Columbia			X	X	PS-5	6-8	9-12	727	207	15:1	13	11	X	
Hilton Head Preparatory School, Hilton Head Island			X	X	1-5	6-8	9-12	433	167	15:1	10	9	X	
Porter-Gaud School, Charleston			X	X	1-5	6-8	9-12	838	299	14:1	9	11		X
Shannon Forest Christian School, Greenville			X	X	PK-6	7-8	9-12	590	116	17:1	5	13		
The Spartanburg Day School, Spartanburg			X	X	PK-4	5-8	9-12	562	136	9:1	16	7		
Trident Academy, Mt. Pleasant		X	X	X	K-6	7-8	9-12	117	31	4:1		3		
Wilson Hall, Sumter			X	X	PS-5	6-8	9-12	698	207	12:1	10	13		
South Dakota														
Dakota Christian High School, New Holland			X	X			9-12	62	62	8:1		6		
Tennessee														
Battle Ground Academy, Franklin			X	X	PK-4	5-8	9-12	923	403	11:1		15		X
Baylor School, Chattanooga	X	X	X	X	7-8		9-12	808	607	7:1	17	28	X	
The Bodine School, Germantown			X	X	1-6		7-12	75	25	6:1				
Chattanooga Christian School, Chattanooga			X	X	K-5	6-8	9-12	1,042	386	18:1	4	16		
Columbia Academy, Columbia			X	X	K-6		7-12	640	320	17:1	1	8		
David Lipscomb High School, Nashville			X	X	PK-4	5-8	9-12	1,589	520	16:1		13		
Donelson Christian Academy, Nashville			X	X	K-6		7-12	1,005	503	15:1	4	10		
Evangelical Christian School, Cordova			X	X	K-5	6-8	9-10	1,285	495	11:1	5	13		X
Father Ryan High School, Nashville			X	X			9-12	1,000	1,000	13:1	6	14		
First Assembly Christian School, Cordova			X	X	PK-6			400		12:1	2	5		
Franklin Road Academy, Nashville			X	X	PK-4	5-8	9-12	901	281	9:1	10	11		X
Friendship Christian School, Lebanon			X	X	PK-5	6-8	9-12	694	247	15:1	2	10		
Girls Preparatory School, Chattanooga				X		6-8	9-12	734	425	15:1	11	12		X
The Harpeth Hall School, Nashville				X		5-8	9-12	539	348	9:1	12	39		X
Hutchison School, Memphis				X	PK-5	6-8	9-12	840	237	18:1	13	4		X
The King's Academy of Greater Knoxville, Seymour	X	X	X	X	K-6	7-8	9-12	254	85	20:1	2	22		

Visit Peterson's Private Schools channel at www.petersons.com

PETERSON'S PRIVATE SCHOOL RESOURCES

	STUDENTS ACCEPTED				GRADES			STUDENT/FACULTY			SCHOOL OFFERINGS (number)		SSAT or ISEE REQUIRED	
	Boarding		Day											
	Boys	Girls	Boys	Girls	Lower	Middle	Upper	Total	Upper	Student/Faculty Ratio	Advanced Placement Subject Areas	Sports	SSAT	ISEE
Tennessee—continued														
The McCallie School, Chattanooga	X		X			6–8	9–12	835	585	8:1	14	40	X	X
Montgomery Bell Academy, Nashville			X			7–8	9–12	625	437	9:1	13	30		X
St. Andrew's-Sewanee School, Sewanee	X	X	X	X		7–8	9–12	252	200	7:1	6	16	X	X
St. Benedict at Auburndale, Cordova			X	X	PK–6	7–8	9–12	965	386	7:1	4	13		
Saint Cecilia Academy, Nashville				X			9–12	208	208	12:1	10	17		X
St. Mary's Episcopal School, Memphis				X	PK–4	5–8	9–12	826	210	10:1	12	3		X
University School of Jackson, Jackson			X	X	PK–4	5–8	9–12	1,343	324	16:1	8	15		
University School of Nashville, Nashville			X	X	K–4	5–8	9–12	975	322	12:1	20	19		X
Washington College Academy, Washington College	X	X	X	X	5–6	7–8	9–12	54	50	8:1		14		
The Webb School, Bell Buckle	X	X	X	X		7–8	9–12	271	202	9:1	6	17	X	X
Webb School of Knoxville, Knoxville			X	X	K–5	6–8	9–12	992	420	10:1	14	19	X	
Texas														
Allen Academy, Bryan	X		X	X	PK–6	7–8	9–12	405		8:1	3	12		
All Saints' Episcopal School of Fort Worth, Fort Worth			X	X	K–6	7–8	9–12	763	213	9:1	9	18		X
The Awty International School, Houston			X	X	PK–5	6–8	9–12	965	257	10:1		8		
Bishop Lynch Catholic High School, Dallas			X	X			9–12	1,033	1,033	14:1	9	21		
Central Catholic High School, San Antonio			X				9–12	491	491	14:1	8	17		
Cistercian Preparatory School, Irving			X			5–8	9–12	336	159	9:1	18	7		
Cliffwood School, Houston			X	X	K–5	6–8	9–12	70	23	10:1				
Dallas Academy, Dallas			X	X		7–8	9–12	134	97	8:1		8		
Dallas Christian School, Mesquite			X	X	PK–5	6–8	9–12	883	267	20:1		11		
Duchesne Academy of the Sacred Heart, Houston				X	PK–4	5–8	9–12	636	218	7:1	10	12		X
Episcopal High School, Bellaire			X	X			9–12	568	568		9			
The Episcopal School of Dallas, Dallas			X	X	PK–4	5–8	9–12	1,090	360			15		X
Fairhill School, Dallas			X	X	1–5	6–8	9–12	220	88	12:1		5		
Fort Worth Christian School, Fort Worth			X	X	PK–5	6–8	9–12	832	265	15:1		14		
Gateway School, Arlington			X	X		7–8	9–12	46	41	10:1		7		
Greenhill School, Addison			X	X	PK–4	5–8	9–12	1,245	411	18:1	14	16		X
The Hockaday School, Dallas		X		X	PK–4	5–8	9–12	1,012	426		14	10		
Houston Christian High School, Houston			X	X			9–12	258	258	15:1	6	12		X
Hyde Park Baptist School, Austin			X	X	K–6	7–8	9–12	632	53	18:1	3	9		

More information on these schools can be found in
Peterson's Guide to Private Secondary Schools 2000–2001

PRIVATE SCHOOL SNAPSHOTS

	STUDENTS ACCEPTED				GRADES			STUDENT/FACULTY			SCHOOL OFFERINGS (number)		SSAT or ISEE REQUIRED	
	Boarding		Day											
	Boys	Girls	Boys	Girls	Lower	Middle	Upper	Total	Upper	Student/Faculty Ratio	Advanced Placement Subject Areas	Sports	SSAT	ISEE
Texas—*continued*														
Incarnate Word High School, San Antonio		X		X			9–12	590	590	13:1	18			
Keystone School, San Antonio			X	X	K–5	6–8	9–12	392	113	7:1	10	4		
Lakehill Preparatory School, Dallas			X	X	K–4	5–8	9–12	290	94	8:1	6	9		
Lubbock Christian Schools, Lubbock			X	X	PK–6	7–8	9–12	365	111	10:1		7		
Lutheran High School of Dallas, Dallas			X	X		7–8	9–12	282	190	14:1		11		
Marine Military Academy, Harlingen	X									14:1	6	29		
The Oakridge School, Arlington			X	X	PK–4	5–8	9–12	671	218	10:1	11	11		
Saint Agnes Academy, Houston				X			9–12	733	733	14:1	11	3		X
St. Augustine High School, Laredo			X	X		6–8	9–12	604	425	20:1	3	8		
St. John's School, Houston			X	X	K–5	6–8	9–12	1,212	522	6:1	12	16		X
St. Joseph High School, Victoria			X	X			9–12	389	389	14:1		11		
St. Mark's School of Texas, Dallas			X		1–4	5–8	9–12	804	350	7:1	19	14		X
Saint Mary's Hall, San Antonio	X	X	X	X	PK–5	6–8	9–PG	910	349	12:1	20	16	X	X
St. Michael's Academy, Austin			X	X			9–12	403	403	11:1	12			X
St. Stephen's Episcopal School, Austin	X	X	X	X		6–8	9–12	607	411	6:1	12	12		X
San Marcos Baptist Academy, San Marcos	X	X	X	X		6–8	9–12	311	230	10:1	5	16		X
Strake Jesuit College Preparatory, Houston			X					741	742	13:1	5	13		
Texas Military Institute, San Antonio	X	X	X	X		6–8	9–12	314	192	7:1	11			X
Trinity Christian Academy, Addison			X	X	K–4	5–8	9–12	1,455	464	11:1	14	9		X
Trinity Valley School, Fort Worth			X	X	K–4	5–8	9–12	889	307	8:1	13	11		X
The Ursuline Academy of Dallas, Dallas				X			9–12	783	783	10:1	13	13		X
Walden Preparatory School, Dallas			X	X			9–12	55	55	6:1				
Westbury Christian School, Houston			X	X	PK–5	6–8	9–12	592	191	11:1		10		
The Winston School, Dallas			X	X	1–6	7–8	9–12	231	120	8:1		13		
Utah														
Aspen Ranch, Loa	X	X					8–12	70	70					
Cross Creek Manor, LaVerkin	X	X				7–8	9–12	215	209	5:1		7		
Intermountain Christian School, Salt Lake City			X	X	PK–5	6–8	9–12	319	106		4	3		
Provo Canyon School, Provo	X	X								10:1		9		
Realms of Inquiry, Salt Lake City			X	X	K–5	6–8	9–12	92	40	8:1		47		
Rowland Hall-St. Mark's School, Salt Lake City			X	X	PK–5	6–8	9–12	899	262	12:1	14	18		
Salt Lake Lutheran High School, Salt Lake City			X	X					68	8:1	2	7		
Sorenson's Ranch School, Koosharem	X	X					7–12	116	116	10:1		25		
Wasatch Academy, Mt. Pleasant	X	X	X	X			9–12	165	165	5:1	6	29		

Visit Peterson's Private Schools channel at **www.petersons.com**

Peterson's: www.petersons.com

PETERSON'S PRIVATE SCHOOL RESOURCES

	STUDENTS ACCEPTED				GRADES			STUDENT/FACULTY			SCHOOL OFFERINGS (number)		SSAT or ISEE REQUIRED	
	Boarding		Day											
	Boys	Girls	Boys	Girls	Lower	Middle	Upper	Total	Upper	Student/Faculty Ratio	Advanced Placement Subject Areas	Sports	SSAT	ISEE
Utah—continued														
The Waterford School, Sandy			X	X	PK-5	6-8	9-12	956	221	5:1	15	3		X
Vermont														
Burke Mountain Academy, East Burke	X	X	X	X			8-PG	80	80	7:1	2	8		
Green Mountain Valley School, Waitsfield	X	X	X	X			8-PG	81	81	6:1		30		
The Greenwood School, Putney	X									3:1		12		
King George School, Sutton	X	X					9-PG	35	35	5:1	10	17	X	
Long Trail School, Dorset	X	X	X	X		6-8	9-12	127	61	3:1	1	27		
Pine Ridge School, Williston	X	X	X	X					88			6		
The Putney School, Putney	X	X	X	X			9-PG	198	198	6:1		32		
Rock Point School, Burlington	X	X	X	X			9-12	33	33					
St. Johnsbury Academy, St. Johnsbury	X	X	X	X			9-PG	930	930	10:1	11	23		
Stratton Mountain School, Stratton Mountain	X	X	X	X		7-8	9-PG	101	88	6:1		11		
Vermont Academy, Saxtons River	X	X	X	X			9-PG	256	256	7:1	8	69	X	X
Virginia														
Benedictine High School, Richmond			X				9-12	276	276	9:1	4	13		
The Blue Ridge School, St. George	X						9-12	180	180	5:1		13		
Broadwater Academy, Exmore			X	X	PK-5	6-8	9-12	490	108		7	6		
Cape Henry Collegiate School, Virginia Beach			X	X	PK-5	6-8	9-12	860	245	10:1	12	28		X
Chatham Hall, Chatham		X		X			9-12	126	126	4:1	9	18	X	
Christchurch Episcopal School, Christchurch	X		X	X			8-PG	205	205	7:1	13	14		
The Collegiate School, Richmond			X	X	K-4	5-8	9-12	1,521	476	17:1	14	15	X	
Eastern Mennonite High School, Harrisonburg			X	X		6-8	9-12	307	231	11:1		10		
Episcopal High School, Alexandria	X	X					9-12	400	400	7:1	14	9	X	
Fishburne Military School, Waynesboro	X		X							9:1	3	39		
Flint Hill School, Oakton			X	X	JK-5	6-8	9-12	652	257		16	10	X	
Fork Union Military Academy, Fork Union	X		X			6-8	9-PG	650	544	14:1	5	20		
Foxcroft School, Middleburg		X		X			9-PG	153	153	5:1	11	9	X	
Fuqua School, Farmville			X	X	PK-5	6-8	9-12	607	203	17:1	5	10		
Hampton Roads Academy, Newport News			X	X		6-8	9-12	471	267		13	13		
Hargrave Military Academy, Chatham	X		X	X		7-8	9-PG	418	368	12:1	1	28		
Little Keswick School, Keswick	X								16	4:1		10		
The Madeira School, McLean		X		X			9-12	308	308	6:1	14	16	X	
Massanutten Military Academy, Woodstock	X	X	X	X		6-8	9-PG	233	195	9:1		18		
Miller School, Charlottesville	X	X	X	X	5-6	7-8	9-PG	140	94	6:1	5	47		

More information on these schools can be found in
Peterson's Guide to Private Secondary Schools 2000–2001

PRIVATE SCHOOL SNAPSHOTS

| | STUDENTS ACCEPTED | | | | GRADES | | | STUDENT/FACULTY | | | SCHOOL OFFERINGS (number) | | SSAT or ISEE REQUIRED | |
| | Boarding | | Day | | | | | | | | | | | |
	Boys	Girls	Boys	Girls	Lower	Middle	Upper	Total	Upper	Student/Faculty Ratio	Advanced Placement Subject Areas	Sports	SSAT	ISEE
Virginia—*continued*														
Nansemond-Suffolk Academy, Suffolk			X	X						12:1		4		
New Dominion School, Dillwyn	X	X							120			6		
Norfolk Academy, Norfolk			X	X	1-6	7-9	10-12	1,180	332	11:1	16	23		X
Norfolk Collegiate School, Norfolk			X	X	K-5	6-8	9-12	805	292	11:1	15	16		X
North Cross School, Roanoke			X	X	JK-5	6-8	9-12	573	160	12:1	11	14		
Notre Dame Academy, Middleburg			X	X			9-12	197	197	10:1	8	25	X	
Oak Hill Academy, Mouth of Wilson	X	X	X	X		8	9-12	131	125	8:1		17		
Oakland School, Keswick	X	X	X	X					80	4:1		24		
The Potomac School, McLean			X	X	PK-3	4-8	9-12	875	304	7:1	14	20	X	X
Randolph-Macon Academy, Front Royal	X	X	X	X		6-8	9-PG	455	383	7:1	3	65		
St. Anne's-Belfield School, Charlottesville	X	X	X	X	PK-4	5-8	9-12	819	275	10:1	11	14		X
St. Catherine's School, Richmond		X		X	PK-5	6-8	9-12	738	237	6:1	17	18	X	
St. Christopher's School, Richmond			X		JK-5	6-8	9-12	880	250	7:1	13	12		
St. Margaret's School, Tappahannock		X		X			8-12	151	151	6:1	5	18	X	
St. Stephen's & St. Agnes School, Alexandria			X	X	JK-5	6-8	9-12	1,154	445	6:1	20	21		X
Stuart Hall, Staunton		X	X	X		6-8	9-12	132	68	6:1	4	12	X	
Thornton Friends School/N.V.A., Alexandria			X	X		6-8	9-12	82	43	6:1		7		
Timber Ridge School, Cross Junction	X													
Trinity Episcopal School, Richmond			X	X		8	9-12	351	323	10:1	13	19		
Virginia Episcopal School, Lynchburg	X	X	X	X			9-12	222	222	8:1	12	21	X	
The Wakefield School, The Plains			X	X	PK-7		8-12	344	148	8:1	13	8	X	
Woodberry Forest School, Woodberry Forest	X									7:1	19	4	X	
Washington														
Annie Wright School, Tacoma		X	X	X	PK-5	6-8	9-12	431	122	8:1	2	10	X	
Auburn Adventist Academy, Auburn	X	X	X	X						12:1		10		
Bellarmine Preparatory School, Tacoma			X	X			9-12	987	987	20:1	8	15		
The Bush School, Seattle			X	X	K-5	6-8	9-12	545	204	8:1	8	26		X
Charles Wright Academy, Tacoma			X	X	PK-5	6-8	9-12	690	283		12	14		X
Chrysalis School, Woodinville			X	X						1:1				
Explorations High School, Bellingham			X	X					25	4:1	1	9		
Forest Ridge School of the Sacred Heart, Bellevue				X		5-8	9-12	330	140	8:1	3	8		X
Gonzaga Preparatory School, Spokane			X	X			9-12	976	976	24:1	7	17		

Visit Peterson's Private Schools channel at **www.petersons.com**

PETERSON'S PRIVATE SCHOOL RESOURCES

	STUDENTS ACCEPTED				GRADES			STUDENT/FACULTY			SCHOOL OFFERINGS (number)		SSAT or ISEE REQUIRED	
	Boarding		Day											
	Boys	Girls	Boys	Girls	Lower	Middle	Upper	Total	Upper	Student/Faculty Ratio	Advanced Placement Subject Areas	Sports	SSAT	ISEE
Washington—continued														
John F. Kennedy Memorial High School, Burien	X	X	X	X			9–12	805	805	21:1	2	16		
King's High School, Seattle			X	X	PK–6	7–8	9–12	1,274	394	17:1	6	6		
King's West School, Bremerton			X	X	K–6		7–12	437	255	14:1	1	7		
Lakeside School, Seattle			X	X		5–8	9–12	708	452	9:1		13		X
The Northwest School, Seattle	X	X	X	X		6–8	9–12	406	296	8:1		17		X
The Overlake School, Redmond			X	X		5–8	9–12	444	236	9:1		17		X
Saint George's School, Spokane			X	X	K–6	7–8	9–12	322	126	9:1	9	8		
Seattle Academy of Arts and Sciences, Seattle			X	X		6–8	9–12	389	211	8:1		4		X
Seattle Christian Schools, Seattle			X	X	K–6	7–8	9–12	730	263		3	4		
Seattle Lutheran High School, Seattle			X	X						8:1		8		
University Prep, Seattle			X	X		6–8	9–12	399	218	9:1	6	3		X
Upper Columbia Academy, Spangle	X	X	X	X			9–12	305	305	9:1	4	5		
West Virginia														
The Linsly School, Wheeling	X	X	X	X	5–8		9–12	414	282	13:1	7	47		
Wisconsin														
Aquinas Schools, La Crosse			X	X		7–8	9–12	730	509	16:1	1	15		
Milwaukee Lutheran High School, Milwaukee			X	X			9–12	785	783	14:1	6	29		
The Prairie School, Racine			X	X	N–4	5–8	9–12	619	215	8:1	11	10		
St. John's Northwestern Military Academy, Delafield	X					7–8	9–12	325	275	12:1		25	X	
University Lake School, Hartland			X	X	K–5	6–8	9–12	300	70	9:1	5	5		
University School of Milwaukee, Milwaukee			X	X	PK–4	5–8	9–12	1,068	308	10:1	19	15		X
Wayland Academy, Beaver Dam	X	X	X	X			9–12	193	193		9	24	X	
Puerto Rico														
American School, Bayamon			X	X	PK–4	5–8	9–12	1,000				4		
Caribbean Preparatory School, San Juan			X	X	PK–4	5–8	9–12	732	155	8:1	6	5		
Robinson School, Condado			X	X	PK–6	7–8	9–12	487	115	18:1	8	8		
Virgin Islands														
The Antilles School, Saint Thomas			X	X	N–5	6–8	9–12	453	144	12:1	10	20		X
Aruba														
International School of Aruba, Seroe Colorado			X	X	PK–5	6–8	9–12	173	62	8:1	5	6		
Austria														
The American International School, 1190 Vienna			X	X	PK–5	6–8	9–12	764	253	5:1	9	20		

More information on these schools can be found in
Peterson's Guide to Private Secondary Schools 2000–2001

PRIVATE SCHOOL SNAPSHOTS

	STUDENTS ACCEPTED				GRADES			STUDENT/FACULTY			SCHOOL OFFERINGS (number)		SSAT or ISEE REQUIRED	
	Boarding		Day											
	Boys	Girls	Boys	Girls	Lower	Middle	Upper	Total	Upper	Student/Faculty Ratio	Advanced Placement Subject Areas	Sports	SSAT	ISEE
Austria—*continued*														
American International School Salzburg, A-5020 Salzburg	X	X	X	X		7–8	9–PG	113	105	9:1	13	18		
Belgium														
Antwerp International School, 2180 Ekeren			X	X	PS–5	6–8	9–12	576	162	6:1		2		
International School of Brussels, Brussels			X	X	N–6	7–9	10–13	1,345	323	10:1	7	15		
Bolivia														
American Cooperative School, La Paz			X	X	PK–5	6–8	9–12	552	162	10:1	6	13		
Cochabamba Cooperative School, Cochabamba			X	X	PK–6	7–8	9–12	410	135	15:1	5	3		
Brazil														
Associacao Escola Graduada de Sao Paulo, Sao Paulo			X	X	K–5	6–8	9–12	1,125	323	8:1	1	12		X
Chapel School, Sao Paulo			X	X	PK			700						
Escola Americana de Campinas, Campinas-SP			X	X	PK–5	6–8	9–12	454	79		5	6		
Pan American School of Bahia, Salvador, Bahia			X	X	N–4	5–8	9–12	408	80	14:1	2	6		
Canada														
Albert College, Belleville, ON	X	X	X	X	1–6	7–8	9–13	308	221	8:1	5	29	X	
Appleby College, Oakville, ON	X	X	X	X		7–8	9–12	560	440	8:1		32	X	
Armbrae Academy, Halifax, NS			X	X						10:1	5	8		
Ashbury College, Ottawa, ON	X	X	X	X	4–8		9–13	641	486	15:1		29		
Balmoral Hall School, Winnipeg, MB		X	X	X	PK–5	6–8	9–12	523	154	11:1	6	21		
Bishop's College School, Lennoxville, PQ	X	X	X	X		7–9	10–12	252	152	8:1	13	18		
The Bishop Strachan School, Toronto, ON		X	X	X						17:1	10	27	X	
Brentwood College School, Mill Bay, BC	X	X	X	X			8–12	420	420					
Columbia International College of Canada, Hamilton, ON	X	X	X	X	9–10	11–11	12	681	513		5	2		
Concordia High School, Edmonton, AB	X	X	X	X					133					
Crescent School, Willowdale, ON			X		3–6	7–8	9–12	635	323	12:1	6	21	X	
Crofton House School, Vancouver, BC				X	1–6		7–12	663	430	11:1	5	17		
Elmwood School, Rockcliffe Park, Ottawa, ON			X	X	JK–6	7–9	10–13	444	124	8:1		30		
Glencairn Academy, Cayuga, ON	X	X	X	X		6–8	9–13	27	18	2.5:1		19		
Glenlyon-Norfolk School, Victoria, BC			X	X	K–7		8–12	700	315	10:1		15		

Visit Peterson's Private Schools channel at **www.petersons.com**

PETERSON'S PRIVATE SCHOOL RESOURCES

	STUDENTS ACCEPTED				GRADES			STUDENT/FACULTY			SCHOOL OFFERINGS (number)		SSAT or ISEE REQUIRED	
	Boarding		Day											
	Boys	Girls	Boys	Girls	Lower	Middle	Upper	Total	Upper	Student/Faculty Ratio	Advanced Placement Subject Areas	Sports	SSAT	ISEE
Canada—continued														
Grenville Christian College, Brockville, ON	X	X	X	X	PK-6	7-8	9-13	317	174	5:1	4	12	X	
Halifax Grammar School, Halifax, NS			X	X	K-4	5-8	9-12	430	165	10:1		11		
Havergal College, Toronto, ON		X		X	JK-6	7-8	9-13	927	496	10:1	2	44	X	
Hillfield Strathallan College, Hamilton, ON			X	X	PK-4	5-8	9-13	1,113	394			15		
Lakefield College School, Lakefield, ON	X	X	X	X			7-13	337	337	7:1	7	22	X	
Landmark East School, Wolfville, NS	X	X	X	X		5-9	10-12	45		2:1		20		
Lower Canada College, Montreal, PQ			X	X	K-6	7-8	9-12	714	291	21:1	8	62		
Luther College High School, Regina, SK	X	X	X	X			9-12	429	429	16:1		19		
Malaspina International Collegiate, Nanaimo, BC	X	X	X	X			10-12	48	48	8:1	5	12		
Maxwell International Baha'i School, Shawnigan Lake, BC	X	X	X	X		7-9	10-12	200	127					
Miss Edgar's and Miss Cramp's School, Montreal, PQ				X	K-5	6-8	9-11	316	94	9:1	2	16		
Pickering College, Newmarket, ON	X	X	X	X	JK-8		9-13	329	177	9:1		19	X	
Queen Margaret's School, Duncan, BC		X	X	X	K-6		7-12	266	156	10:1	7	42		
RCS Netherwood, Rothesay, NB	X	X	X	X		6-9	10-12	200	120	8:1	10	39		
Ridley College, St. Catharines, ON	X	X	X	X		5-8	9-13	623	506	9:1	12	42	X	
Robert Land Academy, Wellandport, ON	X				7-9	10	11-13	136	50	12:1		9		
Rocklyn Academy, Meaford, ON		X										11		
Rosseau Lake College, Rosseau, ON	X	X	X	X			9-13		123	8:1		59		
Rundle College, Calgary, AB			X	X						12:1		18		
Sacred Heart School of Halifax, Halifax, NS			X	X	K-6	7-9	10-12	445	75	13:1		13		
St. Andrew's College, Aurora, ON	X		X			6-8	9-13	493	390	10:1	5	23	X	
St. George's School, Vancouver, BC	X		X							10:1	13	26		
St. George's School of Montreal, Montreal, PQ			X	X	PK-6		7-11	521	325	17:1	8	12		
St. John's-Ravenscourt School, Winnipeg, MB	X	X	X	X	1-6	7-9	10-12	714	255	7:1	10	35		
Saint John's School of Alberta, Stony Plain, AB	X		X			7-9	10-12	117	59	10:1		54		
St. Margaret's School, Victoria, BC		X		X	K-6		7-12	408	265	8:1	3	53		
St. Michaels University School, Victoria, BC	X	X	X	X	K-5	6-8	9-12	867	511	10:1	13	37		
St. Mildred's-Lightbourn School, Oakville, ON				X	JK-6		7-13	594	272	10:1	5	16		
St. Paul's High School, Winnipeg, MB			X							16:1	2	11		
Sedbergh, Montebello, PQ	X	X	X	X	4-6	7-8	9-12	98	70	6:1		59		

More information on these schools can be found in
Peterson's Guide to Private Secondary Schools 2000–2001

PRIVATE SCHOOL SNAPSHOTS

	STUDENTS ACCEPTED				GRADES			STUDENT/FACULTY			SCHOOL OFFERINGS (number)		SSAT or ISEE REQUIRED	
	Boarding		Day											
	Boys	Girls	Boys	Girls	Lower	Middle	Upper	Total	Upper	Student/ Faculty Ratio	Advanced Placement Subject Areas	Sports	SSAT	ISEE
Canada—*continued*														
Selwyn House School, Westmount, QC			X		K-6	7-8	9-11	561	179	20:1		25		
Shawnigan Lake School, Shawnigan Lake, BC	X	X	X	X		8	9-12	390	355		7	4		
Stanstead College, Stanstead, PQ	X	X	X	X	7-9		9-12	228	159	8:1	7	34		
Strathcona-Tweedsmuir School, Okotoks, AB			X	X	1-6	7-9	10-12	663	236		5	7		
The Study, Westmount, PQ				X	K-3	4-6	7-11	371	135			10	X	
Trafalgar Castle School, Whitby, ON		X		X				210	200	8:1		20		
Trinity College School, Port Hope, ON	X	X	X	X		7-8	9-12	479	449	8:1	9	32	X	
Upper Canada College, Toronto, ON	X		X		1-8		9-13	1,081	674	11:1	1	24	X	
York House School, Vancouver, BC				X	K-6		7-12	596	302		9	10		
Chile														
Lincoln International Academy, Santiago			X	X								8		
Santiago College, Santiago			X	X	PK-4	5-8	9-12	1,814	511	22:1		1		
China														
Shanghai American School, Shanghai	X	X	X	X	PK-5	6-8	9-12	1,104	281	14:1	7	7		
Colombia														
Colegio Karl C. Parrish, Barranquilla			X	X	N-5	6-8	9-12	805	210	8:1	3	13		
Colegio Nueva Granada, Santafe de Bogota			X	X	PK-5	6-8	9-12	1,373	395	13:1	7	14		
Costa Rica														
American International School of Costa Rica, San Jose			X	X	PK-6	7-8	9-12	190	70	8:1	7	9		
Cyprus														
American International School in Cyprus, Nicosia	X	X	X	X	K-5	6-8	9-12	184	71	10:1	1	8		
Czech Republic														
International School of Prague, 16400 Prague 6, Nebusice			X	X	PK-5	6-8	9-12	572	145	9:1	10	6		
Denmark														
Copenhagen International School, 2900 Hellerup			X	X	PK-6		7-12	450	210	4:1		2		

Visit Peterson's Private Schools channel at www.petersons.com

Peterson's: www.petersons.com

PETERSON'S PRIVATE SCHOOL RESOURCES

	STUDENTS ACCEPTED				GRADES			STUDENT/FACULTY			SCHOOL OFFERINGS (number)		SSAT or ISEE REQUIRED	
	Boarding		Day											
	Boys	Girls	Boys	Girls	Lower	Middle	Upper	Total	Upper	Student/Faculty Ratio	Advanced Placement Subject Areas	Sports	SSAT	ISEE
Dominican Republic														
The Carol Morgan School, Santo Domingo			X	X	PK-5	6-8	9-12	935	217	8:1	9	8		
Ecuador														
Alliance Academy, Quito	X	X	X	X	PK-6	7-8	9-12	533	199	7:1	10	10		
Inter-American Academy of Guayaquil, Guayaquil			X	X	PK-5	6-8	9-12	319	129	12:1	3	15		
Egypt														
Schutz American School, Alexandria			X	X	PK-4	5-8	9-12	231	66	5:1	5	7		
Finland														
International School of Helsinki, Helsinki 00180			X	X	K-5	6-8	9-12	320	101	8:1		5		
France														
American School of Paris, 92216 Saint Cloud			X	X	PK-5	6-8	9-13	745	308	18:1	10	13		
Germany														
Black Forest Academy, 79396 Kandern	X	X	X	X	1-6	7-8	9-12	340	234	11:1	12	5		
The Frankfurt International School, 61440 Oberursel			X	X	PK-5	6-8	9-12	1,299	439	10:1	10	21		
Munich International School, Starnberg			X	X	PK-4	5-8	9-12	930	250	10:1		21		
Schule Schloss Salem, D-88682 Salem	X	X	X	X	5-7		12-13	575	210			17		
Greece														
American Community Schools of Athens, Athens			X	X	JK-5	6-8	9-12	772	382	13:1	12	10		
Campion School, Athens, Ekali-Athens			X	X	PK-6	7-9	10-13	544	204			18		
TASIS Hellenic International School, Kifissia - Athens	X	X	X	X	PK-5	6-8	9-12	352	231	13:1	8	7		
Honduras														
Mazapan School, La Ceiba			X	X	1-6	7-8	9-12	302	102	8:1	3	18		
India														
Kodaikanal International School, Kodaikanal	X	X	X	X	PS-6	7-8	9-12	484	299	8:1		20		
Woodstock School, Uttar Pradesh	X	X	X	X	1-5	6-8	9-12	456	280		16	14		

More information on these schools can be found in
Peterson's Guide to Private Secondary Schools 2000-2001

PRIVATE SCHOOL SNAPSHOTS

	STUDENTS ACCEPTED				GRADES			STUDENT/FACULTY			SCHOOL OFFERINGS (number)		SSAT or ISEE REQUIRED	
	Boarding		Day											
	Boys	Girls	Boys	Girls	Lower	Middle	Upper	Total	Upper	Student/Faculty Ratio	Advanced Placement Subject Areas	Sports	SSAT	ISEE
Indonesia														
Jakarta International School, Jakarta-Selatan			X	X	PK-5	6-8	9-12	2,399	871	11:1	14	29		
Surabaya International School, Surabaya			X	X	PK-5	6-8	9-12	276	80	11:1	6	10		
Ireland														
Sutton Park School, Dublin	X	X	X	X	K-P1	4-6	7-12	435	272	12:1		18		
Italy														
American Overseas School of Rome, 00189 Rome	X	X	X	X	PK-5	6-8	9-13	467	158	18:1	9	6		
American School of Milan, Noverasco di Opera, Milan			X	X	N-5	6-8	9-12	485	100	7:1	7	14		
Canadian College Italy (CCI International School), Lanciano	X	X	X	X			10-13	110	110	7:1	1	25		
Marymount International School, 00191 Rome			X	X	PK-5	6-8	9-12	800	200	12:1		6		
St. Stephen's School, Rome, Rome	X	X	X	X			9-PG	180	180	7:1	10	6		
Japan														
Canadian Academy, Kobe	X	X	X	X	K-5	6-8	9-10	772	240	11:1	8	8		
Columbia International College of Japan, Tokorozawa	X	X	X	X			7-12	168	168					
Marist Brothers International School, Kobe			X	X	PK-6		7-12	260	132	6:1	4	3		
Nagoya International School, Nagoya			X	X	PK-5	6-8	9-12	281	56	7:1	2	23		
Okinawa Christian School International, Yomitan-son, Okinawa			X	X	K-5	6-8	9-12	392	125	8:1		2		
Osaka International School, Mino City, Osaka			X	X	PK-5	6-8	9-13	256	74	9:1		1		
St. Mary's International School, Tokyo 158			X		K-6	7-8	9-12	900	262	10:1		19		
St. Maur International School, Yokohama			X	X	PK-5	6-8	9-12	501	104	4:1	8	8		
Seisen International School, Tokyo 158-0097			X	X		7-8	9-12	677	144	5:1	5	12		
Yokohama International School, Yokohama			X	X	N-8		9-12	560	115			5		
Kuwait														
The American School of Kuwait, Hawalli 32042			X	X						11:1	10	17		
The Universal American School, Khalidya			X	X	K-5	6-8	9-12	909	277	10:1	8	16		

Visit Peterson's Private Schools channel at www.petersons.com

PETERSON'S PRIVATE SCHOOL RESOURCES

	STUDENTS ACCEPTED				GRADES			STUDENT/FACULTY			SCHOOL OFFERINGS (number)		SSAT or ISEE REQUIRED	
	Boarding		Day											
	Boys	Girls	Boys	Girls	Lower	Middle	Upper	Total	Upper	Student/Faculty Ratio	Advanced Placement Subject Areas	Sports	SSAT	ISEE
Luxembourg														
International School of Luxembourg, L-1511			X	X	PK-6		7-12	429	162	7:1	2	5		
Malaysia														
The International School of Kuala Lumpur, Ampang			X	X	PK-5	6-8	9-13	1,128	454	9:1	10	19		
Mexico														
American School Foundation of Monterrey, Monterrey			X	X	N-5	6-8	9-12	2,005	349	12:1	4	22		
Colegio Peterson, Mexico City			X	X			9-12	181	181			5		
Morocco														
Rabat American School, Rabat			X	X	N-5	6-8	9-12	416	114	15:1	2	8		
Netherlands														
The American School of The Hague, 2241 BX Wassenaar			X	X	PK-4	5-8	9-13	1,010	330	9:1	16	10		
International School of Amsterdam, 1180 AX Amstelveen			X	X	PS-5	6-8	9-13	794	187	11:1		13		
Pakistan														
International School of Karachi, Karachi			X	X	N-5	6-8	9-12	342	117	8:1	10			
Peru														
Colegio Franklin D. Roosevelt, Lima 12			X	X	N-5	6-8	9-12	1,351	362	11:1		2		
Philippines														
Brent School-Baguio, 2600 Baguio City	X	X	X	X	PK-6		7-12	194	111	4:1		5		
Qatar														
American School of Doha, Doha ...			X	X	K-5	6-8	9-12	493	149	17:1	7	17		
Republic of Korea														
International Christian School, Uijongbu			X	X	PK-6	7-8	9-12	215	56	8:1	3	4		
International Christian School, Songtan, Songtan			X	X	1-6	6-8	9-12	217	28	13:1	1	5		
Seoul Foreign School, Seoul			X	X	PK-5	6-8	9-12	1,226	333	9:1	13	9		
Seoul International School, Seoul ...			X	X	PK-5	6-8	9-12	879	321	11:1	16	7		

More information on these schools can be found in
Peterson's Guide to Private Secondary Schools 2000–2001

PRIVATE SCHOOL SNAPSHOTS

	STUDENTS ACCEPTED				GRADES			STUDENT/FACULTY			SCHOOL OFFERINGS (number)		SSAT or ISEE REQUIRED	
	Boarding		Day											
	Boys	Girls	Boys	Girls	Lower	Middle	Upper	Total	Upper	Student/Faculty Ratio	Advanced Placement Subject Areas	Sports	SSAT	ISEE
Singapore														
International School Singapore, Singapore			X	X	PK–4	5–8	9–12	606	230	10:1	6	3		
Overseas Family School, Singapore 238515			X	X	K–5	6–8	9–12	1,645						
Spain														
The American School of Madrid, 28080 Madrid			X	X	PK–6	7–8	9–12	712	254	10:1	10	8		
International College Spain, Madrid			X	X	PK–5	6–8	9–12	553	166	10:1		17		
Switzerland														
Aiglon College, 1885 Chesieres-Villars	X	X	X	X						7:1		10		
The American International School of Zurich, 8802 Kilchberg			X	X		7–8	9–13	248	173		17	14		
American School of Institut Montana, 6300 Zug	X	X	X	X	4–6	7–8	9–13	82	69	6:1	4	38		
College du Leman International School, Versoix	X	X	X	X	K–5	6–8	9–13	1,206	473	9:1	15	26		
Ecole d'Humanite, CH 6085 Hasliberg-Goldern	X	X	X					149	129			28		
Gstaad International School, GSTAAD	X	X	X			8–9	10–12	28	20	4:1		15		
International School of Basel, Bottmingen			X	X	PK–5	6–8	9–12	525	103	8:1	5	1		
The International School of Geneva, Geneva			X	X	PK–4	5–8	9–13	1,709	662	13:1	7	13		
International School of Geneva La Chataigneraie, Founex			X	X	K–6		7–13	1,110	760	12:1		16		
Leysin American School in Switzerland, Leysin	X	X					9–13	289	289	12:1	12	17		
Rosehill International School-Anglo-American Section, CH-9000 St. Gallen	X	X	X	X	2–6	7–8	9–13	151	134	5:1	10	40		
Saint George's School in Switzerland, 1815 Clarens/Montreux		X	X	X	K–5	6–8	9–12	210	77	7.5:1		7		
TASIS American School in Switzerland, CH6926 Montagnola-Lugano	X	X	X	X		7–8	9–PG	273	249	6:1	13	17		
Taiwan														
Taipei American School, Taipei			X	X	K–5	6–8	9–12	2,132	823	10:1	13	10		
Thailand														
Ruamrudee International School, Bangkok			X	X	K–5	6–8	9–12	1,877	760	10:1	12	10		

Visit Peterson's Private Schools channel at **www.petersons.com**

Peterson's: www.petersons.com

PETERSON'S PRIVATE SCHOOL RESOURCES

| | STUDENTS ACCEPTED | | | | GRADES | | | STUDENT/FACULTY | | | SCHOOL OFFERINGS (number) | | SSAT or ISEE REQUIRED | |
| | Boarding | | Day | | | | | | | | | | | |
	Boys	Girls	Boys	Girls	Lower	Middle	Upper	Total	Upper	Student/ Faculty Ratio	Advanced Placement Subject Areas	Sports	SSAT	ISEE
United Arab Emirates														
The American School of Dubai, Dubai			X	X	K-5	6-8	9-12	875	250		8	15		
United Kingdom														
The American Community School–Middlesex Campus, Hillingdon			X	X	N-4	5-8	9-13	672	206	8:1	6	10		
The American Community School–Surrey Campus, Cobham, Surrey	X	X	X	X	N-4	5-8	9-13	1,222	416	10:1	10	8		
The American School in London, London			X	X	PK-5	6-8	9-12	1,264	441	11:1	17	13		
Marymount International School, Surrey		X		X							4	5		
Merchiston Castle School, Edinburgh	X		X						193	7:1		25		
St. Clare's, Oxford, Oxford	X	X	X	X						7:1		12		
TASIS The American School in England, Thorpe	X	X	X	X	PK-5	6-8	9-12	739	321	8:1	19	20		
Windermere St. Anne's School, Windermere		X		X				157				22		

More information on these schools can be found in
Peterson's Guide to Private Secondary Schools 2000–2001

SSAT Diagnostic Test

Part I: Writing Sample
Writing the Essay...................... 50

Part II: Multiple Choice
Verbal 53
Quantitative Mathematics 56
Reading Comprehension.................. 60

Explanatory Answers to the
   SSAT Diagnostic Test 64
     Verbal............................ 64
     Quantitative Mathematics 67
     Reading Comprehension 71

Part I
WRITING SAMPLE

WRITING THE ESSAY

Directions: Using two sheets of lined theme paper, plan and write an essay on the topic assigned below. DO NOT WRITE ON ANOTHER TOPIC. AN ESSAY ON ANOTHER TOPIC IS NOT ACCEPTABLE.

Topic: Winter comes fast on the lazy.

Assignment: Do you agree or disagree with the topic statement? Support your position with one or two specific examples from personal experience, the experience of others, current events, history, or literature.

WRITING THE ESSAY

Name: _____

Write your essay here.

Part II

MULTIPLE CHOICE

Verbal   30 Questions

Directions: Each of the following questions consists of one word followed by five words or phrases. You are to select the one word or phrase whose meaning is closest to the word in capital letters.

1. DISCOVER
    (A) detect
    (B) botch
    (C) verify
    (D) falsify
    (E) assure

2. FIDELITY
    (A) pleasantness
    (B) purity
    (C) faithlessness
    (D) sympathy
    (E) loyalty

3. HOSTILE
    (A) kind
    (B) friendly
    (C) sorry
    (D) antagonistic
    (E) generous

4. PROMPT
    (A) organized
    (B) timely
    (C) distant
    (D) tardy
    (E) tidy

5. AFFIRMATIVE
    (A) unwise
    (B) relevant
    (C) ancient
    (D) positive
    (E) negative

6. POTENT
    (A) powerful
    (B) disorderly
    (C) resentful
    (D) brave
    (E) clumsy

7. STEADFAST
    (A) faithful
    (B) slow
    (C) disloyal
    (D) immovable
    (E) arrogant

8. PASSIVE
    (A) unfriendly
    (B) doubtful
    (C) narrow
    (D) participate
    (E) active

9. HAPHAZARD
    (A) lucky
    (B) clever
    (C) aimless
    (D) planned
    (E) instant

Peterson's: www.petersons.com

10. LUSTROUS

    (A) dull
    (B) wicked
    (C) inaccurate
    (D) candid
    (E) glossy

11. ASSESSMENT

    (A) total
    (B) tax
    (C) evaluation
    (D) bill
    (E) due

12. CHANGE

    (A) alter
    (B) church
    (C) complete
    (D) decide
    (E) agree

13. BOUNTIFUL

    (A) miserly
    (B) considerate
    (C) faulty
    (D) lovely
    (E) generous

14. DREAM

    (A) hope
    (B) vision
    (C) demand
    (D) wealth
    (E) scared

15. VIRTUE

    (A) relationship
    (B) marriage
    (C) prosperity
    (D) happiness
    (E) goodness

Directions: The following questions ask you to find relationships between words. For each question, select the answer that best completes the meaning of the sentence.

16. Song is to recital as episode is to

    (A) bibliography
    (B) series
    (C) team
    (D) agile
    (E) prose

17. Bald is to hirsute as anemic is to

    (A) tiny
    (B) fat
    (C) robust
    (D) loud
    (E) redundant

18. Remove is to out as

    (A) abbreviate is to in
    (B) annotate is to out
    (C) interpolate is to in
    (D) duplicate is to out
    (E) emulate is to in

19. Oblivious is to awareness as

    (A) comatose is to consciousness
    (B) serene is to composure
    (C) erudite is to knowledge
    (D) adroit is to skill
    (E) palpitate is to ignorance

20. Explain is to clarity as

    (A) illuminate is to light
    (B) deracinate is to precision
    (C) invigorate is to energy
    (D) refine is to purity
    (E) coagulate is to gel

VERBAL

21. Poltroon is to pusillanimous as

    (A) jester is to lachrymose
    (B) dynamo is to supine
    (C) optimist is to sanguine
    (D) progressive is to hidebound
    (E) cower is to coward

22. Gold is to Midas as wisdom is to

    (A) eagle
    (B) Satan
    (C) conquest
    (D) Athena
    (E) Shakespeare

23. Tone is to deaf as

    (A) arm is to lift
    (B) touch is to smell
    (C) paint is to brush
    (D) sight is to sound
    (E) color is to blind

24. Radius is to diameter as

    (A) 3 is to 8
    (B) 4 is to 6
    (C) 12 is to 15
    (D) 5 is to 10
    (E) 9 is to 13

25. Oak is to acorn as

    (A) stable is to barn
    (B) tree is to branch
    (C) tulip is to bulb
    (D) library is to book
    (E) ruler is to line

26. $12\frac{1}{2}\%$ is to $\frac{1}{8}$ as

    (A) decade is to century
    (B) 100% is to 1
    (C) $\frac{6}{10}$ is to $\frac{1}{2}$
    (D) $66\frac{2}{3}\%$ is to $\frac{2}{3}$
    (E) second is to minute

27. Bibliophile is to library as

    (A) dog is to biscuit
    (B) neutron is to scientist
    (C) philatelist is to post office
    (D) machinist is to repair
    (E) infant is to adult

28. Galley is to kitchen as

    (A) fabric is to yarn
    (B) teeth is to stomach
    (C) ship is to house
    (D) box is to package
    (E) roof is to walls

29. Retina is to eye as

    (A) wagon is to car
    (B) chair is to leg
    (C) sun is to earth
    (D) piston is to engine
    (E) spur is to horse

30. Ballet is to choreographer as

    (A) paper is to ream
    (B) people is to elect
    (C) pistol is to trigger
    (D) play is to director
    (E) dove is to peace

Quantitative Mathematics

25 Questions

Directions: Following each problem in this section, there are five suggested answers. Work each problem in your head or in the space provided (there will be space for scratchwork in your test booklet). Then look at the five suggested answers and decide which is best.

1. The average of three numbers is 15. What is two times the sum of the three numbers?

   (A) 6
   (B) 15
   (C) 30
   (D) 45
   (E) 90

2. How many factors does the number 12 have?

   (A) 2
   (B) 3
   (C) 4
   (D) 6
   (E) 8

3. John owns $\frac{1}{3}$ of the CDs in the collection. If there are a total of 120 CDs, how many does John own?

   (A) 20
   (B) 40
   (C) 60
   (D) 120
   (E) 360

4. What is the perimeter of an equilateral triangle, one side of which measures 6 inches?

   (A) 18 inches
   (B) 12 inches
   (C) 6 inches
   (D) 3 inches
   (E) It cannot be determined.

5. Tyler, Sharice, and James want to put their money together in order to buy a $270 radio. If Sharice agrees to pay twice as much as James, and Tyler agrees to pay three times as much as Sharice, how much will Sharice contribute?

   (A) $30
   (B) $60
   (C) $90
   (D) $150
   (E) $180

6. The price of a jacket is reduced in half, and the resulting price is then reduced by 10%. The final price is what percentage of the original price?

   (A) 10%
   (B) 40%
   (C) 45%
   (D) 55%
   (E) 60%

7. In a jar of gumdrops, the ratio of green gumdrops to red gumdrops is 5:3. If only green and red gumdrops are in the jar and the total number of gumdrops is 56, how many green gumdrops are in the jar?

   (A) 5
   (B) 8
   (C) 15
   (D) 28
   (E) 35

8. A stop sign has eight equal sides and a perimeter of 64. What is the length of each individual side?

    (A) 2
    (B) 4
    (C) 8
    (D) 12
    (E) It cannot be determined.

9. Two cardboard boxes have equal volume. The dimensions of one box are $3 \times 8 \times 10$. If the length of the other box is 4 and the width is 6, what is the height of the second box?

    (A) 2
    (B) 5
    (C) 10
    (D) 12
    (E) 16

10. At a fundraiser, 300 people each donated y dollars. In terms of y, what was the total number of dollars donated?

    (A) 300
    (B) $300y$
    (C) $\dfrac{y}{300}$
    (D) $\dfrac{300}{y}$
    (E) $300 + y$

11. If a harvest yields 120 bushels of corn, 40 bushels of wheat, and 80 bushels of soybeans, what percent of the total harvest is corn?

    (A) 25%
    (B) 30%
    (C) 33%
    (D) 40%
    (E) 50%

12. Which of the following is a multiple of 6?

    (A) 1
    (B) 2
    (C) 3
    (D) 9
    (E) 12

13. A 3-foot, 2-inch board is how many times bigger than a 2-foot board?

    (A) 1.5
    (B) 1.6
    (C) 1.7
    (D) $\dfrac{19}{12}$
    (E) $\dfrac{17}{12}$

14. What is the distance between $(-14, -11)$ and $(-20, -7)$ along the line connecting them?

    (A) 5
    (B) 10
    (C) $2\sqrt{13}$
    (D) $4\sqrt{13}$
    (E) 13

15. What is the perimeter of a regular pentagon whose sides measure three units?

    (A) 7.5
    (B) 9
    (C) 12
    (D) 15
    (E) 18

16. What is 60 expressed as the product of its prime factors?

    (A) (15)(6)
    (B) (5)(12)
    (C) (5)(3)(3)(2)
    (D) (4)(5)(3)
    (E) (2)(5)(3)(2)

17. Mike bought 25 shares of Zooko stock at the closing price on Tuesday and sold them at the closing price on Friday. How much money did Mike lose on his investment?

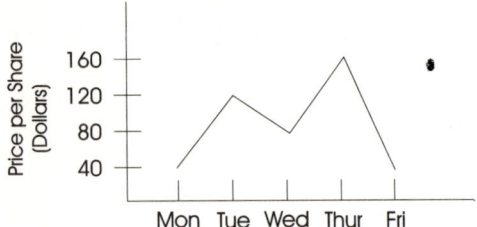

(A) $80
(B) $200
(C) $800
(D) $2,000
(E) $95

18. The hypotenuse of a right triangle is 10 and one leg is 6. Find the length of the other leg of the triangle.

(A) 16
(B) 10
(C) 8
(D) 12
(E) 4

19. Calculate the area of the hexagon.
$OP = 4\sqrt{3}$, $AB = 8$

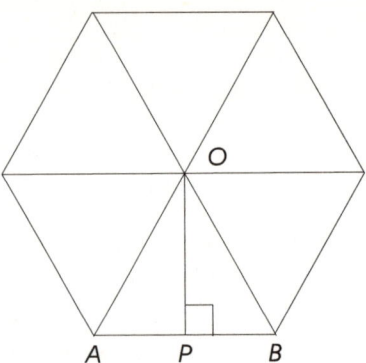

(A) $96\sqrt{3}$
(B) $32\sqrt{3}$
(C) 32
(D) $16\sqrt{3}$
(E) 16

20. If $|3a - 1| = 5$, which of the following is a possible value for a?

(A) -2
(B) -1
(C) 0
(D) 1
(E) 2

21. A coat is on sale for $128 after a discount of 20%. Find the original price.

(A) $102.40
(B) $153.60
(C) $160
(D) $180
(E) $148

22. Rachel worked one Saturday from 7:30 a.m. until 3 p.m. at the rate of $4.65 per hour. How much did she receive?

(A) $19.88
(B) $22.53
(C) $19.00
(D) $22.00
(E) $34.88

23.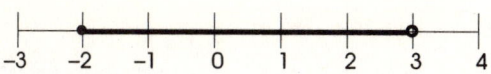

The graph shown above is of which inequality?

(A) $-2 < x < 3$
(B) $-2 \leq x < 3$
(C) $-2 \leq x \leq 3$
(D) $-2 < x \leq 3$
(E) $-2 < x$

24. How many socks would you need to remove from a drawer containing 10 blue socks, 15 black socks, and 5 red socks, to insure that you have at least 2 matching socks?

(A) 3
(B) 4
(C) 16
(D) 17
(E) 28

25. What is the sum of $\dfrac{a}{b}$ and $\dfrac{b}{a}$?

(A) $\dfrac{a+b}{ab}$
(B) $\dfrac{a^2+b^2}{ab}$
(C) $\dfrac{(a+b)^2}{ab}$
(D) $\dfrac{a^2+b^2}{2ab}$
(E) 1

SSAT DIAGNOSTIC TEST

Reading Comprehension

20 Questions

Directions: Read each passage carefully and then answer the questions about it. For each question, decide on the basis of the passage which one of the choices best answers the question.

PASSAGE 1

Line Although the special coloring of moths will hide them from most other insects and birds that want to eat them, it will not protect them from bats, since bats locate their prey
5   by hearing rather than by sight. Bats continually make high-pitched noises that reflect off a moth's body as echoes. These echoes inform the bats of their prey's location, and hunting bats follow these
10 echoes until they find the moth. To protect themselves from bats, some species of moths have developed defenses based on sound. These moths have ears that allow them to hear the sounds the bat makes. If the bat is
15 far enough away, the moth will hear it, but the bat is too far from it to receive the echo from the moth. The moth can then simply swerve out of the bat's path. But if the bat is closer to the moth, the moth is in immediate
20 danger. In order to avoid the bat, it flies wildly, moving in many directions and avoiding any ordered pattern. This tactic tends to confuse the bat. Other species of moths use sound to avoid the bats by
25 producing high-pitched sounds of their own. The many echoes from these sounds make it difficult for the bats to find the moths.

1. According to the passage, some moths escape from bats by

   (A) secreting a substance with a distracting odor.
   (B) making their own high-pitched sounds.
   (C) hiding in small crevices.
   (D) gathering under bright lights.
   (E) flying in circles.

2. Which of the following can be inferred from the passage about insects and birds that eat moths?

   (A) They hunt by sight rather than sound.
   (B) They are confused by the moths' sounds.
   (C) They have no need to protect themselves.
   (D) They fly in circles to find the moths.
   (E) They are often colorful.

3. The sounds bats hear when hunting are

   (A) made by the flapping of the moths' wings.
   (B) echoes of the sounds they make themselves.
   (C) echoes of the sounds made by the moths.
   (D) echoes of the sounds of other bats.
   (E) created by the movement of the air and wind.

4. Moths trying to escape from bats

   (A) always fly in the same direction.
   (B) may not know in which direction to fly.
   (C) do not always use the same strategy.
   (D) fly in an orderly pattern.
   (E) get as far from the bat as they can.

5. According to the passage, bats and some moths are alike because they rely on which of the following to help them survive?

   (A) sight.
   (B) color.
   (C) odor.
   (D) sound.
   (E) taste.

PASSAGE 2

Line   One day, a thirsty fox fell into a well as she was getting a drink of water. She could not find a way to climb back up. After a short time, a thirsty goat came to the edge of the
5   well, and seeing the fox below him, he asked if the water was safe to drink. Thinking quickly, the fox said the water was pure and delicious and suggested that the goat come down to have a drink. The goat
10   immediately jumped into the well. After he had enough to drink, he asked the fox how he could get back up and out of the well. The fox replied, "I have a plan. Put your front legs against the wall, and hold your
15   horns up. I will climb up your back, onto your horns, and then I will jump out of the well. Once I'm out, I'll help you get out." The goat agreed, and the fox quickly got out of the well. The goat called out to her: "Oh
20   Ms. Fox, you said you would help me get out of the well." The fox called down to the goat, "Friend, if you had half as many brains as you have hairs on your chin, you would not have jumped into the well without first
25   thinking about how you would get out."

6. The fox told the goat the water was pure and delicious because

   (A) she had tasted it and knew that it was good.
   (B) she wanted to be kind to the goat.
   (C) she was lonely and wanted company.
   (D) she was afraid the goat would not drink it if she said it was bad.
   (E) she had thought of a plan to get out of the well.

7. The fox's last words suggest that she thinks the goat is

   (A) angry.
   (B) amused.
   (C) unintelligent.
   (D) clumsy.
   (E) uncomfortable.

8. All of the following describes the fox except for which word?

   (A) clever.
   (B) helpful.
   (C) lying.
   (D) inconsiderate.
   (E) selfish.

9. The fox gets out of the well by

   (A) climbing up the walls.
   (B) jumping out.
   (C) using the goat as a ladder.
   (D) calling for help until someone comes.
   (E) using a rope.

10. The best way to state the lesson the fox's last words suggest is:

    (A) think before you act.
    (B) take advantage of opportunities.
    (C) drink before you get too thirsty.
    (D) never trust a fox.
    (E) all goats are foolish.

PASSAGE 3

Line The wealthy hunting societies of Europe at the end of the age of the glaciers did not have their future under their own control. The environment would determine their
5   fate, as it would the fate of the animals. But the humans had an advantage the animals did not. Although people did not notice it, the climate had changed. Summers grew longer and warmer, ice sheets shrank, and
10 glaciers retreated. Because of the changes in climate, plant and animal life changed. The mammoth, rhinoceros, and reindeer disappeared from western Europe, their going perhaps hastened by the human hunters
15 themselves. On what had been open grassland or tundra with dwarf birch and willow trees, great forests spread, stocked with the appropriate forest animals—red deer, aurochs, and wild pigs. Because the
20 great herds of beasts on which they had preyed disappeared, the economic basis of the hunting societies was cut away. But this provided a moment when early humans were able to prove their advantage over the
25 biological specialization of animals: the reindeer found his coat too hot to wear and had to leave; humans merely took their coats off and readjusted their habits.

11. The title that best expresses the idea of this passage is

    (A) Humans Conflict With Their Environment
    (B) Human Adaptation to Climate Change
    (C) Changes in Plant and Animal Life
    (D) Primitive Hunting Tribes
    (E) Extinct Prehistoric Animals

12. From the context of the passage, "auroch" most likely refers to

    (A) the name of one of the hunting societies.
    (B) a type of bird.
    (C) an animal that left Europe.
    (D) an animal that became extinct.
    (E) an animal that survived in Europe.

13. The disappearance of certain animals from western Europe was

    (A) caused mostly by human hunting.
    (B) disastrous to primitive humans.
    (C) the direct result of humans' equipment.
    (D) the immediate result of a more advanced culture.
    (E) a result of changes in climate.

14. The writer apparently believes that a society's future course may be determined by

    (A) economic abundance.
    (B) adapting to changes.
    (C) the ambitions of the people.
    (D) cultural enrichment.
    (E) the clothing worn.

15. In the passage's last sentence, the word "coat" means

    (A) the same thing both times it is used.
    (B) different things to different readers.
    (C) something different each time it is used.
    (D) to cover with a substance.
    (E) a thick layer of fur or hair.

READING COMPREHENSION

PASSAGE 4

Line Although eating too much fat has been shown to be harmful, some fat is essential in the human diet. Fat helps in the absorption of some vitamins, it provides our bodies
5 with insulation, and it is a source of energy. And eating some fat in a meal helps people to feel full for a longer period of time, so they will not want to snack between meals. But not all fat is healthful. There are two
10 kinds of fat, saturated and unsaturated. Saturated fat is the kind of fat that is usually solid at room temperature. It is found in meat and dairy products. This kind of fat is very high in calories, and it raises the blood
15 cholesterol level. High blood cholesterol can clog the arteries, which may lead to heart attacks. There are two types of unsaturated fat. One type, called polyunsaturated, or "essential fatty acid," is found in fish,
20 sunflower seeds, corn oil, and walnuts. Some research suggests that essential fatty acids help to prevent heart disease and aid in healthy brain function and vision. Monounsaturated fat is found in foods like olives,
25 avocados, and peanuts. Diets high in monounsaturated fat can lower cholesterol levels. However, even though some fat is needed, dietary guidelines suggest that no more than 30% of calories in a person's diet
30 should come from fat.

16. According to the passage, essential fatty acids

   (A) can be eaten in unrestricted amounts.
   (B) raise the level of cholesterol in the blood.
   (C) may aid in having good vision.
   (D) lower cholesterol levels.
   (E) are found in peanuts.

17. The best title for this passage is

   (A) The Role of Fat
   (B) Types of Fat
   (C) Foods High in Saturated Fat
   (D) Why Fat is Harmful
   (E) Benefits of Eating Fat

18. Saturated fats could be found in all of the following except

   (A) grilled cheese sandwich.
   (B) tuna fish salad.
   (C) hamburgers and butter.
   (D) a pepperoni pizza.
   (E) sausages and bacon.

19. Monounsaturated fat

   (A) is an essential fatty acid.
   (B) helps to prevent heart disease.
   (C) is found in sunflower seeds and walnuts.
   (D) can lower cholesterol levels.
   (E) is solid at room temperature.

20. According to the passage,

   (A) all fats contain the same amount of calories.
   (B) monounsaturated fat has the smallest number of calories.
   (C) saturated fats are very high in calories.
   (D) calories from fat are always harmful.
   (E) counting calories is not important.

Peterson's: www.petersons.com

EXPLANATORY ANSWERS TO THE SSAT DIAGNOSTIC TEST

VERBAL

1. The correct answer is (A).
2. The correct answer is (E).
3. The correct answer is (D).
4. The correct answer is (B).
5. The correct answer is (D).
6. The correct answer is (A).
7. The correct answer is (A).
8. The correct answer is (B).
9. The correct answer is (C).
10. The correct answer is (E).
11. The correct answer is (C).
12. The correct answer is (A).
13. The correct answer is (E).
14. The correct answer is (B).
15. The correct answer is (E).
16. The correct answer is (B). A song is performed as part of a recital. The relationship is part to whole. An episode is part of a series. Answer (A) is incorrect because an author is not part of a bibliography. The relationship of author to bibliography is item to category. Answer (C) is incorrect because the relationship is leader to group. Answer (D) is incorrect because the relationship of dancer to agile is type to characteristic. Answer (E) is incorrect because the relationship of poetry to prose is similar to item to category. Both are genres of literature.
17. The correct answer is (C). Bald and hirsute are antonyms. Anemic and robust are antonyms. Answers (A) and (E) are incorrect because the words are synonyms. Answers (B) and (D) are incorrect because the words are not specifically related.

18. The correct answer is (C). The relationship is object to its function. When you remove something, you take material out. The same relationship is in answer (C): when you interpolate something you put the material in.

19. The correct answer is (A). Someone who is oblivious lacks awareness. The relationship is word to antonym or opposites. The same relationship is in answer (A): someone who is comatose lacks consciousness.

20. The correct answer is (D). The relationship is word to antonym: when you explain something, you clarify it. The same relationship is in answer (D). When you refine something, you increase its purity.

21. The correct answer is (C). The relationship is object to its function. A poltroon (coward) is by definition pusillanimous (cowardly). An optimist is by definition sanguine (confident).

22. The correct answer is (D). Gold was important to Midas; wisdom was important to Athena. The relationship is worker and creation. Answers (A) and (C) are incorrect because the relationship is item to category. Answer (B) is incorrect because the relationship is synonymous. Answer (E) is incorrect because the relationship is type to characteristic.

23. The correct answer is (E). One who is deaf cannot perceive tone; one who is blind cannot perceive color. This is the analogy of action of object. The other answers cannot be correct: (B) is incorrect because touch and smell are both senses and equal, therefore they cannot parallel "tone is to deaf." By the same token, answer (D) is incorrect because one uses a brush to paint is close to the proper answer; however, the relationship is object to its function. A brush is used to paint.

24. The correct answer is (D). The radius is half the diameter of a given circle. Similarly, 5 is half of 10. This is the analogy of part to whole. There appears to be no relationship with answers (A) and (E). Answers (B) and (C) do have a relationship of sorts, but it is not one-half of the question.

25. The correct answer is (C). An oak grows from an acorn; a tulip grows from a bulb. This is the cause to effect relationship. Notice that in answer (A), the relationship is word to synonym. Both a stable and a barn are shelters for animals. Answer (B) is whole to part. Part of a tree is a branch. Answer (D) also has the relationship of part to whole. Part of a library is the books. Answer (E) has the relationship of object to its function. A ruler will allow you to make a line.

Peterson's: www.petersons.com

26. The correct answer is (D). $12\frac{1}{2}\%$ is equal to $\frac{1}{8}$ as $66\frac{2}{3}\%$ is equal to $\frac{2}{3}$. Both are fractions. The relationship is one of equals or synonyms. Answer (A) indicates a relationship of part to whole; a decade is one-tenth of a century and is therefore incorrect for the relationship being sought; the same is true for answer (E). A second is part of a minute. Answer (B) is incorrect because there is not the relationship of equality that we need for the question. Answer (C) is incorrect because $\frac{6}{10}$ does NOT equal $\frac{1}{2}$. The premise is incorrect.

27. The correct answer is (C). A bibliophile, one who loves books, will spend time in the library. A philatelist, one who collects stamps, will spend time in the post office. The relationship is worker to workplace. Answer (A) is incorrect because the relationship is object to its function. A dog should eat a biscuit. Answers (B) and (D) are both the worker and creation relationship. None of these other answers have the worker to workplace relationship of the question.

28. The correct answer is (C). A galley is a kitchen, but on a ship, not in a house. The relationship is synonymous. Answer (A) is incorrect because it is part to whole. Yarn makes fabric. Answer (B) has no relationship that can fit with the question. Both items are part of the human body, but without the relationship of the question. Answer (D) has the relationship of object to its function: a box makes a package. Answer (E) is incorrect because a roof holds up the walls and is the relationship of object to function.

29. The correct answer is (D). The retina helps the eye function. A piston helps an engine to work. The relationship is cause to effect. Answer (A) is not correct because while both a wagon and a car are modes of transportation, their actual function is totally different. The relationship is item to category. Answer (B) has the relationship of part to whole. A leg is part of the chair. Answer (C) names two celestial objects: the relationship would be item to category. Answer (E) has the relationship of object to its function. One uses a spur to manipulate a horse.

30. The correct answer is (D). A choreographer directs a ballet as a director directs a play. The relationship is worker and creation. Answer (A) is not correct because the relationship is part to whole: 500 pages equal a ream. Answer (B) is worker and creation: the people elect. Answer (C) is part to whole: a trigger is part of a piston. Answer (E) is symbolic: a dove is the sign of peace.

QUANTITATIVE MATHEMATICS

1. The correct answer is (E). If the average of three numbers is 15, then the SUM ÷ 3 = 15. Therefore, the SUM of the three numbers is 15 × 3 = 45. Two times the SUM of 45 is 90.

2. The correct answer is (D). Factors are all the numbers that divide evenly into a number.

    The factors of 12 are:

    1 and 12

    2 and 6

    3 and 4

    which results in a total of 6 factors in all.

3. The correct answer is (B). This is a problem of multiplication by fractions. To find the number of CDs owned by John, multiply the total number by the fraction he owns.

    $\frac{1}{3} \times 120 = 40$

4. The correct answer is (A). An equilateral triangle is made up of three congruent, or equal, sides. To determine the perimeter of a triangle, sum the measure of all three sides.

    6 + 6 + 6 = 18

5. The correct answer is (B). There are three unknown pieces in this question. The contribution made by Tyler (T), the contribution made by Sharice (S), and the contribution made by James (J).

    The total of all contributions is $270, so $T + S + J = 270$.

    Sharice pays twice as much as James: $S = 2J$

    Tyler pays three times what Sharice does: $T = 3S = 6J$ (from previous statement).

    In terms of J, $6J + 2J + J = 270$. Solving for J, $9J = 270$ so $J = 30$ (amount paid by James). Since James pays $30, Sharice pays twice that, or $60.

6. The correct answer is (C). If the jacket originally costs x dollars, when it is reduced in half, it costs $x - .5x$ dollars or simply $.5x$ dollars (original price minus discounted amount). If the new price of $.5x$ is then discounted another 10%, the resulting price is $.5x - .1(.5x)$ which equals $.45x$, or 45% of the original price.

SSAT DIAGNOSTIC TEST

7. The correct answer is (E). Since the ratio of green to red gumdrops is 5:3, there are $5x$ green gumdrops and $3x$ red ones.

    $3x + 5x = 56$
    $8x = 56$
    $x = 7$

    so there are $5(7) = 35$ green gumdrops.

8. The correct answer is (C). The perimeter is equal to the sum of each of the sides. Since all the sides are equal, to determine the length of one side, divide the perimeter by the total number of sides.

    $64 \div 8 = 8$

9. The correct answer is (C). Volume = length × width × height. The volume of both boxes is $3 \times 8 \times 10 = 240$. The volume of the second box is $4 \times 6 \times$ height = 240; therefore, the height of the box is $\frac{240}{4 \times 6} = \frac{240}{24} = 10$.

10. The correct answer is (B). Since each of the 300 attendees donated the same dollar amount, the total amount donated is the product of 300 and y.

11. The correct answer is (E). First, determine the total number of bushels in the harvest. $120 + 40 + 80 = 240$

    To find the percentage of corn, divide the bushels of corn by the total number of bushels.

    $\frac{120}{240} = \frac{1}{2} = 50\%$

12. The correct answer is (E). Multiples result when you multiply a number by an integer. Multiples are always greater than or equal to the original number. 12 is the multiple of 6 in this case because $6 \times 2 = 12$.

13. The correct answer is (D). Convert to common units. Inches are a good choice. The ratio then becomes 38:24, which is 19:12.

14. The correct answer is (C). Use the distance formula (the Pythagorean theorem in disguise).

    The difference in x coordinates is $(-20) - (-14) = -6$. The difference in y coordinates is $(-7) - (-11) = 4$.

    You can use the Pythagorean theorem:

    Distance = $\sqrt{(-6)^2 + (4)^2} = \sqrt{36 + 16} = \sqrt{52} = \sqrt{2 \times 2 \times 13} = 2\sqrt{13}$

15. The correct answer is (D). A pentagon has five sides. A regular pentagon has five congruent sides. To get the perimeter, multiply the length of each side by the number of sides.

$3 \times 5 = 15$

16. The correct answer is (E). To break a number into its prime factors, break it into factors, and break those factors into factors, until you cannot go any further. It doesn't matter what factors you begin with; you will reach the same prime factors.
$60 = 10 \times 6 = 2 \times 5 \times 3 \times 2$. 5, 3, and 2 are prime numbers (they have no factors other than 1 and themselves).

Another way to approach this problem is to rule out the answers that have composite (non-prime) numbers. This rules out (A), (B), and (D). Test the remaining answers by multiplying them out. Only (E) comes to 60.

17. The correct answer is (D). First find the amount Mike paid for the shares.

$\$120 \times 25 = \$3,000$

Then find the amount Mike sold the shares for.

$\$40 \times 25 = \$1,000$

Then subtract. $\$3,000 - \$1,000 = \$2,000$

18. The correct answer is (C). By the Pythagorean theorem:

$a^2 + b^2 = c^2$
$a^2 + 6^2 = 10^2$
$a^2 + 36 = 100$
$\sqrt{a^2} = \sqrt{64}$
$a = 8$

19. The correct answer is (A).

$A = \frac{1}{2}(8)(4\sqrt{3}) = 16\sqrt{3} =$ area of one triangle.

There are six triangles in a hexagon.

$6(16\sqrt{3}) = 96\sqrt{3}$

20. The correct answer is (E).

$$|3a - 1| = 5$$
$$3a - 1 = 5$$
$$3a = 6$$
$$a = 2$$

OR

$$3a - 1 = -5$$
$$3a = -4$$
$$a = -\frac{4}{3}$$

a can equal 2 or $-\frac{4}{3}$

21. The correct answer is (C). Since $128 is 80% of the original price, the base price is

$$B = \frac{P}{R} = \frac{128}{.80} = \$160$$

22. The correct answer is (E). The number of hours from 7:30 a.m. to 3 p.m. totals $7\frac{1}{2}$ hours.

Multiply $7\frac{1}{2}$ or $7.5 \times 4.65 = 34.875 = \$34.88$

23. The correct answer is (B). The line graph with a dark circle on -2 includes -2 and all numbers greater than -2. The open circle on 3 indicates all numbers less than 3. Put together: all numbers greater than or equal to -2 and less than 3:

$$-2 \leq x < 3$$

24. The correct answer is (B). It is possible to draw one of each color before getting a match. Three socks can be drawn without getting a matched pair. But if you've gone this far, the fourth sock drawn must match, as there are only three colors.

You *might* have drawn a pair before this, but you are not assured of having done so.

25. The correct answer is (B). Get common denominators to add fractions. Multiply $\frac{a}{b}$ by $\frac{a}{a}$ getting $\frac{a^2}{ab}$.

Multiply $\frac{b}{a}$ by $\frac{b}{b}$ getting $\frac{b^2}{ab}$. Then add the fractions by adding the numerators.

READING COMPREHENSION

Passage 1

1. The correct answer is (B). (A), (C), and (D) provide information not mentioned in the passage. (E) is incorrect because the passage says moths swerve away or fly wildly; it does not say they fly in circles.

2. The correct answer is (A). (B) is incorrect because the passage does not say that insects and birds hear the moths' sounds. (C) and (D) are not stated in the passage, and nothing in the passage implies them. The insects and birds are not described, so answer (E) is incorrect.

3. The correct answer is (B). While moths may flap their wings, that is not what the bats hear, and while some moths make sounds, it is the echoes, not the sounds, that bats hear. So (A) and (D) are incorrect. (C) is wrong because the passage states specifically that the bats hear the echoes of their own high-pitched noises. The passage does not mention air or wind sounds, so (E) is incorrect.

4. The correct answer is (C). The passage describes two ways that moths fly away from bats: they swerve or they fly in many directions. Each of the other answers names only one way in which the moths try to escape.

5. The correct answer is (D). (A) and (B) refer to how some moths are protected from insects and birds. Nothing in the passage discusses how scent or taste is used by bats or moths, so (C) and (E) are incorrect.

Passage 2

6. The correct answer is (E). While (A) may be a true statement, it is not the reason she tells this to the goat. (B), (C), and (D) are not suggested by the content of the passage.

7. The correct answer is (C). While the goat may be angry (A), clumsy (D), or uncomfortable (E), the fox's words are about her opinion of the goat, not the goat's feelings. (B) is not consistent with the goat's situation or the fox's opinion of him.

8. The correct answer is (B). While the fox may seem to be helping the goat, she only does this to trick him so that she can get out of the well.

9. The correct answer is (C). Nothing in the passage suggests (D) or (E). And while the fox does climb, (A), she climbs up the goat's back, not up the walls. (B) is incorrect because the fox could not have jumped out without using the goat as a ladder.

Passage 3

10. The correct answer is (A). (D) and (E) are incorrect because while they may be inferred from the story, they are not the lessons implied by the fox's words. (C) is incorrect because it is too specific. The problem was not thirst, but acting without thinking. (B) is wrong because it implies the opposite of what the goat did when he jumped into the well.

11. The correct answer is (B). The passage states humans adapted to the climate change. (C), (D), and (E) describe only part of the content of the passage. (A) is incorrect because the passage is not about a conflict.

12. The correct answer is (E). Because "auroch" is included in a list of "appropriate forest animals" that "stocked" the forest, it is a surviving animal. The other answers ignore this information.

13. The correct answer is (E). Although the passages states the animals' disappearance was "perhaps hastened" by hunting, hunting is not given as the major cause, so (A) is incorrect. The conclusion of the passage contradicts (B). The contents of (C) and (D) do not appear in the passage.

14. The correct answer is (B). While (A), (C), and (D) may determine what happens to a society, these are not discussed in the passage. (E) is incorrect because the reference to coats in the passage's last sentence is an adaptation, not a cause.

15. The correct answer is (C). The first time it is used, "coat" refers to an animal's fur or hide; the second time it is used, it refers to an article of clothing worn by a person. Thus, (A) and (E) are incorrect. (D) is incorrect because it refers to an action, not an object. (B) is incorrect because the sentence does not require individual interpretation.

Passage 4

16. The correct answer is (C). (A) is contradicted by the last sentence in the passage. (B) is about saturated fat. (D) and (E) apply to monounsaturated fat according to the passage.

17. The correct answer is (A). The other answers describe only part of the passage's content. (A) is the most general, and it describes all of the content of the passage.

18. The correct answer is (B). The passage says saturated fat is found in meat and dairy products. All of the answers except (B) mention a meat or a dairy product.

19. The correct answer is (D). According to the passages, (A), (B), and (C) are true of polyunsaturated fat, and (E) is true of saturated fat.

20. The correct answer is (C). The passage contradicts (A). The passage does not state whether (B) is a fact. (D) is contradicted by the first three sentences of the passage, and (E) is contradicted by the last sentence of the passage.

ISEE Diagnostic Test

Verbal Ability 74
Quantitative Ability 76
Reading Comprehension. 78
Mathematics Achievement 82
Writing the Essay. 85

**Explanatory Answers to the
ISEE Diagnostic Test**. 88
   Verbal Ability. 88
   Quantitative Ability. 90
   Reading Comprehension 93
   Mathematics Achievement. 95

Verbal Ability

20 Questions

DIRECTIONS: Each question is made up of a word in capital letters followed by four choices. You should circle the one word that is most nearly the same in meaning as the word in capital letters.

1. DISCREDIT:
   - (A) disengage
   - (B) flaunt
   - (C) disbelieve
   - (D) please

2. SUCCULENT:
   - (A) crucial
   - (B) tasty
   - (C) clear
   - (D) wicked

3. EXPLICIT:
   - (A) definite
   - (B) rational
   - (C) vital
   - (D) inventive

4. DELETE:
   - (A) display
   - (B) descend
   - (C) invest
   - (D) remove

5. INTEGRATE:
   - (A) merge into a whole
   - (B) repeat endlessly
   - (C) prove false
   - (D) remain untouched

6. AMNESTY:
   - (A) loss of memory
   - (B) comprehensive pardon
   - (C) long angry speech
   - (D) shortage of supplies

7. ASSET:
   - (A) insult
   - (B) loss
   - (C) agreement
   - (D) benefit

8. SERENITY:
   - (A) sympathy
   - (B) self-confidence
   - (C) peacefulness
   - (D) sweetness

9. CONFOUND:
   - (A) confuse
   - (B) contain
   - (C) eliminate
   - (D) reproduce

10. BLIGHT:
    - (A) satisfy
    - (B) strengthen
    - (C) subtract
    - (D) damage

DIRECTIONS: Each question below is made up of a sentence with one or two blanks. The sentences with one blank indicate that one word is missing. The sentences with two blanks indicate that two words are missing. Each sentence is followed by four choices. You should circle the one word or pair of words that will best complete the meaning of the sentence as a whole.

11. No one anticipated that if the king should _____ his throne there would be such _____ results throughout the country.

    (A) dovetail . . adventurous
    (B) abdicate . . calamitous
    (C) inverse . . venerable
    (D) abut . . incredulous

12. The surgeon was well-respected for her _____, unlike her colleague who was known for his clumsiness.

    (A) philanthropy
    (B) arrogance
    (C) dexterity
    (D) pallor

13. Although she pleaded that she loved him, his _____ made him doubt her _____.

    (A) skepticism . . verity
    (B) flippancy . . enmity
    (C) stoicism . . trepidation
    (D) drudgery . . fabrication

14. The judge stopped the trial when he declared that, "Since the petition has been filed _____ it is _____."

    (A) belatedly . . repugnant
    (B) erroneously . . fallacious
    (C) despicably . . sprightly
    (D) respectively . . insightful

15. The principal told the parents that their son was _____, and, therefore, he behaved in a _____ manner.

    (A) incognito . . pert
    (B) tractable . . vigilant
    (C) curt . . adept
    (D) pugnacious . . belligerent

16. After the legal _____, the loser of the case was required to pay _____.

    (A) precursor . . gallantry
    (B) confrontation . . reparation
    (C) parable . . prospectus
    (D) affray . . jurisdiction

17. Upset by the treachery of his general, the king planned his _____ with great rancor.

    (A) accord
    (B) foreboding
    (C) vengeance
    (D) repercussion

18. During the performance of the play, the audience cheered, applauded, and gave several standing ovations, a true _____ of _____.

    (A) embargo . . plunder
    (B) fiasco . . negation
    (C) sequel . . tedium
    (D) potpourri . . acclamation

19. After reading his student's research paper, the teacher was shocked that his student had no scruples about _____ from his resources.

    (A) terminating
    (B) pilfering
    (C) defraying
    (D) embezzling

20. After being convicted of shoplifting, the _____ pleaded with the judge to be _____.

    (A) rubble . . disarming
    (B) loiterer . . churlish
    (C) envoy . . brazen
    (D) brigand . . lenient

ISEE DIAGNOSTIC TEST

QUANTITATIVE ABILITY — 20 QUESTIONS

DIRECTIONS: Any figures that accompany questions in this section may be assumed to be drawn as accurately as possible EXCEPT when it is stated that a particular figure is not drawn to scale. Letters such as x, y, and n stand for real numbers.

For Questions 1–10, work each in your head or on the space available on these pages. Then select the correct answer.

1. Rounded to the nearest tenth, 46.97 would equal
   - (A) 46.0
   - (B) 46.10
   - (C) 46.9
   - (D) 47.0

2. $2^3 + 5^2 =$
   - (A) 16
   - (B) 29
   - (C) 33
   - (D) 200

3. From a work force of 500,000 employed last year, 8% of the employees had to be fired. How many were dismissed at that time?
   - (A) 100,000
   - (B) 40,000
   - (C) 30,000
   - (D) 8,000

4. If $3a - 5 = 7$, then $a =$
   - (A) -4
   - (B) 4
   - (C) $-\dfrac{2}{3}$
   - (D) $\dfrac{2}{3}$

5. What is .03 expressed as a percent?
   - (A) .0003%
   - (B) 3%
   - (C) .3%
   - (D) .03%

6.

   What percent of the entire figure is shaded?
   - (A) $\dfrac{1}{4}\%$
   - (B) 40%
   - (C) 25%
   - (D) 50%

QUANTITATIVE ABILITY

7. If the fractions

   $$\frac{x+y}{3}$$

   and

   $$\frac{x-y}{4}$$

   are added, the result is:

   (A) $\frac{7x+y}{12}$

   (B) $\frac{2x}{7}$

   (C) $\frac{7x-y}{12}$

   (D) $\frac{5x+4y}{12}$

8. If 35% of a number is 70, what is the number?

   (A) 24.5
   (B) 200
   (C) 50
   (D) 65

9. The solution set of the inequality $3x - 4 > 8$ is:

   (A) $x > 4$
   (B) $x < 4$
   (C) $x > \frac{4}{3}$
   (D) $x < -\frac{4}{3}$

10. The circumference of a circle whose diameter is 7 inches is approximately:

    (A) 22 inches
    (B) 28 inches
    (C) 38 inches
    (D) 154 inches

Directions: For Questions 11–20 note the given information, if any, and then compare the quantity in Column A to the quantity in Column B. Next to the number of each question, write

   A   if the quantity in Column A is greater
   B   if the quantity in Column B is greater
   C   if the two quantities are equal
   D   if the relationship cannot be determined from the information given

	Column A	Column B
11.	$.025 \times 1,000$	250
12.	$\frac{4}{9}$	44%
13.	$\sqrt{106}$	11

14.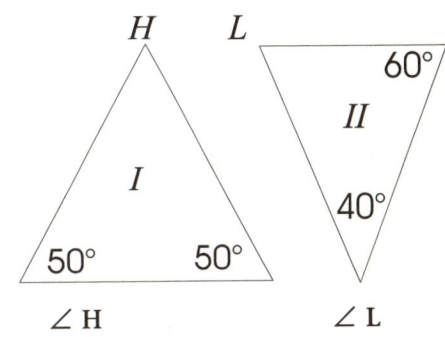

	Column A	Column B
	∠H	∠L
15.	$(12 + 8) \div 4$	$12 + 8 \div 4$
16.	Average of 0.3, −0.8, −0.2, +0.2, and 0.0	0.1
17.	54 sq. ft.	648 sq. in.
18.	$p < 0, q > 0$	
	pq	0
19.	$10b - 17 = 13$ $9z - 27 = 0$	
	b	z
20.	The radius of a circle when the circumference is 9π	The radius of a circle when the area is 25π

Peterson's: www.petersons.com

Reading Comprehension

16 Questions

Directions: Each passage below is followed by questions based on its content. Answer the questions following a passage on the basis of what is *stated* or *implied* in that passage.

Passage 1

Although most people go through life without ever discovering that there is a subject called "aesthetics," few would find life bearable without some sort of primitive aesthetic enjoyment—the sight of a loved face, the taste of a good meal, or the feel of a comfortable resting place. As civilized beings, we might find it equally unbearable to live in a world, such as that described in George Orwell's *1984*, devoid of the aesthetic pleasures derivable from art. Fortunately, our world still contains an almost infinite variety of natural and created phenomena from which we can derive aesthetic pleasure. Most people usually take these phenomena and the pleasures associated with them for granted. Those who do not take them for granted, but who seek to understand their nature and value, are engaged in the task (whether they know it or not) that was initiated by Socrates and Plato more than two thousand years ago and that has kept aesthetics ever since an ongoing concern.

But is the task really meaningful? Is it worth the effort? Can its goal ever be attained? There are critics of aesthetics who would without hesitation answer "No!" Some of these critics hold that aesthetic experience is ineffable, completely beyond the reach of rational description and analysis, and that consequently aesthetics as the theoretical study of this experience is impossible. Others claim that aesthetics must be by its nature such an abstract form of speculation that it can have little or nothing to do with real art and with "the blood and guts" of creative endeavor. Still others are afraid to study aesthetics for fear that it might "clog up the springs of creativity" with its obscure ideas about art and beauty. Among these are some artists who would as soon have a lobotomy as take a course in aesthetics, and even a book on the subject is to them, in William James's phrase, an "abomination of desolation." Aesthetics has also been criticized by poets for being too unfeeling and critical, by art critics for being too general and ill-informed, by psychologists for being immoral, by economists for being useless, by politicians for being undemocratic, by philosophers for being dreary, desolate, and dull, and by students for being "anesthetics in disguise."

1. In the context of the passage, the word ineffable most likely means:

   (A) indescribable
   (B) intellectual
   (C) ineffective
   (D) inescapable

2. According to the passage, the study of aesthetics was begun by:

   (A) psychologists
   (B) William James
   (C) Socrates and Plato
   (D) Dr. Samuel Jackson

3. The primary purpose of the second paragraph is to:

   (A) specifically criticize aesthetics
   (B) describe the criticisms of aesthetics
   (C) argue that aesthetics is unimportant
   (D) discuss the value of aesthetics

4. According to the passage, poets criticize aesthetics for:

   (A) being immoral
   (B) being unfeeling
   (C) being scientific
   (D) being useless

Passage 2

Line   We lived in a small town in Monmouthshire, at the head of one of the coal valleys. Unemployment was endemic there, and enforced leisure gave rise to protracted
5   bouts of philosophy and politics. Most men leaned toward politics, since it gave an appearance of energy and deceived some people into believing they possessed power and influence. It was, if you like, political
10   theory, imaginative and vituperative. The hills about our town were full of men giving their views an airing; eloquence was commonplace.
            True power lay in the hands of a small
15   group—the aldermen and councilors of the town. To a man, they sold insurance and were prosperous. This was because they ran the municipal transport, the public parks and gardens, the collection of taxes, the
20   whole organization of local government in the town and its surrounding villages. They hired and fired, dispensed and took away. They were so corrupt that the Mafia never got a toehold among us. Those Italian boys
25   would have starved.
            In order to get anywhere in our town you had to buy insurance. When teachers, for example, got their salaries at the end of the month, most of them paid heavy
30   insurance. The remainder of the teachers were the sons and daughters of councilors.

5. In the context of the passage, the word protracted (sentence 2) means:

   (A) circular
   (B) lengthy
   (C) complicated
   (D) unintelligible

6. In the context of the passage, the statement "those Italian boys would have starved" (end of paragraph 2) means:

   (A) the townspeople were prejudiced against other ethnic groups
   (B) there was no work in town for the Italians either
   (C) the Italians were not corrupt like the town councilors
   (D) organized crime would not have been able to prosper in the town

7. The discussion of "political theory" in paragraph 1:

   (A) serves as a contrast to the "true power" described in paragraph 2
   (B) provides the setting for the confrontation that occurs later
   (C) prepares the reader for the eloquent political discussion that follows
   (D) explains the townspeople's fascination with the town hall

8. According to the passage, the powerful people in town all:

   (A) sell insurance
   (B) smoke cigars
   (C) teach school
   (D) own antiques

Passage 3

Line A colloid is larger than a molecule but small enough to be "suspended" in a solvent. It is a particle having dimensions between 1 micron and 1 millimicron. A micron is
5 one-millionth of a meter. A millimicron, or nanometer, is one-billionth of a meter. Such a particle cannot be seen with a microscope, but when carried in a solution, it will not diffuse through a membrane made from
10 parchment paper. In contrast, salt molecules or sugar molecules will diffuse. A colloid may consist of grains of a solid, bubbles of a gas, or droplets of a liquid dispersed in three kinds of mediums: (1) sols: solid colloids in a
15 liquid or a gas in a liquid; (2) gels: oblong shaped colloids forming a branched structure in a liquid; (3) emulsions: minute droplets of a liquid dispersed in a second liquid.
20   Colloids have a random motion (they zigzag) because of collisions with other molecules. They are stable while carrying the same electrical charge, which causes them to repel each other and literally
25 disperse themselves in a solvent or gaseous medium. (This phenomenon is known as Brownian motion.) Colloids will provide a path for a sharp beam of light, but may otherwise reflect normal light as a color.
30 (This is known as the Tyndell effect.) They are capable of absorbing themselves on solid surfaces.

9. A nanometer is:

    (A) larger than a millimicron
    (B) smaller than a millimicron
    (C) larger than a micron
    (D) smaller than a micron

10. A salt molecule is:

    (A) larger than a colloid
    (B) smaller than a colloid
    (C) heavier than a colloid
    (D) lighter than a colloid

11. Colloids are stable when:

    (A) they have the same electrical charge
    (B) they are sols
    (C) they are gels
    (D) they zigzag

12. The Tyndell effect deals with colloid:

    (A) size
    (B) reflection of light
    (C) motion
    (D) shape

Passage 4

Ride a wild horse
with purple wings
striped yellow and black
except his head
Which must be red.

Ride a wild horse
against the sky
hold tight to his wings . . .
Before you die
Whatever else you leave undone,
Once, ride a wild horse
Into the sun.

13. This poem best expresses the power of:

    (A) the imagination
    (B) wild horses
    (C) mythological creatures
    (D) nature

14. This poem primarily uses which one of the following literary techniques?

    (A) rhythm
    (B) assonance
    (C) irony
    (D) hyperbole

15. The poet's use of diction suggests the audience is:

    (A) old people
    (B) young people
    (C) women
    (D) cowboys

16. The best title of the poem is:

    (A) Ride a Wild Horse
    (B) Horses of the Sun
    (C) A Horse of a Different Color
    (D) The Last Round-Up

ISEE DIAGNOSTIC TEST

MATHEMATICS ACHIEVEMENT — 25 QUESTIONS

DIRECTIONS: Each question is followed by four suggested answers. Read each question and then decide which of the four suggested answers is best.

1. How many factors does the number 20 have?

   (A) 6
   (B) 4
   (C) 3
   (D) 2

2. $2^3 + 5^2 =$

   (A) 16,807
   (B) 200
   (C) 33
   (D) 16

3. Mary's investment of $3,500 increased over the course of a year to $5,075. What was the percent increase?

   (A) 31%
   (B) 131%
   (C) 69%
   (D) 45%

4. What is the area of an equilateral triangle, one side of which measures 4 units?

   (A) 16
   (B) $4\sqrt{5}$
   (C) $4\sqrt{3}$
   (D) 12

5. What is the perimeter of an equilateral triangle, one side of which measures 15 inches?

   (A) 15 inches
   (B) 35 inches
   (C) 45 inches
   (D) 225 inches

6. The price of a dining room set is reduced by 10% and then goes on clearance for half of the resulting price. The final price is what percentage of the original price?

   (A) 40
   (B) 45
   (C) 55
   (D) 60

7. In a jar of beads, the ratio of green beads to red beads is 5:3. If only green and red beads are in the jar and the total number of beads is 56, how many red beads are in the jar?

   (A) 28
   (B) 21
   (C) 15
   (D) 8

8. Evaluate $3x^2 - 2x - 1$ when x is equal to -2.

   (A) 15
   (B) -15
   (C) -17
   (D) -7

9. On the following graph, what is the percent increase from the lowest point to the highest point?

   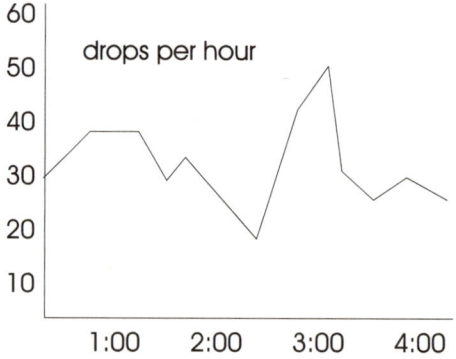

   (A) 60%
   (B) 150%
   (C) 250%
   (D) 300%

10. Which line is parallel to the line $y = 4x - 3$?
    (A) $y = 3x - 4$
    (B) $y + 4x = 3$
    (C) $2y - 8x = -1$
    (D) $x = 4y - 3$

11. Two cardboard boxes have equal volume. The dimensions of one box are $6 \times 8 \times 10$. If the length of the other box is 4 and the width is 6, what is the height of the second box?
    (A) 20
    (B) 3
    (C) 10
    (D) 24

12. At The Wee Little Clubhouse, each of the 12 members donated d dollars to the dues fund. In terms of d, what was the total number of dollars donated?
    (A) 12
    (B) $12d$
    (C) $\dfrac{d}{12}$
    (D) $\dfrac{12}{d}$

13. If a cake mix calls for 2.5 cups of sugar, 4 cups of flour, and 1.5 cups of melted butter, what percent of the recipe calls for flour?
    (A) 31.25%
    (B) 40%
    (C) 50%
    (D) 57%

14. What is the perimeter of a regular nonagon whose sides measure three units?
    (A) 39
    (B) 9
    (C) 12
    (D) 27

15. The hypotenuse of a right triangle is 13 and one leg is 12. Find the length of the other leg of the triangle.
    (A) 1
    (B) 5
    (C) 12
    (D) 25

16. Which number is not a factor of $6 \times 7 \times 12 \times 13 \times 2$?
    (A) 30
    (B) 21
    (C) 39
    (D) 48

17. $(-3)^2 - 4(-3) =$
    (A) 3
    (B) −15
    (C) 108
    (D) 21

18. If $\dfrac{2}{c} = \dfrac{6}{9}$, find the value of c.
    (A) 3
    (B) 2
    (C) 9
    (D) 18

19. If $|2a - 1| = 5$, which of the following is a possible value for a?
    (A) −2
    (B) −1
    (C) 0
    (D) None are possible values.

20. Solve for x: $.02x + .12 = .20$
    (A) 3
    (B) −1
    (C) 4
    (D) 2

21. $|5x - 3| > 7$ is equivalent to:

(A) $-\frac{4}{5} < x < 2$

(B) $-2 < x < \frac{4}{5}$

(C) $\frac{4}{5} < x < 2$

(D) $x > 2$ or $x < -\frac{4}{5}$

22.

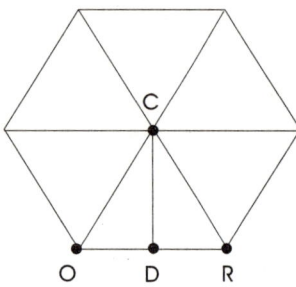

Calculate the area of the hexagon. $OR = 8\sqrt{3}$, $CD = 4$

(A) $96\sqrt{3}$

(B) $32\sqrt{3}$

(C) 32

(D) $16\sqrt{3}$

23. A microwave is on sale for $158 after a discount of 30%. Find the approximate original price.

(A) $205.40
(B) $110.60
(C) $225.70
(D) $268.60

24. Rachel worked one weekend from 9:00 a.m. until 4:30 p.m. at the rate of $9.25 per hour. How much did she receive for both days?

(A) $69.38
(B) $104.06
(C) $138.75
(D) $277.52

25. If $|3a + 1| = 25$, which of the following is a possible value for a?

(A) -8

(B) $-\frac{26}{3}$

(C) $\frac{13}{3}$

(D) 9

WRITING THE ESSAY

Directions: Using two sheets of lined theme paper, plan and write an essay on the topic assigned below. DO NOT WRITE ON ANOTHER TOPIC. AN ESSAY ON ANOTHER TOPIC IS NOT ACCEPTABLE. You have 30 minutes for this section.

There is a saying in Japan that "the nail that sticks out gets hit on the head."

Prompt: Write an essay giving your view of this saying. Do you think that this is valid advice for people? Is it safer to keep a low profile in life? What would be the result of not following this advice? Support your opinion with specific examples from history, current affairs, or personal observations.

ISEE DIAGNOSTIC TEST

Name: _____

Write your essay here.

# WRITING THE ESSAY

EXPLANATORY ANSWERS TO THE ISEE DIAGNOSTIC TEST

VERBAL ABILITY

1. The correct answer is (C).
2. The correct answer is (B).
3. The correct answer is (A).
4. The correct answer is (D).
5. The correct answer is (A).
6. The correct answer is (B).
7. The correct answer is (D).
8. The correct answer is (C).
9. The correct answer is (A).
10. The correct answer is (D).
11. The correct answer is (B). The clue is that *one action resulted in the other*. The word *king* is your trigger. The first word would be "something that a king would do regarding his throne." That eliminates answers (C) and (D). The second word is the "reaction of his subjects to his action." This would eliminate answer (A).
12. The correct answer is (C). The clue is the word *unlike*; it tells you that the words will be opposites. The trigger word is *surgeon*. The missing word is a "quality for which a surgeon would be admired." This eliminates answers (B) and (D). The opposite of *clumsiness* is *dexterity*, which eliminates answer (A).
13. The correct answer is (A). The clue is the word *although*; it tells you that the words will be opposites. The trigger word is *doubt*. He had one quality that made him doubt her love. That eliminates answers (B), (C), and (D). The clue for the second word is that it is "what he doubts about her."
14. The correct answer is (B). The clue is that *one action resulted in the other*. The trigger word is *judge*. The first word would be a "procedural error that would come before a judge." That eliminates answers (C) and (D). The second word would be the "determination the judge would make regarding that error." That would eliminate answer (A).

15. **The correct answer is (D).** The clue is in the words *principal* and *the parents;* the trigger word is *told*. The principal most likely would be having a conference with the parents to "tell them something negative about their son." That is the meaning of the first word. This would eliminate answers (A) and (B). The meaning of the second word is that the "son's behavior is a result of this negative quality; therefore, it is a negative behavior." This would eliminate answer (C).

16. **The correct answer is (B).** The clue for the first word is in the word *loser*. A word that reflects the notion of winning and losing is "contest." This eliminates answers (A) and (C). The trigger for the second word is *pay*. In court "contests," the loser often has to pay "damages" to the winner, as in the word *reparation*. This would eliminate answer (D).

17. **The correct answer is (C).** The clue word is *treachery,* and the trigger word is *planned*. The missing word will be a "reaction, on the part of the king, to treachery." This eliminates answers (A) and (B). The word *repercussion* in answer (D) implies a consequence of an action, but in the context of this sentence, it is just poor grammar. This eliminates answer (D).

18. **The correct answer is (D).** The clue for the first word is the series of words, "cheered, applauded, and gave several standing ovations." The first word would be a "mixture" or "group." The clue for the second word is "kinds of commendation" or "adulation." This eliminates all but answer (D).

19. **The correct answer is (B).** The clue is in the words "after reading his student's research paper." A teacher would look to see if a student "plagiarized" any of the resources. This would eliminate answers (A) and (C). The word *embezzling* in answer (D) is related to stealing. However, the clue from the word *scruples* would be that the student has "no conscience" about using someone else's work as his or her own. That would eliminate answer (D).

20. **The correct answer is (D).** The clue is *shoplifting*. The first word would describe someone who is "criminal." This eliminates answers (A) and (C). The trigger for the second word is *pleaded*. The second word would describe what a criminal would beg for from a judge, a quality like "mercy." This would eliminate answer (B).

QUANTITATIVE ABILITY

1. The correct answer is (D). Begin by writing down as many digits of the given decimal number as required and drop the other digits. Then, starting from the left and going to the right, if the first digit dropped is 4 or less, the number obtained is correct as is. If the first digit dropped is 5 or more, increase by one the last digit in the number as written. Thus,

   46.97 is 46.9 to the nearest tenth. Since we dropped a 7, and 7 > 5, increase the tenths digits by 1.

   $46.9 + .1 = 47.0$

2. The correct answer is (C). First calculate powers, then add.

   $2^3 = 2 \times 2 \times 2 = 8$
   $5^2 = 5 \times 5 = 25$
   $8 + 25 = 33$

3. The correct answer is (B). The word "of" typically indicates multiplication in a percent problem. 8% = .08.

   $500,000 \times .08 = 40,000$ dismissed

4. The correct answer is (B). Begin by adding 5 to both sides of the equation.

   $3a - 5 = 7$
   $+ 5 \quad +5$
   $\overline{3a \quad\quad = 12}$

   Then, divide both sides by 3.

   $\frac{3a}{3} = \frac{12}{3}$

   $a = 4$

5. The correct answer is (B). To convert a decimal to a percent, multiply the decimal by 100

   $.03 \times 100 = 3.00 = 3\%$

6. The correct answer is (C). The total number of triangles is 16; the total number of shaded triangles is 4.

   Ratio of $\frac{\text{shaded}}{\text{total}} = \frac{4}{16} = \frac{1}{4} = 25\%$.

EXPLANATORY ANSWERS TO THE ISEE DIAGNOSTIC TEST

7. The correct answer is (A). The least common denominator of the two fractions is 12.

$$\frac{x+y}{3} = \frac{4x+4y}{12} \qquad \frac{x-y}{4} = \frac{3x-3y}{12}$$

Now, combine like terms in the numerator:

$$\frac{4x+4y+3x-3y}{12} = \frac{7x+y}{12}$$

8. The correct answer is (B). 35% of $N = 70$. Rewrite 35% as .35

$$.35 \times N = 70$$

Divide both sides by .35

$$N = 70 \div .35 = 200$$

9. The correct answer is (A). $3x - 4 > 8$

$$3x > 8 + 4$$
$$3x > 12$$
$$x > 4$$

10. The correct answer is (A). The formula for the circumference of a circle is $C = \pi D$.

Thus, $C = \pi(7) \approx (3.14)(7) = 21.98$, which is almost 22.

11. The correct answer is (B). $.025 \times 1,000 = 25$, which is less than 250.

12. The correct answer is (A). Begin by changing $\frac{4}{9}$ into a decimal by dividing 9 into 4. The result of this division is .444444.... To write this decimal as a percent, move the decimal point two places to the right to obtain 44.4444...%. This percent is clearly larger than 44%.

13. The correct answer is (B). $\sqrt{106}$ is between the integers 10 and 11. That is, $10 < \sqrt{106} < 11$, since $\sqrt{100} < \sqrt{106} < \sqrt{121}$

14. The correct answer is (C). The sum of the angles in a triangle is equal to 180°. Therefore,

$$\angle H + 50° + 50° = 180°$$
$$\angle H + 100° = 180°, \quad \text{which means that}$$
$$\angle H = 80°. \quad \text{Similarly,}$$
$$\angle L + 40° + 60° = 180°$$
$$\angle L + 100° = 180°, \quad \text{so that}$$
$$\angle L = 80°$$

Peterson's: www.petersons.com

15. The correct answer is (B). In Column A, according to the order of operations, simplify within parentheses first:

    $(12 + 8) \div 4 = 20 \div 4 = 5$

    In Column B, according to the order of operations, divide before adding:

    $12 + 8 \div 4 = 12 + 2 = 14$

16. The correct answer is (B). To find the average, we begin by finding the sum of the five numbers in Column A. The easiest way to do this is to add the positive numbers, then the negative numbers, then find the sum of the results.

    $(+0.3) + (0.2) + (0.0) = +0.5$
    $(-0.2) + (-0.8) = -1.0$

    Thus, the total of the five numbers is

    $(+0.5) + (-1.0) = -0.5$

    To find the average, we divide this number by 5.
    $-0.5 \div 5 = -0.1$.

    Thus, the entry in Column B is larger.

17. The correct answer is (A). Since 1 sq. ft. is 12 in. × 12 in. = 144 sq. in., 54 sq. ft. is 54 × 144 = 7776 sq. in.

18. The correct answer is (B). Since p is negative and q is positive, the product pq is negative. The number 0 is larger than any negative number.

19. The correct answer is (C). We must use the given information to solve for b and z.

    $10b - 17 = 13$ Add 17 to both sides
    $10b = 30$ Divide by 10
    $b = 3$. Similarly,
    $9z - 27 = 0$ Add 27 to both sides
    $9z = 27$ Divide by 9
    $z = 3$

20. The correct answer is (B). The formula for the circumference of a circle is $C = \pi D$. Thus, if the circumference of a circle is 9π, the diameter is 9 and the radius is 4.5.

    The formula for the area of a circle is $A = \pi r^2$. Thus, if the area is 25π, the radius is 5.

READING COMPREHENSION

Passage 1

1. The correct answer is (A). (B) is an unlikely answer, since the fact that something is intellectual would not make "the theoretical study of (aesthetic pleasure) . . . impossible" (sentence 4). (C) and (D) are unlikely for the same reason. Note that right after the author first uses the word *ineffable,* he includes an explanation of what it means: *completely beyond the reach of rational description and analysis;* thus, *indescribable* is the correct answer.

2. The correct answer is (C). Although (A), (B), and (D) are all people listed in the passage, the last sentence of paragraph 1 notes that those who study aesthetics "are engaged in the task . . . initiated by Socrates and Plato more than two thousand years ago."

3. The correct answer is (B). (D) is unlikely since the fourth sentence of paragraph 2 begins, "There are critics of aesthetics who . . . " and then lists the complaints of critics. Although (C) is a more likely answer, the author is careful to note that these negative opinions about aesthetics are other people's opinions rather than his own opinion. (A), though another likely possibility, is also incorrect—again, because the author is not criticizing aesthetics but describing the criticisms of other people, the correct answer is (B).

4. The correct answer is (B). (A), (C), and (D) are all listed as criticisms of aesthetics in the passage, but the last sentence of paragraph 2 notes that "poets (criticize aesthetics) for being . . . unfeeling."

Passage 2

5. The correct answer is (B). Choice (A) may seem like a possibility because of the word *protracted;* however, it is a less likely answer based on the context. (C) and (D), similarly, are less likely based on context. Men who are unemployed, with nothing to fill their time, are most likely to engage in lengthy discussions to pass the time.

6. The correct answer is (D). (A) is incorrect because there is no suggestion of prejudice in the passage. In (B) and (C), since paragraph 2 mentions the Mafia, the implication is that the Italians being discussed are also corrupt and that they would not be seeking regular employment. The line suggests that since the town councilors are so corrupt, no other corrupt group would be able to operate in the town. Thus, the correct answer is (D).

7. The correct answer is (A). (C) and (D) do not relate to the passage: the discussion that follows is not a political discussion, and the passage does not suggest that the townspeople are fascinated with the town hall. Although (B) is accurate, it is too general a description of the usual function of opening paragraphs in fiction. Note that sentence 3 in paragraph 1 states that the discussions of political theory "deceived some people into believing they possessed power and influence;" paragraph 2, in contrast, opens with the words "True power," line 14.

8. The correct answer is (A). Although many of the powerful people may have smoked cigars (B) and owned antiques (D), the passage does not mention this as a characteristic of all the powerful people in the town. (C) is incorrect because teachers are hired by the powerful people; they are not powerful people themselves. (A) is correct because paragraph 2 states that the powerful people in town "sold insurance."

Passage 3

9. The correct answer is (D). A nanometer is equal to a millimicron, which is one billionth of a meter. A micron is one millionth of a meter. Therefore, a nanometer is smaller than a micron.

10. The correct answer is (B). The reading contrasts the fact that a colloid cannot be seen with a microscope but cannot diffuse through a membrane made from parchment paper. The use of the phrase "but despite its size" following the statement that a colloid is too small to see implies that the colloid is too big to diffuse through the membrane. Therefore, the salt molecule is smaller than the colloid, and (B) is the correct answer. Nothing was mentioned about weight; therefore (C) and (D) are incorrect.

11. The correct answer is (A). Paragraph 2 states "they are stable while carrying the same electrical charge."

12. The correct answer is (B). Paragraph 2 states that the Tyndell effect is the property of colloids that provides a path for a sharp beam of light, but otherwise reflect normal light as color.

Passage 4

13. The correct answer is (A). One needs imagination to create the vehicle that will take you to unknown places. (B) is a literal response and (C) and (D) are too one-dimensional.

14. The correct answer is (D). This word means exaggeration. The poem uses (A) (rhythm) but it is not a primary tool. (B) and (C) are inappropriate.

15. The correct answer is (B). The words chosen, diction, are simple and direct and are aimed at young people. The poet, of course, wants all people to read the poem but (A) is not the primary audience. (C) and (D) are both inappropriate.

16. The correct answer is (A). This is based on the repetition of the line. (C) is close but is not as central as (A). (B) and (D) are inappropriate.

MATHEMATICS ACHIEVEMENT

1. The correct answer is (A). Factors are all the numbers that divide evenly into a number.

The factors of 20 are:

1 and 20

2 and 10

4 and 5,

which results in a total of 6 factors.

2. The correct answer is (C).

First calculate powers, then add.

$$2^3 = 2 \times 2 \times 2 = 8$$
$$5^2 = 5 \times 5 = +25$$
$$33$$

3. The correct answer is (D).

$$\frac{\$5,075}{\$3,500} = 1.45$$

This represents a 45% increase (while retaining 100% of the original investment).

You could also subtract the original investment of $3,500 from the present value of $5,075 (getting the amount of increase, which is $1,575). Then, the percent increase is $1,575 over the original investment of $3,500.

$$\frac{\$1,575}{\$3,500} = .45 \text{ which is } 45\%$$

4. The correct answer is (C). An equilateral triangle can be divided into two congruent right triangles by bisecting any vertex.

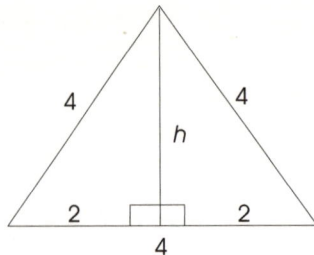

By the Pythagorean theorem,

$4^2 = h^2 + 2^2$

$16 = h^2 + 4$

$12 = h^2$

$h = \sqrt{12} = 2\sqrt{3}$

(You can also get this result by realizing that this forms a 30-60-90 triangle, whose sides are in the ratio $1 : \sqrt{3} : 2$)

Area = one half base times height, so

$A = (2)(2\sqrt{3}) = 4\sqrt{3}$

5. The correct answer is (C). An equilateral triangle is made up of three congruent, or equal, sides. To determine the perimeter of a triangle, sum the measure of all three sides.

$15 + 15 + 15 = 45$

6. The correct answer is (B). If the dining room set originally costs x dollars, when it is reduced by 10%, it costs $x - .1x$ dollars or simply $.9x$ dollars (original price minus discounted amount). If the new price of $.9x$ is then discounted in half, the resulting price is $.9x - .5(.9x)$ which equals $.45x$, or 45% of the original price.

7. The correct answer is (B). Since the ratio of green to red beads is 5:3, there are $5x$ green beads and $3x$ red ones.

$3x + 5x = 56$

$8x = 56$

$x = 7,$

so there are $3(7) = 21$ red beads.

8. The correct answer is (A).

$$3x^2 - 2x - 1 =$$
$$3(-2)^2 - 2(-2) - 1 =$$
$$3(4) - (-4) - 1 =$$
$$12 + 4 - 1 = 15$$

9. The correct answer is (B). The lowest point is around 2:30 and has about 20 drops per hour. The highest point is around 3:00 with 50 drops per hour.

The increase is 30 drops per hour. The base is at the lowest point (20 drops per hour) since we are looking for the percent increase from that point.

$$\frac{30}{20} = 1.5 = 150\%$$

10. The correct answer is (C). Parallel lines have the same slope. The given line has a slope of 4. The slopes of the other answers are easiest to see if the equations are turned into slope-intercept form:

$$y = mx + b$$
$$2y - 8x = -1$$
$$2y = 8x - 1$$
$$y = 4x - \frac{1}{2} \quad \text{which has a slope of 4.}$$

The other answers all have different slopes.

11. The correct answer is (A). Volume = length × width × height.

The volume of both boxes is $6 \times 8 \times 10 = 480$.

The volume of the second box is $4 \times 6 \times \text{height} = 480$; therefore, the height of the box is $\frac{480}{4 \times 6} = \frac{480}{24} = 20$.

12. The correct answer is (B). Since each of the 12 members donated the same dollar amount, the total amount donated is the product of 12 and d.

13. The correct answer is (C). First, determine the total number of cups in the recipe.

$$2.5 + 4 + 1.5 = 8$$

To find the percentage of flour, divide the cups of flour by the total number of cups. $\frac{4}{8} = \frac{1}{2} = 50\%$

14. The correct answer is (D). A nonagon has nine sides. A regular nonagon has nine congruent sides. To get the perimeter, multiply the length of each side by the number of sides.

$3 \times 9 = 27$

15. The correct answer is (B).

By the Pythagorean theorem:

$a^2 + b^2 = c^2$
$a^2 + 12^2 = 13^2$
$a^2 + 144 = 169$
$\sqrt{a^2} = \sqrt{25}$
$a = 5$

16. The correct answer is (A). 30 has a factor of 5. (It is 6×5.) The given number does not have a factor of 5 anywhere. (None of the prime factors is 5 and none of the composite numbers contains a factor of 5.) The other answers can be made from factors contained in the given number. For example, 39 is 13×3, both of which are found in the given number (3 is a factor of 12).

17. The correct answer is (D).

Follow the correct order of operations.

$(-3)^2 - 4(-3) = 9 - (-12)$
$\qquad\qquad\qquad = 9 + (+12)$
$\qquad\qquad\qquad = 21$

18. The correct answer is (A).

Reduce $\frac{6}{9}$ to the equivalent of $\frac{2}{3}$.

Hence, $c = 3$.

19. The correct answer is (A).

$|2a - 1| = 5$
$2a - 1 = 5$
$\quad 2a = 6$
$\quad\quad a = 3$
OR
$2a - 1 = -5$
$\quad 2a = -4$
$\quad\quad a = -2$

a can equal 3 or -2

20. The correct answer is (C).

$$.02x + .12 = .20$$
$$\underline{ .12 = -.12}$$
$$.02x = .08$$
$$2x = 8$$
$$x = 4$$

21. The correct answer is (D).

$$5x - 3 > 7 \qquad -5x + 3 < 7$$
$$5x > 10 \qquad -5x < 4$$
$$x > 2 \qquad x < -\frac{4}{5}$$

Thus, x must be less than $-\frac{4}{5}$ or greater than 2.

22. The correct answer is (A).

$$A = \frac{1}{2}(4)(8\sqrt{3}) = 16\sqrt{3} = \text{area of one triangle.}$$

There are six triangles in a hexagon.

$$6(16\sqrt{3}) = 96\sqrt{3}$$

23. The correct answer is (C). Since $158 is 70% of the original price, the base price is

$$B = \frac{P}{R} = \frac{158}{.70} = \$225.70$$

24. The correct answer is (C).

The number of hours from 9:00 a.m. to 4:30 p.m. totals $7\frac{1}{2}$ hours.

Multiply: $7\frac{1}{2}$ or $7.5 \times 9.25 = 69.375$

Since a total of two days were spent working, the total will be $2 \times 69.375 = \$138.75$.

25. The correct answer is (B).

$$|3a + 1| = 25$$
$$3a + 1 = 25$$
$$3a = 24$$
$$a = 8$$

OR

$$3a + 1 = -25$$
$$3a = -26$$
$$a = -\frac{26}{3}$$

a can equal 8 or $-\frac{26}{3}$

Subject Reviews

Red Alert: Verbal Analysis 103
   Verbal Analysis Review 105
Red Alert: Mathematics 115
   Mathematics Review 135
Red Alert: Reading Comprehension 287
   Sample Passage and Questions 291
   Answers and Explanations 296
Red Alert: Writing Strategies and
Grammar Review 299
   English Grammar Review 310

RED ALERT

VERBAL ANALYSIS/REASONING

One of the most important skills you must have in order to do well on either the SSAT or ISEE Verbal Analysis/Reasoning section is a strong vocabulary. At this point you already have some level of skill in order to have gone this far in school. However, you can always improve, and there are several steps that you can take in order to do so.

DEVELOPING YOUR VOCABULARY

Reading

The single best way to improve your vocabulary skills is to read as much as you can, and take note of the words that you don't know or are unsure of their meaning. Read your local or national newspapers. Read magazines; whether you read *People Weekly* or *Scientific American,* you're sure to encounter unfamiliar words. Write them down on an index card and then look them up.

Index Cards

This is step two in the vocabulary development process. Once you have written down the words you don't know, look them up. Then write the definitions on the back of the card. Essentially, you will create a set of vocabulary flash cards. Now, you can review the words yourself, or have someone test you. Once you feel comfortable with the word, you can discard the card. Continue to review the words you don't know, even as you add to your pile of flash cards.

Practice

It is an accepted fact that the more you practice, the better you will do on an actual exam. Therefore you should answer the questions on the practice exams in this book, and if you missed any of the verbal questions, take extra time to read the answers so that you fully understand *why* you answered them incorrectly. And of course, if you don't know some of the words, make flash cards.

Read and Learn the Directions

Almost all of the written tests that you will take in your lifetime will be timed. It is to your advantage to spend as much time as possible on answering the questions, rather than trying to figure out *how* to answer the questions. If you have to read and reread the directions in

Peterson's: www.petersons.com   RED ALERT

SUBJECT REVIEWS

order to understand what is being asked of you, you will lose time from the overall test. Thus, take the time to understand what is required of you on the SSAT or ISEE before you take the test.

Q&A Techniques

There are several techniques or tricks to help you do well on these tests. If you combine these techniques with your vocabulary knowledge, you should do well on the exam.

Answering Multiple-Choice Questions

The first technique in answering a multiple-choice question is to guess at the answer. We don't mean a pie-in-the-sky guess but an educated one. If you are being asked to find a word that means almost the same as a given word, try to define the word yourself before reading the answers. If you can do that, you are more than halfway to the correct answer. Then read the answers. Which of the answers is the same or similar to your own definition? You'll quickly find that if you can define the word yourself (or fill in the blanks in a sentence completion question) you will have very little trouble with that question.

The second technique is the process of elimination. Start by finding the word or words that you are fairly sure have no relationship to the given word. Eliminate them and that will reduce the number of choices. If you can eliminate two or three choices from the list, you've then got about a 50-50 chance of getting the correct answer.

The third technique is to use context clues. If you are given a sentence, try to find the description of the action that takes place, or the hidden definition within the sentence, or even a synonym that will give you a clue as to what the correct answer might be. You may find words that express positive or negative actions, happy or sad feelings, and so on. Use those clues to eliminate choices that don't fit with the action.

Check your answers. You may not have a lot of time when you go through the test, but that doesn't mean you should be careless. If you have extra time after finishing that section, go back and double-check your answers. However, keep in mind that your first answer is usually your correct answer.

Finally, make sure that you put your marks in the right place on the answer sheet. If you omit an answer, please be careful to answer the next question in the appropriate space. Once you fill in the wrong answer grid, all the rest of your answers will be incorrect. Check the answer number against the question you are answering to make sure you get it right.

Once again, remember that the key to success in answering synonym questions, sentence completion questions, and analogy questions is to have a strong vocabulary. Building your vocabulary requires a day-by-day effort but will be well worth it in the end—when you take the actual SSAT or ISEE examination.

RED ALERT *Peterson's SSAT/ISEE Success*

VERBAL ANALYSIS/REASONING REVIEW

A good way to prepare for the SSAT or ISEE examination is to familiarize yourself with the types of questions that these tests contain. These include vocabulary questions dealing with synonyms, sentence completion, and analogies. The review that follows is designed to further your understanding of the material covered on these two examinations.

SYNONYMS

The questions appear on both the SSAT and the ISEE. The only difference is that the SSAT questions have five answers, while the ISEE questions have four answers. In both, there is a capitalized word given, followed by answers. One of those answers is most nearly the same in meaning as the word in capital letters.

The most important way to study for this section is to read as much as you can, in all types of books, magazines, newspapers, and even this book. Always look up words that you don't know. Then write down the definition. You may never look at the paper again, but just the act of writing the word and definition will help it to stay in your mind. Of course, it's not possible to predict what words will be given on the exams, but the greater your vocabulary, the better your chance of getting the right answer.

One technique that's helpful is to look at the word and try to give your own definition of it, before you look at the answers. That's your own measure of whether or not you know the meaning of the word. Then look at the answers given and determine whether your definition is among them, or even close. Remember that the directions on the ISEE say "most nearly the same in meaning" and the directions on the SSAT say "whose meaning is closest to the word." Those phrases—"most nearly" and "is closest"—are key to answering synonym questions. It's not likely you will get an exact definition, but there is one that is fairly close.

Let's try some practice questions.

1. DAWDLE

    (A) hang loosely
    (B) waste time
    (C) fondle
    (D) splash
    (E) paint

SUBJECT REVIEWS

2. ANGUISH

    (A) torment
    (B) boredom
    (C) resentment
    (D) stubbornness
    (E) clumsiness

3. IMPARTIAL

    (A) unlawful
    (B) incomplete
    (C) unprejudiced
    (D) unfaithful
    (E) unimportant

4. EMBROIL

    (A) explain
    (B) entangle
    (C) swindle
    (D) greet
    (E) imitate

5. INCANDESCENT

    (A) insincere
    (B) melodious
    (C) electrical
    (D) magical
    (E) glowing

The correct answers are:

1. (B)
2. (A)
3. (C)
4. (B)
5. (E)

VERBAL ANALYSIS/REASONING REVIEW

How did you do? How many did you get right? Here's a suggestion if you got more than one wrong. Learn the meaning of the following words:

anguish	incomplete
boredom	insincere
clumsiness	magical
dawdle	melodious
electrical	paint
embroil	resentment
entangle	splash
explain	stubbornness
fondle	swindle
glowing	torment
greet	unfaithful
imitate	unimportant
impartial	unlawful
incandescent	unprejudiced

If they look familiar, they should. These are words that were given in the five questions above. If you had known the meaning of all of these words, you would have gotten all of the correct answers.

Another technique that is important in any kind of multiple-choice question is using the process of elimination. What this means is that you should eliminate—cross off—any words that you know are incorrect. If you can cross off enough answers, you may narrow down your choices to only a few. In the ISEE, where there are only four choices, it makes it much easier.

SENTENCE COMPLETION

These questions appear only on the ISEE. In a sentence completion question, one or more words has been removed. You are required to supply a missing word or words that will best complete a sentence. These questions demand skill in figuring out meanings from context. Choose words that *best* fit the meaning of the sentence. In order to handle this type of question, you should first read the sentence as you see it without trying to fill in the word or words. After reading, consider the *main idea* of the sentence and *then* read the choices. Remember, *both* words must fit into the meaning of the sentence; therefore, read your choice into the sentence by supplying and evaluating *both* words.

SUBJECT REVIEWS

Example

Choose words that best fit the meaning of the sentence:

> The zoology students sat quietly in their observation post; they were pleasantly surprised to observe, over the course of two days, a band of gorillas build a _____ camp each night. This always followed a day of _____ for the berries and leaves that constitute their diet.

(A) solid, trading
(B) sturdy, roaming
(C) interesting, seeking
(D) makeshift, foraging
(E) circular, farming

Your knowledge of the meanings of words and the ability to use those words appropriately within a given context will help you answer sentence completion questions. In addition, each sentence provides key words, specific examples, or an overall logic that helps direct you to the correct answer, regardless of your knowledge of the subject. The rules listed below are also useful:

1. As you read the sentence, note key words that show relationships. For example, *but, although, however,* and *on the other hand* indicate contrasting ideas. *And, another,* and *the same as* denote similarity. *Therefore, as a result, consequently, since,* and *because* signify a cause-effect relationship. In the example, the word *followed* indicates a time relationship.

2. Eliminate any answers that make no sense or that are grammatically incorrect. Answer (C) cannot be correct because the first blank requires a word beginning with a consonant. Answer (E) cannot be correct, because farming does not apply to gorillas or their food.

3. Do not be misled by answers that contain only one word that fits well into the sentence. *Both* words must make sense. For example, in answer (A), *solid* could be logically used to fill the first blank; however, *trading* is a human activity and does not fit logically into the context of the sentence.

4. Be guided by the logic and the meaning of the passage, when two answers could be used to create a sensible thought. Answers (B) and (D) both list words that could be used to complete the sentence. However, since the camp is remade each night, it is probably *makeshift* rather than *sturdy*. Also, while the gorillas may be said to be *roaming* for food, *foraging* is a more specific and suitable word, because it means "searching for food."

VERBAL ANALYSIS/REASONING REVIEW

Example

I attend the local college games, especially the one with our arch rival, State College. The game this year was extremely tough for us. State led throughout the game; but, after the _____ of a strong rally late in the ball game, we really thought we had a great chance of winning. Therefore, we were doubly _____ when our team lost.

- (A) lack, surprised
- (B) threat, amused
- (C) dispute, annoyed
- (D) excitement, disappointed
- (E) skill, doubtful

Using the aforementioned clues and procedures, select the answer you think is best. The key words in the sentence that help you determine this answer are *strong, rally,* and *lost.* You can determine that by looking at the entire selection to see what its intent is.

Rule 2 indicates that answer (A) is not possible because it would make sense ONLY if the team had won.

Rule 3 indicates that answer (B) cannot be correct. While the word *threat* seems reasonable, the word *amused* does not.

Rule 4 applies to answer (D) and tells you that in the context of *strong, rally,* and *lost,* logically this is the correct answer.

In answers (C) and (E), the meanings are incorrect in the context; therefore, rule 4 would fit.

Example

Traditionally, countries with _____ borders requiring _____ must maintain a large army and support it by imposing taxes.

- (A) historic, markers
- (B) vulnerable, defense
- (C) vague, exploration
- (D) unwanted, elimination
- (E) contested, estimation

Now, employing the four rules again, did you choose (B)?

Rule 3 fits here. While *historic* will work in the sentence, *markers* does not work because it makes no sense. A country does NOT employ an army to maintain its markers.

Rule 4 shows us that answer (B) is correct. Logic tells us that vulnerable borders need an army for defense.

Rule 4 also applies to answers (C) and (D) because they are NOT logical. A vague border would not require exploring. An unwanted border does not require an army to eliminate the border.

Rule 2 applies to answer (E), which makes no sense.

ANALOGIES

An analogy question presents two words that are related in some way, and it requires you to first discover the relationship, then find another pair of words that is related in the same way.

Example

Advertising is to selling as

(A) reporting is to informing
(B) training is to helping
(C) discovering is to exploring
(D) marketing is to research
(E) creating is to destroying

To answer analogy questions, use the following strategies:

1. First, determine the relationship between the first pair of words and state that relationship in sentence form: "Advertising is a means of selling products to an audience."

2. Then, find the pair of words in the answers that can be substituted for the original pair: "Reporting is a means of informing an audience." None of the other answers expresses quite the same relationship. Although you can say, "Training is a means of helping an audience," the context is much more general. Answer (A) is the best answer.

VERBAL ANALYSIS/REASONING REVIEW

The following table illustrates some of the most common types of relationships you will encounter in analogy questions:

Type of Analogy	Example
Action of Object	PLAY is to CLARINET as incise is to knife
Cause to Effect	SUN is to SUNBURN as overeating is to indigestion
Item to Category	IGUANA is to REPTILE as cat is to mammal
Object to Its Function	PENCIL is to WRITING as tractor is to plowing
Object to Its Material	CURTAINS is to CLOTH as windows is to glass
Part to Whole	PAGE is to BOOK as limb is to tree
Time Sequence	RECENT is to CURRENT as antique is to obsolete
Word to Antonym	ASSIST is to HINDER as enthrall is to bore
Word to Synonym	PROVISIONS is to SUPPLIES as portent is to omen
Worker and Creation	ARTIST is to SKETCH as composer is to etude
Worker and Workplace	CHEF is to KITCHEN as judge is to courtroom
Word and Word Derived From	ACT is to ACTION as image is to imagine

Now, using the two previously described procedures and the preceding table, look at these examples:

Mnemonic is to memory as

(A) trousers is to speech
(B) glasses is to vision
(C) earmuffs is to movement
(D) blinders is to hearing
(E) glove is to hand

Now, consider the relationship between the words MNEMONIC and MEMORY. A mnemonic device helps one to remember; therefore, a mnemonic device is designed to produce memory or to help one to remember.

Answers (A), (C), (D), and (E) could not fit because each defies the relationship. Speech has no relationship to trousers. Earmuffs have no relationship to movement, and blinders have no relationship to hearing. While a glove covers a hand, it does not help to produce a hand.

Peterson's: www.petersons.com

Answer (B) is correct because glasses are designed to aid vision or to help one to see. The relationship is identical. It is a Cause to Effect relationship.

Example

Waggish is to laughs as

(A) risible is to yawns
(B) bilious is to smiles
(C) lachrymose is to tears
(D) ribald is to moans
(E) frown is to grin

Again, using the previously described procedures, one can determine that a remark that is waggish is designed to produce laughs.

Looking at answers (A), (B), (D), and (E), you can see that they are incorrect because they do not produce the same relationship. (A) and (E) are incorrect because the relationship is Word to Antonym. (B) and (D) are incorrect because the relationship is not Cause to Effect. Therefore, the correct answer is (C).

Example

Phillipic is to vituperative as

(A) liturgy is to ribald
(B) encomium is to complimentary
(C) harangue is to restrained
(D) paean is to scurrilous
(E) anecdote is to story

The relationship is Word to Synonym since a *phillipic* is a kind of speech that is, by definition, vituperative.

Answers (A), (C), and (D) all have the relationship of Word to Antonym. Answer (B) is correct. An encomium is a kind of speech that is, by definition, complimentary.

Example

Act is to action as

(A) therapy is to thermometer
(B) oblivion is to obvious
(C) liturgy is to literature
(D) image is to imagine
(E) bowl is to bowdlerize

The correct answer is (D). The relationship is word and word derived from. The word "action" derives from the word "act." Answer (A) is incorrect: thermometer (temperature measure) does not derive from the word therapy. There is no relationship. Answer (B) is incorrect: the relationship is antonyms or opposites. Oblivion means forgotten: obvious means apparent. The relationship is different. Answer (C) is incorrect: liturgy (ritual) does not provide the root for the word literature, which means a body of work. Answer (E) is incorrect: bowl (goblet) does not form the root for bowdlerize, which means to modify. There is no relationship.

Here's a slightly different version of an analogy question. These have three stem words in the question and only one word to find.

Example

Height is to mountain as depth is to

(A) trench
(B) tree
(C) age
(D) highway
(E) mine

Like the earlier examples, the first step to take is to determine the relationship between the first pair of words and state that relationship in sentence form:

One of the characteristics of a mountain is its height. One of the characteristics of a trench is its depth. Therefore, the correct answer is (A). Answer (B) will not work. While shade is often a characteristic of a tree it is not a persistent characteristic, meaning that a tree does not always give shade. In addition, a mountain possesses height, but a tree gives shade. Answer (C) is incorrect: a characteristic of age is not always weight. The relationship is not the same as height and mountain. Answer (D) is incorrect: while we often associate speed with a highway, speed is *not* a characteristic of the highway. Answer (E) is incorrect: while a mineral comes from a mine, it is not a characteristic of the mine. It is a product of the mine. The relationship is not the same as height and mountain.

These three sections are the basis of the Verbal Analysis section on both the SSAT and ISEE examinations. Once you have mastered this material, go back to the diagnostic tests and check your answers again. Then, go to the Grammar Review section that follows to give yourself an overview of basic grammatical principles. These will help you with many of the questions you will encounter on these exams, since more than vocabulary is involved with these tests. A strong grounding in the basics of proper grammar and usage will make your work a lot easier.

RED ALERT

STRATEGIES FOR TAKING THE MATHEMATICS TEST

GENERAL SUGGESTIONS

Much of the success in test taking comes from being comfortable both physically and mentally with the test you are taking. Physical comfort is very easy to achieve. Just remember a few important points:

1. **Be on time.** Actually, being a few minutes early doesn't hurt. No one is helped by feeling rushed when beginning a test.

2. **Have a supply of #2 pencils with good erasers.** There will be no time for borrowing or sharpening a pencil once the test begins.

3. **Wear comfortable clothing.** Layers of clothing are the best since they can be removed or put on, depending on the temperature of the room. Don't wear shoes that pinch or a belt that is too tight.

4. **Avoid cramming.** Finish your preparation ahead of time, and relax the night before the test. Cramming just before the test begins is not helpful and often leads to panic and confusion. Be sure to get a good night's sleep before taking the test.

5. **Calculators are not permitted** for the test, so there is no need to bring one with you. Be sure that you remember how to perform all mathematical computations by hand!

Mental comfort is a little more difficult to achieve. *Preparation* is the key and comes with study and practice in the weeks and months before the test. Mental comfort is gained by becoming familiar with the test format, instructions, and the types of problems that will appear.

KNOW THE TEST FORMAT AND INSTRUCTIONS

Although the math topics that you will be responsible for on the ISEE and the SSAT are essentially the same, the format and strategy for the math sections on these tests are somewhat different. Be certain that you are familiar with the structure of the test that you are going to take before you take it.

Peterson's: www.petersons.com

RED ALERT

SUBJECT REVIEWS

On the ISEE there are two math sections, *Quantitative Reasoning* and *Mathematics Achievement.* The Mathematics Achievement section contains 45 questions, and you will have 40 minutes to answer them. The Quantitative Reasoning section contains 35 questions, and you will have 35 minutes to answer them.

All 45 of the questions in the Mathematics Achievement section will be in the standard multiple-choice format, with four possible answers. On the other hand, only about half of the questions in the Quantitative Reasoning section are standard multiple-choice; the remaining questions are in the special *Quantitative Comparison* format. The format and strategies for these special questions are discussed later in this section. In general, the Mathematics Achievement section of the ISEE tests your knowledge of the various subject areas in mathematics, while the Quantitative Reasoning section measures general mathematical aptitude.

It is extremely important to remember that on the ISEE there is no penalty for an incorrect answer. You will receive one point for a correct answer and nothing for an incorrect answer or a question left blank. Clearly, then, it is to your advantage to answer every question. If you are not certain of the correct answer, try to eliminate as many of the incorrect answers as possible and make a guess from the remaining answers. Even if you cannot eliminate any answers, you might as well guess. Do not leave any questions blank on the ISEE.

The subject areas covered on the test include basic arithmetic skills (computations with fractions, decimals, and percents; ratios and proportions; and set of numbers), beginning algebra (algebraic representation, numerical evaluation, and solving equations and inequalities), geometry (lines and angles, geometric figures, areas and perimeters, and coordinate geometry), and some miscellaneous topics, such as set theory, the metric system, and graph reading. All of these topics are covered in detail, with many solved examples, later in this book.

On the SSAT, there are also two math sections, but each section contains only 25 questions. You will be allotted 25 minutes for each of these two sections. Unlike the ISEE, all of the questions on the SSAT are in the standard multiple-choice format. Thus, there are not any quantitative comparison questions on this test. Also note that on the SSAT every question will have five possible answers. As on the ISEE, the math questions test your knowledge of mathematical subject areas as well as general mathematical aptitude.

Note that the SSAT does have an incorrect answer penalty. While you will receive one point for each correct answer, you will lose ¼ point for each incorrect answer. There is no penalty for leaving an answer blank. Students taking the SSAT often ask if they should guess on questions that they are not sure of. The general strategy is this: if you guess randomly on a series of questions, you are as likely to hurt as to help your score. However, on any question for which you are able to eliminate *one or more* answers as incorrect, the odds of guessing the correct answer tip in your favor, and you should guess.

The subject areas on the SSAT are the same as those listed above for the ISEE and will be covered in detail later in this book.

Whether you are taking the ISEE or the SSAT, be sure that you have taken enough sample tests to be thoroughly familiar with the instructions. The instructions are a part of the timed test. DO NOT spend valuable time reading them as if you have never seen them before. Simply skim them to refresh your memory each time you start a new section of the test.

PACE YOURSELF

Before you begin any specific section on the exam, remind yourself how long you have to finish the section, and pace yourself accordingly. If you spend too much time on each question, you will not complete enough questions to receive a good score. Many very intelligent students work too slowly and spend too much time on details or neatness. As a result, they end up with a lower score than they should. As you work, put a mark next to the problems that would take too long and a different mark next to those that you don't know how to solve, so that you can go back to them later if you have time.

Bring a watch to the test and thus eliminate worry about how much time is left. When time is almost up, you should look over the rest of the problems and do those you know you can do most quickly.

All questions count the same. Allot your time accordingly. Remember that hard questions count the same as easy ones. Don't miss out on one that might be easy for you by stubbornly sticking to one that might be more difficult.

USE THE TEST BOOKLET SCRATCH AREA

For many problems, a simple sketch on the scratch area of the test booklet will make the solution readily apparent and will thus save time. Also, do not attempt to do all computation work in your head. Remember to use the scratch area of the test booklet; mark only answers on the answer sheet.

Subject Reviews

Specific Suggestions

All of the general suggestions will not help you if you are not prepared to solve the problems and arrive at the correct answers.

As we have seen, the exam requires the knowledge of arithmetic, algebra, and plane and coordinate geometry. Many of the problems require some insight and originality—that is, you will need to know not only *how* to perform certain operations but also *when* to perform them.

Vocabulary is very important. A problem that asks you to find a *quotient* will be hard to do if you do not know the meaning of this term. Some basic terms you should know:

> *sum:* the answer to an addition problem
> *product:* the answer to a multiplication problem
> *quotient:* the answer to a division problem
> *difference:* the answer to a subtraction problem
> *integer:* a whole number, either positive or negative or 0
> *prime number:* a number with no factors other than 1 and itself
> *even integers:* 2, 4, 6, 8, etc.
> *odd integers:* 1, 3, 5, 7, etc.
> *consecutive integers:* numbers in order, 1, 2, 3 or 7, 8, 9, etc.

Different types of problems call for different attacks. Of course, the most desirable situation is to know how to do all problems, work them out, and then fill in the letter space for the correct answer. But what if the answer you get is not among the choices, or you don't know how to do the problem in the first place? Then perhaps the following suggestions will help. However, remember these are only suggested methods for problem solving. Always do a problem your way if you are more comfortable with it and if it will solve the problem just as quickly.

Look for Shortcuts

Rarely will a problem on your test involve a long, cumbersome computation. If you find yourself caught up in a maze of large numbers, you have probably missed a shortcut.

Example

Which is larger?

$$\frac{5}{23} \times \frac{7}{33} \quad \text{or} \quad \frac{7}{23} \times \frac{5}{31}$$

RED ALERT

Peterson's SSAT/ISEE Success

RED ALERT: STRATEGIES FOR TAKING THE MATHEMATICS TEST

Solution

Examination of the problem will let you see that after multiplying, in each case the numerators of the resulting fractions will be the same (5 × 7 and 7 × 5). When the numerators of two fractions are the same, the fraction with the smaller denominator will be the larger fraction. In this case, the denominators are 23 × 33 and 23 × 31. It is not necessary to do the actual multiplication to see that 23 × 31 will be the smaller product (or denominator), making the larger fraction.

Example

If 6 × 6 × (x) = 12 × 12 × 12, then x =

(A) 12   (B) 18   (C) 24   (D) 48

Solution

Use factoring and cancellation to eliminate the need to cube 12 and then divide by 36 (6 × 6). Factor and cancel:

$$x = \frac{\cancel{12}^{2} \cdot \cancel{12}^{2} \cdot 12}{\cancel{6} \cdot \cancel{6}} = 48$$

The correct answer is D.

Estimate

On any timed competitive examination, it is necessary that you be able to estimate. Sometimes it is helpful to round off all numbers to a convenient power of 10 and estimate the answer. This will often enable you to pick the correct answer quickly without performing a lot of time-consuming computations. In some cases it will eliminate one or more of the answers right away, thus improving your chances if you have to guess.

Example

Which of the following is closest to the value of

$$\frac{3654 \times 248}{1756}?$$

(A) 50   (B) 500   (C) 5,000   (D) 5

Peterson's: www.petersons.com

Solution

3,654 is about 4,000. 248 is about 200 (or 300) and 1,756 is about 2,000. The problem then becomes:

$$\frac{\cancel{4000}^{2} \cdot 200}{\cancel{2000}_{1}} \cong 400$$

Therefore, choose answer B.

Substitute

Change confusing problems to more meaningful ones by substituting simple numbers for letters. Many students get confused by problems containing letters in place of numbers. These letters are called *variables*. Just remember that the letters stand for numbers; therefore, the same operations can be performed on them. Just think of how you would do the problem if there were numbers, and then perform the same operations on the letters.

Example

If John's allowance is $x a week and he saves $m a week, what part of his allowance does he spend?

Solution

Substituting some numbers for the letters in the problem, we get: If John's allowance is $5 a week and he saves $1 a week, then he spends $5 − $1, or $4 a week. This represents $4 (part) out of $5 (whole) or $\frac{4}{5}$ of his allowance. Transferring the number computation to the original problem, we get:

$\frac{5-1}{5}$ or $\frac{x-m}{x}$ for the correct answer.

Example

If a man was x years old y years ago, how many years old will he be z years from now?

Solution

Substitute small numbers for the letters. If a man was 20 years old 5 years ago, how many years old will he be 8 years from now? The man is now 25 years old (20 + 5). Eight years from now he will be 20 + 5 + 8, or 33 years old. Back in the original problem, substitute letters for numbers in your solution:

$20 + 5 + 8 = x + y + z$

Work Backward

Some experts advise against this, but in some cases it can be advantageous for you to look at the answers first. You can save valuable time by knowing that all the answers are in common fractional or decimal form. Then you will want to work only in the form in which the answers are given.

Are all the answers the same except for one digit or placement of a decimal? Knowing this can save you time.

Example

The square root of 106.09 is exactly:

(A) .103   (B) 1.03   (C) 10.3   (D) 103

Solution

Don't use your time to find the square root of 106.09. Work backward from the answers, which are all the same except for the placement of the decimal. Using the definition of square root (the number that when multiplied by itself will produce a given number), you can see that answer C is the only one that will give an answer of 106.09 when multiplied by itself.

Another type of problem in which it is helpful to work backward is the problem that contains an equation to solve. Trying each answer in the equation to see which one fits will help, especially if you are unsure of how to solve the equation.

Example

$x\sqrt{.16} = 4$. Find the value of x:

(A) 1   (B) .4   (C) .64   (D) 10

SUBJECT REVIEWS

Solution

Examination of the equation reveals that it is really $.4x = 4$ ($\sqrt{.16} = .4$). Checking each answer will reveal that $10 \times .4 = 4$; therefore, (D) is the correct answer.

Answer the Question

Always check to see if you have answered the question asked. You can be sure, for instance, that if you are doing a problem involving two angles, the values for both angles will be among the answers listed. Be sure that you have found the right value.

Example

If $3x + 2 = 12$, find $x - \frac{1}{3}$

(A) $3\frac{1}{3}$ (B) 3   (C) 10   (D) 4

Solution

Solving the equation:

add -2 to both sides $\quad 3x + 2 = 12$
$\qquad\qquad\qquad\qquad\qquad\quad -2 = -2$
$\qquad\qquad\qquad\qquad\qquad\overline{\quad 3x = 10\quad}$

Divide by 3 $\qquad\qquad\qquad x = \frac{10}{3} = 3\frac{1}{3}$

Notice that $x = 3\frac{1}{3}$ and that this answer is (A). However, the problem asked us to find $x - \frac{1}{3}$. Therefore, the correct answer is (B).

SPECIAL HELP FOR PROBLEM AREAS

Fractions

Comparing Fractions

Many problems will require that you know how to compare fractions. A few simple steps will ensure that you can do this.

1. If the *denominators* of two fractions are the *same,* the fraction with the *larger numerator* will be the fraction with the *larger* value.

RED ALERT

Peterson's SSAT/ISEE Success

Example

Compare $\frac{3}{5}$ and $\frac{2}{5}$

Solution

$3 > 2$, therefore $\frac{3}{5} > \frac{2}{5}$

2. If the *numerators* of two fractions are the *same,* the fraction with the *larger denominator* will be the *smaller* fraction.

Example

Compare $\frac{2}{13}$ and $\frac{2}{15}$

Solution

$13 < 15$, therefore $\frac{2}{13} > \frac{2}{15}$

3. If the numerators and denominators are different, the fractions can be compared by cross multiplying. Cross multiplying eliminates the need to find a common denominator in order to use method 1.

Example

Compare $\frac{9}{13}$ and $\frac{11}{15}$

Solution

Cross multiply, putting the products above the numerators used in the products.

$$\overset{\displaystyle{135}}{}\overset{\displaystyle{143}}{}$$
$$\frac{9}{13}\frac{11}{15}$$

$135 < 143$, therefore $\frac{9}{13} < \frac{11}{15}$

SUBJECT REVIEWS

Complex Fractions

If complex fractions (a fraction within a fraction) cause your mind to go blank, try this little routine. Whenever you have a complex fraction, find the least common denominator for all the denominators within the fraction and multiply all *terms* by this denominator. This will reduce the complex fraction to a simple one and make it easier to handle.

Example

$$\frac{\frac{2}{3} + \frac{3}{4}}{1 - \frac{1}{3}}$$

Solution

The least common denominator is 12. Multiply all terms by 12.

$$\frac{12\left(\frac{2}{3}\right) + \left(\frac{3}{4}\right)12}{12(1) - \frac{1}{3}(12)} = \frac{8 + 9}{12 - 4} = \frac{17}{8} = 2\frac{1}{8}$$

This routine can also be of use if the complex fraction contains letters or variables.

Example

Simplify

$$\frac{1 - \frac{1}{x}}{1 + \frac{1}{x}}$$

Solution

The least common denominator is x. Multiply all terms by x.

$$\frac{x(1) - \frac{1}{x}(x)}{x(1) + \frac{1}{x}(x)} = \frac{x - 1}{x + 1}$$

Percent

Percent problems are another source of trouble for many students. First, you should be sure you know how to change a decimal to a percent (multiply by 100) and to change a percent to a decimal or common fraction (divide by 100).

Examples

$$.35 = 35\% \ (.35 \times 100)$$

$$6\tfrac{1}{2}\% = 6.5\% = .065$$

$$(6\tfrac{1}{2}\% \div 100 = .065) \text{ or } (6.5\% \div 100 = 0.65)$$

It is also a good idea to memorize the equivalent fractions for certain percents. This will save you time, as they will typically come up several times on your test.

$$\tfrac{1}{2} = .50 = 50\% \qquad \tfrac{1}{6} = .16\tfrac{2}{3} = 16\tfrac{2}{3}\%$$

$$\tfrac{1}{4} = .25 = 25\% \qquad \tfrac{5}{6} = .83\tfrac{1}{3} = 83\tfrac{1}{3}\%$$

$$\tfrac{3}{4} = .75 = 75\% \qquad \tfrac{1}{8} = .12\tfrac{1}{2} = 12\tfrac{1}{2}\%$$

$$\tfrac{1}{5} = .20 = 20\% \qquad \tfrac{3}{8} = .37\tfrac{1}{2} = 37\tfrac{1}{2}\%$$

$$\tfrac{2}{5} = .40 = 40\% \qquad \tfrac{5}{8} = .62\tfrac{1}{2} = 62\tfrac{1}{2}\%$$

$$\tfrac{3}{5} = .60 = 60\% \qquad \tfrac{7}{8} = .87\tfrac{1}{2} = 87\tfrac{1}{2}\%$$

$$\tfrac{4}{5} = .80 = 80\% \qquad \tfrac{1}{10} = .10 = 10\%$$

$$\tfrac{1}{3} = .33\tfrac{1}{3} = 33\tfrac{1}{3}\% \qquad \tfrac{3}{10} = .30 = 30\%$$

$$\tfrac{2}{3} = .66\tfrac{2}{3} = 66\tfrac{2}{3}\% \qquad \tfrac{7}{10} = .70 = 70\%$$

$$1 = 100\% \qquad \tfrac{9}{10} = .90 = 90\%$$

Remembering that *of* in a mathematical problem usually means that you have to multiply, algebraic equations can then be set up to solve the three types of percent problems.

Example

What is 15% of 32?

Solution

$x = 15\% \times 32$

$x = (.15)(32)$ (change 15% to a decimal fraction)

$x = 4.80$

Example

9 is 30% of what number?

Solution

$9 = 30\% \times x$

(a) $9 = (.30)x$ (change 30% to a decimal fraction)

or (b) $9 = \left(\dfrac{3}{10}\right)x$ (change 30% to a common fraction)

(a) $30 = x$ (divide by .3)

or (b) $30 = x$ (multiply by $\dfrac{10}{3}$)

Example

12 is what percent of 72?

Solution

$12 = x\% \times 72$

$12 = \left(\dfrac{x}{100}\right) 72$ (change $x\%$ to a fraction)

$\dfrac{12}{72} = \dfrac{x}{100}$ (divide by 72)

$\dfrac{1}{6} = \dfrac{x}{100}$ (reduce $\dfrac{12}{72}$ to $\dfrac{1}{6}$)

$100 = 6x$ (cross multiply)

$16\dfrac{2}{3} = x$ (divide by 6)

or, if you have memorized your fractional equivalent chart, you will know that $16\dfrac{2}{3}\% = \dfrac{1}{6}$.

Geometry

Many of the questions in the geometry area of your test will require recall of the numerical relationships learned in an informal geometry course. You will not be asked to do a formal proof! If you are thoroughly familiar with these relationships, you should not find the geometry questions difficult.

Be very careful with units, especially when finding area, perimeter, or volume. Change all dimensions to a common unit before doing the calculations.

Important Properties and Formulas

Memorize the following geometric properties to help speed your ability to solve the problems.

Properties of a Triangle

The sum of the angles of a triangle equals 180°.

An exterior angle of a triangle is equal to the sum of the remote interior angles.

An equilateral triangle has equal sides and all angles equal to 60°.

An isosceles triangle has two equal sides. The angles opposite these sides are also equal.

In a right triangle, $a^2 + b^2 = c^2$, where a and b are the legs and c is the hypotenuse (Pythagorean theorem).

Properties of Parallel Lines

Pairs of alternate interior angles are equal.

Pairs of corresponding angles are equal.

Pairs of interior angles on the same side of the transversal are supplementary (their sum is 180°).

Properties of a Parallelogram

Opposite sides are parallel.

Opposite sides are congruent.

Opposite angles are congruent.

Diagonals bisect each other.

Properties of a Rectangle

The same properties as a parallelogram, plus:

All angles are right angles.

The diagonals are congruent.

Properties of a Rhombus

The same properties as a parallelogram, plus:

All sides are congruent.

The diagonals are perpendicular to each other.

The diagonals bisect the angles.

Properties of a Square

The same properties as a parallelogram, plus those of a rectangle, plus those of a rhombus.

Peterson's: www.petersons.com

SUBJECT REVIEWS

Important Area Formulas

Area of a triangle: $A = \frac{1}{2}bh$ (b is the base, h is the height)

Area of a parallelogram: $A = bh$ (b is the base, h is the height)

Area of a square: $A = s^2$ (s is a side of the square)

Area of a circle: $A = \pi r^2$ (r is the radius of the circle)

Area of a rectangle: $A = lw$ (l is the length, w is the width)

or $A = bh$ (since a rectangle is a parallelogram)

Area of a trapezoid: $A = \frac{1}{2}h(b_1 + b_2)$ (h is the height, b_1 and b_2 are the bases)

Volume

The volume of most solids is found by finding the area of the base and multiplying by the height.

Volume of a rectangular solid: $V = lwh$ (base is a rectangle)

Volume of a cube: $V = s^3$ (base is a square)

Volume of a cylinder: $V = \pi r^2 h$ (base is a circle)

If you learn to recognize the relationships and formulas given above and the cases in which they apply, you will have the key to doing most of the problems involving geometry on the test.

QUANTITATIVE COMPARISON STRATEGIES FOR THE ISEE

Recall that on the ISEE, there are two math sections, *Quantitative Reasoning* and *Mathematics Achievement*. While all 50 of the questions in the Mathematics Achievement section will be in the standard multiple-choice format, only the first 20 questions in the Quantitative Ability section are standard multiple-choice. The remaining 20 questions are in the special *Quantitative Comparison* format. *Note that there are no Quantitative Comparison sections on the SSAT, so if you are taking that test, you may skip this section of the book.*

Quantitative Comparison questions are the only questions on the entire test that are not arranged in the standard multiple-choice format. Instead, in each of these questions, you are given two quantities, one in Column A and one in Column B. Your job, simply put, is to determine which of these two quantities is larger.

The answer scheme is simple. If the quantity in Column A is larger, you should answer (A). If the quantity in Column B is larger, you should answer (B). If the two quantities are of identical size, the answer is (C). Finally, if it is not possible to tell which quantity is larger, the answer is (D).

Occasionally there will be some additional information given to help you determine the relative size of the two quantities. This information, when given, will be centered just above the Column A and Column B entries.

RED ALERT: STRATEGIES FOR TAKING THE MATHEMATICS TEST

Following are the directions as they appear on the ISEE. They should be memorized so that you do not waste time reading them when you take the actual test.

> **Directions:** For the following questions note the given information, if any, and then compare the quantity in Column A to the quantity in Column B. Next to the number of each question, write:
>
> A   if the quantity in Column A is greater
> B   if the quantity in Column B is greater
> C   if the two quantities are equal
> D   if the relationship cannot be determined from the information given

To gain a better understanding of the answers (A) through (D), we will now look at four examples. These examples have been selected so that the answer to the first one is (A), the answer to the second is (B), and so on.

	Column A	Column B
	\	$\frac{1}{x} = 4$	
1.	1	x

Solution: The equation given in the common information can be solved to determine that $x = \frac{1}{4}$. Since $1 > \frac{1}{4}$, the answer is (A).

	Column A	Column B
2.	$\sqrt{26} - \sqrt{10}$	$\sqrt{26-10}$

Solution: The entry in Column B is equal to 4. While we cannot exactly determine the value of Column A, if we estimate $\sqrt{26}$ and $\sqrt{10}$, we can see that its value is close to 2. The correct answer is (B).

3.

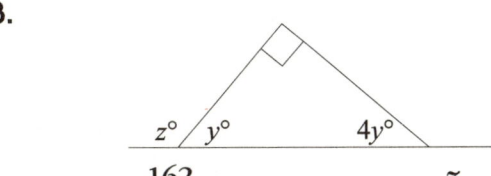

Solution: Since a triangle contains 180°, $y + 4y + 90° = 180°$. Thus, $5y° = 90°$ and $y° = 18°$. Since $z + y = 180$, z must be 162, and the answer is (C).

SUBJECT REVIEWS

	Column A	Column B
4.	$x^6 = 64$	
	2	x

Solution: Solving the equation given as common information, we can determine that x is either 2 or -2. Thus, x is either less than or equal to 2. The answer is (D).

HINTS AND STRATEGIES FOR QUANTITATIVE COMPARISON QUESTIONS

Before we look at some specific problem-solving strategies for Quantitative Comparison questions, let's examine some general strategies.

General Strategies

1. Remember that your goal is to do as little work as possible to answer the question. You frequently don't need to determine the actual size of the quantities in Columns A and B to know which one is larger. As a simple example, if you have enough information to determine that the quantity in Column A is positive and the quantity in Column B is negative, then the quantity in Column A is bigger, regardless of its actual value.

2. Be sure that you understand the meaning of the answers. For example, an answer of (A) indicates that the quantity in Column A is always bigger than the quantity in Column B. If A is sometimes, but not always, bigger, the answer is (D). Similarly, (C) is the answer only if the quantities are always equal.

3. Be sure that you only do as much math as is absolutely necessary to determine which quantity is bigger. Estimate and approximate as much as possible. You can often answer a question correctly by doing very little actual mathematical computation.

4. While you are asked to answer 35 questions in 35 minutes in the Quantitative Reasoning section, it is not a good idea to figure that you should average slightly less than a minute a question. The Quantitative Comparison questions can generally be answered much more quickly than the other multiple-choice questions. A good guideline is that you should average about 30 seconds for each of these questions, which will allow you to average about a minute and a half for the more time-consuming multiple-choice questions.

5. Whenever both of the given quantities are purely numerical (contain only numbers, no letters), then both quantities have a definite size, and the answer cannot be (D). If you are not sure how to answer a problem with two purely numerical entities, be sure to guess either (A), (B), or (C).

RED ALERT: STRATEGIES FOR TAKING THE MATHEMATICS TEST

Specific Mathematical Strategies for Quantitative Comparison Questions

Whenever you can, eliminate common factors and terms from Column A and Column B. Then simply compare the remaining quantities. Often, sums and products can be combined term by term, or factor by factor.

	Column A	Column B
1.	$(108)^2 - (13)^2$	$(108 - 13)^2$

Solution: The quantity in Column A, when factored, becomes $(108 - 13)(108 + 13)$. The quantity in Column B is equal to $(180 - 13)(180 - 13)$. Upon canceling the common factor of $(180 - 13)$, we see that we are comparing $(108 + 13)$ in Column A to $(108 - 13)$ in Column B. The answer is clearly (A).

2.	$\frac{5}{6} + \frac{6}{7} + \frac{7}{8}$	$\frac{5}{7} + \frac{6}{8} + \frac{7}{9}$

Solution: Simply note that each term in Column A is bigger than the corresponding term in Column B. The answer is (A).

3.	$6(125)4$	$2(125)12$

Solution: Cancel the common factor of 125 from both sides. Then, both sides become equal to 24. The answer, therefore, is (C).

Remember that you can often determine which quantity is bigger by simply estimating sizes.

4.	$\frac{221}{333}$	$\frac{667}{999}$

Solution: Note that the quantity in Column A is less than $\frac{2}{3}$ and that the quantity in Column B is greater than $\frac{2}{3}$. The answer is (B).

A Quantitative Comparison question can be treated as if it were an algebraic inequality, with your job being to position the correct inequality sign (=, <, >) between entries. As such, you may perform any operation to both columns of the question that you can perform on both sides of an inequality. This means, whenever you wish, you can add or subtract the same number to Column A and Column B, multiply or divide both columns by the same positive number, or square both numbers (if both entries are positive). This strategy can be used to change the operations of subtraction and division to the relatively less confusing operations of addition and multiplication.

SUBJECT REVIEWS

	Column A	Column B
5.	$\sqrt{89{,}905}$	300

Solution: Square both sides. Column A becomes 89,905 and Column B becomes 90,000. The answer is (B).

6.	$\sqrt{3}$	$\dfrac{4}{\sqrt{3}}$

Solution: Do not waste any time estimating the values of the quantities. Simply multiply both entries by $\sqrt{3}$. Column A is then equal to $\sqrt{3} \times \sqrt{3} = 3$, while Column B is equal to $\dfrac{4}{\sqrt{3}}\sqrt{3} = 4$. Since $4 > 3$, the answer is (B).

7.	$9\dfrac{5}{6} + \dfrac{1}{7}$	$10\dfrac{5}{6} - \dfrac{6}{7}$

Solution: Eliminate the subtraction in Column B by adding $\dfrac{6}{7}$ to both entries. Column A then becomes $9\dfrac{5}{6} + \dfrac{1}{7} + \dfrac{6}{7} = 9\dfrac{5}{6} + 1 = 10\dfrac{5}{6}$. Column B becomes $10\dfrac{5}{6} - \dfrac{6}{7} + \dfrac{6}{7} = 10\dfrac{5}{6}$. The answer is (C).

Whenever you are comparing quantities containing variables, remember to consider both positive and negative values of the variables. Similarly, remember that the variables could have fractional values.

8.	$3 < x < 5$	
	$4 < y < 6$	
	x	y

Solution: Many people might answer (B) for this, assuming that $x = 4$ and $y = 5$. However, remember that x and y could also be fractional. For example, x could be 4.5, while y is 4.1. The correct answer is (D).

RED ALERT: STRATEGIES FOR TAKING THE MATHEMATICS TEST

If the column entries contain algebraic operations, it frequently helps to begin by performing these operations.

	Column A	Column B
9.	$a = -2, c = 5$	
	$3a(2b + 5c)$	$2a(3b + 5c)$

Solution: To begin, expand both expressions. The entry in Column A becomes $6ab + 15ac$. Column B becomes $6ab + 10ac$. Cancel the common factor of $6ab$ and you'll see that we are actually comparing $15ac$ in Column A to $10ac$ in Column B. We know that $a = -2$ and $c = 5$. Thus the entry in Column A becomes -150, while Column B becomes -100. The answer is (B).

See if the common information can be manipulated to a form that is similar in appearance to the entry in one of the columns.

10.	$5p + 7q = 13$	
	40	$15p + 21q$

Solution: If you multiply both sides of the equation given as common information by 3, you will obtain $15p + 21q = 39$. Thus, the value of the expression in Column B is 39. The answer is (A).

When either of the column entries contains variables, it is often very helpful to substitute numerical values for these variables and observe what happens. Any substitution you make will enable you to eliminate two of the possible answers. Suppose, for example, that you plug a value into the quantities, and for this particular value the quantity in Column A turns out to be bigger. This means that the answer cannot be (B) or (C). Either Column A is always larger (A), or sometimes larger (D).

SUBJECT REVIEWS

	Column A	Column B
11.		$s \neq 1$
		$s \neq 0$
	$\dfrac{r}{s}$	$\dfrac{r-1}{s-1}$

Solution: Try to substitute values for r and s. If, for example, $r = s = 2$, $\dfrac{r}{s} = \dfrac{r-1}{s-1}$. Thus we know that the answer is either (C) or (D). Now let $r = 0$ and $s = 2$. Then, the value in Column A becomes 0, and the value in Column B becomes $-\dfrac{1}{2}$. This result indicates that the answer is (D).

Remember that the powers of, roots of, and divisions by numbers between 0 and 1 behave differently than those with numbers greater than 1. For example, if you square a number larger than 1, the resulting number is larger than the original; yet, if you square a number less than 1, the resulting number is smaller than the original. Also, remember that powers of even and odd numbers behave differently. The following examples illustrate some of these variations.

	Column A	Column B
12.		$x > 0$
	x^2	x^3

Solution: While intuition tells us that cubing a positive number yields a larger result than squaring the number, this result is actually true only for numbers bigger than 1. In fact, $x^2 = x^3$ if $x = 1$, and if $x < 1$, $x^2 > x^3$. For example, if $x = \dfrac{1}{2}$, then $x^2 = \dfrac{1}{4}$ and $x^3 = \dfrac{1}{8}$. Thus, there is no way to tell if x^2 or x^3 is larger, and the answer is (D).

	Column A	Column B
13.		$x > 1$
	x^2	x^3

Solution: As long as we know that $x > 1$, we have $x^3 > x^2$. The answer is (B).

	Column A	Column B
14.		$0 < z < 1$
	$\dfrac{12}{z}$	$12z$

Solution: When 12 is divided by z, $0 < z < 1$ will yield a number *greater* than 12, and when 12 is multiplied by z, $0 < z < 1$ will yield a number *smaller* than 1. The answer is (A).

Remember the above strategies and guidelines as you try your hand at the quantitative comparison questions in the upcoming practice tests.

MATHEMATICS REVIEW

Properties of Numbers

Systems of Numbers

All of the numbers that are used in the mathematics sections of the SSAT/ISEE are *real numbers*. In order to understand the real number system, it is easiest to begin by looking at some familiar systems of numbers that lie within the real number system.

The numbers that are used for counting

$$1, 2, 3, 4, 5, \ldots$$

are called the *natural numbers*, the *counting numbers*, or, most commonly, the *positive integers*. The positive integers, together with the number 0, are called the set of *whole numbers*. Then, the positive integers, together with 0 and the *negative integers*

$$-1, -2, -3, -4, -5, \ldots$$

make up the set of *integers*.

A real number is said to be a *rational number* if it can be written as the ratio of two integers, where the denominator is not 0. Thus, for example, numbers such as

$$-16\frac{2}{3}, \frac{-5}{6}, 0, 25, 12\frac{5}{8}$$

are rational numbers. Clearly, then, all integers and fractions are rational numbers. Percents and decimal numbers are rational as well, since they can also be written as the ratio of two integers. For example,

$$25\% = \frac{1}{4}, \text{ and } 9.125 = 9\frac{1}{8}.$$

Any real number that cannot be expressed as the ratio of two integers is called an *irrational number*. The most common irrational numbers that you will see on your test are square roots, such as $\sqrt{3}$ or $-\sqrt{5}$, and the number π, which represents the ratio of the circumference of a circle to its diameter.

Finally, the set of rational numbers, together with the set of irrational numbers, is called the set of *real numbers*.

Example

The number −257 is an integer. It is also rational since it can be written as $\frac{-257}{1}$, and is, of course, real.

The number $\frac{5}{8}$ is rational and real, and the number $\sqrt{7}$ is irrational and real.

Rounding of Numbers

From time to time, a test question will ask you to round an answer to a specific decimal place. The rules for the rounding of numbers are very simple. In the case of whole numbers, begin by locating the digit to which the number is being rounded. Then, if the digit just to the right is 0, 1, 2, 3, or 4, leave the located digit alone. Otherwise, increase the located digit by 1. In either case, replace all digits to the right of the one located with 0's.

When rounding decimal numbers, the rules are similar. Again, begin by locating the digit to which the number is being rounded. As before, if the digit just to the right is 0, 1, 2, 3, or 4, leave the located digit alone. Otherwise, increase the located digit by 1. Finally, drop all the digits to the right of the one located.

Example

Round the following numbers as indicated.

6,342 to the nearest 10

Begin by locating the ten's digit, which is a 4. The number to the right of the 4 is a 2. Thus, drop the 2 and replace it with a 0, yielding 6,340.

392.461 to the nearest tenth

The tenth's digit is 4. The digit just to the right of it is 6, so increase the tenth's digit by 1, making it a 5. Drop the two digits to the right of this. The answer is 392.5.

.0472 to the nearest thousandth

Following the rules above, we obtain .047.

MATHEMATICS REVIEW

Properties of Numbers Problems

1. Classify each of the following numbers as whole, integer, rational, irrational, and real.

   a. -7

   b. $\frac{1}{7}$

   c. $5\frac{2}{3}$

   d. 0

   e. $\sqrt{13}$

2. Round each of the numbers below to the indicated number of decimal places.

   a. 57,380 to the nearest hundred
   b. 1,574,584 to the nearest hundred thousand
   c. 847.235 to the nearest hundredth
   d. 9.00872 to the nearest thousandth

Solutions

1. a. -7 is real, rational, and an integer

   b. $\frac{1}{7}$ is real and rational

   c. $5\frac{2}{3}$ can be written as $\frac{17}{3}$ and is thus real and rational

   d. 0 is real, rational, an integer, and a whole number

   e. $\sqrt{13}$ is real and irrational

2. a. Begin by locating the hundred's digit, which is 3. The digit to the right of it is 8, so increase the hundred's digit by 1, and replace all digits to the right with 0's. The answer is 57,400.

   b. The hundred thousandth's digit is 5. The digit to the right of it is 7, so increase the 5 by 1, and replace all digits to the right with 0's. The answer is 1,600,000.

   c. The hundredth's digit is 3. The digit just to the right of it is 5, so increase the hundredth's digit by 1, making it a 4. Drop the digit to the right of this. The answer is 847.24.

   d. The thousandth's digit is 8. The digit just to the right of it is 7, so increase the thousandth's digit by 1, making it a 9. Drop the digits to the right of this. The answer is 9.009.

Peterson's: www.petersons.com

SUBJECT REVIEWS

Set Theory and Venn Diagrams

Definitions

A *set* is any collection of objects. The objects in a particular set are called the *members* or the *elements* of the set. In mathematics, sets are usually represented by capital letters, and their members are represented by lower case letters. Braces, { and }, are usually used to enclose the members of a set. Thus, the set A, which has members $a, b, c, d,$ and e and no other members, can be written as $A = \{a, b, c, d, e\}$. Note that the order in which the elements of a set are listed is not important; thus the set $\{1, 2, 3\}$ and the set $\{2, 3, 1\}$ represent identical sets.

The symbol used to indicate that an element belongs to a particular set is $\in$, and the symbol that indicates an element does not belong to a set is $\notin$. Thus, if $B = \{2, 4, 6, 8\}$, we can say $6 \in B$ and $7 \notin B$. If is a set is defined so that it does not contain any elements, it is called the *empty* set, or the *null* set, and can be written as $\{\ \}$, or $\emptyset$.

There are several different notational techniques that can be used to represent a set. The simplest one is called *numeration*, in which all of the elements of the set are listed within braces. For example, if C is the set of all odd integers between 10 and 20, we can use numeration to represent the set as $C = \{11, 13, 15, 17, 19\}$. The other is called set-builder notation. In this notation, a short vertical bar is used to stand for the phrase "such that." For example, the set of all integers less than 15 can be written as

$$\{\chi \mid \chi < 15, \chi \text{ is an integer}\}$$

and is read, "The set of all χ such that χ is less than 15, and χ is an integer."

A set that contains a finite number of elements is called a *finite* set. A set that is neither finite nor empty is called an *infinite* set. When using the method of numeration to describe a set, we can use three dots to indicate "and so on." Thus, the infinite set containing all positive integers can be written as $\{1, 2, 3, 4, \ldots\}$. The finite set containing all of the even integers between 2 and 200 can be numerated as $\{2, 4, 6, \ldots, 200\}$.

Example 1

Use numeration to express the set of whole numbers.

$\{0, 1, 2, 3, 4, 5, \ldots\}$

Example 2

Use set-builder notation to express the set of integers that are greater than or equal to 200.

$\{\chi \mid \chi \geq 200, \chi \text{ is an integer}\}$

Subsets and the Universal Set

Suppose that J is the set containing everyone who lives in New Jersey, and K is the set of all people living in New Jersey who are older that 65. Then, clearly, all members of K are also members of J, and we say "K is a subset of J." This relationship is written symbolically as $K \subseteq J$. In general, A is a *subset* of B if every element of A is also an element of B. For example, the set $A = \{2, 4, 6\}$ is a subset of the set $B = \{0, 2, 4, 6, 8, 10\}$. By convention, we agree that the null set is a subset of every other set. Thus, we can write $\emptyset \subseteq A$, where A is any set. Also note that if A and B contain exactly the same elements, then $A \supseteq B$ and $B \supseteq A$. In such a case, we write $A = B$. If $A \subseteq B$ but $A \neq B$, we call A a *proper subset* of B. This is written $A \subset B$. Thus, if A is a subset of B, and B contains at least one element that is not in A, then A is a proper subset of B and we write $A \subset B$.

In a particular discussion, the *universal set* represents the largest possible set, that is, it is the set that contains all of the possible elements under consideration. All other sets in the discussion must therefore be subsets of the universal set, which is usually represented by the letter U. If N is a subset of U, then N', which is called the *complement* of N, is the set of all elements from the universal set that are not in N. For example, if, in a particular problem, U is the set of all integers and N is the set of negative integers, then N' is the set of all nonnegative integers.

Example 1

List all of the subsets of $\{2, 4, 6\}$.

$\{2\}, \{4\}, \{6\}, \{2, 4\}, \{2, 6\} \{4, 6\}, \{2, 4, 6\}, \emptyset$

Example 2

If $U = \{7, 8, 9, 10, 11\}$, and $N = \{9, 11\}$, find N'

N' contains all of the elements of U that are not in N. Thus, $N' = \{7, 8, 10\}$

Venn Diagrams, Union and Intersection

Let U be a universal set, and N a subset of U. Then, the drawing below, called a *Venn diagram*, illustrates the relationship between U, N, and N'.

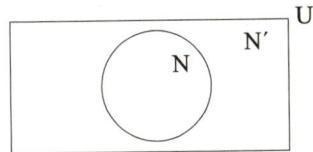

The *union* of two sets A and B, indicated $A \cup B$, is the set of all elements that are in either A or B. The *intersection* of two sets, indicated $A \cap B$, is the set of all elements that are in both A and B. Thus, if $A = \{2, 4, 6, 8, 10\}$ and $B = \{1, 2, 3, 4\}$, we have $A \cap B = \{1, 2, 3, 4, 6, 8, 10\}$ and $A \cap B = \{2, 4\}$. If $A \cap B = \emptyset$, then A and B are said to be *disjoint*.

The Venn diagrams below represent the operations of union and intersection.

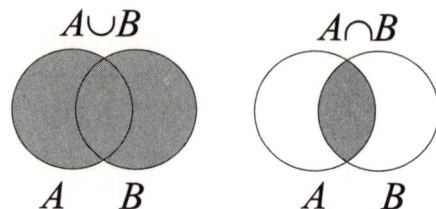

Set Problems

1. Use set-builder notation to describe the set of all integers greater than 12 and less than 48.

2. Use numeration to describe the set of negative integers

3. List all of the subsets of the set $\{a, b, c, d\}$.

4. If $A = \{2, 4, 6\}$, $B = \{1, 3, 5\}$, and $C = \{2, 3, 4\}$, find $A \cup B, A \cup C, A \cap C, A \cap B,$ and $A \cap (B \cup C)$.

5. If $U = \{2, 4, 6, 8, 10, 12, 14, 16, 18, 20\}$ and $W = \{2, 6, 12, 18\}$, find W'.

In problems 6–9, describe the sets listed in terms of D, E, and F and intersections, unions, and complements.

6. $\{\chi \mid \chi \in D \text{ and } \chi \notin E\}$

7. $\{\chi \mid \chi \in F \text{ or } \chi \in E\}$

8. $\{\chi \mid \chi \in D \text{ and } \chi \in E\}$

9. $\{\chi \mid \chi \in D \text{ and } X \text{ is not an element of either } E \text{ or } F\}$

10. Draw a Venn diagram to represent the set $(A \cap B) \cap C$.

Solutions

1. $\{x \mid 12 < x < 48, x \text{ is an integer}\}$
2. $\{\ldots, -4, -3, -2, -1\}$
3. $\emptyset$, {a}, {b}, {c}, {d}, {a, b}, {a, c}, {a, d}, {b, c}, {b, d}, {c, d}, {a, b, c}, {a, b, d}, {a, c, d}, {b, c, d}, {a, b, c, d}.
4. $A \cup B = \{1, 2, 3, 4, 5, 6\}$, $A \cup C = \{2, 3, 4, 6\}$, $A \cap C = \{2, 4\}$, $A \cap B = \emptyset$, $A \cap (B \cup C) = \{2, 4\}$.
5. $W' = \{4, 8, 10, 14, 16, 20\}$
6. $D \cap E'$
7. $F \cup E$
8. $D \cap E$
9. $D \cap (E \cup F)'$
10.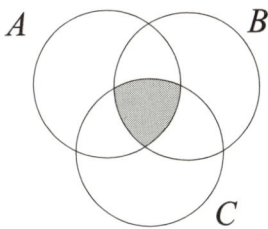

ARITHMETIC

Whole Numbers

Definitions
As we have already seen, the set of positive integers (natural numbers, counting numbers) can be written as the set $\{1, 2, 3, 4, 5, \ldots\}$. The set of positive integers, together with the number 0, are called the set of *whole numbers*, and can be written as $\{0, 1, 2, 3, 4, \ldots\}$.

Place Value
Whole numbers are expressed in a system of tens, called the *decimal* system. Ten *digits*—0, 1, 2, 3, 4, 5, 6, 7, 8, and 9—are used. Each digit differs not only in *face* value but also in *place* value, depending on where it stands in the number.

Example 1

237 means:

$$(2 \cdot 100) + (3 \cdot 10) + (7 \cdot 1)$$

The digit 2 has face value 2 but place value of 200.

Example 2

35,412 can be written as:

$$(3 \cdot 10{,}000) + (5 \cdot 1{,}000) + (4 \cdot 100) + (1 \cdot 10) + (2 \cdot 1)$$

The digit in the last place on the right is said to be in the units or ones place, the digit to the left of that in the tens place, the next digit to the left of that in the hundreds place and so on.

When we take a whole number and write it out as in the two examples above, it is said to be written in *expanded form*.

Odd and Even Numbers

A whole number is *even* if it is divisible by 2; it is *odd* if it is not divisible by 2. Zero is thus an even number.

Example

2, 4, 6, 8, and 320 are even numbers; 3, 7, 9, 21, and 45 are odd numbers.

Prime Numbers

The positive integer p is said to be a prime number (or simply *a prime*) if $p \neq 1$ and the only positive divisors of p are itself and 1. The first ten primes are 2, 3, 5, 7, 11, 13, 17, 19, 23, and 29. All other positive integers that are neither 1 nor prime are *composite numbers*. Composite numbers can be *factored*, that is, expressed as products of their divisors or factors; for example, $56 = 7 \cdot 8 = 7 \cdot 4 \cdot 2$. In particular, composite numbers can be expressed as products of their *prime* factors in just one way (except for order).

To factor a composite number into its prime factors, proceed as follows. First try to divide the number by the prime number 2. If this is successful, continue to divide by 2 until an odd number is obtained. Then attempt to divide the last quotient by the prime number 3 and by 3 again, as many times as possible. Then move on to dividing by the prime number 5, and other successive primes until a prime quotient is obtained. Express the original number as a product of all its prime divisors.

Example

Find the prime factors of 210.

$$\begin{array}{r} 2\,)\overline{210} \\ 3\,)\overline{105} \\ 5\,)\overline{35} \\ 7 \end{array}$$

Therefore:

   $210 = 2 \cdot 3 \cdot 5 \cdot 7$ (written in any order)

and 210 is an integer multiple of 2, of 3, of 5, and of 7.

Consecutive Whole Numbers

Numbers are consecutive if each number is the successor of the number that precedes it. In a consecutive series of whole numbers, an odd number is always followed by an even number, and an even number by an odd. If three consecutive whole numbers are given, either two of them are odd and one is even or two are even and one is odd.

Examples

7, 8, 9, 10, and 11 are consecutive whole numbers.

8, 10, 12, and 14 are consecutive even numbers.

21, 23, 25, and 27 are consecutive odd numbers.

21, 23, and 27 are *not* consecutive odd numbers because 25 is missing.

The Number Line

A useful method of representing numbers geometrically makes it easier to understand numbers. It is called the *number line*. Draw a horizontal line, considered to extend without end in both directions. Select some point on the line and label it with the number 0. This point is called the *origin*. Choose some convenient distance as a unit of length. Take the point on the number line that lies one unit to the right of the origin and label it with the number 1. The point on the number line that is one unit to the right of 1 is labeled 2, and so on. In this way, every whole number is associated with one point on the line, but it is not true that every point on the line represents a whole number.

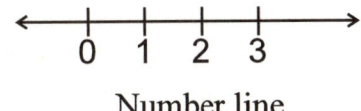

Number line

SUBJECT REVIEWS

Ordering of Whole Numbers

On the number line, the point representing 8 lies to the right of the point representing 5, and we say $8 > 5$ (read "8 is greater than 5"). One can also say $5 < 8$ ("5 is less than 8"). For any two whole numbers a and b, there are always three possibilities:

$$a < b, \quad a = b, \quad \text{or} \quad a > b.$$

If $a = b$, the points representing the numbers a and b coincide on the number line.

Operations with Whole Numbers

The basic operations on whole numbers are addition (+), subtraction (−), multiplication (· or ×), and division (÷). These are all *binary* operations—that is, one works with two numbers at a time in order to get a unique answer. The operations of addition and multiplication on whole numbers are said to be *closed* because the answer in each case is also a whole number. The operations of subtraction and division on whole numbers are not closed because the unique answer is not necessarily a member of the set of whole numbers.

Examples

$3 + 4 = 7$ a whole number
$4 \cdot 3 = 12$ a whole number
$2 - 5 = -3$ not a whole number
$3 \div 8 = \frac{3}{8}$ not a whole number

Addition

If addition is a binary operation, how are three numbers—say, 3, 4, and 8—added? One way is to write:

$$(3 + 4) + 8 = 7 + 8 = 15$$

Another way is to write:

$$3 + (4 + 8) = 3 + 12 = 15$$

The parentheses merely group the numbers together. The fact that the same answer, 15, is obtained either way illustrates the *associative property* of addition:

$$(r + s) + t = r + (s + t)$$

The order in which whole numbers are added is immaterial—that is, $3 + 4 = 4 + 3$. This principle is called the *commutative property* of addition. Most people use this property without realizing it when they add a column of numbers from the top down and then check their result by beginning over again from the bottom. (Even though

Peterson's SSAT/ISEE Success

there may be a long column of numbers, only two numbers are added at a time.)

If 0 is added to any whole number, the whole number is unchanged. Zero is called the *identity element* for addition.

Subtraction

Subtraction is the inverse of addition. The order in which the numbers are written is important; there is no commutative property for subtraction.

$$4 - 3 \neq 3 - 4$$

The $\neq$ is read "not equal."

Multiplication

Multiplication is a commutative operation:

$$43 \cdot 73 = 73 \cdot 43$$

The result or answer in a multiplication problem is called the *product*.

If a number is multiplied by 1, the number is unchanged; the *identity element* for multiplication is 1.

Zero times any number is 0:

$$42 \cdot 0 = 0$$

Multiplication can be expressed with several different symbols:

$$9 \cdot 7 \cdot 3 = 9 \times 7 \times 3 = 9(7)(3)$$

Besides being commutative, multiplication is *associative*:

$$(9 \cdot 7) \cdot 3 = 63 \cdot 3 = 189$$

and

$$9 \cdot (7 \cdot 3) = 9 \cdot 21 = 189$$

A number can be quickly multiplied by 10 by adding a zero at the right of the number. Similarly, a number can be multiplied by 100 by adding two zeros at the right:

$$38 \cdot 10 = 380$$

and

$$100 \cdot 76 = 7{,}600$$

SUBJECT REVIEWS

Division

Division is the inverse of multiplication. It is not commutative:

$$8 \div 4 \neq 4 \div 8$$

The parts of a division example are named as follows:

$$\text{divisor} \overline{\smash{\big)}\, \text{dividend}}^{\text{quotient}}$$

If a number is divided by 1, the quotient is the original number.

Division by 0 is not defined (has no meaning). Zero divided by any number other than 0 is 0:

$$0 \div 56 = 0$$

Divisors and Multiples

The whole number b *divides* the whole number a if there exists a whole number k such that $a = bk$. The whole number a is then said to be an integer *multiple* of b, and b is called a *divisor* (or *factor*) of a.

Examples

3 divides 15 because $15 = 3 \cdot 5$. Thus, 3 is a divisor of 15 (and so is 5), and 15 is an integer multiple of 3 (and of 5).

3 does not divide 8 because $8 \neq 3k$ for a whole number k.

Divisors of 28 are 1, 2, 4, 7, 14, and 28.

Multiples of 3 are 3, 6, 9, 12, 15, . . .

Whole Number Problems

1. What is the prime factorization of 78?
2. What are the divisors of 56?
3. Which property is illustrated by the following statement?

    $(3 + 5) + 8 = 3 + (5 + 8)$

4. Which property is illustrated by the following statement?

    $(5 \cdot 7) \cdot 3 = (7 \cdot 5) \cdot 3$

5. Find the first five multiples of 7.
6. Find all of the common prime factors of 30 and 105.
7. Give an example to show that subtraction on the set of real numbers is not commutative.
8. List all of the prime numbers between 50 and 90.

9. Write the number 786,534 in expanded notation.

10. In each of the statements below, replace the # with either <, >, or = to make a true statement.

    a. −12 # 13

    b. $\frac{1}{16}$ # 0.0625

    c. $3\frac{1}{2}$ # $3\frac{2}{5}$

Solutions:

1. $78 = 2 \cdot 39 = 2 \cdot 3 \cdot 13$

2. The divisors of 56 are 1, 2, 4, 7, 8, 14, 28, 56

3. The Associative Property of Addition

4. The Commutative Property of Multiplication

5. 7, 14, 21, 28, 35

6. 30 can be factored as 2 × 3 × 5. 105 can be factored as 3 × 5 × 7. Thus, the common factors are 3 and 5.

7. $4 - 5 \neq 5 - 4$

8. The prime numbers between 50 and 90 are 53, 59, 61, 67, 71, 73, 79, 83, 87, and 89

9. $786{,}534 = 7(100{,}000) + 8(10{,}000) + 6(1{,}000) + 5(100) + 3(10) + 4$

10. a. $-12 < 13$

    b. $\frac{1}{16} = 0.0625$

    c. $3\frac{1}{2} > 3\frac{2}{5}$

Peterson's: www.petersons.com

Fractions

Definitions

If a and b are whole numbers and $b \neq 0$, the symbol $\frac{a}{b}$ (or a/b) is called a fraction. The upper part, a, is called the *numerator*, and the lower part, b, is called the *denominator*. The denominator indicates into how many parts something is divided, and the numerator tells how many of these parts are taken. A fraction indicates division:

$$\frac{7}{8} = 8\overline{)7}$$

If the numerator of a fraction is 0, the value of the fraction is 0. If the denominator of a fraction is 0, the fraction is not defined (has no meaning):

$$\frac{0}{17} = 0 \qquad \frac{17}{0} \text{ not defined (has no meaning)}$$

If the denominator of a fraction is 1, the value of the fraction is the same as the numerator:

$$\frac{18}{1} = 18$$

If the numerator and denominator are the same number, the value of the fraction is 1:

$$\frac{7}{7} = 1$$

Equivalent Fractions

Fractions that represent the same number are said to be *equivalent*.

If m is a counting number and $\frac{a}{b}$ is a fraction, then: $\frac{m \times a}{m \times b} = \frac{a}{b}$

because $\frac{m}{m} = 1$ and $1 \times \frac{a}{b} = \frac{a}{b}$

Example

$$\frac{2}{3} = \frac{4}{6} = \frac{6}{9} = \frac{8}{12}$$

These fractions are all equivalent.

Inequality of Fractions

If two fractions are not equivalent, one is smaller than the other. The ideas of "less than" and "greater than" were previously defined and used for whole numbers.

For the fractions $\frac{a}{b}$ and $\frac{c}{b}$: $\frac{a}{b} < \frac{c}{b}$ if $a < c$

That is, if two fractions have the same denominator, the one with the smaller numerator has the smaller value.

If two fractions have different denominators, find a common denominator by multiplying one denominator by the other. Then use the common denominator to compare numerators.

Example 1

Which is smaller, $\frac{5}{8}$ or $\frac{4}{7}$?

$8 \cdot 7 = 56 =$ common denominator

$$\frac{5}{8} \times \frac{7}{7} = \frac{35}{56} \qquad \frac{4}{7} \times \frac{8}{8} = \frac{32}{56}$$

Since $32 < 35$,

$$\frac{32}{56} < \frac{35}{56} \text{ and } \frac{4}{7} < \frac{5}{8}$$

Example 2

Which of the fractions, $\frac{2}{5}$, $\frac{3}{7}$, or $\frac{4}{11}$, is the largest?

We begin by comparing the first two fractions. Since $\frac{2}{5} = \frac{14}{35}$ and $\frac{3}{7} = \frac{15}{35}$, we can see that $\frac{3}{7}$ is bigger. Now, we compare $\frac{3}{7}$ to $\frac{4}{11}$. Since $\frac{3}{7} = \frac{33}{77}$ and $\frac{4}{11} = \frac{28}{77}$, we can see that $\frac{3}{7}$ is the biggest of the three fractions.

Reducing to Lowest Terms

The principle that

$$\frac{m \times a}{m \times b} = \frac{a}{b}$$

can be particularly useful in reducing fractions to lowest terms. Fractions are expressed in *lowest terms* when the numerator and denominator have no common factor except 1. To reduce a fraction to an equivalent fraction in lowest terms, express the numerator and denominator as products of their prime factors. Each time a prime appears in the numerator over the same prime in the denominator, $\frac{p}{p}$, substitute its equal value, 1.

Example 1

Reduce $\frac{30}{42}$ to an equivalent fraction in lowest terms:

$$\frac{30}{42} = \frac{2 \cdot 3 \cdot 5}{2 \cdot 3 \cdot 7} = 1 \cdot 1 \cdot \frac{5}{7} = \frac{5}{7}$$

In practice, this can be done even more quickly by dividing numerator and denominator by any number, prime or not, that will divide both evenly. Repeat this process until there is no prime factor remaining that is common to both numerator and denominator:

$$\frac{30}{42} = \frac{15}{21} = \frac{5}{7}$$

Example 2

Reduce $\frac{77}{197}$ to an equivalent fraction in lowest terms:

$$\frac{77}{197} = \frac{7 \times 11}{3 \times 5 \times 13}$$

Since the numerator and the denominator have no common factors, the fraction is already in lowest terms.

Proper Fractions, Improper Fractions, and Mixed Numbers

Definitions

A *proper fraction* is a fraction whose numerator is smaller than its denominator. Proper fractions always have a value less than 1:

$$\frac{3}{4} \quad \frac{5}{8} \quad \frac{121}{132} \quad \frac{0}{1}$$

An *improper fraction* is a fraction with numerator equal to or greater than the denominator. Improper fractions always have a value equal to or greater than 1:

$$\frac{3}{2} \quad \frac{17}{17} \quad \frac{9}{1} \quad \frac{15}{14}$$

A *mixed number* is a number composed of a whole number and a proper fraction. It is always greater than 1 in value:

$$3\frac{7}{8} \quad 5\frac{1}{4} \quad 11\frac{3}{14}$$

The symbol $3\frac{7}{8}$ means $3 + \frac{7}{8}$ and is read "three and seven-eighths."

To Change a Mixed Number into an Improper Fraction

Multiply the denominator by the whole number and add this product to the numerator. Use the sum so obtained as the new numerator, and keep the original denominator.

Example

Write $9\frac{4}{11}$ as an improper fraction:

$$9\frac{4}{11} = \frac{(11 \times 9) + 4}{11} = \frac{99 + 4}{11} = \frac{103}{11}$$

Note: In any calculations with mixed numbers, first change the mixed numbers to improper fractions.

SUBJECT REVIEWS

To Change an Improper Fraction into a Mixed Number

Divide the numerator by the denominator. The result is the whole-number part of the mixed number. If there is a remainder in the division process because the division does not come out evenly, put the remainder over the denominator (divisor). This gives the fractional part of the mixed number:

$$\frac{20}{3} = 3\overline{)20} = 6\frac{2}{3}$$
(quotient 6, 18, 2 remainder)

Multiplication

Proper and Improper Fractions

Multiply the two numerators and then multiply the two denominators. If the numerator obtained is larger than the denominator, divide the numerator of the resulting fraction by its denominator:

$$\frac{3}{8} \times \frac{15}{11} = \frac{45}{88} \qquad \frac{3}{8} \times \frac{22}{7} = \frac{66}{56} = 1\frac{10}{56}$$

Multiplication of fractions is commutative.

Three or more fractions are multiplied in the same way; two numerators are done at a time, and the result is multiplied by the next numerator.

The product in the multiplication of fractions is usually expressed in lowest terms.

Canceling

In multiplying fractions, if any of the numerators and denominators have a common divisor (factor), divide each of them by this common factor and the value of the fraction remains the same. This process is called *canceling* or *cancellation*.

Example

$$\frac{\cancel{27}^{9}}{\cancel{18}_{2}} \times \frac{\cancel{90}^{10}}{\cancel{300}_{100}} = ?$$

$$\frac{27}{18} \times \frac{90}{300} = \frac{27}{18} \times \frac{9}{30} \qquad \text{Divide second fraction by } \frac{10}{10}$$

$$= \frac{\overset{9}{\cancel{27}}}{\underset{2}{\cancel{18}}} \times \frac{\overset{1}{\cancel{9}}}{\underset{10}{\cancel{30}}}$$
Cancel: 18 and 9 each divisible by 9; 27 and 30 each divisible by 3

$$= \frac{9 \times 1}{2 \times 10} = \frac{9}{20}$$
Multiply numerators; multiply denominators

Another method:

$$\frac{\overset{3}{\cancel{27}}}{\underset{2}{\cancel{18}}} \times \frac{\overset{3}{\cancel{9}}}{\underset{10}{\cancel{30}}} = \frac{3 \times 3}{2 \times 10} = \frac{9}{20}$$

Cancel: 27 and 18 have common factor 9; 9 and 30 have common factor 3

Note: Canceling can take place only between a numerator and a denominator in the same or a different fraction, never between two numerators or between two denominators.

Mixed Numbers

Mixed numbers should be changed to improper fractions before multiplying. Then multiply as described above.

Example

To multiply

$$\frac{4}{7} \times 3\frac{5}{8}$$

change $3\frac{5}{8}$ to an improper fraction:

$$3\frac{5}{8} = \frac{(8 \times 3) + 5}{8} = \frac{24 + 5}{8} = \frac{29}{8}$$

Multiply

$$\frac{\overset{1}{\cancel{4}}}{7} \times \frac{29}{\underset{2}{\cancel{8}}} = \frac{29}{14}$$

The answer can be left in this form or changed to a mixed number: $2\frac{1}{14}$

SUBJECT REVIEWS

Fractions with Whole Numbers

Write the whole number as a fraction with a denominator of 1 and then multiply:

$$\frac{3}{4} \times 7 = \frac{3}{4} \times \frac{7}{1} = \frac{21}{4} = 5\frac{1}{4}$$

Note: When any fraction is multiplied by 1, its value remains unchanged. When any fraction is multiplied by 0, the product is 0.

Division

Reciprocals

Division of fractions involves reciprocals. One fraction is the *reciprocal* of another if the product of the fractions is 1.

Example 1

$\frac{3}{4}$ and $\frac{4}{3}$ are reciprocals since

$$\frac{\cancel{3}}{\cancel{4}} \times \frac{\cancel{4}}{\cancel{3}} = \frac{1 \times 1}{1 \times 1} = 1$$

Example 2

$\frac{1}{3}$ and 3 are reciprocals since

$$\frac{1}{\cancel{3}} \times \frac{\cancel{3}}{1} = 1$$

To find the reciprocal of a fraction, interchange the numerator and denominator—that is, invert the fraction, or turn it upside down.

Proper and Improper Fractions

Multiply the first fraction (dividend) by the reciprocal of the second fraction (divisor). Reduce by cancellation if possible. If you wish to, change the answer to a mixed number when possible:

Example

$$\frac{9}{2} \div \frac{4}{7} = \frac{9}{2} \times \frac{7}{4} \quad \text{The reciprocal of } \frac{4}{7} \text{ is } \frac{7}{4} \text{ because } \frac{4}{7} \times \frac{7}{4} = 1$$

$$= \frac{63}{8}$$

$$= 7\frac{7}{8}$$

Mixed Numbers and/or Whole Numbers

Both mixed numbers and whole numbers must first be changed to equivalent improper fractions. Then proceed as described above.

Note: If a fraction or a mixed number is divided by 1, its value is unchanged. Division of a fraction or a mixed number by 0 is not defined. If a fraction is divided by itself or an equivalent fraction, the quotient is 1:

$$\frac{19}{7} \div \frac{19}{7} = \frac{19}{7} \times \frac{7}{19} \qquad \text{Reciprocal of } \frac{19}{7} \text{ is } \frac{7}{19}$$

$$= 1 \times 1 = 1$$

Addition

Fractions can be added only if their denominators are the same (called the *common denominator*). Add the numerators; the denominator remains the same. Reduce the sum to the lowest terms:

$$\frac{3}{8} + \frac{2}{8} + \frac{1}{8} = \frac{3+2+1}{8} = \frac{6}{8} = \frac{3}{4}$$

When the fractions have different denominators, you must find a common denominator. One way of doing this is to find the product of the different denominators.

Example

$$\frac{5}{6} + \frac{1}{4} = ?$$

A common denominator is $6 \cdot 4 = 24$.

$$\frac{5}{6} \times \frac{4}{4} = \frac{20}{24} \quad \text{and} \quad \frac{1}{4} \times \frac{6}{6} = \frac{6}{24}$$

$$\frac{5}{6} + \frac{1}{4} = \frac{20}{24} + \frac{6}{24}$$

$$= \frac{20+6}{24}$$

$$= \frac{26}{24}$$

$$= \frac{13}{12}$$

$$= 1\frac{1}{12}$$

Least Common Denominator

A denominator can often be found that is smaller than the product of the different denominators. If the denominator of each fraction will divide into such a number evenly and it is the *smallest* such number, it is called the *least* (or *lowest*) *common denominator*, abbreviated as LCD. Finding a least common denominator may make it unnecessary to reduce the answer and enables one to work with smaller numbers. There are two common methods.

First Method: By Inspection

$$\frac{5}{6} + \frac{1}{4} = ?$$

LCD = 12 because 12 is the smallest number into which 6 and 4 divide evenly. Therefore:

$12 \div 6 = 2$ multiply $\frac{5}{6} \times \frac{2}{2} = \frac{10}{12}$

$12 \div 4 = 3$ multiply $\frac{1}{4} \times \frac{3}{3} = \frac{3}{12}$

Then:

$$\frac{5}{6} + \frac{1}{4} = \frac{10}{12} + \frac{3}{12}$$
$$= \frac{13}{12}$$
$$= 1\frac{1}{12}$$

Second Method: By Factoring

This method can be used when the LCD is not recognized by inspection. Factor each denominator into its prime factors. The LCD is the product of the highest power of each separate factor, where *power* refers to the number of times a factor occurs.

Example

$$\frac{5}{6} + \frac{1}{4} = ?$$

Factoring denominators gives:

$6 = 2 \cdot 3$ and $4 = 2 \cdot 2$

LCD $= 2 \cdot 2 \cdot 3$

$ = 12$

Convert to LCD:

$$\frac{5}{6} \times \frac{2}{2} = \frac{10}{12} \qquad \frac{1}{4} \times \frac{3}{3} = 12$$

$$\frac{5}{6} + \frac{1}{4} = \frac{10}{12} + \frac{3}{12}$$

$$= \frac{13}{12}$$

$$= 1\frac{1}{12}$$

The denominators 4 and 6 factor into 2 · 2 and 2 · 3, respectively. Although the factor 2 *appears* three times, its power is 2^2 from factoring 4. The factor 3 appears once, so its power is 3^1. Therefore, the LCD as a *product* of the *highest power of each separate factor* is 2 × 2 × 3.

The factoring method of adding fractions can be extended to three or more fractions.

Example

$$\frac{1}{4} + \frac{3}{8} + \frac{1}{12} = ?$$

Factoring denominators gives:

$$4 = 2 \cdot 2 \qquad 8 = 2 \cdot 2 \cdot 2 \qquad 12 = 2 \cdot 2 \cdot 3$$

$$\text{LCD} = 2 \cdot 2 \cdot 2 \cdot 3$$

$$= 24$$

Convert to LCD:

$$\frac{1}{4} \times \frac{6}{6} = \frac{6}{24} \qquad \frac{3}{8} \times \frac{3}{3} = \frac{9}{24}$$

$$\frac{1}{12} \times \frac{2}{2} = \frac{2}{24}$$

$$\frac{1}{4} + \frac{3}{8} + \frac{1}{12} = \frac{6}{24} + \frac{9}{24} + \frac{2}{24}$$

$$= \frac{6 + 9 + 2}{24}$$

$$= \frac{17}{24}$$

SUBJECT REVIEWS

Addition of Mixed Numbers

Change any mixed numbers to fractions. If the fractions have the same denominator, add the numerators. If the fractions have different denominators, find the LCD of the several denominators and then add numerators. Reduce the answer if possible. Write the answer as a mixed number if you wish.

Example

$$2\frac{2}{3} + 5\frac{1}{2} + 1\frac{2}{9} = ?$$

Factoring denominators gives:

$3 = 3 \qquad 2 = 2 \qquad 9 = 3 \cdot 3$

$\text{LCD} = 2 \cdot 3 \cdot 3$

$\phantom{\text{LCD}} = 18$

Convert to LCD:

$$\frac{8}{3} \times \frac{6}{6} = \frac{48}{18} \qquad \frac{11}{2} \times \frac{9}{9} = \frac{99}{18} \qquad \frac{11}{9} \times \frac{2}{2} = \frac{22}{18}$$

$$2\frac{2}{3} + 5\frac{1}{2} + 1\frac{2}{9} = \frac{8}{3} + \frac{11}{2} + \frac{11}{9}$$

$$= \frac{48}{18} + \frac{99}{18} + \frac{22}{18}$$

$$= \frac{48 + 99 + 22}{18}$$

$$= \frac{169}{18} = 9\frac{7}{18}$$

Subtraction

Fractions can be subtracted only if the denominators are the same. If the denominators are the same, find the difference between the numerators. The denominator remains unchanged.

Example

$$\frac{19}{3} - \frac{2}{3} = ?$$

$$= \frac{19 - 2}{3}$$

$$= \frac{17}{3}$$

$$= 5\frac{2}{3}$$

When fractions have different denominators, find equivalent fractions with a common denominator and then subtract numerators.

Example

$$\frac{7}{8} - \frac{3}{4} = ?$$

Factoring denominators gives:

$8 = 2 \cdot 2 \cdot 2 \qquad 4 = 2 \cdot 2$

$\text{LCD} = 2 \cdot 2 \cdot 2$

$\qquad = 8$

Convert to LCD:

$$\frac{7}{8} = \frac{7}{8} \qquad \frac{3}{4} \times \frac{2}{2} = \frac{6}{8}$$

$$\frac{7}{8} - \frac{3}{4} = \frac{7}{8} - \frac{6}{8}$$

$$= \frac{7-6}{8}$$

$$= \frac{1}{8}$$

Mixed Numbers

To subtract mixed numbers, change each mixed number to a fraction. Find the LCD for the fractions. Write each fraction as an equivalent fraction whose denominator is the common denominator. Find the difference between the numerators.

Example

$$3\frac{3}{8} - 2\frac{5}{6} = ?$$

$\text{LCD} = 24$

$$3\frac{3}{8} - 2\frac{5}{6} = \frac{27}{8} - \frac{17}{6}$$

$$= \frac{81}{24} - \frac{68}{24}$$

$$= \frac{13}{24}$$

If zero is subtracted from a fraction, the result is the original fraction:

$$\frac{3}{4} - 0 = \frac{3}{4} - \frac{0}{4} = \frac{3}{4}$$

SUBJECT REVIEWS

Fraction Problems

In the following problems, perform the indicated operations and reduce the answers to lowest terms.

1. $\dfrac{5}{12} \times \dfrac{4}{15}$

2. $\dfrac{1}{2} \div \dfrac{3}{8}$

3. $\dfrac{5}{12} + \dfrac{2}{3}$

4. $\dfrac{2}{3} - \dfrac{5}{11}$

5. $3\dfrac{1}{3} \times \dfrac{4}{5}$

6. $7\dfrac{4}{5} - 2\dfrac{1}{3}$

7. $2\dfrac{3}{5} + 7\dfrac{3}{5}$

8. $\dfrac{6}{7} \times \dfrac{3}{4} \times \dfrac{2}{3}$

9. $6 \times \dfrac{2}{3} \times 2\dfrac{5}{6}$

10. $2\dfrac{2}{3} \div 1\dfrac{7}{9}$

Solutions

1. $\dfrac{5}{12} \times \dfrac{4}{15} = \dfrac{\cancel{5}^{1}}{\cancel{12}_{3}} \times \dfrac{\cancel{4}^{1}}{\cancel{15}_{3}} = \dfrac{1}{9}$

2. $\dfrac{1}{2} \div \dfrac{3}{8} = \dfrac{1}{2} \times \dfrac{8}{3} = \dfrac{1}{\cancel{2}_{1}} \times \dfrac{\cancel{8}^{4}}{3} = \dfrac{4}{3}$

3. $\dfrac{5}{12} + \dfrac{2}{3} = \dfrac{5}{12} + \dfrac{8}{12} = \dfrac{13}{12} = 1\dfrac{1}{12}$

4. $\dfrac{2}{3} - \dfrac{5}{11} = \dfrac{22}{33} - \dfrac{15}{33} = \dfrac{7}{33}$

5. $3\dfrac{1}{3} \times \dfrac{4}{5} = \dfrac{10}{3} \times \dfrac{4}{5} = \dfrac{\cancel{10}^{2}}{3} \times \dfrac{4}{\cancel{5}_{1}} = \dfrac{8}{3} = 2\dfrac{2}{3}$

6. $7\dfrac{4}{5} - 2\dfrac{1}{3} = \dfrac{39}{5} - \dfrac{7}{3} = \dfrac{117}{15} - \dfrac{35}{15} = \dfrac{82}{15} = 5\dfrac{7}{15}$

7. $2\frac{3}{5} + 7\frac{3}{5} = \frac{13}{5} + \frac{38}{5} = \frac{51}{5} = 10\frac{1}{5}$

8. $\frac{6}{7} \times \frac{3}{4} \times \frac{2}{3} = \frac{6}{7} \times \frac{2}{4} \times \frac{3}{3} = \frac{6}{7} \times \frac{1}{2} \times \frac{1}{1} = \frac{3}{7} \times \frac{1}{1} \times \frac{1}{1} = \frac{3}{7}$

9. $6 \times \frac{2}{3} \times 2\frac{5}{6} = \frac{6}{1} \times \frac{2}{3} \times \frac{17}{6} = \frac{34}{3} = 11\frac{1}{3}$

10. $2\frac{2}{3} \div 1\frac{7}{9} = \frac{8}{3} \div \frac{16}{9} = \frac{8}{3} \times \frac{9}{16} = \frac{9}{3} \times \frac{8}{16} = \frac{3}{1} \times \frac{1}{2} = \frac{3}{2}$

Decimals

Earlier, we stated that whole numbers are expressed in a system of tens, or the decimal system, using the digits from 0 to 9. This system can be extended to fractions by using a period called a *decimal point*. The digits after a decimal point form a *decimal fraction*. Decimal fractions are smaller than 1—for example, .3, .37, .372, and .105. The first position to the right of the decimal point is called the *tenths' place,* since the digit in that position tells how many tenths there are. The second digit to the right of the decimal point is in the *hundredths' place*. The third digit to the right of the decimal point is in the *thousandths' place,* and so on.

Example 1

.3 is a decimal fraction that means

$$3 \times \frac{1}{10} = \frac{3}{10}$$

read "three-tenths."

Example 2

The decimal fraction of .37 means

$$3 \times \frac{1}{10} + 7 \times \frac{1}{100} = 3 \times \frac{10}{100} + 7 \times \frac{1}{100}$$
$$= \frac{30}{100} + \frac{7}{100} = \frac{37}{100}$$

read "thirty-seven hundredths."

Example 3

The decimal fraction .372 means

$$\frac{300}{1,000} + \frac{70}{1,000} + \frac{2}{1,000} = \frac{372}{1,000}$$

read "three hundred seventy-two thousandths."

Whole numbers have an understood (unwritten) decimal point to the right of the last digit (i.e., 4 = 4.0). Decimal fractions can be combined with whole numbers to make *decimals*—for example, 3.246, 10.85, and 4.7.

Note: Adding zeros to the right of a decimal after the last digit does not change the value of the decimal.

Decimals and Fractions

Changing a Decimal to a Fraction
Place the digits to the right of the decimal point over the value of the place in which the last digit appears and reduce if possible. The whole number remains the same.

Example

Change 2.14 to a fraction or mixed number. Observe that 4 is the last digit and is in the hundredths' place.

$$.14 = \frac{14}{100} = \frac{7}{50}$$

Therefore:

$$2.14 = 2\frac{7}{50}$$

Changing a Fraction to a Decimal
Divide the numerator of the fraction by the denominator. First put a decimal point followed by zeros to the right of the number in the numerator. Add and divide until there is no remainder. The decimal point in the quotient is aligned directly above the decimal point in the dividend.

Example

Change $\frac{3}{8}$ to a decimal.

Divide

$$\begin{array}{r} .375 \\ 8\overline{)3.000} \\ \underline{24} \\ 60 \\ \underline{56} \\ 40 \\ \underline{40} \end{array}$$

When the division does not terminate with a 0 remainder, two courses are possible.

First Method

```
    .833
  ┌─────
6)5.000
   48
   ──
    20
    18
    ──
    20
    18
    ──
     2
```

The 3 in the quotient will be repeated indefinitely. It is called an *infinite decimal* and is written .833 . . . .

Second Method

Divide until there are two decimal places in the quotient and then write the remainder over the divisor.

Example

Change $\frac{5}{6}$ to a decimal.

$$6\overline{)5.000} = .83\frac{1}{3}$$

```
    .833
  ┌─────
6)5.000
   48
   ──
    20
    18
    ──
    20
```

Addition

Addition of decimals is both commutative and associative. Decimals are simpler to add than fractions. Place the decimals in a column with the decimal points aligned under each other. Add in the usual way. The decimal point of the answer is also aligned under the other decimal points.

Example

$43 + 2.73 + .9 + 3.01 = ?$

```
43.
 2.73
  .9
 3.01
─────
49.64
```

Subtraction

For subtraction, the decimal points must be aligned under each other. Add zeros to the right of the decimal point if desired. Subtract as with whole numbers.

Examples

$$\begin{array}{r} 21.567 \\ -9.4 \\ \hline 12.167 \end{array} \qquad \begin{array}{r} 21.567 \\ -9.48 \\ \hline 13.087 \end{array} \qquad \begin{array}{r} 39.00 \\ -17.48 \\ \hline 21.52 \end{array}$$

Multiplication

Multiplication of decimals is commutative and associative:

$$5.39 \times .04 = .04 \times 5.39$$
$$(.7 \times .02) \times .1 = .7 \cdot (.02 \times .1)$$

Multiply the decimals as if they were whole numbers. The total number of decimal places in the product is the sum of the number of places (to the right of the decimal point) in all of the numbers multiplied.

Example

$8.64 \times .003 = ?$

$$\begin{array}{rll} 8.64 & 2 & \text{places to right of decimal point} \\ \times .003 & +\ 3 & \text{places to right of decimal point} \\ \hline .02592 & 5 & \text{places to right of decimal point} \end{array}$$

A zero had to be added to the left of the product before writing the decimal point to ensure that there would be five decimal places in the product.

Note: To multiply a decimal by 10, simply move the decimal point one place to the right; to multiply by 100, move the decimal point two places to the right.

Division

To divide one decimal (the dividend) by another (the divisor), move the decimal point in the divisor as many places as necessary to the right to make the divisor a whole number. Then move the decimal point in the dividend (expressed or understood) a corresponding number of places, adding zeros if necessary. Then divide as with whole numbers. The decimal point in the quotient is placed above the decimal point in the dividend after the decimal point has been moved.

Example

Divide 7.6 by .32.

$$.32\overline{)7.60} = 32\overline{)760.00}$$

$$\begin{array}{r} 23.75 \\ 64 \\ \hline 120 \\ 96 \\ \hline 240 \\ 224 \\ \hline 160 \\ 160 \end{array}$$

Note: "Divide 7.6 by .32" can be written as $\frac{7.6}{.32}$. If this fraction is multiplied by $\frac{100}{100}$, an equivalent fraction is obtained with a whole number in the denominator:

$$\frac{7.6}{.32} \times \frac{100}{100} = \frac{760}{32}$$

Moving the decimal point two places to the right in both divisor and dividend is equivalent to multiplying each number by 100.

Special Cases

If the dividend has a decimal point and the divisor does not, divide as with whole numbers and place the decimal point of the quotient above the decimal point in the divisor.

If both dividend and divisor are whole numbers but the quotient is a decimal, place a decimal point after the last digit of the dividend and add zeros as necessary to get the required degree of accuracy. (*See* Changing a Fraction to a Decimal, page 162.)

Note: To divide any number by 10, simply move its decimal point (understood to be after the last digit for a whole number) one place to the left; to divide by 100, move the decimal point two places to the left; and so on.

Decimal Problems

1. Change the following decimals into fractions and reduce.

    a. 1.16
    b. 15.05

2. Change the following fractions into decimals.

    a. $\dfrac{3}{8}$

    b. $\dfrac{2}{3}$

In the following problems, perform the indicated operations.

3. 3.762 + 23.43

4. 1.368 − .559

5. 8.7 × .8

6. .045 ÷ .5

7. 73 − .46

8. 5.43 + .154 + 17

9. 7.2 × .002

10. 2.2 ÷ 8

11. Which of the three decimals .09, .769, and .8 is the smallest?

Solutions

1. a. $1.16 = 1\dfrac{16}{100} = 1\dfrac{8}{50} = 1\dfrac{4}{25}$

    b. $15.05 = 15\dfrac{5}{100} = 15\dfrac{1}{20}$

2. a. $\dfrac{3}{8} = 8\overline{)3.000}.375$

    $\underline{24}$
    60
    $\underline{-56}$
    40

    b. $\dfrac{2}{3} = 3\overline{)2.00}.666\ldots$

    $\underline{18}$
    20
    $\underline{-18}$
    20

MATHEMATICS REVIEW

3. 3.762
    $+23.43$
    $\overline{27.192}$

4. 1.368
    $-.559$
    $\overline{.809}$

5. 8.7
    $\times.8$
    $\overline{6.96}$

6. $.5\overline{)0.0.45}^{0.09}$

7. 73.00
    $-.46$
    $\overline{72.54}$

8. 5.43
    $.154$
    $+17.000$
    $\overline{22.584}$

9. 7.2 (One digit to the right of the decimal point)
    $\times.002$ (Three digits to the right of the decimal point)
    $\overline{.0144}$ (Four digits to the right of the decimal point)

10. $8\overline{)2.2}^{0.275}$

11. The easiest way to determine the smallest decimal number is to append 0's to the end of each of the numbers until they all have the same number of digits. Then, ignore the decimal points and see which number is the smallest. Thus, .09 = .090, .769 = .769, .8 = .800. Clearly, the smallest number is .09

Percents

Percents, like fractions and decimals, are ways of expressing parts of whole numbers, as 93%, 50%, and 22.4%. Percents are expressions of hundredths—that is, of fractions whose denominator is 100. The symbol for percent is "%".

Example

$$25\% = \text{twenty-five hundredths} = \frac{25}{100} = \frac{1}{4}$$

The word *percent* means *per hundred*. Its main use is in comparing fractions with equal denominators of 100.

Relationship with Fractions and Decimals

Changing a Percent to a Decimal

Divide the percent by 100 and drop the symbol for percent. Add zeros to the left when necessary:

$$30\% = .30 \qquad 1\% = .01$$

Remember that the short method of dividing by 100 is to move the decimal point two places to the left.

Changing a Decimal to a Percent

Multiply the decimal by 100 by moving the decimal point two places to the right, and add the symbol for percent:

$$.375 = 37.5\% \qquad .001 = .1\%$$

Changing a Percent to a Fraction

Drop the percent sign. Write the number as a numerator over a denominator of 100. If the numerator has a decimal point, move the decimal point to the right the necessary number of places to make the numerator a whole number. Add the same number of zeros to the right of the denominator as you moved places to the right in the numerator. Reduce where possible.

Examples

$$20\% = \frac{20}{100} = \frac{2}{10} = \frac{1}{5}$$

$$36.5\% = \frac{36.5}{100} = \frac{365}{1{,}000} = \frac{73}{200}$$

Changing a Fraction to a Percent

Use either of two methods.

First Method

Change the fraction into an equivalent fraction with a denominator of 100. Drop the denominator (equivalent to multiplying by 100) and add the % sign.

Example

Express $\frac{6}{20}$ as a percent.

$$\frac{6}{20} \times \frac{5}{5} = \frac{30}{100} = 30\%$$

Second Method

Divide the numerator by the denominator to get a decimal with two places (express the remainder as a fraction if necessary). Change the decimal to a percent.

Example

Express $\frac{6}{20}$ as a percent.

$$\frac{6}{20} = 20\overline{)6.00}^{.30} = 30\%$$
$$\phantom{\frac{6}{20} = 20)}\underline{60}$$

Percent Problems

1. Change the following percents into decimals:

   a. 37.5%
   b. 0.5%

2. Change the following decimals into percents:

   a. 0.625
   b. 3.75

3. Change the following fractions into percents:

   a. $\frac{7}{8}$
   b. $\frac{73}{200}$

4. Change the following percents into fractions:

   a. 87.5%
   b. 0.02%

5. Change $12\frac{1}{4}\%$ to a decimal.

6. Write .07% as both a decimal and a fraction.

7. Write $\frac{11}{16}$ as both a decimal and a percent.

8. Write 1.25 as both a percent and a fraction.

9. Which of the following is the largest: $\frac{5}{8}$, 62%, or .628?

SUBJECT REVIEWS

Solutions

1. a. 37.5% = 0.375

   b. 00.5% = 0.005

2. a. 0.625 = 62.5%

   b. 3.75 = 375%

3. a. $\frac{7}{8} = 8\overline{)7.000} = 87.5\%$ (quotient 0.875)

   b. $\frac{73}{200} = 200\overline{)73.000} = 36.5\%$ (quotient 0.365)

4. a. $87.5\% = 0.875 = \frac{875}{1,000} = \frac{35}{40} = \frac{7}{8}$

   b. $0.02\% = 0.0002 = \frac{2}{10,000} = \frac{1}{5,000}$

5. $12\frac{1}{4}\% = 12.25\% = 0.1225$

6. $.07\% = 0.0007 = \frac{7}{10,000}$

7. $\frac{11}{16} = 16\overline{)11.0000} = 68.75\%$ (quotient .6875)

8. $1.25 = 125\% = \frac{125}{100} = \frac{5}{4}$

9. In order to determine the largest number, we must write them all in the same form. Writing $\frac{5}{8}$ as a decimal, we obtain .625. If we write 62% as a decimal, we get .62. Thus, .628 is the largest of the three numbers.

Solving Percent Problems

There are several different types of word problems involving percents that might appear on your test. In addition to generic percent problems, other applications you might be asked to solve involve taxation, commission, profit and loss, discount, and interest. All of these problems are solved in essentially the same way, as the examples that follow illustrate.

Note that when solving percent problems, it is often easier to change the percent to a decimal or a fraction before computing. When we take a percent of a certain number, that number is called the *base*, the percent we take is called the *rate*, and the result is called the part. If we let B represent the base, R represent the rate, and P represent the part, the relationship between these three quantities can be expressed by the following formula

$$P = R \times B$$

All percent problems can be solved with the help of this formula.

The first four examples below show how to solve all types of generic percent problems. The remaining examples involve specific financial applications.

Example 1

In a class of 24 students, 25% received an A. How many students received an A?

The number of students (24) is the base, and 25% is the rate. Change the rate to a fraction for ease of handling and apply the formula.

$$25\% = \frac{25}{100} = \frac{1}{4}$$

$$P = R \times B$$

$$= \frac{1}{4} \times \frac{24}{1}$$

$$= 6 \text{ students}$$

To choose between changing the percent (rate) to a decimal or a fraction, simply decide which would be easier to work with. In Example 1, the fraction is easier to work with because cancellation is possible. In Example 2, the situation is the same except for a different rate. This time the decimal form is easier.

Example 2

In a class of 24 students, 29.17% received an A. How many students received an A? Changing the rate to a fraction yields

$$\frac{29.17}{100} = \frac{2917}{10,000}$$

You can quickly see that the decimal is the better choice.

$$29.17\% = .2917$$
$$P = R \times B$$
$$= .2917 \times 24$$
$$= 7 \text{ students}$$

```
  .2917
×   24
 1.1668
 5.834
 7.0008
```

Example 3

What percent of a 40-hour week is a 16-hour schedule?

40 hours is the base and 16 hours is the part. $P = R \times B$
$$16 = R \times 40$$

Divide each side of the equation by 40.

$$\frac{16}{40} = R$$

$$\frac{2}{5} = R$$

$$40\% = R$$

Example 4

A woman paid $15,000 as a down payment on a house. If this amount was 20% of the price, what did the house cost?

The part (or percentage) is $15,000, the rate is 20%, and we must find the base. Change the rate to a fraction.

$$20\% = \frac{1}{5}$$

$$P = R \times B$$

$$\$15,000 = \frac{1}{5} \times B$$

Multiply each side of the equation by 5.

$$\$75,000 = B = \text{cost of house}$$

Example 5

A salesperson sells a new car for $24,800 and receives a 5% commission. How much commission does he receive?

The cost of the car ($24,800) is the base, and the rate is 5%. We are looking for the amount of commission, which is the part.

$$P = 5\% \times \$24,800 = .05 \times \$24,800 = \$1,240$$

Thus, the salesperson receives a commission of $1,240.

Example 6

Janet buys a laptop computer for $1,199 and has to pay 7% sales tax. What is the amount of sales tax she owes, and what is the total price of the computer?

The cost of the computer ($1,199) is the base, and the rate is 7%. We are looking for the amount of sales tax, which is the part.

$P = 7\% \times \$1{,}199 = .07 \times \$1{,}199 = \$83.93$

Thus, the sales tax is $83.93, and the total cost of the computer is $1,199 + $83.93 = $1,282.93.

Discount

The amount of discount is the difference between the original price and the sale, or discount, price. The rate of discount is usually given as a fraction or as a percent. Use the formula of the percent problems $P = R \times B$, but now P stands for the part or discount, R is the rate, and B, the base, is the original price.

Example 7

A table listed at $160 is marked 20% off. What is the sale price?

$P = R \times B$
$ = .20 \times \$160 = \$32$

This is the amount of discount, or how much must be subtracted from the original price. Then:

$160 − $32 = $128 sale price

Example 8

A car priced at $9,000 was sold for $7,200. What was the rate of discount?

Amount of discount = $9,000 − $7,200
$ = \$1{,}800$

Discount = rate × original price
$\quad \$1{,}800 = R \times \$9{,}000$

Divide each side of the equation by $9,000:

$$\frac{\cancel{1{,}800}^{\,20}}{\cancel{9{,}000}_{\,100}} = \frac{20}{100} = R = 20\%$$

SUBJECT REVIEWS

Successive Discounting

When an item is discounted more than once, it is called successive discounting.

Example 9

In one store, a dress tagged at $40 was discounted 15%. When it did not sell at the lower price, it was discounted an additional 10%. What was the final selling price?

$$\text{Discount} = R \times \text{original price}$$
$$\text{First discount} = .15 \times \$40 = \$6$$
$$\$40 - \$6 = \$34 \text{ selling price after first discount}$$
$$\text{Second discount} = .10 \times \$34 = \$3.40$$
$$\$34 - \$3.40 = \$30.60 \text{ final selling price}$$

Example 10

In another store, an identical dress was also tagged at $40. When it did not sell, it was discounted 25% all at once. Is the final selling price lower or higher than in Example 1?

$$\text{Discount} = R \times \text{original price}$$
$$= .25 \times \$40$$
$$= \$10$$

$40 - $10 = $30 final selling price

This is a lower selling price than in Example 9, where two successive discounts were taken. Although the two discounts from Example 9 add up to the discount of Example 10, the final selling price is not the same.

Interest

Interest problems are similar to discount and percent problems. If money is left in the bank for a year and the interest is calculated at the end of the year, the usual formula $P = R \times B$ can be used, where P is the *interest*, R is the *rate*, and B is the *principal* (original amount of money borrowed or loaned).

Example 11

A certain bank pays interest on savings accounts at the rate of 4% per year. If a man has $6,700 on deposit, find the interest earned after 1 year.

$$P = R \times B$$

Interest = rate · principal

$$P = .04 \times \$6,700 = \$268 \text{ interest}$$

Interest problems frequently involve more or less time than 1 year. Then the formula becomes:

Interest = rate × principal × time

Example 12

If the money is left in the bank for 3 years at simple interest (the kind we are discussing), the interest is

3 × $268 = $804

Example 13

Suppose $6,700 is deposited in the bank at 4% interest for 3 months. How much interest is earned?

Interest = rate × principal × time

Here the 4% rate is for 1 year. Since 3 months is $\frac{3}{12} = \frac{1}{4}$

Interest = .04 × $6,700 × $\frac{1}{4}$ = $67

Percent of Change Problems

The percent of change problem is a special, yet very common, type of percent problem. In such a problem, there is a quantity that has a certain starting value (usually called the "original value"). This original value changes by a certain amount (either an increase or a decrease), leading to what is called the "new value." The problem is to express this increase or decrease as a percent.

Percent of change problems are solved by using a method analogous to that used in the problems above. First calculate the *amount* of the increase or decrease. This amount plays the role of the part P in the formula $P = R \times B$. The base, B, is the original amount regardless of whether there was a gain or a loss.

Example 14

By what percent does Mary's salary increase if her present salary is $20,000 and she accepts a new job at a salary of $28,000?

Amount of increase is:

$28,000 − $20,000 = $8,000

$$P = R \times B$$

$$\$8,000 = R \times \$20,000$$

Divide each side of the equation by $20,000. Then:

$$\frac{\cancel{8,000}^{\,40}}{\cancel{20,000}_{\,100}} = \frac{40}{100} = R = 40\% \text{ increase}$$

SUBJECT REVIEWS

Example 15

On Tuesday, the price of Alpha stock closed at $56 a share. On Wednesday, the stock closed at a price that was $14 higher than the closing price on Tuesday. What was the percent of increase in the closing price of the stock?

In this problem, we are given the amount of increase of $14. Thus,

$P = R \times B$

$14 = R \times 56$. Thus,

$R = \dfrac{14}{56} = \dfrac{1}{4} = 25\%.$

The percent of increase in the closing price of the stock is 25%.

Percent Word Problems

1. Janet received a rent increase of 15%. If her rent was $785 monthly before the increase, what is her new rent?

2. School bus fares rose from $25 per month to $30 per month. Find the percent of increase.

3. A dress originally priced at $90 is marked down 35%, then discounted a further 10%. What is the new, reduced price?

4. Dave delivers flowers for a salary of $45 a day, plus a 12% commission on all sales. One day his sales amounted to $220. How much money did he earn that day?

5. A certain bank pays interest on money market accounts at a rate of 6% a year. If Brett deposits $7,200, find the interest earned after one year.

6. A small business office bought a used copy machine for 75% of the original price. If the original price was $3,500, how much did they pay for the copy machine?

7. A lawyer who is currently earning $42,380 annually receives a 6.5% raise. What is his new annual salary?

8. An industrial plant reduces its number of employees, which was originally 3,760, by 5%. How many employees now work at the plant?

9. The value of a mutual fund investment of $3,750 increased $500. What is the percent of increase in the price of the mutual fund?

10. Due to a decrease in demand for a particular computer printer, a computer supply store reduces the number of orders for the printer from 35 per month to 20 per month. What percent of decrease does this represent? Round off your answer to the nearest whole number percent.

Solutions

1. Amount of increase = $785 × 15% = $785 × .15 = $117.75

   New rent = $902.75

2. Amount of increase = $30 − $25 = $5

   Percent of increase = $\frac{5}{25} = \frac{1}{5} = 20\%$

3. Amount of first markdown = $90 × 35% = $90 × .35 = $31.50

   Reduced price = $90 − $31.50 = $58.50

   Amount of second markdown = $58.50 × 10%
   $$= \$58.50 \times .1$$
   $$= \$5.85$$

   Final price = $58.50 − $5.85 = $52.65

4. Commission = $220 × 12% = $220 × .12 = $26.40

   Money earned = $45 + $26.40 = $71.40

5. Interest = $7,200 × 6% = $7,200 × .06 = $432

6. Cost = $3,500 × 75% = $2,625

7. Amount of raise = $42,380 × 6.5% = $2,754.70

   New salary = $42,380 + $2,754.70 = $45,134.70

8. Number of employees who lost their jobs = 3,760 × 5% = 188

   Number of employees who now work at the plant
   = 3,760 − 188 = 3,572

9. Percent of increase = change/original value = $\frac{500}{3750}$ = 13.33%

10. The amount of the decrease is 35 − 20 = 15

    The percent of decrease is $\frac{15}{35}$ = 42.857%, which rounds off to 43%

Signed Numbers

In describing subtraction of whole numbers, we said that the operation was not closed—that is, $4 - 6$ will yield a number that is not a member of the set of counting numbers and zero. The set of *integers* was developed to give meaning to such expressions as $4 - 6$. The set of integers is the set of all *signed* whole numbers and zero. It is the set $\{\ldots, -4, -3, -2, -1, 0, 1, 2, 3, 4, \ldots\}$

The first three dots symbolize the fact that the negative integers go on indefinitely, just as the positive integers do. Integers preceded by a minus sign (called *negative integers*) appear to the left of 0 on a number line.

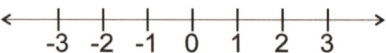

Decimals, fractions, and mixed numbers can also have negative signs. Together with positive fractions and decimals, they appear on the number line in this fashion:

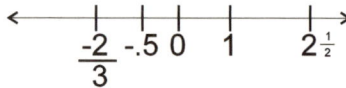

All numbers to the right of 0 are called *positive numbers*. They have the sign +, whether it is actually written or not. Business gains or losses, feet above or below sea level, and temperature above and below zero can all be expressed by means of signed numbers.

Addition

If the numbers to be added have the same sign, add the numbers (integers, fractions, decimals) as usual and use their common sign in the answer:

$$+9 + (+8) + (+2) = +19 \text{ or } 19$$
$$-4 + (-11) + (-7) + (-1) = -23$$

If the numbers to be added have different signs, add the positive numbers and then the negative numbers. Ignore the signs and subtract the smaller total from the larger total. If the larger total is positive, the answer will be positive; if the larger total is negative, the answer will be negative. The answer may be zero. Zero is neither positive nor negative and has no sign.

Example

$$+3 + (-5) + (-8) + (+2) = ?$$
$$+3 + (+2) = +5$$
$$-5 + (-8) = -13$$
$$13 - 5 = 8$$

Since the larger total (13) has a negative sign, the answer is -8.

Subtraction

The second number in a subtraction problem is called the *subtrahend*. In order to subtract, change the sign of the subtrahend and then continue as if you were *adding* signed numbers. If there is no sign in front of the subtrahend, it is assumed to be positive.

Examples

Subtract the subtrahend (bottom number) from the top number.

15	5	−35	−35	42
5	15	−42	42	35
10	−10	7	−77	7

Multiplication

If two and only two signed numbers are to be multiplied, multiply the numbers as you would if they were not signed. Then, if the two numbers have the *same sign*, the product is *positive*. If the two numbers have *different signs*, the product is *negative*. If more than two numbers are being multiplied, proceed two at a time in the same way as before, finding the signed product of the first two numbers, then multiplying that product by the next number, and so on. The product has a positive sign if all the factors are positive or there is an even number of negative factors. The product has a negative sign if there is an odd number of negative factors.

Example

$-3 \cdot (+5) \cdot (-11) \cdot (-2) = -330$

The answer is negative because there is an odd number (three) of negative factors.

The product of a signed number and zero is zero. The product of a signed number and 1 is the original number. The product of a signed number and −1 is the original number with its sign changed.

Examples

$$-5 \cdot 0 = 0$$
$$-5 \cdot 1 = -5$$
$$-5 \cdot (-1) = +5$$

Division

If the divisor and the dividend have the same sign, the answer is positive. Divide the numbers as you normally would. If the divisor and the dividend have different signs, the answer is negative. Divide the numbers as you normally would.

Examples

$$-3 \div (-2) = \frac{3}{2} = 1\frac{1}{2}$$

$$8 \div (-.2) = -40$$

If zero is divided by a signed number, the answer is zero. If a signed number is divided by zero, the answer does not exist. If a signed number is divided by 1, the number remains the same. If a signed number is divided by −1, the quotient is the original number with its sign changed.

Examples

$$0 \div (-2) = 0$$

$$-\frac{4}{3} \div 0 \quad \text{not defined}$$

$$\frac{2}{3} \div 1 = \frac{2}{3}$$

$$4 \div -1 = -4$$

Signed Numbers Problems

Perform the indicated operations:

1. $+6 + (-5) + (+2) + (-8) =$
2. $-5 - (-4) + (-2) - (+6) =$
3. $-3 \cdot (+5) \cdot (-7) \cdot (-2) =$
4. $9 \div (-.3) =$
5. $(-3) + (-12) + 7 + (-13)$
6. $(-8) - (-5) + (-1) - (+3)$
7. $(3)(2)(1)(0)(-1)(-2)(-3)$
8. $\dfrac{(-8)(+3)}{(-6)(-2)(5)}$
9. $\dfrac{6}{15} \div \left(\dfrac{-12}{5}\right)$
10. $\dfrac{(+5) - (-13)}{(-4) + (-5)}$

Solutions

1. $+6 + (-5) = +1$
   $+1 + (+2) = +3$
   $+3 + (-8) = -5$

2. $-5 - (-4) = -5 + 4 = -1$
   $-1 + (-2) = -3$
   $-3 - (+6) = -9$

3. $-3 \cdot (+5) = -15$
   $-15 \cdot (-7) = +105$
   $+105 \cdot (-2) = -210$

4. $9 \div (-.3) = -30$

5. $(-3) + (-12) = -15$
   $-15 + 7 = -8$
   $-8 + (-13) = -21$

6. $(-8) - (-5) = -8 + 5 = -3$
   $-3 + -1 = -4 - (+3)$
   $-4 - (+3) = -7$

7. $(3)(2)(1)(0)(-1)(-2)(-3) = 0$, since, if 0 is a factor in any multiplication, the result is 0

8. $\dfrac{(-8)(+3)}{(-6)(-2)(5)} = \dfrac{-24}{60} = -\dfrac{2}{5}$

9. $\dfrac{6}{15} \div \left(\dfrac{-12}{5}\right) = \dfrac{6}{15} \times \dfrac{5}{-12} = -\dfrac{1}{6}$

10. $\dfrac{(+5) - (-13)}{(-4) + (-5)} = \dfrac{5 + 13}{-9} = \dfrac{18}{-9} = -2$

SUBJECT REVIEWS

POWERS, EXPONENTS, AND ROOTS

Exponents

The product $10 \times 10 \times 10$ can be written 10^3. We say 10 is raised to the *third power*. In general, $a \times a \times a \ldots a$ n times is written a^n. The *base a* is raised to the *n*th power, and n is called the *exponent*.

Examples

$3^2 = 3 \times 3$ read "3 squared"
$2^3 = 2 \times 2 \times 2$ read "2 cubed"
$5^4 = 5 \times 5 \times 5 \times 5$ read "5 to the fourth power"

If the exponent is 1, it is usually understood and not written; thus, $a^1 = a$.

Since

$a^2 = a \times a$ and $a^3 = a \times a \times a$

then

$a^2 \times a^3 = (a \times a)(a \times a \times a) = a^5$

There are three rules for exponents. In general, if k and m are any counting numbers or zero, and a is any number,

Rule 1: $a^k \times a^m = a^{k+m}$
Rule 2: $a^m \times b^m = (ab)^m$
Rule 3: $(a^k)^n = a^{kn}$

Examples

Rule 1: $2^2 \times 2^3 = 4 \times 8 = 32$
and
$2^2 \times 2^3 = 2^5 = 32$

Rule 2: $3^2 \times 4^2 = 9 \times 16 = 144$
and
$3^2 \times 4^2 = (3 \times 4)^2 = 12^2 = 144$

Rule 3: $(3^2)^3 = 9^3 = 729$
and
$(3^2)^3 = 3^6 = 729$

Roots

The definition of roots is based on exponents. If $a^n = c$, where a is the base and n the exponent, a is called the nth *root* of c. This is written $a = \sqrt[n]{c}$. The symbol $\sqrt{}$ is called a *radical sign*. Since $5^4 = 625$, $\sqrt[4]{625} = 5$ and 5 is the fourth root of 625. The most frequently used roots are the second (called the square) root and the third (called the cube) root. The square root is written $\sqrt{}$ and the cube root is written $\sqrt[3]{}$.

Square Roots

If c is a positive number, there are two values, one negative and one positive, which when multiplied together will produce c.

Example

$+4 \times (+4) = 16$ and $-4 \times (-4) = 16$

The positive square root of a positive number c is called the *principal* square root of c (briefly, the *square root* of c) and is denoted by $\sqrt{c}$:

$\sqrt{144} = 12$

If $c = 0$, there is only one square root, 0. If c is a negative number, there is no real number that is the square root of c:

$\sqrt{-4}$ is not a real number

Cube Roots

Both positive and negative numbers have real cube roots. The cube root of 0 is 0. The cube root of a positive number is positive; that of a negative number is negative.

Example

$2 \times 2 \times 2 = 8$

Therefore $\sqrt[3]{8} = 2 - 3 \times (-3) \times (-3) = -27$

Therefore $\sqrt[3]{-27} = -3$

Each number has only one real cube root.

Expanded Form

We previously have seen how to write whole numbers in expanded form. Recall, for example, that the number 1,987 can be written as

$1,987 = 1(1,000) + 9(100) + 8(10) + 7$

Thus, 1,987 represents a number containing 7 "ones," 8 "tens," 9 "hundreds," and 1 "thousand." Using exponential notation, 1,987 can be written somewhat more compactly as

$1,987 = 1(10^3) + 9(10^2) + 8(10^1) + 7$

Example 1

Write the number 50,127 in expanded form using exponential notation.

$50,127 = 5(10^4) + 0(10^3) + 1(10^2) + 2(10^1) + 7$

SUBJECT REVIEWS

Example 2

What number is represented by the expanded form
$7(10^5) + 3(10^3) + 2(10^2) + 5(10^1) + 4?$

Note that there is no term corresponding to 10^4. Thus, the answer is 703,254.

Simplification of Square Roots

Certain square roots can be written in a "simplified" or "reduced" form. Just as all fractions should be simplified if possible, all square roots should also be simplified if possible. To simplify a square root means to remove any perfect square factors from under the square root sign.

The simplification of square roots is based on the *Product Rule for Square Roots*:

$$\sqrt{a \times b} = \sqrt{a} \times \sqrt{b}.$$

To illustrate the technique, let us simplify $\sqrt{12}$. Begin by writing 12 as 4×3, thus transforming the number under the square root sign into a product containing the perfect square factor 4

$$\sqrt{12} = \sqrt{4 \times 3}$$

Then, using the Product Rule, write the square root of the product as the product of the square root

$$\sqrt{12} = \sqrt{4 \times 3} = \sqrt{4} \times \sqrt{3}$$

Finally, compute $\sqrt{4}$ to obtain the simplified form

$$\sqrt{12} = \sqrt{4 \times 3} = \sqrt{4} \times \sqrt{3} = 2\sqrt{3}$$

Example 1

Simplify $\sqrt{98}$

$$\begin{aligned}\sqrt{98} &= \sqrt{2 \times 49} \\ &= \sqrt{2} \times \sqrt{49} \quad \text{where 49 is a square number} \\ &= \sqrt{2} \times 7\end{aligned}$$

Therefore, $\sqrt{98} = 7\sqrt{2}$ and the process terminates because there is no whole number whose square is 2. $7\sqrt{2}$ is called a radical expression or simply a *radical*.

MATHEMATICS REVIEW

Example 2

Which is larger, $\left(\sqrt{96}\right)^2$ or $\sqrt{2^{14}}$?

$\left(\sqrt{96}\right)^2 = \sqrt{96} \times \sqrt{96} = \sqrt{96 \times 96} = 96$

$\sqrt{2^{14}} = 2^7 = 128$ because $2^{14} = 2^7 \times 2^7$ by Rule 1

or because $\sqrt{2^{14}} = (2^{14})^{1/2} = 2^7$ by Rule 3

Since $128 > 96$, $\sqrt{2^{14}} > \left(\sqrt{96}\right)^2$

Example 3

Which is larger, $2\sqrt{75}$ or $6\sqrt{12}$?

These numbers can be compared if the same number appears under the radical sign. Then the greater number is the one with the larger number in front of the radical sign.

$\sqrt{75} = \sqrt{25 \times 3} = \sqrt{25} \times \sqrt{3} = 5\sqrt{3}$

Therefore:

$2\sqrt{75} = 2(5\sqrt{3}) = 10\sqrt{3}$

$\sqrt{12} = \sqrt{4 \times 3} = \sqrt{4} \times \sqrt{3} = 2\sqrt{3}$

Therefore:

$6\sqrt{12} = 6(2\sqrt{3}) = 12\sqrt{3}$

Since $12\sqrt{3} > 10\sqrt{3}$, $6\sqrt{12} > 2\sqrt{75}$

Radicals can be added and subtracted only if they have the same number under the radical sign. Otherwise, they must be reduced to expressions having the same number under the radical sign.

Example 4

Add $2\sqrt{18} + 4\sqrt{8} - \sqrt{2}$.

$\sqrt{18} = \sqrt{9 \times 2} = \sqrt{9} \times \sqrt{2} = 3\sqrt{2}$

Therefore:

$2\sqrt{18} = 2(3\sqrt{2}) = 6\sqrt{2}$

and

$\sqrt{8} = \sqrt{4 \times 2} = \sqrt{4} \times \sqrt{2} = 2\sqrt{2}$

Therefore:

$4\sqrt{8} = 4(2\sqrt{2}) = 8\sqrt{2}$

giving

$2\sqrt{18} + 4\sqrt{8} - \sqrt{2} = 6\sqrt{2} + 8\sqrt{2} - \sqrt{2} = 13\sqrt{2}$

Radicals are multiplied using the rule that

$\sqrt[k]{a \times b} = \sqrt[k]{a} \times \sqrt[k]{b}$

Example 5

$\sqrt{2}\left(\sqrt{2} - 5\sqrt{3}\right) = \sqrt{4} - 5\sqrt{6} = 2 - 5\sqrt{6}$

A quotient rule for radicals similar to the Product Rule is:

$\sqrt[k]{\dfrac{a}{b}} = \dfrac{\sqrt[k]{a}}{\sqrt[k]{b}}$

Example 6

$\sqrt{\dfrac{9}{4}} = \dfrac{\sqrt{9}}{\sqrt{4}} = \dfrac{3}{2}$

Exponents, Powers, and Roots Problems

1. Simplify $\sqrt{162}$
2. Find the sum of $\sqrt{75}$ and $\sqrt{12}$
3. Combine $\sqrt{80} + \sqrt{45} - \sqrt{20}$
4. Simplify $\sqrt{5}(2\sqrt{2} - 3\sqrt{5})$
5. Divide and simplify $\dfrac{15\sqrt{96}}{5\sqrt{2}}$
6. Calculate $5^2 \times 2^3$
7. Simplify $(\sqrt{15})^2$

MATHEMATICS REVIEW

8. Simplify $\sqrt{216}$
9. Combine $5\sqrt{18} + 7\sqrt{27}$
10. Simplify $\sqrt{6}\sqrt{3}\sqrt{2}$

Solutions

1. $\sqrt{162} = \sqrt{2 \times 81} = \sqrt{2} \times \sqrt{81} = 9\sqrt{2}$
2. $\sqrt{75} + \sqrt{12} = 5\sqrt{3} + 2\sqrt{3} = 7\sqrt{3}$
3. $\sqrt{80} + \sqrt{45} - \sqrt{20} = 4\sqrt{5} + 3\sqrt{5} - 2\sqrt{5} = 5\sqrt{5}$
4. $\sqrt{5}(2\sqrt{2} - 3\sqrt{5}) = 2\sqrt{10} - 3\sqrt{25} = 2\sqrt{10} - 3(5)$
   $= 2\sqrt{10} - 15$
5. $\dfrac{15\sqrt{96}}{5\sqrt{2}} = \dfrac{15(4\sqrt{6})}{5\sqrt{2}} = \dfrac{60\sqrt{6}}{5\sqrt{2}} = 12\sqrt{3}$
6. $5^2 \times 2^3 = 25 \times 8 = 200$
7. $(\sqrt{15})^2 = 15$, since squares and roots are inverse operations
8. $\sqrt{216} = \sqrt{2 \times 2 \times 2 \times 3 \times 3 \times 3} = \sqrt{4 \times 9 \times 6}$
   $= \sqrt{4}\sqrt{9}\sqrt{6} = 2 \times 3\sqrt{6} = 6\sqrt{6}$
9. $5\sqrt{18} + 7\sqrt{27} = 5\sqrt{9 \times 2} + 7\sqrt{9 \times 3}$
   $= 5\sqrt{9}\sqrt{2} + 7\sqrt{9}\sqrt{3} = 15\sqrt{2} + 21\sqrt{3}$
10. $\sqrt{6}\sqrt{3}\sqrt{2} = \sqrt{6 \times 3 \times 2} = \sqrt{36} = 6$

Systems of Measurements

The English System

When taking the SSAT/ISEE, you will need to be able to compute using both the English system of measurement and the metric system. It may also be necessary for you to convert measurements from one system to the other, but in such cases, you will be given the appropriate conversion factors.

Make sure you have the following relationships within the English system memorized:

Conversion Factors for Length

36 inches = 3 feet = 1 yard

12 inches = 1 foot

5,280 feet = 1,760 yards = 1 mile

Conversion Factors for Volume

2 pints = 1 quart

16 fluid ounces = 1 pint

8 pints = 4 quarts = 1 gallon

Conversion Factors for Weight

16 ounces = 1 pound

2,000 pounds = 1 ton

These conversion factors enable you to change units within the English system.

Examples

1. How many feet are in 5 miles?

    5 miles × (5,280 feet/1 mile) = 26,400 feet

    Notice how the unit of "miles" cancels out of the numerator and denominator.

2. How many ounces are in 2 tons?

    2 tons × (2,000 pounds/1 ton) × (16 ounces/1 pound) = 64,000 ounces

    Notice how the units of "tons" and "pounds" cancel out of the numerator and denominator.

The Metric System

In the metric system, distance or length is measured in meters. Similarly, volume is measured in liters, and mass is measured in grams. The prefixes below are appended to the beginning of these basic units to indicate other units of measure with sizes equal to each basic unit multiplied or divided by powers of 10.

$$\text{giga} = 10^9$$
$$\text{mega} = 10^6$$
$$\text{kilo} = 10^3$$
$$\text{hecto} = 10^2$$
$$\text{deka} = 10^1$$
$$\text{deci} = 10^{-1}$$
$$\text{centi} = 10^{-2}$$
$$\text{milli} = 10^{-3}$$
$$\text{micro} = 10^{-6}$$
$$\text{nano} = 10^{-9}$$
$$\text{pico} = 10^{-12}$$

From the table above, we can see, for example, that a kilometer is 1,000 times as long as a meter, 100,000 times as long as a centimeter, and 1,000,000 times as a long as a millimeter. Similarly, a centigram is $\frac{1}{100}$ the size of a gram.

Conversions among metric units can be made quickly by moving decimal points.

Examples

1. Convert 9.43 kilometers to meters.

   Since meters are smaller than kilometers, our answer will be larger than 9.43. There are 1,000 meters in a kilometer, so we move the decimal point three places over to the right. 9.43 kilometers is equal to 9,430 meters.

2. Convert 512 grams to kilograms.

   Since kilograms are more massive than grams, our answer must be less than 512. There are 10^{-3} kilograms in a gram, so we move the decimal point three places to the left. 512 grams are equal to .512 kilograms.

Conversions between the English and the Metric Systems

Conversions between the English and metric systems are accomplished in the same way as conversions within the English system. Recall that any problem that requires you to make such a conversion will include the necessary conversion factors.

Examples

1. If 1 meter is equivalent to 1.09 yards, how many yards are in 10 meters?

    10 meters × (1.09 yards/1 meter) = 10.9 yards

2. If 1 yard is equivalent to .914 meters, how many meters are there in 24 yards?

    24 yards × (.914 meters/1 yard) = 21.936 meters

Systems of Measurement Problems

1. Express 38 meters in millimeters.
2. Express 871 millimeters in centimeters.
3. Which measurement is greater, 8,000 millimeters or 7 meters?
4. Arrange the following from smallest to biggest: 6,700 meters, 672,000 centimeters, and 6.6 kilometers.
5. Express 49 milligrams in centigrams.
6. 4.6 liters is how many milliliters?
7. A package weighing 32.5 kilograms is shipped to the U.S. What is its weight in pounds? There are 2.2 pounds in a kilogram.
8. A line drawn on a blueprint measures 1.5 yards. What is its length in meters? There are .914 meters in a yard.
9. If the distance between two exits on a highway is 40 kilometers, what is the distance in miles? There are .62 miles in a kilometer.
10. A particular brand of bottled water is available in two different bottle size—a 2.25 quart bottle and a 2.1 liter bottle. Which bottle contains more water? There are 1.06 quarts in a liter.

Solutions

1. Since meters are larger than millimeters, our answer will be larger than 38. There are 1,000 millimeters in a meter, so we move the decimal point three places over to the right. 38 meters is equal to 38,000 millimeters.

2. Since millimeters are smaller than centimeters, our answer will be smaller than 871. There are 10 millimeters in a centimeter, so we move the decimal point one place over to the left. 871 millimeters is equal to 87.1 centimeters.

3. In order to answer this question, we must express both measures in the same units. Since, for example, 8,000 millimeters is equal to 8 meters, we can see that 8,000 millimeters is larger than 7 meters.

4. Let's start by expressing all measurements in meters.

    672,000 centimeters = 6,720 meters
    6.6 kilometers = 6,600 meters
    6,700 meters = 6,700 meters

    Thus, from smallest to largest, we have 6.6 kilometers, 6,700 meters, and 672,000 centimeters.

5. Since there are 10 milligrams in a centigram, 49 milligrams is equal to 4.9 centigrams.

6. Since there are 1,000 milliliters in a liter, there are 4,600 milliliters in 4.6 liters.

7. 32.5 kgs = 32.5 kgs × (2.2 lbs/1 kg) = 71.5 lbs

8. 1.5 yards = 1.5 yards × (.914 meters/1 yard) = 1.371 meters

9. 40 kilometers = 40 kilometers × (.62 miles/1 kilometer) = 24.8 miles

10. Express 2.1 liters in quarts.

    2.1 liters = 2.1 liters × (1.06 quarts/1 liter) = 2.226 quarts. Thus, the quart bottle holds more.

Algebra

Algebra is a generalization of arithmetic. It provides methods for solving problems that cannot be done by arithmetic alone or that can be done by arithmetic only after long computations. Algebra provides a shorthand way of reducing long verbal statements to brief formulas, expressions, or equations. After the verbal statements have been reduced, the resulting algebraic expressions can be simplified. Suppose that a room is 12 feet wide and 20 feet long. Its perimeter (measurement around the outside) can be expressed as:

$$12 + 20 + 12 + 20 \text{ or } 2(12 + 20)$$

If the width of the room remains 12 feet but the letter l is used to symbolize length, the perimeter is:

$$12 + l + 12 + l \text{ or } 2(12 + l)$$

Further, if w is used for width, the perimeter of *any* rectangular room can be written as $2(w + l)$. This same room has an area of 12 feet by 20 feet, or 12×20. If l is substituted for 20, any room of width 12 has area equal to $12l$. If w is substituted for the number 12, the area of any rectangular room is given by wl or lw. Expressions such as wl and $2(w + l)$ are called *algebraic expressions*. An *equation* is a statement that two algebraic expressions are equal. A *formula* is a special type of equation.

Evaluating Formulas

If we are given an expression and numerical values to be assigned to each letter, the expression can be evaluated.

Example 1

Evaluate $2x + 3y - 7$ if $x = 2$ and $y = -4$.

Substitute given values.

$2(2) + 3(-4) - 7 = ?$

Multiply numbers using rules for signed numbers.

$4 + -12 - 7 = ?$

Collect numbers.

$4 - 19 = -15$

We have already evaluated formulas in arithmetic when solving percent, discount, and interest problems.

Example 2

Evaluate each of the following expressions if $a = 3$, $b = -2$, and $c = 0$.

    a. $-a^2$
    b. $3b - 4b^2$
    c. $ab + 4c$

a. $-a^2 = -(3)^2 = -(9) = -9$

b. $b - 4b^2 = 3(-2) - 4(-2)^2 = -6 - 4(4) = -6 - 16 = -22$

c. $ab + 4c = (3)(-2) + 4(0) = -6 + 0 = -6$

Example 3

If $x = 1$ and $y = -2$, find the value of $-x^2y^2$

$-x^2y^2 = -(1)^2(-2)^2 = -(1)(4) = -(4) = -4$

Example 4

The formula for temperature conversion is:

$$F = \frac{9}{5}C + 32$$

where C stands for the temperature in degrees Celsius and F for degrees Fahrenheit. Find the Fahrenheit temperature that is equivalent to 20°C.

$$F = \frac{9}{5}(20°C) + 32 = 36 + 32 = 68°F$$

Example 5

The formula for the area of a triangle is $A = \frac{bh}{2}$. Find A if $b = 12$ and $h = 7$.

$$A = \frac{bh}{2} = \frac{12 \times 7}{2} = 42$$

Algebraic Expressions

Formulation

A more difficult problem than evaluating an expression or formula is translating from a verbal expression to an algebraic one:

Verbal	Algebraic
Thirteen more than x	$x + 13$
Six less than twice x	$2x - 6$
The square of the sum of x and 5	$(x + 5)^2$
The sum of the square of x and the square of 5	$x^2 + 5^2$
The distance traveled by a car going 50 miles an hour for x hours	$50x$
The average of 70, 80, 85, and x	$\dfrac{70 + 80 + 85 + x}{4}$

Simplification

After algebraic expressions have been formulated, they can usually be simplified by means of the laws of exponents and the common operations of addition, subtraction, multiplication, and division. These techniques will be described in the next section. Algebraic expressions and equations frequently contain parentheses, which are removed in the process of simplifying. If an expression contains more than one set of parentheses, remove the inner set first and then the outer set. Brackets, [ ], which are often used instead of parentheses, are treated the same way. Parentheses are used to indicate multiplication. Thus, $3(x + y)$ means that 3 is to be multiplied by the sum of x and y. The *distributive law* is used to accomplish this:

$$a(b + c) = ab + ac$$

The expression in front of the parentheses is multiplied by each term inside. Rules for signed numbers apply.

Example

Simplify $3[4(2 - 8) - 5(4 + 2)]$.

This can be done in two ways.

Method 1: Combine the numbers inside the parentheses first:

$$3[4(2 - 8) - 5(4 + 2)] = 3[4(-6) - 5(6)]$$
$$= 3[-24 - 30]$$
$$= 3[-54] = -162$$

Method 2: Use the distributive law:

$$3[4(2 - 8) - 5(4 + 2)] = 3[8 - 32 - 20 - 10]$$
$$= 3[8 - 62]$$
$$= 3[-54] = -162$$

If there is a (+) before the parentheses, the signs of the terms inside the parentheses remain the same when the parentheses are removed. If there is a (−) before the parentheses, the sign of each term inside the parentheses changes when the parentheses are removed.

Once parentheses have been removed, the order of operations is multiplication and division, then addition and subtraction from left to right.

Example

$(-15 + 17) \times 3 - [(4 \times 9) \div 6] = ?$

Work inside the parentheses first: $(2) \times 3 - [36 \div 6] = ?$

Then work inside the brackets: $2 \times 3 - [6] = ?$

Multiply first, then subtract, proceeding from left to right: $6 - 6 = 0$

The placement of parentheses and brackets is important. Using the same numbers as above with the parentheses and brackets placed in different positions can give many different answers.

Example

$-15 + [(17 \times 3) - (4 \times 9)] \div 6 = ?$

Work inside the parentheses first:
$-15 + [(51) - (36)] \div 6 = ?$

Then work inside the brackets:
$-15 + [15] \div 6 = ?$

Since there are no more parentheses or brackets, proceed from left to right, dividing before adding:

$$-15 + 2\frac{1}{2} = -12\frac{1}{2}$$

Operations

When letter symbols and numbers are combined with the operations of arithmetic (+, −, ×, ÷) and with certain other mathematical operations, we have an *algebraic expression*. Algebraic expressions are made up of several parts connected by a plus or a minus sign; each part is called a *term*. Terms with the same letter part are called *like terms*. Since algebraic expressions represent numbers, they can be added, subtracted, multiplied, and divided.

When we defined the commutative law of addition in arithmetic by writing $a + b = b + a$, we meant that a and b could represent any number. The expression $a + b = b + a$ is an *identity* because it is true for all numbers. The expression $n + 5 = 14$ is not an identity because it is not true for all numbers; it becomes true only when the number 9 is substituted for n. Letters used to represent numbers are called *variables*. If a number stands alone (the 5 or 14 in $n + 5 = 14$), it is called a *constant* because its value is constant or unchanging. If a number appears in front of a variable, it is called a *coefficient*. Because the letter x is frequently used to represent a variable, or *unknown*, the times sign ×, which can be confused with it in handwriting, is rarely used to express multiplication in algebra. Other expressions used for multiplication are a dot, parentheses, or simply writing a number and letter together:

$5 \cdot 4$ or $5(4)$ or $5a$

Of course, 54 still means fifty-four.

Addition and Subtraction

Only like terms can be combined. Add or subtract the coefficients of like terms, using the rules for signed numbers.

Example 1

Add $x + 2y − 2x + 3y$.

$x − 2x + 2y + 3y = −x + 5y$

Example 2

Perform the subtraction:

$$-30a - 15b + 4c$$
$$-(-5a + 3b - c + d)$$

Change the sign of each term in the subtrahend and then add, using the rules for signed numbers:

$$-30a - 15b + 4c$$
$$\underline{5a - 3b + c - d}$$
$$-25a - 18b + 5c - d$$

Example 3

Perform the following subtraction:

$(h^2 + 6hk - 7k^2) - (3h^2 + 6hk - 10k^2)$

Once again, change the sign of each term in the subtrahend and then add.

$(h^2 + 6hk - 7k^2) - (3h^2 + 6hk - 10k^2)$
$= (h^2 + 6hk - 7k^2) + (3h^2 - 6hk + 10k^2)$
$= -2h^2 + 3k^2$

Multiplication

Multiplication is accomplished by using the *distributive property*. If the multiplier has only one term, then

$a(b + c) = ab + bc$

Example

$9x(5m + 9q) = (9x)(5m) + (9x)(9q)$
$= 45mx + 81qx$

When the multiplier contains more than one term and you are multiplying two expressions, multiply each term of the first expression by each term of the second and then add like terms. Follow the rules for signed numbers and exponents at all times.

Example 1

$(2x - 1)(x + 6)$
$= 2x(x + 6) - 1(x + 6)$
$= 2x^2 + 12x - x - 6$
$= 2x^2 + 11x - 6$

Example 2

$(3x + 8)(4x^2 + 2x + 1)$
$= 3x(4x^2 + 2x + 1) + 8(4x^2 + 2x + 1)$
$= 12x^3 + 6x^2 + 3x + 32x^2 + 16x + 8$
$= 12x^3 + 38x^2 + 19x + 8$

If more than two expressions are to be multiplied, multiply the first two, then multiply the product by the third factor, and so on, until all factors have been used.

Algebraic expressions can be multiplied by themselves (squared) or raised to any power.

Example 1

$$(a + b)^2 = (a + b)(a + b)$$
$$= a(a + b) + b(a + b)$$
$$= a^2 + ab + ba + b^2$$
$$= a^2 + 2ab + b^2$$

since $ab = ba$ by the commutative law.

Example 2

$$(a + b)(a - b) = a(a - b) + b(a - b)$$
$$= a^2 - ab + ba - b^2$$
$$= a^2 - b^2$$

Factoring

When two or more algebraic expressions are multiplied, each is called a factor and the result is the *product*. The reverse process of finding the factors when given the product is called *factoring*. A product can often be factored in more than one way. Factoring is useful in multiplication, division, and solving equations.

One way to factor an expression is to remove any single-term factor that is common to each of the terms and write it outside the parentheses. It is the distributive law that permits this.

Example 1

$$3x + 12 = 3(x + 4)$$

The result can be checked by multiplication.

Example 2

$$3x^3 + 6x^2 + 9x = 3x(x^2 + 2x + 3)$$

The result can be checked by multiplication.

Expressions containing squares can sometimes be factored into expressions containing letters raised to the first power only, called *linear factors*. We have seen that

$$(a + b)(a - b) = a^2 - b^2$$

Therefore, if we have an expression in the form of a difference of two squares, it can be factored as:

$$a^2 - b^2 = (a + b)(a - b)$$

Example 1

Factor $x^2 - 16$.

$$x^2 - 16 = (x)^2 - (4)^2 = (x - 4)(x + 4)$$

Example 2

Factor $4x^2 - 9$.

$$4x^2 - 9 = (2x)^2 - (3)^2 = (2x + 3)(2x - 3)$$

Again, the result can be checked by multiplication.

A third type of expression that can be factored is one containing three terms, such as $x^2 + 5x + 6$. Since

$$\begin{aligned}(x + a)(x + b) &= x(x + b) + a(x + b) \\ &= x^2 + xb + ax + ab \\ &= x^2 + (a + b)x + ab\end{aligned}$$

an expression in the form $x^2 + (a + b)x + ab$ can be factored into two factors of the form $(x + a)$ and $(x + b)$. We must find two numbers whose product is the constant in the given expression and whose sum is the coefficient of the term containing x.

Example 1

Find factors of $x^2 + 5x + 6$.

First find two numbers which, when multiplied, have +6 as a product. Possibilities are 2 and 3, −2 and −3, 1 and 6, −1 and −6. From these select the one pair whose sum is 5. The pair 2 and 3 is the only possible selection, and so:

$$x^2 + 5x + 6 = (x + 2)(x + 3) \quad \text{written in either order}$$

SUBJECT REVIEWS

Example 2

Factor $x^2 - 5x - 6$.

Possible factors of -6 are -1 and 6, 1 and -6, 2 and -3, -2 and 3. We must select the pair whose sum is -5. The only pair whose sum is -5 is $+1$ and -6, and so

$$x^2 - 5x - 6 = (x + 1)(x - 6)$$

In factoring expressions of this type, notice that if the last sign is plus, both a and b have the same sign and it is the same as the sign of the middle term. If the last sign is minus, the numbers have opposite signs.

Many expressions cannot be factored.

Example 3

Factor $2x^3 - 8x^2 + 8x$.

In expressions of this type, begin by factoring out the largest common monomial factor, then try to factor the resulting trinomial.

$$2x^3 - 8x^2 + 8x = 2x(x^2 - 4x + 4) = 2x(x-2)(x-2) = 2x(x-2)^2$$

Division

$$\frac{36mx^2}{9m^2x} = 4m^1x^2m^{-2}x^{-1}$$

$$= 4m^{-1}x^1 = \frac{4x}{m}$$

Method 2

Cancellation

$$\frac{36mx^2}{9m^2x} = \frac{\overset{4}{\cancel{36}}m\cancel{x}x}{\underset{1}{\cancel{9}\cancel{m}xm}} = \frac{4x}{m}$$

This is acceptable because

$$\frac{ab}{bc} = \frac{a}{b}\left(\frac{c}{c}\right) \text{ and } \frac{c}{c} = 1$$

so that $\dfrac{ac}{bc} = \dfrac{a}{b}$

Example 1

If the divisor contains only one term and the dividend is a sum, divide each term in the dividend by the divisor and simplify as you did in Method 2.

$$\frac{9x^3 + 3x^2 + 6x}{3x} = \frac{9x^3}{3x} + \frac{3x^2}{3x} + \frac{6x}{3x}$$
$$= 3x^2 + x + 2$$

This method cannot be followed if there are two terms or more in the denominator since

$$\frac{a}{b+c} \neq \frac{a}{b} + \frac{a}{c}$$

In this case, write the example as a fraction. Factor the numerator and denominator if possible. Then use laws of exponents or cancel.

Example 2

Divide $x^3 - 9x$ by $x^3 + 6x^2 + 9x$.

Write as:

$$\frac{x^3 - 9x}{x^3 + 6x^2 + 9x}$$

Both numerator and denominator can be factored to give:

$$\frac{x(x^2 - 9)}{x(x^2 + 6x + 9)} = \frac{\cancel{x(x+3)}(x - 3)}{\cancel{x(x+3)}(x + 3)} = \frac{x - 3}{x + 3}$$

Algebra Problems

1. Simplify: $4[2(3-7) - 4(2+6)]$
2. Subtract: $(-25x + 4y - 12z) - (4x - 8y - 13z)$
3. Multiply: $(5x + 2)(3x^2 - 2x + 1)$
4. Factor completely: $2x^3 + 8x^2 - 90x$
5. Factor completely: $32x^2 - 98$
6. Divide: $\dfrac{x^2 + 2x - 8}{x^2 - x - 20}$
7. Simplify: $6x - 2(3 - 3x)$
8. Add: $(a - b - c) + (a - b - c) - (a - b - c)$
9. Multiply: $(9a^2 - 12)(9a^2 + 12)$
10. Factor completely: $4a^2b + 12ab - 72b$

Solutions

1. $4[2(3-7) - 4(2+6)] = 4[2(-4)-4(8)] = 4[-8 - 32]$
   $= 4(-40) = -160$

2. $(-25x + 4y - 12z) - (4x - 8y - 13z)$
   $= -25x + 4y - 12z - 4x + 8y + 13z$
   $= -29x + 12y + z$

3. $(5x + 2)(3x^2 - 2x + 1)$
   $= 5x(3x^2 - 2x + 1) + 2(3x^2 - 2x + 1)$
   $= 15x^3 - 10x^2 + 5x + 6x^2 - 4x + 2$
   $= 15x^3 - 4x^2 + x + 2$

4. $2x^3 + 8x^2 - 90x = 2x(x^2 + 4x - 45) = 2x(x + 9)(x - 5)$

5. $32x^2 - 98 = 2(16x^2 - 49) = 2(4x - 7)(4x + 7)$

6. $\dfrac{x^2 + 2x - 8}{x^2 - x - 20} = \dfrac{(x + 4)(x - 2)}{(x - 5)(x + 4)}$

   $= \dfrac{\cancel{(x + 4)}(x - 2)}{(x - 5)\cancel{(x + 4)}} = \dfrac{x - 2}{x - 5}$

7. $6x - 2(3 - 3x) = 6x - 6 + 6x = 12x - 6$

8. $(a - b - c) + (a - b - c) - (a - b - c)$
   $= a - b - c + a - b - c - a + b + c = a - b - c$

9. $(9a - 12)(9a + 12)$
   $= 81a^2 + 108a - 108a - 144 = 81a^2 - 144$

10. $4a^2b + 12ab - 72b = 4b(a^2 + 3a - 18) = 4b(a + 6)(a - 3)$

SUBJECT REVIEWS

Equations

Solving equations is one of the major objectives in algebra. If a variable x in an equation is replaced by a value or expression that makes the equation a true statement, the value or expression is called a *solution* of the equation. (Remember that an equation is a mathematical statement that one algebraic expression is equal to another.)

An equation may contain one or more variables. We begin with one variable. Certain rules apply to equations whether there are one or more variables. The following rules are applied to give equivalent equations that are simpler than the original:

Addition: If $s = t$, then $s + c = t + c$.
Subtraction: If $s + c = t + c$, then $s = t$.
Multiplication: If $s = t$, then $cs = ct$.
Division: If $cs = ct$ and $c \neq 0$, then $s = t$.

To solve for x in an equation in the form $ax = b$ with $a \neq 0$, divide each side of the equation by a:

$$\frac{ax}{a} = \frac{b}{a} \quad \text{yielding} \quad x = \frac{b}{a}$$

Then, $\frac{b}{a}$ is the solution to the equation.

Example 1

Solve $x + 5 = 12$

Subtract 5 from both sides.

$$\begin{array}{r} x + 5 = 12 \\ -5 \quad -5 \\ \hline x = 7 \end{array}$$

Example 2

Solve $4x = 8$.

Write $\frac{4x}{4} = \frac{8}{4}$

$x = 2$

Example 3

Solve $\frac{x}{4} = 9$.

Write $4 \times \frac{x}{4} = 9 \times 4$.

Thus, $x = 36$.

MATHEMATICS REVIEW

Example 4

Solve $3x + 7 = 19$.

$3x = 12$ Subtract 7 from both sides.

$x = 4$ Divide each side by 3.

Example 5

Solve $2x - (x - 4) = 5(x + 2)$ for x.

$2x - (x - 4) = 5(x + 2)$

$2x - x + 4 = 5x + 10$ Remove parentheses by distributive law.

$x + 4 = 5x + 10$ Combine like terms.

$x = 5x + 6$ Subtract 4 from each side.

$-4x = 6$ Subtract $5x$ from each side.

$x = \dfrac{6}{-4}$ Divide each side by -4.

$= -\dfrac{3}{2}$ Reduce fraction to lowest terms.

Negative sign now applies to the entire fraction.

Check the solution for accuracy by substituting in the original equation:

$2(-\dfrac{3}{2}) - (-\dfrac{3}{2} - 4) \stackrel{?}{=} 5(-\dfrac{3}{2} + 2)$

$-3 - \left(-\dfrac{11}{2}\right) \stackrel{?}{=} 5\left(\dfrac{1}{2}\right)$

$-3 + \dfrac{11}{2} \stackrel{?}{=} \dfrac{5}{2}$

$-\dfrac{6}{2} + \dfrac{11}{2} \stackrel{?}{=} \dfrac{5}{2}$ check

SUBJECT REVIEWS

Equations Problems

Solve the following equations for x:

1. $3x - 5 = 3 + 2x$
2. $3(2x - 2) = 12$
3. $4(x - 2) = 2x + 10$
4. $7 - 4(2x - 1) = 3 + 4(4 - x)$
5. $7x + 6 = 4x + 6$
6. $3(x - 2) - 4(x - 3) = 8$
7. $\dfrac{2x + 3}{5} - 10 = \dfrac{4 - 3x}{2}$
8. $3(2x + 1) + 2(3x + 1) = 17$
9. $(w + 6) - (5 - 2w) = -2$
10. $(x - 5)^2 = 4 + (x + 5)^2$

Solutions

1. $3x - 5 = 3 + 2x$
   $-2x \qquad\quad -2x$
   $x - 5 = 3$
   $\quad +5 \ +5$
   $x = 8$

2. $3(2x - 2) = 12$
   $6x - 6 = 12$
   $6x = 18$
   $x = 3$

3. $4(x - 2) = 2x + 10$
   $4x - 8 = 2x + 10$
   $4x = 2x + 18$
   $2x = 18$
   $x = 9$

4. $7 - 4(2x - 1) = 3 + 4(4 - x)$
   $7 - 8x + 4 = 3 + 16 - 4x$
   $11 - 8x = 19 - 4x$
   $11 = 19 + 4x$
   $-8 = 4x$
   $x = -2$

5. $7x + 6 = 4x + 6$
   $7x = 4x$
   $3x = 0$
   $x = 0.$

6. $3(x - 2) - 4(x - 3) = 8$
   $3x - 6 - 4x + 12 = 8$
   $-x + 6 = 8$
   $-x = 2$
   $x = -2$

7. $\dfrac{2x + 3}{5} - 10 = \dfrac{4 - 3x}{2}$
   $\left(10 \times \dfrac{2x + 3}{5}\right) - (10 \times 10) = \left(\dfrac{4 - 3x}{2} \times 10\right)$
   $2(2x + 3) - 100 = 5(4 - 3x)$
   $4x + 6 - 100 = 20 - 15x$
   $4x - 94 = 20 - 15x$
   $4x = 114 - 15x$
   $19x = 114$
   $x = 6$

8. $3(2x + 1) + 2(3x + 1) = 17$
   $6x + 3 + 6x + 2 = 17$
   $12x + 5 = 17$
   $12x = 12$
   $x = 1$

9. $(w + 6) - (5 - 2w) = -2$
   $w + 6 - 5 + 2w = -2$
   $3w + 1 = -2$
   $3w = -3$
   $w = -1$

10. $(x - 5)^2 = 4 + (x + 5)^2$
    $x^2 - 10x + 25 = 4 + x^2 + 10x + 25$ Subtract x^2 from both sides and combine terms.
    $-10x + 25 = 10x + 29$
    $20x = -4$
    $x = \dfrac{-1}{5}$

SUBJECT REVIEWS

Word Problems Involving One Unknown

In many cases, if you read a word problem carefully, assign a letter to the quantity to be found, and understand the relationships between known and unknown quantities, you can formulate an equation with one unknown.

Number Problems and Age Problems

These two kinds of problems are similar to each other.

Example 1

One number is 3 times another, and their sum is 48. Find the two numbers.

Let x = second number. Then the first is $3x$. Since their sum is 48,

$3x + x = 48$
$4x = 48$
$x = 12$

Therefore, the first number is $3x = 36$.

$36 + 12 = 48$ check

Example 2

Art is now three times older than Ryan. Four years ago, Art was five times as old as Ryan was then. How old is Art now?

Let R = Ryan's age

Then $3R$ = Art's age

Four years ago, Ryan's age was $R - 4$, and Art's age was $3R - 4$.

Since at that time Art was five times as old as Ryan, we have

$5(R - 4) = 3R - 4$
$5R - 20 = 3R - 4$
$2R = 16$
$R = 8, 3R = 24.$

Art is 24 years old now.

Distance Problems

The basic concept is:

$$\text{Distance} = \text{rate} \cdot \text{time}$$

Example 1

In a mileage test, a man drives a truck at a fixed rate of speed for 1 hour. Then he increases the speed by 20 miles per hour and drives at that rate for 2 hours. He then reduces that speed by 5 miles per hour and drives at that rate for 3 hours. If the distance traveled was 295 miles, what are the rates of speed over each part of the test?

Let x be the first speed, $x + 20$ the second, and $x + (20 - 5) = x + 15$ the third. Because distance = rate · time, multiply these rates by the time and formulate the equation by separating the two equal expressions for distance by an equals sign:

$$1x + 2(x + 20) + 3(x + 15) = 295$$
$$x + 2x + 3x + 40 + 45 = 295$$
$$6x = 210$$
$$x = 35$$

The speeds are 35, 55, and 50 miles per hour.

Example 2

Two trains leave the Newark station at the same time traveling in opposite directions. One travels at a rate of 60 mph, and the other travels at a rate of 50 mph. In how many hours will the trains be 880 miles apart?

The two trains will be 880 miles apart when the sum of the distances that they both have traveled is 880 miles.

Let r_1 = the rate of the first train; r_2 = the rate of the second train

Let t_1 = the time of the first train; t_2 = the time of the second train

Then, the distance the first train travels is $r_1 t_1$, and the distance the second train travels is $r_2 t_2$. Our equation will be $r_1 t_1 + r_2 t_2 = 880$. Since $r_1 = 60$, $r_2 = 50$, and $t_1 = t_2$, we can rewrite the equation as

$$60t + 50t = 880$$
$$110t = 880$$
$$t = 8$$

It will take 8 hours for the trains to get 880 miles apart.

SUBJECT REVIEWS

Consecutive Number Problems

This type usually involves only one unknown. Two numbers are consecutive if one is the successor of the other. Three consecutive numbers are of the form x, $x + 1$, and $x + 2$. Since an even number is divisible by 2, consecutive even numbers are of the form $2x$, $2x + 2$, and $2x + 4$. An odd number is of the form $2x + 1$.

Example 1

Find three consecutive whole numbers whose sum is 75.

Let the first number be x, the second $x + 1$, and the third $x + 2$. Then:

$$x + (x + 1) + (x + 2) = 75$$
$$3x + 3 = 75$$
$$3x = 72$$
$$x = 24$$

The numbers whose sum is 75 are 24, 25, and 26. Many versions of this problem have no solution. For example, no three consecutive whole numbers have a sum of 74.

Example 2

Find three consecutive even integers whose sum is 48.

We can express three consecutive even integers as x, $x + 2$, and $x + 4$. Thus, we have

$$x + (x + 2) + (x + 4) = 48$$
$$3x + 6 = 48$$
$$3x = 42$$
$$x = 14$$

The integers are 14, 16, and 18.

Work Problems

These problems concern the speed with which work can be accomplished and the time necessary to perform a task if the size of the work force is changed.

Example 1

If Joe can type a chapter alone in 6 days and Ann can type the same chapter in 8 days, how long will it take them to type the chapter if they both work on it?

We let x = number of days required if they work together and then put our information into tabular form:

	Joe	Ann	Together
Days to type chapter	6	8	x
Part typed in 1 day	$\frac{1}{6}$	$\frac{1}{8}$	$\frac{1}{x}$

Since the part done by Joe in 1 day plus the part done by Ann in 1 day equals the part done by both in 1 day, we have

$$\frac{1}{6} + \frac{1}{8} = \frac{1}{x}$$

Next we multiply each member by $48x$ to clear the fractions, giving:

$$8x + 6x = 48$$
$$14x = 48$$
$$x = 3\frac{3}{7} \text{ days}$$

Example 2

Working alone, one pipe can fill a pool in 8 hours, a second pipe can fill the pool in 12 hours, and a third can fill it in 24 hours. How long would it take all three pipes, working at the same time, to fill the pool?

Using the same logic as in the previous problem, we obtain the equation

$$\frac{1}{8} + \frac{1}{12} + \frac{1}{24} = \frac{1}{x}$$

To clear the fractions, we multiply each side by $24x$, giving

$$3x + 2x + x = 24$$
$$6x = 24$$
$$x = 4$$

It would take the pipes 4 hours to fill the pool.

Word Problems in One Unknown Problems

1. If 18 is subtracted from six times a certain number, the result is 96. Find the number.

2. A 63-foot rope is cut into two pieces. If one piece is twice as long as the other, how long is each piece?

3. Peter is now three times as old as Jillian. In six years, he will be twice as old as she will be then. How old is Peter now?

4. Lauren can clean the kitchen in 30 minutes. It takes Kathleen 20 minutes to complete the same job. How long would it take to clean the kitchen if they both worked together?

5. A train travels 120 miles at an average rate of 40 mph, and it returns along the same route at an average rate of 60 mph. What is the average rate of speed for the entire trip?

6. The sum of two consecutive odd integers is 68. Find the integers.

7. On election day, the winning candidate received 100 votes more than his opponent. If there were 8,574 votes cast in total, how many votes did the winning candidate get?

8. Ten less than four times a number is equal to the difference between the number and 1. What is the number?

9. Tony is now three years older than Karen. If seven years from now the sum of their ages is 79, how old is Karen now?

10. A freight train and a passenger train leave the same station at noon and travel in opposite directions. If the freight train travels at 52 mph and the passenger train travels at 84 mph, at what time are they 680 miles apart?

Solutions

1. Let x = the number.

   Then, $6x - 18 = 96$

   $6x = 114$

   $x = 19$

   The number is 19.

2. Let x = the length of the short piece.

   Then, $2x$ = the length of the longer piece.

   And $x + 2x = 63$

   $3x = 63$

   $x = 21$

   $2x = 42$

   The pieces are 21 feet and 42 feet.

3. Let J = Jillian's age now;

   $3J$ = Peter's age now;

   $J + 6$ = Jillian's age in 6 years;

   $3J + 6$ = Peter's age in 6 years.

   Then,

   $3J + 6 = 2(J + 6)$

   $3J + 6 = 2J + 12$

   $3J = 2J + 6$

   $J = 6$

   $3J = 18$

   Peter is currently 18 years old.

4. Let x = the number of minutes to do the job working together.

   Lauren does $x/30$ of the job.

   Kathleen does $x/20$ of the job.

   $x/30 + x/20 = 1$ (Multiply by 60)

   $2x + 3x = 60$

   $5x = 60$

   $x = 12$

   It would take 12 minutes to do the job together.

SUBJECT REVIEWS

5. The train takes 120/40 = 3 hours out, and the train takes 120/60 = 2 hours back. The total trip takes 5 hours. The total distance traveled is 240 miles. Then,

   Rate = Distance/Time = 240/5 = 48

   The average rate is 48 mph.

6. Let x = the first odd integer.

   Then, $x + 2$ = the second odd integer, and

   $$x + x + 2 = 68$$
   $$2x + 2 = 68$$
   $$2x = 66$$
   $$x = 33$$
   $$x + 2 = 35$$

   The numbers are 33 and 35.

7. Let x = the number of votes the winning candidate got. Then, $x - 100$ = the number of votes the losing candidate got, and

   $$x + x - 100 = 8{,}574$$
   $$2x - 100 = 8{,}574$$
   $$2x = 8{,}674$$
   $$x = 4{,}337$$

   The winning candidate got 4,337 votes.

8. Let x = the number. Then,

   $$4x - 10 = x - 1$$
   $$3x = 9$$
   $$x = 3$$

   The number is 3.

9. Let K = Karen's age.

   Then, $K + 3$ = Tony's age.

   In seven years, Karen's age will be $K + 7$, and Tony's will be $K + 10$.

   Therefore, in 7 years, we will have

   $$(K + 7) + (K + 10) = 79$$
   $$2K + 17 = 79$$
   $$2K = 62$$
   $$K = 31$$

   Karen is 31 now.

10. Let $t =$ the amount of time each train travels. Then, the distance the freight train travels is $52t$, and the distance the passenger train travels is $84t$. Thus,

$$52t + 84t = 680$$
$$136t = 680$$
$$t = 5$$

The trains each travel for 5 hours, so they will be 680 miles apart at 5 p.m.

Literal Equations

An equation may have other letters in it besides the variable (or variables). Such an equation is called a *literal equation*. An illustration is $x + b = a$, with x being the variable. The solution of such an equation will not be a specific number but will involve letter symbols. Literal equations are solved by exactly the same methods as those involving numbers, but we must know which of the letters in the equation is to be considered the variable. Then the other letters are treated as constants.

Example 1

Solve $ax - 2bc = d$ for x.

$$ax = d + 2bc$$
$$x = \frac{d + 2bc}{a} \text{ if } a \neq 0$$

Example 2

Solve $ay - by = a^2 - b^2$ for y.

$y(a - b) = a^2 - b^2$	Factor out common term.
$y(a - b) = (a + b)(a - b)$	Factor expression on right side.
$y = a + b$	Divide each side by $a - b$ if $a \neq b$.

Example 3

Solve for S the equation

$$\frac{1}{R} = \frac{1}{S} + \frac{1}{T}$$

Multiply every term by RST, the LCD:

$$ST = RT + RS$$
$$ST - RS = RT$$
$$S(T - R) = RT$$
$$S = \frac{RT}{T - R} \quad \text{If } T \neq R$$

Quadratic Equations

An equation containing the square of an unknown quantity is called a *quadratic* equation. One way of solving such an equation is by factoring. If the product of two expressions is zero, at least one of the expressions must be zero.

Example 1

Solve $y^2 + 2y = 0$.

$y(y + 2) = 0$ Remove common factor.

$y = 0$ or $y + 2 = 0$ Since product is 0, at least one of the factors must be 0.

$y = 0$ or $y = -2$

Check by substituting both values in the original equation:

$$(0)^2 + 2(0) = 0$$
$$(-2)^2 + 2(-2) = 4 - 4 = 0$$

In this case there are two solutions.

Example 2

Solve $x^2 + 7x + 10 = 0$.

$x^2 + 7x + 10 = (x + 5)(x + 2) = 0$

$x + 5 = 0$ or $x + 2 = 0$

$x = -5$ or $x = -2$

Check:

$(-5)^2 + 7(-5) + 10 = 25 - 35 + 10 = 0$
$(-2)^2 + 7(-2) + 10 = 4 - 14 + 10 = 0$

Not all quadratic equations can be factored using only integers, but solutions can usually be found by means of a formula. A quadratic equation may have two solutions, one solution, or occasionally no real solutions. If the quadratic equation is in the form $Ax^2 + Bx + C = 0$, x can be found from the following formula:

$$x = \frac{-B \pm \sqrt{B^2 - 4AC}}{2A}$$

MATHEMATICS REVIEW

Example 3

Solve $2y^2 + 5y + 2 = 0$ by formula. Assume $A = 2$, $B = 5$, and $C = 2$.

$$x = \frac{-5 \pm \sqrt{5^2 - 4(2)(2)}}{2(2)}$$

$$= \frac{-5 \pm \sqrt{25 - 16}}{4}$$

$$= \frac{-5 \pm \sqrt{9}}{4}$$

$$= \frac{-5 \pm 3}{4}$$

This yields two solutions:

$$x = \frac{-5 + 3}{4} = \frac{-2}{4} = \frac{-1}{2} \quad \text{and}$$

$$x = \frac{-5 - 3}{4} = \frac{-8}{4} = -2$$

So far, each quadratic we have solved has had two distinct answers, but an equation may have a single answer (repeated), as in

$$x^2 + 4x + 4 = 0$$
$$(x + 2)(x + 2) = 0$$
$$x + 2 = 0 \text{ and } x + 2 = 0$$
$$x = -2 \text{ and } x = -2$$

The only solution is -2.

It is also possible for a quadratic equation to have no real solution at all.

Example

If we attempt to solve $x^2 + x + 1 = 0$ by formula, we get:

$$x = \frac{-1 \pm \sqrt{1 - 4(1)(1)}}{2} = \frac{-1 \pm \sqrt{-3}}{2} \text{ Since } \sqrt{-3} \text{ is not}$$

defined, this quadratic has no real answer.

Rewriting Equations

Certain equations written with a variable in the denominator can be rewritten as quadratics.

Example

Solve $-\dfrac{4}{x} + 5 = x$

$-4 + 5x = x^2$ Multiply both sides by $x \neq 0$.

$-x^2 + 5x - 4 = 0$ Collect terms on one side of equals and set sum equal to 0.

$x^2 - 5x + 4 = 0$ Multiply both sides by -1.

$(x - 4)(x - 1) = 0$ Factor

$x - 4 = 0$ or $x - 1 = 0$

$x = 4$ or $x = 1$

Check the result by substitution:

$-\dfrac{4}{4} + 5 \stackrel{?}{=} 4$ and $-\dfrac{4}{1} + 5 \stackrel{?}{=} 1$

$-1 + 5 = 4$ $-4 + 5 = 1$

Some equations containing a radical sign can also be converted into a quadratic equation. The solution of this type of problem depends on the principle that

If $A = B$ then $A^2 = B^2$
and If $A^2 = B^2$ then $A = B$ or $A = -B$

Equations Involving Square Roots

To solve equations in which the variable appears under a square root sign, begin by manipulating the equation so that the square root is alone on one side. Then square both sides of the equation. Since squares and square roots are inverses, the square root will be eliminated from the equation.

Example 1

Solve $\sqrt{12x + 4} + 2 = 6$

Rewrite the equation as $\sqrt{12x + 4} = 4$. Now square both sides.

$(\sqrt{12x + 4})^2 = 4^2$

$12x + 4 = 16$

$12x = 12$

$x = 1$

It is easy to check that 1 is a solution to the equation by plugging the 1 into the original equation. However, sometimes when we use this procedure, the solution obtained will not solve the original equation. Thus, it is crucial to check your answer to all square root equations.

Example 2

Solve $y = \sqrt{3y + 4}$

$$y = \sqrt{3y + 4}$$
$$y^2 = 3y + 4$$
$$y^2 - 3y - 4 = 0$$
$$(y - 4)(y + 1) = 0$$
$$y = 4 \text{ or } y = -1$$

Check by substituting values into the original equation:

$4 \stackrel{?}{=} \sqrt{3(4) + 4}$ and
$-1 \stackrel{?}{=} \sqrt{3(-1) + 4}$
$4 \stackrel{?}{=} \sqrt{16} \quad\quad -1 \stackrel{?}{=} \sqrt{1}$
$4 = 4 \quad\quad\quad -1 \neq 1$

The single solution is $y = 4$; the false root $y = -1$ was introduced when the original equation was squared.

Equation Solving Problems

Solve the following equations for the variable indicated:

1. Solve for W: $P = 2L + 2W$
2. Solve for x: $ax + b = cx + d$
3. Solve for x: $8x^2 - 4x = 0$
4. Solve for x: $x^2 - 4x = 21$
5. Solve for y: $\sqrt{y + 1} - 3 = 7$
6. Solve for x: $4\sqrt{\dfrac{2x}{3}} = 48$
7. Solve $A = P + Prt$ for r
8. Solve for x: $3x^2 - x - 4 = 0$
9. Solve $\dfrac{q}{x} + \dfrac{p}{x} = 1$ for x
10. Solve for x: $3x^2 - 5 = 0$

SUBJECT REVIEWS

Solutions

1. $P = 2L + 2W$
    $2W = P - 2L$
    $W = \dfrac{P - 2L}{2}$

2. $ax + b = cx + d$
    $ax = cx + d - b$
    $ax - cx = d - b$
    $x(a - c) = d - b$
    $x = \dfrac{d - b}{a - c}$

3. $8x^2 - 4x = 0$
    $4x(x - 2) = 0$
    $x = 0, 2$

4. $x^2 - 4x = 21$
    $x^2 - 4x - 21 = 0$
    $(x - 7)(x + 3) = 0$
    $x = 7, -3$

5. $\sqrt{y + 1} - 3 = 7$
    $\sqrt{y + 1} = 10$
    $(\sqrt{y + 1})^2 = 10^2$
    $y + 1 = 100$
    $y = 99$

6. Begin by dividing both sides by 4 to get $\sqrt{\dfrac{2x}{3}} = 12$. Then, square both sides.
    $\left(\sqrt{\dfrac{2x}{3}}\right)^2 = 12^2$
    $\dfrac{2x}{3} = 144$ Now, multiply both sides by 3.
    $2x = 432$
    $x = 216$

7. $A = P + Prt$
    $A - P = Prt$
    $\dfrac{A - P}{Pt} = r$

8. $3x^2 - x - 4 = 0$ Here, $A = 3$, $B = -1$, and $C = -4$. Using the quadratic formula, we get

$$x = \frac{-B \pm \sqrt{B^2 - 4AC}}{2A} = \frac{1 \pm \sqrt{1 - 4(3)(-4)}}{6}$$

$$= \frac{1 \pm \sqrt{1+48}}{6} = \frac{1 \pm \sqrt{49}}{6} = \frac{1 \pm 7}{6} = \frac{8}{6}, \frac{-6}{6}$$

Thus, $x = \frac{4}{3}$ or -1. Note that this equation could have been solved by factoring as well. The quadratic formula, however, can be used to solve all quadratic equations, including those that cannot be factored.

9. $\frac{q}{x} + \frac{p}{x} = 1$ Multiply both sides by x to clear the fraction, and obtain

$q + p = x$

10. $3x^2 - 5 = 0$

This equation can easily be solved for x by first solving for x^2 and then taking the square root of both sides.

$$3x^2 = 5$$
$$x^2 = \frac{5}{3}$$
$$\sqrt{x^2} = \pm\sqrt{\frac{5}{3}}.$$

Since $\sqrt{x^2} = x$, we have $x = \pm\sqrt{\frac{5}{3}}$.

Linear Inequalities

For each of the sets of numbers we have considered, we have established an ordering of the members of the set by defining what it means to say that one number is greater than the other. Every number we have considered can be represented by a point on a number line.

An *algebraic inequality* is a statement that one algebraic expression is greater than (or less than) another algebraic expression. If all the variables in the inequality are raised to the first power, the inequality is said to be a *linear inequality*. We solve the inequality by reducing it to a simpler inequality whose solution is apparent. The answer is not unique, as it is in an equation, since a great number of values may satisfy the inequality.

SUBJECT REVIEWS

There are three rules for producing equivalent inequalities:

1. The same quantity can be added or subtracted from each side of an inequality.

2. Each side of an inequality can be multiplied or divided by the same *positive* quantity.

3. If each side of an inequality is multiplied or divided by the same *negative* quantity, the sign of the inequality must be reversed so that the new inequality is equivalent to the first.

Example 1

Solve $5x - 5 > -9 + 3x$.

$5x > -4 + 3x$ Add 5 to each side.
$2x > -4$ Subtract $3x$ from each side.
$x > -2$ Divide by +2.

Any number greater than -2 is a solution to this inequality.

Example 2

Solve $2x - 12 < 5x - 3$.

$2x < 5x + 9$ Add 12 to each side.
$-3x < 9$ Subtract $5x$ from each side.
$x > -3$ Divide each side by -3, changing sign of inequality.

Any number greater than -3—for example, $-2\frac{1}{2}$, 0, 1, or 4—is a solution to this inequality.

Example 3

$$\frac{x}{3} - \frac{x}{2} > 1$$

Begin by multiplying both sides by 6 to clear the fractions. We then obtain

$2x - 3x > 6$
$-x > 6$

Now, divide both sides by -1, and reverse the inequality.

$x < -6$

Linear Equations in Two Unknowns

Graphing Equations

The number line is useful in picturing the values of one variable. When two variables are involved, a coordinate system is effective. The Cartesian coordinate system is constructed by placing a vertical number line and a horizontal number line on a plane so that the lines intersect at their zero points. This meeting place is called the *origin*. The horizontal number line is called the x axis, and the vertical number line (with positive numbers above the x axis) is called the y axis. Points in the plane correspond to ordered pairs of real numbers.

Example

The points in this example are:

x	y
0	0
1	1
3	−1
−2	−2
−2	1

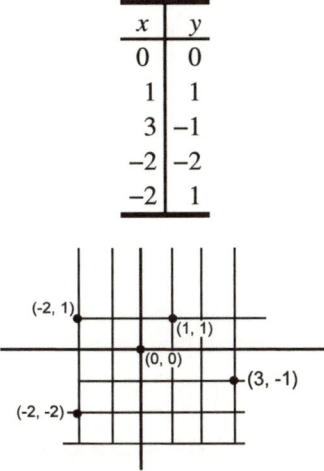

A first-degree equation in two variables is an equation that can be written in the form $ax + by = c$, where a, b, and c are constants. *First-degree* means that x and y appear to the first power. *Linear* refers to the graph of the solutions (x, y) of the equation, which is a straight line. We have already discussed linear equations of one variable.

Example

Graph the line $y = 2x - 4$.

First make a table and select small integral values of x. Find the value of each corresponding y and write it in the table:

x	y
0	-4
1	-2
2	0
3	2

If $x = 1$, for example, $y = 2(1) - 4 = -2$. Then plot the four points on a coordinate system. It is not necessary to have four points; two would do, since two points determine a line, but plotting three or more points reduces the possibility of error.

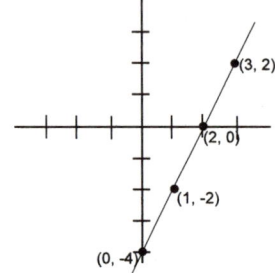

After the points have been plotted (placed on the graph), draw a line through the points and extend it in both directions. This line represents the equation $y = 2x - 4$.

Solving Simultaneous Linear Equations

Two linear equations can be solved together (simultaneously) to yield an answer (x, y) if it exists. On the coordinate system, this amounts to drawing the graphs of two lines and finding their point of intersection. If the lines are parallel and therefore never meet, no solution exists.

Simultaneous linear equations can be solved in the following manner without drawing graphs. From the first equation, find the value of one variable in terms of the other; substitute this value into the second equation. The second equation is now a linear equation in one variable and can be solved. After the numerical value of the one variable has been found, substitute that value into the first equation to find the value of the second variable. Check the results by putting both values into the second equation.

Example 1

Solve the system

$2x + y = 3$
$4x - y = 0$

From the first equation, $y = 3 - 2x$. Substitute this value of y into the second equation to get

$$4x - (3 - 2x) = 0$$
$$4x - 3 + 2x = 0$$
$$6x = 3$$
$$x = \frac{1}{2}$$

Substitute $x = \frac{1}{2}$ into the first of the original equations:

$$2\left(\frac{1}{2}\right) + y = 3$$
$$1 + y = 3$$
$$y = 2$$

Check by substituting both x and y values into the second equation:

$$4\left(\frac{1}{2}\right) - 2 = 0$$
$$2 - 2 = 0$$

Example 2

The sum of two numbers is 87 and their difference is 13. What are the numbers?

Let $x =$ the larger of the two numbers and y the smaller. Then,

$x + y = 87$
$x - y = 13$.

Rewrite the second equation as $x = y + 13$ and plug it into the first equation.

$$(y + 13) + y = 87$$
$$2y + 13 = 87$$
$$2y = 74$$
$$y = 37$$

Then, $x = 13 + 37 = 50$.

The numbers are 50 and 37.

Example 3

A change-making machine contains $30 in dimes and quarters. There are 150 coins in the machine. Find the number of each type of coin.

Let x = number of dimes and y = number of quarters. Then:

$x + y = 150$

Since $.25y$ is the product of a quarter of a dollar and the number of quarters and $.10x$ is the amount of money in dimes,

$.10x + .25y = 30$

Multiply the last equation by 100 to eliminate the decimal points:

$10x + 25y = 3000$

From the first equation, $y = 150 - x$. Substitute this value into the equivalent form of the second equation.

$$10x + 25(150 - x) = 3000$$
$$-15x = -750$$
$$x = 50$$

This is the number of dimes. Substitute this value into $x + y = 150$ to find the number of quarters, $y = 100$.

Check:

$$.10(50) + .25(100) = 30$$
$$\$5 + \$25 = \$30$$

Linear Inequalities and Equations Problems

1. Solve for x: $12x < 5(2x + 4)$

2. Solve for y: $6y + 2 < 8y + 14$

3. Find the common solution:

   $x - 3y = 3$
   $2x + 9y = 11$

4. A coin collection consisting of quarters and nickels has a value of $4.50. The total number of coins is 26. Find the number of quarters and the number of nickels in the collection.

5. Mr. Linnell bought 3 cans of corn and 5 cans of tomatoes for $3.75. The next week, he bought 4 cans of corn and 2 cans of tomatoes for $2.90. Find the cost of a can of corn.

6. Solve for z: $6z + 1 \leq 3(z - 2)$

7. Find the common solution:

   $y = 3x + 1$

   $x + y = 9$

8. Find the common solution:

   $2x + y = 8$

   $x - y = 1$

9. A 20-foot piece of wood is cut into 2 pieces, one of which is 4 feet longer than the other. How long is each piece of wood?

10. A printer and monitor together cost $356. The monitor costs $20 more than two times the printer. How much do the printer and monitor cost separately?

Solutions

1. $12x < 5(2x + 4)$

   $12x < 10x + 20$

   $2x < 20$

   $x < 10$

2. $6y + 2 < 8y + 14$

   $6y < 8y + 12$

   $-2y < 12$

   $y > -6$

3. $x - 3y = 3$

   $2x + 9y = 11$

   Multiply the first equation by 3.

   $3(x - 3y) = 3(3)$

   $2x + 9y = 11$

   $3x - 9y = 9$

   $2x + 9y = 11$

   $5x = 20$

   $x = 4$

   Now substitute this answer for x in the second equation.

   $2(4) + 9y = 11$

   $8 + 9y = 11$

   $9y = 3$

   $y = \dfrac{1}{3}$

4. Let Q = the number of quarters in the collection.

   Let N = the number of nickels in the collection.

   Then $.25Q + .05N = 4.50$
   $$Q + N = 26$$

   Multiply the top equation by 100 to clear the decimals:

   $25Q + 5N = 450$
   $$Q + N = 26$$

   Multiply the bottom equation by -5 and add:

   $25Q + 5N = 450$
   $\underline{-5Q - 5N = -130}$
   $20Q = 320$
   $Q = 16$
   $N = 10$

   There are 16 quarters and 10 nickels.

5. Let c = the cost of a can of corn

   t = the cost of a can of tomatoes

   Then

   $3c + 5t = 3.75$
   $4c + 2t = 2.90$

   Multiply the top equation by 2, the bottom one by -5, and add:

   $6c + 10t = 7.50$
   $\underline{-20c - 10t = -14.50}$
   $-14c = -7.00$
   $c = .50$

   A can of corn costs 50¢.

6. $6z + 1 \leq 3(z - 2)$
   $6z + 1 \leq 3z - 6$
   $3z \leq -7$
   $z \leq -\dfrac{7}{3}$

   Note that even though the answer is negative, we do not reverse the inequality sign since we never multiplied or divided by a negative number.

7. $y = 3x + 1 \qquad x + y = 9$

   Begin by substituting $y = 3x + 1$ into the second equation

   $x + (3x + 1) = 9$
   $4x + 1 = 9$
   $4x = 8$
   $x = 2$

   If $x = 2$, $y = 3(2) + 1 = 6 + 1 = 7$

8. $2x + y = 8 \qquad x - y = 1$

   From the second equation, we can see $x = y + 1$. Then, substituting into the first equation

   $2(y + 1) + y = 8$
   $3y + 2 = 8$
   $3y = 6$
   $y = 2$

   If $y = 2$, then $x = y + 1 = 2 + 1 = 3$

9. Let L = the length of the longer piece of wood.

   Let S = the length of the shorter piece of wood. Then the equations are

   $L + S = 20$
   $L - S = 4$

   From the second equation, we obtain $L = S + 4$. Substituting into the first equation, we get

   $(S + 4) + S = 20$
   $2S + 4 = 20$
   $2S = 16$
   $S = 8$

   The shorter piece of wood is 8 feet, so the longer piece is 12 feet.

10. The printer and monitor together cost $356. The monitor cost $20 more than two times the printer.

Let P = the cost of the printer.

Let M = the cost of the monitor. Then
$P + M = 356$
$M = 20 + 2P$

Substituting for M in the first equation, we get
$P + (20 + 2P) = 356$
$3P + 20 = 356$
$3P = 336$
$P = 112$

Then $M = 20 + 2(112) = 244$

The printer costs $112, and the monitor costs $244.

Ratio and Proportion

Many problems in arithmetic and algebra can be solved using the concept of *ratio* to compare numbers. The ratio of a to b is the fraction $\frac{a}{b}$. If the two ratios $\frac{a}{b}$ and $\frac{c}{d}$ represent the same comparison, we write:

$$\frac{a}{b} = \frac{c}{d}$$

This equation (statement of equality) is called a *proportion*. A proportion states the equivalence of two different expressions for the same ratio.

Example 1

In a class of 39 students, 17 are men. Find the ratio of men to women.

39 students − 17 men = 22 women

Ratio of men to women is 17/22, also written 17:22.

Example 2

The scale on a map is $\frac{3}{4}$ inch = 12 miles. If the distance between City A and City B on the map is $4\frac{1}{2}$ inches, how far apart are the two cities actually?

Let x = the distance between the two cities in miles.

Begin by writing a proportion that compares inches to miles.

$$\frac{Inches \rightarrow}{Miles \rightarrow} \frac{\frac{3}{4}}{12} = \frac{\frac{9}{2}}{x} \quad \text{Cross multiply to solve the equation.}$$

$$\left(\frac{3}{4}\right)x = 12\left(\frac{9}{2}\right)$$

$$\left(\frac{3}{4}\right)x = 54 \quad \text{Multiply by 4}$$

$$3x = 216$$

$$x = 72$$

The two cities are 72 miles apart.

Example 3

A fertilizer contains 3 parts nitrogen, 2 parts potash, and 2 parts phosphate by weight. How many pounds of fertilizer will contain 60 pounds of nitrogen?

The ratio of pounds of nitrogen to pounds of fertilizer is 3 to 3 + 2 + 2 = 3/7. Let x be the number of pounds of mixture. Then:

$$\frac{3}{7} = \frac{60}{x}$$

Multiply both sides of the equation by $7x$ to get:

$$3x = 420$$

$$x = 140 \text{ pounds}$$

SUBJECT REVIEWS

Computing Averages and Medians

Mean

Several statistical measures are used frequently. One of them is the *average* or *arithmetic mean*. To find the average of N numbers, add the numbers and divide their sum by N.

Example 1

Seven students attained test scores of 62, 80, 60, 30, 50, 90, and 20. What was the average test score for the group?

$$62 + 80 + 60 + 30 + 50 + 90 + 20 = 392$$

Since there are 7 scores, the average score is

$$\frac{392}{7} = 56$$

Example 2

Brian has scores of 88, 87, and 92 on his first three tests. What grade must he get on his next test to have an overall average of 90?

Let x = the grade that he needs to get. Then we have

$$\frac{88 + 87 + 92 + x}{4} = 90 \text{ Multiply by 4 to clear the fraction.}$$

$$88 + 87 + 92 + x = 360$$
$$267 + x = 360$$
$$x = 93$$

Brian needs to get a 93 on his next test.

Example 3

Joan allotted herself a budget of $50 a week, on the average, for expenses. One week she spent $35, the next $60, and the third $40. How much can she spend in the fourth week without exceeding her budget?

Let x be the amount spent in the fourth week. Then:

$$\frac{35 + 60 + 40 + x}{4} = 50$$

$$35 + 60 + 40 + x = 200$$
$$135 + x = 200$$
$$x = 65$$

She can spend $65 in the fourth week.

Median

If a set of numbers is arranged in order, the number in the middle is called the *median*.

Example

Find the median test score of 62, 80, 60, 30, 50, 90, and 20. Arrange the numbers in increasing (or decreasing) order

20, 30, 50, 60, 62, 80, 90

Since 60 is the number in the middle, it is the median. It is not the same as the arithmetic mean, which is 56.

If the number of scores is an even number, the median is the arithmetic mean of the middle two scores.

COORDINATE GEOMETRY

We have already seen that a coordinate system is an effective way to picture relationships involving two variables. In this section, we will learn more about the study of geometry using coordinate methods.

Lines

Recall that the general equation of a line has the following form:

$$Ax + By + C = 0$$

where A and B are constants and are not both 0. This means that if you were to find all of the points (x, y) that satisfy the above equation, they would all lie on the same line as graphed on a coordinate axis.

If the value of B is not 0, a little algebra can be used to rewrite the equation in the form

$$y = mx + b$$

where m and b are two constants. Since the two numbers m and b determine this line, let's see what their geometric meaning is. First of all, note that the point $(0, b)$ satisfies the above equation. This means that the point $(0, b)$ is one of the points on the line; in other words, the line crosses the y-axis at the point b. For this reason, the number b is called the *y-intercept* of the line.

To interpret the meaning of m, choose any two points on the line. Let us call these points (x_1, y_1) and (x_2, y_2). Both of these points must satisfy the equation of the line above, and so:

$$y_1 = mx_1 + b \text{ and } y_2 = mx_2 + b.$$

If we subtract the first equation from the second, we obtain

$$y_2 - y_1 = m(x_2 - x_1)$$

and solving for m, we find

$$m = (y_2 - y_1)/(x_2 - x_1).$$

The above equation tells us that the number m in the equation $y = mx + b$ is the ratio of the difference of the y-coordinates to the difference of the x-coordinates. This number is called the *slope* of the line. Therefore, the ratio $m = (y_2 - y_1)/(x_2 - x_1)$ is a measure of the number of units the line rises (or falls) in the y direction for each unit moved in the x direction. Another way to say this is that the slope of a line is a measure of the rate at which the line rises (or falls). Intuitively, a line with a positive slope rises from left to right; one with a negative slope falls from left to right.

Because the equation $y = mx + b$ contains both the slope and the y-intercept, it is called the *slope-intercept* form of the equation of the line.

Example

Write the equation $2x - 3y = 6$ in slope-intercept form.

To write the equation in slope-intercept form, we begin by solving for y.

$$-3y = 6 - 2x$$
$$3y = 2x - 6$$
$$y = \frac{2x}{3} - \frac{6}{3} \text{ or}$$
$$y = \frac{2x}{3} - 2$$

Thus, the slope of the line is $\frac{2}{3}$, and the y-intercept is -2.

This, however, is not the only form in which the equation of the line can be written.

If the line contains the point (x_1, y_1), its equation can also be written as:

$$y - y_1 = m(x - x_1).$$

This form of the equation of a line is called the *point-slope* form of the equation of a line, since it contains the slope and the coordinates of one of the points on the line.

Example

Write the equation of the line that passes through the point (2, 3) with slope 8 in point-slope form.

In this problem, $m = 8$, and $(x_1, y_1) = (2, 3)$. Substituting into the point-slope form of the equation, we obtain

$$y - 3 = 8(x - 2)$$

Two lines are parallel if and only if they have the same slope. Two lines are perpendicular if and only if their slopes are negative inverses of each other. This means that if a line has a slope m, any line perpendicular to this line must have a slope of $-1/m$. Also note that a horizontal line has a slope of 0. For such a line, the slope-intercept form of the equation reduces to $y = b$.

Finally, note that if $B = 0$ in the equation $Ax + By + C = 0$, the equation simplifies to

$$Ax + C = 0$$

and represents a vertical line (a line parallel to the y-axis) that crosses the x-axis at $-C/A$. Such a line is said to have no slope.

Example 1

Find the slope and the y-intercept of the following lines.

    a. $y = 5x - 7$

    b. $3x + 4y = 5$

a. $y = 5x - 7$ is already in slope-intercept form. The slope is 5, and the y-intercept is -7.

b. Write $3x + 4y = 5$ in slope-intercept form:

$$4y = -3x + 5$$

$$y = \left(-\frac{3}{4}\right)x + \left(\frac{5}{4}\right)$$

The slope is $\frac{-3}{4}$, and the y-intercept is $\frac{5}{4}$. This means that the line crosses the y-axis at the point $\frac{5}{4}$, and for every 3 units moved in the x direction, the line falls 4 units in the y direction.

Example 2

Find the equations of the following lines:

    a. the line containing the points (4, 5) and (7,11)

    b. the line containing the point (6, 3) and having slope 2

    c. the line containing the point (5, 2) and parallel to $y = 4x + 7$

    d. the line containing the point (−2, 8) and perpendicular to $y = -2x + 9$

Solutions

a. First, we need to determine the slope of the line.

$$m = (11 - 5)/(7 - 4) = 6/3 = 2.$$

Now, using the point-slope form:

$$y - 5 = 2(x - 4).$$

If desired, you can change this to the slope-intercept form: $y = 2x - 3$.

b. Since we know the slope and a point on the line, we can simply plug into the point-slope form:

$$y - 3 = m(x - 6) \text{ to obtain}$$

$$y - 3 = 2(x - 6).$$

c. The line $y = 4x + 7$ has a slope of 4. Thus, the desired line can be written as $y - 2 = 4(x - 5)$.

d. The line $y = -2x + 9$ has a slope of -2. The line perpendicular to this one has a slope of $\frac{1}{2}$. The desired line can be written as $y - 8 = \left(\frac{1}{2}\right)(x + 2)$.

Circles

From a geometric point of view, a circle is the set of points in a plane, each of whose members is the same distance from a particular point called the center of the circle. We can determine the equation of a circle by manipulating the distance formula.

Suppose that we have a circle whose radius is a given positive number r and whose center lies at the point (h, k). If (x, y) is a point on the circle, then its distance from the center of the circle would be

$$\sqrt{(x - h)^2 + (y - k)^2}$$

and since this distance is r, we can say

$$\sqrt{(x - h)^2 + (y - k)^2} = r.$$

Squaring both sides, we get the following result: the equation of a circle whose center is at (h, k) and whose radius is r is given by:

$$(x - h)^2 + (y - k)^2 = r^2$$

Example 1

Find the equation of the circle with radius 7, and center at (0, −5).

Substituting into the formula above, we obtain $x^2 + (y + 5)^2 = 49$.

Example 2

Describe the set of points (x, y) with the property that $x^2 + y^2 > 25$.

The equation $x^2 + y^2 = 25$ describes a circle, centered at the origin, with radius 5. The given set contains all of the points that are *outside* this circle.

Coordinate Geometry Problems

1. Find the y-intercept of the line $3x − 5y = 15$.
2. Find the equation of the line whose slope is −2 and whose y-intercept is 5.
3. Find the slope of the line $2x + 3y = 8$.
4. Find the equation of the line containing the points (2, 4) and (10, 9).
5. Find the equation of the line containing the point (6, 3) and parallel to $y = 6x − 8$.
6. Find the equation of the line containing the point (2, 3) and perpendicular to $y = -\frac{1}{3}x + 7$.
7. Find the equation of the circle centered at (−2, 3) with radius 7.
8. Write the equation $4x − 5y = 12$ in slope-intercept form.
9. Find the equation of the line parallel to $x = 7$ and containing the point (3, 4).
10. Write an inequality that represents all of the points inside the circle centered at (4, 5) with radius 4.
11. Find the equation of the line perpendicular to $x = −3$, containing the point (−3, −6).
12. Find the slope of the line containing the points (−4, 6) and (2, 6).

SUBJECT REVIEWS

Solutions

1. A line crosses the *y*-axis at the point where $x = 0$.
   $$3(0) - 5y = 15$$
   $$-5y = 15$$
   $$y = -3$$
   The *y*-intercept is $(0, -3)$.

2. Using the slope-intercept formula for the equation of a line: $y = -2x + 5$.

3. Put the equation in slope-intercept form:
   $$2x + 3y = 8$$
   $$3y = -2x + 8$$
   $$y = -\frac{2}{3}x + \frac{8}{3}$$
   The slope is $-\frac{2}{3}$.

4. The slope of the line would be $\frac{9-4}{10-2} = \frac{5}{8}$. Using the point-slope form:
   $$(y - 4) = \frac{5}{8}(x - 2)$$
   $$8(y - 4) = 5(x - 2)$$
   $$8y - 32 = 5x - 10$$
   $$5x - 8y = -22$$

5. The slope of $y = 6x - 8$ is 6.
   Using the point-slope form:
   $$y - 3 = 6(x - 6)$$
   $$y - 3 = 6x - 36$$
   $$6x - y = 33$$

6. The slope of $y = -\frac{1}{3}x + 7$ is $-\frac{1}{3}$.
   The slope of the perpendicular line would be 3.
   Using the point-slope formula:
   $$y - 3 = 3(x - 2)$$
   $$y - 3 = 3x - 6$$
   $$3x - y = 3$$

7. Using the general formula for the equation of a circle:

   $(x - (-2))^2 + (y - 3)^2 = 7^2$

   or $(x + 2)^2 + (y - 3)^2 = 49$

8. To write the equation in slope-intercept form, we begin by solving for y:

   $4x - 5y = 12$

   $-5y = -4x + 12$

   $y = \dfrac{-4x}{-5} + \dfrac{12}{-5} = \dfrac{4x}{5} - \dfrac{12}{5}$

   Thus, the equation in slope-intercept form is:

   $y = \dfrac{4x}{5} - \dfrac{12}{5}$. The slope is $\dfrac{4}{5}$, and the y-intercept is $\dfrac{-12}{5}$.

9. Since $x = 7$ is horizontal, any line parallel to $x = 7$ will be horizontal also. The line horizontal to $x = 7$ through (3, 4) is $x = 3$.

10. The equation of the circle with center at (4, 5) with radius 4 is

    $(x - 4)^2 + (y - 5)^2 = 4^2 = 16$.

    The points inside this circle are given by the inequality:
    $(x - 4)^2 + (y - 5)^2 < 16$.

11. The line $x = -3$ is horizontal, so any line perpendicular to it is vertical. The vertical line through the point $(-3, -6)$ is $y = -6$.

12. The slope of the line containing the points $(-4, 6)$ and $(2, 6)$ is

    $m = \dfrac{6 - 6}{2 - (-4)} = \dfrac{0}{6} = 0$. Thus, the line is vertical.

PLANE GEOMETRY

Plane geometry is the science of measurement. Certain assumptions are made about undefined quantities called points, lines, and planes, and then logical deductions about relationships between figures composed of lines, angles, and portions of planes are made based on these assumptions. The process of making the logical deductions is called a *proof.* In this summary, we are not making any proofs but are giving the definitions frequently used in geometry and stating relationships that are the results of proofs.

Lines and Angles

Angles

A line in geometry is always a straight line. When two straight lines meet at a point, they form an *angle*. The lines are called *sides* or *rays* of the angle, and the point is called the *vertex*. The symbol for angle is ∠. When no other angle shares the same vertex, the name of the angle is the name given to the vertex, as in angle *A*:

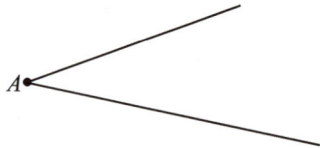

An angle may be named with three letters. In the following example, *B* is a point on one side and *C* is a point on the other. In this case, the name of the vertex must be the middle letter, and we have angle *BAC*.

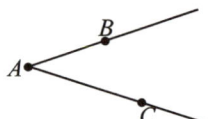

Occasionally, an angle is named by a number or small letter placed in the angle.

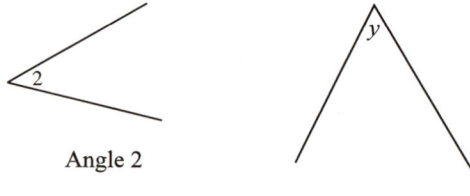

Angle 2

Angle *y*

Angles are usually measured in degrees. An angle of 30 degrees, written 30°, is an angle whose measure is 30 degrees. Degrees are divided into minutes; 60' (read "minutes") = 1°. Minutes are further divided into seconds; 60" (read "seconds") = 1'.

Vertical Angles

When two lines intersect, four angles are formed. The angles opposite each other are called *vertical angles* and are equal to each other.

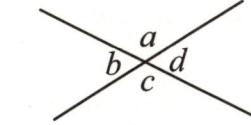

a and *c* are vertical angles.
∠a = ∠c
b and *d* are vertical angles.
∠b = ∠d

Straight Angle

A *straight angle* has its sides lying along a straight line. It is always equal to 180°.

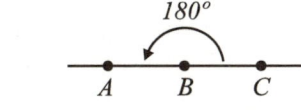

∠ABC = ∠B = 180°
∠B is a straight angle.

Adjacent Angles

Two angles are *adjacent* if they share the same vertex and a common side but no angle is inside another angle. ∠ABC and ∠CBD are adjacent angles. Even though they share a common vertex B and a common side AB, ∠ABD and ∠ABC are not adjacent angles because one angle is inside the other.

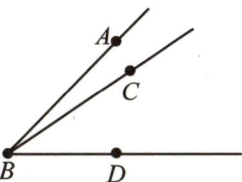

Supplementary Angles

If the sum of two angles is a straight angle (180°), the two angles are *supplementary* and each angle is the supplement of the other.

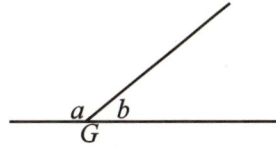

∠G is a straight angle = 180°.
∠a + ∠b = 180°
∠a and ∠b are supplementary angles.

Right Angles

If two supplementary angles are equal, they are both *right angles*. A right angle is one half a straight angle. Its measure is 90°. A right angle is symbolized by ⌐.

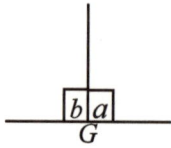

∠G is a straight angle.
∠b + ∠a = ∠G, and ∠a = ∠b. ∠a and ∠b are right angles.

Complementary Angles

Complementary angles are two angles whose sum is a right angle (90°).

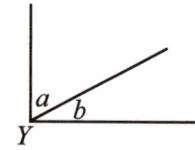

∠Y is a right angle.
∠a + ∠b = ∠Y = 90°.
∠a and ∠b are complementary angles.

Acute Angles

Acute angles are angles whose measure is less than 90°. No two acute angles can be supplementary angles. Two acute angles can be complementary angles.

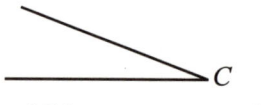

∠C is an acute angle.

Obtuse Angles

Obtuse angles are angles that are greater than 90° and less than 180°.

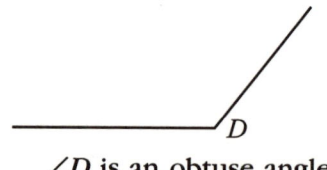

∠D is an obtuse angle.

Example 1

In the figure, what is the value of *x*?

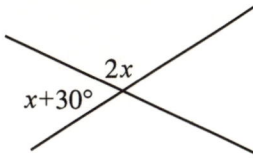

Since the two labeled angles are supplementary angles, their sum is 180°.

$(x + 30°) + 2x = 180°$
$3x = 150°$
$x = 50°$

Example 2

Find the value of *x* in the figure.

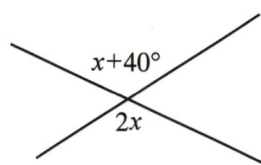

Since the two labeled angles are vertical angles, they are equal.

$x + 40° = 2x$
$40° = x$

Example 3

If angle *Y* is a right angle and angle *b* measures 30°15′, what does angle *a* measure?

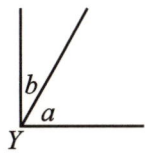

Since angle *Y* is a right angle, angles *a* and *b* are complementary angles and their sum is 90°.

$\angle a + \angle b = 90°$
$\angle a + 30°15′ = 90°$
$\angle a = 59°45′$

Example 4

In the figure below, what is the value of *x*?

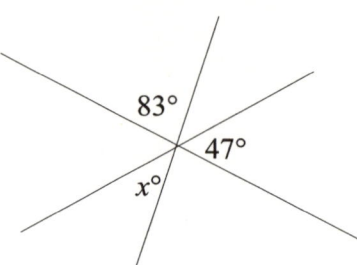

The angle that is vertical to the angle labeled *x*° also has a measure of *x*°. This angle, along with those labeled 83° and 47°, form a straight line and are thus supplementary. Therefore,

$$83 + 47 + x = 180$$
$$130 + x = 180$$
$$x = 50$$

The value of *x* is 50°.

Lines

A *line* in geometry is always assumed to be a straight line. It extends infinitely far in both directions. It can be determined if two of its points are known. It can be expressed in terms of the two points, which are written as capital letters. The following line is called *AB*.

Or a line may be given one name with a small letter. The following line is called line *k*.

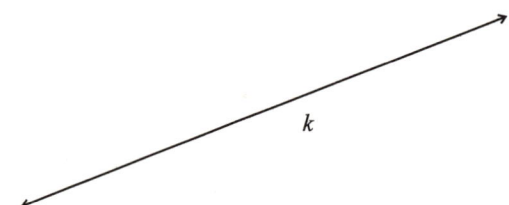

A *line segment* is a part of a line between two *endpoints*. It is named by its endpoints, for example, *A* and *B*.

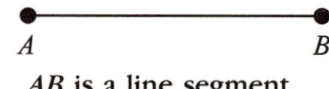

AB is a line segment.
It has a definite length.

If point *P* is on the line and is the same distance from *A* as from *B*, then *P* is the *midpoint* of segment *AB*. When we say *AP* = *PB*, we mean that the two line segments have the same length.

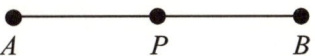

A part of a line with one endpoint is called a *ray*. *AC* is a ray, of which *A* is an endpoint. The ray extends infinitely far in the direction away from the endpoint.

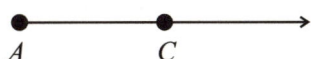

Parallel Lines

Two lines meet or intersect if there is one point that is on both lines. Two different lines may either intersect in one point or never meet, but they can never meet in more than one point.

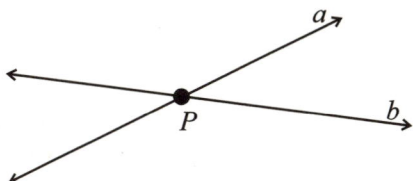

Two lines in the same plane that never meet no matter how far they are extended are said to be *parallel*, for which the symbol is ∥. In the following diagram, *a* ∥ *b*.

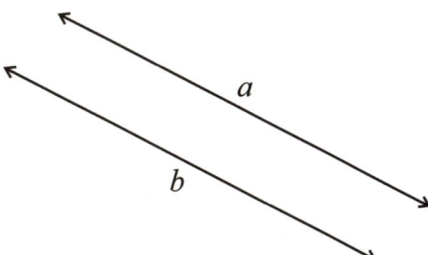

If two lines in the same plane are parallel to a third line, they are parallel to each other. Since *a* ∥ *b* and *b* ∥ *c*, we know that *a* ∥ *c*.

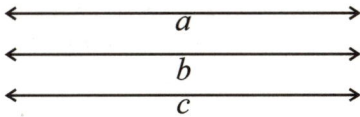

Two lines that meet each other at right angles are said to be *perpendicular,* for which the symbol is ⊥. Line *a* is perpendicular to line *b*.

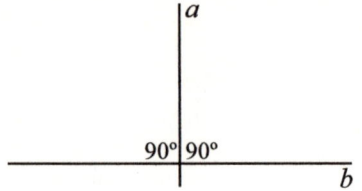

Two lines in the same plane that are perpendicular to the same line are parallel to each other.

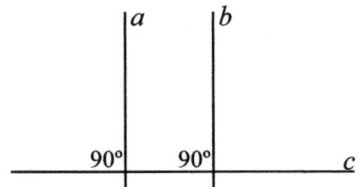

Line *a* ⊥ line *c* and line *b* ⊥ line *c*.
Therefore, *a* ∥ *b*.

A line intersecting two other lines is called a *transversal.* Line *c* is a transversal intersecting lines *a* and *b*.

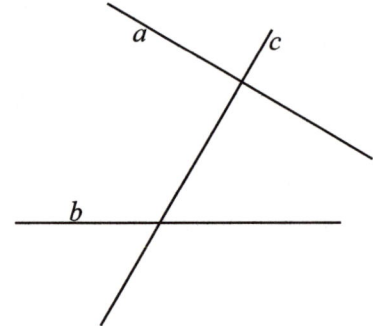

The transversal and the two given lines form eight angles. The four angles between the given lines are called *interior angles;* the four angles outside the given lines are called *exterior angles.* If two angles are on opposite sides of the transversal, they are called *alternate angles.*

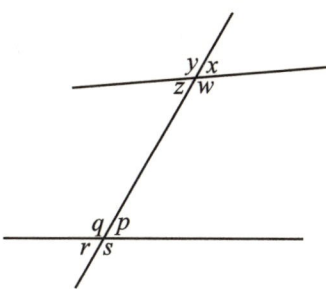

∠z, ∠w, ∠q, and ∠p are interior angles.
∠y, ∠x, ∠s, and ∠r are exterior angles.
∠z and ∠p are alternate interior angles; so are ∠w and ∠q.
∠y and ∠s are alternate exterior angles; so are ∠x and ∠r.

Pairs of *corresponding* angles are ∠y and ∠q, ∠z and ∠r, ∠x and ∠p, and, ∠w and ∠s. Corresponding angles are sometimes called exterior-interior angles.

When the two given lines cut by a transversal are parallel lines:

1. the corresponding angles are equal.
2. the alternate interior angles are equal.
3. the alternate exterior angles are equal.
4. interior angles on the same side of the transversal are supplementary.

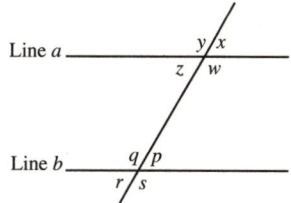

If line *a* is parallel to line *b:*

1. ∠y = ∠q, ∠z = ∠r, ∠x = ∠p, and ∠w = ∠s.
2. ∠z = ∠p and ∠w = ∠q.
3. ∠y = ∠s and ∠x = ∠r.
4. ∠z + ∠q = 180° and ∠p + ∠w = 180°.

Because vertical angles are equal, ∠p = ∠r, ∠q = ∠s, ∠y = ∠w, and ∠x = ∠z. If any one of the four conditions for equality of angles holds true, the lines are parallel; that is, if two lines are cut by a transversal and one pair of the corresponding angles is equal, the lines are parallel. If a pair of alternate interior angles or a pair of alternate exterior angles is equal, the lines are parallel. If interior angles on the same side of the transversal are supplementary, the lines are parallel.

SUBJECT REVIEWS

Example 1

In the figure, two parallel lines are cut by a transversal. Find the measure of angle y.

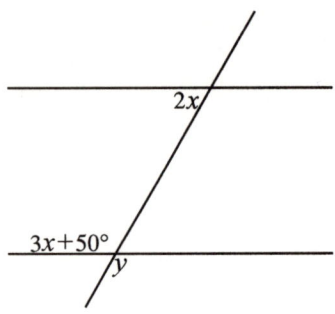

The two labeled angles are supplementary.

$2x + (3x + 50°) = 180°$
$5x = 130°$
$x = 26°$

Since $\angle y$ is vertical to the angle whose measure is $3x + 50°$, it has the same measure.

$y = 3x + 50° = 3(26°) + 50° = 128°$

Example 2

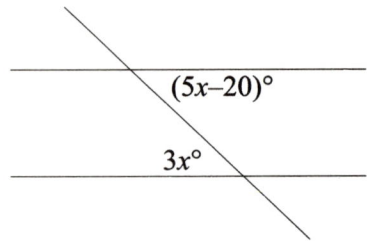

In the figure above, two parallel lines are cut by a transversal. Find the measure of angle x.

The two labeled angles are alternate interior angles and thus are congruent. Therefore,

$5x - 20 = 3x$
$2x = 20$
$x = 10$

The measure of angle x is $10°$.

Polygons

A *polygon* is a closed plane figure composed of line segments joined together at points called *vertices* (singular, *vertex*). A polygon is usually named by giving its vertices in order.

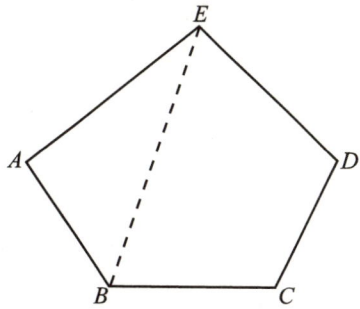

Polygon *ABCDE*

In the figure, points *A, B, C, D,* and *E* are the vertices, and the sides are *AB, BC, CD, DE,* and *EA*. *AB* and *BC* are *adjacent* sides, and *A* and *B* are adjacent vertices. A *diagonal* of a polygon is a line segment joining any two nonadjacent vertices. *EB* is a diagonal.

Polygons are named according to the number of sides or angles. A *triangle* is a polygon with three sides, a *quadrilateral* a polygon with four sides, a *pentagon* a polygon with five sides, and a *hexagon* a polygon with six sides. The number of sides is always equal to the number of angles.

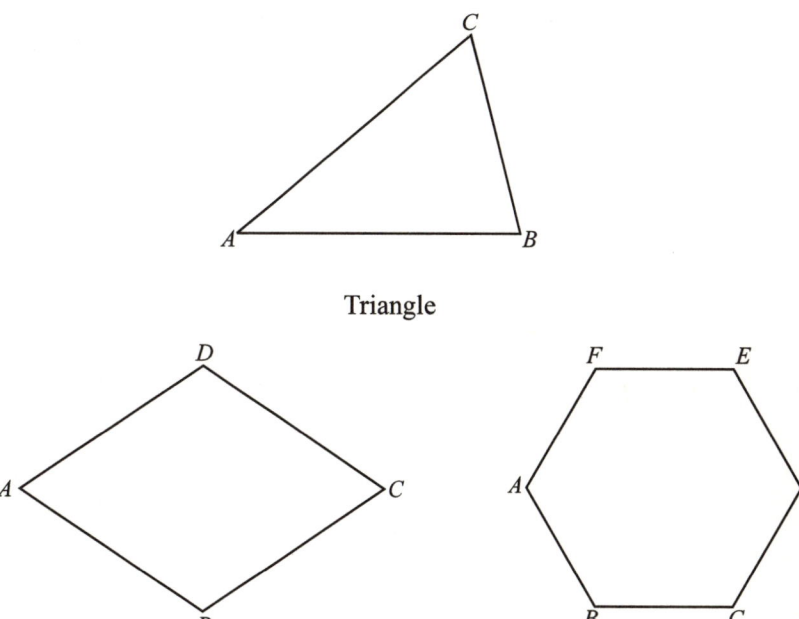

Triangle

Quadrilateral

Hexagon

The *perimeter* of a polygon is the sum of the lengths of its sides. If the polygon is regular (all sides equal and all angles equal), the perimeter is the product of the length of *one* side and the number of sides.

SUBJECT REVIEWS

Congruent and Similar Polygons

If two polygons have equal corresponding angles and equal corresponding sides, they are said to be *congruent*. Congruent polygons have the same size and shape. They are the same in all respects except possibly position. The symbol for congruence is ≅.

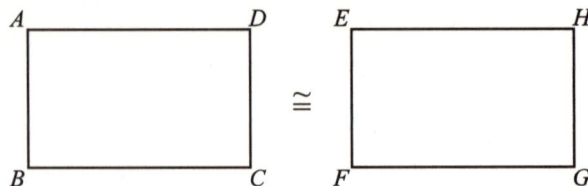

When two sides of congruent or different polygons are equal, we indicate the fact by drawing the same number of short lines through the equal sides.

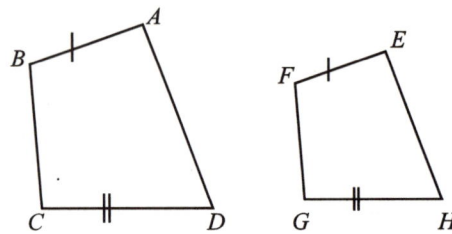

This indicates that *AB* = *EF* and *CD* = *GH*.

Two polygons with equal corresponding angles and corresponding sides in proportion are said to be *similar*. The symbol for similar is ∼.

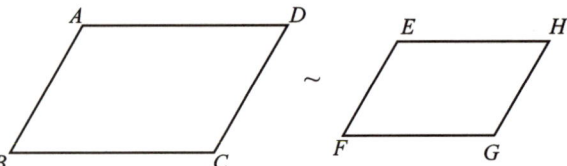

Similar figures have the same shape but not necessarily the same size.

A *regular polygon* is a polygon whose sides are equal and whose angles are equal.

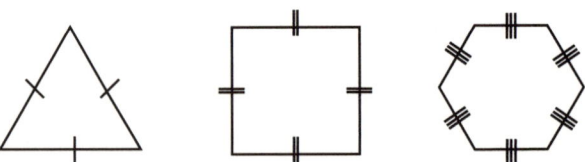

Triangles

A *triangle* is a polygon of three sides. Triangles are classified by measuring their sides and angles. The sum of the angles of a plane triangle is always 180°. The symbol for a triangle is △. The sum of any two sides of a triangle is always greater than the third side.

Equilateral

Equilateral triangles have equal sides and equal angles. Each angle measures 60° because $\frac{1}{3}(180°) = 60°$.

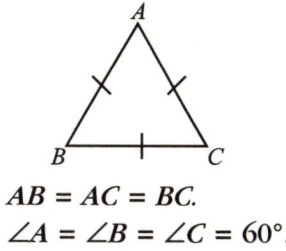

$AB = AC = BC$.
$\angle A = \angle B = \angle C = 60°$.

Isosceles

Isosceles triangles have two equal sides. The angles opposite the equal sides are equal. The two equal angles are sometimes called the *base* angles and the third angle is called the *vertex* angle. Note that an equilateral triangle is isosceles.

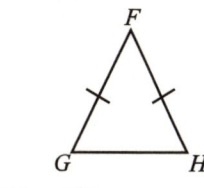

$FG = FH$.
$FG \neq GH$.
$\angle G = \angle H$.
$\angle F$ is the vertex angle.
$\angle G$ and $\angle H$ are base angles.

Scalene

Scalene triangles have all three sides of different length and all angles of different measure. In scalene triangles, the shortest side is opposite the angle of smallest measure, and the longest side is opposite the angle of greatest measure.

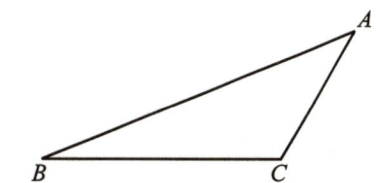

$AB > BC > CA$; therefore $\angle C > \angle A > \angle B$.

SUBJECT REVIEWS

Example 1

In triangle *XYZ*, ∠*Y* is twice ∠*X*, and ∠*Z* is 40° more than ∠*Y*. How many degrees are in the three angles?

Solve this problem just as you would an algebraic word problem, remembering that there are 180° in a triangle.

Let x = the number of degrees in ∠X

Then $2x$ = the number of degrees in ∠Y

and $2x + 40$ = the number of degrees in ∠Z

Thus,

$$x + 2x + (2x + 40) = 180$$
$$5x + 40 = 180$$
$$5x = 140$$
$$x = 28°$$

Therefore, the measure of ∠X is 28°, the measure of ∠Y is 56°, and the measure of ∠Z is 96°.

Example 2

In the figure below, the two lines are parallel. What is the value of x?

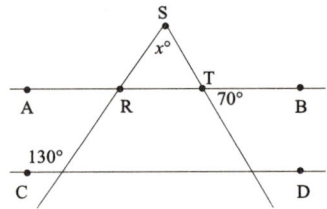

Corresponding angles are equal, so ∠ARS is also 130°. ∠SRT is the supplement of ∠ARS and thus is 50°. By the property of vertical angles, we have ∠STR = 70°. Finally, since the sum of the angles in triangle SRT is 180°, we have

$$x + 50 + 70 = 180$$
$$x + 120 = 180$$
$$x = 60°.$$

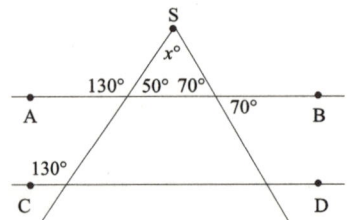

Right

Right triangles contain one right angle. Since the right angle is 90°, the other two angles are complementary. They may or may not be equal to each other. The side of a right triangle opposite the right angle is called the *hypotenuse*. The other two sides are called *legs*. The *Pythagorean theorem* states that the square of the length of the hypotenuse is equal to the sum of the squares of the lengths of the legs.

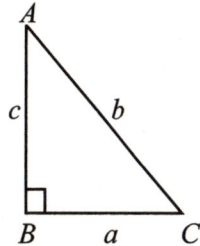

AC is the hypotenuse.
AB and BC are legs.
$\angle B = 90°$.
$\angle A + \angle C = 90°$.
$a^2 + c^2 = b^2$.

Example 1

If ABC is a right triangle with right angle at B, and if $AB = 6$ and $BC = 8$, what is the length of AC?

$$AB^2 + BC^2 = AC^2$$
$$6^2 + 8^2 = 36 + 64 = 100 = AC^2$$
$$AC = 10$$

If the measure of angle A is 30°, what is the measure of angle C?

Since angles A and C are complementary:

$$30° + C = 90°$$
$$C = 60°$$

If the lengths of the three sides of a triangle are a, b, and c and the relation $a^2 + b^2 = c^2$ holds, the triangle is a right triangle and side c is the hypotenuse.

Example 2

Show that a triangle of sides 5, 12, and 13 is a right triangle. The triangle will be a right triangle if $a^2 + b^2 = c^2$.

$5^2 + 12^2 = 13^2$
$25 + 144 = 169$

Therefore, the triangle is a right triangle and 13 is the length of the hypotenuse.

Example 3

A plane takes off from the airport in Buffalo and flies 600 miles to the north and then flies 800 miles to the east to City C. What is the straight-line distance from Buffalo to City C?

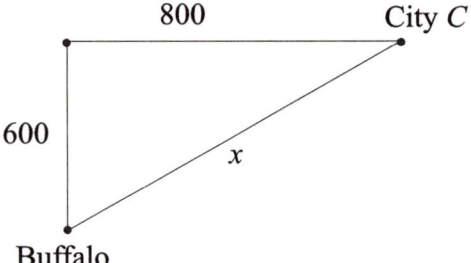

As the diagram above shows, the required distance x is the hypotenuse of the triangle. Thus,

$(600)^2 + (800)^2 = x^2$
$3,600 + 6,400 = x^2$
$10,000 = x^2$
$x = \sqrt{100,000} = 1,000$

Thus, the distance from Buffalo to City C is 1,000 miles.

Area of a Triangle

An *altitude* (or height) of a triangle is a line segment dropped as a perpendicular from any vertex to the opposite side. The area of a triangle is the product of one half the altitude and the base of the triangle. (The base is the side opposite the vertex from which the perpendicular was drawn.)

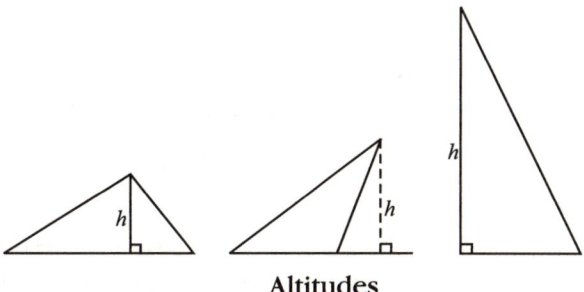
Altitudes

Example 1

What is the area of a right triangle with sides 5, 12, and 13?

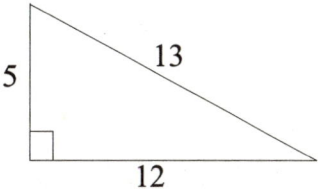

As the picture above shows, the triangle has hypotenuse 13 and legs 5 and 12. Since the legs are perpendicular to each other, we can use one as the height and one as the base of the triangle. Therefore, we have

$$A = \frac{1}{2}bh$$

$$A = \frac{1}{2}(12)(5)$$

$$A = 30$$

The area of the triangle is 30.

SUBJECT REVIEWS

Example 2

Find the area A of the following isosceles triangle.

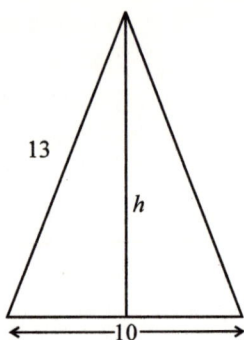

In an isosceles triangle, the altitude from the vertex angle bisects the base (cuts it in half).

The first step is to find the altitude. By the Pythagorean theorem, $a^2 + b^2 = c^2$; $c = 13$, $a = h$, and $b = \frac{1}{2}(10) = 5$.

$$h^2 + 5^2 = 13^2$$
$$h^2 + 25 = 169$$
$$h^2 = 144$$
$$h = 12$$
$$A = \frac{1}{2} \cdot \text{base} \cdot \text{height}$$
$$= \frac{1}{2} \cdot 10 \cdot 12$$
$$= 60$$

Similarity

Two triangles are *similar* if all three pairs of corresponding angles are equal. The sum of the three angles of a triangle is 180°; therefore, if two angles of triangle I equal two corresponding angles of triangle II, the third angle of triangle I must be equal to the third angle of triangle II and the triangles are similar. The lengths of the sides of similar triangles are in proportion to each other. A line drawn parallel to one side of a triangle divides the triangle into two portions, one of which is a triangle. The new triangle is similar to the original triangle.

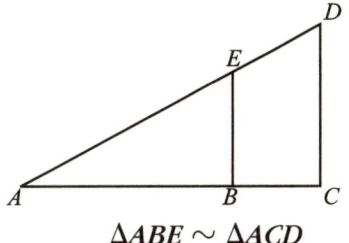

$\triangle ABE \sim \triangle ACD$

Example 1

In the following figure, if $AC = 28$ feet, $AB = 35$ feet, $BC = 21$ feet, and $EC = 12$ feet, find the length of DC if $DE \parallel AB$.

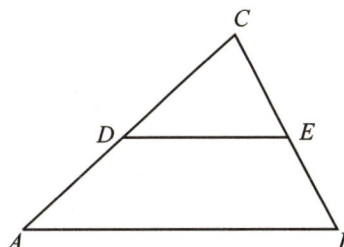

Because $DE \parallel AB$, $\triangle CDE \sim \triangle CAB$. Since the triangles are similar, their sides are in proportion:

$$\frac{DC}{AC} = \frac{EC}{BC}$$

$$\frac{DC}{28} = \frac{12}{21}$$

$$DC = \frac{12 \cdot 28}{21} = 16 \text{ feet}$$

Example 2

A pole that is sticking out of the ground vertically is 10 feet tall and casts a shadow of 6 feet. At the same time, a tree next to the pole casts a shadow of 24 feet. How tall is the tree?

Below is a diagram of the tree and the pole. At the same time of the day, nearby objects and their shadows form similar triangles.

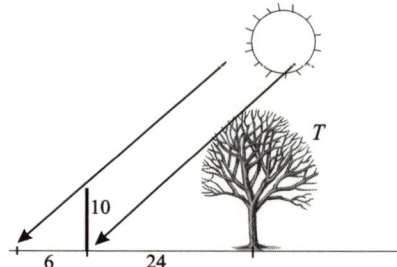

Call the height of the tree T. Then we can write a proportion between the corresponding sides of the triangles.

$$\frac{10}{T} = \frac{6}{24}$$

To solve this proportion, multiply by $24T$.

$$24 \times 10 = 6T$$
$$240 = 6T$$
$$T = 40$$

The tree is 40 feet tall.

Quadrilaterals

A quadrilateral is a polygon of four sides. The sum of the angles of a quadrilateral is 360°. If the opposite sides of a quadrilateral are parallel, the quadrilateral is a *parallelogram*. Opposite sides of a parallelogram are equal and so are opposite angles. Any two consecutive angles of a parallelogram are supplementary. A diagonal of a parallelogram divides the parallelogram into congruent triangles. The diagonals of a parallelogram bisect each other.

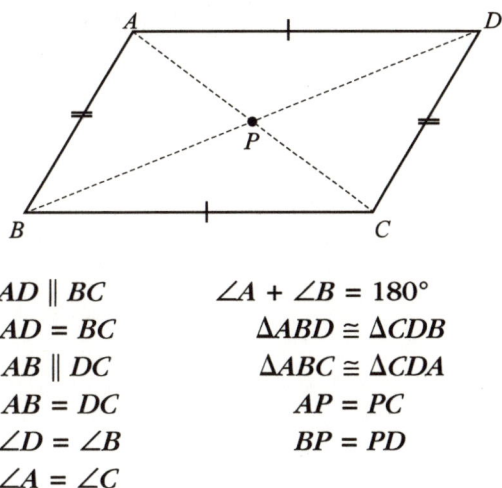

$AD \parallel BC$ $\angle A + \angle B = 180°$
$AD = BC$ $\triangle ABD \cong \triangle CDB$
$AB \parallel DC$ $\triangle ABC \cong \triangle CDA$
$AB = DC$ $AP = PC$
$\angle D = \angle B$ $BP = PD$
$\angle A = \angle C$

Definitions

A *rhombus* is a parallelogram with four equal sides. The diagonals of a rhombus are perpendicular to each other.

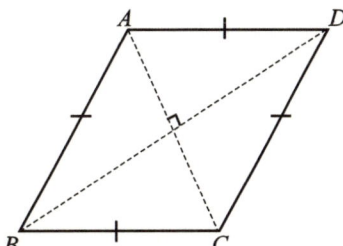

A *rectangle* is a parallelogram with four right angles. The diagonals of a rectangle are equal and can be found using the Pythagorean theorem if the sides of the rectangle are known.

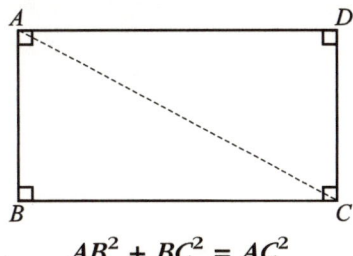

$$AB^2 + BC^2 = AC^2$$

A *square* is a rectangle with four equal sides.

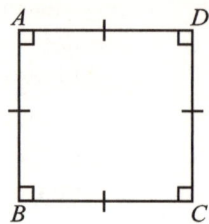

A *trapezoid* is a quadrilateral with only one pair of parallel sides, called *bases*. The nonparallel sides are called *legs*.

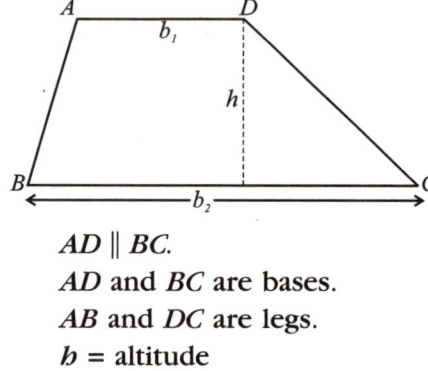

$AD \parallel BC$.
AD and BC are bases.
AB and DC are legs.
h = altitude

Finding Areas

The area of any *parallelogram* is the product of the base and the height, where the height is the length of an altitude, a line segment drawn from a vertex perpendicular to the base.

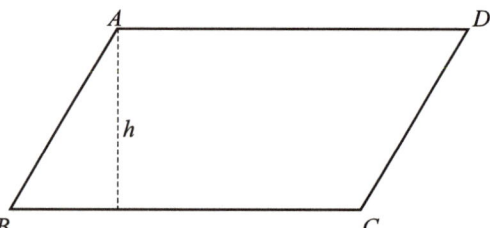

Since rectangles and squares are also parallelograms, their areas follow the same formula. For a *rectangle*, the altitude is one of the sides, and the formula is length times width. Since a *square* is a rectangle for which length and width are the same, the area of a square is the square of its side.

The area of a *trapezoid* is the height times the average of the two bases. The formula is:

$$A = h\frac{b_1 + b_2}{2}$$

The bases are the parallel sides, and the height is the length of an altitude to one of the bases.

Example 1

Find the area of a square whose diagonal is 12 feet. Let s = side of square. By the Pythagorean theorem:

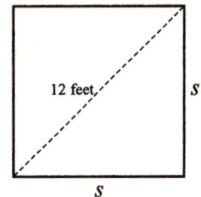

$$s^2 + s^2 = 12^2$$
$$2s^2 = 144$$
$$s^2 = 72$$
$$s = \sqrt{72}$$

Use only the positive value because this is the side of a square.

Since $A = s^2$

$A = 72$ square feet

Example 2

Find the altitude of a rectangle if its area is 320 and its base is 5 times its altitude.

Let altitude = h. Then base = $5h$. Since $A = bh$,

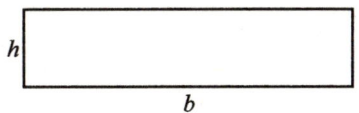

$$A = (5h)(h) = 320$$
$$5h^2 = 320$$
$$h^2 = 64$$
$$h = 8$$

If a quadrilateral is not a parallelogram or trapezoid but is irregularly shaped, its area can be found by dividing it into triangles, attempting to find the area of each, and adding the results.

Example 3

The longer base of a trapezoid is 4 times the shorter base. If the height of the trapezoid is 6 and the area is 75, how long is the longer base?

Recall that the area of a trapezoid is given by the formula

$$A = h\frac{b_1 + b_2}{2}.$$

Let b_1 represent the shorter base. Then the longer base is $b_2 = 4b_1$, and we have

$$A = 6\frac{b_1 + 4b_1}{2} = 6\frac{5b_1}{2} = 15b.$$ Since the area is 72, we get

$$75 = 15b_1$$
$$b_1 = 5.$$

Thus, the short base is 5 and the long base is 20.

Circles

Definitions

Circles are closed plane curves with all points on the curve equally distant from a fixed point called the *center*. The symbol ⊙ indicates a circle. A circle is usually named by its center. A line segment from the center to any point on the circle is called the *radius* (plural, radii). All radii of the same circle are equal.

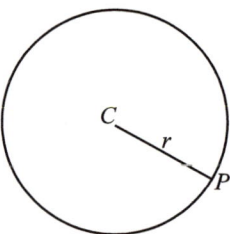

C = center
CP = radius = r

A *chord* is a line segment whose endpoints are on the circle. A *diameter* of a circle is a chord that passes through the center of the circle. A diameter, the longest distance between two points on the circle, is twice the length of the radius. A diameter perpendicular to a chord bisects that chord.

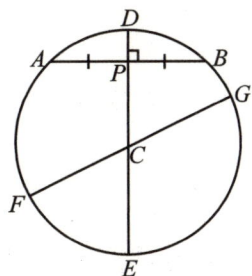

AB is a chord.
C is the center.
DCE is a diameter.
FCG is a diameter.
AB ⊥ DCE so AP = PB.

A *central angle* is an angle whose vertex is the center of a circle and whose sides are radii of the circle. An *inscribed angle* is an angle whose vertex is on the circle and whose sides are chords of the circle.

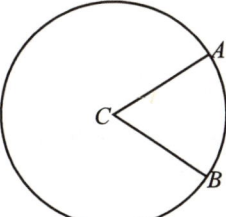 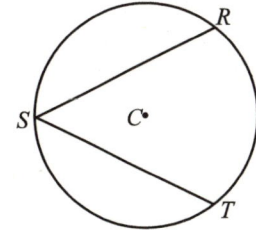

∠ACB is a central angle
∠RST is an inscribed angle

An *arc* is a portion of a circle. The symbol ⌒ is used to indicate an arc. Arcs are usually measured in degrees. Since the entire circle is 360°, a semicircle (half a circle) is an arc of 180°, and a quarter of a circle is an arc of 90°.

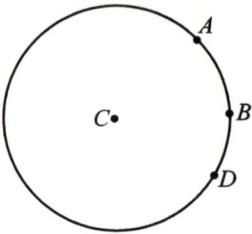

$\overset{\frown}{ABD}$ is an arc.

$\overset{\frown}{AB}$ is an arc.

$\overset{\frown}{BD}$ is an arc.

A central angle is equal in measure to its intercepted arc.

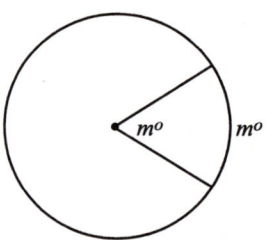

An inscribed angle is equal in measure to one half its intercepted arc. An angle inscribed in a semicircle is a right angle because the semicircle has a measure of 180°, and the measure of the inscribed angle is one half of that.

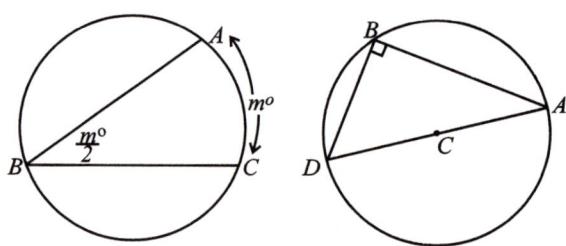

$\overset{\frown}{DA} = 180°$; therefore,
$\angle DBA = 90°$.

Perimeter and Area

The perimeter of a circle is called the *circumference*. The length of the circumference is πd, where d is the diameter, or $2\pi r$, where r is the radius. The number π is irrational and can be approximated by 3.14159..., but in problems dealing with circles, it is best to leave π in the answer. There is no fraction exactly equal to π.

Example 1

If the circumference of a circle is 8π feet, what is the radius?

Since $C = 2\pi r = 8\pi$, $r = 4$ feet.

The length of an arc of a circle can be found if the central angle and radius are known. Then the length of the arc is $\dfrac{n°}{360°}(2\pi r)$, where the central angle of the arc is $n°$. This is true because of the proportion:

$$\frac{\text{Arc}}{\text{Circumference}} = \frac{\text{central angle}}{360°}$$

Example 2

If a circle of radius 3 feet has a central angle of 60°, find the length of the arc intercepted by this central angle.

$$\text{Arc} = \frac{60°}{360°}(2\pi 3) = \pi \text{ feet}$$

The area A of a circle is πr^2, where r is the radius. If the diameter is given instead of the radius,

$$A = \pi \left(\frac{d}{2}\right)^2 = \frac{\pi d^2}{4}.$$

Example 3

Find the area of a circular ring formed by two concentric circles of radii 6 and 8 inches, respectively. (Concentric circles are circles with the same center.)

The area of the ring will equal the area of the large circle minus the area of the small circle.

$$\text{Area of ring} = \pi 8^2 - \pi 6^2$$
$$= \pi(64 - 36)$$
$$= 28\pi \text{ square inches}$$

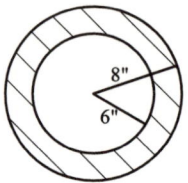

Example 4

A square is inscribed in a circle whose diameter is 10 inches. Find the difference between the area of the circle and that of the square.

If a square is inscribed in a circle, the diagonal of the square is the diameter of the circle. If the diagonal of the square is 10 inches, then, by the Pythagorean theorem,

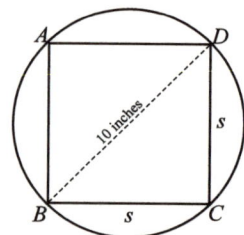

$$2s^2 = 100$$
$$s^2 = 50$$

The side of the square s is $\sqrt{50}$, and the area of the square is 50 square inches. If the diameter of the circle is 10, its radius is 5 and the area of the circle is $\pi 5^2 = 25\pi$ square inches. Then the difference between the area of the circle and the area of the square is:

$25\pi - 50$ square inches
$= 25(\pi - 2)$ square inches

Distance Formula

In the arithmetic section, we described the Cartesian coordinate system when explaining how to draw graphs representing linear equations. If two points are plotted in the Cartesian coordinate system, it is useful to know how to find the distance between them. If the two points have coordinates (a, b) and (p, q), the distance between them is:

$$d = \sqrt{(a-p)^2 + (b-q)^2}$$

This formula makes use of the Pythagorean theorem.

Example 1

Find the distance between the two points $(-3, 2)$ and $(1, -1)$.

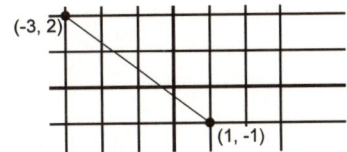

Let $(a, b) = (-3, 2)$ and $(p, q) = (1, -1)$. Then:

$$d = \sqrt{(-3-1)^2 + [2-(-1)]^2}$$
$$= \sqrt{(-4)^2 + (2+1)^2}$$
$$= \sqrt{(-4)^2 + 3^2}$$
$$= \sqrt{16 + 9} = \sqrt{25} = 5$$

Example 2

What is the area of the circle that passes through the point $(10, 8)$ and has its center at $(2, 2)$?

We can use the distance formula to find the radius of the circle.

$$r = \sqrt{(10-2)^2 + (8-2)^2} = \sqrt{8^2 + 6^2} = \sqrt{100} = 10$$

Thus, the radius of the circle is 10. The area would be $A = \pi r^2 = \pi(10)^2 = 100\pi$.

Volume

Definitions

The volume of any three-dimensional solid figure represents the amount of space contained within it. While area, as we have seen, is measured in square units, the volume of an object is measured in cubic units, such as cubic feet, cubic meters, and cubic centimeters. One cubic foot is defined as the amount of space contained within a cube that is 1 foot on each side.

There are several volume formulas for common solid figures that you should be familiar with.

A rectangular solid is a six-sided figure whose sides are rectangles. The volume of a rectangular solid is its length times its width times its height.

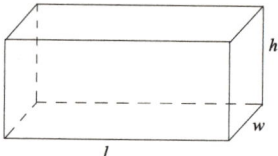

A cube is a rectangular solid whose sides are all the same length. The volume of a cube is the cube of its side.

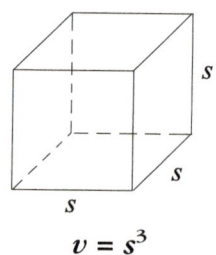

$v = s^3$

The volume of a cylinder is equal to the area of its base times its height. Since the base is a circle, the volume is $V = \pi r^2 h$.

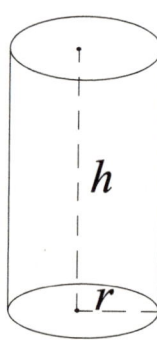

A pyramid has a rectangular base and triangular sides. Its area is given by the formula $V = \frac{1}{3}lwh$.

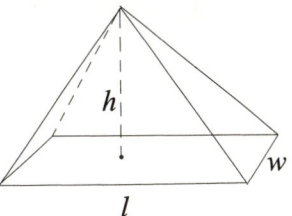

The volume of a cone is given by the formula $V = \frac{1}{3}\pi r^2 h$.

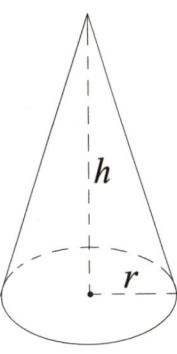

Finally, the formula for the volume of a sphere is given by the formula $V = \frac{4}{3}\pi r^3$.

Example 1

What is the surface area of a cube whose volume is 125 cubic centimeters?

Since the formula for the volume of a cube is $V = s^3$, we have $V = s^3 = 125$. Thus, $s = \sqrt[3]{125} = 5$ centimeters.

If the side of the cube is 5 centimeters, the area of one of its faces is $5^2 = 25$ square centimeters. Since the cube has 6 faces, its surface area is $6 \times 25 = 150$ square centimeters.

Example 2

The volume of a cylinder having a height of 12 is 144π. What is the radius of its base?

The formula for the volume of a cylinder is $V = \pi r^2 h$. Since $V = 144\pi$ and $h = 12$, we have

$144\pi = \pi r^2 (12)$.

Divide both sides by π.

$144 = 12r^2$
$12 = r^2$
$r = \sqrt{12} = 2\sqrt{3}$.

Thus, the radius of the base is $2\sqrt{3}$.

Geometry Problems

1. In triangle QRS, $\angle Q = \angle R$ and $\angle S = 64°$. Find the measures of $\angle Q$ and $\angle R$.

2. In parallelogram $ABCD$, $\angle A$ and $\angle C$ are opposite angles. If $\angle A = 12x°$ and $\angle C = (10x + 12)°$, find the measures of $\angle A$ and $\angle C$.

3. What is the area of a trapezoid whose height is 5 feet and whose bases are 7 feet and 9 feet?

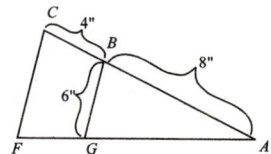

4. In the preceding figure, $CF \parallel BG$. Find the length of CF.

5. The hypotenuse of a right triangle is 25 feet. If one leg is 15 feet, find the length of the other leg.

6. Find the area of a circle whose diameter is 16 inches.

7. Find the distance between the points $(-1, -2)$ and $(5, 7)$.

8. In the diagram below, AB is parallel to CD. Find the measures of x and y.

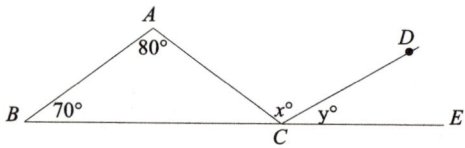

MATHEMATICS REVIEW

9. In the triangle below, find the measures of the angles.

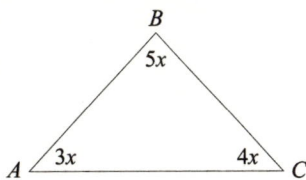

10. If the base of a parallelogram decreases by 20% and the height increases by 40%, by what percent does the area increase?

11. In the circle below, $AB = 9$ and $BC = 12$. If AC is the diameter of the circle, what is the radius?

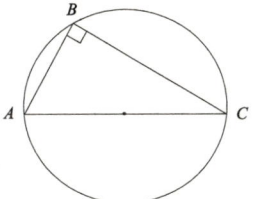

12. In the right triangle below, AB is twice BC. What is the length of BC?

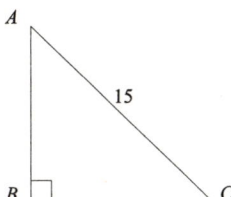

Solutions

1. $\angle Q + \angle R + \angle S = 180°$
   $\angle Q + \angle R + 64° = 180°$
   $\angle Q + \angle R = 116°$

   Since $\angle Q = \angle R$, they must each have measures of 58°.

2. The opposite angles in a parallelogram are equal. Thus,

   $12x = 10x + 12$
   $2x = 12$
   $x = 6$

   Thus, $12x = 12(6) = 72$.

   $\angle A$ and $\angle C$ both measure 72°.

3. $A = h\left(\dfrac{b_1 + b_2}{2}\right)$

$= 5\left(\dfrac{7+9}{2}\right) = 5\left(\dfrac{16}{2}\right) = 5(8) = 40$

The area of the trapezoid is 40.

4. Since $CF \parallel BG$, $\triangle ACF \sim \triangle ABG$.

Therefore, $\dfrac{6}{CF} = \dfrac{8}{12}$

$8\,CF = 72$

$CF = 9$ inches.

5. Using the Pythagorean theorem,

$a^2 + 15^2 = 25^2$

$a^2 + 225 = 625$

$a^2 = 400$

$a = \sqrt{400} = 20$

The length of the other leg is 20.

6. If $d = 16$, $r = 8$. $A = \pi r^2 = \pi(8)^2 = 64\pi$ The area of the triangle is 64π.

7. $d = \sqrt{(5-(-1))^2 + (7-(-2))^2}$

$= \sqrt{6^2 + 9^2} = \sqrt{36 + 81} = \sqrt{117}$

The distance between the points is equal to $\sqrt{117}$.

8. Since AB and CD are parallel, $\angle BAC$ and $\angle ACD$ are alternate interior angles and are therefore equal. Thus, $x = 80$. Similarly, $\angle ABC$ is a corresponding angle to $\angle DCE$, and so $y = 70$.

9. Since there are 180° in a triangle, we must have

$3x + 4x + 5x = 180$

$12x = 180$

$x = 15$, and $3x = 45$, $4x = 60$, and $5x = 75$. Thus, the angles in the triangle measure 45°, 60°, and 75°.

10. Let b = the length of the base and h = the height in the original parallelogram. Then the area of the original parallelogram is $A = bh$. If the base decreases by 20%, it becomes $.8b$. If the height increases by 40%, it becomes $1.4h$. The new area, then, is $A = (.8b)(1.4h) = 1.12bh$, which is 12% bigger than the original area.

11. Note that triangle ABC is a right triangle. Call the diameter d. Then we have

$$9^2 + 12^2 = d^2, \text{ or}$$
$$81 + 144 = d^2$$
$$225 = d^2$$
$$d = 15.$$

If the diameter is 15, the radius is $7\frac{1}{2}$.

12. Let the length of BC be x. Then the length of AB is $2x$. By the Pythagorean theorem, we have

$$x^2 + (2x)^2 = 15^2$$
$$x^2 + 4x^2 = 225$$
$$5x^2 = 225$$
$$x^2 = 45$$
$$x = \sqrt{45} = \sqrt{9 \times 5} = 3\sqrt{5}$$

The length of BC is $3\sqrt{5}$.

TABLES AND GRAPHS

Tables and graphs give visual comparisons of amount. They show relationships between two or more sets of information. It is essential to be able to read tables and graphs correctly.

Tables

Tables present data corresponding to classifications by row and column. Tables always state the units (thousands of people, years, or millions of dollars, for example) in which the numbers are expressed. Sometimes the units are percents. Both specific and general questions can be answered by using the information in the table.

Persons 5 Years Old and Over Speaking Various Languages at Home, by Age: November 1995

(Numbers in thousands: civilian noninstitutional population)

Language spoken at home	Persons 5 years old and over	Total %	5 to 13 years	14 to 17 years	18 to 24 years	25 to 44 years	45 to 64 years	65 to 74 years	75 years and over
Total	200,812	*	30,414	15,955	27,988	59,385	43,498	15,053	8,519
Percent	*	100.0	15.1	7.9	13.9	29.6	21.7	7.5	4.2
Speaking									
English only	176,319	100.0	15.4	8.0	14.1	29.5	21.5	7.4	4.0
Speaking other language	17,985	100.0	14.4	6.9	12.6	30.8	21.8	7.5	6.0
Chinese	514	100.0	12.5	5.8	15.8	34.8	21.2	6.8	3.1
French	987	100.0	8.1	5.5	10.2	29.9	30.4	9.9	6.0
German	1,261	100.0	5.4	7.1	10.8	24.3	27.4	12.8	12.2
Greek	365	100.0	16.7	4.9	10.4	38.1	21.9	4.4	3.6
Italian	1,354	100.0	7.5	4.9	8.1	19.3	31.5	15.1	13.7
Japanese	265	100.0	7.9	6.8	7.9	27.2	36.6	9.4	3.8
Korean	191	100.0	16.2	5.8	17.8	35.6	19.9	3.7	1.0
Philippine languages	419	100.0	10.7	5.3	8.6	40.8	20.3	7.2	6.9
Polish	731	100.0	2.7	1.4	3.7	13.8	45.7	21.6	10.9
Portuguese	245	100.0	15.9	8.6	12.2	33.9	22.0	3.7	3.3
Spanish	8,768	100.0	20.2	8.8	15.4	34.6	15.8	3.1	2.2
Yiddish	234	100.0	8.5	0.4	3.0	15.8	20.9	29.1	21.8
Other	2,651	100.0	10.0	4.9	10.8	30.3	23.3	10.1	10.6
Not reported	6,508	100.0	11.1	8.4	13.5	26.9	25.1	9.5	5.6

(Notice that in this table, the numbers are given in thousands, so that the number speaking German at home, for example, is not 1261 but 1,261,000.)

Example 1

What language is spoken at home by almost one half of those not speaking English at home?

Spanish; 8,768/17,985 is about 48%.

Example 2

What language has the highest percent of its speakers in the 45- to 64-year-old age bracket?

Polish, with 45.7%.

Example 3

How many persons between the ages of 18 and 24 speak Korean at home?

There are 191,000 of all ages speaking Korean, of whom 17.8% are between 18 and 24:

$.178 \times 191,000 = 33,998$ persons

Example 4

Of the people between the ages of 14 and 17, which is greater, the number who speak German at home or the number who speak Italian at home?

The number of 14- to 17-year-olds speaking German at home is $1,261,000 \times .071 = 89,531$.

The number of 14- to 17-year-olds speaking Italian at home is $1,354,000 \times .049 = 66,346$.

Therefore, more people in the 14- to 17-year-old group speak German even though, overall, more people speak Italian.

Graphs

Bar Graphs

Bar graphs may be horizontal or vertical, but both axes are designed to give information. The height (or width) of the bar is proportional to the number or percent represented. Bar graphs are less accurate than tables but give a quick comparison of information. There may be only two variables, as in the following graph. One is the year and the other is the percentage of the labor force made up of women.

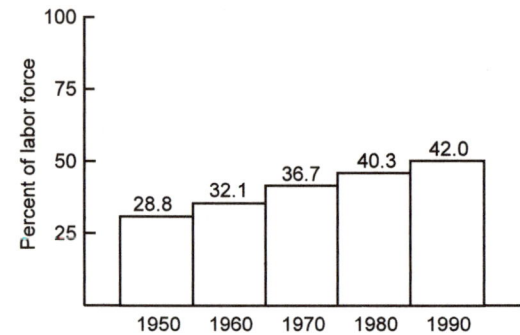

WOMEN AS A PERCENTAGE OF THE LABOR FORCE

Example 1

Between which 10 years does the chart show the greatest percent increase of women in the labor force?

For each of the 10-year periods, there is some increase. Subtract each percent from the one to the right of it; four subtractions. The greatest increase, 4.6%, occurs between 1960 and 1970.

Example 2

In 1990, what was the ratio of women in the labor force to men in the labor force?

Since, in 1990, 42% of the labor force were women, it follows that 58% of the labor force were men. Therefore,

$$\frac{Women}{Men} \to \frac{42}{58}$$

This ratio can be reduced.

$$\frac{42}{58} = \frac{21}{29}$$

Thus, the ratio of women to men is 21 to 29. If we take the top and bottom of $\frac{21}{29}$ and divide by 21, we get $\frac{1}{1.38}$. Thus, another way to express this ratio is as 1 to 1.38. This means that, for every 1 woman in the labor force, there are 1.38 men.

In this bar graph, percents are written at the top of each bar. This is not always the case. If the numbers are not given, you must read across, using a ruler or card, to the relevant axis and estimate the height.

Bar graphs such as the following can compare two sets of data for varying years. This graph shows, for example, that 86.8% of the male population 16 years old and over was in the labor force in 1950. In that same year, 33.9% of the female population was in the labor force. It gives different information from the previous graph.

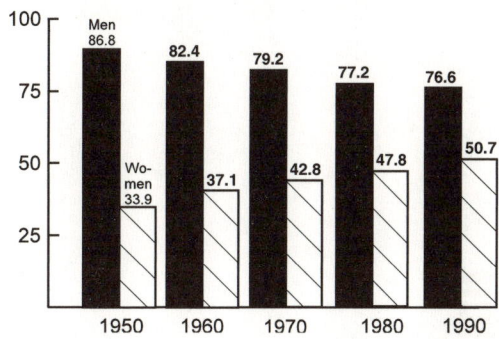

PERCENTAGE OF POPULATION 16 YEARS OLD AND OVER IN THE LABOR FORCE

Example 1

Explain the apparent discrepancy for the year 1980 between the percentage for women in this graph (47.8%) and that in the previous graph (40.3%).

This graph shows that 47.8% of all women were in the labor force in 1980—that is, 47.8 of 100 women were working. The previous graph showed that 40.3 of 100 *workers,* or 40.3%, were women. There is no discrepancy. The populations are different.

Example 2

If, in 1980, there were 90,000,000 women 16 years old or older, approximately how many of these women were not in the labor force?

In 1980, 47.8% of women 16 and over were in the labor force. Since there were 90,000,000 women in this age group, we have

90,000,000 × .478 = 43,020,000 women in the labor force. Then the number of women not in the labor force was

90,000,000 − 43,020,000 = 46,980,000.

Cumulative Bar Graphs

These graphs are similar to bar graphs, but each bar contains more than one kind of information and the total height is the sum of the various components. The following graph gives percentages of college graduates on the bottom and high school graduates on the top. There might well be other gradations, such as "some college" above the college section and "some high school" above the high school section.

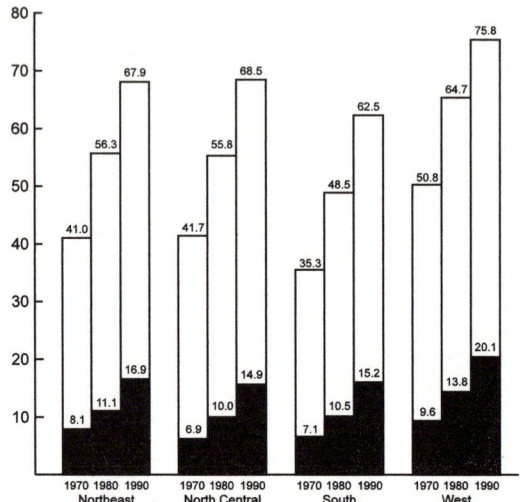

Percent of persons 25 years old and over who were high school graduates and college graduates, by region: 1970, 1980, and 1990

Example 1

For each of the 3 years, which region consistently has the lowest percentage of college graduates?

North Central

Example 2

Which region has the lowest *total* educational attainment for each of the 3 years?

The South

Example 3

In 1990, which region had the highest percentage of high school graduates, and what was it?

For 1990, subtract the percent of college graduates from the total percent; four subtractions. The highest is the West, with 75.8% − 20.1% = 55.7%.

Example 4

Which region had the greatest increase in the percentage of college graduates between 1980 and 1990?

The West, with 20.1% − 13.8% = 6.3%.

Example 5

In 1990, which of the four regions had the highest percentage of persons 25 years old and over who were neither high school nor college graduates?

Since the South had the lowest percentage (62.5%) of persons 25 years old and over who were either high school or college graduates, then it must have the highest percentage of persons 25 years old and over who were neither high school nor college graduates. In fact, 100% − 62.5% = 37.5% were neither high school nor college graduates in the South.

SUBJECT REVIEWS

Circle Graphs

Circle graphs, also known as pie charts, show the breakdown of an entire quantity, such as a college budget, into its component parts. The circle representing 100% of the quantity is cut into pieces, each piece having a certain percentage value. The sum of the pieces is 100%. The size of the piece is proportional to the size of the percentage. To make a circle graph, you must have an instrument called a protractor, which measures degrees. Suppose the measured quantity is 10% of the whole. Because 10% of 360° is 36°, a central angle of 36° must be measured and radii drawn. This piece now has an area of 10% of the circle. When answering questions on circle graphs, compare percentages.

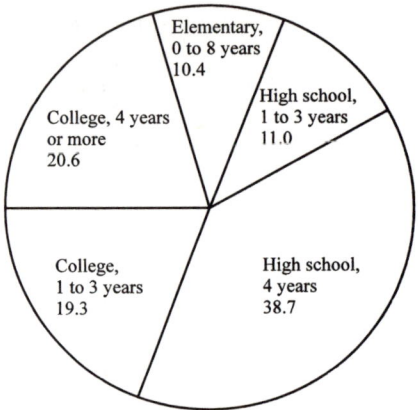

Years of school completed

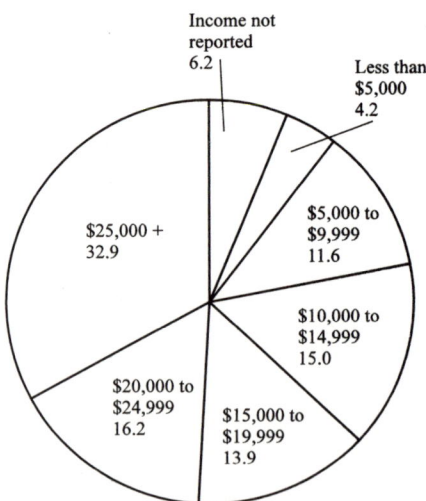

Family Income
(restricted to persons living in primary families)

Percent distribution of voters in the last election by years of school completed and family income

Peterson's SSAT/ISEE Success

Example 1

Of those who voted in the last election, what percentage attended college at some time?

This information is in the first graph. Add 20.6% to 19.3% to get 39.9%.

Example 2

Of those who voted in the last election and who reported their income levels, what percentage had a family income below $10,000?

This information is in the second graph. Add 4.2% to 11.6% to get 15.8%.

Example 3

If 36,000 people voted in the last election, how many of these people had family incomes of $20,000 or greater?

To answer this question, we use the second circle graph. First note that 16.2% + 32.9% = 49.1% of the voters had family incomes of $20,000 or greater. Since there were 36,000 voters, we have

$36,000 \times .491 = 17,676.$

Therefore, 17,676 of the voters had family incomes of $20,000 or greater.

Line Graphs

Like bar graphs, line graphs follow vertical and horizontal information axes, but the line graph is continuous. There may be a single broken line or there may be several, comparing three or four stocks or incomes or, as in the case of this graph, numbers of workers in selected occupations. The line graph shows trends: increasing, decreasing, or not changing.

MILLIONS OF WORKERS IN SELECTED OCCUPATIONS

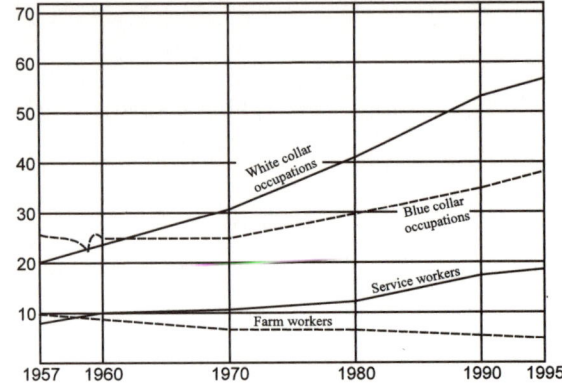

In this graph, the actual number of people in an occupation in a given year must be estimated. For example, the number of service workers in 1980 seems to be 14 million, and the number of white-collar workers for the same year about 40 million.

Example 1

In 1990, what was the total number of workers in all four occupations?

Estimate each number by comparison with the values at the left. Then add the four. Estimates: farm workers 3 million, service workers 18 million, blue-collar workers 33 million, and white-collar workers 52 million, total 106 million.

Example 2

In which year were the number of service workers and the number of farm workers approximately equal?

The number of workers is equal at the point on the graph where the lines representing service and farm workers cross. Looking at the graph, the point where the lines cross appears to be approximately 1959. Prior to that, the number of service workers is less than the number of farm workers; after that, it is more.

MATHEMATICS REVIEW

Since the scale on graphs is usually marked in large increments, since the lines used are often thick, and since the estimates must often be made on the side of the graph far from the scale, use whole numbers as much as possible when estimating. Use only the fraction one half (1/2) if your judgment tells you something less than a whole number should be used. Because all the information must be estimated, units less than one half will not significantly affect your answer. Do not spend time trying to figure the precise number on the scale. A reasonable estimate should let your answer be within 1 or 2 percent on either side of the correct answer choice. As part of your strategy for dealing with graphs, look at the answer choices to get an idea of the magnitude of your estimate before doing the estimating. Choose the answer choice closest to your estimate.

Example

If your estimate is 97 million and the answer choices are 3 million, 0.5 million, 90 million, 103 million, and 98 million, choose 98 million as your answer.

Tables and Graphs Problems

Use this bar graph to answer the following questions:

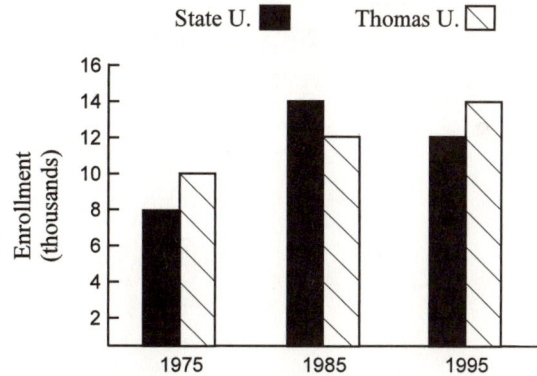

STUDENT ENROLLMENTS: STATE U. VS. THOMAS U.

1. What was the enrollment at State U. in 1975?

2. In 1985, how many more students were enrolled at State U. than at Thomas U.?

3. If the average tuition at State U. in 1995 was $6,500, what was the total revenue received in tuition at State U. that year?

4. In 1985, 74% of the students enrolled at State U. were males. How many males attended State U. in 1985?

5. Find the percent of increase in enrollment at Thomas U. from 1975 to 1985.

Use this circle graph to answer the following questions.

**ADULT EDUCATION COURSES
Based on 250,000 Courses Offered—1998**

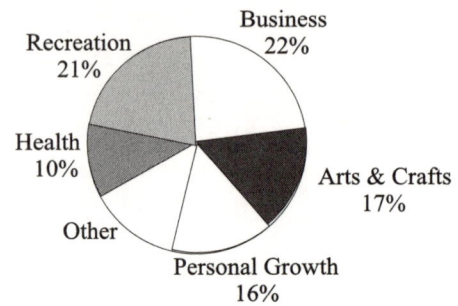

6. How many personal growth courses are offered?

7. How many health courses and business courses are offered?

8. How many courses offered are in the "other" category?

9. How many more business courses are offered than recreation courses?

10. If 20% of the arts & crafts courses offered are painting courses, how many painting courses are offered?

Solutions

1. 8,000 students

2. 14,000 − 12,000 = 2,000 students

3. 12,000 × $6,500 = $78,000,000

4. 14,000 × 74% = 14,000 × .74 = 10,360 students

5. Increase in enrollment = 12,000 − 10,000 = 2,000
   Percent of increase in enrollment = 2,000 ÷ 10,000 = 1/5 = 20%

6. 250,000 × .16 = 40,000 personal growth courses

7. Health and business together account for 10% + 22% = 32% of the courses. Thus, 250,000 × .32 = 80,000 health and business courses.

8. Note that the percentage of courses for the "other" category is missing. To determine it, add the percentages for all of the other courses and subtract from 100%. The sum of all of the percentages shown is 86%, so 14% of the courses are in the "other" category. Thus, 250,000 × .14 = 35,000 courses are in the "other" category.

9. The easiest way to solve this problem is to subtract the percentage that represents business courses from the percentage that represents recreation courses. 22% − 21% = 1%. Thus, there is a 1% difference. 250,000 × .01 = 2,500.

10. The number of arts and crafts courses is 250,000 × .17 = 42,500. The number of painting courses is 20% of this number: 42,500 × .20 = 8,500.

RED ALERT

READING COMPREHENSION

The Reading Comprehension portion of ISEE is composed of nine passages with a total of 40 questions to be answered in 35 minutes. Each question has four choices (A–D). The SSAT Reading Comprehension section is 25 minutes long and also has 40 questions, each of which has five choices (A–E).

The kinds of questions fall into these categories:

- Science—biology, general science, history of science
- Social studies—history, politics, current events
- Personal narrative—someone's story or opinion ("How camping taught me independence")
- Fiction or poetry—a short excerpt from a book or a short poem

As you can see, if you have to answer 40 questions in 25 or 35 minutes, you have less than a minute to answer each one, not even counting the time it will take to read each passage. Pacing yourself, therefore, is important. You need to move at a fairly steady pace; it is not necessary, however, that you answer the questions in the order in which they appear in the test. Just be sure when you skip a section that you put your answers in the proper location on your answer sheet. Answering more questions *correctly* is more important than merely answering questions. You do not need to have any special knowledge to answer any of these questions. Choose an answer based on the information provided in the passages.

The ISEE and the SSAT reading comprehension questions test your ability to handle the kinds of information you will meet in high school classes.

TYPES OF QUESTIONS

Factual These questions test whether you understood the information presented in the passage. The subject matter can deal with humanities (arts, biographies, and poetry), social studies (history, economics, and sociology), and science (medicine, astronomy, chemistry, physics, anthropology, and psychology). Remember, however, your answer is based solely on the information presented in the passage.

> *Example:* According to the passage, the kinds of relics located in the South American digs were (A) . . . (B) . . . , etc.

Vocabulary These questions are designed to determine your grasp of key terms used in the selection. Typically these words are defined through examples, synonyms, or explanations.

> *Example:* As used in the sentence, "infusion" most nearly means (A) . . . (B) . . . , etc.

Implications or inferences These questions test your ability to draw logical conclusions based on the material presented in the passage. Since the author of the passage tells us _____, then _____ must also be true.

> *Example:* The passage implies that (A) . . . (B) . . . , etc.
>
> The reader can infer from the passage that (A) . . . (B) . . . , etc.
>
> Which of the following can be deduced from the passage? (A) . . . (B) . . . , etc.

Author's attitude Questions of this type test your ability to recognize the author's judgment toward the subject matter. Is the attitude one of approval or disapproval? Is the attitude toward the subject matter humorous? Doubtful? Serious?

> *Example:* Which of the following best describes the author's attitude toward the subject? (A) . . . (B) . . . , etc.

Best title These questions test your ability to recognize the difference between the main idea and supporting ideas in a passage.

> *Example:* Which of these titles is the most appropriate for the passage? (A) . . . (B) . . . , etc.

Narrative Excerpts from novels, short stories, essays

> *Example:* According to the passage, where does the action occur?

READING SKILLS: SQ3R

An important part of improving your reading skills is finding a dependable method or approach. The SQ3R method is one that many students have found to be beneficial. This approach gives you a logical way to boost your reading comprehension and maximize your time. The SQ3R study technique, developed in 1941 by Francis Robinson, can improve your reading comprehension in virtually all areas. Here are its components:

S = Survey		This first step, survey or preview, requires you to do a quick overview of what you're reading. Check the title of the passage (if there is one), read the first paragraph or introduction, and read the first sentence of each of the other paragraphs. Read the last paragraph or the conclusion. This approach gives you a glimpse of the material as well as an estimation of the time you'll need to complete the task.
Q = Question		Knowing the questions before you read a passage can give you a better sense of purpose as you read. You can quickly scan the questions that follow the selection to be a more actively involved reader. It's not necessary at this point to preview the choices of answers.
R = Read		This stage is definitely an important one. Don't rush! Completing the first two steps in this method should give you a clear sense of purpose. Read at a steady pace.
R = Recite		Although you cannot recite aloud the important ideas as you take a standardized test, you should make every effort to repeat them mentally. Studies have shown that reciting can increase your retention rate from 20% to 80%. Try to summarize the main idea in each paragraph.
R = Review		Although this step is more effective for remembering information over a long period of time, you can review the details mentally, thus reassuring yourself that you have read and understood the material.

Useful Reading Techniques

As you read your test questions silently, keep these points in mind. *Vocalization* or moving your lips while you read can slow your reading rate. It takes too much time to say the words with your lips. To break this habit, try practicing reading with a pencil clenched between your teeth or chewing gum while you read. *Subvocalizing* is another problematic reading habit that is similar except that the reader isn't forming words with his or her lips; the reader forms words in his or her larynx. Practice reading rapidly under timed conditions to eliminate this habit. *Pointing* is also a problem that can slow a reader's progress. Keep your hands in your lap to break yet another habit that interferes with your development.

SUBJECT REVIEWS

The movement of your eyes across the page is another important component in the way you read. Instead of reading in a straight line across the page and looking at each word separately, your eyes should move in arcs across the page in a sort of "bouncing" pattern. Your brain "sees" the words, but you are unaware of these arcs and fixations. Fast readers take in 2.5 to 3 words per fixation. Practicing speed and comprehension drills can also be beneficial in saving you time and helping you become a better reader. Try to read more rapidly by focusing on key words in each line.

Pre-reading a passage on a standardized test can provide a sense of purpose to your reading. You can have a clear sense of what kinds of details are important. Often reading the first and last sentences of the passage as well as the topic sentences in the body paragraphs can clarify the important points. Just taking a few minutes can be useful; however, you must preview rapidly. Even if you don't use the other steps in the SQ3R approach, previewing (or surveying) can help.

Skimming and *scanning* are two other reading methods that can be profitable. Both of these skills can help you become a better reader. In *scanning,* you glance at material, usually looking from the top to the bottom of the page, until you locate a particular piece of information. For instance, when you look up a number in a telephone book, you scan the entries until you find the number. *Skimming,* on the other hand, gives you an overview of the major points of a passage. You look over material quickly, just seeking main ideas. Of these two skills, skimming is probably more useful when you take a standardized reading comprehension test. In only a very few instances can you scan a passage to find as specific a detail as the answer to a question. Most questions, on the other hand, require inferences or conclusions that the reader must formulate after having read and understood the passage. The restrictions of time may be an important factor in deciding whether you can rely on skimming; a more deliberate pace is usually more suitable. In some instances, however, you'll need to read at a fast rate to finish the test.

Now it's time to put it all together. Following are three reading selections and accompanying questions. Using the reading skills and techniques we've given you, read the passages. Then, try to identify the types of questions that follow the passages. Answering the questions should now be an easy task.

SAMPLE PASSAGES AND QUESTIONS

> **Directions:** Each passage below is followed by questions. Answer the questions following each passage on the basis of what is stated or implied in that passage.

Passage 1

Line One of the attractions of a new car is its showroom shine. Eventually, however, exposure to light, water, air pollution, and other kinds of destructive factors begin to age the shine, and the gloss starts to fade. To restore the sheen you can use an auto polish. Choices include
5 liquid, paste, and even spray forms of polish, also known as wax or sealants. Whichever form you choose, be sure to wash your car thoroughly beforehand. Rubbing tough road dirt into the surface will probably scratch the paint on your car.
   Regardless of the type of polish you select, applying the polish
10 should be easy. Perhaps the easiest to apply are liquids because they spread better than paste polishes. Be careful not to get polish on any kind of vinyl because the polish may affect the appearance of the vinyl. Instructions for polishing also include explanation for burnishing the car once the polish has dried. Usually you can use a soft, dry
15 cotton cloth to restore that attractive showroom luster.

1. Types of car polish include

   (A) paste.
   (B) liquid.
   (C) spray-on.
   (D) all of the above.

2. According to the passage, a car's showroom finish can be dulled because of

   (A) parking under trees.
   (B) exposure to pollution.
   (C) poor paint coverage.
   (D) hail.

3. The word "burnishing" in the passage is used to mean

   (A) degree of physical fitness needed to polish a car.
   (B) removing dirt before you polish the car.
   (C) washing the car.
   (D) rubbing the polish to restore the shine.

SUBJECT REVIEWS

4. Which of the following is the best title for this passage?

   (A) Waxing and Waning Your Car
   (B) Renewing the Sheen
   (C) Washing Your Car
   (D) How to Use a Sealant

Passage 2

Line Historians believe that American science fiction movies popular in the 1950s were a manifestation of a general fear of invasion of the country. The Red Scare of the McCarthy era made American citizens aware of the possible presence of Communist spies who were
5 virtually impossible to detect. The original version of *Invasion of the Body Snatchers* depicted the ease with which outsiders could infiltrate our society. Besides this general fear of aliens, the movies also reflected concerns about the effects of radiation such as the aftermath of the atomic bomb dropped to end World War II. *Attack*
10 *of the Fifty-foot Woman* was a typical movie of this type. Even a film version of *War of the Worlds* generated anxiety not unlike the chaos Orson Welles created with his infamous radio broadcast on October 30, 1938, when thousands of New Jersey citizens were convinced that Martians were landing in their state. Space was still mysterious.
15 Who knew what or who was out there? Writers with vivid imaginations such as Isaac Asimov and Robert Heinlein offered thrilling possibilities. Readers envisioned little green men who might be real—or the "purple people eater" made famous by a popular song that attempted to poke fun at the obsession with aliens.

5. The writer of this passage implies that

   (A) science fiction served as an outlet for fears in the fifties.
   (B) science fiction was based on some real UFO sightings.
   (C) it was easy for writers to fool Americans obsessed with invaders.
   (D) all Americans feared invaders from space.

6. The term "infamous" most nearly means

   (A) not famous.
   (B) notorious.
   (C) well-known.
   (D) unpopular.

7. It is possible to infer that science fiction experienced such popularity because

   (A) the public was worried about invasion from Communist Russia.
   (B) the public enjoyed being scared by outrageous sci-fi films.
   (C) sci-fi literature appealed to a population tired of radio as entertainment but not quite ready for television.
   (D) the sci-fi available played on obsessions with little green men.

8. The McCarthy "Red Scare" of the 1950s relates to the popularity of science fiction because

   (A) the hearings revealed the truth about Joseph McCarthy.
   (B) Americans learned of the existence of Communist spies in America.
   (C) movies were made about the hearings.
   (D) the hearings suggested a connection between Communist spies and invaders from space.

9. Which of the following was based directly on popular fears?

   (A) *Invasion of the Body Snatchers*
   (B) *War of the Worlds*
   (C) *The Attack of the Fifty-foot Woman*
   (D) all of the above.

Passage 3

Line   The earliest British settlers who came to what became the United States of America can be divided into two groups. First, there were those like Sir Walter Raleigh, who was intent on using the fertile soil of the area now known as Virginia to raise tobacco. Some of the men
5   who came with Raleigh were "second sons"; according to British law, the eldest son would inherit the bulk of the estate. Second and subsequent sons had to look elsewhere for livelihood. Some chose to enter the ministry; others came to Virginia, never intending to stay. Captain John Smith is a well-known figure from this era. These men
10   planned to turn tobacco into cash when they came back to Britain with their harvested crops. He and other entrepreneurs came to be known as "planters." Some even believed that they could easily turn the Native Americans into slaves. The facts, of course, are that none of this fledgling tobacco business was easy. While the area was
15   remarkably arable, clearing the land required time and manpower. Many of the planters did not plan to do the manual labor themselves. They tended, however, to stake claims to huge acres of land. Eventually, a work force was brought in. Some of these workers were convicts; some were indentured servants; some were African natives.

20 This southern area of the New World would eventually become the American South; the beginning of slavery was already in kernel form.

The second group, the earliest arrivals in the North, were mostly British citizens who sought the freedom to practice religion as they wished. This religious group had fled Great Britain and moved to
25 Holland where they lived briefly, but they chose to move to the New World. They landed in the New England area, where the land was rocky and not very fertile. These settlers tended to form small communities because they shared religious beliefs and sought to establish a theocracy, a society in which civil law is the same as
30 religious law. They also feared the wilderness, which was believed to be the home of Satan. John Bradford, the first governor of this area, recorded much of the early history. These settlers came to America to stay; they worked together to create a community. Because of these qualities, their settlements thrived.
35 The basic differences in these two groups laid the foundation for the War Between the States, which did not occur until almost 200 years later.

10. The best title for this passage is

    (A) Tobacco for Today
    (B) Early Settlers in America
    (C) Religion in Early America
    (D) Second Sons Settling the South
    (E) The First Slaves

11. In sentence nine of the first paragraph, the word "arable" most nearly means

    (A) fertile
    (B) clear of trees
    (C) dry, desert-like
    (D) swampy
    (E) unprofitable

12. The writer implies that the group who came to Virginia

    (A) were all members of the aristocracy.
    (B) was unwilling to do any physical labor.
    (C) was not as unified as the northern group.
    (D) planned to rely on tobacco for income.
    (E) tended to settle near the coast.

SAMPLE PASSAGES AND QUESTIONS

13. What was the writer's purpose in this passage?

    (A) to show how slavery began
    (B) to contrast the beginnings of two sections of America
    (C) to point out the stronger settlers
    (D) to explain why tobacco was such an important crop
    (E) to describe the religious roots of the North

ANSWERS AND EXPLANATIONS

Passage 1

1. This is a factual question. The correct answer is (D). All three types of car polish are mentioned in the passage.

2. This is a factual question. The correct answer among the options is (B). Answer (A), though probably true, is incorrect because it is not included in the passage. Remember that you must answer the questions based solely on the information provided or implied in the passage. Answer (C) is incorrect; there is no mention of paint coverage. Answer (D) is incorrect. Although it may be a true statement, it is not mentioned in the passage.

3. This is a vocabulary-in-context question. The correct answer is (D). Answer (A) is incorrect; physical fitness is not mentioned in the passage. Answer (B) is incorrect; the sentence in which "burnishing" appears makes it clear that "burnishing" occurs after the polish has been applied. Answer (C) is incorrect; again, "burnishing" occurs after the polish has been applied. Logically, the car must be washed before the polish can be applied.

4. This is a main idea question. The correct answer is (B). Even if you were unsure of the meaning of "sheen," by process of elimination, you should select this answer because the other three are not appropriate. Answer (A) is incorrect; "waning" does not apply here. It means to reduce. For example, the moon "waxes" and "wanes" as it goes through its cycle. Answer (C) is incorrect because it is incomplete. Washing is only part of the process. Answer (D) is incorrect because there is only one mention of sealant.

Passage 2

5. This is an implications question. The correct answer is (A). Answer (B) is incorrect; there is no mention of UFOs. Answer (C) is incorrect; there is no evidence that writers were trying to "fool Americans." Answer (D) is incorrect; this sentence is an unsupported generalization.

6. This is a vocabulary-in-context question. The correct answer is (B). "Infamous" and "notorious" mean well known for bad reasons. Answer (A) is incorrect; the "in-" prefix here does not mean "not." Answer (C) is incorrect; "well-known" has a positive connotation. Answer (D) is incorrect; "unpopular" is not relevant.

7. This is an inference question. The correct answer is (A). Answer (B) is incorrect because the passage offers no supporting evidence that the public enjoyed being scared. Answer (C) is incorrect; there is no mention of sci-fi as entertainment. Answer (D) is incorrect; there is no evidence of "obsessions with little green men."

ANSWERS AND EXPLANATIONS

8. This is an inference question. The correct answer is (B). Answer (A) is incorrect. Although probably true, this statement is not relevant. Answer (C) is incorrect; there is no mention of movies made about the hearings. Answer (D) is incorrect; no such connection was suggested.

9. This is a factual question. The correct answer is (D). All of these movies are cited in the passage.

Passage 3

10. This is a main idea question. The correct answer is (B). Answer (A) is incorrect because it is too narrow. Answer (C) is incorrect because it also is too narrow. Answer (D) is incorrect because it is not a main idea. Answer (E) is incorrect; it is another option that is too restricted.

11. This is a vocabulary-in-context question. The correct answer is (A); "arable" means that the land can be easily farmed because the soil is fertile. Answer (B) is incorrect because lack of trees does not necessarily mean the land can be plowed and planted. Answers (C), (D), and (E) are virtually the opposite in meaning.

12. This is an implications question. The correct answer is (D). Although several of the other options are included in the passage, the best answer is (D). Answer (A) is incorrect because only some were aristocratic. Answer (B) is incorrect; again, only some fell into this category. Answer (C) is incorrect. Although perhaps true, nothing in the passage offers compelling evidence to support this answer. Answer (E) is incorrect; the coast is not mentioned at all.

13. This is a primary purpose question. The correct answer is (B). Answer (A) is incorrect because the comments made about slavery are not the main focus of the passage. Answer (C) is incorrect; there is no mention of "stronger" settlers. Answer (D) is incorrect; there is no mention of the importance of the tobacco crop. Answer (E) is incorrect; this answer is too limited.

These passages and questions should give you a good idea of the types of questions that you will encounter on the actual exams. We have given you enough examples of question types so that you can recognize these on the exams. If you answered any reading comprehension questions incorrectly on the Diagnostic tests, go back to those again, reread the passages using your newly learned techniques, and try the questions again. You should now have improved scores, and these will also be evident when you take the practice tests at the end of this book.

RED ALERT

WRITING STRATEGIES AND GRAMMAR REVIEW

HOW TO WRITE AN ESSAY—STRATEGIES FOR SUCCESS

An essay is a way to express your ideas in writing rather than by speaking. To do so effectively, you focus on a specific topic, roughly organize your ideas, and write as clearly and logically as possible in the time allotted. You will be provided with a "prompt" or topic about which to write. Be sure that you read the topic carefully, preferably twice. Then take a few minutes to organize your ideas and begin to write. Don't spend too much time organizing a rough outline; more ideas may occur to you as you write. While the readers at the schools to which you apply realize that you have a limited amount of time in which to write, you are expected to write logically and clearly.

Typically, an essay has three parts: an introduction, body, and conclusion. Writing the introduction is sometimes the most difficult part of the writing process. On the SSAT you usually will be asked to agree or disagree with a statement, while on the ISEE you will be given a broad topic about which to write, and you have 30 minutes in which to write your essay. Your opening sentence should be a response to this statement.

WRITING THE ESSAY FOR THE SSAT

Here is a sample topic for the SSAT:

> **Topic:** Nothing can be gained without some loss. Do you agree or disagree with this topic sentence? Support your position with one or two specific examples from personal experience, the experience of others, current events, history, or literature.

Introduction

You must introduce your topic and establish your focus, that is, the point you want to prove about this topic. Strive to be concise and clear. Be sure that your first sentence responds *directly* to the topic. For the topic suggested, your opening sentence can be as simple as merely repeating the sentence; however, a paraphrasing of the statement, which means you summarize the statement in your own

Peterson's: www.petersons.com   RED ALERT

words, can show more clearly that you understand the question. If you disagree with the statement, your sentence can be as follows: "Some things can be gained without some loss." Check this opening sentence carefully to avoid making any errors. This first sentence will make a big impression on the admissions officers who read your essay. Be sure that this first sentence conveys a positive image of you. If you think you may be misspelling a word, choose another word that you know you can spell correctly.

Body

This is the substance or main content of your essay. In this section of your essay, you will discuss the topic, offer supporting examples, and draw conclusions—in other words, prove your point. In this main part of your essay, you must be careful to develop your ideas as logically and smoothly as possible, trying to avoid major composition errors such as comma splices and sentence fragments. Typically, the body of an essay contains three paragraphs with one main idea per paragraph.

Fluency of expression and sentence variety are two areas the admissions officers or committee will evaluate when they read your essay. These skills, which refer to your ability to develop your ideas smoothly by using an array of types of sentences, are best produced by practicing; the more you write, the better you should become at expressing your ideas clearly and effectively. Another important quality necessary for a successful essay is sufficient evidence. Be sure that you have included enough evidence to prove your point. You will need at least two and possibly three pieces of evidence to support your view. Each of your supporting details also requires discussion to show its significance. While the admissions readers will read your essay to evaluate your writing skills to see how well you respond to the topic, they realize, of course, that your essay is a rough draft.

Conclusion

This is the final section of your essay, the place in which you remind your reader of the point you set out to prove. This last part may be only a sentence, or it could be several sentences. Just as there are a number of ways to write the opening paragraph or introduction, the conclusion can take many forms. Re-emphasizing your focus is the main purpose of this section. It is important, though, to offer some kind of conclusion to provide a sound essay.

RED ALERT: WRITING STRATEGIES AND GRAMMAR REVIEW

Serious Grammar Errors to Avoid

Comma splices occur when a writer attempts to connect two independent clauses with only a comma to join them. To connect these independent clauses correctly, a writer must use a coordinating conjunction, such as "and" or "but," and a comma, or the writer may use a semicolon instead of a comma, in which case the coordinating conjunction is unnecessary. Of course, a third choice is to treat the two independent clauses as two separate complete sentences.

Here are some examples of these errors:

> Winning is something everyone wants to do, we all enjoy winning.

This sentence illustrates a **comma splice.** Two simple sentences (or independent clauses) are connected by a comma, which is not a strong enough mark of punctuation to join these constructions. To correct a comma splice, you have three options:

1. Change the comma to a semicolon (;), which is strong enough to connect independent clauses. Winning is something everyone wants *to do; we all* enjoy winning.

2. Add a conjunction such as "and," "but," "or," or "nor." These are known as coordinate conjunctions. Winning is something everyone wants to *do, and we all* enjoy winning.

3. Change the comma to a period and begin a new sentence with the second clause. Winning is something everyone wants *to do. We all* enjoy winning.

Next is another example of an error: a **sentence fragment.**

> Everyone has a chance. To win the contest.

This sentence fragment can be corrected in a number of ways. Here are some illustrations:

1. Make the fragment a sentence by completing the idea. To win the contest *will be exciting.* This sample has added a predicate, which the original construction lacked.

2. Attach the fragment to a nearby sentence. Everyone has a *chance to win the contest.* Here the fragment is attached to a simple sentence that already has a subject and a predicate.

Here is a sample step-by-step example for writing the essay

1. Read the topic or question "prompt." Be sure that you understand the topic. Do not write on any other topic.

2. Take a few minutes to generate some ideas. This process is sometimes called "brainstorming." Your goal here is to develop a sound approach to support your response to the topic.

Compose your thesis, which is a statement of the topic and your focus—that is, the point you are setting out to prove in your essay. For instance, if the topic is the one mentioned previously, you may choose to agree or to disagree with the statement. Your thesis, then, can be one of these: "Nothing can be gained without some loss" or " "Some things can be gained without some loss." If you agree with the original statement, you are setting out to prove inevitably some loss occurs with every gain. Remember, however, you can choose to write an essay that supports the opposite position.

Let's continue the process and assume that you have decided to agree with the original statement. Begin writing the essay. Try to move into the body as quickly as possible.

3. Write the body of the essay. The actual number of paragraphs is not as important as the **content** in the body. Each of these body paragraphs should include a strong topic sentence that clearly establishes the main idea of the paragraph; each paragraph is designed to help you build an effective discussion of your topic and focus. You can choose to compose three body paragraphs, but you are not restricted to three. The admissions officers who read your essay will primarily evaluate it for content and logical development.

4. Write the conclusion or closing section of your essay. Remind the reader of what you set out to prove—your focus. Did you succeed in defending your approach?

5. Take a few minutes—if you have any time remaining—to review and proofread your essay.

Now, let's try part of this process with a sample topic.

Topic or Question Prompt

> **Nothing can be gained without some loss.** Do you agree or disagree with this topic sentence? Support your position with one or two specific examples from personal experience, the experience of others, current events, history, or literature. Develop your response into a well-written essay.

1. For our sample, let's assume that you decide to **agree** with the statement.

2. "Brainstorm" to come up with some ideas that will support or illustrate the statement. Make some notes, if you would like, in the test booklet, not on the page designated for the essay. Maybe you think of ideas like these:

   - gaining years to become an adult means a loss of innocence
   - gaining new friends sometimes means losing others
   - gaining independence from your parents means losing dependence on them for money
   - learning more about current events means losing some innocence
   - Huck Finn gains independence from Pap but loses his connection with the town
   - The Allies won World War II but suffered many devastating losses of life and property.

   Notice that the last two in the list refer to a specific piece of literature and to history. Don't forget that you can write about literature or history—or even personal experience.

3. Assume you decide to write about World War II because you know some facts about it. After you devise an opening sentence or copy the topic sentence as your opening sentence, you can begin offering evidence or supporting details to illustrate the truth of the statement. You will offer examples to show that although the Allies did indeed win the war, they suffered great losses as well. Remember—you need three major pieces of evidence.

4. If time allows, try to proofread your essay. Remember that the admissions officers will read your essay, but it will not be scored. Write it as legibly as possible.

Review

To recap the process of writing an essay, review these important steps:

1. Decide how you want to respond to the topic.

2. "Brainstorm" to generate some relevant details.

3. Write a topic sentence or thesis that clearly indicates your purpose. This sentence can be just a copy of the question prompt, or you may compose your own topic sentence. Just be sure that your response to the statement is clear. You will take a position and defend it.

4. Write the body of the essay, making sure to include enough evidence to prove your point.

5. If you have time left, proofread your essay and make any corrections as neatly as possible.

Sample Essay Topics for SSAT

Choose one of these, agree or disagree with it, and write a practice essay:

1. We have become too dependent on technology in our lives today.

2. "Education means developing the mind, not stuffing the memory." (Anon.)

3. The most important qualities of a hero are bravery, compassion, and selflessness.

4. We can reduce the level of violence in society today by stronger gun control.

5. The event that most changed my life was _____. Explain why.

6. Sports in a school should be considered as important as academics.

Writing the Essay for ISEE

Writing an essay for the ISEE is similar. You will have 30 minutes in which to write the essay. The topics, on the other hand, are different. For the ISEE, your choices are usually more personal. You will have the opportunity to write about yourself in most instances.

Here are some sample topics for the ISEE test:

- My most important dream
- The most important change I have made in my life
- The person I admire most
- The word that describes me best
- The most important or significant book I have read

You may also have to respond to a statement similar to those on the SSAT; you have to agree or disagree with the statement and then offer evidence to support or prove your position.

This kind of statement may resemble the following:

> **DIRECTIONS:** Using the paper provided, write an essay in which you express your point of view on the topic presented in the following prompt:
>
> Contrary to earlier times in American history, no true American role models exist today to serve as inspiration for teens. Most of what contemporary teens are exposed to is too violent, crime-related, and self-centered to provide a genuine hero that teens can admire and try to model their own lives after.
>
> Your response will be evaluated for organization and development of ideas, appropriateness of examples and supporting details, and technique (spelling, punctuation, and usage).

The process for writing the essay is essentially the same for the ISEE. For the question prompt provided above, you will have to decide if you agree or disagree and what supporting details you can offer. Then you write your essay and strive to allow enough time to proofread the essay.

Another kind of ISEE question is an open-ended prompt in which you must decide how to complete the prompt. Instead of agreeing or disagreeing with a statement, you will be asked to complete a statement and explain your reasons. This kind of question will allow you to set up a more personal essay, writing that is based on your experience. After this beginning, the procedure for writing the essay is the same. Aim for developing your ideas logically and for including enough reasons to explain your response to the question.

SUBJECT REVIEWS

HINTS FOR SUCCESS IN WRITING THE ESSAY

1. Practice writing whenever you can. Success in writing is achieved just as success is in any other field—sports, art, games, scouting, music, community service, or spiritual life. You have to practice to improve your skills. Consider how long the members of a sports team train every day after school to prepare for one game. And what about the cast members of a play as they rehearse for a production? Your skill as a writer is every bit as important—and not merely in anticipation of this standardized test. You will need to have strong writing skills throughout high school and college. The more you write, therefore, the better writer you can become.

2. Try to simulate test conditions when you practice writing. Limit yourself to 30 minutes. Be sure that you will not be interrupted. Arrange to write at a desk that is clear of other materials.

3. If you are unable to complete your essay by the end of 30 minutes, mark this point in your essay and then complete your writing. Afterward, look at the essay to see how you could have saved some time and finished within the 30-minute limit. Did you take too long to make up your mind about the topic? Did you try to offer too much evidence? Can you actually form the letters of the words more rapidly to write faster but still legibly?

4. Now try to evaluate your writing. While we are all usually most critical of our own writing, try to make a fair assessment of what you have written. Check for grammatical errors, especially those noted earlier as particularly serious mistakes—the comma splice and the sentence fragment. It is also a good idea to put the essay away for a while, maybe no more than a few hours, and then re-read it to see if your evaluation has changed. Consider what you can do to improve your writing.

5. Practice writing more often. One way to practice is to keep a daily journal. Of course, the contents of your journal are private, but for the purposes we are focusing on here, the contents are not actually the most important part of the journal. The journal is a way to drill and polish your writing skills in a nonthreatening way. After all, no one except you will see this journal. You can even choose to write about the sample topics in your journal. Aim to be as objective as possible when you evaluate your compositions.

RED ALERT

Peterson's SSAT/ISEE Success

RED ALERT: WRITING STRATEGIES AND GRAMMAR REVIEW

FURTHER PRACTICE WITH ESSAY WRITING

Let's look at some additional sample topics for the SSAT and the ISEE and go through the steps needed to write a successful essay.

Topics

- Traveling is one way to learn about other cultures.
- Studying the past is one way to prepare for the future.
- I never felt better than when I . . . .
- If I could visit another city, I would choose . . . .
- Pets provide more for owners than owners provide for the animals.
- Students should wear uniforms to school.
- Everyone should be computer literate.

Assume that you decide to write about the topic, "Students should wear uniforms to school."

1. Brainstorm to generate some ideas related to school uniforms. If you want to make a rough list, jot these points down in the test booklet, not on the paper provided for you to write the essay. Some sample ideas may be these:

eliminates distraction of clothes	minimizes competition about appearance
minimizes economic differences	makes student preparation for school fast
can be passed down for siblings	encourages students to behave with dignity

   These are probably enough to get you started. Now, what about your opening sentence? You can use the sentence provided by the topic: Students should wear uniforms to school. You can, on the other hand, revise this sentence without changing its meaning. For instance, you can write, "In schools today, both public and private, students should wear uniforms." Be careful not to lapse into needless wordiness. Be concise. Develop an opening paragraph, which may be no more than a few sentences related to your topic sentence. Another sentence could be, "In schools today student dress has sometimes become bizarre. Some students seem to be more concerned about their appearance than about academics. Uniforms can be a solution for some problems." Do not say something as blunt as "In this essay I will discuss school uniforms."

2. Next, you need to set up the body paragraphs. Looking at your rough list, you can select these points: economic differences, competition about appearance, and student behavior. In your opinion, these are the strongest choices you have. Decide in what order you wish to present these points. You can organize ideas from least to most important, from most to least important, or in chronological order (which is not an option with this topic), among other choices. Your decisions mean that you will write the first body paragraph about competition about appearance or peer pressure to dress a certain way. The second body paragraph can deal with economic differences, because this point ties in well with the first one. Students sometimes feel pressure to wear certain labels, often expensive brands. Finally, you can discuss how student dress affects student behavior.

Remember, each paragraph must include explanation of the topic and supporting details or evidence to prove each of your ideas.

3. Finally, you should write a brief conclusion. Remind your reader of the most important points of your essay.

4. If you have any time remaining, try to proofread your essay. Look for the kinds of errors you know you are likely to make. For instance, check spelling, use of commas, or tense consistency.

Now let's repeat the process for a topic like those for the SSAT in which you agree or disagree with a statement. Let's assume that you select this topic:

> Contrary to earlier times in American history, <u>no true American role models exist today to serve as inspiration for teens</u>. Most of what contemporary teens are exposed to is too violent, crime-related, and self-centered to provide a genuine hero that teens can admire and try to model their own lives after.

The underlined sentence is the key statement. Decide if you agree or disagree with it.

1. The first step, then, is deciding whether you agree or disagree with the statement. You choose to disagree.

RED ALERT: WRITING STRATEGIES AND GRAMMAR REVIEW

2. Again, brainstorm to generate a rough list of possible ideas relevant to the position you have chosen.

   Possible ideas include these:

   > Is there a difference between a hero and a role model? What differentiates the two?
   >
   > Positive role models in a number of areas—sports, entertainment, education, family, church, government, family friends—name some
   >
   > Volunteer work, community service, and other selfless actions performed by role models
   >
   > List some well-known American figures, such as Christopher Reeve, Oprah Winfrey, Michael Jordan, and others.
   >
   > Consider "ordinary" heroes, such as firefighters, police officers, soldiers, and teachers.

3. This topic is somewhat more involved than the one above because you have to make more decisions before you begin to write. You can save some time by determining whether you want to focus on "ordinary" heroes or celebrity heroes. Let's assume you focus on "ordinary" heroes.

4. Establish three major ideas for the body paragraphs: (1) public servants, (2) elected officials, and (3) family members. Decide the order in which you want to present these ideas. Then write a paragraph about each, offering a few specific examples to illustrate each type. In the paragraph about public servants, for instance, you can discuss firefighters and police officers, who risk their lives daily to protect society.

5. The danger of a topic like this one is that it is easy to be tempted into writing more than you need and be unable to complete the essay in the time allotted. Be sure that you write concisely at a steady pace.

6. Finally, close your essay with a sentence or two that concludes your argument.

Now that we have gone over the process a few times, you should actually write a practice essay or two, following the suggestions offered. When you really take the SSAT or ISEE, you will feel more confident about this aspect of the test because you have practiced and you have a reliable strategy for success.

Peterson's: www.petersons.com

ENGLISH GRAMMAR REVIEW

USAGE REVIEW

Parts of Speech

NOUN

A NOUN is the name of a person, place, or thing.

actor,   city,   lamp

There are three kinds of nouns, according to the type of person, place, or thing the noun names.

1. A *common* noun refers to a general type: girl, park, army.

2. A *proper* noun refers to a particular person, place, or thing, and always begins with a capital letter: Mary, Central Park, U.S. Army.

3. A *collective* noun signifies a number of individuals organized into one group: team, crowd, Congress.

Singular/Plural

Every noun has number. That means every noun is either singular or plural. The singular means only one; the plural means more than one. There are four ways to form the plurals of nouns:

1. by adding *s* to the singular (horses, kites, rivers)

2. by adding *es* to the singular (buses, churches, dishes, boxes, buzzes)

3. by changing the singular (*man* becomes *men*, *woman* becomes *women*, *child* becomes *children*, *baby* becomes *babies*, *alumnus* becomes *alumni*)

4. by leaving the singular as it is (moose, deer, and sheep are all plural as well as singular).

Note: When forming the plural of letters and numbers, add 's: A's, 150's. Otherwise, 's denotes possession.

Case

Nouns also have case, which indicates the function of the noun in the sentence. There are three cases—the nominative case, the objective case, and the possessive case.

(1) Nominative Case

A noun is in the nominative case when it is the subject of a sentence: The *book* fell off the table. The *boys* and *girls* ran outside.

The subject of a sentence is the person, place, or thing that the sentence is about. Thus, the *book* fell off the table is about the book.

A noun is in the nominative case when it is a predicate noun. This is a noun used after a linking verb. In such cases, the predicate noun means the same as the subject.

Einstein was a *scientist*. (Einstein = scientist)

Judith was a brilliant *scholar* and gifted *teacher*. (Judith = scholar and teacher)

A noun is in the nominative case when it is used in direct address. A noun in direct address shows that someone or something is being spoken to directly. This noun is set off by commas.

Claudel, please answer the phone.

Go home, *Fido*, before you get hit by a car.

A noun is in the nominative case when it is a nominative absolute. This is a noun with a participle (see verbs) that stands as an independent idea but is part of a sentence.

The *rain* having stopped, we went out to play.

The *bike* having crashed, the race was stopped.

A noun is in the nominative case when it is a nominative in apposition. This is one of a pair of nouns. Both nouns are equal in meaning and are next to each other. The noun in apposition is set off from the rest of the sentence by commas.

Steve, *my son*, is going to college.

That man is Syd, the *musician*.

(2) Objective Case

A noun is in the objective case when it is the direct object of a verb. A direct object is the receiver of the action of a verb. A verb that has a direct object is called a transitive verb.

The team elected *David*.

The team won the *game*.

A noun is in the objective case when it is the indirect object of a verb. This is a noun that shows *to* whom or *for* whom the action is taking place. The words *to* and *for* may not actually appear in the sentence, but they are understood. An indirect object *must* be accompanied by a direct object.

Pedro threw *Mario* the ball. (Pedro threw the ball to Mario).

Anya bought her *mother* a gift. (Anya bought a gift for her mother).

A noun is in the objective case when it is an objective complement. An objective complement is a noun that explains the direct object. The word *complement* indicates that this noun *completes* the meaning of the direct object.

> The team elected Terry *captain*.

A noun is in the objective case when it is an objective by apposition. An objective by apposition is very much like a nominative in apposition. Again we have a pair of nouns that are equal in meaning and are next to each other. The noun in apposition explains the other noun, but now the noun being explained is in the objective case. Therefore, the noun in apposition is called the objective by apposition. The objective by apposition is set off from the rest of the sentence by commas.

> The bully pushed Steve, the little *toddler*, into the sandbox.

> He gave the money to Sam, the *banker*.

A noun is in the objective case when it is an adverbial objective. This is a noun that denotes distance or time.

> The storm lasted an *hour*.

> The troops walked five *miles*.

A noun is in the objective case when it is an object of a preposition.

> The stick fell into the *well*. (*Into* is the preposition.)

> The picture fell on the *table*. (*On* is the preposition.)

See the section on prepositions.

(3) Possessive Case

A noun is in the possessive case when it shows ownership. The correct use of the possessive case is often tested on the exam. The following rules will help you answer such questions correctly.

A. The possessive case of most nouns is formed by adding an apostrophe and s to the singular.

> The *boy's* book
>
> *Emile's* coat

B. If the singular ends in *s* add an apostrophe, or apostrophe *s*.

> The *bus's* wheels
>
> or
>
> The *bus'* wheels
>
> *Charles'* books
>
> or
>
> *Charles's* books

C. The possessive case of plural nouns ending in *s* is formed by adding just an apostrophe.

>The *dogs'* bones

Note: If *dog* was singular, the possessive case would be *dog's*.

D. If the plural noun does not end in *s* then add an apostrophe and *s*.

>The *children's* toys

>The *men's* boots

E. The possessive case of compound nouns is formed by adding an apostrophe and *s* to the last word if it is singular, or by adding an *s* and an apostrophe if the word is plural.

>My *brother-in-law's* house

>My *two brothers'* house

F. To show individual ownership, add an apostrophe and *s* to each owner.

>*Joe's* and *Jim's* boats (They each own their own boat.)

G. To show joint ownership, add an apostrophe and *s* to the last name.

>Joe and *Jim's* boat (They both own the same boat.)

PRONOUNS

A pronoun is used in place of a noun. The noun for which a pronoun is used is called the *antecedent*. The use of pronouns, particularly the relationship between a pronoun and its antecedent, is one of the most common items found on the test. Always make sure a pronoun has a clear antecedent.

>John had a candy bar and a cookie. He ate *it* quickly. (Ambiguous) (What is the antecedent of *it* — *candy bar* or *cookie*?)

>The boy rode his bike through the hedge, *which* was very large. (Ambiguous) (What was very large — the *bike* or the *hedge*?)

>The captain was very popular. *They* all liked him. (Ambiguous) (Who liked him? *They* has no antecedent.)

There are ten kinds of pronouns:

1. Expletive pronoun. The words *it* and *there* followed by the subject of the sentence are expletive pronouns.

   There were only a few tickets left.

   It was a long list of chores.

   When using an expletive, the verb agrees with the subject.

   There *remains* one *child* on the bus.

   There *remain* many *children* on the bus.

2. Intensive pronoun. This is a pronoun, ending in *self* or *selves*, which follows its antecedent and emphasizes it.

   He *himself* will go.

   The package was delivered to the boys *themselves*.

3. A reflexive pronoun. This is a pronoun, ending in *self* or *selves*, which is usually the object of a verb or preposition, or the complement of a verb.

   I hate *myself*.

   They always laugh at *themselves*.

   Myself, yourself, himself, herself, and *itself* are all singular. *Ourselves, yourselves*, and *themselves* are all plural. There is no such pronoun as hisself or theirselves. Do not use *myself* instead of *I* or *me*.

4. Demonstrative pronoun. This is used in place of a noun and points out the noun. Common demonstrative pronouns are *this, that, these*, and *those*.

   I want *those*.

5. Indefinite pronoun. This pronoun refers to any number of persons or objects. Following is a list of some singular and plural indefinite pronouns.

   SINGULAR

   anybody, anyone, each, everybody, everyone, no one, nobody, none, somebody, someone

   PLURAL

   all, any, many, several, some

   If the singular form is used as a subject, the verb must be singular.

   Everyone of *them* sings. (One person sings.)

If the singular form is used as an antecedent, its pronoun must be singular.

>Did *anybody* on any of the teams lose *his* sneakers? (One person lost *his* sneakers.)

6. Interrogative pronoun. This pronoun is used in asking a question. Such pronouns are *who, whose, whom, what,* and *which*. *Whose* shows possession. *Whom* is in the objective case. *Whom* is used only when an object pronoun is needed.

7. Reciprocal pronoun. This pronoun is used when referring to mutual relations. The reciprocal pronouns are *each other* and *one another*.

>They love *one another*.

>They often visit *each other's* houses.

Note that the possessive is formed by an *'s* after the word *other*.

8. Possessive pronoun. This pronoun refers to a noun that owns something. The possessive pronouns are as follows:

>SINGULAR

>mine (my), yours, his, hers, its

>PLURAL

>ours, yours, theirs

Notice that possessive pronouns do not use an 's. *It's* is a contraction meaning *it is*; *its* denotes possession.

9. Relative pronoun.

>Nominative case — who, that, which

>Objective case — whom, that, which

>Possessive case — whose

A relative pronoun used as the *subject* of a dependent clause is in the nominative case.

>I know *who* stole the car.

>Give the prize to *whoever* won it.

A relative pronoun used as the *object* of a dependent clause is in the objective case.

>He is the thief *whom* I know. (Object of verb *know*)

Note that the difficulty always comes when choosing *who* or *whom*. Remember that *who* is in the nominative case and is used for the appropriate situations discussed under nominative case in the section on nouns. *Whom* is in the objective case and is used for the appropriate situations discussed under objective case in the section on nouns.

>Who is coming? (*Who* is the subject.)

>Whom are you going with? (*Whom* is the object of the preposition *with*.)

The relative pronoun in the possessive case is *whose*. Notice there is no apostrophe in this word. The contraction *who's* means *who is*.

>I know *whose* book it is. (Denotes possession)

>I know *who's* on first base. (*who's* means *who is*)

10. Personal pronouns.

	Singular	*Plural*
NOMINATIVE CASE		
First person	I	we
Second person	you	you
Third person	he, she, it	they
OBJECTIVE CASE		
First person	me	us
Second person	you	you
Third person	him, her, it	them
POSSESSIVE CASE		
First person	mine (my)	ours (our)
Second person	yours (your)	yours (your)
Third person	his, hers, its (his, her, its)	theirs (their)

Personal pronouns denote what is called *person*. First-person pronouns show the person or thing that is speaking.

>I am going. (First person speaking)

Second-person pronouns show the person or thing being spoken to.

>*You* are my friend. (Second person spoken to)

Third-person pronouns show the person or thing being spoken about.

>Bea did not see *her*. (Third person spoken about)

ENGLISH GRAMMAR REVIEW

IMPORTANT FOR EXAM

1. *Who* refers to persons only.
2. *Which* refers to animals or objects.
3. *That* refers to persons, animals, or objects.

> I don't know *who* the actor is. (Person)
>
> They missed their dog, *which* died. (Animal)
>
> I finished the book *which* (or *that*) you recommended. (Object)
>
> They are the people *who* started the fight. (Person)
>
> That is the tiger *that* ran loose. (Animal)
>
> The light *that* failed was broken. (Object)

Note that the singular indefinite antecedents always take a singular pronoun.

> *Everyone* of the girls lost *her* hat.
>
> *None* of the boys lost *his*.
>
> *Someone* left *his* bike outside.

Note that collective singular nouns take singular pronouns; collective plural nouns take plural pronouns.

> The choir sang *its* part beautifully.
>
> The choirs sang *their* parts beautifully.

Note that two or more antecedents joined by *and* take a plural pronoun.

> Dave *and* Steve lost *their* way.

Note that two or more singular antecedents joined by *or* or *nor* take a singular pronoun.

> Tanya or Charita may use *her* ball.
>
> Neither Tanya nor Charita may use *her* ball.

If two antecedents are joined by *or* or *nor*, and if one is plural and the other is singular, the pronoun agrees in number with the nearer antecedent.

> Neither the *ball* nor the *rackets* were in *their* place.

Case

Remember that pronouns must also be in the correct case.

1. A pronoun must be in the nominative case when it is the subject of a sentence.

    James and *I* went to the airport.

    We freshmen helped the seniors.

    Peter calls her more than *I* do.

    Peter calls her more than *I*. (Here, the verb *do* is understood, and *I* is the subject of the understood verb *do*.)

2. A pronoun is in the objective case when it is a direct object of the verb.

    Leaving James and *me*, they ran away.

    John hit *them*.

    The freshman helped *us* seniors.

    A pronoun is in the objective case when it is the indirect object of a verb.

    Give *us* the ball.

3. A pronoun is in the objective case when it is an object of a preposition.

    To Ben and *me*

    With Sheila and *her*

    Between you and *them*

4. A pronoun is in the possessive case when it shows ownership.

    Her car broke down.

    Theirs did also.

    A pronoun is in the possessive case when it appears before a gerund (see verbals).

    His going was a sad event.

    For a more detailed analysis of the three cases, see the section on cases of nouns.

ADJECTIVES

An adjective describes or modifies a noun or a pronoun. An adjective usually answers the question *which one?* Or *what kind?* Or *how many?* There are a number of types of adjectives you should know.

1. Articles (a, an, the)

    An article must agree in number with the noun or pronoun it modifies.

    A boy

    An apple

    The girls

    If the noun or pronoun begins with a consonant, use *a*. If the noun or pronoun begins with a vowel, use *an*.

    A pear

    An orange

2. Limiting adjectives point out definite nouns or tell how many there are.

    Those books belong to John.

    The *three* boys didn't see *any* birds.

3. Descriptive adjectives describe or give a quality of the noun or pronoun they modify.

    The *large* chair

    The *sad* song

4. Possessive, demonstrative, and indefinite adjectives look like the pronouns of the same name. However, the adjective does not stand alone. It describes a noun or pronoun.

    This is *mine*. (Demonstrative and possessive pronouns)

    This book is *my* father's. (Demonstrative and possessive adjectives)

5. Interrogative and relative adjectives look the same, but they function differently. Interrogative adjectives ask questions.

    Which way should I go?

    Whose book is this?

    What time is John coming?

    Relative adjectives join two clauses and modify some word in the dependent clause.

    I don't know *whose* book it is.

IMPORTANT FOR EXAM

An adjective is used as a predicate adjective after a linking verb. If the modifier is describing the verb (a non-linking verb) we must use an adverb.

> The boy is *happy*. (Adjective)
> Joe appeared *angry*. (Adjective)
> The soup tasted *spicy*. (Adjective)
> Joe looked *angrily* at the dog. (Adverb — *angrily* modifies *looked*)

Positive, Comparative, and Superlative Adjectives

1. The positive degree states the quality of an object.

2. The comparative degree compares two things. It is formed by using *less* or *more* or adding *er* to the positive.

3. The superlative degree compares three or more things. It is formed by using *least* or *most* or adding *est* to the positive.

Positive	Comparative	Superlative
Easy	easier; more easy; less easy	easiest; most easy; least easy
Pretty	prettier; more pretty; less pretty	prettiest; least pretty; most pretty

Do Not Use Two Forms Together

> She is the most prettiest. (Incorrect)
>
> She is the prettiest. (Correct)
>
> She is the most pretty. (Correct)

VERBS

A verb either denotes action or a state of being. There are four major types of verbs: transitive, intransitive, linking, and auxiliary.

1. Transitive verbs are action words that must take a direct object. The direct object, which receives the action of the verb, is in the objective case.

    > Joe *hit* the ball. (*Ball* is the direct object of *hit*.)
    >
    > Joe *killed* Bill. (*Bill* is the direct object of *killed*.)

2. Intransitive verbs denote action but do not take a direct object.

    > The glass *broke*.
    >
    > The boy *fell*.

IMPORTANT FOR EXAM

Set, lay, and *raise* are always transitive and take an object. *Sit, lie*, and *rise* are always intransitive and do not take a direct object.

Set the book down, *lay* the pencil down, and *raise* your hands. (*Book, pencil*, and *hands* are direct objects of *set, lay*, and *raise*.)

Sit in the chair.

She *lies* in bed all day.

The sun also *rises*.

The same verb can be transitive or intransitive, depending on the sentence.

The pitcher *threw* wildly. (Intransitive)

The pitcher *threw* the ball wildly. (Transitive)

3. Linking verbs have no action. They denote a state of being. Linking verbs mean "equal." Here are some examples: *is, are, was, were, be, been, am* (any form of the verb *to be*), *smell, taste, feel, look, seem, become, appear*.

    Sometimes, these verbs are confusing because they can be linking verbs in one sentence and action verbs in another. You can tell if the verb is a linking verb if it means equal in the sentence.

    He felt nervous. (*He* equals *nervous*.)

    He felt nervously for the door bell. (*He* does not equal *door bell*.)

    Linking verbs take a predicate nominative or predicate adjective. (See sections on nouns, pronouns, and adjectives.)

    It *is I*.

    It *is she*.

4. Auxiliary verbs are sometimes called "helping" verbs. These verbs are used with an infinitive verb (*to* plus the verb) or a participle to form a verb phrase.

    The common auxiliary verbs are:

    All forms of *to be, to have, to do, to keep*.

    The verbs *can, may, must, ought to, shall, will, would, should*.

    He *has to go*. (Auxiliary *has* plus the infinitive *to go*)

    He *was going*. (Auxiliary *was* plus the present participle *going*)

    He *has gone*. (Auxiliary *has* plus the past participle *gone*)

There is no such form as *had ought*. Use *ought to have* or *should have*.

He *ought to have gone*.

He *should have gone*.

Every verb can change its form according to five categories. Each category adds meaning to the verb. The five categories are: *tense, mood, voice, number,* and *person*.

Tense: This indicates the *time*, or *when* the verb occurs. There are six tenses. They are:

present	past	future
present perfect	past perfect	future perfect

Three principal parts of the verb — the present, the past, and the past participle — are used to form all the tenses.

The *present tense* shows that the action is taking place in the present.

The dog *sees* the car and *jumps* out of the way.

The present tense of a regular verb looks like this:

	SINGULAR	PLURAL
First person	I jump	We jump
Second person	You jump	You jump
Third person	He, she, it jumps	They jump

Notice that an *s* is added to the third-person singular.

The *past tense* shows that the action took place in the past.

The dog *saw* the car and *jumped* out of the way.

The past tense of a regular verb looks like this:

	SINGULAR	PLURAL
First person	I jumped	We jumped
Second person	You jumped	You jumped
Third person	He, she, it jumped	They jumped

Notice that *ed* is added to the verb. Sometimes just *d* is added, as in the verb *used*, for example. In regular verbs the past participle has the same form as the past tense, but it is used with an auxiliary verb.

The dog *had jumped*.

The *future tense* shows that the action is going to take place in the future. The future tense needs the auxiliary verbs *will* or *shall*.

The dog *will see* the car and *will jump* out of the way.

The future tense of a regular verb looks like this:

	SINGULAR	PLURAL
First person	I shall jump	We shall jump
Second person	You will jump	You will jump
Third person	He, she, it will jump	They will jump

Notice that *shall* is used in the first person of the future tense.

To form the *three perfect tenses,* the verb *to have* and the past participle are used.

- The present tense of *to have* is used to form the *present perfect.*

    The dog *has seen* the car and *has jumped* out of the way.

- The present perfect tense shows that the action has started in the past and is continuing or has just been implemented in the present.

- The past tense of *to have* is used to form the *past perfect.*

    The dog *had seen* the car and *jumped* out of the way.

- The past perfect tense shows that the action had been completed in the past.

- The future tense of *to have* is used to form the *future perfect.*

    The dog *will have seen* the car and *will have jumped* out of the way.

- The future perfect tense shows that an action will have been completed before a definite time in the future.

Following is a table that shows the present, past, and future tenses of *to have*.

PRESENT TENSE

	SINGULAR	PLURAL
First person	I have	We have
Second person	You have	You have
Third person	He, she, it has	They have

PAST TENSE

	SINGULAR	PLURAL
First person	I had	We had
Second person	You had	You had
Third person	He, she, it had	They had

FUTURE TENSE

	SINGULAR	PLURAL
First person	I shall have	We shall have
Second person	You will have	You will have
Third person	He, she, it will have	They will have

The perfect tenses all use the past participle. Therefore, you must know the past participle of all the verbs. As we said, the past participle usually is formed by adding *d* or *ed* to the verb. However, there are many irregular verbs. Following is a table of the principal parts of some irregular verbs.

ENGLISH GRAMMAR REVIEW

PRESENT	PAST	PAST PARTICIPLE
arise	arose	arisen
awake	awoke, awaked	awoke, awaked, awakened
awaken	awakened	awakened
be	was	been
bear	bore	borne
beat	beat	beaten
become	became	become
begin	began	begun
bend	bent	bent
bet	bet	bet
bid (command)	bade, bid	bidden, bid
bind	bound	bound
bite	bit	bitten
bleed	bled	bled
blow	blew	blown
break	broke	broken
bring	brought	brought
build	built	built
burn	burned	burned, burnt
burst	burst	burst
buy	bought	bought
catch	caught	caught
choose	chose	chosen
come	came	come
cost	cost	cost
dig	dug	dug
dive	dived, dove	dived
do	did	done
draw	drew	drawn
dream	dreamed	dreamed
drink	drank	drunk
drive	drove	driven
eat	ate	eaten
fall	fell	fallen
fight	fought	fought
fit	fitted	fitted
fly	flew	flown
forget	forgot	forgotten, forgot
freeze	froze	frozen
get	got	got, gotten
give	gave	given
go	went	gone
grow	grew	grown
hang (kill)	hanged	hanged
hang (suspended)	hung	hung
hide	hid	hidden
hold	held	held

PRESENT	PAST	PAST PARTICIPLE
know	knew	known
lay	laid	laid
lead	led	led
lend	lent	lent
lie (recline)	lay	lain
lie (untruth)	lied	lied
light	lit	lit
pay	paid	paid
raise (take up)	raised	raised
read	read	read
rid	rid	rid
ride	rode	ridden
ring	rang	rung
rise (go up)	rose	risen
run	ran	run
saw (cut)	sawed	sawed
say	said	said
see	saw	seen
set	set	set
shake	shook	shaken
shine (light)	shone	shone
shine (to polish)	shined	shined
show	showed	shown, showed
shrink	shrank	shrunk, shrunken
sing	sang	sung
sit	sat	sat
slay	slew	slain
speak	spoke	spoken
spend	spent	spent
spit	spat, spit	spat, spit
spring	sprang	sprung
stand	stood	stood
steal	stole	stolen
swear	swore	sworn
swim	swam	swum
swing	swung	swung
take	took	taken
teach	taught	taught
tear	tore	torn
throw	threw	thrown
wake	waked, woke	waked, woken
wear	wore	worn
weave	wove, weaved	woven, weaved
weep	wept	wept
win	won	won
write	wrote	written

Another aspect of tense that appears on the test is the *correct sequence* or *order of tenses*. *Be sure if you change tense you know why you are doing so. Following are some rules to help you.*

When using the perfect tenses remember:

- The present perfect tense goes with the present tense.

  present
  As Dave *steps* up to the plate,

  present perfect
  the pitcher *has thrown* the ball to

  present perfect
  first and I *have caught* it.

- The past perfect tense goes with the past tense.

  past
  Before Dave *stepped* up to the

  past perfect
  plate, the pitcher *had thrown*

  past perfect
  the ball to first and I *had caught* it.

- The future perfect goes with the future tense.

  future
  Before Dave *will step* up to the plate, the pitcher

  future perfect
  will have thrown the ball to first

  future perfect
  and I *shall have caught* it.

- The present participle (verb + *ing*) is used when its action occurs at the same time as the action of the main verb.

  John, *answering* the bell, *knocked* over the plant. (*Answering* and *knocked* occur at the same time.)

- The past participle is used when its action occurs before the main verb.

  The elves, *dressed* in costumes, will *march* proudly to the shoemaker. (The elves dressed *before* they will march.)

Mood

The mood or mode of a verb shows the manner of the action. There are three moods.

1. The *indicative mood* shows the sentence is factual. Most of what we way is in the indicative mode.

2. The *subjunctive mood* is used for conditions contrary to fact or for strong desires. The use of the subjunctive mood for the verb *to be* is a test item.

Following is the conjugation (list of forms) of the verb *to be* in the subjunctive mood:

	PRESENT TENSE	
	SINGULAR	PLURAL
First person	I be	We be
Second person	You be	You be
Third person	He, she, it be	They be

	PAST TENSE	
	SINGULAR	PLURAL
First person	I were	We were
Second person	You were	You were
Third person	He, she, it were	They were

If I *be* wrong, then punish me.

If he *were* king, he would pardon me.

Also, *shall* and *should* are used for the subjunctive mood.

If he *shall* fail, he will cry.

If you *should* win, don't forget us.

3. The *imperative mood* is used for commands.

Go at once!

If strong feelings are expressed, the command ends with an exclamation point. In commands, the subject *you* is not stated but is understood.

Voice

There are two voices of verbs. The active voice shows that the subject is acting upon something or doing something *to* something else. The active voice has a direct object.

      subject   object
The *car* hit the *boy*.

The passive voice shows that the subject is acted upon *by* something. Something was done *to* the subject. The direct object becomes the subject. The verb *to be* plus the past participle is used in the passive voice.

      subject
The *boy* was hit by the car.

Number

This, as before, means singular or plural. A verb must agree with its subject in number.

    The *list was* long. (Singular)

    The *lists were* long. (Plural)

Nouns appearing between subject and verb do not change subject/verb agreement.

    The *list* of chores *was* long. (Singular)

    The *lists* of chores *were* long. (Plural)

Subjects joined by *and* are singular if the subject is one person or unit.

    My *friend and colleague has* decided to leave. (Singular)

    Five and five is ten. (Singular)

    Tea and milk is my favorite drink. (Singular)

Singular subjects joined by *or, either-or,* and *neither-nor* take singular verbs.

    Either Alvin or Lynette *goes* to the movies.

If one subject is singular and one is plural, the verb agrees with the nearer subject.

    Either Alvin or the girls *go* to the movies.

The use of the expletive pronouns *there* and *it* do not change subject/verb agreement.

> There *is no one* here.
>
> There *are snakes* in the grass.
>
> Think: No one is there; snakes are in the grass.

A relative pronoun takes a verb that agrees in number with the pronoun's antecedent.

> It is the *electrician who suggests* new wiring. (Singular)
>
> It is the *electricians who suggest* new wiring. (Plural)

Singular indefinite pronouns take singular verbs.

> Everybody *buys* tickets.

It is hard to tell if some nouns are singular. Following is a list of tricky nouns that take singular verbs.

> Collective nouns — *army, class, committee, team*
>
> Singular nouns in plural form — *news, economics, mathematics, measles, mumps, news, politics*
>
> Titles, although plural in form, refer to a single work — *The New York Times*, Henry James's *The Ambassadors*
>
> The *army is* coming.
>
> *News travels* fast.
>
> *Jaws is* a good movie.

Don't (do not) is incorrect for third-person singular. *Doesn't (does not)* is correct.

> He *doesn't* agree.

Person

Person, as before, refers to first person (speaking), second person (spoken to), and third person (spoken about). A verb must agree with its subject in person.

> I study. (First person)
>
> He studies. (Third person)

Intervening nouns or pronouns do not change subject/verb agreement.

> *He* as well as I *is* going. (Third person)

If there are two or more subjects joined by *or* or *nor*, the verb agrees with the nearer subject.

> Either John or *we are* going. (First-person plural)

ADVERBS

An adverb describes or modifies a verb, an adjective, or another adverb. Adverbs usually answer the questions *why?*, *where?*, *when?*, *how?* and *to what degree?* Many adverbs end in *ly*. There are two types of adverbs similar in use to the same type of adjective.

1. *Interrogative adverbs* ask questions.

    Where are you going?

    When will you be home?

2. *Relative adverbs* join two clauses and modify some word in the dependent clause.

    No liquor is sold *where* I live.

As with adjectives, there are three degrees of comparison for adverbs and a corresponding form for each.

1. The positive degree is often formed by adding *ly* to the adjective.

    She was *angry*. (Adjective)

    She screamed *angrily*. (Adverb)

2. The *comparative* is formed by using *more* or *less* or adding *er* to the positive.

3. The *superlative* is formed by using *most* or *least* or adding *est* to the positive.

Here are two typical adverbs:

POSITIVE DEGREE	COMPARATIVE DEGREE	SUPERLATIVE DEGREE
easily	easier, more easily, less easily	easiest, most easily, least easily
happily	happier, more happily, less happily	happiest, most happily, least happily

SUBJECT REVIEWS

CONJUNCTIONS

Conjunctions connect words, phrases, or clauses. Conjunctions can connect equal parts of speech.

>   and
>   but
>   for
>   or

Some conjunctions are used in pairs:

>   either . . . or
>   neither . . . nor
>   not only . . . but also

Here are some phrases and clauses using conjunctions:

>   John *or* Mary (Nouns are connected.)
>
>   On the wall *and* in the window (Phrases are connected.)
>
>   Mark had gone *but* I had not. (Clauses are connected)
>
>   *Either* you go *or* I will. (Clauses are connected.)

If the conjunction connects two long clauses, a comma is used in front of the coordinating conjunction:

>   Julio had gone to the game in the afternoon, but Pedro had not.

Some conjunctions are transitional:

>   therefore
>   however
>   moreover
>   finally
>   nevertheless

These conjunctions connect the meaning of two clauses or sentences.

IMPORTANT FOR EXAM

Be aware of *comma splices*. Comma splices occur when one connects two independent clauses with a comma, rather than with a semicolon or with a comma followed by a coordinating conjunction. An independent clause is a clause that can stand alone as a complete sentence.

>   His bike was broken; therefore, he could not ride. (Correct)
>
>   His bike was broken. Therefore he could not ride. (Correct)
>
>   His bike was broken, and, therefore, he could not ride. (Correct)
>
>   His bike was broken, therefore, he could not ride. (Incorrect)
>
>   He found his wallet, however he still left the auction. (Incorrect)

The last two sentences are comma splices and are incorrect. *Remember, two independent clauses cannot be connected by a comma.*

ENGLISH GRAMMAR REVIEW

PREPOSITIONS

A preposition shows the relationship between a noun or pronoun and some other word in the sentence.

The following are all prepositions:

about	for	through
above	in	to
across	inside	under
around	into	up
behind	of	upon
beneath	off	within
during	over	without

Sometimes groups of words are treated as single prepositions. Here are some examples:

according to

ahead of

in front of

in between

The preposition together with the noun or pronoun it introduces is called a prepositional phrase.

Under the table

In front of the oil painting

Behind the glass jar

Along the waterfront

Beside the canal

Very often on the test, idiomatic expressions are given that depend upon prepositions to be correct. Following is a list of idioms showing the correct preposition to use:

Abhorrence of: He showed an *abhorrence of* violence.

Abound in (or *with*): The lake *abounded with* fish.

Accompanied by (a person): He was *accompanied by* his friend.

Accompanied with: He *accompanied* his visit *with* a house gift.

Accused by, of: He was *accused by* a person *of* a crime.

Adept in: He is *adept in* jogging.

Agree to (an offer): I *agree to* the terms of the contract.

Agree with (a person): I *agree with* my son.

Agree upon (or *on*) (a plan): I *agree upon* that approach to the problem.

SUBJECT REVIEWS

Angry at (a situation): I was *angry at* the delay.

Available for (a purpose): I am *available for* tutoring.

Available to (a person): Those machines are *available to* the tenants.

Burden with: I won't *burden* you *with* my problems.

Centered on (or *in*): His efforts *centered on* winning.

Compare to (shows similarity): An orange can be *compared to* a grapefruit.

Compare with (shows difference): An orange can't be *compared with* a desk.

Conform to (or *with*): He does not *conform to* the rules.

Differ with (an opinion): I *differ with* his judgement.

Differ from (a thing): The boss's car *differs from* the worker's car.

Different from: His book is *different from* mine. (Use *different than* with a clause.)

Employed at (salary): He is *employed at* $25 a day.

Employed in (work): He is *employed in* building houses.

Envious of: She is *envious of* her sister.

Fearful of: She is *fearful of* thunder.

Free of: She will soon be *free of* her burden.

Hatred of: He has a *hatred of* violence.

Hint at: They *hinted at* a surprise.

Identical with: Your dress is *identical with* mine.

Independent of: I am *independent of* my parents.

In search of: He went *in search of* truth.

Interest in: He was not *interested in* his friends.

Jealous of: He was *jealous of* them.

Negligent of: He was *negligent of* his responsibilities.

Object to: I *object to* waiting so long.

Privilege of: He had the *privilege of* being born a millionaire.

Proficient in: You will be *proficient in* grammar.

Wait for: We will *wait for* them.

Wait on (service): The maid *waited on* them.

Like is used as a preposition. He wanted his dog to act *like* Lassie.

VERBALS

Sometimes verbs can change their form and be used as nouns, adverbs, or adjectives. These forms are called verbals.

1. The infinitive is formed by adding *to* in front of the verb. The infinitive may act as a noun, adjective, or adverb.

    I love *to sing*. (Noun)

    Music *to sing* is my favorite kind. (Adjective)

    He went *to sing* in the choir. (Adverb)

    An infinitive phrase is used as a noun, adjective, or adverb.

    I love *to sing songs*. (Noun)
    Music *to sing easily* is my favorite. (Adjective)
    He went *to sing very often*. (Adverb)

2. The participle can be either present or past. The present participle is usually formed by adding *ing* to a verb. The past participle is usually formed by adding *n, en, d,* or *ed* to a verb. The participle is used as an adjective.

    The *swaying* crane struck the *fallen* boy.

    (*Swaying* is a present participle; *fallen* is a past participle.)

    A participle phrase is used as an adjective.

    Blowing the crane fiercely, the wind caused much danger.

IMPORTANT FOR EXAM

Beware of dangling participle phrases.

Blowing the crane fiercely, the crowd ran.

(The wind is blowing the crane, not the crowd.)

3. The gerund is formed by adding *ing* to a verb. Although the gerund may look like a present participle, it is used only as a noun.

    Seeing clearly is important for good *driving*.

    (*Seeing* is the subject; *driving* is the object of the preposition *for*.)

    A participle phrase is used as a noun.

    Seeing traffic signals is important for good driving.

PHRASES

A prepositional phrase begins with a preposition. A prepositional phrase can also be a noun phrase or an adjective phrase or an adverbial phrase.

> *"Over the hill"* was the slogan of the geriatric club. (Noun phrase)
>
> The top *of the statue* was broken. (Adjective phrase)
>
> The owl sat *in the nest*. (Adverbial phrase)

See the previous section on *verbals* for infinitive phrases, participle phrases, and gerund phrases.

IMPORTANT FOR EXAM

A dangling or misplaced modifier is a word or phrase acting as a modifier that does not refer clearly to the word or phrase it modifies.

> A bright light blinded his eyes *over the door*. (Misplaced modifier — his eyes were not over the door.)
>
> *Blowing the crane fiercely*, the crowd ran. (Misplaced participle phrase — the crowd was not blowing the crane.)
>
> *Watching television*, cookies were eaten. (Dangling gerund phrase — cookies were not watching television.)
>
> *Not able to stop*, the man jumped out of my way. (Dangling infinitive phrase — is it the man who could not stop?)

The following modifying phrases clearly show what they modify.

> A bright light over the door blinded his eyes.
>
> Because the wind was blowing the crane fiercely, the crowd ran.
>
> Watching television, Laura ate the cookies.
>
> Since I was not able to stop, the man jumped out of my way.

CLAUSES

Clauses are groups of words that contain a subject and a predicate (verb part of the sentence). There are two main kinds of clauses. One kind is the *independent clause*, which makes sense when it stands alone. Independent clauses are joined by coordinating conjunctions.

> I know how to clean silver, *but* I never learned how to clean copper.
>
> (The two independent clauses could stand alone as complete sentences.)
>
> I know how to clean silver. I never learned how to clean copper.

The other kind of clause is a *dependent or subordinate clause*. Although this type of clause has a subject and a predicate, it cannot stand alone.

When I learn to clean copper, I will keep my pots sparkling.

When I learn to clean copper, by itself, does not make sense. Dependent clauses are always used as a single part of speech in a sentence. They function as nouns or adjectives or adverbs. When they function as nouns they are called *noun clauses*. When they function as adjectives they are called *adjective clauses*. When they are adverbs, they are called *adverbial clauses*. Since a dependent or subordinate clause cannot stand alone, it must be joined with an independent clause to make a sentence. A *subordinating conjunction* does this job. A relative pronoun (*who, that, which, what, whose,* and *whom*) may act as the subordinating conjunction. For adjective and adverbial clauses, a relative adverb (*while, when*) may act as the subordinating conjunction.

I noticed *that he was very pale*.

That he was very pale is a noun clause — the object of the verb *noticed*. *That* is the subordinating conjunction.

Who was guilty is not known.

Who was guilty is a noun clause — subject of the verb *is*. *Who* is the subordinating conjunction.

She lost the belt *which was a present*.

Which was a present is an adjective clause — describing *belt*. *Which* is the subordinating conjunction.

She lost the belt *when she dropped the bag*.

When she dropped the bag is an adverbial clause answering the question *when* about the predicate. *When* is the subordinating conjunction.

Clauses should refer clearly and logically to the part of the sentence they modify.

We bought a dress at Bloomingdale's *which was expensive*.

(Misplaced adjective clause. Did the writer mean Bloomingdale's was expensive?)

Correct: We bought a dress *which was expensive* at Bloomingdale's.

When finally discovered, not a sound was heard.

(Misplaced adverbial clause. Who or what is discovered?)

Correct: *When finally discovered*, the boys didn't make a sound.

SUBJECT REVIEWS

SENTENCES

A sentence is a group of words that expresses a complete thought. An independent clause can stand by itself and may or may not be a complete sentence.

> Beth and Terry rode the Ferris wheel; they enjoyed the ride. (Two independent clauses connected by a semicolon)
>
> Beth and Terry rode the Ferris wheel. They enjoyed the ride. (Two independent clauses — each is a sentence)

1. A simple sentence has one independent clause. A dependent clause is never a sentence by itself. Here are some simple sentences:

   > John and Fred played.
   >
   > John laughed and sang.
   >
   > John and Fred ate hot dogs and drank beer.

   The following is not an independent clause:

   > Fred said. (Incorrect — *said* is a transitive verb. It needs a direct object.)
   >
   > Fred said hello. (Correct)

2. A compound sentence has at least two independent clauses.

   > *Darryl bought the meat*, and *Laverne bought the potatoes*.

3. A complex sentence has one independent clause and at least one dependent clause.

   > Because she left early, she missed the end.
   >
   > (*Because she left early* is the dependent clause. *She missed the end* is an independent clause.)

4. A compound-complex sentence has two independent clauses and one or more dependent clauses.

   > You prefer math and I prefer music, although I am the math major.
   >
   > (*You prefer math* and *I prefer music* are the independent clauses. The dependent clause is *although I am the math major*.)

Common Sentence Errors

SENTENCE FRAGMENTS

These are parts of sentences that are incorrectly written with the capitals and punctuation of a sentence.

> Around the corner.
>
> Because she left early.
>
> Going to the movies.
>
> A terrible tragedy.

Remember that sentences must have at least a subject and a verb.

RUN-ON SENTENCES

These are sentences that are linked incorrectly.

> The rain was heavy, lightning was crackling he could not row the boat. (Incorrect)
>
> Because the rain was heavy and lightning was crackling, he could not row the boat. (Correct)
>
> The rain was heavy. Lightning was crackling. He could not row the boat. (Correct)

FAULTY PARALLELISM

Elements of equal importance within a sentence should have parallel structure or similar form.

> To sing, *dancing*, and to laugh make life happy. (Incorrect)
>
> To sing, to dance, and to laugh make life happy. (Correct)
>
> He wants health, wealth, and *to be happy*. (Incorrect)
>
> He wants health, wealth, and happiness. (Correct)

Watch Arbitrary Tense Shifts

> He *complained* while his father *listens*. (Incorrect)
>
> He *complained* while his father *listened*. (Correct)

Watch Non-pronoun Agreements

> A *person* may pass if *they* study. (Incorrect)
>
> A *person* may pass if *he* studies. (Correct)

Watch These Don'ts

DON'T use *being that*; use *since* or *because*.

DON'T use *could of, should of, would of*; use *could have, should have, would have*.

DON'T use the preposition *of* in the following: off *of* the table, inside *of* the house.

DON'T use *this here* or *that there*; use just *this* or *that*.

DON'T misuse *then* as a coordinating conjunction; use *than* instead.

> He is better *than* he used to be. (Correct)
>
> He is better *then* he used to be. (Incorrect)

CAPITALIZATION

1. Capitalize all proper nouns.

    Capitalize names of specific people, places, things, peoples, and their languages: Americans, America, Spanish. Note: Henry takes Spanish three times a week. Henry takes math three times a week.

2. Capitalize religions and holy books: Islam, Koran, Bible

3. Capitalize calendar words: Monday, April

4. Capitalize historical periods and events: Renaissance, Civil War

5. Always capitalize the first word in a sentence: It is Henry.

6. Capitalize the first word in a letter salutation: Dear John, Dear Sir

7. Capitalize the first word of a letter closing: Very truly yours,

8. Capitalize the first word in a direct quote: He said, "Go away."

9. Capitalize the first, last, and important words in titles: *The Man Without a Country*

    Note: *A, an, and, the* are usually not capitalized unless they are the first word.

    Note also that conjunctions and prepositions with fewer than five letters are usually not capitalized.

10. Capitalize words used as part of a proper noun: Hudson Street, Uncle Fritz

11. Capitalize specific regions: I want to move to the South.

12. Capitalize abbreviations of capitalized words: D. B. Edelson

13. Capitalize acronyms formed from capitalized words: NASA, NATO

14. Capitalize the pronoun *I*: I beseech you to hear my prayer.

    Note that capitals are not used for seasons (summer, winter).

    Note that capitals are not used for compass directions (east, northeast).

    Note that capitals are not used for the second part of a quote: "I see," she said, "how smart Henry is."

PUNCTUATION

THE PERIOD

1. Use the period to end full sentences.

    Harry loves candy.

    Although John knew the course was difficult, he did not expect to fail.

2. Use the period with abbreviations:

    Mr.

    Ph.D.

THE QUESTION MARK

1. Use the question mark to end a direct question:

    Are you going to the store?

2. Note that indirect questions end with a period:

    He asked how Sue knew the right answer.

THE EXCLAMATION POINT

1. Use the exclamation point to denote strong feeling:

    Act now!

THE COLON

1. The colon can introduce a series or an explanation, but it must always follow an independent clause.

    The following sciences are commonly taught in college: biology, chemistry, and physics. (Correct)

    The sciences are: biology, chemistry, and physics. (Incorrect)

    The sciences are is not an independent clause.

SUBJECT REVIEWS

2. The colon is used after the salutation in a business letter.

   Dear Sir:

3. The colon is used to express the time:

   It is 1:45.

THE SEMICOLON

1. The semicolon is used to link related independent clauses not linked by *and, but, or, nor, for, so,* or *yet*:

   No person is born prejudiced; prejudice must be taught.

2. The semicolon is used before conjunctive adverbs and transitional phrases placed between independent clauses:

   No person is born prejudiced; however, he has been taught well.

   No person is born prejudiced; nevertheless, he has always appeared bigoted.

3. The semicolon is used to separate a series that already contains commas:

   The team had John, the pitcher; Paul, the catcher; and Peter, the shortstop.

THE COMMA

1. The comma is used before long independent clauses linked by *and, but, or, nor, for, so,* or *yet*:

   No person is born prejudiced, but some people learn quickly.

2. The comma is used following clauses, phrases, or expressions that introduce a sentence:

   As I was eating, the waiter cleared the table.

   In a great country like ours, people enjoy traveling.

3. The comma is used with nonrestrictive, or parenthetical, expressions (not essential to the meaning of the main clause).

   He pulled the ice cream sundae, topped with whipped cream, toward him.

   John is afraid of all women who carry hand grenades. *Notice there is no comma.* John is not afraid of all women. He is afraid of all women who carry hand grenades (restrictive clauses).

4. Use commas between items in a series:

    Beth loves cake, candy, cookies, and ice cream.

5. Use the comma in direct address:

    Pearl, come here.

6. Use the comma before and after terms in apposition:

    Give it to Pearl, our good friend.

7. Use the comma in dates or addresses:

    June 3, 1996

    Freeport, Long Island

8. Use the comma after the salutation in a friendly letter:

    Dear Henry,

9. Use the comma after the closing in letters:

    Sincerely yours,

10. Use a comma between a direct quotation and the rest of the sentence:

    "Our fudge," the cook bragged, "is the best in town."

11. Be sure to use two commas when needed:

    A good dancer, generally speaking, loves to dance.

12. Do not separate subjects and verbs with a comma:

    Students and teachers, receive rewards. (Incorrect)

13. Do not separate verbs and their objects with a comma:

    He scolded and punished, the boys. (Incorrect)

THE APOSTROPHE

1. Use the apostrophe to denote possession (see nouns).

    John's friend

2. Use the apostrophe in contractions:

    Didn't (did not)

    There's (there is)

3. Do not use an apostrophe with his, hers, ours, yours, theirs, or whose. Use an apostrophe with *its* if *its* is a contraction:

    The dog chewed *its* bone; *it's* hard for a little dog to chew such a big bone. (*It's* means it is; *its* is a pronoun that denotes possession.)

SUBJECT REVIEWS

QUOTATION MARKS

1. Use quotation marks in direct quotes:

    "Get up," she said.

2. Use single quotes for a quote within a quote:

    Mark said, "Denise keeps saying 'I love you' to Ralph."

PARENTHESES

1. Use parentheses to set off nonrestrictive or unnecessary parts of a sentence:

    This book (an excellent review tool) will help students.

THE DASH

1. Use the dash instead of parentheses:

    This book—an excellent review tool—will help students.

2. Use the dash to show interruption in thought:

    There are eight—remember, eight—parts of speech.

RHETORICAL REVIEW

STYLE

Good writing is clear and economical.

AVOID AMBIGUOUS PRONOUN REFERENCES

Tom killed Jerry. I feel sorry for *him*. (Who is *him*? Tom? Jerry?)

Burt is a nice man. I don't know why *they* insulted him. (Who does *they* refer to?)

AVOID CLICHÉS

Betty is *sharp as a tack*.

The math exam was *easy as pie*.

It will be *a cold day in August* before I eat dinner with Louisa again.

AVOID REDUNDANCY

Harry is a man who loves to gamble. (Redundant—we know that Harry is a man.)

Harry loves to gamble. (Correct)

Claire is a strange one. (Redundant— *one* is not necessary.)

Claire is strange.

This July has been particularly hot in terms of weather. (Redundant—*in terms of weather* is not necessary.)

This July has been particularly hot. (Correct)

AVOID WORDINESS

The phrases on the left are wordy. Use the word on the right.

WORDY	PREFERABLE
the reason why is that	because
the question as to whether	whether
in a hasty manner	hastily
be aware of the fact that	know
due to the fact that	because
in light of the fact that	since
regardless of the fact that	although
for the purpose of	to

AVOID VAGUE WORDS OR PHRASES

It is always preferable to use specific, concrete language rather than vague words and phrases:

The reality of the situation necessitated action. (Vague)

Bill shot the burglar before the burglar could shoot him. (Specific)

BE ARTICULATE. USE THE APPROPRIATE WORD OR PHRASE

The following are words or phrases that are commonly misused:

1. Accept: to receive or agree to (verb)
   I *accept* your offer.

   Except: preposition that means to leave out
   They all left *except* Dave.

2. Adapt: to change (verb)
   We must *adapt* to the new ways.

   Adopt: to take as one's own, to incorporate (verb)
   We will *adopt* a child.

SUBJECT REVIEWS

3. **Affect:** to influence (verb)
   Their attitude may well *affect* mine.

   Effect: result (noun)
   What is the *effect* of their attitude?

4. **Allusion:** a reference to something (noun)
   The teacher made an *allusion* to Milton.

   Illusion: a false idea (noun)
   He had the *illusion* that he was king.

5. **Among:** use with more than two items (preposition)
   They pushed *among* the soldiers.

   Between: use with two items (preposition)
   They pushed *between* both soldiers.

6. **Amount:** cannot be counted (noun)
   Sue has a large *amount* of pride.

   Number: can be counted (noun)
   Sue bought a *number* of apples.

7. **Apt:** capable (adjective)
   She is an *apt* student.

   Likely: probably (adjective)
   We are *likely* to receive the prize.

8. **Beside:** at the side of (preposition)
   He sat *beside* me.

   Besides: in addition to (preposition)
   There were others there *besides* Joe.

9. **Bring:** toward the speaker (verb)
   Bring that to me.

   Take: away from the speaker (verb)
   Take that to him.

10. **Can:** to be able to (verb)
    I *can* ride a bike.

    May: permission (verb)
    May I ride my bike?

11. **Famous:** well known (adjective)

He is a *famous* movie star.

Infamous: well known but not for anything good (adjective)

He is the *infamous* criminal.

12. **Fewer:** can be counted (adjective)

I have *fewer* pennies than John.

Less: cannot be counted (adjective)

I have *less* pride than John.

13. **Imply:** the speaker or writer is making a hint or suggestion (verb)

He *implied* in his book that women were inferior.

Infer: to draw a conclusion from the speaker or writer (verb)

The audience *inferred* that he was a woman-hater.

14. **In:** something is already there (preposition)

He is *in* the kitchen.

Into: something is going there (preposition)

He is on his way *into* the kitchen.

15. **Irritate:** to annoy (verb)

His whining *irritated* me.

Aggravate: to make worse (verb)

The soap *aggravated* his rash.

16. **Teach:** to provide knowledge (verb)

She *taught* him how to swim.

Learn: to acquire knowledge (verb)

He *learned* how to swim from her.

17. **Uninterested:** bored (adjective)

She is *uninterested* in everything.

Disinterested: impartial (adjective)

He wanted a *disinterested* jury at his trial.

SUBJECT REVIEWS

ORGANIZATION

A paragraph, like an essay, must have some organization plan. Each paragraph should represent the development of some point the author is making. Learn to recognize topic sentences, which often come at the beginning or end of a paragraph. Topic sentences tell the reader the main point of the paragraph.

Here are some sample topic sentences:

- De Tocqueville is also concerned with the conflict between individual liberty and equality.
- Another of the social institutions that leads to disaster in *Candide* is the aristocracy.
- The Fortinbras subplot is the final subplot that points to Hamlet's procrastination.

Read the following paragraph and answer the appropriate questions.

(1) Throughout history, writers and poets have created countless works of art. (2) The result is Paul's failure to pursue Clara and establish a meaningful relationship with her. (3) Paul's mother loves him, but the love is smothering and overprotective. (4) Although Paul feels free to tell his mother almost everything, he fails to tell her he is sexually attracted to Clara. (5) His feelings for Clara obviously make him feel he is betraying his mother. (6) Paul Morel's relationship with his mother in *Sons and Lovers* interferes with his relationship with Clara.

1. Which sentence does not belong in the above paragraph?

   The correct answer is (1). The first sentence is inappropriate to the idea of the paragraph, which concerns Paul's relationship with his mother and with Clara. The first sentence is also vague and virtually meaningless. Obviously, many works of art have been created throughout history. So what?

2. Unscramble the above paragraph and put the sentences in the correct order.

   (A) 2, 4, 3, 6, 5
   (B) 6, 5, 2, 4, 3
   (C) 3, 4, 5, 6, 2
   (D) 6, 3, 4, 5, 2

   The correct answer is (D). Obviously, sentence 1 does not fit the paragraph. Sentence 6 mentions Paul by his full name, the name of the work, and his relationships with both women, all of which are covered in the paragraph. It is the topic sentence. Sentence 2 sums up the paragraph; the clue is in the phrase "the result is." Logically sentence 2 should end the paragraph.

ENGLISH GRAMMAR REVIEW

Since the paragraph concerns Paul's relationship with his mother and its effect on his relationship with Clara, the other sentences should fall in place.

This section has covered a lot of the basic rules of grammar. It is primarily a reference section and you will not be expected to know everything on the exam. However, we suggest you use this section as a handy guide to help you understand many of the answers that might involve certain grammar principles with which you may not be familiar. Feel free to highlight certain portions of these principles so you can go back to them from time to time, especially when confronted with more difficult explanations of some of the problems in the Strategy section and in any of the exams in the book.

SSAT Practice Test 1

Part I: Writing Sample
Writing the Essay........................ 352

Part II: Multiple Choice
Verbal................................. 355
Quantitative Mathematics 1 361
Reading Comprehension.................... 364
Quantitative Mathematics 2 372

**Explanatory Answers to the
SSAT Practice Test 1 .... 376**
   Verbal.............................. 376
   Quantitative Mathematics 1............ 380
   Reading Comprehension 384
   Quantitative Mathematics 2............ 389

Part I
WRITING SAMPLE

| **WRITING THE ESSAY** | **TIME: 25 MINUTES** |

Directions: Using two sheets of lined theme paper, plan and write an essay on the topic assigned below. DO NOT WRITE ON ANOTHER TOPIC. AN ESSAY ON ANOTHER TOPIC IS NOT ACCEPTABLE.

Topic: Speech is great, but silence is greater.

Assignment: Do you agree or disagree with the topic statement? Support your position with one or two specific examples from personal experience, the experience of others, current events, history, or literature.

WRITING THE ESSAY

Name: _____

Write your essay here.

Part II

MULTIPLE CHOICE

| VERBAL | TIME: 25 MINUTES | 60 QUESTIONS |

Directions: Each of the following questions consists of one word followed by five words or phrases. You are to select the one word or phrase whose meaning is closest to the word in capital letters.

1. QUANDARY

    (A) predicament
    (B) decision
    (C) requirement
    (D) community
    (E) information

2. PROTECT

    (A) retain
    (B) intend
    (C) require
    (D) defend
    (E) secure

3. OVERDUE

    (A) impending
    (B) appointment
    (C) including
    (D) late
    (E) library

4. VERBOSE

    (A) wordy
    (B) aloud
    (C) orate
    (D) speech
    (E) complete

5. DIMINISH

    (A) grow
    (B) impede
    (C) lessen
    (D) forecast
    (E) disappear

6. TRANSPARENT

    (A) opaque
    (B) filmy
    (C) serene
    (D) glass
    (E) motivation

7. PLIABLE

    (A) tool
    (B) flexible
    (C) useful
    (D) rigid
    (E) thrill

8. PROPHECY

    (A) anticipation
    (B) prediction
    (C) fortune
    (D) crystal
    (E) seer

9. DEJECTED

    (A) gifted
    (B) rewarded
    (C) concerned
    (D) serious
    (E) sad

Peterson's: www.petersons.com

10. BENEVOLENT
    (A) charitable
    (B) courageous
    (C) bravery
    (D) contest
    (E) seek

11. RECEDE
    (A) surrender
    (B) retreat
    (C) decline
    (D) lose
    (E) requite

12. FASTIDIOUS
    (A) chaos
    (B) unkempt
    (C) precise
    (D) classify
    (E) sanitary

13. SURLY
    (A) strong
    (B) wily
    (C) anticipate
    (D) rude
    (E) prodigal

14. FRUGAL
    (A) facility
    (B) careful
    (C) poverty
    (D) wealth
    (E) increase

15. DEPLETE
    (A) continue
    (B) guide
    (C) utilize
    (D) proceed
    (E) exhaust

16. FORCE
    (A) military
    (B) might
    (C) power
    (D) require
    (E) increase

17. EXTINCT
    (A) brief
    (B) clear
    (C) inactive
    (D) imperfect
    (E) poor

18. THWART
    (A) love
    (B) frustrate
    (C) defend
    (D) grow
    (E) advance

19. STIPEND
    (A) plant
    (B) financier
    (C) fluid
    (D) bank
    (E) payment

20. PRECLUDE
    (A) prevent
    (B) avoid
    (C) promise
    (D) listen
    (E) imagine

21. FOIBLE
    (A) story
    (B) flaw
    (C) strength
    (D) tradition
    (E) goodbye

VERBAL

22. MEDITATE
   - (A) compromise
   - (B) reject
   - (C) agree
   - (D) ponder
   - (E) repair

23. PARADOX
   - (A) occurrence
   - (B) heaven
   - (C) approval
   - (D) contradiction
   - (E) example

24. SURMISE
   - (A) guess
   - (B) daybreak
   - (C) provide
   - (D) shock
   - (E) govern

25. PSEUDONYM
   - (A) falsehood
   - (B) forgery
   - (C) elephant
   - (D) pen name
   - (E) writer

26. ECCENTRIC
   - (A) trustworthy
   - (B) truthful
   - (C) prompt
   - (D) earnest
   - (E) unusual

27. PRISON
   - (A) contain
   - (B) penal
   - (C) judge
   - (D) captivity
   - (E) justice

28. LITTLE
   - (A) periphery
   - (B) minute
   - (C) multiple
   - (D) confection
   - (E) gladden

29. ROBUST
   - (A) florid
   - (B) contained
   - (C) healthy
   - (D) considerable
   - (E) weak

30. SPHERE
   - (A) globe
   - (B) balloon
   - (C) orb
   - (D) radial
   - (E) horizon

Directions: The following questions ask you to find relationships between words. For each question, select the answer that best completes the meaning of the sentence.

31. Astute is to acumen as
   - (A) indigent is to wealth
   - (B) diplomatic is to tact
   - (C) clumsy is to skill
   - (D) vacuous is to intelligence
   - (E) rainbow is to hue

32. Judge is to adjudicate as
   - (A) lawyer is to propitiate
   - (B) bodyguard is to guide
   - (C) doctor is to sublimate
   - (D) champion is to defend
   - (E) suburb is to neighborhood

33. Imperceptible is to notice as
    (A) intangible is to touch
    (B) insoluble is to discern
    (C) invisible is to sense
    (D) enviable is to foresee
    (E) assuage is to repair

34. Claustrophobic is to enclosure as
    (A) miser is to money
    (B) narcissist is to sell
    (C) misogynist is to women
    (D) glutton is to food
    (E) myth is to tragedy

35. Fresh is to frozen as water is to
    (A) wax
    (B) crest
    (C) fish
    (D) ice cubes
    (E) white

36. Gullible is to bilk as
    (A) valiant is to cow
    (B) confident is to perturb
    (C) docile is to lead
    (D) affluent is to impoverish
    (E) vanquish is to disappear

37. Overblown is to exaggerated as
    (A) warrant is to justify
    (B) anachronism is to timely
    (C) malapropism is to accurate
    (D) requirement is to optional
    (E) sine die is to tomorrow

38. Arson is to fire as
    (A) pulverize is to dust
    (B) incinerate is to ashes
    (C) debilitate is to air
    (D) inundate is to water
    (E) indigo is to transport

39. Clown is to zany as
    (A) zealot is to patrician
    (B) showoff is to flamboyant
    (C) jester is to lugubrious
    (D) spy is to effusive
    (E) canvas is to paint

40. Horn is to blow as harp is to
    (A) democracy
    (B) play
    (C) denounce
    (D) pluck
    (E) pants

41. Inveigle is to flattery as
    (A) cozen is to encouragement
    (B) browbeat is to intimidation
    (C) reassure is to censure
    (D) cajole is to criticism
    (E) whine is to mourn

42. Trite is to insincere as
    (A) obloquy is to complimentary
    (B) empathy is to callous
    (C) persiflage is to abrasive
    (D) hypocrisy is to deceit
    (E) mold is to surround

43. Devotee is to fervid as
    (A) pundit is to apathetic
    (B) sycophant is to caustic
    (C) connoisseur is to discriminating
    (D) pessimist is to sanguine
    (E) optimist is to persuade

44. Mule is to stubborn as
    (A) pig is to idleness
    (B) horse is to iconoclastic
    (C) fox is to maladroit
    (D) elephant is to oblivious
    (E) turkey is to gullible

45. Repetitive is to redundant as
    (A) lampoon is to prolix
    (B) vignette is to noisome
    (C) homily is to incoherent
    (D) incorrect is to erroneous
    (E) ennui is to energize

46. Virtuoso is to éclat as
    (A) gallant is to panache
    (B) proselyte is to untruth
    (C) harbinger is to conclusion
    (D) klutz is to tact
    (E) casual is to plan

47. Bilious is to queasy as
    (A) quizzical is to content
    (B) contumelious is to elated
    (C) dangerous is to alarm
    (D) ambivalent is to sleepy
    (E) adroit is to able

48. Disorganized is to form as
    (A) ineffable is to size
    (B) empty is to substance
    (C) epical is to scope
    (D) immediacy is to duration
    (E) idolize is to confound

49. Midget is to minuscule as
    (A) accomplished is to abortive
    (B) dictum is to risible
    (C) serious is to waggish
    (D) colossus is to gargantuan
    (E) enigma is to original

50. Prude is to fastidious as
    (A) puritan is to simple
    (B) prodigy is to lackluster
    (C) witness is to truth
    (D) hedonist is to malcontent
    (E) heathen is to adoration

51. Waggish is to laughs as
    (A) risible is to yawns
    (B) bilious is to smiles
    (C) sad is to tears
    (D) ribald is to sneers
    (E) morbid is to concern

52. Diaphanous is to veils as
    (A) noisome is to clouds
    (B) gossamer is to cobwebs
    (C) bulky is to showers
    (D) abortive is to breezes
    (E) fishing is to net

53. Microcosm is to macrocosm as
    (A) plenty is to lack
    (B) glutton is to craven
    (C) understand is to orbit
    (D) granite is to touchstone
    (E) diameter is to edge

54. Homily is to church as
    (A) sermon is to air show
    (B) diatribe is to game show
    (C) aria is to horse show
    (D) monologue is to talk show
    (E) eulogy is to celebrate

55. Mnemonic is to memory as
    (A) trousers is to speech
    (B) glasses is to vision
    (C) earmuffs is to movement
    (D) blinders is to hearing
    (E) denim is to jacket

56. Healing is to health as
    (A) pragmatic is to avidity
    (B) eleemosynary is to profit
    (C) tendentious is to justice
    (D) therapeutic is to recovery
    (E) mercury is to speed

57. Uncaring is to concern as

(A) oblivious is to consciousness
(B) sanguine is to optimism
(C) quizzical is to erudition
(D) portentous is to intrepidity
(E) puzzlement is to understand

58. Tearjerker is to maudlin as

(A) opera is to prurient
(B) tragedy is to risible
(C) farce is to hilarious
(D) satire is to heartrending
(E) comedy is to wrenching

59. Passion is to devotion as

(A) liturgy is to ribald
(B) concern is to interest
(C) harangue is to restrained
(D) feisty is to mousy
(E) rapidity is to movement

60. Klutz is to inept as

(A) bigot is to intolerant
(B) dynamo is to supine
(C) aficionado is to blase
(D) pundit is to ignorant
(E) learned is to possess

Quantitative Mathematics 1   Time: 25 Minutes   25 Questions

Directions: Following each problem in this section, there are five suggested answers. Work each problem in your head or in the space provided (there will be space for scratchwork in your test booklet). Then look at the five suggested answers and decide which is best.

1. A gas tank is $\frac{1}{3}$ empty. When full, the tank holds 18 gallons. How many gallons are in the tank now?

   (A) 3
   (B) 6
   (C) 8
   (D) 12
   (E) 18

2. Which of the following is the smallest?

   (A) $\frac{1}{4} + \frac{2}{3}$
   (B) $\frac{3}{4} - \frac{1}{3}$
   (C) $\frac{1}{12} \div \frac{1}{3}$
   (D) $\frac{3}{4} \times \frac{1}{3}$
   (E) $\frac{1}{12} \times 2$

3. If the sum of x and $x + 3$ is greater than 20, which is a possible value for x?

   (A) -10
   (B) -8
   (C) -2
   (D) 8
   (E) 10

4. If a square has a perimeter of 88, what is the length of each side?

   (A) 4
   (B) 11
   (C) 22
   (D) 44
   (E) 110

5. If a Set R contains four positive integers whose average is 9, what is the largest number Set R could contain?

   (A) 4
   (B) 9
   (C) 24
   (D) 33
   (E) 36

6. Which of the following is *not* a multiple of 4?

   (A) 20
   (B) 30
   (C) 36
   (D) 44
   (E) 96

Questions 7 and 8 refer to the following definition: For all real numbers m, $*m = 10m - 10$.

7. $*7 =$

   (A) 70
   (B) 60
   (C) 17
   (D) 7
   (E) 0

8. If $*m = 120$, then $m =$

   (A) 11
   (B) 12
   (C) 13
   (D) 120
   (E) 130

9. At Nifty Thrifty Buy 'N Sell, an item that usually sells for $9 is on sale for $6. What approximate discount does that represent?

   (A) 10%
   (B) 25%
   (C) 33%
   (D) 50%
   (E) 66%

10. In Jackie's golf club, 8 of the 12 members are right-handed. What is the ratio of left-handed members to right-handed members?

    (A) 1:2
    (B) 2:1
    (C) 2:3
    (D) 3:4
    (E) 4:3

11. The sum of five consecutive positive integers is 35. What is the square of the largest of these integers?

    (A) 5
    (B) 9
    (C) 25
    (D) 81
    (E) 100

12. $2^2 \times 2^3 \times 2^3 =$

    (A) 24
    (B) 64
    (C) 2^8
    (D) 2^{10}
    (E) 2^{18}

13. If the area of a square is $100s^2$, what is the length of one side of the square?

    (A) $100s^2$
    (B) $10s^2$
    (C) $100s$
    (D) $10s$
    (E) 10

14. If 10 books cost d dollars, how many books can be purchased for 4 dollars?

    (A) $\dfrac{4d}{10}$
    (B) $40d$
    (C) $\dfrac{d}{40}$
    (D) $\dfrac{40}{d}$
    (E) $\dfrac{10d}{4}$

15. If g is an even integer, h is an odd integer, and j is the product of g and h, which of the following must be true?

    (A) j is a fraction
    (B) j is an odd integer
    (C) j is divisible by 2
    (D) j is between g and h
    (E) j is greater than 0

16. If a class of 6 students has an average grade of 78 before a seventh student joins, what must the seventh student get as a grade in order to raise the class average to 80?

    (A) 80
    (B) 84
    (C) 88
    (D) 92
    (E) 96

17. If 6 is a factor of a certain number, what must also be factors of that number?

    (A) 1, 2, 3, and 6
    (B) 2 and 3 only
    (C) 6 only
    (D) 2 and 6 only
    (E) 1, 2, and 3

18.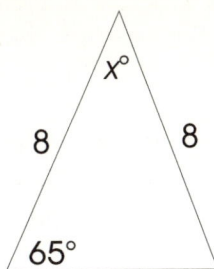

    $x =$

    (A) 8
    (B) 30
    (C) 50
    (D) 65
    (E) 70

19. For what priced item does 40% off equal a $2.00 discount?

    (A) $5.00
    (B) $4.00
    (C) $10.00
    (D) $80.00
    (E) $40.00

20. On Monday, Gerri ate $\frac{1}{4}$ of an apple pie. On Tuesday, she ate $\frac{1}{2}$ of what was left of the pie. What fraction of the entire pie did Gerri eat on both days?

    (A) $\frac{3}{8}$
    (B) $\frac{1}{2}$
    (C) $\frac{5}{8}$
    (D) $\frac{3}{4}$
    (E) $\frac{7}{8}$

21. If the area of a square is equal to its perimeter, what is the length of one side of that square?

    (A) 1
    (B) 2
    (C) 4
    (D) 8
    (E) 10

22. If $6x - 4 = 38$, then $x - 5 =$

    (A) 2
    (B) 3
    (C) 5
    (D) 7
    (E) 9

23. $3(x^2y^{-4}z)^4x^3y =$

    (A) $3x^{11}y^{-15}z^4$
    (B) $81x^{-1}yz^4$
    (C) $81x^{11}y^{-15}z^4$
    (D) $3x^9yz^4$
    (E) $3x^3y^{-5}z$

24. What is not a prime factor of 360?

    (A) 2
    (B) 3
    (C) 4
    (D) 5
    (E) All of the above are prime factors of 360

25. What is the area of an equilateral triangle whose altitude is 4?

    (A) 16
    (B) $4\sqrt{3}$
    (C) $8\sqrt{3}$
    (D) $\frac{16\sqrt{3}}{3}$
    (E) 8

Reading Comprehension   Time: 25 Minutes   40 Questions

Directions: Read each passage carefully and then answer the questions about it. For each question, decide on the basis of the passage which one of the choices best answers the question.

Passage 1

Line In the spring of 1963, Martin Luther King Jr., a leader of the American civil rights movement, was invited by the Birmingham, Alabama, branch of the Southern Christian
5 Leadership Conference, an organization fighting for civil rights for African-Americans, to lead a demonstration supporting their cause. King applied for a permit to hold a peaceful march through Birmingham, but
10 the city officials denied his request. Nevertheless, he scheduled the march. Because the marchers had no permit, their action was illegal, and the march was broken up by police. King and many of the marchers were
15 arrested. While King was in jail, eight clergymen signed a letter that was published in the local newspaper. The letter, while it asked the community to work to end racial problems, opposed marches and demonstra-
20 tions as the means of working toward a solution. After King read the letter, he wrote a response, replying to each point the clergymen raised. His response, published as "Letter from Birmingham Jail," includes an
25 analysis of when it is proper to act in violation of a law. He believed that if a law is unjust or unfair, people have not only a right but also a positive moral duty to oppose it, so long as their opposition
30 remains peaceful and non-violent. Because of its balanced sentence structure, appropriate references to the Bible and historical fact, and its powerful wording, "Letter from Birmingham Jail" is considered to be a
35 masterpiece of rhetoric.

1. King went to Birmingham because he
   (A) wanted to lead a march.
   (B) believed desegregation was important.
   (C) could ask for a permit to demonstrate.
   (D) was asked to do so by an organization.
   (E) wanted to reply to the clergymen.

2. The march led by King was illegal because
   (A) the city officials did not favor civil rights.
   (B) the demonstrators did not have permission to march.
   (C) the letter from eight clergymen presented a case against it.
   (D) the marchers were arrested by the police.
   (E) the community was working to end racial problems.

3. King believed that breaking a law
   (A) is always wrong.
   (B) is always the right thing to do.
   (C) is one's duty if one dislikes the law.
   (D) is a proper way to oppose an unjust law.
   (E) is always proper if the opposition is not violent.

4. The clergymen who wrote the letter wanted to
   (A) stop the marches and demonstrations.
   (B) be sure King remained in jail.
   (C) oppose the ending of racial problems.
   (D) provide civil rights for African-Americans.
   (E) help King get out of jail.

5. In the last sentence of the passage, "rhetoric" means

   (A) advertisement.
   (B) excellent writing.
   (C) an emotional speech.
   (D) poetry.
   (E) religious teaching.

Passage 2

Line When you buy a house plant, if the plant is healthy, it is likely to grow successfully in your home. How do you decide if a plant is sound? First, look at the leaves. If they are
5   brown at the edges, the plant has been given too much fertilizer or has been kept in temperatures that are too warm for its species. If the leaves are pale or yellow, the plant has been given too much or too little
10   water. If the leaves are very far apart from each other on the stem, this may mean the plant has been pushed to grow abnormally fast, and new leaves will not grow to fill in the gaps. You should look for a plant whose
15   foliage is dense.
     After checking the leaves' general appearance, look carefully at the underside of the leaves and the places where the leaves join the stem for evidence of insects.
20   Because the insects that infest house plants are very tiny, it may be hard to see them. But they leave clues that they are living on the plant. Some secrete a shiny sticky substance called honeydew on the plant.
25   Others leave behind tiny fine white webs.
     Finally, check to see if the plant's roots are growing out through the drainage hole in the bottom of the pot. If the roots are growing through the hole, the plant has
30   outgrown its pot, and it may not be the healthiest plant, even if you repot it in a larger container.

6. If a plant has been given too much fertilizer,

   (A) its leaves may have brown edges.
   (B) its leaves may be yellow.
   (C) there will be tiny webs on the leaves.
   (D) the foliage will be dense.
   (E) the soil will appear dry.

7. To check a plant's health, examine

   (A) leaf color.
   (B) leaf density.
   (C) the bottom of the pot.
   (D) the stem.
   (E) all of the above.

8. In context, "infest" most likely means

   (A) infect.
   (B) eat.
   (C) grow from.
   (D) live on.
   (E) secrete.

9. Too much or too little water will cause

   (A) dark-colored foliage.
   (B) large gaps between the leaves.
   (C) yellow or pale leaves.
   (D) roots to grow out of the drainage hole.
   (E) shiny spots on the stem.

10. Based on this passage, a reader can infer that

    (A) all growers of plants for sale raise them in perfect conditions.
    (B) some plants for sale have not been cared for properly.
    (C) plants are forced to grow abnormally fast.
    (D) it is difficult to care for a plant at home.
    (E) a plant's health is based on its environment.

Passage 3

Line Some myths are stories told by early
civilizations to explain the origins of natural
phenomena. The Greek myth that explains
the origin of the seasons is about Demeter,
5   the goddess of the harvest. She had a
daughter, Persephone, whom she loved very
much. Hades, god of the underworld, fell in
love with Persephone, and he asked Zeus,
the ruler of the gods, to give Persephone to
10 him as his wife. Zeus did not want to offend
either Hades or Persephone, so he said he
would not agree to the marriage, but neither
would he forbid it. Hades, therefore, decided
to take the girl without permission. As she
15 was picking flowers in a meadow, he seized
her and took her the underworld. When
Demeter found out what happened to
Persephone, she became so angry that she
caused all plants to stop growing. People
20 were in danger of starving. But Demeter
swore that no food would grow until
Persephone was returned to her. Zeus, still
not wanting to offend Hades, set a condition
for Persephone's return. She could go back
25 to her mother if she had not eaten anything
while she was in the underworld. Demeter
did not know it, but Persephone had eaten
several pomegranate seeds in the underworld. When Zeus discovered this, he
30 permitted a compromise. Persephone could
spend part of the year with her mother, but
because she had eaten the seeds, she must
spend part of the year in the underworld.
And when Persephone is in the underworld,
35 Demeter is sad, and therefore will not let the
crops grow. That is why we have winter,
when plants do not grow. When Persephone
returns, Demeter is happy, it is spring, and
plants begin to grow again.

11. Demeter is the goddess of
    (A) food plants.
    (B) the underworld.
    (C) marriage.
    (D) humanity.
    (E) the weather.

12. Myths are stories which
    (A) are always about gods and goddesses.
    (B) try to explain nature.
    (C) tell about mysteries.
    (D) have a religious purpose.
    (E) explain the origin of the seasons.

13. According to the story of Demeter, winter occurs because
    (A) Hades stole Persephone from her mother.
    (B) Zeus did not give Hades permission to marry Persephone.
    (C) Demeter is sad.
    (D) Persephone is unhappy.
    (E) Demeter disliked Hades.

14. Zeus did not give permission to Hades to marry Persephone because he
    (A) disliked him.
    (B) did not want to upset him.
    (C) wanted Persephone to be his wife.
    (D) thought this might make Demeter angry.
    (E) was the ruler of all the gods and goddesses.

15. Demeter stopped the growth of crops when
    (A) Zeus did not forbid the marriage.
    (B) Hades took Persephone to the underworld.
    (C) she discovered what Hades had done.
    (D) Persephone ate some pomegranate seeds.
    (E) Persephone was returned to her.

READING COMPREHENSION

Passage 4

Line　The Big Bang theory, an explanation of the origins of our universe, is one of the greatest intellectual achievements of the twentieth century. According to this theory, about ten
5　to twenty million years ago, the matter of which the universe is made was infinitely tightly compressed. Something—called the Big Bang—turned this matter into a gigantic fireball. As the matter was set into motion
10　and flew away from its compressed state, bits of it became glued together to create galaxies and later, stars and planets. The motion of the matter that flew out of the fireball continues today, and the universe
15　appears to be expanding. The theory grew out of observations of the Doppler effect. It explains that the frequency of radiation given off by a moving body decreases as the sources get further from the observer. In
20　1965, scientists discovered that the radiation bathing the earth is at the precise microwave frequency that would be expected if the universe began with a big bang. Some scientists think the expansion of the
25　universe will continue to infinity, while others theorize that gravity will, at some point in the far distant future, collapse back onto itself in a "big crunch," returning it to a state of compressed matter.

16. The best title for this passage is
    (A) The Big Bang
    (B) The Big Crunch
    (C) Our Expanding Universe
    (D) The Doppler Effect
    (E) Scientific Discoveries

17. As a moving object gets further from its source, its radiation frequency
    (A) stays the same.
    (B) grows larger.
    (C) grows smaller.
    (D) expands.
    (E) collapses.

18. The matter of which the universe is made was originally
    (A) expanding.
    (B) loosely connected.
    (C) decreasing.
    (D) tightly packed.
    (E) growing.

19. According to the passage, which of the following is true?
    (A) Scientists believe the universe will expand infinitely.
    (B) The Doppler effect created the universe.
    (C) Gravity will cause the universe to collapse.
    (D) Stars and planets grew out of galaxies.
    (E) Scientists do not agree about the universe's future.

20. The author of this passage thinks the Big Bang theory
    (A) has not been proven.
    (B) does not explain the creation of the universe.
    (C) is a very important contribution to knowledge.
    (D) explains what happens when a moving body gets further from its source.
    (E) shows the frequency of radiation bathing the earth.

Passage 5

Line Although the First World War had been
fought as the "war to make the world safe
for democracy," and the "war to end all
wars," the world's problems were not solved
5 when fighting was stopped by the cease fire
agreement signed on November 11, 1918.
The world was not yet at peace. In Russia,
there was a civil war among various factions
wishing to replace the monarchy, which had
10 been lead by the Czar. Greece was fighting
Turkey over territory that had belonged to
the former Turkish Empire. In the Middle
East, the Jews were asking for the establish-
ment of a national homeland, and the Arabs
15 in the area were opposing them. In India, at
that time a colony of the British Empire,
educated Indians thought their contributions
to the war meant their nation was ready for
more self-rule and some independence from
20 Great Britain. And throughout the world,
populations had been reduced by the 1918
influenza epidemic, which, most public
health experts believe, killed more people
than were killed in the war's battles. When
25 the Paris Peace Conference began in January
1919, the defeated nations were not invited.
They would simply be notified of the terms
of the peace treaty and asked to sign it. In
the United States, Americans' disgust about
30 the huge human costs of the war lead to
isolationism, the desire to avoid international
political situations and focus only on
problems within the country. Thus it is not
surprising that the League of Nations,
35 formed while the Peace Conference was in
session as an international organization to
create a better world, did not succeed in its
goals of achieving world disarmament and
preventing nations from invading one
40 another.

21. As used in the passage, the word "factions" means
    (A) fractions.
    (B) international terrorists.
    (C) nationalists.
    (D) disagreeing groups.
    (E) followers of the king.

22. The influenza epidemic of 1918
    (A) was a result of the war.
    (B) increased the misery of the soldiers.
    (C) killed vast numbers of civilians.
    (D) surprised public health experts.
    (E) was localized in a few nations.

23. The conflict between Greece and Turkey and the conflict between Jews and Arabs were similar because both
    (A) were about control over land.
    (B) involved a new homeland.
    (C) arose from the terms of the peace treaty.
    (D) led to revolutions.
    (E) were settled by the League of Nations.

24. Wishing to withdraw from international politics is called
    (A) organization.
    (B) monarchy.
    (C) factionalism.
    (D) isolationism.
    (E) home rule.

25. The fighting of World War I ended
    (A) after the world was made safe for democracy.
    (B) in January 1919.
    (C) in November 1918.
    (D) when the League of Nations as founded.
    (E) by the terms of the peace treaty.

Passage 6

Line I was flying from Los Angeles to Tucson, Arizona, to celebrate New Year's weekend with some friends. Because of the holiday and winter weather delays, the airport was
5 crowded, and many flights were canceled or late. Boarding for my flight began at 1:15 p.m., the time originally scheduled for departure. The airline personnel appeared to be in a hurry. As passengers boarded, the
10 pilot announced on the public address system, "O.K. folks, we're cleared for departure at 1:35. If you'll all take your seats, we'll take off at that time." Cabin attendants guided people to their seats and
15 helped them stow baggage. "Are we all okay?" a cabin attendant asked.

Across the aisle from where I sat, a woman said, "Where are my son and grandson? They're supposed on be on the
20 plane with me. They came to the airport with me." She was an older woman with well-cut white hair. Her face, although lined, was carefully but not overly made up. She wore a stylish suit and small earrings. The
25 attendant leaned over and spoke to her, and then made an announcement. "Passengers Stuart and John Miller, please let me know where you are seated." There was no reply. She repeated her announcement. Again, no
30 one responded. She told Mrs. Miller that her son was not on the plane. "But they came with me," Mrs. Miller said. "They're supposed to be here."

The attendant went to the cockpit to
35 consult the flight officers. Returning to Mrs. Miller, she said, "Ma'am, I'm sorry. We need to have you deplane. I'm sure the airport personnel will be able to help you find your son." Then she guided Mrs. Miller to the
40 exit.

The doors closed; the engines fired; the plane began to taxi. A passenger seated next to me said, "Oh, dear! That woman was wrong. Her son left her with airline person-
45 nel and told them to be sure to escort her onto the plane." My heart sank. Mrs. Miller probably suffered from confusion that sometimes affects older people. Someone, no doubt, would be waiting to meet her in
50 Tucson. Clearly, that person would be worried. And what of Mrs. Miller? Her son and grandson had probably left the airport by now. Would she remember their telephone number? And if she did, was it likely
55 they had already arrived home? Who would care for Mrs. Miller in a crowded, busy airport where passengers were trying to locate flights to replace canceled ones, and airline personnel were concerned about
60 sticking to a schedule? I thought I might weep.

26. As a result of bad weather,

   (A) passengers were in a hurry.
   (B) Mrs. Miller's son had not arrived home.
   (C) flights were late or canceled.
   (D) the flight attendant was rude to Mrs. Miller.
   (E) Mrs. Miller was escorted onto the plane.

27. The reader can infer the plane took off

   (A) on time.
   (B) half an hour late.
   (C) at some unknown time.
   (D) in the morning.
   (E) in the early afternoon.

28. The description of Mrs. Miller suggests that she

   (A) cannot take care of herself.
   (B) is a very wealthy woman.
   (C) loves her son and grandson.
   (D) has a sense of humor.
   (E) cares about her appearance.

29. The airline people asked Mrs. Miller to leave the plane because.

    (A) she was confused.
    (B) she didn't know her son's telephone number.
    (C) they wanted to help her find her son.
    (D) they wanted to take off as soon as possible.
    (E) other passengers were in a hurry.

30. Words that describe the author of this passage are:

    (A) observant.
    (B) compassionate.
    (C) sensitive.
    (D) None of the above.
    (E) (A), (B), and (C).

Passage 7

Line An intelligent and daring young woman who spoke many languages, Alexandrine Tinne seems to have been one of the more unusual explorers who ever lived. She was the
5   daughter of a wealthy Dutch merchant and a member of the Dutch aristocracy. Her father died when she was five, leaving her the richest heiress in the Netherlands at that time.
10   When she was grown up, after traveling throughout Europe, Tinne explored various parts of north central Africa. In 1863 and 1864, she charted the area around Bahr el Ghazal, a river system that flows into the
15   Nile. During this expedition, the group was struck with illness. One of the scientists died of fever in April of 1864, and Tinne's mother, who was also with the group, died in June. Tinne must have been a healthy
20   young woman to survive. Her expedition provided scientists with new and valuable information about the plants, animals, geology, and climate of this part of Africa. Later, traveling in Algeria and Tunisia, Tinne
25   became fascinated by the desert and the people who lived there. In 1869, she set out on an expedition across the Sahara Desert. Unfortunately, this remarkable explorer was murdered by inhabitants of the desert during
30   these travels. It was reported that they believed that her iron water tanks were filled with gold.

31. As used in the passage, "charted" means

    (A) mapped.
    (B) erased.
    (C) invented.
    (D) changed.
    (E) carried.

32. The passage suggests Tinne's expeditions were important mainly because she

    (A) could communicate in many languages.
    (B) enjoyed the warmth of the desert and meeting interesting people.
    (C) collected new scientific information.
    (D) died before she could finish her work.
    (E) took her mother along with her.

33. The Bahr el Ghazal river system is in

    (A) Europe.
    (B) South America.
    (C) Asia.
    (D) Antarctica.
    (E) Africa.

34. The passage implies Tinne was murdered

    (A) because the murderers did not like Europeans.
    (B) because she was careless about guarding her group.
    (C) because it was thought she had wealth that could be stolen.
    (D) so that her scientific knowledge could be stolen.
    (E) so that no one would ever explore the area again.

35. Which of the following best describes the author's attitude toward Tinne's actions?

(A) envy.
(B) indifference.
(C) sadness.
(D) skepticism.
(E) admiration.

Passage 8

Line My father's family name being Pirrip, and my first being Philip, my infant tongue could make of both names nothing longer or more explicit than Pip. So, I called myself Pip, and
5 came to be called Pip.

I give Pirrip as my father's family name, on the authority of his tombstone and my sister—Mrs. Joe Gargery, who married the blacksmith. As I never saw my father or my
10 mother and never saw any likeness of either of them (for their days were long before the days of photographs), my first fancies regarding what they were like were unreasonably derived from their tombstones. The
15 shape of the letters on my father's gave me an odd idea that he was a square, stout dark man, with curly black hair.

36. This passage was most probably written

(A) last year.
(B) about five years ago.
(C) less than 25 years ago.
(D) more than 100 years ago.
(E) about 2,000 years ago.

37. In the passage, the word "fancies" means

(A) elaborate lettering.
(B) hopes and dreams.
(C) imagined ideas.
(D) writing on tombstones.
(E) grown-up thoughts.

38. Pip never saw his birth parents because

(A) he was adopted.
(B) he ran away from home.
(C) they abandoned him.
(D) they died when he was an infant.
(E) his sister prevented their meeting.

39 Pip's sister's name is

(A) Mrs. Pirrip.
(B) Mrs. Gargery.
(C) Mrs. Philip.
(D) Mrs. Pip.
(E) Mrs. Stout.

40. Pip's sister's husband works as a

(A) stonecutter.
(B) gravedigger.
(C) blacksmith.
(D) photographer.
(E) barber.

QUANTITATIVE MATHEMATICS 2   TIME: 25 MINUTES   25 QUESTIONS

Directions: Following each problem in this section, there are five suggested answers. Work each problem in your head or in the space provided (there will be space for scratchwork in your test booklet). Then look at the five suggested answers and decide which is best.

1. At the start of the year Terry invested $6,000 in South Bend Oil Corp. At the end of the year his stock was worth $4,500. What was the percent decline in the value of his investment?

    (A) 25%
    (B) $33\frac{1}{3}$%
    (C) $66\frac{2}{3}$%
    (D) 75%
    (E) 125%

2. What is $\frac{a}{b} - \frac{b}{a}$?

    (A) $\frac{a-b}{ab}$
    (B) $\frac{a^2 - b^2}{ab}$
    (C) $\frac{(a-b)^2}{ab}$
    (D) $\frac{a^2 - b^2}{2ab}$
    (E) 1

3. Tracy has a test average of 90 after five tests. She only knows the scores of four of her tests: they are 80, 87, 94, and 89. What was the score on her other test?

    (A) 100
    (B) 98
    (C) 97
    (D) 90
    (E) 87

4. What is 4 percent expressed as a decimal?

    (A) 40
    (B) 4
    (C) .4
    (D) .04
    (E) .25

5. Express in simplest form the following ratio: 15 hours to 2 days.

    (A) $7\frac{1}{2}$
    (B) $\frac{16}{5}$
    (C) $\frac{5}{8}$
    (D) $\frac{15}{2}$
    (E) $\frac{5}{16}$

6. .58 × .14 =

    (A) 812
    (B) 8.12
    (C) 81.2
    (D) .812
    (E) .0812

7. If $3a - 5 = 7$, then $a =$
   - (A) -4
   - (B) 4
   - (C) $-\frac{2}{3}$
   - (D) $\frac{2}{3}$
   - (E) $\frac{5}{3}$

8. A gumball machine contains five red and three blue gumballs. If one gumball is removed, what is the probability that it will be red?
   - (A) $\frac{5}{3}$
   - (B) $\frac{3}{5}$
   - (C) $\frac{5}{8}$
   - (D) $\frac{3}{8}$
   - (E) $\frac{8}{3}$

9. How long is chord AB of circle O?

   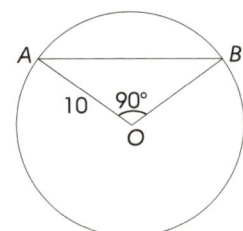

   - (A) $\sqrt{10}$
   - (B) $10\sqrt{2}$
   - (C) 100
   - (D) 10
   - (E) $\sqrt{50}$

10. $(2x^2 - 3x + 5) + (3x - 2) =$
    - (A) $2x^2 + 3$
    - (B) $2x^2 + 6x + 3$
    - (C) $2x^2 + 6x + 7$
    - (D) $2x + 3$
    - (E) $2x^2 - 6x + 3$

11. Using the formula $A = p + prt$, find A when $p = 500$, $r = .04$, and $t = 2\frac{1}{2}$.
    - (A) 700
    - (B) 600
    - (C) 550
    - (D) 500
    - (E) 450

12.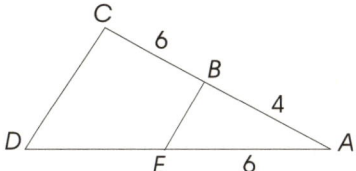

    Triangles ABE and ACD are similar. Find the length of DE.
    - (A) 9
    - (B) 15
    - (C) 4
    - (D) 11
    - (E) 8

13. The expression $(3K^2)^3$ is equivalent to:
    - (A) $9K^6$
    - (B) $27K^6$
    - (C) $27K^5$
    - (D) $9K^5$
    - (E) $3K^5$

14. Find the value of y in the proportion:
$$\frac{20}{12} = \frac{5}{y}$$

   (A) $\frac{3}{8}$
   (B) 3
   (C) 15
   (D) 8
   (E) $8\frac{1}{3}$

15. If $\frac{3}{x}$ is subtracted from $\frac{4}{x}$, the result is:

   (A) 1
   (B) $\frac{7}{x}$
   (C) $-\frac{1}{x}$
   (D) $\frac{1}{x}$
   (E) $\frac{1}{x^2}$

16. The markdown price of a computer game was $36.75, which represented 75% of the original selling price. What was the original selling price?

   (A) $27.56
   (B) $42.35
   (C) $45.94
   (D) $49.00
   (E) $45.35

17. Use this chart to answer question 17.

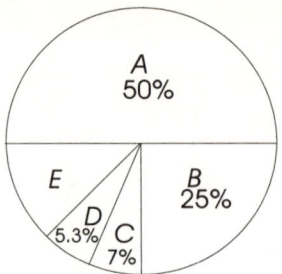

Freddie's Budget
Weekly net income = $350

A. Food
B. Rent and Utilities
C. Entertainment
D. Clothing
E. Miscellaneous

How much money does Freddie spend on miscellaneous items each week?

   (A) $43.05
   (B) $19.05
   (C) $130.95
   (D) $18.55
   (E) $44.45

18. What is the x-intercept of the line described by the equation $y = 3x + 7$?

   (A) 7
   (B) -7
   (C) $-\frac{3}{7}$
   (D) $-\frac{7}{3}$
   (E) 0

19. What is 60 expressed as the product of its prime factors?

   (A) (5)(13)
   (B) (5)(12)
   (C) (5)(3)(2)(2)
   (D) (4)(4)(3)
   (E) (15)(6)

20. If $|12a-7| = 3$, what is a possible value of a?

(A) 3
(B) -3
(C) 29
(D) $-\dfrac{1}{3}$
(E) $\dfrac{5}{6}$

21. What is the graph of the inequality $4 \leq x \leq 7$?

(A) [number line with closed dots at 4 and 7, segment between]
(B) [number line with open dots at 4 and 7, segment between]
(C) [number line with closed dot at 4 going left, closed dot at 7 going right]
(D) [number line with open dot at 4 going left, open dot at 7 going right]
(E) [number line with closed dot at 7 going left]

22. $11^2 - 9^2 =$

(A) 2
(B) 4
(C) -4
(D) 40
(E) 16

23. Eric's test scores were 98, 95, 84, 100, and 92. What would he need on his next test to have an average of 94?

(A) 90
(B) 92
(C) 95
(D) 100
(E) It is not possible to get that average.

24. Where does the line $y = x - 3$ cross the y-axis?

(A) (0,3)
(B) (0, -3)
(C) (-3, 0)
(D) (-3, (3)
(E) (0,0)

25.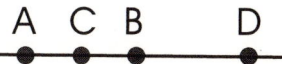

If points A, B, C, and D are distinct collinear points, and AC is congruent to BC, and B lies between A and D, and the length of AC is 7, what is the length of CD?

(A) 7
(B) 14
(C) 21
(D) 28
(E) It cannot be determined.

EXPLANATORY ANSWERS TO THE SSAT PRACTICE TEST 1

VERBAL

1. The correct answer is (A).
2. The correct answer is (D).
3. The correct answer is (D).
4. The correct answer is (A).
5. The correct answer is (C).
6. The correct answer is (B).
7. The correct answer is (B).
8. The correct answer is (B).
9. The correct answer is (E).
10. The correct answer is (A).
11. The correct answer is (B).
12. The correct answer is (C).
13. The correct answer is (D).
14. The correct answer is (B).
15. The correct answer is (E).
16. The correct answer is (C).
17. The correct answer is (C).
18. The correct answer is (B).
19. The correct answer is (E).
20. The correct answer is (A).
21. The correct answer is (B).
22. The correct answer is (D).
23. The correct answer is (D).
24. The correct answer is (A).
25. The correct answer is (D).
26. The correct answer is (E).
27. The correct answer is (D).

28. The correct answer is (B)

29. The correct answer is (C)

30. The correct answer is (C)

31. The correct answer is (B). The relationship is possession. Someone who is *astute* possesses *acumen*. Therefore, only answer (B) has the same relationship. Someone who is *diplomatic* possesses a great deal of *tact*.

32. The correct answer is (D). The relationship is one of object to its function: a *judge* would by definition *adjudicate*. A *champion* is a person who by definition would *defend* a matter.

33. The correct answer is (A). The relationship is word to antonym: if something is *imperceptible*, a person cannot *notice* it. The only answer that is an antonym is (A): if something is *intangible*, a person cannot *touch* it.

34. The correct answer is (C). The relationship is object to its function. A *claustrophobic* by definition hates *enclosure*. The only answer that is object to function is item (C): a *misogynist* is a person who by definition dislikes *women*.

35. The correct answer is (D). Something fresh, like water, can be frozen. In this case, frozen water makes ice cubes. The relationship is cause and effect. Answer (A) is incorrect because there is no relationship. Answer (B) and (E) are incorrect because the relationship is type to characteristic. A wave has a crest and a cloud may be white. Answer (C) is incorrect because there is no specific relationship.

36. The correct answer is (C). The relationship is cause to effect. One who is *gullible* is easy to *bilk*. The only cause to effect relationship is (C): if you are *docile*, it would be easy to *lead* you.

37. The correct answer is (A). The relationship is word to definition. An *overblown* situation is *exaggerated*. Answer (A) has the same relationship: a *warrant* is by definition *justified*.

38. The correct answer is (D). The relationship is cause to effect. If you wanted to commit *arson*, you would use *fire*. Answer (D) has the same relationship: if you wanted to *inundate* something, you would use *water*.

39. The correct answer is (B). The relationship is action of object. A *clown* acts *zany*. A *showoff* is a person whose actions could aptly be described as *flamboyant*.

40. The correct answer is (D). A horn is blown and a harp is plucked to make music.

41. The correct answer is (B). The relationship is cause to effect. You would *inveigle* someone by using *flattery*. Answer (B) has the same relationship: you would try to *browbeat* someone by using *intimidation*.

42. The correct answer is (D). The relationship is word to synonym. *Trite* is by definition *insincere*. Answer (D) has the same effect. *Hypocrisy* is by definition a form of *deceit*.

43. The correct answer is (C). The relationship is action of object. A *devotee* is a person who by definition is *fervid*. Answer (C) has the same relationship: a *connoisseur* is a person who is by definition *discriminating*.

44. The correct answer is (A). The relationship is action of object. A *mule* is an animal that is proverbially *stubborn*. Answer (A) has the same relationship: a *pig* is an animal that is proverbially *idle*.

45. The correct answer is (D). The relationship is word to synonym. *Repetition* is by definition *redundant*. Answer (D) has the same relationship: something that is *incorrect* is by definition *erroneous*.

46. The correct answer is (A). The relationship is action to object. A *virtuoso* is a person who would by definition perform with *éclat* (great brilliance). Answer (A) has the same relationship. A *gallant* is a person who would by definition perform with *panache* (dash).

47. The correct answer is (C). The relationship is cause to effect. Something that is *bilious* would by definition make a person feel *queasy*. Answer (C) has the same relationship: something that is *dangerous* would by definition make a person feel *alarmed*.

48. The correct answer is (B). The relationship is word to antonym. Something that is *disorganized* is lacking in *form*. Answer (B) has the same relationship: something that is *empty* is by definition lacking in *substance*.

49. The correct answer is (D). The relationship is word to synonym. A *midget*, by definition, is *minuscule*. Answer (D) has the same relationship: a *colossus* is by definition *gargantuan*.

50. The correct answer is (A). The relationship is object to its function. A *prude* is a person whose tastes could aptly be described as *fastidious*. Answer (A) has the same effect: a puritan is a person whose tastes could aptly be described as *simple*.

51. The correct answer is (C). The relationship is cause and effect. A remark that is *waggish* is designed to produce *laughs*. Answer (C) has the same effect: a remark that is *sad* is designed to produce *tears*.

52. The correct answer is (B). The relationship is word to synonym. Clothing that is *diaphanous* is reminiscent of *veils*. Answer (B) has the same relationship. Clothing that is *gossamer* is reminiscent of *cobwebs*.

53. The correct answer is (A). The relationship is word to antonym. A *microcosm* (small system) is the opposite of a *macrocosm* (universe). The same relationship is in answer (A): *plenty* means the opposite of *lack*.

54. The correct answer is (D). The relationship is object to its function. You would hear a *homily* at a *church*. The same relationship is in answer (D): you would be likely to hear a *monologue* in a *talk show*.

55. The correct answer is (B). The relationship is object to its function. A *mnemonic* is designed to help one's *memory*. The same relationship is in answer (B). *Glasses* are designed to help one's *vision*.

56. The correct answer is (D). The relationship is cause and effect. Something that is *healing* is conducive to one's *health*. Answer (D) has the same relationship: something that is *therapeutic* is conducive to one's *recovery*.

57. The correct answer is (A). The relationship is word to its antonym. Someone who is *uncaring* lacks *concern* about something. The same relationship is in answer (A): someone who is *oblivious* lacks *consciousness* about something.

58. The correct answer is (C). The relationship is word to its synonym. A *tearjerker* is a literary form that is by definition *maudlin*. The same relationship is found in answer (C): a *farce* is a literary form that is by definition *hilarious*.

59. The correct answer is (B). The relationship is word to its synonym: one who has *passion* has *devotion*. The same relationship is in answer (B): one who has *concern* has *interest*.

60. The correct answer is (A). The relationship is object to its function. A *klutz* is a type of person who is *inept*. The same relationship is in answer (A): a *bigot* is a type of person who is *intolerant*.

QUANTITATIVE MATHEMATICS 1

1. The correct answer is (D). If the tank is $\frac{1}{3}$ empty, it must be $\frac{2}{3}$ full. $\frac{2}{3}$ the total capacity of 18 gallons is 12.

2. The correct answer is (E). The value of A is $\frac{11}{12}$; the value of B is $\frac{5}{12}$; the value of C is $\frac{1}{4}$ or $\frac{3}{12}$; the value of (D) is $\frac{1}{4}$ or $\frac{3}{12}$; and the value of (E) is $\frac{1}{6}$ or $\frac{2}{12}$. Therefore, (E) has the smallest value.

3. The correct answer is (E). If $x + (x + 3) > 20$, then $2x > 17$. So $x > 8.5$. The only answer that is appropriate is 10.

4. The correct answer is (C). The perimeter of a square is found by summing the lengths of each side. Because the lengths are equal on a square, you can multiply one side by 4 to get the perimeter. Therefore, $4s = 88$, so $s = 22$.

5. The correct answer is (D). To find the largest value of the four, assume the remaining three values are the smallest possible positive integer, 1. The average then is $\frac{1+1+1+x}{4}=9$.

    Solve for x. $3 + x = 36$, so $x = 33$.

6. The correct answer is (B). Multiples of 4 include: 4, 8, 12, 16, 20, 24, 28, 32, 36, 40, 44, etc. Comparing these with the answers provided, notice that the number 30 is not a multiple of 4.

7. The correct answer is (B). Substitute 7 for m. *7 = 10(7) − 10 = 70 − 10 = 60.

8. The correct answer is (C). If *m = 10m − 10 and *m = 120, then $10m - 10 = 120$.

    Solve for m: $10m = 130$, $m = 13$.

9. The correct answer is (C). The total discounted amount is $3 or ($9 − $6). The original amount × the discounted percent = the total discounted amount.

    $9 × discounted percent = $3.

    The discounted percent $= \frac{3}{9} = \frac{1}{3} = 33\%$.

10. The correct answer is (A). The number of left-handed members is equal to $12 - 8$, or 4. The ratio of left-handers to right-handers is 4:8, which simplifies to 1:2.

11. The correct answer is (D). Let the five consecutive integers be: $x, x + 1, x + 2, x + 3,$ and $x + 4$.

Then $x + x + 1 + x + 2 + x + 3 + x + 4 = 35$;
$5x + 10 = 35; 5x = 25; x = 5$

Since the smallest of the five integers is 5, the largest is $5 + 4$, or 9. $9^2 = 81$.

12. The correct answer is (C). When multiplying like values raised to a power, add the integers.

$$2^3 \times 2^3 \times 2^3 = 2^{2+3+3} = 2^8$$

13. The correct answer is (D). The area of a square is equal to the (length of the side)^2, or L^2.

$$100s^2 = L^2$$
$$\sqrt{100s^2} = \sqrt{L^2}$$
$$10s = L$$

14. The correct answer is (D). Set up a ratio for this problem and solve:

Let x represent the number of books purchased with 4 dollars.

$$\frac{10}{d} = \frac{x}{4}$$

$10 \times 4 = d \times x$ (using cross-multiplication)

$$\frac{40}{d} = x$$

15. The correct answer is (C). Since integers can be both positive and negative, and the product of a positive and negative integer is always negative, answer (E) must be false. Looking further at the answers, notice that (B) and (C) are opposites of one another. Therefore, one of those must be true and the other false. Substitute two numbers in for g and h and see which of the two is true. If $g = -4$ and $h = 5$, $g \times h = -4 \times 5 = -20$. Since -20 is even, answer (C) is correct.

SSAT PRACTICE TEST 1

16. The correct answer is (D). The sum of the first six grades is $78 \times 6 = 468$. (To find the average grade of 78, divide the sum of the six grades by 6.)

    The average with seven students is $468 + x = 80 \times 7$.

    $468 + x = 560; x = 92$

17. The correct answer is (A).

    All factors of 6 are factors of the number.

    The factors of 6 are: 1×6

    2×3

18. The correct answer is (C). Since this is an isosceles triangle, the angles opposite the congruent sides are also congruent. The sum of the angles in a triangle equal 180°. So $65° + 65° + x° = 180°$ and $x = 50°$.

19. The correct answer is (A).

    Let p equal the price of the item.

    Price × Discount Rate = Discount Amount

    So $p \times 40\% = \$2.00; p \times .40 = 2.00; p = \dfrac{2.00}{.40} = 5$

20. The correct answer is (C). On Monday, $\dfrac{1}{4}$ of the pie was eaten. On Tuesday, there was $\dfrac{3}{4}$ of the pie left.

    $\dfrac{1}{2} \times \dfrac{3}{4} = \dfrac{3}{8}$ And $\dfrac{1}{4} + \dfrac{3}{8} = \dfrac{5}{8}$.

21. The correct answer is (C). The perimeter of a square equals $4s$. The area of a square equals s^2. Setting them equal will determine the length of one side, s.

    $s^2 = 4s$
    $s^2 - 4s = 0$
    $s(s - 4) = 0$
    $s = 0 \text{ or } s = 4$

    Since it would make no sense for the length to be 0, the correct answer is 4.

EXPLANATORY ANSWERS TO THE SSAT PRACTICE TEST 1

22. The correct answer is (A).

$$6x - 4 = 38$$
$$6x = 42$$
$$x = 7 \text{ so}$$
$$7 - 5 = 2$$

23. The correct answer is (A).

$$3(x^2 y^{-4} z)^4 x^3 y =$$
$$3x^8 y^{-16} z^4 x^3 y =$$
$$3x^{11} y^{-15} z^4$$

24. The correct answer is (C). They are all factors of 360, but 4 is not prime. (A prime number is a number that has no factors other than 1 and itself.)

25. The correct answer is (D). The altitude of an equilateral triangle bisects the vertex, forming a 30-60-90 triangle with sides in the ratios shown.

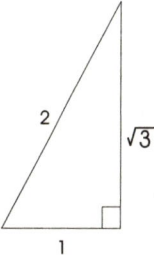

(This also comes from the Pythagorean theorem, and the fact that the base of an equilateral triangle has been bisected to form this 30-60-90 triangle.)

The sides will be in the same ratio for the given triangle:

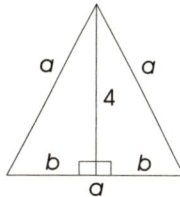

So, with the ratios $1:\sqrt{3}:2$ equaling the ratios $b:4:a$ we find $b = \dfrac{4}{\sqrt{3}}$ and $a = \dfrac{8}{\sqrt{3}}$.

Area = one half base times height, so
$$A = (4)\left(\dfrac{4}{\sqrt{3}}\right) = \dfrac{16}{\sqrt{3}} = \dfrac{16\sqrt{3}}{3}.$$

READING COMPREHENSION

Passage 1

1. The correct answer is (D). The word "invited" in the first sentence indicates he was asked to come to Birmingham. (A) is incorrect because the passage does not say what King wanted to do. While (B) may be a true statement, the passage does not state that was his reason. (C) and (E) refer to events after he had arrived, so they are incorrect.

2. The correct answer is (B). (A), (C), and (E) are not related to any laws. Answer (D) is the result of an illegal action, not a reason that the action was illegal.

3. The correct answer is (D). (A) is incorrect because the passage states he analyzes when a law can be broken. (B) and (C) are incorrect because the passage states only unjust laws could be violated. (E) is incorrect because according to King, if the law is not unfair, breaking the law is wrong even if the opposition is nonviolent.

4. The correct answer is (A). (B) is incorrect because the letter did not discuss King's situation. (C) is incorrect because it is contradicted by the passage. (D) and (E) are incorrect because they name specific actions that are not in the letter.

5. The correct answer is (B). (A) is incorrect because the letter does not try to sell a product, which is what an advertisement does. (C) is incorrect because it is a letter, not a speech, and (D) is incorrect because the letter is not a poem. (E) is incorrect because there is no mention of religion as part of the letter.

Passage 2

6. The correct answer is (A). (B) applies to leaves that have not had the proper amount of water. (C) applies to plants infested with insects. (D) describes a healthy plant, and (E) is about the soil, not the leaves.

7. The correct answer is (E). All of the answers above it are discussed at some point in the passage.

8. The correct answer is (D). The sentence after the one in which "infest" appears gives the phrase "live on" to explain what infest means.

9. The correct answer is (C). (A) is not mentioned in the passage. (B) is a result of forcing the plant to grow too quickly. (D) is a symptom of a plant that has outgrown its pot. (E) is a sign of insects on the plant.

EXPLANATORY ANSWERS TO THE SSAT PRACTICE TEST 1

10. The correct answer is (B). If all plants were cared for properly, there would be no need to see if they were healthy before purchasing them. (A) is incorrect because if all plants were raised perfectly, they all would be healthy. (C) applies to some plants, not all of them. The passage does not discuss caring for plants at home or a plant's environment, so (D) and (E) are incorrect.

Passage 3

11. The correct answer is (A). Since Demeter is the goddess of the harvest, she oversees crops planted for food. (B), (C), and (D) are contradicted by the passages because Hades is the god of the underworld, and the passage does not state who rules over marriage or humanity. (E) is incorrect, because while the weather affects the growth of crops, Demeter rules the growth of plants, not what causes them to grow or not grow.

12. The correct answer is (B). The passages does not say myths always involved gods and goddesses, so (A) is incorrect. The passage does not indicate whether (C) and (D) are true or false statements. (E) is true of the Demeter myth, but it would not be true of all myths.

13. The correct answer is (C). (A) and (B) are true statements about the story, but they are not the reason Demeter causes winter to occur. (D) and (E) might be inferred from the story, but they are not the reason given for winter.

14. The correct answer is (D). (A) is incorrect because the passage does not state Zeus' feelings about Hades. (B) is incorrect because if Zeus did not want to upset Hades, he would have given his permission. (C) is incorrect because it was Hades, not Zeus, who wanted Persephone as his wife. (E) is a true statement, but it is not the reason Zeus did not give permission to Hades.

15. The correct answer is (C). Although answers (A), (B), (D) and (E) state events that happened in the story, these events are not when according to the story, Demeter first stopped the growth of crops.

Passage 4

16. The correct answer is (A). (B) is a theory which only some scientists believe to be true. (C) and (D) are about part of the passage's content, but they do not describe the whole passage. (E) is too general; the passage deals with a specific scientific discovery.

17. The correct answer is (C). The passage states the radiation frequency "decreases," so (A), (B), and (D) are incorrect. (E) is incorrect because "collapse" does not mean the same as "decrease."

18. The correct answer is (D). The passage states the matter was "tightly compressed." (A) is incorrect, because while the matter may be expanding after the Big Bang, it was not expanding originally. (B) means the opposite of "tightly compressed," so it is incorrect. (C) and (E) refer to what may have happened after the Big Bang, so they are incorrect.

19. The correct answer is (E). The passage states some scientists think the universe will continue to expand, while others think it will collapse. Since both views are given, (A) and (C) are incorrect. (B) and (D) are contradicted by the passage.

20. The correct answer is (C), as indicated by the first sentence of the passage. That sentence also contradicts (B), and information in the passage about the 1965 discovery also suggests that the theory has been proven, so (A) is incorrect. (D) is about the Doppler effect, not the Big Bang, so it is incorrect. (E) is about evidence for the theory, not what the author thinks about the theory.

Passage 5

21. The correct answer is (D). (A) is incorrect, because fractions means "parts," but it does not indicate they do not agree with each other. (B) is incorrect because the factions are within a nation, so they cannot be "international." (C) refers to people who believe in their nation, so it does not fit the passage. (E) is contradicted because the factions wished to "replace" the monarchy.

22. The correct answer is (C). (A) and (B) may or may not be true, but the passage does not state that they are true. (D) is incorrect because the passage does not say how the experts felt about their discovery. (E) is contradicted by the phrase "throughout the world."

23. The correct answer is (A). (B) is incorrect because the conflict between Greece and Turkey did not involve a new land. (C) is incorrect because it refers to events after the occurrence of these conflicts. (D) and (E) are incorrect because the passage does not explain what these conflicts led to or how they were settled.

24. The correct answer is (D). The term is defined in the passage by the words occurring immediately after it.

25. The correct answer is (C). The passage gives November 1918 as the time when the "cease fire" was signed. Only after 1918 did the peace conference of January 1919 begin (B), during which the League of Nations was founded (D), and the peace treaty was not signed until the end of the conference (E). (A) is incorrect because while this was a slogan about the war, its hopes never came into existence.

Passage 6

26. The correct answer is (C). The passage does not say the passengers were hurrying (A). Nor does it explain why Mrs. Miller's son had not arrived home (B). (D) is incorrect, because the flight attendant's words include "I'm sorry," so she is not being rude. (E) is incorrect because the weather would not affect passengers inside the airport who were going to board a plane.

27. The correct answer is (E). (A) is incorrect because the author was boarding the plane at the scheduled take-off time. (B) is incorrect because the reader is not told exactly when the plane left. While this would make (C) a possibility, there is enough information in the passage to make it clear the plane took off some short time after 1:15 in the afternoon, so (D) would be incorrect.

28. The correct answer is (E). (A) is contradicted by the description; she is well dressed and carefully made up. (B) is incorrect, because the details of her appearance do not have examples of things which are very expensive. (C) may be true about Mrs. Miller, but it is not suggested by what she looks like. Nothing in the passage reveals her sense of humor or lack of it, so (D) is incorrect.

29. The correct answer is (D). While (A) may be a correct statement about Mrs. Miller, and (E) might be inferred from the passage, neither explains the motives of the airline personnel. (B) may or may not be true. The author asks if Mrs. Miller knows the number, but does not know if she does or does not. (C) is incorrect because they take her off the plane so that they will not have to help her find her son.

30. The correct answer is (E). The author notices the details of Mrs. Miller's appearance, which is observant (A). The author feels sorry for Mrs. Miller, which is compassionate (B), and the author is moved to great sadness when considering the situation, which shows sensitive feelings (C).

Passage 7

31. The correct answer is (A). None of the other answers makes sense in context because an area of land cannot be "erased" (B), "invented" (C), "changed" (D), or "carried" (E).

32. The correct answer is (C). (A) and (B) may be true, but these reasons would not be important for anyone but Ms. Tinne. (E) is also a personal statement. (D) is incorrect because her death caused her work to end rather than made it important.

33. The correct answer is (E). The passage states in the sentence before Bahr el Gazal is mentioned that she explored "parts of north central Africa." Thus, the other answers are incorrect.

34. The correct answer is (C). Nothing in the passage suggests (A), (B), (D), or (E). (C) may be inferred because the people who killed her believed she was carrying gold, according to the last sentence in the passage.

35. The correct answer is (E). Words like "intelligent," "daring," and "remarkable" and the statement that her information was valuable show the author's *admiration*. While the author calls her death "unfortunate," the overall tone of the passage is not sad, so (C) is incorrect.

Passage 8

36. The correct answer is (D). Since Pip's parents were alive "long before" photography was invented, (A), (B), and (C) are not probable. (E) is incorrect because the reference to photography shows that the writer lived when the process was known.

37. The correct answer is (C). (A) is incorrect because elaborate lettering would not indicate something in Pip's mind. (B) is incorrect because since his parents are dead, he would have no "hopes" about them. (D) is incorrect because it is the source of his fancies. (E) is incorrect because Pip was a child when he had the fancies.

38. The correct answer is (D). None of the other answers is implied by anything in the passage.

39. The correct answer is (B). Since she is married, her name would not be Pirrip, so (A) is incorrect. (C) and (D) refer to the speaker's first names, so they are not correct, and no Mrs. Stout appears in the passage, so (E) is incorrect.

40. The correct answer is (C). It is explicitly stated in the passage. While the passage talks about tombs and tombstones, neither stone-cutting nor grave digging is mentioned in connection with the husband, so (A) and (B) are incorrect. (D) cannot be correct because the passage concerns a time before photography was invented. (E) is incorrect because the passage does not mention a barber.

QUANTITATIVE MATHEMATICS 2

1. The correct answer is (A). The stock declined in value by $1,500, from an initial value of $6,000. The fractional decline in value is $\frac{1500}{6000} = \frac{1}{4}$ which is 25%.

2. The correct answer is (B). Get common denominators to add fractions. Multiply $\frac{a}{b}$ by $\frac{a}{a}$ getting $\frac{a^2}{ab}$. Multiply $\frac{b}{a}$ by $\frac{b}{b}$ getting $\frac{b^2}{ab}$. Subtract the fractions by subtracting the numerators.

3. The correct answer is (A). To have an average of 90 after five tests, the total of all the scores must be $90 \times 5 = 450$. The known scores add up to $80 + 87 + 94 + 89 = 350$, so she needs 100 points on the last test.

4. The correct answer is (D). Percent means "per 100". 4 percent means $\frac{4}{100}$.

5. The correct answer is (E). Put time in like units. $\frac{15 \text{ hours}}{48 \text{ hours}}$ Canceling out the common factor of 3 results in $\frac{5}{16}$.

6. The correct answer is (E). When multiplying decimals, be sure the final decimal point is in the correct place.

   ```
     .58      2 places
    ×.14      2 places
    ----
     232
     58
    ----
    .0812     4 places
   ```

7. The correct answer is (B). To solve equations, use inverse operations. First add 5 to both sides.

   $3a - 5 = 7$
   $+ 5 = +5$
   $3a = 12$

   Then divide both sides by 3.

   $\frac{3a}{3} = \frac{12}{3}$

   $a = 4$

8. The correct answer is (C). There are eight outcomes (total gumballs), of which five are successes (red).

9. The correct answer is (B). $OA = OB$ because the radii in the same circle are equal. The triangle AOB is a right triangle. By the Pythagorean theorem:

$$a^2 + b^2 = c^2$$

$$(\text{leg})^2 + (\text{leg})^2 = (\text{hypotenuse})^2$$

$$(10)^2 + (10)^2 = c^2$$

$$100 + 100 = c^2$$

$$200 = c^2$$

$$\sqrt{2 \times 100} = \sqrt{c^2}$$

$$10\sqrt{2} = c$$

10. The correct answer is (A). To add algebraic expressions, combine like terms.

$$\begin{array}{r} 2x^2 - 3x + 5 \\ +3x - 2 \\ \hline 2x^2 + 0 + 3 = 2x^2 + 3 \end{array}$$

11. The correct answer is (C). Substitute values $p = 500$, $r = .04$, and $t = 2\frac{1}{2}$.

$$A = 500 + (500)(.04)2\frac{1}{2} = 500 + 50 = 550$$

12. The correct answer is (A). Corresponding parts of similar triangles are in proportion:

$$\frac{AB}{AC} = \frac{AE}{AD}$$

$$\frac{4}{4+6} = \frac{6}{6+x}$$

$$4(6 + x) = 6(4 + 6)$$

$$24 + 4x = 60$$

$$-24 \quad\quad = -2$$

$$4x = 36$$

$$x = 9$$

13. The correct answer is (B).

$$(3K^2)^3 = (3K^2)(3K^2)(3K^2)$$
$$= (3)(3)(3)(K^2)(K^2)(K^2)$$
$$= 27K^{2+2+2} \quad \text{(multiply numbers;}$$
$$= 27K^6 \qquad \text{add exponents)}$$

14. The correct answer is (B).

$$\frac{20}{12} = \frac{5}{y}$$
$$20y = 12 \times 5 \text{ (cross-multiply)}$$
$$20y = 60$$
$$y = 3$$

15. The correct answer is (D).

$$\frac{4}{x} - \frac{3}{x} = \frac{1}{x}$$

The problem is written with all common denominators. Simply subtract the numerators.

16. The correct answer is (D).

$$75\% \text{ of } N = 36.75$$
$$75\% = \frac{75}{100} = .75 \qquad .75 \text{ of } N \text{ means } .75 \times N$$
$$.75 \times N = 36.75 \qquad \text{Divide both sides by .75 to isolate } N$$
$$\frac{.75 \times N}{.75} = \frac{36.75}{.75}$$
$$N = \frac{36.75}{.75} = 49$$

17. The correct answer is (E). First find what percent of Freddie's income is spent on miscellaneous items.

$$50\% + 25\% + 7\% + 5.3\% = 87.3\%$$
$$100\% - 87.3\% = 12.7\%$$

Then find 12.7% of $350.

Amount = Weekly Net Income × Miscellaneous Percent

$$= 350 \times .127 = \$44.45$$

18. The correct answer is (D). The line described by the equation crosses the x-axis when $y = 0$.

$$0 = 3x + 7$$
$$-7 = 3x$$
$$-\frac{7}{3} = x$$

19. The correct answer is (C). To break a number into its prime factors, break it into factors, and break those factors into factors, until you cannot go any further. It doesn't matter what factors you begin with. You will reach the same prime factors.

$$60 = 10 \times 6 = 5 \times 2 \times 3 \times 2$$

5, 3, and 2 are prime numbers (they have no factors other than themselves and 1), and multiplication is commutative (can be performed in any order).

Another way to approach the problem is to rule out the answers that have composite (non-prime) numbers. This rules out B, D, and E. Test the remaining answers by multiplying them out. Only C comes to 60.

20. The correct answer is (E).

$$12a - 7 \text{ can be 3 or } -3.$$

In the first case:

$$12a - 7 = 3$$
$$12a = 10$$
$$a = \frac{5}{6}$$

In the second case:

$$12a - 7 = -3$$
$$12a = 4$$
$$a = \frac{1}{3}$$

The only solution that fits the given answers is $\frac{5}{6}$.

21. The correct answer is (A). x is less than or equal to 7, and at the same time, x is greater than or equal to 4. An open circle would indicate a less than or a greater than condition at the endpoint, while filled-in-circles indicate a "less than or equal to" or a "greater than or equal to" condition at the endpoint.

22. The correct answer is (D).

$$11^2 = 121$$
$$9^2 = 81$$
$$121 - 81 = 40$$

23. The correct answer is (C). To have an average of 94 after six tests, Eric's total score would need to be $94 \times 6 = 564$. He already has a total score of $98 + 95 + 84 + 100 + 92$, which equals 469, so he needs $564 - 469$ points, which is 95.

24. The correct answer is (B). In the form $y = mx + b$, the slope is given by m and the y-intercept is given by b. The y-intercept is the value of y when $x = 0$.

25. The correct answer is (E).

AC and CB are congruent, making C the midpoint of AB. AC is 7 so BC is 7 and AB is 14. It is not given that B is the midpoint of AD, just that it lies between A and D. Therefore, AB and BD are not necessarily congruent. There is no other relationship that will give the length of segment BD or of CD.

SSAT Practice Test 2

Part I: Writing Sample
Writing the Essay........................ 396

Part II: Multiple Choice
Verbal................................. 399
Quantitative Mathematics 1 405
Reading Comprehension................... 409
Quantitative Mathematics 2 418

Explanatory Answers to the
   SSAT Practice Test 2 422
    Verbal............................... 422
    Quantitative Mathematics 1............ 428
    Reading Comprehension 433
    Quantitative Mathematics 2............ 437

Part I
WRITING SAMPLE

| **WRITING THE ESSAY** | **TIME: 25 MINUTES** |

Directions: Using two sheets of lined theme paper, plan and write an essay on the topic assigned below. DO NOT WRITE ON ANOTHER TOPIC. AN ESSAY ON ANOTHER TOPIC IS NOT ACCEPTABLE.

Topic: Money is a good servant, but a dangerous master.

Assignment: Do you agree or disagree with the topic statement? Support your position with one or two specific examples from personal experience, the experience of others, current events, history, or literature.

WRITING THE ESSAY

Name: _____

Write your essay here.

Part II

MULTIPLE CHOICE

VERBAL	TIME: 25 MINUTES	60 QUESTIONS

Directions: Each of the following questions consists of one word followed by five words or phrases. You are to select the one word or phrase whose meaning is closest to the word in capital letters.

1. PREMONITION
   - (A) payment
   - (B) ghost
   - (C) forewarning
   - (D) reward
   - (E) greeting

2. DECREE
   - (A) quantity
   - (B) loss
   - (C) challenge
   - (D) order
   - (E) joke

3. RELINQUISH
   - (A) release
   - (B) conquer
   - (C) discourage
   - (D) excite
   - (E) announce

4. IMMATERIAL
   - (A) untidy
   - (B) false
   - (C) unimportant
   - (D) wicked
   - (E) substantial

5. CONTOUR
   - (A) journey
   - (B) outline
   - (C) gathering
   - (D) agency
   - (E) photograph

6. THESIS
   - (A) guess
   - (B) hypothesis
   - (C) debate
   - (D) theme
   - (E) definition

7. HABITAT
   - (A) sleep
   - (B) cushion
   - (C) yarn
   - (D) promise
   - (E) home

8. INTERVENE
   - (A) come between
   - (B) withdraw
   - (C) contact
   - (D) construct
   - (E) require

9. ASPHYXIATION
   - (A) suffocation
   - (B) extension
   - (C) loss
   - (D) delivery
   - (E) breathing

10. ANTIDOTE
    - (A) poison
    - (B) story
    - (C) opponent
    - (D) cure
    - (E) predecessor

11. BATTERY
    - (A) ambush
    - (B) corner
    - (C) precarious
    - (D) group
    - (E) delirium

12. PATIENT
    - (A) tolerant
    - (B) irregular
    - (C) leisure
    - (D) multiple
    - (E) military

13. PAINSTAKING
    - (A) disease
    - (B) scrupulous
    - (C) delicate
    - (D) medicine
    - (E) generic

14. PRELUDE
    - (A) symphony
    - (B) soprano
    - (C) postlude
    - (D) beginning
    - (E) drama

15. REVERENCE
    - (A) nonfiction
    - (B) simplicity
    - (C) respect
    - (D) love
    - (E) glory

16. UNUSUAL
    - (A) ordinary
    - (B) rare
    - (C) pedantic
    - (D) sincere
    - (E) common

17. NOISE
    - (A) music
    - (B) locomotive
    - (C) sound
    - (D) siren
    - (E) crowd

18. EXPRESS
    - (A) verbalize
    - (B) quickly
    - (C) overnight
    - (D) careful
    - (E) holster

19. KIND
    - (A) significant
    - (B) quality
    - (C) equal
    - (D) hermitage
    - (E) good

20. SHAMEFUL
    - (A) ridiculous
    - (B) deceitful
    - (C) hurtful
    - (D) significant
    - (E) meaningless

21. HAPPY
    - (A) wild
    - (B) delighted
    - (C) forthright
    - (D) satisfied
    - (E) scuttle

22. FRACTION
    - (A) splinter
    - (B) sect
    - (C) piece
    - (D) share
    - (E) slice

23. GREAT
    - (A) historical
    - (B) famous
    - (C) hearth
    - (D) renown
    - (E) immense

24. TALENTED
    - (A) gifted
    - (B) musical
    - (C) artistic
    - (D) dramatic
    - (E) reputable

25. REPUTABLE
    - (A) star
    - (B) capable
    - (C) fame
    - (D) honest
    - (E) significant

26. LUCKY
    - (A) happy
    - (B) gleeful
    - (C) hilarious
    - (D) useful
    - (E) fortunate

27. IRRESPONSIBLE
    - (A) inconclusive
    - (B) unsure
    - (C) unreliable
    - (D) incisive
    - (E) unrealistic

28. JEOPARDY
    - (A) entertaining
    - (B) endangerment
    - (C) vocabulary
    - (D) journey
    - (E) archival

29. MOIST
    - (A) swamp
    - (B) damp
    - (C) saturate
    - (D) sponge
    - (E) fresh

30. SHAMEFUL
    - (A) evil
    - (B) bewildering
    - (C) caustic
    - (D) willful
    - (E) humiliating

Directions: The following questions ask you to find relationships between words. For each question, select the answer that best completes the meaning of the sentence.

31. Height is to mountain as
    - (A) depth is to trench
    - (B) shade is to tree
    - (C) weight is to age
    - (D) speed is to highway
    - (E) mineral is to mine

32. Oblivious is to awareness as
    - (A) comatose is to consciousness
    - (B) serene is to composure
    - (C) erudite is to knowledge
    - (D) adroit is to skill
    - (E) invigorate is to energy

33. Bellwether is to barometer as
    (A) proselyte is to spark plug
    (B) panhandler is to kill
    (C) embezzler is to abduct
    (D) cynosure is to magnet
    (E) morass is to catalyst

34. Act is to action as
    (A) therapy is to thermometer
    (B) oblivion is to obvious
    (C) liturgy is to literature
    (D) image is to imagine
    (E) bowl is to bowdlerize

35. Bibulous is to drink as
    (A) rapacious is to clothing
    (B) gluttonous is to food
    (C) altruistic is to money
    (D) vegetarian is to meat
    (E) controversy is to reconcile

36. Venison is to deer as veal is to
    (A) calf
    (B) cow
    (C) steer
    (D) sheep
    (E) lamb

37. Cursory is to superficial as
    (A) dismal is to cheerful
    (B) approbation is to consecration
    (C) death is to victory
    (D) desultory is to aimless
    (E) heroism is to reward

38. Bacchus is to drink as
    (A) Orpheus is to Eurydice
    (B) Amazon is to ruler
    (C) Diana is to hunt
    (D) Zeus is to Olympus
    (E) Plato is to Aristotle

39. Bald is to hairy as
    (A) small is to tiny
    (B) broad is to fat
    (C) anemic is to robust
    (D) fatuous is to loud
    (E) repetitive is to redundant

40. Gold is to Midas as
    (A) bird is to eagle
    (B) devil is to Satan
    (C) hero is to conquest
    (D) wisdom is to Athena
    (E) genius is to Shakespeare

41. Philanthropist is to generous as
    (A) dentist is to teeth
    (B) iconoclast is to conformist
    (C) rider is to horse
    (D) teacher is to educated
    (E) plagiarist is to robber

42. Fresh is to frozen as
    (A) clean is to wax
    (B) wave is to crest
    (C) jungle is to fish
    (D) water is to ice cubes
    (E) cloud is to white

43. Nazis is to Nuremburg as
    (A) judge is to jury
    (B) guard is to prison
    (C) communist is to Marx
    (D) persecute is to prosecution
    (E) gun is to death

44. Politics is to bribe as
    (A) parking is to meter
    (B) business is to contract
    (C) examinations is to cheat
    (D) nesting is to leaving
    (E) painting is to commission

45. Fraud is to cheater as

(A) infatuation is to love
(B) obsession is to interest
(C) impostor is to impersonator
(D) ignominy is to disloyalty
(E) castigation is to praise

46. Bacon is to pound as

(A) gun is to lead
(B) dime is to silver
(C) ceiling is to chandelier
(D) eggs is to dozen
(E) puppet show is to puppet maker

47. Horn is to blow as

(A) anarchy is to democracy
(B) game is to play
(C) reprove is to denounce
(D) harp is to pluck
(E) pocket is to pants

48. Limousine is to car as

(A) house is to cave
(B) railroad is to bus
(C) fur is to animal
(D) mansion is to house
(E) stone is to pebble

49. Warts is to moles as mildew is to

(A) dirt
(B) grass
(C) weeds
(D) alcohol
(E) gold

50. Bass is to soprano as

(A) art is to music
(B) light is to shading
(C) govern is to dictate
(D) low is to high
(E) chorus is to solo

51. Braid is to hair as wind is to

(A) run
(B) movie
(C) joke
(D) bow
(E) clock

52. Blade is to grass as

(A) air is to gas
(B) grain is to sand
(C) metal is to rod
(D) plant is to leaves
(E) roof is to house

53. Athlete is to training as

(A) mercenary is to money
(B) porpoise is to sea
(C) student is to studying
(D) child is to parent
(E) adult is to child

54. Novel is to author as

(A) rain is to flood
(B) form is to shape
(C) light is to switch
(D) opera is to composer
(E) song is to tape

55. Miser is to gold as

(A) engine is to caboose
(B) toastmaster is to dinner
(C) general is to victories
(D) prison is to criminal
(E) button is to zipper

56. Horse is to centaur as

(A) Pegasus is to fly
(B) cat is to lion
(C) unicorn is to tapestry
(D) worm is to snake
(E) fish is to mermaid

57. Bat is to ball as

    (A) stove is to pan
    (B) foot is to pedal
    (C) theater is to seats
    (D) glove is to hand
    (E) fist is to mitt

58. Ignition is to start as

    (A) radio is to antenna
    (B) shut is to door
    (C) brake is to stop
    (D) air is to tire
    (E) gas is to tank

59. Touch is to push as

    (A) water is to milk
    (B) angry is to choleric
    (C) glass is to water
    (D) translucent is to opaque
    (E) sip is to gulp

60. Bananas is to bunch as

    (A) capon is to rooster
    (B) ram is to ewe
    (C) chicken is to duck
    (D) lettuce is to head
    (E) surgeon is to operation

Quantitative Mathematics 1 — Time: 25 Minutes — 25 Questions

Directions: Following each problem in this section, there are five suggested answers. Work each problem in your head or in the space provided (there will be space for scratchwork in your test booklet). Then look at the five suggested answers and decide which is best.

1. Which of the following is a multiple of both 4 and 5?

    (A) 10
    (B) 45
    (C) 50
    (D) 60
    (E) 90

2. Four less than a number is two-thirds of that number. What is the number?

    (A) 12
    (B) 4
    (C) $\frac{12}{5}$
    (D) $\frac{5}{3}$
    (E) 6

3. On a test with 25 questions, Mark scored an 84%. How many questions did Mark answer correctly?

    (A) 22
    (B) 21
    (C) 16
    (D) 5
    (E) 4

4. $\frac{1}{2} + \frac{2}{3} + \frac{3}{4} - \frac{1}{2} - \frac{1}{3} + \frac{1}{4} - \frac{1}{3} =$

    (A) $\frac{1}{2}$
    (B) $\frac{2}{3}$
    (C) 1
    (D) 2
    (E) $\frac{3}{4}$

5. The perimeter of a square with a side length of 4 is how much less than the perimeter of a rectangle with sides of length 6 and width 4?

    (A) 8
    (B) 6
    (C) 4
    (D) 2
    (E) 0

6. Which of the following is most nearly 40% of $19.95?

    (A) $8.00
    (B) $4.00
    (C) $14.50
    (D) $12.00
    (E) $6.75

7. One-fifth of a class chose electricity for the topic of a science project. If 2 students chose this topic, how many students are in the class?

    (A) 20
    (B) 10
    (C) 8
    (D) 5
    (E) 2

Peterson's: www.petersons.com

8. Don is 5 years older than Peter is. In 5 years, Don will be twice as old as Peter is now. How old is Peter now?

   (A) 5
   (B) 10
   (C) 15
   (D) 25
   (E) 35

9. If p pieces of candy cost c cents, 20 pieces of candy will cost

   (A) $\dfrac{pc}{20}$ cents
   (B) $\dfrac{20c}{p}$ cents
   (C) $20pc$ cents
   (D) $\dfrac{20p}{c}$ cents
   (E) $20 + p + c$ cents

10. Durant's Trading Company earned profits of $750,000 in 1990. In 1998, their profit was $4,500,000. The profit from 1998 was how many times as great as it was in 1990?

    (A) 2
    (B) 4
    (C) 6
    (D) 10
    (E) 60

11.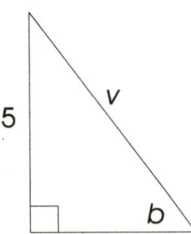

    If $b = 45°$, then $v^2 =$

    (A) 64
    (B) 50
    (C) 25
    (D) 10
    (E) It cannot be determined.

12. A pet goat eats 2 pounds of oats and one pound of grass each day. When the goat has eaten a total of 30 pounds, how many pounds of grass has been eaten?

    (A) 6
    (B) 8
    (C) 10
    (D) 30
    (E) 60

13. If $3x - 9 = 18$, what is $x \div 9$?

    (A) 6
    (B) 3
    (C) 0
    (D) 9
    (E) 1

14. One-half the difference between the number of degrees in a rectangle and the number of degrees in a triangle is

    (A) 360
    (B) 240
    (C) 180
    (D) 90
    (E) 45

15. A zoo has 4 times as many gorillas as tigers. There are 4 more tigers than there are zebras at the zoo. If z represents the number of zebras, in terms of z, how many gorillas are in the zoo?

    (A) $4z$
    (B) $z + 4$
    (C) $z + 8$
    (D) $4z + 4$
    (E) $4z + 16$

16. If cats sleep $\frac{3}{4}$ of every day, how many full days would a cat sleep in a four-day period?

    (A) $\frac{1}{4}$

    (B) $\frac{3}{4}$

    (C) 1
    (D) 3
    (E) 4

17. What is the smallest number that can be added to 2,042 to produce a result divisible by 9?

    (A) 1
    (B) 2
    (C) 3
    (D) 5
    (E) 6

18. An art club of 5 boys and 4 girls makes craft projects. If the girls average 2 projects each and the boys average 3 projects each, what is the total number of projects produced by this group?

    (A) 5
    (B) 9
    (C) 22
    (D) 23
    (E) 26

19. The area of a rectangle with width 3 and length 8 is equal to the area of a triangle with base 6 and height of

    (A) 1
    (B) 2
    (C) 3
    (D) 4
    (E) 8

Questions 20 and 21 refer to the following definition: For all real numbers r and s, $r \clubsuit s = (r \times s) - (r + s)$.

20. $10 \clubsuit 2 =$

    (A) 20
    (B) 16
    (C) 12
    (D) 8
    (E) 4

21. If $L(4 \clubsuit 3) = 30$, then $L =$

    (A) 3
    (B) 4
    (C) 5
    (D) 6
    (E) 7

22. Jessie scores an 88, 86, and 90 on her first 3 exams. What must she score on her fourth exam to receive an average of 91?

    (A) 92
    (B) 95
    (C) 98
    (D) 99
    (E) 100

23. Solve for x: $3x - 8 = 10x - 13$

    (A) $\frac{5}{7}$

    (B) $-\frac{5}{7}$

    (C) -35
    (D) -3
    (E) 3

24. If the price of a handbag is $75.00 before a discount of 15%, what is the final discounted price?

(A) $11.25
(B) $60.00
(C) $63.75
(D) $75.00
(E) $86.25

25. Find the height of a triangle whose base is 15 inches and whose area is 75 square inches.

(A) 5 inches
(B) 5 square inches
(C) 10 inches
(D) 10 square inches
(E) 20 inches

READING COMPREHENSION

| READING COMPREHENSION | TIME: 25 MINUTES | 40 QUESTIONS |

Directions: Read the passage carefully and then answer the questions about it. For each question, decide on the basis of the passage which one of the choices best answers the questions.

Passage 1

Line Most people living between 1400 and 1600 lived in complete ignorance of science. They continued to accept superstitions and nonsensical beliefs and lived in a world in
5 which spirits, demons, and witches were very real for them. Even professional men were not noted for their use of reason. One French playwright, Molière, had so little faith in the knowledge of doctors that he
10 made one of the characters in a play say: "What will you do, sir, with four physicians? Is not one enough to kill any one body?"
   Certainly the majority of men and women—educated or not—were not
15 constantly "scientific" in their attitudes. Talented individuals, rather than the mass of people, were responsible for the gains in the sciences. These individuals did outstanding work, not only in science and medicine but
20 also in the field of invention (the application of abstract scientific principles to produce something of concrete use). Johann Gutenberg (c. 1390-1468), a German, was one of several people who helped advance the art
25 of printing in a practical way. He constructed a workable press about the middle of the fifteenth century. By that date, paper and printer's ink were available for the printing process.
30   Gutenberg must not be called the "inventor" of the printing press. Printing developed too gradually for any one man to receive all of the credit. People living in China and Korea had movable type as early
35 as the eleventh century A.D., and several Europeans in the Rhineland area of Germany experimented with printing during the early fifteenth century.
   The invention of printing was one of
40 the greatest achievements in the history of civilization. Books could now be published in large numbers and sold at lower costs. Remember that in the Middle Ages each book was copied by hand on expensive
45 parchment (made from the stretched skin of a sheep or goat). A monk, illustrating and decorating the pages as he went, would take months or years on a single book. When paper was introduced to Europe, books
50 became cheaper, but they were still very scarce. Movable type meant that each letter or type was a tiny engraving. The letters could be arranged in words, then sentences, then a whole page. After ink had been
55 applied to the type and many impressions of the page made, the type was disassembled and could be used over and over. Hundreds or thousands of copies of each book or newspaper or sheet could easily be printed.
60 Books declined in price as a result, and the number of people who could afford to buy books increased greatly.
   Statistics show the importance of the printing press. In 1400, when each book
65 was copied by hand and was very expensive, few men could afford to buy books. Yet by 1966 over 300 million paperback books were bought annually in the United States alone! The printed page became a
70 major bond in communication.

Peterson's: www.petersons.com

1. Which one of the following areas is not mentioned as a birthplace of printing?

    (A) The Rhineland
    (B) China
    (C) Korea
    (D) Germany
    (E) France

2. Which one of the following did most people living between 1400 and 1600 not believe in?

    (A) science
    (B) witches
    (C) superstition
    (D) spirits
    (E) demons

3. Which invention allowed the creation of books in great number?

    (A) parchment
    (B) printing press
    (C) typewriter
    (D) movable type
    (E) printer's ink

4. The best meaning of the word "disassembled" is

    (A) taken apart.
    (B) put together.
    (C) a large gathering.
    (D) destroyed.
    (E) erased.

5. The best title for this passage is

    (A) The Problems of the Dark Ages
    (B) Great Progress in Invention
    (C) The Story of Gutenberg
    (D) Inventions Across the Continents
    (E) The Ignorance of the Dark Ages

Passage 2

Line Bananas ripe and green, and gingerroot,
     Cocoa in pods and alligator pears,
     And tangerines and mangoes and grapefruit,
     Fit for the highest prize at parish fairs.
5   Set in the window, bringing memories
     Of fruit trees laden by low-singing rills,
     And dewy dawns, and mystical blue skies
     In benediction over nunlike hills.
     My eyes grew dim, and I could no more gaze;
10 A wave of longing through my body swept,
     And, hungry for the old, familiar ways,
     I turned aside and bowed my head and wept.

6. The first three lines of the poem mention fruits grown in the tropics. Where exactly does the poet find himself?

    (A) at a church fair
    (B) in the West Indies
    (C) in a dream
    (D) on a city street
    (E) on a farm

7. In lines 7 and 8 the poet uses the words "mystical," "benediction," and "nunlike" to create which of the following images?

    (A) a collection of fruit in a store
    (B) a church fair
    (C) an almost religious experience
    (D) a forest
    (E) a stage set

8. Why does the poet "weep" at the end of the poem?

    (A) The fruits have been eaten.
    (B) He is cut off from the past.
    (C) He did not win the prize.
    (D) The future appears to be difficult.
    (E) He has become ill.

9. What is the best meaning of "rills" in line 6?

    (A) singers
    (B) trees
    (C) winds
    (D) streams
    (E) birds

10. The tone of this poem can best be described as

    (A) humorous
    (B) indifferent
    (C) ironic
    (D) sad
    (E) happy

Passage 3

Line Is Earth flat or round? Until 1522, most people believed Earth was flat. In that year one of Magellan's ships completed the first trip all the way around Earth. Long before
5 the explorer Magellan, however, early scientists thought that Earth was shaped like a ball. In geometry the ball shape is called a sphere, so the earth scientists said that Earth is spherical.
10   The spherical model of Earth is based on such evidence as the following:
       The mast of a ship was the first part to appear over the horizon. It was the last part to disappear. The traditional cry of the
15 lookout in a sailing vessel is, "I see a mast."
       When ships sailed north or south, sailors observed that the nighttime sky changed in appearance. The North Star rose higher in the sky as they sailed northward. It
20 sank in the sky as they sailed southward. The position of the North Star changed so gradually and so evenly that it could only be explained in one way. The ship was sailing on a spherical surface. When ships sailed far
25 enough south, constellations such as the Big Dipper could no longer be seen, but new ones such as the Southern Cross appeared in the sky. Would this be true on a flat Earth?

    An eclipse of the moon occurs when
30 Earth's shadow falls on the moon. During an eclipse of the moon, the edge of Earth's shadow as it moves across the moon is always the arc of a circle. Only a sphere casts a circular shadow, no matter what
35 position it is in.
       The evidence listed above is, of course, still visible today, although a lookout is much more likely to see a smokestack than a mast. But now everyone can see the
40 evidence. Many photographs of Earth have been taken by orbiting spacecraft. Other photographs of Earth have been taken from the moon by the Apollo astronauts.

11. In the context of the passage, the word "constellation" most likely means:

    (A) a group of planets.
    (B) a number of spheres.
    (C) a pattern of stars.
    (D) the Big Dipper.
    (E) the North Star.

12. When a ship sails north the North Star

    (A) stays in the same place in the sky.
    (B) rises higher in the sky.
    (C) sinks lower in the sky.
    (D) becomes the Southern Cross.
    (E) changes shape.

13. In the paragraph describing an eclipse of the moon we can infer that

    (A) the Earth is flat.
    (B) the moon is closer to the Earth than the sun.
    (C) the Earth is in shadow.
    (D) the moon has an orbit.
    (E) the Earth is spherical.

14. The title that best expresses the idea of this passage is

    (A) Magellan's Trip Around the World
    (B) What We Need from the Moon
    (C) Science Has All the Answers
    (D) The Earth Is Spherical
    (E) The Meaning of a Lunar Eclipse

15. The deduction that the Earth is round is based on all of the following except:

    (A) observation of eclipse
    (B) observation of sailors
    (C) observation of constellations
    (D) observations of philosophers
    (E) observations of astronauts

Passage 4

Line Each town is built in a given site and situation. If the surrounding terrain is mountainous, a town's accessibility and, therefore, much of its potential growth are
5 limited. Most of our large cities have grown on fairly flat land. Here they have ready accessibility as well as the important advantage of the low cost of developing and servicing flat land. Thus topographic
10 differences between towns, affecting accessibility and cost, can help some communities grow at the expense of others.

  Nevertheless, landforms are more often important in determining how (that is, in
15 what shape) towns and cities grow than why they grow. For example, Amsterdam, a city virtually built on water, and San Francisco, which is built on steep hills and surrounded on three sides by water,
20 continue to grow and prosper. Each of these has developed a unique character, partly because of its physical setting. In the early days of town building, when sites were chosen for defense (for example the island
25 location of Montreal), the landforms limited the towns' outward growth. Although these original limitations have ceased to affect any but the downtown areas, some modern communities must still adapt to their sites.
30 The outposts of western Newfoundland, which are limited to a narrow strip of land between the mountains and the ocean, provide one picturesque example.

  It has often been observed by conserva-
35 tionists that cities such as Vancouver, Toronto, and Los Angeles have grown at the expense of some of our best farmland. This phenomenon does not mean, however, that good soils are a prerequisite for urban
40 growth. Many of these cities were originally agricultural market towns and grew because farming prospered. Only when transportation improvements enabled long-distance shipping of food could the city afford to
45 "bite off the land that feeds it." The ease and low cost of building on flat land were also significant factors.

  An example of this conflict between urban and agricultural land uses is found in
50 the Niagara Peninsula fruit belt of Ontario. This district has both sandy, well-drained soils and a moderate climate suited for tender-fruit growing, a very rare combination in Canada. However, the soils and climate,
55 combined with its proximity to the Toronto-Hamilton urban industrial complex, make this region ideal for urban growth. As a result, some of the most valuable and irreplaceable farmland in southern Ontario
60 has been taken out of production and built on.

  A pleasant climate has played a significant role in the growth of some towns and cities. Many Florida cities have pros-
65 pered because of an almost year-round tourist trade. Arizona's warm dry winters attract many people, often with respiratory diseases, to Tucson, Phoenix, and other urban centers. The famous climate of
70 southern California has been one of the major factors in its rapid urbanization and general population growth. Much of the

California boom was also due to the fact that the film and airplane industries located there to take advantage of the sunshine and warm winters. Thus, some urban growth can best be explained by environmental factors.

16. The main idea of this passage is

    (A) important cities are built by water
    (B) a town should be built on flat land
    (C) Los Angeles grew at the expense of farmland
    (D) climate is crucial to urban growth
    (E) town growth is affected by environmental factors

17. From this passage one can assume that a "conservationist" is interested in

    (A) the creation of cities
    (B) determining the growth of cities
    (C) the best use of land
    (D) transportation of goods and services
    (E) the creation of parks

18. What is most unusual about the Niagara Peninsula?

    (A) it has mountains and desert
    (B) its warm, dry winters
    (C) its location to cultural centers
    (D) its sandy soil and moderate climate
    (E) its abundance of flat land

19. In building a town today which of the following can be inferred to be least important based on the passage?

    (A) accessibility
    (B) flat land
    (C) climate
    (D) transportation
    (E) defense

20. The best title of this passage is

    (A) Population Growth
    (B) Great Cities of the World
    (C) The Suburb Versus the Inner City
    (D) Vancouver, Toronto, and Los Angeles: Great Cities
    (E) Environment and Its Effects on City Growth

Passage 5

Line A single flow'r he sent me, since we met.
All tenderly his messenger he chose;
Deep-hearted, pure, with scented dew still wet—
One perfect rose.

5 I knew the language of the floweret;
"My fragile leaves," it said, "his heart enclose."
Love long has taken for his amulet
One perfect rose

Why is it no one ever sent me yet
10 One perfect limousine, do you suppose?
Ah no, it's always just my luck to get
One perfect rose.

21. What is the tone of the first two stanzas?

    (A) sarcastic
    (B) ironic
    (C) angry
    (D) irritation
    (E) serious

22. Which word changes the meaning of the poem?

    (A) tenderly
    (B) floweret
    (C) scented
    (D) language
    (E) limousine

23. The first two lines of stanza two use which of the following literary devices?

(A) alliteration
(B) realism
(C) personification
(D) dialect
(E) hyperbole

24. The best meaning for "scented" (line 3) is

(A) attractive to the sense of smell
(B) wet
(C) rose colored
(D) attractive to touch
(E) pure

25. What event is being described in the poem?

(A) a dream
(B) a mixed reaction to a gift
(C) a tale of miscommunication
(D) the story of all love affairs
(E) a tale of a flower-delivery service

Passage 6

Line   The major intellectual change of the eighteenth century was the widespread acceptance among educated people of the idea that reason could achieve solutions to
5   problems of many kinds, whether scientific or social. It is easy to see the origins of this attitude in the rationalism of Descartes, the scientific method of Francis Bacon, the achievements of Newton and other
10   seventeenth-century scientists, and the writing of John Locke on psychology.
        The Enlightenment thinkers applied Newtonian methods to problems in such areas as psychology and education, govern-
15   ment, religion, law codes, treatment of criminals, the slave trade, and economic life. They acted on the assumption that the universe operated according to natural law, similar to the all-embracing law of gravita-
20   tion, which Newton had discovered. They believed that individuals, using a rational approach, could discover these natural laws. As in science, this would not necessarily be easy, for these laws had been obscured by
25   an accumulation of centuries-old customs, prejudices, and superstitions, which did not accord with natural laws. However, with education and a clear-headed approach, people could rid themselves of their
30   superstitions and prejudices. Then reform in many areas of human relations could bring laws and customs into a harmonious relationship in a naturally orderly universe.
        What has just been said is a very broad
35   generalization. Not all thinkers in the eighteenth century had unquestioning faith in reason and natural law. There were limits to human reasoning powers, as some pointed out. Emotion, or feelings, also
40   played a great part in governing human behavior. These thinkers were not in the majority, but they were read and respected.
        The majority attitude described above was basically optimistic in the outlook
45   toward life. It saw people as moving forward, making progress toward a better life (and even toward perfection) through use of reason. Some writers felt that progress was almost inevitable under these
50   circumstances. Others thought it was necessary to work for progress along many different lines. Those who denied that the use of reason was the answer to all problems were viewed as skeptics. The faith in
55   progress caused eighteenth-century individuals to undertake many crusades for reform—the elimination of slavery, the end of religious intolerance, the reform of criminal codes, and the guarantee of permanent
60   world peace, for example.

26. Which of the following is not an element of "natural law?"

    (A) superstition
    (B) rationalism
    (C) the scientific method
    (D) reason
    (E) observation and discovery

27. Someone who believes in "natural law" would suggest humans should not be guided by

    (A) intellect
    (B) the wish for an orderly universe
    (C) a sense of optimism
    (D) science
    (E) emotions

28. The best meaning of "inevitable" in paragraph four is

    (A) rational
    (B) reasonable
    (C) necessary
    (D) impossible
    (E) improbable

29. The best title for this passage is

    (A) The Newtonian Age
    (B) Reason Versus Emotion
    (C) Descartes, Bacon, and Locke
    (D) Faith in Progress
    (E) Ideas in the Age of Enlightenment

30. An "enlightened" approach to government would yield all of the following except

    (A) a constitution
    (B) separation of powers
    (C) the rule of law
    (D) totalitarianism
    (E) democracy

Passage 7

Line   Although land and soil are generally thought to be renewable, several problems limit their renewability. One problem is that the areas with the most fertile soil are often the areas
5   with the greatest population density. Few crops are grown in mountain areas, deserts, or polar regions; few people live in those same areas. Most crops are grown on level land in moderate climates. Most people live
10   on fairly level land in moderate climates. In some areas of the world, the conflict between land for housing and land for crops is a critical problem. In Japan, about 85 percent of the land surface is mountainous.
15   The amount of land suitable for farming, is therefore, quite limited. The bulk of the Japanese population, including farmers, lives in the same 15 percent of the country. As a result, the conflict between using land for
20   housing and for farming is a critical one.
       A second problem in land and soil use is soil depletion. Crop plants use certain nutrients in the soil, as do natural grasses. When natural grasses die, the nutrients are
25   returned to the soil. When crops are harvested, however, the nutrients are removed from the soil. In time, the soil can become so lacking in nutrients that it will no longer grow a usable crop. The problem of
30   soil depletion can be managed through good farming practices. Fields can be left to rest. A crop can be allowed to return to the soil. Or, the kind of crop grown on a field can be changed from year to year. These practices
35   are not always followed, however, because they can be very expensive in the short term.
       A third problem in soil use is desertification. This occurs in areas where plant
40   cover has been removed by farming or by farm animals. When this happens, the bare soil can be easily removed by wind or rain, like the soil in a desert. The lost soil is

difficult to replace. The land has become
nonrenewable.
    Salinization is a problem in desert areas. With water, some desert soils are very fertile. However, water brought in to irrigate a desert contains minerals. The dry air of the desert causes water to evaporate rapidly. When this happens, minerals in the water, such as salt, are left behind on the soil surface. In time, the soil surface has so much mineral matter that crops can no longer be grown. Such soil is difficult to reclaim.

31. Which one of the following is not a problem in land and soil use?

    (A) salinization
    (B) desertification
    (C) soil depletion
    (D) natural grasses
    (E) population density

32. From the passage we can infer the following:

    (A) soil depletion is too difficult a problem to control
    (B) desertification only occurs in mountainous areas
    (C) in the future the Japanese may have difficulty growing enough crops for the people
    (D) soil depletion increases nutrients in the land
    (E) salinization is good for crops

33. The best meaning of salinization is:

    (A) an increase of water in the desert
    (B) detoxification
    (C) plant cover removed by farm animals
    (D) the loss of nutrients
    (E) an increase of minerals and soil due to loss of water

34. The best title for this passage is:

    (A) Problems in Land and Soil Use
    (B) Desertification and Salinization
    (C) Japan and Its Land
    (D) The Best Crops to Grow
    (E) How to Renew the Land

35. A solution to all the problems mentioned in the passage would be

    (A) good farming practices
    (B) developing a better import system
    (C) setting wind screens around farms
    (D) growing all food in moderate climates
    (E) changing one's diet

Passage 8

Whose woods these are I think I know
His house is in the village, though;
He will not see me stopping here
To watch his woods fill up with snow.

My little horse must think it queer
To stop without a farmhouse near
Between the woods and frozen lake
The darkest evening of the year.

He gives his harness bells a shake
To ask if there is some mistake.
The only other sound's the sweep
Of easy wind and downy flake.

The woods are lovely, dark and deep.
But I have promises to keep,
And miles to go before I sleep,
And miles to go before I sleep.

36. The speaker's horse "must think it queer to stop" because

    (A) the horse is used to completing its journey
    (B) it is late at night
    (C) it is too cold
    (D) they have run out of food
    (E) the horse is cold

37. What is the author's purpose in repeating the last line twice?

    (A) to reinforce the rhyme
    (B) to catch the attention of the horse
    (C) to show the contrast between the village and the farm
    (D) to add meaning to the word "sleep"
    (E) to wake the reader

38. The woods seem to have a special meaning for the speaker. Which is most likely?

    (A) He is interested in buying them.
    (B) He wants to build a new house there.
    (C) They seem to pull him in.
    (D) He is thinking about their owner in the village.
    (E) He is interested in farming.

39. Which literary technique is used to define the relationship between the speaker and the horse?

    (A) alliteration
    (B) rhyme
    (C) irony
    (D) exaggeration
    (E) contrast

40. The best meaning for "downy" in line 12 is

    (A) frozen
    (B) soft
    (C) clean
    (D) wind-swept
    (E) cold

SSAT PRACTICE TEST 2

QUANTITATIVE MATHEMATICS 2 **TIME: 25 MINUTES** **25 QUESTIONS**

Directions: Following each problem in this section, there are five suggested answers. Work each problem in your head or in the space provided (there will be space for scratchwork in your test booklet). Then look at the five suggested answers and decide which is best.

1. What is .03 expressed as a percent?

   (A) 30%
   (B) 3%
   (C) .3%
   (D) .03%
   (E) .003%

2. What is 72 expressed as the product of prime factors?

   (A) (2)(3)
   (B) (2)(3)(12)
   (C) (2)(2)(2)(3)(3)
   (D) (8)(9)
   (E) (6)(6)(2)

3. Fred invested $4,000 at a simple interest rate of 5.75%. What is the total value of his investment after one year?

   (A) $200
   (B) $230
   (C) $4,200
   (D) $4,230
   (E) $4,400

4. The area of a circle is the same as the area of a square whose side is 5 centimeters. The radius of the circle is closest to:

   (A) 25 centimeters
   (B) 3 centimeters
   (C) 3 square centimeters
   (D) 8 centimeters
   (E) 16 centimeters

5. Solve for x: $7x - 3 = 4x + 6$

   (A) 3
   (B) -1
   (C) 4
   (D) 2
   (E) -4

6. The length of a side of a square is represented by $x + 2$, and the length of a side of an equilateral triangle by $2x$. If the square and the equilateral triangle have equal perimeters, find x.

   (A) 24
   (B) 16
   (C) 12
   (D) 8
   (E) 4

7. A bag has five green marbles and four blue marbles. If one marble is drawn at random, what is the possibility that it is *not* green?

   (A) $\frac{1}{9}$
   (B) $\frac{4}{9}$
   (C) $\frac{5}{9}$
   (D) $\frac{5}{20}$
   (E) $\frac{4}{20}$

8. The expression $\sqrt{162}$ is equivalent to:

   (A) $4\sqrt{2}$
   (B) $4 + \sqrt{2}$
   (C) $9\sqrt{2}$
   (D) $3\sqrt{2}$
   (E) $9 + \sqrt{2}$

9.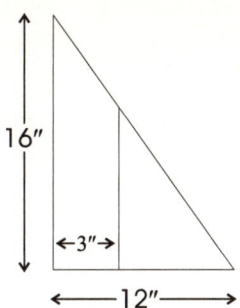

In the accompanying figure, the legs of a right triangle are 16 inches and 12 inches. Find the number of inches in the length of the line segment parallel to the 16-inch side and 3 inches from it.

(A) 16
(B) 12
(C) 9
(D) 15
(E) 10

10. On a map, 2 inches represents 15 miles. How many miles would 5 inches represent?

(A) 6
(B) 8
(C) 30
(D) $37\frac{1}{2}$
(E) 75

11.

Three congruent squares are arranged in a row. If the perimeter of ABCD is 80, the area of ABCD is:

(A) 240
(B) 320
(C) 640
(D) 300
(E) 160

12. Express as a ratio in simplest form: 5 feet to 3 inches

(A) $\frac{5}{3}$
(B) $\frac{3}{5}$
(C) $\frac{60}{3}$
(D) $\frac{1}{20}$
(E) 20

13. What is the slope of the line that passes through the point (2,6) and the point (7, −7)?

(A) $-\frac{13}{5}$
(B) $\frac{5}{13}$
(C) $-\frac{1}{5}$
(D) $\frac{13}{5}$
(E) $\frac{21}{7}$

14. 423,252 × 835,234 =

(A) 353,534,359,987
(B) 983,414,460,968
(C) 989,353,414,426
(D) 353,514,425,972
(E) 353,514,460,968

15. If points A, B, C, and D are collinear, and C is the midpoint of AB, and B is the midpoint of AD, and the length of AD is 24, what is the length of CD?

(A) 12
(B) 24
(C) 18
(D) 6
(E) It cannot be determined.

16. If $x = 4$ on the graph of $y = -5x + 4$, what does y equal?

    (A) -1
    (B) 5
    (C) -5
    (D) 16
    (E) -16

17. What is the graph of the inequality $6 < x \leq 9$?

    (A)
    (B)
    (C)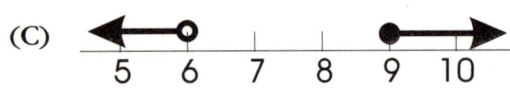
    (D)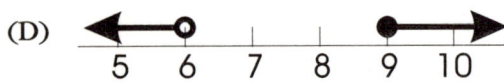
    (E)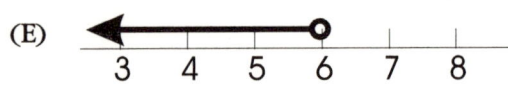

18. $3x^5$ divided by $4x^7$ is

    (A) $7x^{12}$
    (B) $12x^{12}$
    (C) $\dfrac{3}{4x^2}$
    (D) $12x^{35}$
    (E) $\dfrac{4x^2}{3}$

19. .075 expressed as a percent is

    (A) 75%
    (B) 7.5%
    (C) .75%
    (D) .075%
    (E) 8%

20. A scale model of a cube has sides that are one-fortieth of the length of the original. If the scale model required three gallons of paint to coat, how much paint is required to coat the original with the same thickness of paint?

    (A) $\dfrac{40}{3}$ gallons
    (B) 7,280 gallons
    (C) 4,800 gallons
    (D) 240 gallons
    (E) 120 gallons

21. Dinner (plus tax and tip) cost $93.60. The tax rate is 5% and Mr. Simmons left a 15% tip. Both tax and tip are calculated on the base amount of the check. What was the base amount of Mr. Simmons' bill?

    (A) $78.00
    (B) $113.32
    (C) $77.41
    (D) $112.00
    (E) $81.30

22. What is the area of a square whose diagonal is 6?

(A) 36
(B) 24
(C) 18
(D) 12
(E) $6\sqrt{2}$

23. Which fraction lies between $\frac{2}{3}$ and $\frac{4}{5}$?

(A) $\frac{5}{6}$
(B) $\frac{17}{20}$
(C) $\frac{7}{10}$
(D) $\frac{13}{15}$
(E) $\frac{9}{10}$

24. The circumference of a circle whose diameter is 7 inches is approximately

(A) 22 inches
(B) 28 inches
(C) 38 inches
(D) 154 inches
(E) 14 inches

25.

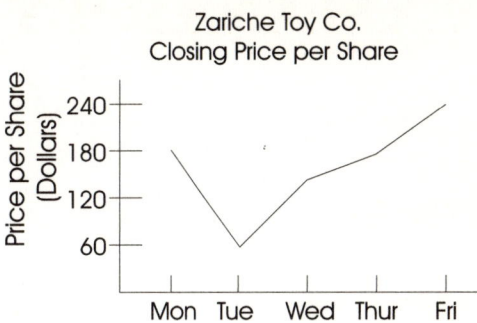

Josie bought 16 shares of Zariche stock at the closing price Monday and sold them at the closing price on Friday. What was Josie's profit on this investment?

(A) $60
(B) $96
(C) $600
(D) $960
(E) None of these

EXPLANATORY ANSWERS TO THE SSAT PRACTICE TEST 2

VERBAL

1. The correct answer is (C).
2. The correct answer is (D).
3. The correct answer is (A).
4. The correct answer is (C).
5. The correct answer is (B).
6. The correct answer is (D).
7. The correct answer is (E).
8. The correct answer is (A).
9. The correct answer is (A).
10. The correct answer is (D).
11. The correct answer is (D).
12. The correct answer is (A).
13. The correct answer is (B).
14. The correct answer is (D).
15. The correct answer is (C).
16. The correct answer is (B).
17. The correct answer is (C).
18. The correct answer is (A).
19. The correct answer is (E).
20. The correct answer is (C).
21. The correct answer is (B).
22. The correct answer is (C).
23. The correct answer is (E).
24. The correct answer is (A).
25. The correct answer is (D).
26. The correct answer is (E).
27. The correct answer is (C).

28. The correct answer is (B).

29. The correct answer is (B).

30. The correct answer is (E).

31. The correct answer is (A). One of the characteristics of a *mountain* is its *height*. One of the characteristics of a *trench* is its *depth*. Answer (B) will not work. While shade is often a characteristic of a tree it is not a persistent characteristic, meaning that a tree does not always give shade. In addition, a mountain possesses height, but a tree GIVES shade. Answer (C) is incorrect: a characteristic of age is not always weight. The relationship is not the same as height and mountain. Answer (D) is incorrect: while we often associate speed with a highway, speed is NOT a characteristic of the highway. Answer (E) is incorrect: while a mineral comes from a mine, it is not a characteristic of the mine. It is a product of the mine. The relationship is not the same as height and mountain.

32. The correct answer is (A). Someone who is *oblivious* lacks *awareness*. The relationship is word to antonym or opposites. Answer (B) is incorrect. The relationship here is synonyms. One who is serene is composed. Answer (C) is incorrect. Again, the relationship is synonyms. One who is erudite possesses knowledge. Answer (D) is incorrect: one who is adroit possesses skill. The relationship is synonymous. Answer (E) is incorrect: the relationship is that of synonyms. One who is invigorated possesses energy.

33. The correct answer is (D). A *cynosure* functions as a *magnet*. A cynosure is the center of attention, or a magnet: a magnet attracts attention. The relationship is object to its function. A *bellwether* is a *barometer*. Answer (A) is incorrect: a proselyte does not function as a spark plug. Answer (B) is incorrect: a panhandler does not kill. Answer (C) is incorrect: an embezzler does not abduct. Answer (E) is incorrect: a morass (swamp) does not function as a catalyst (leavening).

34. The correct answer is (D). The relationship is word and derived form. The word "action" derives from the word "act." Answer (A) is incorrect: thermometer (temperature measure) does not derive from the word therapy. There is no relationship. Answer (B) is incorrect: the relationship is antonyms or opposites. Oblivion means forgotten and obvious means apparent. The relationship is different. Answer (C) is incorrect: Liturgy (ritual) does not provide the root for the word literature, which means a body of work. Answer (E) is incorrect: bowl (goblet) does not form the root for bowdlerize, which means to modify. There is no relationship.

35. The correct answer is (B). The relationship is object to its function. One who is *bibulous* consumes more *drink* than is advisable. Answer (B) is the correct answer because one who is *gluttonous* consumes more *food* than is advisable. Answer (A) is incorrect: rapacious (taken by force) has no relationship to clothing. Answer (C) is incorrect: one who is altruistic (concerned for the welfare of others) would not have more money than was advisable. The relationship is not the same. Answer (D) is incorrect. A vegetarian would not consume more meat than advisable. Answer (E) is incorrect: controversy and reconcile have the relationship of opposites.

36. The correct answer is (A). *Venison* is the meat of a *deer*. The relationship is part to whole. *Veal* is the meat of a *calf*. Answers (B), (C), (D), and (E) are incorrect because although they are animals from which we get meat, we do not get veal from any of them.

37. The correct answer is (D). *Cursory* and *superficial* are both adjectives and are synonyms—they have same meaning. (A), (B), and (C) are incorrect because the answers, while both adjectives, are antonyms—they have opposite meanings. Answer (E) is incorrect because the relationship is cause to effect.

38. The correct answer is (C). *Bacchus* is the god of *wine; Diana* is the goddess of the *hunt.* This is a worker and creation relationship. Answer (A) is incorrect because both Orpheus and Eurydice are mythological gods. Answers (B) and (D) are incorrect because the relationship is unclear. Answer (E) is incorrect because the relationship is item to category.

39. The correct answer is (C). *Bald* and *hairy* are antonyms. *Anemic* and *robust* are antonyms. Answers (A) and (E) are incorrect because the words are synonyms. Answers (B) and (D) are incorrect because the words are not related specifically.

40. The correct answer is (D). *Gold* was important to *Midas; wisdom* was important to *Athena.* The relationship is worker and creation. Answers (A) and (C) are incorrect because the relationship is item to category. Answer (B) is incorrect because the relationship is synonymous. Answer (E) is incorrect because the relationship is type to characteristic.

41. The correct answer is (D). A *philanthropist* is very *generous*. A *teacher* is usually very *educated*. The relationship is type to characteristic. Answer (A) is incorrect because the relationship is worker to workplace, a dentist works on teeth. Answer (B) is incorrect because the words are antonyms. Answer (C) is incorrect because the relationship is worker and workplace, a rider rides on a horse. Answer (E) is incorrect because the words are synonyms.

42. The correct answer is (D). Something fresh, like water, can be frozen. In this case, frozen water makes ice cubes. The relationship is cause and effect. Answer (A) is incorrect because there is no relationship. Answers (B) and (E) are incorrect because the relationship is type to characteristic. A wave has a crest: a cloud may be white. Answer (C) is incorrect because there is no specific relationship.

43. The correct answer is (D). The Nazis persecuted many during the Nuremburg trials, the place of prosecution. The relationship is object to its function. Answer (A) is incorrect because the judge and jury work together. Answer (B) is incorrect because the relationship is worker to workplace: a guard works in a prison. Answer (C) is incorrect because the relationship is type to characteristic. Marx was a communist. Answer (E) is incorrect because it is cause to effect. A gun causes death.

44. The correct answer is (C). A wrongdoing connected with politics is bribery as cheating is a wrongdoing connected with examinations. The relationship is type to characteristic. Answers (A) and (B) are incorrect because the relationship is object to function: one parks at a meter; one may use contracts in a business. Answer (D) is incorrect because it is time sequence. Birds nest then leave. Answer (E) is incorrect because the relationship is cause and effect: a painting earns a commission.

45. The correct answer is (C). A fraud, a cheater, an impostor, and an impersonator refer to people who are fakes. The relationship is synonymous. Answers (A), (B), and (D) are incorrect because while similar in many ways, the words are not synonyms. Answer (E) is incorrect because the words are antonyms.

46. The correct answer is (D). *Bacon* is sold by the *pound*; *eggs* are sold by the *dozen*. The relationship is part to whole. Answers (A) and (B) are incorrect because the relationship is item to category: a gun is made of lead; a dime is made of silver. Answer (C) is incorrect because the relationship is worker and workplace: a chandelier is located in the ceiling. Answer (E) is incorrect because the relationship is worker to creation. A puppet show is the work of the puppet maker.

47. The correct answer is (D). A horn is blown; a harp is plucked to make music. Answer (A) is incorrect because anarchy and democracy are antonyms. Answer (B) is incorrect because while a game is played, there is no connection with music. Answer (C) is incorrect because reprove and denounce are synonyms. Answer (E) is incorrect because a pocket is located within pants, making the relationship part to whole.

48. The correct answer is (D). A *limousine* is a luxurious *car* as a *mansion* is a luxurious *house*. The relationship is item to category. Answer (A) is incorrect because the relationship, while item to category, is not the same relationship. House and cave indicate lack of luxury. Answer (B) is incorrect because the relationship is modes of transportation. Answer (C) is incorrect because the relationship is object to material, an animal is covered with fur. Answer (E) is incorrect: stone and pebble are synonyms.

49. The correct answer is (C). Warts, moles, mildew, and weeds are all unwanted growths. This is a part to whole relationship.

50. The correct answer is (D). A *bass* sings in a *low* register: a *soprano* sings in a *high* register. The words are antonyms. Answer (A) is incorrect because art and music are forms of fine arts; they are a type of synonym. Answer (B) is incorrect: while light and shading are similar, they are not synonyms. Answer (C) is incorrect: while govern and dictate are both forms of government, they are not synonymous. Answer (E) is incorrect because a chorus is made up of many people, while a solo is performed by only one.

51. The correct answer is (C). We *braid hair* as we *wind* a *clock*. To braid and to wind are actions applied to objects.

52. The correct answer is (B). *Blades* make up *grass* as *grains* make up *sand*. The relationship is that of part to whole. Answers (A), (D), and (E) are incorrect because the relationship is type to characteristic. Answer (C) has no obvious relationship other than rods may be made of metal.

53. The correct answer is (C). An *athlete* needs *training* to succeed: a *student* needs *studying* to succeed. The relationship is object to its function. Answer (A) is incorrect because the relationship is worker and creation. Answer (B) is incorrect because the relationship is worker to workplace. Answers (D) and (E) are incorrect because the relationship is that of antonyms.

54. The correct answer is (D). A *novel* is written by an *author*. An *opera* is written by a *composer*. The relationship is worker and creation. Answers (A) and (C) are incorrect because they show cause to effect. Answer (B) is incorrect because the relationship is that of synonyms. Answer (E) is incorrect because the relationship is part to whole. Several songs make up a tape.

55. The correct answer is (C). A *miser* desires *gold* as a *general* desires *victories.* The relationship is cause to effect. Answer (A) is incorrect because the relationship is item to category. Answer (B) is incorrect because it is worker and creation. Answer (D) is incorrect because it is worker to workplace. Answer (E) is incorrect because the relationship is that of synonyms.

56. The correct answer is (E). A *centaur* is a mythological *horse.* A *mermaid* is a mythological *fish.* The relationship is that of synonyms. Answer (A) is incorrect because it is the relationship of worker and creation. Answers (B) and (D) are incorrect because they are both item to category in relationship. Answer (C) is incorrect because there is no relationship.

57. The correct answer is (B). A *foot* moves against a *pedal* as a *bat* hits against a *ball.* The relationship is action to object. Answers (A) and (C) are incorrect because the relationship is worker and workplace. Answers (D) and (E) are incorrect because the relationship is object to material.

58. The correct answer is (C). We *start* a car with the *ignition;* we *stop* a car with the *brake.* The relationship is action to object. Answers (A) and (B) are incorrect since the relationship is object to its function. Answers (D) and (E) are incorrect because the relationship is object to its material. A tire needs air, a tank needs gas.

59. The correct answer is (E). To *push* is an extreme *touch;* to *gulp* is an extreme *sip.* All four words are verbs. The relationship is type to characteristic. Answer (A) is incorrect. While the relationship is similar, the item to category relationship would better fit: both items are drinks. However, the words are nouns and therefore not a true analogy. Answer (B) is incorrect. The words are synonyms. Answer (C) is incorrect; one uses a glass to drink, therefore the relationship is item to function. Answer (D) is incorrect because the words are antonyms.

60. The correct answer is (D). *Bananas* are collected by the *bunch; lettuce* is collected by the *head.* The relationship is type to characteristic. Answer (A) is incorrect because the words are synonyms. Answer (B) is incorrect because the words are antonyms. Answer (C) is incorrect because the relationship is item to category—both words represent members of the fowl family. Answer (E) is incorrect because it is object to function: a surgeon performs an operation.

SSAT PRACTICE TEST 2

QUANTITATIVE MATHEMATICS 1

1. The correct answer is (D).

   Factor out each of the given possibilities.

   The factors of 10 are 2×5.

   The factors of 45 are $3 \times 3 \times 5$.

   The factors of 50 are $2 \times 5 \times 5$.

   The factors of 60 are $2 \times 2 \times 3 \times 5$.

   The factors of 90 are $2 \times 3 \times 3 \times 5$.

   Since $4 = 2 \times 2$, 60 has factors of 4 and 5.

2. The correct answer is (A). Translate the sentence into a mathematical equation, then solve.

$$x - 4 = \frac{2}{3}x$$

$$x - \frac{2}{3}x = 4$$

$$\frac{1}{3}x = 4$$

$$x = 4\left(\frac{3}{1}\right) = 12$$

3. The correct answer is (B).

$$\text{score} = \frac{\# \text{ correct}}{\# \text{ questions}}; 84\% = \frac{84}{100} = .84$$

$$.84 = \frac{n}{25}$$

$$n = .84 \times 25 = 21$$

4. The correct answer is (C). Rearrange the fractions to make it easier to solve by combining fractions with like denominators.

$$\frac{1}{2} - \frac{1}{2} + \frac{2}{3} - \frac{1}{3} - \frac{1}{3} + \frac{3}{4} + \frac{1}{4}$$

The first five fractions cancel each other out, leaving

$$\frac{3}{4} + \frac{1}{4} = \frac{4}{4} = 1.$$

Peterson's SSAT/ISEE Success

EXPLANATORY ANSWERS TO THE SSAT PRACTICE TEST 2

5. **The correct answer is (C).** The perimeter of a square is $4s$. With side length $= 4$, the perimeter is $4(4) = 16$.

    The perimeter of a rectangle is $2L + 2W$. With length $= 6$ and width $= 4$, the perimeter is $2(6) + 2(4) = 12 + 8 = 20$.

    The difference between the perimeters is $20 - 16 = 4$.

6. **The correct answer is (A).**

    Round $19.95 to $20.00 and find 40% of 20.

    $$40\% = \frac{40}{100} = .4$$

    $.4 \times 20 = 8$

7. **The correct answer is (B).** 2 students make up one-fifth of a class.

    Translating this into a mathematical equation, you get $\frac{1}{5}c = 2$.

    $$c = 2\left(\frac{5}{1}\right) = 10$$

8. **The correct answer is (B).**

    Let d represent Don's age now and $d + 5$ represent Don's age 5 years from now.

    Let p represent Peter's age now and $p + 5$ represent Peter's age 5 years from now.

    Set up mathematical equations for the problem.

    $$d = p + 5$$
    $$d + 5 = 2p$$

    Substitute the value of d in the first equation into the second equation to find p.

    $$(p + 5) + 5 = 2p$$
    $$p + 10 = 2p$$
    $$p = 10$$

9. The correct answer is (B). Set up a ratio for this problem and solve:

   p represents the number of pieces of candy purchased with c cents $\left(\dfrac{p}{c}\right)$.

   20 pieces of candy can be purchased for x cents $\left(\dfrac{20}{x}\right)$. So,

   $$\dfrac{p}{c} = \dfrac{20}{x}$$

   $px = 20c$ (using cross-multiplication)

   $$\dfrac{20c}{p} = x$$

10. The correct answer is (C).

    $4,500,000 is t times greater than $750,000.

    $4,500,000 = 750,000t$

    $$t = \dfrac{4,500,000}{750,000} = 6$$

11. The correct answer is (B).

    This is a 45-45-90 triangle. Since this is true, the base is also 5 units long.

    By the Pythagorean theorem, $v^2 = 5^2 + 5^2 = 25 + 25 = 50$.

12. The correct answer is (C).

    Let o represent the amount of oats eaten, and g the amount of grass eaten.

    Since twice as many pounds of oats are eaten as grass, $o = 2g$.

    $o + g = 30$

    Substituting the value for o into $o + g = 30$ gives $2g + g = 30$.

    So, $3g = 30$, and $g = 10$.

13. The correct answer is (E).

    $3x - 9 = 18$
    $3x = 27$
    $x = 9$
    $9 \div 9 = 1$

14. The correct answer is (D). There are 180° in a triangle and 360° in a rectangle (made up of four 90° angles).

    The difference is 360° − 180° = 180°.

    One-half of 180° is 90°.

15. **The correct answer is (E).**

    Let g represent the number of gorillas and let t represent the number of tigers.

    If there are 4 times as many gorillas as tigers, then $g = 4t$.

    If there are 4 more tigers than zebras, then $t = z + 4$.

    To find the number of gorillas in terms of zebras, substitute the first equation into the second.

    Then, $g = 4(z + 4) = 4z + 16$.

16. **The correct answer is (D).** In four days, a cat sleeps $4\left(\frac{3}{4}\right) = 3$ full days.

17. **The correct answer is (A).** To determine if a number is divisible by 9, the sum of the digits in that number will equal 9. The sum of the digits in 2,042 is $2 + 0 + 4 + 2 = 8$. By adding 1 to this number, the sum of the digits will equal 9 and therefore be divisible by 9.

18. **The correct answer is (D).**

    4 girls make 2 projects each for a subtotal of $4 \times 2 = 8$.

    5 boys make 3 projects each for a subtotal of $5 \times 3 = 15$.

    The total number of projects made is $8 + 15 = 23$.

19. **The correct answer is (E).**

    The area of the rectangle is $l \times w = 8 \times 3 = 24$.

    The area of the triangle is $\frac{1}{2}bh = \frac{1}{2}6h$.

    Since the areas are equal, set the equations equal to each other to determine the height of the triangle.

    $$\frac{1}{2}6h = 24$$
    $$3h = 24$$
    $$h = 8$$

20. **The correct answer is (D).** Substitute 10 for r and 2 for s.

    $(10 \times 2) - (10 + 2) = 20 - 12 = 8$

21. The correct answer is (D).

$$(4 \clubsuit 3) = \frac{30}{L}$$
$$(4 \clubsuit 3) = (4 \times 3) - (4 + 3) = 12 - 7 = 5$$
$$5 = \frac{30}{L}$$
$$L = \frac{30}{5} = 6$$

22. The correct answer is (E). To score an average of 91 on 4 exams, the total of the 4 exams added together must be $91 \times 4 = 364$. On her first 3 exams, Jesse has scored a total of $88 + 86 + 90 = 264$. Therefore, she needs 100 points on her last exam.

23. The correct answer is (A).

$$3x - 8 = 10x - 13$$
$$3x = 10x - 5$$
$$-7x = -5$$
$$x = \frac{-5}{-7} = \frac{5}{7}$$

24. The correct answer is (C). 15% expressed as a decimal is .15, so you can either calculate the discount $(.15)(75) = 11.25$ and subtract this from the original price of $75, getting $63.75, or you can calculate the final price directly. It will be 85% of the original price ($100\% - 15\% = 85\%$), $(.85)(75) = 63.75$.

25. The correct answer is (C).

Use the formula

$$A = \frac{1}{2}bh$$
$$75 = \frac{1}{2}(15)h$$
$$\frac{75}{7.5} = \frac{7.5h}{7.5}$$
$$10 \text{ inches} = h$$

READING COMPREHENSION

Passage 1

1. The correct answer is (E). France is mentioned in the passage but not in connection with the emergence of the printing press. (A) is tricky since the Rhineland is part of Germany. (B), (C), and (D) are all clearly mentioned in the passage.

2. The correct answer is (A). They believed in science—stated clearly in the first paragraph. (B), (C), (D), and (E) are listed as beliefs in the same paragraph.

3. The correct answer is (D). Movable type allowed multiple copies to be made. (B) and (E) are close—without them you could not have printing but, by themselves, large amounts of books could not be made. (A) and (C) are inappropriate.

4. The correct answer is (A). (B) is an antonym, which is often used in the vocabulary question. (D) and (E) are both close to (A) in meaning but are still incorrect. (C) is used to trick the student who read half the word or just rushed through this too quickly.

5. The correct answer is (B), the main idea of the passage. (A) is only a reference to the first paragraph. (C) is close but not enough stress is placed on his role to warrant the title. (D) is also close but is too specific. (E) is inappropriate.

Passage 2

6. The correct answer is (D), since these fruits are "set in a window." (A) is a trick answer; these fruits could win a prize at a fair. (B) is where the fruits come from, grown, perhaps, in (E). The experience makes him "dream" (C) but it was quite real.

7. The correct answer is (C). The poet's past is brought back to life for him. (A) is the result of the first three lines which could win at (B), but they are not an image of lines 7 and 8. (D) and (E) are inappropriate.

8. The correct answer is (B); in his new town the poet has lost his tropical past and it grieves him. We, perhaps, can infer (D), but the poem does not support this fully. (A), (C), and (E) are all inappropriate.

9. The correct answer is (D), referring to the babbling sounds water can make. (E) is a trick answer; the birds can be in the trees. (A) and (C) can both "sing" but are inappropriate, as is (B).

10. The correct answer is (D), the poet misses his life in the tropics. There is a touch of (E), which is overwhelmed by the wistful-

SSAT PRACTICE TEST 2

ness of the last 4 lines. (A), (B), and (C) are inappropriate (although they are words you should know).

Passage 3

11. The correct answer is (C). (D) is an example of the definition; therefore, it is not the same as the definition. (A) and (B) describe groupings which are not constellations. (E) refers to one star, not a group of stars.

12. The correct answer is (B). This tests your ability to read for detail. (A) and (C) attempt to confuse the reader by giving the opposite seemingly logical but incorrect responses. (D) refers to a constellation mentioned in the passage which has little to do with the North Star. (E) is not mentioned in the passage.

13. The correct answer is (E). This tests your ability to figure out what is suggested by a passage. (A) is the opposite, and though (B) and (D) are correct ideas, they are not proved by the passage. (C) misstates a fact.

14. The correct answer is (D). (A) and (B) mentioned details from the passage, but they do not tell the whole story. (C) is a false inference, and (E) refers to a possible proof of (D) which is just one of three proofs in the passage.

15. The correct answer is (D). (A), (B), (C), and (E) are all details mentioned in the passage. (D) may be true, but the passage deals only with scientific concepts.

Passage 4

16. The correct answer is (E), a general abstraction which covers the main points of the passage. (A) and (C) are factual examples presented in the passage and thus do not deserve to be called the main ideas. (B) and (D) can be inferred from the passage, but, again, these facts are not large enough to cover the whole passage.

17. The correct answer is (C), which covers the way cities use their resources. (B) is very close and is one part of a conservationist's view, as is (E). (A) and (D) are concepts interesting to conservationists but they are not as central or as broad as (C).

18. The correct answer is (D), a detail clearly stated in the fourth paragraph. (B) and (E) are facts in the passage unconnected to the question, and (A) and (C) are inappropriate.

19. The correct answer is (E). This factor was most important in the "early days of town building", and other factors mentioned above have taken precedence.

Peterson's SSAT/ISEE Success

20. The correct answer is (E). Every paragraph details examples of how environment affects the growth of cities. (A) is a general statement which affects city growth, but it is not the focus of this passage. (D) mentions cities in the passage but this detail does not make it worthy of becoming the title.

Passage 5

21. The correct answer is (E). You have to hear the author's voice to figure out his or her attitude. Given stanza three, one might think (B) is possible. (A), (C), and (D) cannot be found in the poem.

22. The correct answer is (E). "Limousine" changes the poem from serious to amusing. (A), (B), and (C) are words which signify love and its meaning, while (D) refers to what the flower means.

23. The correct answer is (C); the author has the rose speak. This is clearly not an example of (B). (E), hyperbole (which means exaggeration), is the closest to the correct answer. (A) and (D) are incorrect, but well worth looking up.

24. The correct answer is (A); the dew receives its smell from the rose. The dew may be rose-colored but that is not the meaning of "scented." (B), (D), and (E) are all inappropriate.

25. The correct answer is (B). One has to infer the positive response in lines 1–8 as a contrast to the wry response of lines 9–12. (C) is close, but the receiver of the rose just has a different interpretation of what a rose can mean. (A) is off base and (D) and (E) are inappropriate.

Passage 6

26. The correct answer is (A). The concept of natural law is a reaction to superstition and contains aspects of (B), (C), (D), and (E).

27. The correct answer is (E). If you believe in natural law emotions become secondary guides to truth. All the other responses are essential elements of the Age of Enlightenment discussed in the passage.

28. The correct answer is (C), which is closest to the exact meaning of inevitable (something must occur). The other words all "fit" in the sentence, but the larger context yields the best definition.

29. The correct answer is (E). This title is broad enough to cover all the subjects mentioned in the passage. (A), (B), (C), and (D) are all aspects covered in the material, but they are not large enough to cover the concepts mentioned above.

30. The correct answer is (D). You must deduce from the Enlightenment concepts mentioned in the passage (rationalism, natural law, reason) that "totalitarianism" is least compatible. All the other answers can be defended by the ideas presented in the passage.

Passage 7

31. The correct answer is (D); natural grasses help maintain land and soil use. The rest are examples of problems detailed in the passage.

32. The correct answer is (C), given the fact that only 10% of land in Japan is arable. (A) is contradicted by the facts as are (D) and (E). (B) is incorrect even though deserts could occur at high elevations.

33. The correct answer is (E), given in the last paragraph. (A), (C), and (D) are definitions of other terms in the passage. (B) sounds like the word, but is far from defining it.

34. The correct answer is (A) since each paragraph deals with a specific issue of land and soil use. (B) is close, but soil depletion is not mentioned. (C) deals with the lead paragraph only. (D) and (E) refer to topics connected to the passage but not mentioned here.

35. The correct answer is (A), which is mentioned in the second paragraph and implied in the other paragraphs. (B) sounds good but is only a stopgap measure. (C) may be helpful but is only worthwhile on a small scale. (D) sounds correct but doesn't refer to how the food is grown. (E) does not work at all.

Passage 8

36. The correct answer is (A) through inference. To complete its journey is to return or go to a farmhouse. (B) and (C) refer to factual elements of the poem, but neither provides compelling reasons for the horse to "think it queer." (D) is not supported by the poem, and neither is (E).

37. The correct answer is (D); "sleep" is not only rest but eternal rest in this context. (A) is a good answer about the poem's form but not nearly as strong as (D). (B), (C), and (E) are not supported by the poem.

38. The correct answer is (C). The woods seem to pull him in because of their beauty and perhaps for a deeper, undisclosed reason. Even though he mentions the owner, (A) and (D) are not appropriate. (B) and (E) are not supported by the poem.

39. The correct answer is (E). This best explains the difference between the horse and speaker. (D) is the closest of the others but it is used to point out the essential contrast. (A), (B), and (C) are literary terms one should know, but they do not answer the question properly.

40. The correct answer is (B); downy refers to the soft feathers of a swan, for example. (D) is closest since the flakes are "wind-swept" but this does not refer to the feel of the flakes. (A), (C), and (E) are elements in the poem but do not convey the meaning of downy.

QUANTITATIVE MATHEMATICS 2

1. The correct answer is (B). To convert a decimal to a percent, multiply the decimal by 100.

    $.03 \times 100 = 3.00 = 3\%$

2. The correct answer is (C). A prime number is a number that is divisible by itself and by 1. Hence, $72 = 8 \times 9 = 2 \times 2 \times 2 \times 3 \times 3 \rightarrow 2$ and 3 are prime numbers

3. The correct answer is (D).

    First find the amount of interest.

    $I = P \times R \times T$
    $= \$4{,}000 \times .0575 \times 1 = \$230$

    Add the amount of interest to the original amount to get the total amount after one year.

4. The correct answer is (B).

    First find the area of the square.

    $A = s^2$
    $= 5^2 = 25$ sq. cm.

    Then, using the formula,

    $A = \pi r^2$
    $25 \approx (3.14) r^2$
    $7.96 \approx r^2$
    $\sqrt{7.96} \approx r$
    $2.8 \text{ cm} \approx r$

Peterson's: www.petersons.com

5. The correct answer is (A).

    Combine like terms by additive inverse:

    $7x - 3 = 4x + 6$
    $\underline{-4x + 3 = -4x + 3}$
    $3x = 9$

    Divide 9 by 3.

    $x = 3$

6. The correct answer is (E).

    The perimeter of the square = $4s$.

    $P = 4s = 4(x + 2) = 4x + 8$

    The perimeter of the equilateral triangle is $3s$.

    $P = 3s = 3(2)x = 6x$
    $4x + 8 = 6x$
    $8 = 2x$
    $4 = x$

7. The correct answer is (B). There are 4 marbles that are not green out of a total of 9 marbles, so $\frac{4}{9}$.

8. The correct answer is (C).

    Find two factors of 162, one of which is a perfect square.

    $\sqrt{162} = \sqrt{81 \times 2}$
    $= \sqrt{81}\sqrt{2}$ (reduce perfect square)
    $\sqrt{81} = 9$
    $= 9\sqrt{2}$

9. The correct answer is (B).

    If a line is parallel to one side of a triangle and intersects the other two sides, the line divides those sides proportionately.

    $\frac{16}{12} = \frac{x}{9}$

    $12x = (16)(9)$
    $12x = 144$ and $x = 12$

10. The correct answer is (D).

    This problem can very easily be solved using a proportion.

    $$\frac{2 \text{ inches}}{15 \text{ miles}} = \frac{5 \text{ inches}}{x \text{ miles}}$$

    After cross-multiplication, this proportion becomes

    $2x = 75$

    $x = 37\frac{1}{2}$

11. The correct answer is (D). Count all the exterior sides of *ABCD*; 8 sides make up the perimeter, which is 80. So, 1 side = 10.

    area of rectangle = (length) × (width)
    length (*DC*) = 30
    width (*AD*) = 10
    Area = (30)(10) = 300

12. The correct answer is (E). Convert all measurements to the same units, such as inches. 5 feet is 60 inches. We now have the ratio 60 inches to 3 inches, expressed as $\frac{60}{3}$, and this reduces to $\frac{20}{1}$, or 20.

    The ratio $\frac{60}{3}$, while correct, is not in lowest form.

13. The correct answer is (A). Slope is rise over run. Rise is the change in *y* coordinate, run is the change in *x* coordinate. Be sure you use the same point as the "first" point in both cases, or the algebraic sign will be wrong!

    $$\frac{rise}{run} = \frac{6-(-7)}{2-7} = \frac{13}{-5} = -\frac{13}{5}$$

14. The correct answer is (E). No tedious multiplying is necessary. The last digit of each factor determines what the last digit of the product is; in this case it must be 8. There are only two answers that end in 8. A quick approximate multiplication (400,000 × 800,000) yields 320,000,000,000, ruling out answer (B).

15. The correct answer is (C).

    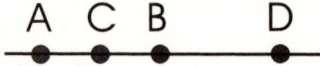

    C is the midpoint of *AB*, so *AC* and *CB* are congruent and each is equal to half the measure of *AB*. *B* is the midpoint of *AD* so *AB* and *BD* are congruent. This makes *AC* equal to one-fourth the measure of *AD*.

    If *AD* is 24, then *AC* is 6, *CB* is 6, and *BD* is 12.

    CD is 6 + 12 = 18.

16. The correct answer is (E).

    $y = -5x + 4$

    $y = -5(4) + 4$

    $y = -20 + 4 = -16$

17. The correct answer is (A). *x* is less than or equal to 9, and at the same time, *x* is greater than 6. The values between 6 and 9 satisfy this condition. The value 9 but not 6 (because 6 is not greater than 9) also satisfies this condition. An open circle would indicate "less than" or "greater than" a condition at an endpoint, while a filled-in circle would indicate an endpoint is "less than or equal to" (or "greater than or equal to") a condition.

18. The correct answer is (C).

    When dividing terms, subtract the exponents. You can see this by expanding. Remember x^5 is $x \times x \times x \times x \times x$ and x^7 is $x \times x \times x \times x \times x \times x \times x$. Then just divide. This is the basis for the rules of exponents.

    $$\frac{3 \times x \times x \times x \times x \times x}{4 \times x \times x \times x \times x \times x \times x \times x} = \frac{3}{4x^2}$$

19. The correct answer is (B). To express a percent as a decimal, divide by 100. To express a decimal as a percent, multiply by 100. Literally, percent ("per cent") means "per hundred".
    .075 × 100 = 7.5

20. The correct answer is (C). The amount of paint needed depends on the area. The given ratios are ratios of length and the figures are similar. Therefore, the ratios of the areas are the squares of the ratios of the lengths.

   1:40 in length

   $1:40^2$ in area (that is, 1:1600 in area)

   Since the model required three gallons, the original will require

   $3 \times 1{,}600 = 4{,}800$ gallons.

21. The correct answer is (A). This one is easier to work backward. The total bill will be more than the base amount, thereby ruling out answers (B) and (D). Since both tax (5%) and tip (15%) are already included in the total, try adding 20% to each answer to see which results in a total of $93.60.

   Or, work from the given $93.60, which represents 120% of the base amount. Divide 93.60 by 1.2 to get $78.00.

22. The correct answer is (C).

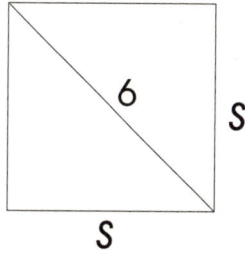

   If the diagonal of a square is 6, then (by the Pythagorean theorem), the sides of the square must be $\dfrac{6}{\sqrt{2}} = \dfrac{6\sqrt{2}}{2} = 3\sqrt{2}$. Square this to get the area of 18.

23. The correct answer is (C). Convert all fractions to decimal equivalents:

$$\frac{2}{3} = .666 \qquad \frac{4}{5} = .800$$

$$\frac{5}{6} = .8333 \qquad \frac{17}{20} = .85$$

$$\frac{7}{10} = .7 \qquad \frac{13}{15} = .8666$$

$$\frac{9}{10} = .9$$

$\frac{7}{10}$ is the only fraction between $\frac{2}{3}$ and $\frac{4}{5}$.

24. The correct answer is (A). Using the formula for circumference,
$C = \pi d$

$= (3.14)(7)$

$= 21.98$ inches

25. The correct answer is (D).

First find the amount Josie bought the shares for:
$180 \times 16 = \$2,880$

Then find the amount Josie sold the shares for:
$240 \times 16 = \$3,840$

Finally, subtract. $\$3,840 - \$2,880 = \$960$

ISEE Practice Test 1

Verbal Reasoning........................ 444
Quantitative Reasoning................. 448
Reading Comprehension.................. 452
Mathematics Achievement................ 462
Writing the Essay...................... 468

**Explanatory Answers to the
ISEE Practice Test 1................... 471**
Verbal Reasoning..................... 471
Quantitative Reasoning............... 476
Reading Comprehension................ 482
Mathematics Achievement.............. 487

Verbal Reasoning

Time: 20 minutes **40 Questions**

DIRECTIONS: Each question is made up of a word in capital letters followed by four choices. You should circle the one word that is most nearly the same in meaning as the word in capital letters.

1. EXORBITANT:
   - (A) essential
   - (B) lacking
   - (C) literal
   - (D) excessive

2. JARGON:
   - (A) opposite
   - (B) decoy
   - (C) terminology
   - (D) membership

3. CHAGRIN:
   - (A) disappointment
   - (B) fabrication
   - (C) acceptance
   - (D) exemption

4. STEALTHY:
   - (A) small
   - (B) sly
   - (C) ashamed
   - (D) tardy

5. PONDEROUS:
   - (A) amazed
   - (B) irregular
   - (C) trembling
   - (D) weighty

6. DAUNTLESS:
   - (A) thoughtful
   - (B) believable
   - (C) brave
   - (D) pure

7. INCORRIGIBLE:
   - (A) incredible
   - (B) immaterial
   - (C) shameless
   - (D) selective

8. FEINT:
   - (A) fool
   - (B) proclaim
   - (C) penalize
   - (D) scavenge

9. CURT:
   - (A) impending
   - (B) fair
   - (C) blunt
   - (D) meek

10. SPURN:
    - (A) reject
    - (B) sew
    - (C) meddle
    - (D) warp

11. SUPPRESS:
    - (A) subdue
    - (B) substitute
    - (C) liberate
    - (D) squander

12. INNOVATION:
    - (A) balance
    - (B) certainty
    - (C) agreement
    - (D) change

13. SUBMISSIVE:
    - (A) deceptive
    - (B) annoying
    - (C) harmless
    - (D) unflinching

14. **CLIENTELE:**
    - (A) militants
    - (B) patrons
    - (C) members
    - (D) combatants

15. **SUCCUMB:**
    - (A) yield
    - (B) irritate
    - (C) echo
    - (D) succeed

16. **EULOGIZE:**
    - (A) attack
    - (B) disable
    - (C) reduce
    - (D) glorify

17. **INFRINGE:**
    - (A) equip
    - (B) trespass
    - (C) strike
    - (D) shrink

18. **PEER:**
    - (A) equal
    - (B) officer
    - (C) beginner
    - (D) patient

19. **COWER:**
    - (A) injure
    - (B) insult
    - (C) misrepresent
    - (D) cringe

20. **SLOTH:**
    - (A) sadness
    - (B) regret
    - (C) laziness
    - (D) forgetfulness

DIRECTIONS: Each question below is made up of a sentence with one or two blanks. The sentences with one blank indicate that one word is missing. The sentences with two blanks indicate that two words are missing. Each sentence is followed by four choices. You should circle the one word or pair of words that will best complete the meaning of the sentence as a whole.

21. The emotions of love and hate, though opposites, can be found even in the most _____ and _____ character in Shakespeare's plays.
    - (A) virtuous . . steadfast
    - (B) wholesome . . despicable
    - (C) contemptible . . decent
    - (D) elderly . . malicious

22. Some experts think that certain psychological conditions are the result of _____; others think it is _____.
    - (A) contagion . . communicability
    - (B) milieu . . surroundings
    - (C) heredity . . environment
    - (D) coincidence . . happenstance

23. Nutritionists say that when eating it is important to _____ completely in order for proper _____ to occur.
    - (A) inhale . . respiration
    - (B) absorb . . rumination
    - (C) repose . . relaxation
    - (D) masticate . . digestion

24. After ruining her carpet when I spilled my dessert, I would have preferred her most sarcastic _____ to the _____ looks she cast in my direction.
    - (A) invectives . . disparaging
    - (B) scurrilous . . amiable
    - (C) civilities . . reproachful
    - (D) amenities . . agreeable

25. During the violent hurricane, the people in its path _____ God for divine _____.

    (A) entreated .. intervention
    (B) disdained .. interaction
    (C) importuned .. wavering
    (D) ostracized .. interference

26. The burglar was successful because he could move in a _____ and _____ manner.

    (A) flagrant .. underhanded
    (B) stealthy .. candid
    (C) furtive .. evasive
    (D) inept .. prominent

27. During commencement, the valedictorian delivered an inspiring _____, and it had a(n) _____ effect on the audience.

    (A) tribulation .. debilitating
    (B) salutation .. invigorating
    (C) oratory .. incapacitating
    (D) defamation .. heartening

28. According to the doctor, some medicines have side effects that can make people extremely _____ and _____.

    (A) dynamic .. slumberous
    (B) vigorous .. zealous
    (C) sluggish .. vigorous
    (D) lethargic .. impassive

29. The author found that her editor was very _____; he made many _____ in her work to make it as good as possible.

    (A) disorderly .. avowals
    (B) fastidious .. emendations
    (C) laggard .. plaudits
    (D) militant .. apparitions

30. The unpredictable nature of the student caused problems; his _____ _____ caused concern among the faculty.

    (A) periodic eruptions
    (B) invariable indiscretions
    (C) leisurely patrimony
    (D) immutable rebuttal

31. In a courtroom proceeding which was shown on television, the _____ heard the testimony and _____ the man to jail.

    (A) turncoat .. committed
    (B) magistrate .. pulverized
    (C) plebeian .. dispatched
    (D) arbitrator .. remanded

32. As a result of his recent accident, the _____ victim was _____ to a wheelchair.

    (A) inventive .. cowered
    (B) auspicious .. restrained
    (C) propitious .. limited
    (D) hapless .. confined

33. In Biology class we discussed animal families, and that farmers need to grow acres of grass because members of the _____ family are _____.

    (A) chivalrous .. benevolent
    (B) porcine .. carnivorous
    (C) bovine .. herbivorous
    (D) patrician .. wrathful

34. Anyone who is new at a job knows that novice _____ can lead to _____.

    (A) ineptitude .. problems
    (B) facility .. expertise
    (C) proficiency .. deficiency
    (D) incapacity .. aptness

35. One of the main concerns of the conservation movement is that we do not have a _____ of energy sources; therefore, we must be _____ with what we do have.

    (A) abundance . . excessive
    (B) paucity . . intemperate
    (C) profusion . . immoderate
    (D) deluge . . frugal

36. In the principal's office, one can often see students _____ for their _____ behavior.

    (A) castigated . . antagonistic
    (B) reprimanded . . laudable
    (C) chided . . exemplary
    (D) reverted . . foreboding

37. Industrial waste products from the nearby factory made the once _____ lake into a _____ cesspool.

    (A) pristine . . contaminated
    (B) tainted . . unsullied
    (C) portent . . mutable
    (D) sullen . . untenable

38. In a tense situation, sometimes _____ remarks can _____ an argument.

    (A) sarcastic . . peruse
    (B) facetious . . precipitate
    (C) deferential . . yield
    (D) acerbic . . beleaguer

39. The political prisoner appealed for at least a _____ of his sentence, if not a total _____.

    (A) filibuster . . guffaw
    (B) collusion . . demurring
    (C) vindication . . diminishing
    (D) reduction . . acquittal

40. Although the judge is _____ to have taken bribes, no _____ evidence has been brought to the authorities.

    (A) alleged . . substantial
    (B) supposed . . deceptive
    (C) desiccated . . credible
    (D) mandated . . redolent

ISEE PRACTICE TEST 1

| QUANTITATIVE REASONING | TIME: 35 MINUTES | 35 QUESTIONS |

DIRECTIONS: Any figures that accompany questions in this section may be assumed to be drawn as accurately as possible EXCEPT when it is stated that a particular figure is not drawn to scale. Letters such as x, y, and n stand for real numbers.

For Questions 1–18, work each in your head or on the space available on these pages. Then select the correct answer.

1. Which of the following fractions is larger than $\frac{3}{5}$?

    (A) $\frac{39}{50}$
    (B) $\frac{7}{25}$
    (C) $\frac{3}{10}$
    (D) $\frac{59}{100}$

2. What is .1 % expressed as a decimal?

    (A) .001
    (B) .01
    (C) .1
    (D) 1

3. Five women had the following amounts of money in their wallets: $12.50, $11.83, $10.40, $0.74, and $0.00. What was the average amount of money carried by these women?

    (A) $7.09
    (B) $7.62
    (C) $9.88
    (D) $35.47

4. Solve for x: $7x - 3 = 4x + 6$

    (A) 2
    (B) 4
    (C) -1
    (D) 3

5. $2\frac{2}{3} + (-8) =$

    (A) $5\frac{1}{3}$
    (B) $-5\frac{1}{3}$
    (C) $10\frac{2}{3}$
    (D) $-10\frac{2}{3}$

6. Find the perimeter of a rectangle whose length is 7 centimeters and whose width is 5 centimeters.

    (A) 35 centimeters
    (B) 70 centimeters
    (C) 12 centimeters
    (D) 24 centimeters

7. The recipe for a cake calls for $\frac{2}{3}$ cup of sugar. How many cakes did Janet bake for a baked-goods sale if she used 4 cups of sugar?

    (A) 3
    (B) 4
    (C) 5
    (D) 6

Peterson's SSAT/ISEE Success

QUANTITATIVE REASONING

8. Solve for x: $1.4x - 0.9 = 3.3$

    (A) 4.2
    (B) 3
    (C) 7.6
    (D) 4.7
    (E) 12.3

9. Brian jogged $\frac{1}{2}$ of a mile, rested, then jogged $\frac{1}{3}$ of a mile. What fractional part of a mile must he jog to complete 1 mile?

    (A) $\frac{2}{5}$
    (B) $\frac{1}{6}$
    (C) $\frac{5}{6}$
    (D) $\frac{1}{12}$

10. $(-4)^2 - 3(-4) =$

    (A) -4
    (B) 52
    (C) -52
    (D) 28

11. The difference between the measures of two complementary angles is 50°. Find in degrees the measure of the smaller angle.

    (A) 50°
    (B) 70°
    (C) 20°
    (D) 10°

12. The expression $2(a + 1) - (1 + 2a)$ is equivalent to

    (A) 1
    (B) -1
    (C) 0
    (D) $4a$

13. Each inch on a map corresponds to a distance of 110 miles. What distance corresponds to 5.5 inches on the map?

    (A) 20 miles
    (B) 550 miles
    (C) 605 miles
    (D) 1100 miles

14. Which of the following is a rational number?

    (A) $\sqrt{2}$
    (B) $\sqrt{3}$
    (C) $\sqrt{5}$
    (D) $\sqrt{9}$

15. An inheritance of $120,000 is divided among 3 people in a ratio of 3:4:5. How much is the largest share?

    (A) $40,000
    (B) $45,000
    (C) $50,000
    (D) $55,000

16. If the price of an item triples, the increase is what percent of the new price?

    (A) $33\frac{1}{3}\%$
    (B) $66\frac{2}{3}\%$
    (C) 200%
    (D) 300%

17. Find the value of $-5S^2T$, when $S = -2$ and $T = -3$.

   (A) -30
   (B) 30
   (C) -60
   (D) 60

18.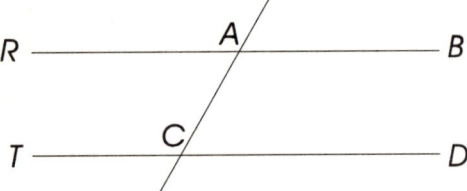

   (*RB* is parallel to *TD*)

   If $\angle BAC = (a + 30)°$, then $\angle ACD$ expressed in terms of a is:

   (A) $(a + 30)°$
   (B) $(150 - a)°$
   (C) $(60 - a)°$
   (D) $(60 + a)°$

Directions: For questions 19–35 note the given information, if any, and then compare the quantity in Column A to the quantity in Column B. Next to the number of each question, write

   A if the quantity in Column A is greater
   B if the quantity in Column B is greater
   C if the two quantities are equal
   D if the relationship cannot be determined from the information given

	Column A	Column B
19.	$12 \times 72 \times 250$	$10 \times 7 \times 200$
20.	Least common denominator of $\dfrac{1}{4}$ and $\dfrac{3}{5}$	Least common denominator of $\dfrac{2}{3}$ and $\dfrac{5}{8}$
21.	$4m - 3n - (3m + 2n)$	$m + 5n$

22.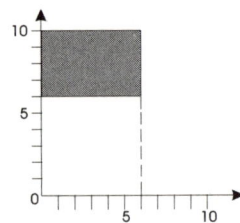

	Area of the shaded figure	Perimeter of the shaded figure
23.	$(12 + 4)5 + 8$	$12 + 4 \times 5 + 8$

24.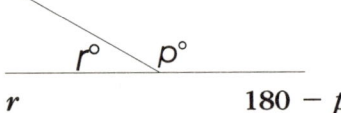

	r	$180 - p$
25.	$x - y$	$y - x$
26.	$5\sqrt{2}$	$2\sqrt{5}$

QUANTITATIVE REASONING

	Column A	Column B
27.	$\left(1 \times \frac{1}{10}\right) + \left(8 \times \frac{1}{100}\right) + \left(3 \times \frac{1}{1000}\right)$	.183
28.	$\left(-\frac{3}{5}\right)^2$	$\frac{6}{10}$
29.	Price of 32 envelopes if purchased at a rate of two for 5 cents	Price of 1 lb. of coffee if a $3\frac{2}{3}$ lb. can costs $3.30
30.	Number of boxes in 12 rows of cartons with 16 cartons in a row and 9 boxes in each carton	1,728

Use this drawing for questions 31 and 32.

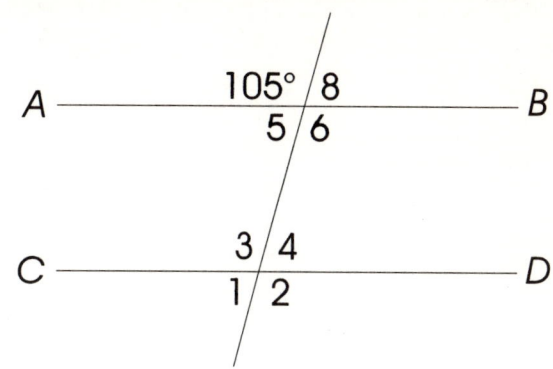

	Column A	Column B
31.	$\angle 1$	$\angle 6$
32.	$\angle 2$	$\angle 8$
33.	x	-18
34.	$\dfrac{7\frac{2}{3}}{\left(\frac{4}{5}\right)\left(\frac{5}{12}\right)}$	$\dfrac{7\frac{1}{3}}{\left(\frac{5}{6}\right)\left(\frac{6}{15}\right)}$
35.	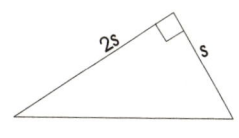 Area of Triangle	 Area of Square

Reading Comprehension   Time: 35 minutes   40 Questions

Directions: Each passage below is followed by questions based on its content. Answer the questions following a passage on the basis of what is *stated* or *implied* in that passage.

Passage 1

Line Beneath the surface of Monterey Bay lies splendor seen only by a lucky few: Monterey Canyon. Hidden from view by thousands of feet of water, this submarine chasm pos-
5   sesses steep rocky cliffs and curving geography inhabited by strange and hard-to-find marine life. West of the Monterey Peninsula, the canyon walls gradually drop an incredible 7,360 feet—a quarter mile more than
10   the highest cliff of Arizona's Grand Canyon.
     Monterey Canyon is part of a much larger geologic feature, the Monterey Canyon System, comparable in size to the 278-mile-long Grand Canyon. The 60-mile-long gorge
15   empties into the gently sloping Monterey Sea Valley. The valley continues out into the Pacific Ocean for an additional 180 miles until it reaches the flat Pacific Ocean plain.
     Even at this size, Monterey Canyon is
20   not the world's largest undersea chasm. But to marine researchers, it is the most convenient. At the port of Moss Landing, the head of the canyon is within yards of the coast. From here, the floor of the canyon begins its
25   gradual descent to a depth of nearly 8,000 feet.
     In the bay's sunless middle depths, otherworldly creatures drift through the darkness feeding on the blizzard of organic
30   material, or "marine snow," from above. In the canyon itself, dense colonies of clams, tube worms, and bacteria feed on chemical-rich fluids oozing from underwater springs.
     Monterey Canyon's geology is a focus
35   of intense study. Although its geologic history is understood in its essentials, the details of how it was carved out of the continental shelf are not yet completely known. When submarine canyons were first
40   discovered, geologists assumed that they started out as canyons on dry land at a time when the sea level was lower. Then, according to this theory, the canyons were flooded by a rise in sea level. But there was
45   one problem: not all undersea canyons lie near a river old and powerful enough to have carved such canyons. A bigger, older knife was needed.
     In the 1930's, geologists found a
50   mechanism that could, given enough time, carve even the grandest undersea canyons: turbidity currents. These are enormously powerful underwater debris flows, made up of a dense mixture of sea water, rock debris,
55   of various sizes, and fine sediments. They flow down underwater slopes at high speed, tearing away rocks and sediments. Most geologists believe that turbidity currents carved undersea canyons as surely as the
60   Colorado River cut the Grand Canyon.

1. According to the passage, Monterey Canyon is convenient for marine researchers because it is

   (A) comparable in size to the Grand Canyon.
   (B) close to shore and easy to reach.
   (C) the world's largest undersea canyon.
   (D) the focus of intense study.

2. The main point of paragraph 5 is that the original theory of how undersea canyons were formed

   (A) had to be abandoned.
   (B) wasn't old enough.
   (C) didn't explain flooding.
   (D) didn't consider erosion.

3. According to the passage, turbidity currents contain all of the following except:

   (A) fine sediments.
   (B) rock debris.
   (C) chemical rich fluids.
   (D) sea water.

4. The "blizzard . . . of marine snow"

   (A) is caused by weather conditions in the atmosphere.
   (B) contains chemical-rich fluids from springs.
   (C) falls from the bay's sunless middle depths.
   (D) is made up of organic matter sea creatures eat.

5. According to the passage, how deep is the Monterey Canyon?

   (A) 7,360 feet.
   (B) 60 miles.
   (C) 278 miles.
   (D) 180 miles.

Passage 2

Line Shut it off, Steiner told himself, and the station wagon was silent. He had pulled into the driveway without the reality of any of it registering, and now he turned to his
5 9-year-old, James, in the seat beside him, and saw the boy's face take on the expression of odd imbalance that Steiner had noticed for the first time this afternoon.

Steiner got out and James bucked
10 against his seat belt, so Steiner eased back in, shoving the unruly hair off his forehead, and took hold of the wheel. He was so used to James being out of the car and heading across the yard the second after he stopped
15 that he felt dazed. His 7-year-old twin daughters, who were in the rear of the car with his wife, Jen, were whispering, and Steiner turned to them with a look that meant "Silence!" Steiner got out again with a
20 heaviness that made him feel that his age, 45, was the beginning of old age, and that the remorse he'd recently been feeling had a focus: it was a remorse that he and Jen hadn't had more children.

25 As he was driving home, a twin had pulled herself forward from the backseat and whispered that James had reached over and honked the horn while Steiner was in the department store, where had gone to look
30 for a shatterproof, full-length mirror and an exercise mat the physical therapist had recommended. And since James hadn't spoken for two weeks, the incident had set the twins to whispering hopefully about
35 James, for most of the long trip.

"I'm sorry," Steiner said, seeing that he was still the only one outside the car, as if he had to apologize for being on his feet. He slid back in, brushing aside his hair again,
40 and began to unbuckle James's seat belt. The boy stared out the windshield with a look Steiner couldn't translate, and, once free,

tried to scoot over to the passenger door by bending his upper body forward and back.

45 "Take it easy, honey," Steiner said. Then, he added for the boy and the others, in the phrase that he'd used since James was an infant, "Here we are home." Silence. Steiner turned to Jen, who was leaning
50 close, and said, "Do you have his other belt?" She nodded.

Steiner got out and looked across the top of the station wagon at their aging house. He hadn't seen it in two weeks. He'd
55 spent that time at the hospital with James, first in intensive care, then in a private room, where physical therapists came and went. At the sight of the white siding that he and James and Jen had scraped and
60 repainted at the beginning of the summer, he had to swallow down the loss that he'd started to feel when he realized he was grieving for a son he might never see again.

The boy's hair was as unruly as
65 Steiner's, and the curls at its edges needed trimming. James's eyes were nearly covered by it, Steiner saw, and then they rested on his father with a dull love.

6. According to the passage, James is

   (A) Jen's stepson.
   (B) younger than the twins.
   (C) Steiner's son.
   (D) 45 years old.

7. Steiner had spent the past two weeks

   (A) scraping and repainting the house.
   (B) looking for an exercise mat.
   (C) in the hospital with James.
   (D) not speaking to anyone at all.

8. In the context of the passage, the statement that Steiner is "grieving for a son he might never see again" most likely means that

   (A) his son, James, has died.
   (B) he fears James may never recover.
   (C) he knows he won't have more children.
   (D) his son is in the hospital.

9. It can be inferred from the passage that Steiner says, "Here we are home" in order to

   (A) begin a conversation with Jen and the twins.
   (B) suggest that James needs help getting out of the car.
   (C) explain they have moved to a new house.
   (D) restore a feeling of normality to the situation.

10. James honked the horn while

    (A) Steiner was talking to the physical therapist.
    (B) the twins were whispering about him.
    (C) Steiner was looking for an exercise mat.
    (D) Jen was getting him out of the car.

11. When in the story does Steiner notice James's hair needs cutting?

    (A) Before Steiner helps James out of the car.
    (B) While the twins are whispering about him.
    (C) When Jen asks him a question.
    (D) As Steiner shuts off the car's engine.

Passage 3

Line Carthage, a city on the Tunisian coast of
North Africa, originally settled by the
Phoenicians, was a major power of the
Mediterranean world in ancient times.
5 Bertold Brecht summed up seven centuries
of its history when he wrote "Great
Carthage made war three times. After the
first, she was powerful. After the second,
she was rich. After the third, no one knew
10 where Great Carthage had been." The last
sentence was a slight exaggeration. The
great general Hannibal, who used elephants
to cross the Alps in 281 BC to start the
Second Punic War with Rome ("Punic"
15 comes from the Roman word for "Phoenician"), was a well-known figure. Knowing
about him was part of Roman history; the
Romans had built a city of their own on the
site of Carthage after defeating it. Roman
20 Carthage was a center of industry, learning,
and luxury, arguably the second greatest city
of the Roman Empire, after Rome itself.

In Carthage there had been great
libraries of books in the Punic language. Not
25 a page, not a line, remains. The works of a
Carthaginian named Magro, the greatest
writer on agriculture in antiquity, were
translated and studied by Roman landown-
ers, but now even the translations are lost.
30 What remains of the Punic language, a
variety of Phoenician, are mostly grave
inscriptions with the names of parents
offering children to a god or a goddess, and
some lines of comic dialogues put into the
35 mouths of Carthaginian merchants and slaves
in the work of a Roman playwright.

One consequence is that practically
everything we know about the Carthaginians
comes from the Greeks and Romans, who
40 made war on Carthage for centuries. Their
historians naturally tended to present a
biased picture of the enemy as cruel and
untrustworthy. But there is no reason to
think the people of ancient Carthage were
45 any more addicted to cruelty than the
Romans, who thought nothing of crucifying
prisoners along the public highways and
leaving them there till their bones were
picked clean by birds. Some scholars
50 challenge the whole idea that Carthaginians
practiced infant sacrifice, claiming that the
charred bones in the urns, when they are
not those of lambs and calves, are of infants
who died of natural causes.

12. The passage notes that our knowledge of
Carthage is incomplete because:

  I. none of the books written by
     Carthaginians has survived.
  II. the Roman portrayals of Carthage were
      inaccurate.
  III. Magro's book was only about agricul-
       ture.

  (A) I only.
  (B) II only.
  (C) I and II.
  (D) I and III.

13. In the context of the passage, what is the
purpose of the statement that the Romans
"thought nothing of crucifying prisoners
along the public highways"?

  (A) The Romans did not practice infant
      sacrifice.
  (B) The Romans were as cruel as the
      Carthaginians.
  (C) The Romans treated the Carthaginians
      cruelly.
  (D) The Romans were even more cruel
      than the Carthaginians.

14. The main idea of the second paragraph is that
    (A) the records of the Carthaginians were almost totally destroyed.
    (B) the city of Carthage was completely destroyed.
    (C) Punic was a form of the Phoenician language.
    (D) a Roman playwright preserved the Punic language.

15. Although the author writes that the claim "no one knew where great Carthage had been" is a "slight exaggeration," which of the following statements from the passage best reveals how completely Carthage was destroyed?
    (A) The Phoenicians who had settled it no longer lived there.
    (B) Hannibal was not a well-known general.
    (C) The only remains of the Punic language are grave inscriptions.
    (D) The Romans built a new city on the site of Carthage.

Passage 4

Line Twas in the merry month of May
      When green leaves began swelling
      Young William on his deathbed lay
      For love of Barbara Allen.

5   He sent his men down through the town
      To the place where she was dwelling

      "O hurry to my master dear
      If you are Barbara Allen."

      Slowly, slowly went she then
10   To the place where William was lying
      And when she saw him to him said,
      "Young man, I think you're dying."

      He turned his face unto the wall
      And death with him was dealing
15   "Good-bye, good-bye, my dear friends all,
      Be kind to Barbara Allen."

      Slowly, slowly rose she up,
      And slowly, slowly left him,
      And sighing said she could not stay
20   Since death from life had reft him.

      She had not gone a mile or two
      When she heard the death bell tolling
      And every stroke the death bell sang
      "Oh woe to Barbara Allen."

25   "O mother, mother, make my bed!
      O make it soft and narrow.
      Since William died for me today;
      I'll die for him tomorrow."

16. The story told by this poem takes place in
    (A) winter.
    (B) spring.
    (C) summer.
    (D) autumn.

17. Lines 7 and 8 of the poem are spoken by
    (A) Young William.
    (B) Barbara Allen.
    (C) William's employee.
    (D) Barbara's mother.

18. The stanza which best demonstrates Barbara Allen's cruelty is
    (A) Stanza 3.
    (B) Stanza 4.
    (C) Stanza 5.
    (D) Stanza 6.

19. Barbara Allen will die because she

    (A) is extremely ill.
    (B) realizes she truly loved William.
    (C) recognizes her cruelty caused his death.
    (D) hears the death bell ringing for William.

20. The word "reft" in line 20 most probably means

    (A) torn.
    (B) revived.
    (C) freed.
    (D) joined.

Passage 5

Line   I was on a visit to seven of Costa Rica's national parks and nature reserves. My first stop, Monteverde Cloud Forest Reserve, taught me a lesson. To see something
5 interesting in this naturalist's paradise of a country, all I had to do was sit down and wait. Something was sure to come by, and it was likely to be something new and wonderful. Names tell the story: quetzals, iguanas,
10 and howler monkeys; sloths; scarlet macaws, and green parrots; yellow toucans, anteaters, roseate spoonbills, giant turtles, and more. Endlessly more.
    Costa Rica is blessed with natural
15 beauty. It claims more than 830 species of birds living in a wide range of habitats, from volcanic summit to white-sand beach, from coral reef to rain forest. A large portion of its land, an amazing 25 percent, has been set
20 aside in one of the world's best systems of reserves and national parks, some 35 in all. And because the country averages only 150 miles across and 300 miles long, it's easy to get from one place to another.
25   For example, Monteverde is less than 100 miles from Costa Rica's capital, San Jose. I drove there in one morning, through the temperate central valley down into hot, dry country along the Pacific coast, and then up
30 to misty forest.
    Monteverde is a prime sample of tropical cloud forest, named for its ability to derive moisture not only from rain but also from the misty touch of clouds, which
35 almost always blankets the area. Entering the trees felt like going underwater, sinking beneath the shimmering surface of a new and alien world. But gradually, I began to see a sort of order, an order defined by the
40 need for sunlight. Great trees had muscled their way skyward, blocking the sun from the forest floor. In their shade, ground-level plants had survived by growing huge leaves, often several feet in diameter, to collect
45 what light they could. I came to a single tree with a cluster of substantial trunks: a strangler fig. Starting as a seedling in the canopy, the fig had dropped shoots that took root in the forest floor and then
50 gradually enveloped and choked their host. The original tree, having served as a ladder to the soil, had long since disappeared.
    The relationships of plants and animals weave into the complex fabric of the forest
55 like vines. I began to think of the forest as an organism itself, growing at a fantastic pace.

21. When the author states that "names tell the story," it means that

    (A) names of Monteverde's animals are unusual.
    (B) there are more giant turtles than other animals in Monteverde.
    (C) Monteverde is a cloud forest.
    (D) Monteverde has many kinds of animals.

22. The author's purpose in paragraph 3 is to

    (A) establish the fact that the capital is close to Monteverde.
    (B) provide examples of climate differences in Costa Rica.
    (C) provide an example supporting ease of getting from place to place.
    (D) support the author's statement that there is a wide range of habitats.

23. What is the author's attitude toward Costa Rica's preserves?

    (A) strongly favorable.
    (B) favorable with reservations.
    (C) neutral.
    (D) unimpressed.

24. The author states that one sort of order in the Monteverde Cloud Forest occurs because of a need for

    (A) sunlight.
    (B) niches.
    (C) tumult.
    (D) recycling.

25. Which statement is not true of the strangler fig?

    (A) It uses the host tree to reach the ground.
    (B) It is a ladder to the soil.
    (C) It has a cluster of trunks.
    (D) It sends out shoots.

26. The best title for this selection is

    (A) Costa Rica: Biologist's Paradise
    (B) Biological Diversity in Monteverde
    (C) Monteverde Cloud Forest
    (D) A Visit to Costa Rica

Passage 6

Line   Although humans think of cockroaches as bothersome, fewer than 1% of cockroach species are pests. These annoying bugs include the American cockroach and the
5   German cockroach, which live in kitchens and bathrooms. They like the dark, and it can be very unnerving to come home at night, turn on a lamp, and see the roaches scuttling across the floor to their homes in
10   cracks and behind the walls. However, most cockroaches live out of doors, where humans tend to ignore them.
        The roaches are one of the most successful species on our planet. Fossil
15   records show that cockroaches were around as long as 300 million years ago. By comparison, flowering plants have only been around for 100 million years, and humans for about two million years. Interestingly, the differ-
20   ences between the fossil cockroaches and today's roaches are very slight; they mainly involve the position of the veins on the wings.
        Why haven't the cockroaches changed?
25   They can live in a wide variety of habitats and temperatures (they are even found in sub-Arctic climates), and they are scavengers. Their food includes plants, animal matter, and debris. Their flat bodies are
30   close to the ground, so they can hide in any tiny space for protection. When they hatch from their egg cases, they are ready to move, although they are very tiny and lack wings. Unlike some other insects, they do
35   not undergo a metamorphosis during which they might be vulnerable. They shed their skins several times before they become

adults, but they are always speedy and mobile. While adults can fly, they usually
40 run.

The cockroach's survival for many eons in an unchanged form is a fact that, oddly, supports the theory of natural selection. If species succeed, there is no need for
45 evolutionary changes to help them survive.

27. Cockroaches have existed for about

(A) 2 million years.
(B) 100 million years.
(C) 200 million years
(D) 300 million years.

28. One reason for their success as a species is that cockroaches

(A) like the cold.
(B) can hide easily.
(C) don't have wings.
(D) hatch from eggs.

29. The American and German cockroach are species that

(A) are not pests.
(B) live outdoors.
(C) are ignored by humans.
(D) dislike light.

30. As used in the passage, the word "vulnerable" means

(A) valuable.
(B) protected.
(C) easy to attack.
(D) confusing to predators.

Passage 7

Line Biosphere 2 was a project designed as an experiment to see if humans could live in a totally self-sustaining sealed environment. A huge glass greenhouse structure, it was
5 meant to duplicate Biosphere 1, our planet, and to show that we could live on another planet by creating such a project there. Eight people lived in Biosphere 2 for two years, and although they emerged in good
10 health, they were extremely thin. While they lived in Biosphere 2, they had complained frequently of hunger, fatigue, and weakness.

One of the reasons for their feeling of hunger was that the food-producing plants
15 and animals in the biosphere did not develop as expected. The chickens laid very few eggs. The pigs did not reproduce, and the goats provided little milk. Not all of the food plant species did well, and the biosphe-
20 rians' diet was composed mostly of beans and sweet potatoes.

The fatigue and weakness partially resulted from the hard physical labor the biospherians' performed many hours a day
25 so that there would be enough food to survive. But later research revealed a more significant problem. The atmosphere of Biosphere 2 was to be maintained by the plants and algae growing inside it and in its
30 simulated ocean; these, it was thought, would produce enough oxygen so the atmosphere would duplicate the 21% oxygen of Earth. In Biosphere 2, the oxygen levels sometimes dropped as low as 14.5%. In
35 addition, the carbon dioxide level was about twice that of the area directly outside Biosphere 2.

But this problem in the original experiment has led to a new mission for the
40 Biosphere 2. According to a brochure given to tourists at the site, "researchers are working to understand how increased carbon dioxide in our atmosphere—such as

that produced by cars, industry, and the burning of forests—will affect us and the plant life we so depend on." So while the Biosphere 2 may not show how to survive on other planets, it may teach us how we can live in the increasingly polluted environment of Biosphere 1.

31. One cause of the bionspherians' fatigue was

    (A) a boring diet.
    (B) too little oxygen.
    (C) not enough to do.
    (D) decreased carbon dioxide.

32. Food-producing animals in Biosphere 2

    (A) did not develop normally.
    (B) ate food meant for humans.
    (C) provided variety in the biospherians' diet.
    (D) died when they were young.

33. Oxygen in Biosphere 2 was to be produced by

    (A) air from outside the sealed environment.
    (B) the ocean inside it.
    (C) chickens, pigs, and goats.
    (D) land and water plants.

34. The carbon dioxide-rich atmosphere in Biosphere 2

    (A) was a cause of the biospherians' weakness.
    (B) provides the possibility of new experiments.
    (C) is twice as high as that of the area surrounding it.
    (D) all of the above.

Passage 8

In the 1890's, Cuba was part of what remained of Spain's once huge empire in the New World. Several times Cuban insurgents had rebelled against Spanish rule, but they had failed to free their country. As discontent with Spanish rule grew, in late February 1895, revolt again broke out.

Cuban insurgents established a military organization in New York City to raise money, purchase weapons, and wage a propaganda war to sway American public opinion in their favor. Conditions in Cuba were grim. The insurgents engaged in a hit-and-run scorched-earth policy to force the Spanish to leave, while the Spanish commander tried to corner the rebels in the eastern end of the island and destroy them.

After initial failures, Spain, in January 1896, sent General Weyler to Cuba. Relentless and brutal, Weyler gave the rebels ten days to lay down their arms. He then put into effect a "reconcentration" policy designed to move the native population into camps and destroy the rebels' popular base. Herded into fortified areas, Cubans died by the thousands—victims of unsanitary conditions, overcrowding, and disease.

There was a wave of sympathy for the insurgents, stimulated by the American newspapers. The so-called yellow press printed gruesome stories of Spanish atrocities. But yellow journalism did not cause the war. It stemmed from larger conflicts in policy between Spain and the United States.

35. The word "insurgents" as used in the passage means

(A) natives.
(B) rebels.
(C) militia.
(D) reconcentrationists.

36. The primary purpose of reconcentration was to

(A) reduce the size of the rebel forces.
(B) relocate the native Cubans.
(C) cause disease among the rebels.
(D) carry out the scorched earth policy.

37. Yellow journalism refers to the newspapers'

(A) cowardliness.
(B) causing conflicts in policies.
(C) sympathy.
(D) use of sensationalism.

Passage 9

Line Cultural anthropologists are scientists who study how members of human societies experience events in their lives. They examine how people in a culture work, find
5 their food, build their shelters, marry, raise their children, care for the ill, and treat their dead. They may find that some cultures have practices unlike those of their own culture. For example, an American anthropologist
10 discovers that in some cultures it is normal to find insects as part of the human diet. The anthropologist also learns that in ancient cultures, human sacrifice was practiced. Most Americans would find these
15 practices abhorrent.

If anthropologists were to condemn such behaviors as "wrong," they would be assuming that their own culture is superior, since it does things the "right" way. But this
20 would lead to the conclusion they should not waste time studying other cultures. If their own way is "right," and others are "wrong," they would then merely be studying "mistakes." Instead, anthropologists
25 try to understand a culture on its own terms. What purpose or meaning do the behaviors have to the people who practice them? The ancient Aztec culture of Mexico believed that the universe was periodically destroyed
30 by the gods, and the only way to prevent this disaster was to sacrifice humans. While this does not mean anthropologists need to approve of human sacrifice, by understanding the role it played in a culture, they can
35 avoid judging it by their society's standards.

38. As used in the passage, "abhorrent" means

(A) illegal.
(B) experimental.
(C) disgusting.
(D) unfamiliar.

39. Cultural anthropologists do not condemn behaviors which seem strange because they

(A) know which behaviors are right and which are wrong.
(B) want to understand how the culture views the behavior.
(C) do not want to make mistakes.
(D) do not think it is right to destroy the universe.

40. The best title for this passage is

(A) The Aztec Culture
(B) What Is an Anthropologist
(C) How Anthropologists Think
(D) Judging Other Cultures

MATHEMATICS ACHIEVEMENT TIME: 40 MINUTES   45 QUESTIONS

DIRECTIONS: Each question is followed by four suggested answers. Read each question and then decide which of the four suggested answers is best.

1. Which of the following is equivalent to .00000072?

   (A) 7.2×10^{-5}
   (B) 7.2×10^{-6}
   (C) 7.2×10^{-7}
   (D) 7.2×10^{-8}

2. The three angles of a triangle are in the ratio 8:9:13. Find the number of degrees in the smallest angle.

   (A) 36°
   (B) 48°
   (C) 54°
   (D) 60°

3. $62\frac{1}{2}\% =$

   (A) $\frac{5}{8}$
   (B) $\frac{8}{5}$
   (C) .62
   (D) 62.5

4. Which of the following is the largest?

   (A) $\frac{1}{2} + \frac{2}{3}$
   (B) $\frac{3}{4} - \frac{1}{3}$
   (C) $\frac{1}{12} \times \frac{1}{3}$
   (D) $\frac{3}{4} \times \frac{1}{3}$

5. If the sum of s and $s + 9$ is greater than 27, which is a possible value for s?

   (A) -10
   (B) -8
   (C) 8
   (D) 10

6. 21.49 is closest to:

   (A) 22
   (B) 21
   (C) 21.5
   (D) 21.45

7.

The perimeter of ABCD is 100. If $AB > AD$, AB may be equal to:

(A) 25
(B) 35
(C) 50
(D) 55

8. $3\frac{1}{3} + (-6) =$

(A) $2\frac{2}{3}$
(B) $-2\frac{2}{3}$
(C) $9\frac{1}{3}$
(D) $-9\frac{1}{3}$

9. Find the value of $-5ST^2$ when $S = -2$ and $T = -3$.

(A) -90
(B) 90
(C) -60
(D) 60

10. If $ab + c = 2$ is solved for a, then a is equal to:

(A) $bc - 2$
(B) $2 - c - b$
(C) $\frac{c+2}{b}$
(D) $\frac{2-c}{b}$

11. Find S using the formula $S = \frac{a(1-r^n)}{1-r}$ if $a = -2$, $r = 2$, and $n = 3$.

(A) 14
(B) -14
(C) 2
(D) -2

12. Find the length of the second leg of a right triangle whose hypotenuse is 30 feet and whose first leg is 18 feet.

(A) 48 feet
(B) 12 feet
(C) 24 feet
(D) 36 feet

13. If the length and the width of a rectangle are both tripled, the ratio of the area of the original rectangle to the area of the enlarged rectangle is:

(A) 1:3
(B) 1:6
(C) 1:9
(D) 1:18

14. Which of the following is *not* a multiple of 8?

    (A) 24
    (B) 72
    (C) 100
    (D) 144

15. On Chuck's softball team, 8 of the 12 players are right-handed. What is the ratio of right-handed members to left-handed members?

    (A) 1:2
    (B) 2:1
    (C) 2:3
    (D) 3:4

16. If 5 books cost *d* dollars, how many books can be purchased for 2 dollars?

    (A) $\frac{10}{d}$
    (B) $10d$
    (C) $\frac{d}{10}$
    (D) $\frac{2d}{5}$

17. If 8 is a factor of a certain number, what numbers must be factors of that number?

    (A) 1, 2, 4, and 8
    (B) 2 and 4 only
    (C) 2, 4, and 8 only
    (D) 1, 2, and 4 only

18. $x =$

    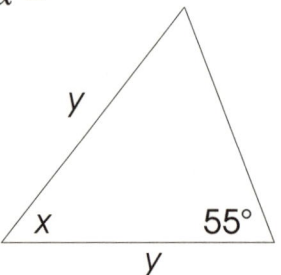

    (A) 80
    (B) 70
    (C) 55
    (D) 50

19. For what priced item does 40% off equal a $4.00 discount?

    (A) $16.00
    (B) $4.00
    (C) $8.00
    (D) $10.00

20. Sally has 3 skirts and 4 blouses ready for wear on a particular day. How many different outfits can Sally choose?

    (A) 12
    (B) 7
    (C) 9
    (D) 16

21. One day Tom completed $\frac{1}{4}$ of his tax returns. The next day he did $\frac{1}{2}$ of what was left. What fraction of his taxes did Tom complete over both days?

    (A) $\frac{3}{8}$
    (B) $\frac{5}{8}$
    (C) $\frac{3}{4}$
    (D) $\frac{7}{8}$

22. If $8x - 14 = 42$, then $x - 5 =$

    (A) 2
    (B) 3
    (C) 5
    (D) 7

23. $2\frac{2}{3} + (-7) =$

(A) $4\frac{1}{3}$
(B) $-4\frac{1}{3}$
(C) $9\frac{2}{3}$
(D) $-9\frac{2}{3}$

24. A carton of milk is $\frac{2}{3}$ empty. When full, the carton holds 60 ounces. How many ounces are in the carton now?

(A) 40
(B) 20
(C) 30
(D) 45

25. What is the area of an equilateral triangle whose altitude is 8?

(A) 16
(B) $\frac{64\sqrt{3}}{3}$
(C) $8\sqrt{3}$
(D) $\frac{16\sqrt{3}}{3}$

26.

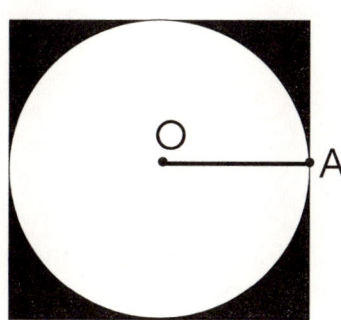

Radius $OA = 3$. Calculate the area of the shaded region.

(A) 9
(B) $36 - 36\pi$
(C) 36π
(D) $36 - 9\pi$

27. At the start of the year Franklyn invested $11,000 in an Internet stock. At the end of the year his stock was worth $9,500. What was the percent of decline in the value of his investment?

(A) 13.64%
(B) 15.79%
(C) 84.21%
(D) 86.36%

28. A radio has a list price of $350. There is a 10% discount sale, and the sales tax is 10%. What is the total paid, including tax?

(A) $350.00
(B) $346.50
(C) $315.00
(D) $365.00

29. What is the equation of a line with slope 8 which intersects the y-axis at $y = -3$?

(A) $y = 3x - 8$
(B) $y = 8x - 3$
(C) $y = 3x + 8$
(D) $y = 8x + 3$

30. Brittany has a test average of 80 after five tests. She only knows the scores of four of her tests: they are 70, 87, 94, and 69. What was the score on her other test?

(A) 90
(B) 96
(C) 80
(D) 82

31. What is $4\frac{1}{2}$ percent expressed as a decimal?

(A) 4.50
(B) .412
(C) .45
(D) .045

32. Express in simplest form the following ratio: 15 hours to 3 days.

    (A) $\dfrac{5}{16}$

    (B) $\dfrac{5}{1}$

    (C) $\dfrac{5}{24}$

    (D) $\dfrac{15}{72}$

33. Solve for x: $5x + 4 = 9x - 2$

    (A) $-\dfrac{1}{2}$

    (B) $\dfrac{1}{2}$

    (C) $-\dfrac{3}{2}$

    (D) $\dfrac{3}{2}$

34. A gumball machine contains five red, six white, and three blue gumballs. If one gumball is removed, what is the probability that it will be red?

    (A) $\dfrac{1}{5}$

    (B) $\dfrac{1}{14}$

    (C) $\dfrac{5}{14}$

    (D) $\dfrac{9}{14}$

35. $(2x^2 - 3x + 5) - (3x + 2) =$

    (A) $2x^2 - 6x + 3$
    (B) $2x^2 + 6x - 3$
    (C) $2x^2 - 6x + 7$
    (D) $2x^2 + 3$

36. Using the formula $A = p + prt$, find A when $p = 1{,}500$, $r = .04$, and $t = 2\dfrac{1}{2}$.

    (A) 1,850
    (B) 1,650
    (C) 1,550
    (D) 1,350

37. Find the value of y in the proportion:
    $$\dfrac{30}{8} = \dfrac{12}{y}$$

    (A) 20
    (B) 6
    (C) $3\dfrac{1}{5}$
    (D) $4\dfrac{3}{4}$

38. If $\dfrac{9}{x}$ is subtracted from $\dfrac{12}{x}$, the result is:

    (A) $\dfrac{3}{x^0}$

    (B) $\dfrac{21}{x}$

    (C) $\dfrac{3}{x^2}$

    (D) $\dfrac{3}{x}$

39. Evaluate $4^3 - 3^4$

    (A) 17
    (B) -17
    (C) 0
    (D) 24

40. What is the x-intercept of the line described by the equation $y = -3x + 7$?

    (A) $\dfrac{7}{3}$

    (B) 7

    (C) $-\dfrac{3}{7}$

    (D) $-\dfrac{7}{3}$

41. What is 50 expressed as the product of its prime factors?

    (A) (5)(10)
    (B) (2)(25)
    (C) (5)(2)(5)(2)
    (D) (5)(5)(2)

42. Find the height of a triangle whose base is 40 and area is 320.

   (A) 16
   (B) 40
   (C) 80
   (D) 160

43. Lines *A* and *B* are parallel. The measure of ∠1 is 49°. What is the measure of ∠2?

   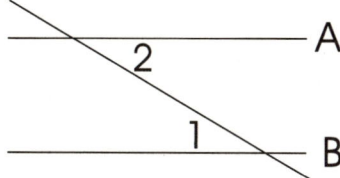

   (A) 49°
   (B) 41°
   (C) 131°
   (D) It cannot be determined.

44. How long of a shadow will a 120-ft. pole cast if a foot-long ruler casts a three-inch shadow?

   (A) 25 feet
   (B) 30 feet
   (C) 350 inches
   (D) 90 feet

45. If points *A*, *B*, *C*, and *D* are distinct collinear points, and *AC* is congruent to *BC*, and *B* lies between *A* and *D*, and the length of *AC* is 10, what is the length of *CD*?

   (A) 10
   (B) 5
   (C) 20
   (D) It cannot be determined.

| WRITING THE ESSAY | TIME: **30** MINUTES |

Directions: Using two sheets of lined theme paper, plan and write an essay on the topic assigned below. DO NOT WRITE ON ANOTHER TOPIC. AN ESSAY ON ANOTHER TOPIC IS NOT ACCEPTABLE.

Critics have said that rock bands rarely create any more, especially after becoming popular. They just recreate.

Prompt: Write an essay giving your view of this. Do you think that this is a true observation? Is money the key factor? Support your opinion with specific examples from history, current music, or personal observations.

WRITING THE ESSAY

Name: _____

Write your essay here.

ISEE PRACTICE TEST 1

EXPLANATORY ANSWERS TO THE ISEE PRACTICE TEST 1

VERBAL REASONING

1. The correct answer is (D).
2. The correct answer is (C).
3. The correct answer is (A).
4. The correct answer is (B).
5. The correct answer is (D).
6. The correct answer is (C).
7. The correct answer is (C).
8. The correct answer is (A).
9. The correct answer is (C).
10. The correct answer is (A).
11. The correct answer is (A).
12. The correct answer is (D).
13. The correct answer is (C).
14. The correct answer is (B).
15. The correct answer is (A).
16. The correct answer is (D).
17. The correct answer is (B).
18. The correct answer is (A).
19. The correct answer is (D).
20. The correct answer is (C).
21. The correct answer is (A). The clue is in the words *though opposites* and *even in the most*. This tells you that the opposite qualities of love and hate can reside in a character who is either very good or very bad. The trigger word is *and* because it shows that the words in the blanks will be synonymous (they will either demonstrate qualities of "goodness" or "badness"). Answers (B) and (C) can be eliminated because they are both good and bad qualities. Answer (D) can be eliminated because age has nothing to do with good or bad qualities.

22. The correct answer is (C). The clue can be found in the words *some experts think* and *others think* because it tells you that there is a difference of opinion. Therefore, the words that go in the blanks will be more opposite than alike. The trigger word is *psychological* because it tells you that the differing opinions are about the origins of mental illness. The debate is whether some of them are "genetic" or "behavioral." Answers (A), (B), and (D) can be eliminated because the two words are the same in each case, referring only to the environment, not genetics.

23. The correct answer is (D). The clue is the word *eating*. This lets you know that the words most likely have to do with the process of eating and getting nutrition ("chewing" and "digestion"). Therefore answer (A) can be eliminated because it is about the breathing process. Similarly, answer (C) can be eliminated because it is about resting. The trigger words are *in order for*. This shows that the relationship between the first word and the second word is that of cause and effect.

24. The correct answer is (A). The clue is in the words *would have preferred*. The trigger word is *looks*. This tells you the first word is something other than looks, for instance, "harshly spoken words." Also, it shows that the looks were "angry." Answer (B) can be eliminated because the second word means friendly looks. Answer (C) can be eliminated because the first word means friendly words. Finally, answer (D) can be ruled out because both words are positive.

25. The correct answer is (A). The clue is in the words *violent hurricane*. They set up a cause and effect relationship between the storm and the action that the people take. The trigger words are *God* and *divine*. People pray to God in times of need. A prayer is a "request." The word "divine" modifies the second word as in divine help. Answers (B) and (D) can be eliminated because the first words are not related to a request. Answer (C) can be eliminated because the second word is not related to help.

26. The correct answer is (C). The clue in the words *successful* and *burglar* shows the blanks will contain words that are the "qualities of a successful burglar." The trigger word is *and*. That shows that the words will be synonyms that relate to those qualities. Answers (A) and (B) can be eliminated because the one word out of the two means to move in an obvious, observable manner. Answer (D) can be eliminated because the two words are not qualities of a successful burglar.

27. The correct answer is (B). The clue is *commencement*. At a graduation ceremony, the valedictorian would deliver a "speech." The trigger words are *inspiring* and *effect*. The second word will be a synonym for "inspiring." Answer (A) can be eliminated because both words are negative. Answer (C) can be eliminated because the second word means the speech was damaging. Also, answer (D) can be ruled out because the first word means to lie.

28. The correct answer is (D). The clue is in the words *medicines* and *side effects*. This shows that the words will be about the "bad effects" of medicines. One common side effect of some medicines is that they can make people "drowsy." The trigger word is *and*. This shows that the words will be synonyms. Answers (A) and (C) can be eliminated because the pairs of words are antonyms (opposites). Answer (B) can be eliminated because even though the words are synonyms, they do not mean "drowsy."

29. The correct answer is (B). The clue is the word *editor*. The job requires a person to be "exacting" in order to correct errors. The trigger word is *many*. It is the work of an editor to make "corrections." So the word in the first blank will be a synonym for "exacting." The word in the second blank will be a synonym for "many." Answers (A) and (C) can be eliminated. The first word in each answer is an opposite of "exacting." Answer (D) can be eliminated. Neither of the words has any relationship to an "exacting" editor making many "corrections."

30. The correct answer is (A). The clue is in the words *unpredictable* and *problems*. The words in the blanks (an adjective and a noun because there is no comma between them) will relate to "unpredictability" and "problems." Answer (B) can be eliminated because the first word means constant, so it does not relate to "unpredictability." Answers (C) and (D) can be eliminated because neither of the words relates to the clue words.

31. The correct answer is (D). The clue word is *courtroom*. It tells you that a judge would be there to hear the testimony, so the first word will be a synonym for "judge." The trigger words are *to jail*. The second word will be a verb that is a synonym for "sending." Answers (A) and (C) can be eliminated because the first word in each answer is not a synonym for "judge." Answer (B) can be eliminated because the second word is not a synonym for "sending."

ISEE PRACTICE TEST 1

32. The correct answer is (D). The clue is in the words *As a result of,* and the trigger word is *accident.* The first word describes the "victim." The second word is a verb that relates to "being in a wheelchair." Answer (A) can be eliminated because neither of the words relates to a "victim" or "being confined in a wheelchair." Answers (B) and (C) can be eliminated because the first word in each answer is not a description suitable for a "victim."

33. The correct answer is (C). The clue words are *animal families.* A term for a "specific animal family" will be the first word. The trigger word is *grass.* The second word is a term for "eating grass." One animal that comes to mind readily is the cow. Answers (A) and (D) can be eliminated because they do not relate to "animal families" or "eating grass." Answer (B) can be eliminated because it describes a different animal family as eating meat.

34. The correct answer is (A). The clue is in the words *new at a job* and *novice.* Therefore, "novice" can be defined as being new on the job. Novice describes the noun that will be the first word. The trigger word is *lead.* Being new on an unfamiliar job would make one "unskilled." This could lead to problems. The second word would be a synonym for "problems." Answer (B) can be eliminated because they are the opposite qualities of a "novice." Answers (C) and (D) can be eliminated because the terms contradict each another.

35. The correct answer is (D). The clue is in the words *conservation movement, do not have,* and *energy sources.* It tells you that the movement is interested in "conserving" energy sources because we don't have many. The first word will be a synonym for "plenty" because it is preceded by "not." The trigger word is *therefore.* It establishes a cause and effect relationship between not having abundant energy sources and what we should do about it. The second word will be a synonym for "sparingly." Answers (A) and (C) can be eliminated because although they provide synonyms of "plenty," the second words are the opposite of "sparingly." Answer (B) can be eliminated because the first word is not a synonym for "plenty" but an opposite.

36. The correct answer is (A). The clue is in the words *principal's office* and *behavior*. The appearance of those words in the same sentence usually points toward "bad behavior." The trigger words are *for their*. They link a result of an action. The first word would be a synonym for "punishment." The second word would be a synonym for "bad." Answers (B) and (C) can be eliminated because the second word in each answer is the opposite of "bad" behavior. Answer (D) can be eliminated because the words have no relationship to "punishment" or "bad."

37. The correct answer is (A). The clue is in the words *industrial waste products*, and the trigger word is *once*. The first word will be an adjective that describes the lake before it was affected by the waste and would be a synonym for "pure." The second word would be a synonym for "polluted." Answer (B) can be eliminated because the order of "pure" and "polluted" synonyms is reversed. Answers (C) and (D) do not relate to the clue and trigger words.

38. The correct answer is (B). The clue is in the words *tense situation* and *an argument*. The trigger word is *remarks*. The first word would be an adjective that describes what kind of remarks would cause an argument. It would be a synonym for "sarcastic." The second word would be a synonym for "cause." Answer (A) can be eliminated because the second word in the answer is not a synonym for "cause." Answer (C) can be eliminated because the first word is an opposite of "sarcastic." The last answer can be eliminated because the second word in the answer is not a synonym for "cause."

39. The correct answer is (D). The clue is in the words *prisoner appealed*. That tells you the first word will be a synonym for "lessening." The trigger words are *if not* and *total*. That tells you the second word will be a synonym for "dismissal." Answers (A) and (B) can be eliminated because they do not relate to the clue words and the trigger words. Answer (C) can be eliminated because it reverses the order of the synonyms for "lessening" and "dismissal."

40. The correct answer is (A). The clue is in the words *although* and *taken bribes*. The first word would be a synonym for "suspected." The trigger words are *no* and *evidence*. The second word would be a synonym for "important." Answer (B) can be eliminated because the second word in the answer is not a synonym for "important." Answer (C) can be eliminated because the first word in the answer is not a synonym for "suspected." Answer (D) can be eliminated because the words in the answer do not relate to "suspected" and "important."

QUANTITATIVE REASONING

1. The correct answer is (A). Convert each fraction to an equivalent fraction with a denominator of 100.

    $$\frac{3}{5} \times \frac{20}{20} = \frac{60}{100}$$

    (A) $\frac{39}{50} \times \frac{2}{2} = \frac{78}{100}$

    (B) $\frac{7}{25} \times \frac{4}{4} = \frac{28}{100}$

    (C) $\frac{3}{10} \times \frac{10}{10} = \frac{30}{100}$

    (D) $\frac{59}{100} \times \frac{1}{1} = \frac{59}{100}$

    Thus, $\frac{39}{50} > \frac{3}{5}$

2. The correct answer is (A). To convert percents to decimals, move the decimal point two places to the left:

    .1 % = .001

3. The correct answer is (A). To find the average, divide the sum of the items by 5.

    12.50 + 11.83 + 10.40 + 0.74 + 0.0 = 35.47

    $35.47 ÷ 5 = $7.09

4. The correct answer is (D). $7x - 3 = 4x + 6$ Add 3 to both sides

    $7x = 4x + 9$ Subtract $4x$ from both sides

    $3x = 9$ Divide both sides by 3

    $x = 3$

5. The correct answer is (B). To add signed numbers with different signs, subtract the numbers and use the sign of the number with the larger absolute value.

    $8 - 2\frac{2}{3} = 5\frac{1}{3}$.

    Since 8 is larger than $2\frac{2}{3}$, the solution will be $-5\frac{1}{3}$.

6. The correct answer is (D). To find the perimeter, use the formula $P = 2l + 2w$.

    $P = 2(7) + 2(5) = 14 + 10 = 24$ cm

7. The correct answer is (D). Since 1 cake uses $\frac{2}{3}$ cup of sugar, let $x =$ the number of cakes for which you would need 4 cups of sugar. Now, set up a proportion:

   $$\frac{1}{x} = \frac{\frac{2}{3}}{4}$$ Now, cross multiply

   $(4)(1) = \frac{2}{3}x$ Multiply both sides by $\frac{3}{2}$ to solve for x

   $$4\left(\frac{3}{2}\right) = \left(\frac{3}{2}\right)\frac{2}{3}x$$

   $6 = x$

8. The correct answer is (B).
   $1.4x - 0.9 = 3.3$ Add 0.9 to both sides
   $1.4x = 4.2$ Divide by 1.4
   $x = 3$

9. The correct answer is (B). Begin by finding out how far Brian has jogged:

   $\frac{1}{2} + \frac{1}{3} = \frac{3}{6} + \frac{2}{6} = \frac{5}{6}$ Subtract this result from 1 mile to determine how much is left to run.

   $1 - \frac{5}{6} = \frac{1}{6}$

10. The correct answer is (D). Follow the order of operations
    $(-4)^2 - 3(-4) = 16 - 3(-4) = 16 - (-12) = 16 + 12 = 28$

11. The correct answer is (C). Let $x =$ the first angle

    Then, $90 - x =$ the second angle. We have

    $x - (90 - x) = 50$

    $x - 90 + x = 50$

    $2x - 90 = 50$

    $2x = 140$

    $x = 70$. Thus, the smaller angle must be 20°

12. The correct answer is (A). $2(a + 1) - (1 + 2a)$ Begin by distributing

    $2a + 2 - 1 - 2a$ Now, combine like terms

    $2a - 2a + 2 - 1 = 1$

13. The correct answer is (C). Set up a proportion:

    $\dfrac{1 \text{ inch}}{110 \text{ miles}} = \dfrac{5.5 \text{ inches}}{x \text{ miles}}$ Now, cross multiply

    $x = 5.5 \times 110 = 605$ miles

14. The correct answer is (D). A rational number is a quotient of two integers x and y, $y \neq 0$. $\sqrt{2}, \sqrt{3}$, and $\sqrt{5}$ are all irrational numbers; they cannot be expressed as the quotient of two integers. However, $\sqrt{9} = 3 = \dfrac{3}{1}$, so it is rational.

15. The correct answer is (C). Picture the inheritance as being divided into $3 + 4 + 5 = 12$ portions, of which the largest share consists of 5 of the 12 portions.

    $\dfrac{5}{12} \times 120{,}000 = 50{,}000$

16. The correct answer is (B). The easiest way to solve this problem is to assume that the original price was some nice number, such as $100. Then, the price increases to $300, which is an increase of $200. Thus,

    $\dfrac{\text{increase}}{\text{new price}} = \dfrac{200}{300} = 66\dfrac{2}{3}\%$

17. The correct answer is (D).

    $-5S^2T = -5(-2)^2(-3) = -5(4)(-3) = 60$

18. The correct answer is (B). $\angle BAC$ and $\angle ACD$ are supplementary angles; hence, $m\angle BAC + m\angle ACD = 180$. Substituting, we obtain

    $(a + 30) + m\angle ACD = 180$ or

    $m\angle ACD = 180 - (a + 30) = 150 - a$.

19. The correct answer is (A). Each factor in Column A is bigger than the corresponding factor in Column B.

20. The correct answer is (B). The least common denominator is the smallest number divisible by both denominators.

    The LCD of $\dfrac{1}{4}$ and $\dfrac{3}{5}$ is 20. The LCD of $\dfrac{2}{3}$ and $\dfrac{5}{8}$ is 24.

EXPLANATORY ANSWERS TO THE ISEE PRACTICE TEST 1

21. The correct answer is (D). $4m - 3n - (3m + 2n) = 4m - 3n - 3m - 2n = m - 5n$. Since we do not have numerical values for m and n, $m - 5n$ and $m + 5n$ cannot be compared.

22. The correct answer is (A). The rectangle depicted is 6 by 4. Since the area of a rectangle is length $\times$ width, the area is $6 \times 4 = 24$. The perimeter is given by the formula $2l + 2w = 2(6) + 2(4) = 12 + 8 = 20$.

23. The correct answer is (A). Follow the order of operations

    $(12 + 4)5 + 8 = (16)5 + 8 = 80 + 8 = 88$

    $12 + 4 \times 5 + 8 = 12 + 20 + 8 = 40$

24. The correct answer is (C).

    Since $r + p = 180$, we have $r = 180 - p$

25. The correct answer is (D). Since we know nothing about the size of either x or y, we cannot determine whether $x - y$ or $y - x$ is bigger.

26. The correct answer is (A).

    $\sqrt{2} \approx 1.4$.

    Thus, $5\sqrt{2} \approx 5 \times 1.4 = 7$. $\sqrt{5} \approx 2.2$.

    Thus, $2\sqrt{5} \approx 2 \times 2.2 = 4.4$.

27. The correct answer is (C).

    $\left(1 \times \dfrac{1}{10}\right) + \left(8 \times \dfrac{1}{100}\right) + \left(3 \times \dfrac{1}{1000}\right) = .1 + .08 + .003 = .183$

28. The correct answer is (B). $\left(-\dfrac{3}{5}\right)^2 = \dfrac{9}{25}$

    $\dfrac{6}{10} = \dfrac{3}{5} = \dfrac{15}{25}$

    $\dfrac{9}{25} < \dfrac{15}{25}$

29. The correct answer is (B). For Column A, let x = the price of 32 envelopes. Then, set up a proportion and cross multiply

$$\frac{2}{32} = \frac{5}{x}$$

$$2x = 5 \times 32$$

$$2x = 160$$

$$x = 80 \text{ cents}$$

For Column B, divide 3.30 by $3\frac{2}{3}$

$$\frac{3.30}{3\frac{2}{3}} = \frac{3.30}{\frac{11}{3}} = 3.30 \times \frac{3}{11} = \frac{9.90}{11} = 90 \text{ cents}$$

30. The correct answer is (C). 9 boxes $\times$ 16 cartons = 144 boxes in one row

144 $\times$ 12 rows = 1,728 boxes in 12 rows

31. The correct answer is (B). First, note that $m\angle 3 = 105°$ since corresponding angles are equal.

Then, since $\angle 1$ is supplementary to $\angle 3$, we have $m\angle 1 = 75°$.

Also, $m\angle 6 = 105°$ since vertical angles are congruent. Thus, $m\angle 6 > m\angle 1$.

32. The correct answer is (A). We have $m\angle 2 = 105°$ since $\angle 2$ and $\angle 3$ are congruent.

Then, since $\angle 8$ is the supplement of a 105° angle, we have $m\angle 8 = 75°$.

33. The correct answer is (B). Solve the inequality for x

$\frac{1}{3}x + 3 > -6$ Subtract 3 from both sides

$\frac{1}{3}x > -9$ Multiply both sides by 3

$x > -27$. Since $-18 > -27$, the answer is (B).

34. The correct answer is (A).

$$\frac{7\frac{2}{3}}{\left(\frac{4}{5}\right)\left(\frac{5}{12}\right)} = \frac{\frac{23}{3}}{\frac{1}{3}} = \frac{23}{3} \times 3 = 23$$

$$\frac{7\frac{1}{3}}{\left(\frac{5}{6}\right)\left(\frac{6}{15}\right)} = \frac{\frac{22}{3}}{\frac{1}{3}} = \frac{22}{3} \times 3 = 22$$

35. The correct answer is (C). The area of a triangle is given by the formula $A = \frac{1}{2}bh$. Since the two legs labeled are perpendicular to each other, we can use one as the height and the other as the base: $A = \frac{1}{2}(2s)(s) = s^2$.

The area of a square is given by the formula $A = s^2$.

READING COMPREHENSION

Passage 1

1. The correct answer is (B). (C) is a poor answer since the passage notes that the canyon "is not the world's largest undersea chasm." Both (A) and (D) are possibilities, since they are mentioned in the passage; however, neither explains the convenience of the canyon.

2. The correct answer is (A). (D) is the poorest answer since the subject of erosion is not mentioned in the passage. (C) is incorrect because the paragraph explains that "the canyons were submerged by a rise in sea level." (B) is a better possibility, since the passage mentions "a bigger, older knife," but the problem was not that the theory wasn't old enough; it was that the mechanism described wasn't old enough.

3. The correct answer is (C). Items (A), (B), and (D) are listed in the passage. Since this is a negative question, the only item not on the list is the correct answer.

4. The correct answer is (D). (A) is not mentioned in the passage. (C) is not correct because the blizzard falls "from above" to the depths, not from the depths. (B) is not correct because it describes another substance some of the creatures feed on.

5. The correct answer is (A). (C) is the length of the Grand Canyon in Arizona. Answers (B) and (D) describe the length, not the depth, of the Monterey Canyon.

Passage 2

6. The correct answer is (C). (A) is a poor answer because nothing in the story suggests that Jen is not James's mother. (B) is contradicted because the passage says James is 9, and the twins are 7. (D) is Steiner's age, not James's.

7. The correct answer is (C). (D) is incorrect because it was James who has not spoken in two weeks, not Steiner. (B) does not make sense since Steiner left the family in the car while he looked for the mat, so he could not have been looking for it for two weeks. (A) refers to a time earlier than this part of the story.

8. The correct answer is (B). (A) is impossible, since we are told of James's actions in the car. (D) is incorrect because the passage states James is being driven home from the hospital. (C) is possible since Steiner is described as feeling bad that he and Jen hadn't had more children; however, the wording of the question implies he is grieving for a son he has already had.

EXPLANATORY ANSWERS TO THE ISEE PRACTICE TEST 1

9. The correct answer is (D). (C) is unlikely since it is clear they are returning to a home they have lived in before. Since he had used the phrase since James was an infant, it is unlikely it is meant to start a conversation, so (A) is incorrect. The phrase is general and does not suggest action is needed, so (B) is incorrect.

10. The correct answer is (C). (A) is unlikely since any talks with a physical therapist happened before this story takes place. (D) is incorrect because James honks the horn while he is still in the car. (B) is incorrect since the twins start whispering about him because he honked the horn.

11. The correct answer is (A). Steiner notices James's long hair at the beginning of the last paragraph in the passage. Answers (B), (C), and (D) occur earlier in the passage, and they do not refer to Steiner's looking at James's hair.

Passage 3

12. The correct answer is (C). Since Magro's book has not survived, the limited subject of his work does not contribute to our lack of knowledge about the Carthaginians; thus (D) is not correct. Since I and II are both correct, neither (A) nor (B) is the right answer.

13. The correct answer is (B). Although (A) may be true, that is not the purpose of the statement about Roman crucifixion. (C) is incorrect since the passage does not suggest that the Romans were cruel to any specific group. And since the passage states "there is no reason to think the people of ancient Carthage were any more addicted to cruelty than the Romans," the purpose of the description is not to show they were more cruel, but that they were equally cruel. Thus, (D) is incorrect.

14. The correct answer is (A). (B) is described in the first paragraph. (C) states a fact, but it is not broad enough to describe the entire paragraph, so it is incorrect. (D) is inaccurate, since the language as a whole was not preserved; the playwright's lines are dialogues in his plays.

15. The correct answer is (D). (A) is incorrect because the passage does not tell what happened to the Phoenicians. (B) is contradicted by the content of the passage, and (C) omits the fact that the playwright uses dialogue in the Punic language, so these answers are incorrect.

Passage 4

16. The correct answer is (B). Since the month is May and the leaves are beginning to swell, it is spring. By summer, the leaves would be full grown, so (C) is incorrect, and leaves are not usually green in winter or autumn, making answers (A) and (D) incorrect.

17. The correct answer is (C). Since the person is talking to Barbara Allen, (B) cannot be correct, and since the person is talking about his master, (A) cannot be correct. Barbara's mother is not mentioned until the poem's last stanza, so (D) is incorrect.

18. The correct answer is (A). Her only words to William are to indicate what he already knows, that he is dying. Stanza 4 describes his death, not her behavior, so (B) is incorrect. Stanzas 5 and 6 occur after William dies, so he would not feel her cruelty. Thus, (C) and (D) are incorrect answers.

19. The correct answer is (C). There is no indication that she is ill, so (A) is incorrect. She does not express love for William, so (B) is incorrect. And while she has heard the death bell, it is not the cause of her death (D). The last two lines of the poem imply she knows she caused William's death, making (C) the correct answer.

20. The correct answer is (A). (B) would not make sense because William dies, so he is not revived. While death could be said to "free" a person from life, the word suggests something positive, which does not fit the context of the poem, so (C) is incorrect. (D) is incorrect because William has been parted from life, not joined to it.

Passage 5

21. The correct answer is (D). The author states that "something was sure to come by." The paragraph ends by referring to endlessly more (wildlife). (A) is incorrect because the story is the story of the animals, not of their names. (B) is incorrect; there are not more turtles, but more animals. (C) is a true statement, but it is unrelated to the names of the animals.

22. The correct answer is (C). The words "for example" send the reader to the previous sentence. The trip from Monteverde to San Jose is an example of how easy it is to get from one place to another. (A) could not be correct because the words "for example" always send the reader to the previous text. (B) is incorrect because the information about the climate is between dashes. Dashes indicate information is not the main part of the sentence. For the same reason, answer (D) is incorrect.

EXPLANATORY ANSWERS TO THE ISEE PRACTICE TEST 1

23. The correct answer is (A). Words such as "blessed," "naturalist's paradise" and "one of the world's best systems of reserves" demonstrate the author's attitude.

24. The correct answer is (A). The author states that the order is "defined by the need for sunlight." (B) is incorrect; although the author mentions niches, there is no stated relationship between niches and order or need. (C) means confusion. (D) is addressed, but not in a context of order.

25. The correct answer is (B); the "original tree" was the ladder for the strangler fig. (A) is true; the original tree disappears after having served as a ladder to the soil. (C) is true; the strangler fig is a single tree with a cluster of trunks. (D) is true; the strangler fig dropped shoots that took root in the forest floor.

26. The correct answer is (C) because the author discusses the origin and size of Monteverde, as well as his personal observations. (A) is too general, since only one aspect of Monteverde is mentioned. (B) is too narrow to be a general title. (D) is too general; the focus of the passage is Monteverde.

Passage 6

27. The correct answer is (D). The passage states humans have been around for two million years (A) and flowering plants for 100 million years (B). (C) is not mentioned in the passage.

28. The correct answer is (B). Paragraph 3 states they can "hide in any tiny space." Although the passage states some cockroaches live in sub-Arctic climates, it does not imply all cockroaches like the cold, so (A) is incorrect. (C) is incorrect because adult cockroaches have wings. While (D) is a true statement, the passage does not state this as a reason they have survived.

29. The correct answer is (D). The passage states they "like the dark" and run to their homes when a light comes on. (A), (B), and (C) refer to cockroaches that are not members of these species, according to the passage.

30. The correct answer is (C). The paragraph in which the word appears is about why cockroaches have survived without change. The sentence in which "vulnerable" appears says the cockroaches do "not" undergo metamorphosis, which might make them "vulnerable." Thus, to be vulnerable is undesirable. So (A), (B), and (D) would not be correct.

ISEE PRACTICE TEST 1

Passage 7

31. The correct answer is (B). (A) is incorrect, because while the diet may have been boring, they did not starve. The passage notes they had a "feeling of hunger," but the fact that they "emerged in good health" means they were getting enough to eat. (C) is contradicted by the fact they had to work hard, and (D) is the opposite of what the passage says about carbon dioxide.

32. The correct answer is (A). The passage does not say what the animals ate, so (B) is incorrect. (C) is contradicted because while that may have been the intent of having the animals in Biosphere 2, they did not produce as expected. (D) is incorrect because the passage does not say what happened to the animals.

33. The correct answer is (D). Since the environment was meant to be sealed, outside air could not be let in, so (A) is incorrect. (B) is incorrect because it is plants in the ocean, not the ocean itself, that would provide oxygen. (C) is incorrect because the passage states the animals were meant to be food producers, and animals consume oxygen rather than produce it.

34. The correct answer is (D). Each of the other answers is stated at some point in the passage.

Passage 8

35. The correct answer is (B). The insurgents had rebelled against Spanish rule, and the Spanish commander tried to corner "the rebels." (A) would include the insurgents, but also many other Cubans not involved in a rebellion. (C) suggests a fighting force. Insurgents based in New York, for example, were not directly involved in fighting. (D) is a word that relates to reconcentration, which was a Spanish policy, so it would not describe Cubans rebelling against Spanish rule.

36. The correct answer is (A). The passage states the policy was "designed to move the native population into camps and destroy the rebel's popular base." That is, to remove the source of new rebel troops. Although native Cubans were relocated into camps, making (B) a possibility, the primary purpose of reconcentration was military. (C) was a result of reconcentration, but not its purpose. (D) refers to insurgent activity, not to the relocation carried out by Spaniards.

37. The correct answer is (D), which is supported by the statement the press printed "gruesome" stories. Although "yellow" may mean cowardly in some contexts, it is incorrect in this passage, so (A) is incorrect. (B) is a paraphrase of the sentence "it stemmed from larger conflicts in policy." "It" refers to the war, not to yellow journalism. (C) refers to the sympathy of the American public, so it is incorrect.

Passage 9

38. The correct answer is (C). The word refers to the practices of normally eating insects and human sacrifice. While murder may be illegal, (A), there are no laws preventing Americans from eating what they choose to. Since the passage states eating insects is "normal," (B), "experimental," is not correct. (D) is incorrect because it is a synonym for "unlike," in the passage's third sentence, so it would not add anything to the passage.

39. The correct answer is (B). (A) is incorrect because it implies anthropologists do condemn some behaviors. (C) is incorrect because the passage says that anthropologists do not condemn other behavior. Condemnation would imply that they were judging other cultures against their own—their own being "right" and others being "wrong," and therefore, wrong cultures were merely mistakes. After all, why waste time studying the mistakes of others. Answer (D) is incorrect because the destruction of the universe is part of an example about Aztec culture and is not about why anthropologists think as they do.

40. The correct answer is (C). (A) only refers to one example in the passage, so it is too narrow. (B) is possible, because the first sentence defines an anthropologist, but the passage's content has a broader purpose, showing how anthropologists go about their work. (D) is incorrect because the focus of the passage is on anthropologists, not on judging other cultures.

MATHEMATICS ACHIEVEMENT

1. The correct answer is (C).

   $7.2 \times 10^{-7} = .00000072$

2. The correct answer is (B).

   First find variable expressions to represent the three angles.

   Let the three angles be $8x$, $9x$, and $13x$.

   Since the sum of the angles of any triangle is 180°,

   $8x + 9x + 13x = 180°$.

   Now solve the equation.

   $30x = 180$

   $x = 6$

   Since the smallest angle is $8x$, $8x = 8(6) = 48°$.

3. The correct answer is (A).

   To change a percent into a fraction, divide by 100.

   $$62\frac{1}{2} \div 100 = \frac{125}{2} \div \frac{100}{1} = \frac{125}{2} \times \frac{1}{100} = \frac{125}{200} = \frac{5}{8}$$

4. The correct answer is (A).

   The value of (A) is $\frac{11}{12}$; the value of (B) is $\frac{5}{12}$; the value of (C) is $\frac{1}{36}$; and the value of (D) is $\frac{1}{4}$ or $\frac{3}{12}$. Therefore, (A) has the largest value.

5. The correct answer is (D).

   If $s + (s + 9) > 27$, then $2s > 18$. So $s > 9$. The only answer that is appropriate is 10.

6. The correct answer is (C). To round a number to the tenths place, look at the digit in the hundreths place. If the digit is 5 or larger, raise the tenths digit by one. 21.49

   Since 9 is 5 or larger, 21.49 becomes 21.5.

7. The correct answer is (B). The perimeter of $ABCD = 2l + 2w = 100$. Divide by 2: $l + w = 50$. If the length $AB >$ the width AD, answer (A) would make $AB = AD$. Answers (C) and (D) are too large. Therefore, answer (B) is correct.

8. The correct answer is (B). To add signed numbers with different signs, subtract and use the sign of the number with the larger absolute value.

   $$3\frac{1}{3} + (-6) = 5\frac{3}{3} - \left(3\frac{1}{3}\right) = 2\frac{2}{3}$$

   Since -6 has the larger absolute value, $-2\frac{2}{3}$ is the answer.

9. The correct answer is (B).

   $$-5ST^2 = (-5)(-2)(-3)^2 = (-5)(-2)(-3)(-3) = 90$$

10. The correct answer is (D).

    $ab + c = 2$

    Subtract c: $ab + c - c = 2 - c$
    $ab = 2 - c$

    Divide by b to get a: $\frac{ab}{b} = \frac{2-c}{b}$ $a = \frac{2-c}{b}$

11. The correct answer is (B).

    Substitute the numerical values for *a, r,* and *n* and compute *S*.

    $$S = \frac{a(1-r^n)}{1-r} = \frac{(-2)(1-2^3)}{1-2} = \frac{(-2)(1-8)}{-1} = \frac{(-2)(-7)}{-1} = \frac{14}{-1} = -14$$

12. The correct answer is (C).

    Using the Pythagorean theorem,

    $$a^2 + b^2 = c^2$$
    $$a^2 + (18)^2 = (30)^2$$
    $$a^2 + 324 = 900$$
    $$a^2 + 324 - 324 = 900 - 324$$
    $$a^2 = 576$$
    $$a = \sqrt{576}$$
    $$a = 24$$

13. The correct answer is (C).

    Let the original rectangle be expressed as:

    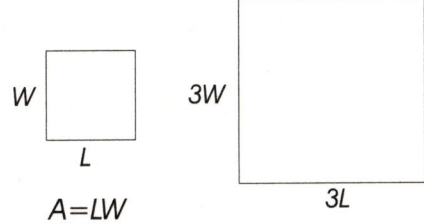

    $$\text{ratio} = \frac{\text{original}}{\text{enlarged}} = \frac{1lw}{9lw} = \frac{1}{9} = 1:9$$

14. The correct answer is (C). Multiples of 8 include: 8, 16, 24, 32, 40, 48, 56, 64, 72, 80, 88, 104, etc. Comparing these with the answers provided, notice that the number 100 is not a multiple of 8. 144 is equal to 8×18.

15. The correct answer is (B). The number of left-handed members is equal to $12 - 8$, or 4. The ratio of right-handers to left-handers is 8:4, which simplifies to 2:1.

16. The correct answer is (A). Set up a ratio for this problem and solve.

    Let x represent the number of books purchased with 2 dollars.

    $$\frac{5}{d} = \frac{x}{2}$$

    $5 \times 2 = d \times x$ (using cross-multiplication)

    $$\frac{10}{d} = x$$

17. The correct answer is (A).

    All factors of 8 are factors of the number.

    The factors of 8 are:

    1×8

    2×4

18. The correct answer is (B). Since this is an isosceles triangle, the angles opposite the congruent sides are also congruent. The sum of the angles in a triangle equal 180°. So $55° + 55° + x° = 180°$ and $x = 70°$.

19. The correct answer is (D).

    Let p equal the price of the item.

    Price × Discount Rate = Discount Amount

    So $p \times 40\% = \$4.00$; $p \times .40 = 4.00$; $p = \frac{4.00}{.40} = 10$

20. The correct answer is (A). There are 12 different outfits since for every skirt there is a choice of four different blouses.

    $3 \times 4 = 12$

21. The correct answer is (B).

    The first day, $\frac{1}{4}$ of the taxes was done, so there were $\frac{3}{4}$ left.

    $$\frac{1}{2} \times \frac{3}{4} = \frac{3}{8}$$

    And

    $$\frac{1}{4} + \frac{3}{8} = \frac{5}{8}$$

22. The correct answer is (A).

    $$8x - 14 = 42$$
    $$8x = 56$$
    $$x = 7, \text{ so}$$
    $$7 - 5 = 2$$

23. The correct answer is (B). To add signed numbers, if the signs are different, subtract and use the sign of the number with the larger absolute value.

    $$2\frac{2}{3} + (-7) = 7 - 2\frac{2}{3} = 4\frac{1}{3}$$

    Because -7 has the larger absolute value, the solution is

    $$-4\frac{1}{3}$$

24. The correct answer is (B). If the carton is $\frac{2}{3}$ empty, it must be $\frac{1}{3}$ full. $\frac{1}{3}$ the total capacity of 60 ounces is 20.

25. The correct answer is (B). The altitude of an equilateral triangle bisects the vertex, forming a 30-60-90 triangle with sides in the ratios shown.

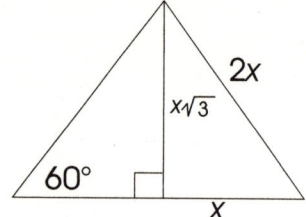

(This also comes from the Pythagorean theorem, and the fact that the base of an equilateral triangle has been bisected to form this 30-60-90 triangle.)

The sides will be in the same ratio for the given triangle.

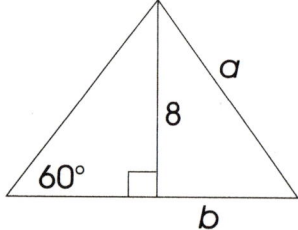

So, with the ratios $1:\sqrt{3}:2$ equaling the ratios $b:8:a$ we find $b = \dfrac{8}{\sqrt{3}}$ and $a = \dfrac{16}{\sqrt{3}}$.

Area = one half base times height, so

$$A = (8)\left(\dfrac{8}{\sqrt{3}}\right) = \dfrac{64}{\sqrt{3}} = \dfrac{64\sqrt{3}}{3}.$$

26. The correct answer is (D). The area of the square minus the area of the circle equals the shaded area.

$OA = 3$

$2OA = 6 =$ diameter = side of square

area of square = s^2

area of circle = πr^2

$A = (6)^2$ $A = \pi(3)^2$
$\quad = 36$ $\quad = 9\pi$

27. The correct answer is (A). The stock declined in value by $1,500, from an initial value of $11,000. The fractional decline in value is $\frac{1500}{11000} = .1364$, which is 13.64%.

28. The correct answer is (B). When you decrease a price by a given percentage, and then increase the (now lowered) price by that same percentage, the actual amount of increase is less than the actual amount of decrease.

After a 10% discount, the sale price is 90% of the original amount. A 10% tax on this sale price means the final price is 110% of the taxable amount. (100% for the item, and 10% for the tax.)

Expressing percents as decimals, we have:

$(350 \times .9) \times 1.1 = 346.50$

It doesn't matter what order the operations are performed in since multiplication is commutative and associative.

$(350 \times 1.1) \times .9$ is still 346.50

29. The correct answer is (B). The equation of a line is given by $y = mx + b$ where m is the slope and b is the y-intercept. In this case, $y = 8x + (-3)$ which is the same as $y = 8x - 3$.

30. The correct answer is (C). To have an average of 80 after five tests, the total of all the scores must be $80 \times 5 = 400$. The known scores add up to $70 + 87 + 94 + 69 = 320$, so she needs $400 - 320 = 80$ points on the last test.

31. The correct answer is (D). Percent means "per 100."

$4\frac{1}{2}$ percent means $\frac{4.5}{100} = .045$

32. The correct answer is (C).

Put time in like units.

$\frac{15 \text{ hours}}{3 \text{ days}} = \frac{15 \text{ hours}}{3 \times 24 \text{ hours}} = \frac{15 \text{ hours}}{72 \text{ hours}}$

Cancel out common factor of $3 = \frac{5}{24}$

Although (D) is correct, it is not expressed in simplest form.

33. The correct answer is (D).

$$5x + 4 = 9x - 2$$
$$5x + 4 - 4 = 9x - 2 - 4$$
$$5x = 9x - 6$$
$$5x - 9x = 9x - 6 - 9x$$
$$-4x = -6$$
$$x = \frac{-6}{-4} = \frac{6}{4} = \frac{3}{2}$$

34. The correct answer is (C). There are 14 outcomes (total gumballs), of which five are successes (red).

35. The correct answer is (A).

To add algebraic expressions, combine like terms.

$$2x^2 - 3x + 5$$
$$\underline{-3x - 2}$$
$$2x^2 - 6x + 3$$

36. The correct answer is (B).

Substitute values $p = 1,500$, $r = .04$, and $t = 2\frac{1}{2}$.

$$A = 1,500 + (1,500)(.04)2\frac{1}{2} = 1,500 + 150 = 1,650$$

37. The correct answer is (C).

$$\frac{30}{8} = \frac{12}{y}$$
$$30y = 12 \times 8 \text{ (cross-multiply)}$$
$$30y = 96$$
$$y = \frac{96}{30} = 3\frac{1}{5}$$

38. The correct answer is (D).

$$\frac{12}{x} - \frac{9}{x} = \frac{3}{x}$$

The problem is written with all common denominators. Simply subtract the numerators.

39. The correct answer is (B).

$$4^3 - 3^4 = 64 - 81 = -17$$

40. The correct answer is (A). The line described by the equation crosses the x-axis when $y = 0$.

$$0 = -3x + 7$$
$$-7 = -3x$$
$$x = \frac{-7}{-3} = \frac{7}{3}$$

41. The correct answer is (D). To break a number into its prime factors, break it into factors, and break those factors into factors, until you cannot go any further. It doesn't matter what factors you begin with. You will reach the same prime factors.

$$50 = 10 \times 5 = 5 \times 2 \times 5$$

5 and 2 are prime numbers (they have no factors other than themselves and 1), and multiplication is commutative (it can be performed in any order).

Another way to approach the problem is to rule out the answers that have composite (non-prime) numbers. This rules out (A) and (B). Test the remaining answers by multiplying them out. Only (D) comes to 50.

42. The correct answer is (A).

$$A = \frac{bh}{2}$$
$$320 = \frac{40h}{2}$$
$$320 = 20h$$
$$16 = h$$

43. The correct answer is (A). If there are two parallel lines cut by a transversal, the alternate interior angles are congruent.

44. The correct answer is (B). Draw a diagram. They form similar triangles, ($\angle A = \angle B$). Therefore, corresponding sides are in the same ratio:

12 inches : 3 inches = 120 feet : 30 feet

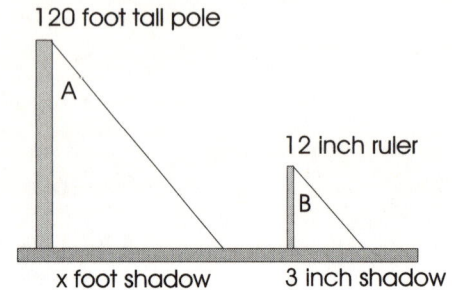

45. The correct answer is (D).

AC and CB are congruent, making C the midpoint of AB. AC is 10 so BC is 10 and AB is 20. It is not given that B is the midpoint of AD, just that it lies between A and D. Therefore, AB and BD are not necessarily congruent. There is no other relationship that will give the length of segment BD or of CD.

ISEE Practice Test 2

Verbal Reasoning 498
Quantitative Reasoning 502
Reading Comprehension 506
Mathematics Achievement 515
Writing the Essay 521

**Explanatory Answers to the
ISEE Practice Test 2** 524
   Verbal Reasoning 524
   Quantitative Reasoning 528
   Reading Comprehension 534
   Mathematics Achievement 538

Verbal Reasoning

Time: 20 minutes **40 Questions**

DIRECTIONS: Each question is made up of a word in capital letters followed by four choices. You should circle the one word that is most nearly the same in meaning as the word in capital letters.

1. APPRAISE:
   - (A) search
   - (B) estimate
   - (C) prove
   - (D) complain

2. AUGMENT:
   - (A) scatter
   - (B) strike
   - (C) honor
   - (D) increase

3. TRITE:
   - (A) ignorant
   - (B) unlikely
   - (C) common
   - (D) unskilled

4. SOLICIT:
   - (A) comfort
   - (B) consent
   - (C) help
   - (D) request

5. VIGILANT:
   - (A) anxious
   - (B) harmful
   - (C) watchful
   - (D) pleasant

6. BIZARRE:
   - (A) greedy
   - (B) strange
   - (C) brief
   - (D) fortunate

7. ANALOGY:
   - (A) contract
   - (B) contest
   - (C) similarity
   - (D) necessity

8. FRUGAL:
   - (A) showy
   - (B) thrifty
   - (C) abundant
   - (D) grateful

9. DEFECTION:
   - (A) desertion
   - (B) denial
   - (C) reduction
   - (D) obsession

10. DILEMMA:
    - (A) citation
    - (B) scheme
    - (C) difficulty
    - (D) decree

11. EMINENT:
    - (A) profane
    - (B) despicable
    - (C) affluent
    - (D) distinguished

12. PERCEIVE:
    - (A) reject
    - (B) understand
    - (C) persist
    - (D) relinquish

13. COLLABORATE:
    - (A) work together
    - (B) deny completely
    - (C) walk briskly
    - (D) leave alone

14. RUTHLESS:
    - (A) careless
    - (B) useless
    - (C) merciless
    - (D) fearless

15. AGGRESSIVE:
    - (A) casual
    - (B) lengthy
    - (C) lenient
    - (D) hostile

16. FIDELITY:
    - (A) timeliness
    - (B) loyalty
    - (C) hatred
    - (D) spite

17. IRATE:
    - (A) enraged
    - (B) dejected
    - (C) economical
    - (D) capable

18. ABDUCT:
    - (A) abbreviate
    - (B) abdicate
    - (C) kidnap
    - (D) relieve

19. GRIMACE:
    - (A) journal
    - (B) grindstone
    - (C) treasure
    - (D) sneer

20. REFUTE:
    - (A) disprove
    - (B) assist
    - (C) postpone
    - (D) demolish

DIRECTIONS: Each question below is made up of a sentence with one or two blanks. The sentences with one blank indicate that one word is missing. The sentences with two blanks indicate that two words are missing. Each sentence is followed by four choices. You should circle the one word or pair of words that will best complete the meaning of the sentence as a whole.

21. After assessing the term of the elderly politician, one could conclude that as he neared _____ he became a(n) _____ leader, as shown by his forgetfulness on the floor of the Congress.
    - (A) feebleness . . competent
    - (B) senility . . unproductive
    - (C) infirmity . . capable
    - (D) polarity . . brackish

22. A refugee fleeing a country may have to _____ his allegiance to that country and _____ his family and friends.
    - (A) anticipate . . constitute
    - (B) evaluate . . abandon
    - (C) renounce . . forsake
    - (D) relinquish . . fluctuate

23. After taking a course in Home and Careers, she could conclude that _____ is a part of the study of _____.
    - (A) anatomy . . optometry
    - (B) fatalism . . etymology
    - (C) ornithology . . criminology
    - (D) autism . . agnosticism

24. Many great thinkers have observed that the lifetime of an individual is _____ when compared to _____, thereby making each of us seem less important in the big picture.

    (A) fatigued . . energy
    (B) momentary . . eternity
    (C) ephemeral . . insignificance
    (D) juvenile . . maturation

25. "When I am _____, I am also _____," explained the student with the downhearted look on her face.

    (A) blissful . . sparkling
    (B) irrational . . insightful
    (C) melancholy . . lamentable
    (D) bellicose . . affable

26. The psychologist could see that his patient suffered from _____ because he always thinks others _____ against him.

    (A) levity . . crusade
    (B) paranoia . . conspire
    (C) renown . . falsify
    (D) finesse . . rally

27. Historically, in witchcraft an evil witch when casting a _____ spell would use a small figurine as a _____.

    (A) malevolent . . fetish
    (B) virtuous . . charm
    (C) malignant . . heretic
    (D) beneficent . . amulet

28. Before the time of the internal combustion machine, during warfare it would not be unusual to see the _____ troops appear on the _____.

    (A) scapegoat . . mercenary
    (B) shiftless . . glut
    (C) sequestered . . epoch
    (D) equestrian . . mesa

29. People who live in large cities have to deal with the rushed pace of metropolitan life; as a relief from _____ pressures, many plan to vacation in _____ locales.

    (A) inert . . kindred
    (B) urban . . bucolic
    (C) rural . . metropolitan
    (D) porous . . ungainly

30. A male who has physically taken advantage of females should realize that his _____ has led him to _____.

    (A) whimsy . . avowal
    (B) kindness . . lechery
    (C) lust . . carnality
    (D) lewdness . . slothfulness

31. Although her natural abilities as an athlete are minimal, she has _____ them to the fullest; whereas her brother, who is a natural athlete, has _____ his.

    (A) maximized . . squandered
    (B) subjugated . . liberated
    (C) awed . . slighted
    (D) breached . . rectified

32. When trying to get the business owner to pay his fair share of taxes, the accountant often finds that _____ business owners are often mainly concerned only with the _____ aspects of life.

    (A) parsimonious . . monetary
    (B) generous . . charitable
    (C) dexterous . . caustic
    (D) ample . . estranged

33. During the summer cold snap, temperatures _____ to freezing, but the next week they _____ back into the nineties.

    (A) nullified . . vied
    (B) evolved . . maimed
    (C) skyrocketed . . plunged
    (D) plummeted . . soared

34. Even though the boxer had _____ a number of powerful punches, he refused to _____ to his opponent.

    (A) endured . . submit
    (B) repelled . . capitulate
    (C) engrossed . . sustain
    (D) obstructed . . infiltrate

35. The earthquake was so powerful that it _____ the entire city, leaving the once majestic skyscraper in piles of _____.

    (A) accorded . . remains
    (B) rued . . wreckage
    (C) enhanced . . rubble
    (D) devastated . . debris

36. The debater did not _____ many proofs to support his argument, but the ones that he did present were _____ enough to make him the winner.

    (A) summon . . noisome
    (B) cite . . cogent
    (C) enumerate . . debilitating
    (D) reference . . deleterious

37. Even though her happy birthday wish to me was _____, it was enough to _____ my hurt feelings.

    (A) churlish . . pacify
    (B) verdant . . bequeath
    (C) belated . . assuage
    (D) punctual . . damaged

38. The musician was _____ that most of the critics gave her concert complimentary reviews; however, she was still _____ by the negative ones.

    (A) elated . . agitated
    (B) irate . . contented
    (C) delighted . . exhilarated
    (D) despondent . . riled

39. In the medical malpractice lawsuit, the _____ was seeking _____ for the pain and suffering he experienced after a failed operation.

    (A) invalid . . absolution
    (B) plaintiff . . recompense
    (C) rustic . . enlightenment
    (D) defrauder . . compensation

40. The love story ended happily when the young husband returns to save his _____ bride from what surely would have been _____ death.

    (A) apex . . flippant
    (B) surly . . unavoidable
    (C) boorish . . inevitable
    (D) cherished . . inescapable

QUANTITATIVE REASONING   TIME: 35 MINUTES   35 QUESTIONS

DIRECTIONS: Any figures that accompany questions in this section may be assumed to be drawn as accurately as possible EXCEPT when it is stated that a particular figure is not drawn to scale. Letters such as x, y, and n stand for real numbers.

For Questions 1-18, work each in your head or on the space available on these pages. Then select the correct answer.

1. 21.49 is closest to:
   - (A) 22
   - (B) 21.4
   - (C) 21.5
   - (D) 21.45

2. Tom's bowling scores were 175, 155, and 210. What is his average score?
   - (A) 540
   - (B) 185
   - (C) 180
   - (D) 175

3. $62\frac{1}{2}\% =$
   - (A) $\frac{5}{8}$
   - (B) $\frac{8}{5}$
   - (C) 62.5
   - (D) $\frac{31}{50}$

4. Find the sum of $2b + 5$, $4b - 4$, and $3b - 6$.
   - (A) $9b - 5$
   - (B) $9b - 10$
   - (C) $24b^2 + 120$
   - (D) $9b - 1$

5. $(-3)^2 - 4(-3) =$
   - (A) 3
   - (B) -15
   - (C) 108
   - (D) 21

6. At the Hoboken Gourmet Company, Karen is baking cookies. The recipe calls for 100 grams of flour per 40 ounces of water. How many ounces of water would be needed for 8,025 grams of flour?
   - (A) 2,006 ounces
   - (B) 1,284 ounces
   - (C) 3,210 ounces
   - (D) 3,325 ounces

7.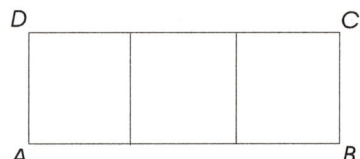

   Three congruent squares are arranged in a row. If the perimeter of ABCD is 80, then the area of ABCD is:
   - (A) 100
   - (B) 193
   - (C) 260
   - (D) 300

8. What is 72 expressed as the product of prime factors?
   - (A) (2)(3)
   - (B) (2)(3)(12)
   - (C) (6)(6)(2)
   - (D) (2)(2)(2)(3)(3)

9. Find the value of $\frac{8}{3-x}$ if $x = -1$.

   (A) $\frac{8}{5}$
   (B) 4
   (C) 2
   (D) $\frac{1}{2}$

10. The sum of two consecutive integers is 39. What is the value of the smaller of these integers?

    (A) 11
    (B) 12
    (C) 18
    (D) 19

11. The perimeter of a square is R meters. The area of the square is:

    (A) $4R$
    (B) $\frac{R^2}{4}$
    (C) $\frac{R^2}{16}$
    (D) $2R^2$

12. Tom's weekly rent increased from $125 to $143.75. Find the percent of increase.

    (A) 1.15%
    (B) 1.5%
    (C) 8.7%
    (D) 15%

13. If $\frac{3}{x}$ is subtracted from $\frac{4}{x}$, the result is:

    (A) 1
    (B) $\frac{7}{x}$
    (C) $\frac{-1}{x}$
    (D) $\frac{1}{x}$

14. Find the value of y in the proportion $\frac{20}{12} = \frac{5}{y}$.

    (A) $8\frac{1}{3}$
    (B) 3
    (C) 15
    (D) 8

15. Express as a trinomial: $(3a + 5)(2a - 3)$

    (A) $6a^2 + 15$
    (B) $6a^2 - 4a - 15$
    (C) $6a^2 + a - 15$
    (D) $6a^2 - a + 15$

16. If two fractions, each of which has a value between 0 and 1, are multiplied together, the product will be:

    (A) Always greater than both of the original fractions
    (B) Always less than both of the original fractions
    (C) Sometimes greater and sometimes less than both of the original fractions
    (D) Never less than both of the original fractions

17. The expression $\sqrt{162}$ is equivalent to:

    (A) $4\sqrt{2}$
    (B) $4 + \sqrt{2}$
    (C) $9\sqrt{2}$
    (D) $9 + \sqrt{2}$

18. If the length and the width of a rectangle are both tripled, the ratio of the area of the original rectangle to the area of the enlarged rectangle is:

    (A) 1:3
    (B) 1:6
    (C) 1:9
    (D) 1:18

Directions: For Questions 19–35 note the given information, if any, and then compare the quantity in Column A to the quantity in Column B. Next to the number of each question, write

A if the quantity in Column A is greater
B if the quantity in Column B is greater
C if the two quantities are equal
D if the relationship cannot be determined from the information given

	Column A	Column B
19.	.01	.0099

20.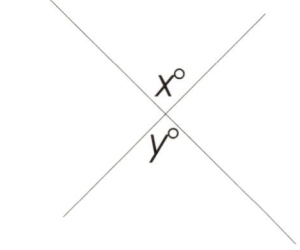
    x y

21. $6 \times 5 + 3$ $(6 + 5)3$

	Column A	Column B
22.	$7y = 28$	
	y	$(-2)^2$
23.	Ratio of $\frac{1}{4}$ to $\frac{3}{8}$	$66\frac{2}{3}\%$

24.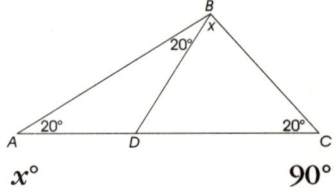
    $x°$ $90°$

25. $\frac{1}{3}$ of $\frac{3}{5}$ .25

26. $r < 0$
    $\frac{1}{r}$ r^2

27. 8^2 2^8

28. $4:6 = m:15$
    m 10

29. $\left(\frac{1}{10}\right)^2$ $\left(\frac{1}{10}\right)^3 \times 10$

30.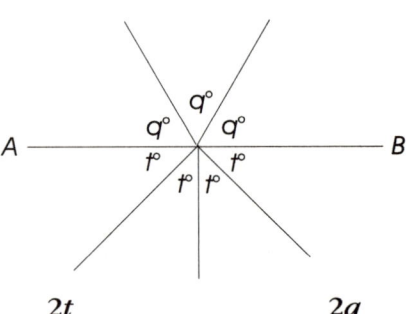
    $2t$ $2q$

31. The average price per pound of a mixture of 3 lbs. of nuts at $1.89 per pound and 2 lbs. of pecans at $1.49 per pound   Average of $1.09, $2.19, and $4.75

QUANTITATIVE REASONING

	Column A	Column B
32.	$x^2 + x$	$\left(\dfrac{\sqrt{3}}{2}\right)^2$

$x = \dfrac{1}{2}$

	Column A	Column B
33.	The area of a circle whose radius is 10 inches	The circumference of a circle whose diameter is 100 inches
34.	$\dfrac{\sqrt{7}}{3}$	$\dfrac{3}{\sqrt{7}}$

	Column A	Column B
35.	$m\angle 4$	$m\angle 2$

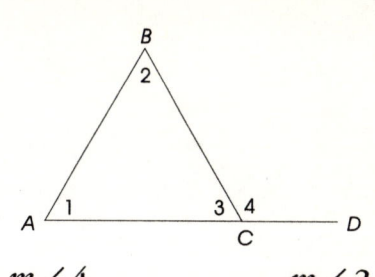

Reading Comprehension   Time: 35 minutes   40 Questions

Directions: Each passage below is followed by questions based on its content. Answer the questions following a passage on the basis of what is *stated* or *implied* in that passage.

Passage 1

Line   Without his particular world of voices, persons, events, the world that both expresses and contains him, Othello is unimaginable. And so, I think, are Antony,
5   King Lear, Macbeth, and Hamlet. We come back then to Hamlet's world, of all the tragic worlds that Shakespeare created, easily the most various and brilliant, the most elusive. It is with no thought of doing justice to it
10   that I have singled out three of its attributes for comment. I know too well, if I may echo a sentiment of Mr. E. M. W. Tillyard's, that no one is likely to accept another man's reading of *Hamlet,* that anyone who tries to
15   throw light on one part of the play throws the rest into deeper shadow, and that what I have to say leaves many problems—to mention only one, the knotty problem of the text. All I would say in defense of the
20   materials I have chosen is that they seem to me interesting, close to the root of the matter even if we continue to differ about what the root of the matter is, and explanatory, in a modest way, of this play's peculiar
25   hold on everyone's imagination, its almost mythic status, one might say, as a paradigm of the life of man.

The first attribute that impresses us, I think, is mysteriousness. We hear often it
30   said, perhaps with truth, that every great work of art has a mystery at the heart; but the mystery of *Hamlet* is something else. We feel its presence in the numberless explanations that have been brought forth for
35   Hamlet's delay, his madness, his ghost, his treatment of Polonius, or Ophelia, or his mother; and in the controversies that still go on about whether the play is "undoubtedly a failure" (Eliot's phrase) or one of the
40   greatest artistic triumphs; whether, if it is a triumph, it belongs to the highest order of tragedy; whether, if it is such a tragedy, its hero is to be taken as a man of exquisite moral sensibility (Bradley's view) or an
45   egomaniac (Madariaga's view).

Doubtless there have been more of these controversies and explanations than the play requires; for in *Hamlet,* to paraphrase a remark of Falstaff's, we have a
50   character who is not only mad in himself but a cause that madness is in the rest of us. Still, the very existence of so many theories and counter-theories, many of them formulated by sober heads, gives food for thought.
55   *Hamlet* seems to lie closer to the illogical logic of life than Shakespeare's other tragedies. And while the causes of this situation may be sought by saying that Shakespeare revised the play so often that
60   eventually the motivations were smudged over, or that the original old play has been here and there imperfectly digested, or that the problems of Hamlet lay so close to Shakespeare's heart that he could not quite
65   distance them in formal terms of art, we have still as critics to deal with effects, not causes. If I may quote again from Mr. Tillyard, the play's very lack of a rigorous type of causal logic seems to be a part of its
70   point.

1. Which one of the names on the following list does not provide an opinion about *Hamlet*?

    (A) Tillyard
    (B) Eliot
    (C) Antony
    (D) Bradley

2. The best meaning of the word "paradigm" is

    (A) example
    (B) highlight
    (C) opinion
    (D) exalted view

3. From this passage we can infer that *Hamlet*

    (A) is open to many interpretations
    (B) is best interpreted by Eliot
    (C) cannot be interpreted
    (D) can be explained only by logic

4. This passage is written by which one of the following types of writers?

    (A) a journalist
    (B) a memoirist
    (C) a critic
    (D) a reviewer

Passage 2

Line   Mechanical weathering happens in many ways. Common mechanical weathering processes are frost action, wetting and drying, action of plant and animals, and the
5   loss of overlying rock and soil.
       Water takes up about 10 percent more space when it freezes. This expansion puts great pressure on a container. For example, think about a pail of water left outdoors in
10   freezing weather. The force of freezing water may split the pail. In the same way, water held in the cracks of rocks wedges the rocks apart when it freezes. This process is called ice wedging or frost action. Ice wedging oc-
15   curs in places where the temperature varies from below the freezing point of water (32 degrees Fahrenheit) to above the freezing point. In the northern United States and in other places in which there are frequent
20   freezes and thaws, ice wedging is the most damaging of all weathering processes.
       Ice wedging occurs mostly in porous rocks and in rocks with cracks in them. Bare mountaintops, especially, are subject to ice
25   wedging. Vast fields of large, sharp-cornered boulders are often found on such mountaintops. Ice wedging also causes potholes on paved streets and highways. Here it is helped by ice heaving. Ice heaving happens
30   when water in the ground freezes and lifts the pavement above it. When the ice thaws, the pavement collapses, leaving the pothole.
       Repeated wetting and drying is especially effective at breaking up rocks that
35   contain clay. Clays swell up when wet and shrink when dry. Constant swelling and shrinking causes rock that contains clay, such as shale, to fall apart.
       Small plants, such as lichens and
40   mosses, grow on rocks. They wedge their tiny roots into pores and crevices. When the roots grow, the rock splits. Larger shrubs and trees may grow through cracks in boulders. Ants, earthworms, rabbits, wood-
45   chucks, and other animals dig holes in the soil. These holes allow air and water to reach the bedrock and weather it.
       Granite is a rock formed far below Earth's surface. It is exposed when the rocks
50   on top of it are worn away. The removal of the rocks reduces the pressure on the granite. When this happens, the relief from the pressure lets the granite expand. Upward expansion leads to long curved
55   breaks, or joints. The joints are parallel to the surface and occur in exposed peaks or outcrops. This process is sheet joining. From time to time, large sheets of loosened rock break away from the outcrop. This process
60   is called exfoliation—the peeling of surface layers. Rounded mountain peaks called exfoliated domes are formed in this way.

5. The best title of this passage is

   (A) Some Geological Basics
   (B) How Rocks Change
   (C) Ice Wedging and Ice Heaving
   (D) Types of Mechanical Weathering

6. The most damaging of all weathering processes is

   (A) ice wedging
   (B) ice heaving
   (C) wetting and drying
   (D) exfoliation

7. Which of the following combinations causes potholes?

   (A) ice wetting and wetting and drying
   (B) ice wedging and sheet joining
   (C) sheet joining and exfoliation
   (D) ice wedging and ice heaving

8. What is an "outcrop"?

   (A) an exfoliated peak
   (B) an exposed peak
   (C) a granite peak
   (D) all exposed rock

9. Frost action is the same as

   (A) ice heaving
   (B) ice wedging
   (C) sheet joining
   (D) exfoliation

Passage 3

Line Unable to subdue Great Britain in the West, Napoleon turned toward the East. In 1812 he invaded Russia. At first, Napoleon's huge army of about 600,000 men was successful.
5   It defeated Russian forces in several engagements and pushed on toward Moscow. However, the Russian emperor, Alexander I, refused to risk the outcome of the war on a single battle. His forces retreated deep into
10   Russia until, as the French General Caulaincourt said: "We (the French) were in the heart of inhabited Russia and yet . . . we were like a vessel without a compass in the midst of a vast ocean, knowing nothing of
15   what was happening around us."
      Napoleon's army entered Moscow in the middle of September and found a deserted city. Napoleon waited for the Russian emperor to surrender. He waited
20   while Russian peasants stole into Moscow at night and set fire to parts of the city. He waited while Russian Cossacks raided his supply routes and cut his lines of communication. He waited while the winds of Russia
25   became colder and colder. He waited, but Emperor Alexander I said nothing.
      With the approach of winter his supplies ran dangerously low. Napoleon therefore decided to move his army out of
30   Russia. On October 19, he left Moscow. Thus began one of the most disastrous retreats. Soldiers starved or froze to death. Horses, kept on the move for 14 and 15 hours a day, collapsed. The wounded fell off
35   carts only to have the drivers of other vehicles ride over their bodies so as not to lose their place in line. The Cossacks waylaid stragglers and raided transport wagons. Brotherhood was forgotten and,
40   according to General Caulaincourt, "every man thought of himself, and himself alone."
      Napoleon, who rarely concerned himself about the men who lost their lives, issued this bulletin: "His Majesty (Napoleon)
45   has never been in better health." The purpose of this was to end rumors in France that he was dead or dying and to stifle any plans to replace him. Then on December 5, he abandoned his doomed army and hurried
50   to Paris to strengthen his position in France. Only 40,000 of Napoleon's troops crossed the border out of Russia.

10. The repetition of "He waited . . ." in paragraph 2 is intended to create which effect on the reader?

(A) boredom
(B) dread
(C) to provide images
(D) suspense

11. The best title of this passage is

(A) Napoleon's Greatest Battle
(B) Napoleon's Disastrous Invasion
(C) In the Middle of the Ocean
(D) The French and Russian War

12. The passage illustrates which one of Napoleon's qualities best?

(A) his strategic brilliance
(B) his ability to negotiate
(C) his disdain for his own soldiers
(D) his ability to transform misfortune into victory

13. The best meaning of the word "stifle" is

(A) suppress
(B) encourage
(C) delay
(D) give voice to

Passage 4

Line Imagine a steep valley high in the mountainous Alps of Switzerland. No river runs in this valley. Instead, the entire valley floor is covered by a mass of snow-covered ice,
5 hundreds of meters thick. This ice mass can be followed up the valley for many kilometers. It begins in huge fields of ice and snow just below the very highest peaks.

Careful study would show that the ice
10 in this valley has moved downhill at the rate of several meters a day. At the lower part of the valley, the thin ice runs out and suddenly ends. Milky-colored water runs from beneath the ice and flows down into the
15 valley. This long, slow-moving, wedge-shaped stream of ice is a valley glacier.

Imagine a great landmass in the polar latitudes of the far north or south. The climate is so cold that only snow falls. For
20 thousands of years snow has been falling, building up, and changing to ice. Almost the whole landmass is covered by the thick mass of ice. Only the highest mountain peaks reach above the ice.

25 The ice is thousands of meters thick, and it moves outward from its center in all directions toward the seacoasts. In some places it reaches the sea by traveling through low valleys. Here great chunks of
30 ice break off to float away as icebergs. This moving mass of ice, far larger than a valley glacier, is called an ice sheet.

Glaciers are born in areas always covered by snow. These are areas where
35 more snow falls than melts each year. Some snow is always left to add to the buildup of previous years. Climates cold enough to cause such conditions may be found in any part of the world. Air temperatures drop
40 with greater height above sea level and with greater distance from the equator.

Even in equatorial areas, then, permanent snows may be found on high mountains. Farther from the equator the moun-
45 tains need not be so high for snow to exist. In the polar areas permanent snows may be found even at sea level. The lowest level that permanent snows reach in summer is called the snow line. A mountain that is
50 completely covered with snow in winter, but from which the snow is all melted by summer, has no snow line.

The snow line is highest near the equator and lowest near the poles. As
55 climates become colder with greater latitude (distance from the equator), less height is needed to reach a snow line. The position of the snow line also changes with the total yearly snowfall and the amount of exposure

60 to the sun. Thus the height of a snow line is not the same for all places in the same latitude.

14. From this passage it is clear that a valley glacier

   (A) is too heavy to move
   (B) runs swiftly like a river
   (C) can run downhill several yards a day
   (D) is stationary

15. In which way does an "ice sheet" compare to a "valley glacier"?

   (A) they both produce icebergs
   (B) an ice sheet is larger
   (C) a valley glacier is larger
   (D) they both are taller than mountains

16. From this passage we can infer that a snow line

   (A) cannot exist near the equator
   (B) is always the same height
   (C) is lowest near the equator
   (D) is lowest near the poles

17. From this passage we can deduce that the latitude of a pole compared to the equator is

   (A) greater
   (B) impossible to determine
   (C) constantly changing
   (D) equal

Passage 5

Line Two roads diverged in a yellow wood,
      And sorry I could not travel both
      And be one traveler, long I stood
      And looked down one as far as I could
5   To where it bent in the undergrowth;

      Then took the other, as just as fair,
      And having perhaps the better claim,
      Because it was grassy and wanted wear;
      Though as for that, the passing there
10   Had worn them really about the same.

      And both that morning equally lay
      In leaves no step had trodden black.
      Oh, I kept the first for another day!
      Yet knowing how way leads on to way,
15   I doubted if I should ever come back.

      I shall be telling this with a sigh
      Somewhere ages and ages hence;
      Two roads diverged in a wood, and I—
      I took the one less traveled by,
20   And that has made all the difference.

18. The best meaning of the word "diverged" in the last stanza is

   (A) came together
   (B) became intertwined
   (C) became indistinct
   (D) branched off

19. The poem is an extended metaphor that deals with the following theme:

   (A) life's choices
   (B) building a roadway
   (C) the battle between life and death
   (D) the loss of the Garden of Eden

20. The choice the speaker makes in Stanza 2 suggests which quality of character?

   (A) conformity
   (B) adventurousness
   (C) indifference
   (D) fear

21. The line "Oh, I kept the first for another day!" suggests which one of the following?

   (A) the speaker will return tomorrow
   (B) an arrogant disdain
   (C) a need for people to maintain options as long as possible
   (D) the speaker will return as an old person

READING COMPREHENSION

22. The speaker says, "I shall be telling this with a sigh" this suggests which possible emotion?

    (A) exasperation
    (B) glee
    (C) depression
    (D) weariness

Passage 6

Line   North Dakota entered the United States as the 39th state on November 2, 1889. South Dakota, which is officially recognized as the 40th state, also became a state the same day.
5   Two other states, Montana and Washington, were added later that same month. Colorado had been named the 38th state 13 years before North Dakota's admittance. North Dakota is located at the geographical center
10 of North America in the great plains. North Dakota is bordered on the north by Canada, on the east by Minnesota, south by South Dakota, and west by Montana.
    North Dakota can be divided into two
15 regions, east and west. The eastern part of the state extends from the Red River Valley. The Red River draws the North Dakota–Minnesota border and is characterized as the central lowlands. The central lowlands
20 consist of the Red River Valley and the Young Drift Plains. These regions were carved out by glaciers in the last ice age. When these glaciers melted, a prehistoric lake named Lake Agassiz was formed. With
25 time, Lake Agassiz dried up and left very fertile soil in this region. The eastern part of the state also gets an average rainfall of about 30 inches. The combination of rich soil and healthy rainfall during the growing
30 season results in farms that have among the highest yield per acre in the world. Of particular fame is the wheat and barley grown in this region.

23. South Dakota:

    (A) is east of North Dakota
    (B) entered the United States after North Dakota
    (C) is the geographical center of North America
    (D) entered the United States before Colorado

24. The Young Drift Plains and the Red River Valley were formed by:

    (A) continental drift
    (B) flooding of the Red River
    (C) an earthquake
    (D) glaciers from the last ice age

25. Factors contributing to the high per-acre yield in eastern North Dakota include:

    I. fertile soil
    II. healthy rainfall during the growing season
    III. a long growing season

    (A) I and II
    (B) II and III
    (C) I and III
    (D) I, II, and III

26. North Dakota is bordered on the east by:

    (A) settlers
    (B) Colorado
    (C) Canada
    (D) The Red River

Passage 7

Line   The word petroleum means "rock oil." Petroleum, like coal, is a sedimentary material of organic origin. It is a mixture made mainly of liquid hydrocarbons, which
5   are compounds of hydrogen and carbon. Gasoline and kerosene are hydrocarbons.
    Scientists think that petroleum was formed by slow chemical changes in plant and animal materials buried under sand and
10 clay in shallow coastal waters. Some of the

Peterson's: www.petersons.com

hydrocarbons formed were liquids and some were gases. As the sediments became compacted, the hydrocarbons were squeezed into pores and cracks of nearby sandstone or limestone. These rocks also contained seawater. The lighter, mixed hydrocarbon liquid (petroleum) rose above the water, and the natural gas collected above the petroleum.

Why haven't the petroleum and gas kept rising and escaped from the rock in the millions of years since they formed? Probably a good deal did. The petroleum found today was sealed in by an impermeable rock layer, such as shale. Such rock structures are called oil traps.

Wells were drilled into oil-bearing rock to release the oil. The pressure of the natural gas helps bring the oil to the surface. Unless the drilling is carefully controlled, the high pressure causes wasteful oil gushers. Even with modern technology, only about 40 percent of the oil is pumped out of a given well.

Natural gas often occurs with petroleum. Yet it may also exist in great deposits of gas alone. It is a mixture of hydrocarbon gases, mostly methane. Natural gas is an efficient fuel for use in heating.

When petroleum is refined, it is separated into many different hydrocarbons. Gasoline is used in automobiles. Kerosene and fuel oil are used for heating. Other oils are used as lubricants. Both petroleum and natural gas are used as raw material in making such substances as plastics, fertilizers, dyes, and medicines.

At the present rate of use, United States reserves of petroleum are expected to last between 30 and 50 years. United States reserves of natural gas are expected to last between 40 and 60 years. Other reserves may be found, but usage is likely to increase.

27. From this passage we can assert that

(A) out of a given well we can pump all its oil
(B) the United States will never run out of oil reserves
(C) petroleum is inorganic
(D) natural gas can be used for heating

28. The word "impermeable" in paragraph 3 best means

(A) sedimentary
(B) impassable
(C) permanent
(D) shale

29. All of the following are examples of hydrocarbons except

(A) seawater
(B) petroleum
(C) gasoline
(D) kerosene

30. From this passage we can infer that petroleum has its origin in

(A) seawater
(B) plant and animal material
(C) crushed rock
(D) gas

Passage 8

When I was 11 years old, my only brother, who had just graduated from Union College, came home to die. A young man of great talent and promise, he was the pride of my father's heart.

I recall going into the large darkened parlor and finding the casket, mirrors, and pictures all draped in white, and my father seated, pale and immovable. As he took no notice of me, after standing a long while, I climbed upon his knee, when he mechanically put his arm about me, and, with my head resting against his beating heart, we both sat in silence, he thinking of the wreck

15 of all his hopes in the loss of a dear son, and I wondering what could be said or done to fill the void in his breast. At length he heaved a deep sigh and said: "Oh, my daughter, I wish you were a boy!"

20 Throwing my arms about his neck, I replied: "I will try to be all my brother was."

All that day and far into the night I pondered the problem of boyhood. I thought that the chief thing to be done in
25 order to equal boys was to be learned and courageous. So I decided to study Greek and learn to manage a horse. I learned to leap a fence and ditch on horseback.

I began to study Latin, Greek, and
30 mathematics with a class of boys in the academy, many of whom were older than I. For three years one boy kept his place at the head of the class, and I always stood next. Two prizes were offered in Greek. I strove
35 for one and took the second. One thought alone filled my mind. "Now," said I, "my father will be satisfied with me."

I rushed breathless into his office, laid down the new Greek Testament, which was
40 my prize, on his table and exclaimed: "There, I got it!" He took up the book, asked me some questions about the class, and, evidently pleased, handed it back to me. Then he kissed me on the forehead and
45 exclaimed with a sigh, "Ah, you should have been a boy!"

31. The best title for this passage is
    (A) American Women of the 19th Century
    (B) The Struggle for Success
    (C) The Prize
    (D) You Should Have Been a Boy

32. The tone of this passage is best stated as
    (A) humorous
    (B) furious
    (C) sorrowful
    (D) indignant

33. The best meaning of the word "void" in paragraph 2 is
    (A) emptiness
    (B) vessel
    (C) blood
    (D) feeling

34. We can infer that the speaker of this passage will
    (A) become angry, depressed, and withdrawn
    (B) go to Greece to study its culture
    (C) go to Union College
    (D) continue to struggle to be seen as equal to men

35. Which word best describes the father's feelings toward his daughter?
    (A) warm
    (B) scornful
    (C) reproachful
    (D) irritated

Passage 9

Line Between 1000 and 1750 A.D. few basic changes were made in the way men lived in England. Most of the people in 1750 were still tilling the soil, and they were doing it
5 about the same way their ancestors had in the year 1000. The "agricultural revolution" was barely under way.

England's population was small, slightly over six million. Her customs were deeply
10 rooted. Her pace of living, according to British historian G. M. Trevelyan, was that of "a slowly moving stream."

There were some industries, but most of them were small. There was some
15 manufacturing, but much of this work was done in private homes under the "domestic system." Under this system a businessman provided workers with equipment for making finished products at home. There
20 were some important business centers, but

none of them had yet felt the frantic rush of modern industrial life.

England was not a rural paradise. If the villagers danced about the Maypole on festival days, they also worked hard on other days. If they breathed free air, they also lacked some of the goods that came with the smoke of factories. If they had sufficient time to eat, they also rarely dined on rich meats and pastry. In short, life in England in 1750 was peaceful but rugged.

In the next hundred years, vast changes took place. By 1850 the English landscape was transformed in many places. There were smoky factories, roaring machinery, crowded towns, and a new way of life. Similar changes were occurring or were about to take place in other parts of Europe and beyond. Our story is concerned with the reasons for this remarkable change.

From about 1750 to 1860, new inventions, new techniques, and new sources of power helped to speed up tremendously the pace of life in England and elsewhere. The many economic and social changes of this period make up what has been caused the "Industrial Revolution."

The term "Industrial Revolution" is far from accurate. It suggests that there was a sudden overthrowing of the past. Such was not the case. Actually, the economic and social changes of this so-called "revolution" grew out of the past and were to extend far into the future. One aspect of culture is technology, defined as "the sum of the ways in which a social group provides its members with the material objects of their civilization." A study of articles, produced by men from ancient times on, shows high levels of design, craftsmanship, and ingenuity in furniture, architecture, mechanical devices, and other fields. Industry had long been in existence, and many of its products were highly sophisticated. The new elements were the changes in methods of production and the resulting extension of the volume of production. Once these changes got underway, there was a tendency for one to bring about the next related change. The Industrial Revolution fed on itself and spread within one industry and from one industry to another.

36. The image "a slowly moving stream" conveys what message about England from 1000 to 1750 A.D.?

(A) it was a land dependent on fishing
(B) there were major changes taking place
(C) change did not come quickly
(D) the countryside was picturesque

37. The sentences in the paragraph beginning "England was not a rural paradise" generally follow which pattern of construction?

(A) the combination of opposites
(B) the use of multiple examples
(C) general and particular
(D) building to an ironic climax

38. The best meaning of the word "ingenuity" is

(A) clever talent
(B) ability to make an engine
(C) furniture design
(D) industry

39. We can infer from the passage that the Industrial Revolution

(A) only occurred in England
(B) took place before the "agricultural revolution"
(C) was a sudden overthrow of the past
(D) grew out of the past

40. From this passage we can assume that ancient people were

(A) slow-witted
(B) incapable of chance
(C) living in an agricultural paradise
(D) sophisticated

Mathematics Achievement

MATHEMATICS ACHIEVEMENT   **TIME: 40 MINUTES**   **45 QUESTIONS**

DIRECTIONS: Each question is followed by four suggested answers. Read each question and then decide which one of the four suggested answers is best.

1. Which of the following is a multiple of both 6 and 5?
   - (A) 20
   - (B) 45
   - (C) 65
   - (D) 90

2. Six less than a number is two-thirds of that number. What is the number?
   - (A) 18
   - (B) 9
   - (C) 4
   - (D) $5\frac{1}{3}$

3. $(3a^3 - 6) - (2a^2 + 1) =$
   - (A) $a - 5$
   - (B) $3a^3 - 2a^2 - 5$
   - (C) $3a^3 - 2a^2 - 7$
   - (D) None of these.

4. On a test with 25 questions, Reyna scored 88%. How many questions did Reyna answer correctly?
   - (A) 21
   - (B) 22
   - (C) 4
   - (D) 5

5. The perimeter of a square with a side length of 5 is how much less than the perimeter of a rectangle with a side length of 6 and width of 5?
   - (A) 6
   - (B) 4
   - (C) 2
   - (D) 1

6. One-fifth of a class voted to go to the science museum for a field trip. If 4 students chose this location, how many students are in the class?
   - (A) 10
   - (B) 20
   - (C) 11
   - (D) 24

7. If 35% of a number is 70, find the number.
   - (A) 24.5
   - (B) 200
   - (C) 50
   - (D) 140

8. The length of the side of an equilateral triangle is 10. Find the area of the triangle.
   - (A) 25
   - (B) 100
   - (C) $25\sqrt{3}$
   - (D) $20\sqrt{3}$

Peterson's: www.petersons.com

9. A father can do a job in a certain number of hours. His son takes twice as long to do the job. Working together, they can do the job in 6 hours. How many hours does it take the father to do the job alone?

   (A) 9
   (B) 18
   (C) 12
   (D) 10

10. How many 12.6-inch strips can be cut from a board 189 inches long?

    (A) 1.5
    (B) 15
    (C) 150
    (D) 176.4

11. David is 5 years older than Paul. In 5 years, David will be twice as old as Paul is now. How old is David now?

    (A) 15
    (B) 10
    (C) 25
    (D) 20

12. If $3x - 9 = 45$, what is $x \div 9$?

    (A) 6
    (B) 3
    (C) 2
    (D) 1

13. $\dfrac{1}{2} + \dfrac{2}{3} + \dfrac{3}{4} - \dfrac{1}{2} - \dfrac{1}{3} - \dfrac{1}{4} - \dfrac{1}{3} =$

    (A) $\dfrac{1}{2}$
    (B) $\dfrac{2}{3}$
    (C) 1
    (D) $\dfrac{3}{4}$

14. Which of the following is most nearly 60% of $19.95?

    (A) $8.00
    (B) $9.00
    (C) $14.50
    (D) $12.00

15. Find the sum of $2b + 5$, $4b - 4$, and $3b - 6$.

    (A) $9b - 5$
    (B) $7b - 10$
    (C) $6b - 1$
    (D) $9b + 5$

16.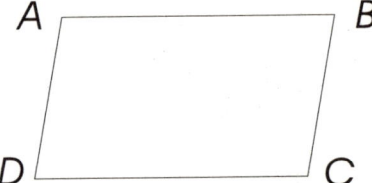

    Figure ABCD is a parallelogram. $A = 105°$. $B = 75°$. Find the measurement of D.

    (A) 105°
    (B) 75°
    (C) 160°
    (D) 150°

17. If *l* laser discs cost *d* dollars, 10 laser discs will cost:

    (A) $\frac{ld}{10}$ dollars

    (B) $\frac{10d}{l}$ dollars

    (C) $10ld$ dollars

    (D) $\frac{10l}{d}$ dollars

18. A salesman earns a commission of 8% of his total sales. How much must he sell to earn a commission of $124?

    (A) $9,920
    (B) $1,550
    (C) $992
    (D) $1,148.15

19. What is the smallest number that can be added to 42,042 to produce a result divisible by 9?

    (A) 6
    (B) 8
    (C) 5
    (D) 7

20. If $5x + 7 \geq x - 1$, then

    (A) $x \leq 2$
    (B) $x \geq 8$
    (C) $x \leq 8$
    (D) $x \geq -2$

21. The expression $\frac{1}{2}\sqrt{28}$ is equivalent to:

    (A) $\sqrt{14}$
    (B) $2\sqrt{7}$
    (C) $\sqrt{7}$
    (D) $4\sqrt{7}$

22.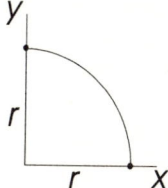

    Determine the area between the curve and the *x* and *y* axes. Assume that $r = 10$.

    (A) 100π
    (B) 25π
    (C) 20π
    (D) 400π

23. Randi scores an 85, 81, and 95 on her first 3 exams. What must she score on her fourth exam to receive an average of 90?

    (A) 90
    (B) 94
    (C) 99
    (D) 100

24. Solve for *x*: $3x - 6 = 10x - 11$

    (A) $\frac{5}{7}$
    (B) $-\frac{5}{7}$
    (C) -3
    (D) 3

25. If $x < y$ and $y < z$, which statement about the integers x, y, and z must be true?

    (A) $x < z$
    (B) $x = z$
    (C) $x > z$
    (D) $y - x = z$

26. If $g(x) = 2x^2 - 4x + 5$, what is the value of $g(3)$?

    (A) 5
    (B) 11
    (C) 12
    (D) 18

27. Find the height of a triangle whose base is 25 inches and whose area is 75 square inches.

    (A) 3 inches
    (B) 3 square inches
    (C) 6 inches
    (D) 6 square inches

28. What is .09 expressed as a percent?

    (A) .009%
    (B) 9%
    (C) .9%
    (D) .09%

29. What is the equation of the line passing through the point (2,3) and parallel to the line: $3x - 6y = 12$?

    (A) $x + 2y = 8$
    (B) $2x - y = 1$
    (C) $-x - 2y = 4$
    (D) $x - 2y = -4$

30. On level ground, a man 6 feet tall casts a shadow 8 feet long at the same time that a tree casts a shadow 20 feet long. Find the number of feet in the height of the tree.

    (A) $46\frac{2}{3}$
    (B) 15
    (C) 8
    (D) 120

31. The average of 2 and x is 7; find the value of x.

    (A) 9
    (B) 12
    (C) 14
    (D) 16

32. $\sqrt{16} - \sqrt[3]{27} =$

    (A) 1
    (B) 7
    (C) -1
    (D) -7

33. What is 64 expressed as the product of prime factors?

    (A) (2)(2)(2)(3)(3)
    (B) (2)(2)(2)(2)(2)(2)
    (C) (2)(2)(2)(2)(2)
    (D) (8)(8)

34. The area of a circle is the same as the area of a square whose side is 4 centimeters. The radius of the circle is closest to:

    (A) 16 centimeters
    (B) 5 centimeters
    (C) 4 centimeters
    (D) 2 centimeters

35. The length of a side of a square is represented by $2x + 2$, and the length of a side of an equilateral triangle by $4x$. If the square and the equilateral triangle have equal perimeters, find x.

(A) 6
(B) 4
(C) 1
(D) 2

36. The expression $\sqrt{250}$ is equivalent to:

(A) $25\sqrt{10}$
(B) $10\sqrt{2}$
(C) $5\sqrt{10}$
(D) $50\sqrt{2}$

37. On a map, 4 inches represents 15 miles. How many miles would 5 inches represent?

(A) 12
(B) $37\frac{1}{2}$
(C) 60
(D) $18\frac{3}{4}$

38. Express as a ratio in simplest form: 5 inches to 3 feet

(A) $\frac{5}{3}$
(B) $\frac{3}{5}$
(C) $\frac{5}{36}$
(D) $\frac{36}{5}$

39. If $x = 1$ on the graph of $y = -5x + 4$, what does y equal?

(A) -1
(B) -5
(C) 4
(D) 9

40. $4x^5$ divided by $3x^7$ is:

(A) $12x^{12}$
(B) $\frac{4}{3x^2}$
(C) $\frac{4x^2}{3}$
(D) $\frac{3x^2}{4}$

41. .0825 expressed as a percent is:

(A) 825%
(B) 8.25%
(C) .825%
(D) .0825%

42. What is the area of a square whose diagonal is 12?

(A) 36
(B) 24
(C) $12\sqrt{2}$
(D) 72

43. Which fraction lies between $\frac{3}{5}$ and $\frac{4}{5}$?

(A) $\frac{5}{6}$
(B) $\frac{17}{20}$
(C) $\frac{7}{10}$
(D) $\frac{13}{15}$

44.

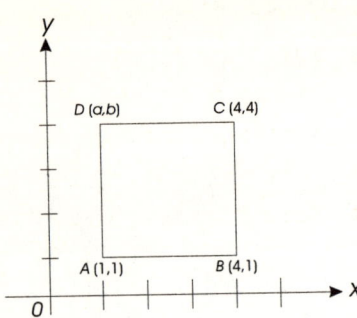

Find the coordinates of point D.

(A) (1,4)
(B) (4,1)
(C) (4,4)
(D) (1,1)

45. The circumference of a circle whose diameter is 9 inches is approximately:

(A) 18 inches
(B) 28 inches
(C) 81 inches
(D) 254 inches

| **WRITING THE ESSAY** | **TIME: 30 MINUTES** |

Directions: Using two sheets of lined theme paper, plan and write an essay on the topic assigned below. DO NOT WRITE ON ANOTHER TOPIC. AN ESSAY ON ANOTHER TOPIC IS NOT ACCEPTABLE. You have 30 minutes for this section.

The playwright, George Bernard Shaw, once said, "Youth is wasted on the young."

Prompt: Write an essay giving your view of this. Do you agree with this statement? Does the computer industry support this concept? Support your opinion with specific examples from history, current events, or personal observations.

Name: _____

Write your essay here.

WRITING THE ESSAY

EXPLANATORY ANSWERS TO THE ISEE PRACTICE TEST 2

VERBAL REASONING

1. The correct answer is (B).
2. The correct answer is (D).
3. The correct answer is (C).
4. The correct answer is (D).
5. The correct answer is (C).
6. The correct answer is (B).
7. The correct answer is (C).
8. The correct answer is (B).
9. The correct answer is (A).
10. The correct answer is (C).
11. The correct answer is (D).
12. The correct answer is (B).
13. The correct answer is (A).
14. The correct answer is (C).
15. The correct answer is (D).
16. The correct answer is (B).
17. The correct answer is (A).
18. The correct answer is (C).
19. The correct answer is (D).
20. The correct answer is (A).
21. The correct answer is (B). The clue is the word *elderly*. As people age, they can become physically and/or mentally impaired. The first word would be a synonym for "impairment." This eliminates answer (D) because the words have nothing to do with impairment. The trigger word is *forgetfulness*. The second word would be a synonym for "ineffective." This would eliminate answers (A) and (C).

EXPLANATORY ANSWERS TO THE ISEE PRACTICE TEST 2

22. The correct answer is (C). The clue is the word *refugee*. The trigger word is *fleeing*. Because the act is hasty and unplanned, both words in the blanks will be synonyms for "surrender" or "give up." That would eliminate answer (A). Answer (B) can be eliminated because the first word isn't a synonym for "surrender." Answer (D) can be eliminated because the second word is not a synonym for "surrender."

23. The correct answer is (A). The clue words are *part of*, and the trigger word is *study*. This shows that you are looking for a part of a whole. All other answers can be eliminated because they don't demonstrate that relationship.

24. The correct answer is (B). The clue is in the words *less important*. The trigger words are *when compared to*. The clue and the trigger tell you that the life of an individual seem less important in relationship to the big picture. The first word will be similar in meaning to the phrase "less important" as in not lasting forever. The second word will be similar to the concept of a "big picture," something larger and longer lasting than an individual. Answers (A) and (D) can be eliminated because the two words do not apply to the clue and trigger. Answer (C) can be eliminated because the second word is not similar to the concept of something larger.

25. The correct answer is (C). The clue is in the words *downhearted look*. This tells you that the person is "sad." The trigger word is *also*. That shows that the second word is related to the first word. Answer (A) can be eliminated because even though the words are related to one another, they do not correspond to the emotion of sadness. Answers (B) and (D) can be eliminated because the words in each answer do not relate to each another.

26. The correct answer is (B). The clue is in the word *psychologist*. That tells you the patient would be described using the terminology of psychology for the first word. The trigger word is *because*. That means the second part of the sentence, including the second word, defines the first word. Answers (A), (C), and (D) can be eliminated because even though the second word in each answer is a synonym for "conspire," the first words are not conditions from which a patient would suffer.

27. The correct answer is (A). The clue word is *evil*. The first word that describes "spell" would be an adjective that is a synonym for "evil." The trigger words are *small figurine*. The second word would represent a "small figurine." Answers (B), (C), and (D) can be eliminated because even though the second words in each answer are similar to "small figurine," the first words are opposites of "evil."

28. The correct answer is (D). The clue is in the words *Before the time of the internal combustion machine.* That would tell you that a means of transportation other than automotive is being used. The first would be a synonym for "horseback." The trigger word is *appear*. The second word would be a noun for "where riders could appear." Answers (A), (B), and (C) can be eliminated because the first words in each answer are not synonyms for "horseback."

29. The correct answer is (B). The clue is in the words *metropolitan life*. The first word would be a word that describes life in the big city, "city-like." The trigger words are *relief from*. The second word will be an adjective that describes settings that are the opposite of city. It would be a synonym for "country-like." Answers (A) and (D) can be eliminated because they don't relate to the clue or the trigger. Answer (C) reverses "city-like" and "country-like."

30. The correct answer is (C). The clue is in the words *physically taken advantage of.* This tells you that the first word will be a synonym for "desire." The trigger words are *has led*. This establishes a cause/effect relationship and tells you that the second word would be the result of his "desire." Answer (A) can be eliminated because neither word relates to "desire." Answers (B) and (D) can be eliminated because only one of the words relates to "desire."

31. The correct answer is (A). The clue is in the words *although* and *minimal*. That tells you the first word is a synonym for the phrase "made the most of." The trigger words are *whereas* and *natural athlete*. That tells you her brother is the opposite. The second word will be a synonym for "wasted." Answers (B), (C), and (D) can be eliminated because they do not relate to the clue and trigger.

EXPLANATORY ANSWERS TO THE ISEE PRACTICE TEST 2

32. **The correct answer is (A).** The clue is in the words *business owners*. They are often concerned with "money" as their profit. The first word would be related to "wanting to retain money." The trigger words are *mainly concerned*. The second word would be related to the "monetary" aspects of life. Answer (B) can be eliminated because it is the opposite of concern for personal wealth. Answers (C) and (D) can be eliminated because they have no relationship to "money."

33. **The correct answer is (D).** The clue is in the words *summer* and *freezing*. The first word would be a synonym for "dropped." The trigger words are *back* and *nineties*. The second word would be a synonym for "rising quickly." Answers (A) and (B) can be eliminated because the words do not relate to the clue and trigger. Answer (C) can be eliminated because the words are in reverse order of "rising" and "dropping."

34. **The correct answer is (A).** The clue is in the words *even though*. This tells you that the first word would refer to the boxer "taking punches." The trigger word is *refused*. The second word would refer to the boxer refusing to "give in." Answer (B) can be eliminated because the first word indicates that the boxer is doing well. Answers (C) and (D) can be eliminated because they do not relate to the clue and trigger words.

35. **The correct answer is (D).** The clue is in the words *powerful* and *earthquake*. That tells you the first word would be a synonym for "destruction." The triggers are the words *skyscrapers* and *piles*. This means that the second word would be a synonym for "ruins." All other answers can be eliminated because the first word in each answer is not a synonym for "destruction."

36. **The correct answer is (B).** The clue is in the words *debater* and *proofs*. The first word would be a synonym for "present." The trigger words are *make him the winner*. The second word would be a synonym for "effective." All other answers can be eliminated because the second words in each answer are the opposites of "effective."

37. **The correct answer is (C).** The clue is in the words *even though*. The trigger words are *it was enough* and *hurt feelings*. The first word will be a synonym for "late," while the second word will be a synonym for "soothing." Answer (A) can be eliminated because the first word is not a synonym for "late." Answer (B) can be eliminated because the words do not relate to the clue and trigger words. Answer (D) can be eliminated because the words are the opposites of the clue and trigger words.

38. The correct answer is (A). The clue is in the words *complimentary reviews*. That tells you the first word is a synonym for "pleased." The trigger words are *however* and *negative ones*. That tells you the second word would be the opposite of pleased, a synonym for "angered." Answers (B) and (C) can be eliminated because the second word in the choice is the opposite of "angered." Answer (D) can be eliminated because the first word in the answer is the opposite of "pleased."

39. The correct answer is (B). The clue is in the words *medical malpractice lawsuit*. That tells you the first word will be a synonym for the "person who is suing the doctor." The trigger words are *was seeking*. The second word will be a synonym for "damages." Answer (A) can be eliminated because the first word in the answer is not a synonym for the "person suing." Answer (C) can be eliminated because the words have no relevance to the clue or trigger. Answer (D) can be eliminated because the first word in the answer misrepresents the person doing the suing.

40. The correct answer is (D). The clue is in the words *love* and *happily*. That tells you the first word that describes the bride would be a synonym for "beloved." The trigger words are *surely would have been*. The second word would be a synonym for "certain." Answer (A) can be eliminated because the words do not match the clue or trigger. Answers (B) and (C) can be eliminated because the first word in each choice is not a synonym for "beloved."

QUANTITATIVE ABILITY

1. The correct answer is (C). To round a number to the tenth's place, look at the digit in the hundredth's place. If this digit is 5 or larger, raise the tenth's digit by one.

   Since 9 is larger than 5, 21.49 becomes 21.5.

2. The correct answer is (C). The find an average of a set of scores, add the scores and divide the sum by the number of scores.

   $$175 + 155 + 210 = 540$$
   $$540 \div 3 = 180$$

3. The correct answer is (A). To change a percent into a fraction, divide by 100.

   $$62\frac{1}{2} \div 100 = \frac{125}{2} \div \frac{100}{1} = \frac{125}{2} \times \frac{1}{100} = \frac{125}{200} = \frac{5}{8}$$

4. The correct answer is (A). $(2b + 5) + (4b - 4) + (3b - 6) = 2b + 4b + 3b + 5 - 4 - 6 = 9b - 5$

5. The correct answer is (D). $(-3)^2 - 4(-3) = 9 - 4(-3) = 9 - (-12) = 9 + 12 = 21$

6. The correct answer is (C). To solve this problem, begin by setting up a proportion. Let x = the number of ounces of water we are looking for. Then,

$$\text{water} \rightarrow \frac{40}{100} = \frac{x}{8{,}025} \quad \text{Cross multiply}$$
$$\text{flour} \rightarrow$$

$$100x = 40 \times 8{,}025$$
$$100x = 321{,}000 \quad \text{Divide by 100}$$
$$x = 3{,}210$$

7. The correct answer is (D). The perimeter of the rectangle is equal in length to 8 sides of the squares. Since the perimeter is 80, each side of the square must be 10.

The area of a rectangle is equal to the length $\times$ width. Since the width is 10, and the length is $3(10) = 30$, we have $A = 10 \times 30 = 300$.

8. The correct answer is (D). A prime number is a number that is divisible by only itself and 1. Hence,

$72 = 2 \times 2 \times 2 \times 3 \times 3$; 2 and 3 are prime numbers

9. The correct answer is (C). Replace the value of x with -1.

$$\frac{8}{3 - x} = \frac{8}{3 - (-1)} = \frac{8}{3 + 1} = \frac{8}{4} = 2$$

10. The correct answer is (D). Let the smaller of the integers equal x. Then, the larger integer is $x + 1$, and we have

$$x + (x + 1) = 39$$
$$2x + 1 = 39 \quad \text{Subtract 1 from both sides}$$
$$2x = 38$$
$$x = 19 \quad \text{The smaller integer is 19}$$

11. The correct answer is (C). The perimeter of a square is 4s. Thus,

$$R = 4s \text{ or}$$
$$\frac{R}{4} = s \quad \text{The area of a square is } s^2. \text{ Therefore,}$$
$$A = s^2 = \left(\frac{R}{4}\right)^2 = \frac{R^2}{16}$$

12. The correct answer is (D). To find the percent of increase, divide the amount of increase by the original amount.

$$143.75 - 125 = 18.75$$
$$\frac{18.75}{125} = .15 = 15\%$$

13. The correct answer is (D). $\frac{4}{x} - \frac{3}{x} = \frac{1}{x}$ When the denominators are the same, subtract the numerators.

14. The correct answer is (B). Begin by cross multiplying:

$$\frac{20}{12} = \frac{5}{y}$$
$$20y = 12 \times 5$$
$$20y = 60$$
$$y = 3$$

15. The correct answer is (C). $(3a + 5)(2a - 3)$
    Multiply the two first terms: $(3a)(2a) = 6a^2$
    Multiply the two outer terms: $(3a)(-3) = -9a$
    Multiply the two inner terms: $(5)(2a) = 10a$
    Multiply the two last terms: $(5)(-3) = -15$

    The sum of the resulting products is
    $6a^2 - 9a + 10a - 15 = 6a^2 + a - 15$

16. The correct answer is (B). The product of two fractions between 0 and 1 is always less than both of the original fractions. For example:

    $\frac{1}{2} \times \frac{3}{4} = \frac{3}{8}$, and $\frac{3}{8}$ is less than both $\frac{1}{2}$ and $\frac{3}{4}$.

    Hence, only (B) can be true.

17. The correct answer is (C). Try to find two factors of 162, one of which is a perfect square:

$$\sqrt{162} = \sqrt{81 \times 2} = \sqrt{81}\sqrt{2} = 9\sqrt{2}$$

18. The correct answer is (C). Let the length of the original rectangle be L and the width be W. Then, the original rectangle has area $A = LW$.

The enlarged rectangle has length $3L$ and width $3W$. Its area is, thus, $(3L)(3W) = 9LW$. Then,

$$\frac{\text{original area}}{\text{enlarged area}} = \frac{LW}{9LW} = \frac{1}{9}.$$ The ratio is 1 to 9

19. The correct answer is (A). Affix zeros to $.01 = .0100$. Now, compare to $.0099$.

$$.0100 > .0099$$

20. The correct answer is (C). All vertical angles are congruent

21. The correct answer is (C). Follow the order of operations:

$$6 \times 5 + 3 = 30 + 3 = 33$$
$$(6 + 5)3 = (11)3 = 33$$

22. The correct answer is (C). Solving for y in the given information, we obtain $y = 4$. Similarly, $(-2)^2 = 4$.

23. The correct answer is (C). $\dfrac{\frac{1}{4}}{\frac{3}{8}} = \dfrac{1}{4} \div \dfrac{3}{8} = \dfrac{1}{4} \times \dfrac{8}{3} = \dfrac{8}{12} = \dfrac{2}{3}$

$$66\frac{2}{3}\% = \frac{66\frac{2}{3}}{100} = \frac{\frac{200}{3}}{100} = \frac{200}{3} \div \frac{100}{1} = \frac{200}{3} \times \frac{1}{100} = \frac{200}{300} = \frac{2}{3}$$

$$\frac{2}{3} = \frac{2}{3}$$

24. The correct answer is (A). The sum of the angles in a triangle is 180.

$$20 + 20 + (20 + x) = 180$$
$$60 + x = 180$$
$$x = 120$$

ISEE PRACTICE TEST 2

25. The correct answer is (B). $\frac{1}{3} \times \frac{3}{5} = \frac{3}{15} = \frac{1}{5}$

Since $.25 = \frac{1}{4}$, the entry in Column B is bigger.

26. The correct answer is (B). We are given that r is negative. This means that $\frac{1}{r}$ is also negative. On the other hand, r^2 will be positive. Any positive number is larger than any negative number.

27. The correct answer is (B). $8^2 = 8 \times 8 = 64$

$2^8 = 2 \times 2 \times 2 \times 2 \times 2 \times 2 \times 2 \times 2 = 256$

28. The correct answer is (C). We are given that $\frac{4}{6} = \frac{m}{15}$. To solve for m, cross multiply

$$4 \times 15 = 6m$$
$$60 = 6m$$
$$10 = m$$

29. The correct answer is (C). $\left(\frac{1}{10}\right)^2 = \frac{1}{10} \times \frac{1}{10} = \frac{1}{100}$

$\left(\frac{1}{10}\right)^3 \times 10 = \frac{1}{10} \times \frac{1}{10} \times \frac{1}{10} \times 10 = \frac{1}{100}$

30. The correct answer is (B). $t° + t° + t° + t° = 180°$

$$4t° = 180°$$
$$t° = 45° \quad \text{Similarly,}$$
$$q° + q° + q° = 180°$$
$$3q° = 180°$$
$$q° = 60°$$
$$2t° = 90° \quad 2q° = 120°$$

31. The correct answer is (B). $1.89 × 3 = $5.67

    $1.49 × 2 = $2.98

    $5.67 + $2.98 = $8.65 = total price of the nuts and pecans. To find the average price per pound divide by 5:

    $8.65 ÷ 5 = $1.73

    In Column B, $1.09 + $2.19 + $4.75 = $8.03. To find the average, divide by 3

    $8.03 ÷ 3 = $2.68

32. The correct answer is (C). Given that $x = \frac{1}{2}$, we compute

    $$x^2 + x = \left(\frac{1}{2}\right)^2 + \frac{1}{2} = \frac{1}{4} + \frac{1}{2} = \frac{3}{4}$$

    $$\left(\frac{\sqrt{3}}{2}\right)^2 = \frac{(\sqrt{3})^2}{2^2} = \frac{3}{4}$$

33. The correct answer is (C). The formula for the area of a circle is $A = \pi r^2$. If the radius is 10, then the area is $A = \pi(10)^2 = 100\pi$.

    The formula for the circumference of a circle is $C = \pi D$. If the diameter is 100, we have $C = 100\pi$

34. The correct answer is (B). If we multiply both sides by $3\sqrt{7}$, then Column A becomes:

    $\frac{\sqrt{7}}{3} \times 3\sqrt{7} = \sqrt{7} \times \sqrt{7} = 7$, while Column B becomes

    $\frac{3}{\sqrt{7}} \times 3\sqrt{7} = 9$. Thus, the answer is (B).

35. The correct answer is (A). Since there are 180° in a triangle, ∠1 + ∠2 + ∠3 = 180.

    Since ∠3 and ∠4 are supplementary, ∠3 + ∠4 = 180. Overall, then,

    ∠1 + ∠2 + ∠3 = ∠3 + ∠4 Subtract ∠3 from both sides

    ∠1 + ∠2 = ∠4. Since ∠1 > 0°, we must have ∠2 < ∠4

READING COMPREHENSION

Passage 1

1. The correct answer is (C). Antony is the name of a character from one of Shakespeare's plays. (A), (B), and (D) are critics mentioned who provide opinions of Hamlet and his character.

2. The correct answer is (A). (D) is the best of the wrong answers but it is not supported by the context. (B) and (C) are inappropriate.

3. The correct answer is (A). The passage provides multiple responses to Hamlet's character. (C) is contradicted at the beginning of the passage, and (B) and (D) are overridden by other details provided.

4. The correct answer is (C). In the last paragraph he refers to "we . . . as critics." (D) is the closest of the other responses, but the passage is not a review of the play. (A) and (B) are inappropriate.

Passage 2

5. The correct answer is (D). The passage illustrates a number of ways mechanical weathering occurs. (A) is too general to be the best title of this passage. (B) is incorrect because there are other ways rocks can change. (C) refers to only two of the four types of changes discussed.

6. The correct answer is (A). This specific detail is provided in paragraph 2. (B), (C), and (D) are examples of weathering processes but none are equal to (A) in damage production.

7. The correct answer is (D). The details are provided for us in paragraph 3. The other answers are all inappropriate.

8. The correct answer is (B). This is discussed in the final paragraph. (A) is close, but it refers to only one type of outcrop. (C) and (D) are both inappropriate.

9. The correct answer is (B). The synonym is provided in the paragraph discussing ice wedging. (A) is often connected to frost action but it is not the same. (C) and (D) are inappropriate.

Passage 3

10. The correct answer is (D). We wait with Napoleon for the Emperor to speak but he says nothing. (C) is the closest of the other responses and is a secondary effect of what was occurring while Napoleon was waiting. (A) and (B) are incorrect.

11. The correct answer is (B). The passage concentrates on the horrors of Napoleon's invasion of Russia. (D) is the best of the wrong answers but it is not specific enough of a title. (A) and (C) are incorrect.

12. The correct answer is (C). The final paragraph provides the necessary information to answer the question. (A), (B), and (D) are all contradicted by details in the passage.

13. The correct answer is (A). (B), (C), and (D) are incorrect.

Passage 4

14. The correct answer is (C). The answer is tricky—meters are converted to yards. (D), stationary, means to stand still and (A) and (B) are incorrect.

15. The correct answer is (B). This tests your ability to read for details. (A), (C), and (D) are inappropriate.

16. The correct answer is (D). The answer is clearly stated in the last paragraph. (A), (B), and (C) confuse the details.

17. The correct answer is (A). The information that gives us this answer is in the last paragraph. (B), (C), and (D) are inappropriate.

Passage 5

18. The correct answer is (D). This reflects the theme of the entire poem. (C) is inappropriate, while (A) and (B) are virtual synonyms.

19. The correct answer is (A). The roads are the "roads of life"—one can never return to the same time when one has made a choice. There are tinges of loss in this poem, and (D) is close to the right answer. (B) and (C) are inappropriate.

20. The correct answer is (B). The speaker will take the road that "wanted wear"—in other words, was less traveled. (A), (C), and (D) do not reflect the tone of the poem.

21. The correct answer is (C). The speaker wants to believe that the road is still available even though he knows he may never return. (B) is closest to the correct answer; the speaker thinks he is special for going down a "less traveled" road. (A) and (D) are inappropriate.

ISEE PRACTICE TEST 2

22. The correct answer is (D). The speaker laments having to make choices. (A) and (C) are close but are not confirmed by the rest of the stanza. (B) is inappropriate.

Passage 6

23. The correct answer is (B). The answer is provided in the first paragraph, which states that South Dakota became the 40th state after North Dakota became the 39th. (A) is contradicted in the same paragraph, and (C) and (D) are incorrect.

24. The correct answer is (D). The detail is provided in paragraph 2. (A), (B), and (C) are inappropriate.

25. The correct answer is (A). The question determines your ability to couple details to provide an answer. (B), (C), and (D) are incorrect.

26. The correct answer is (D). This question demands an ability to seek a second level of response. In paragraph 1 we are told that Minnesota is east, but paragraph 2 tells us that the Red River is on the North Dakota-Minnesota border. (A), (B), and (C) are incorrect.

Passage 7

27. The correct answer is (D). This question asks if you can read for the right detail. (A), (B), and (C) are all contradicted by facts in the passage.

28. The correct answer is (B). In order for rock to contain the oil it must be equivalent to a closed lid. (A) and (D) refer to types of rock mentioned in the passage and (C) plays on the root of the word.

29. The correct answer is (A). Seawater and oil may be lodged in the same area but they are not both hydrocarbons. (B), (C), and (D) are listed in paragraph 1.

30. The correct answer is (B). This tests your ability to read for detail; this fact is mentioned in the second paragraph. (A), (C), and (D) are inappropriate.

Passage 8

31. The correct answer is (D). The use of repetition underscores the power of this phrase. (A) is too general; this is the tale of one woman. (B) and (C) refer to elements in the passage only.

32. The correct answer is (C). The author is eager for her father to see her as more than just a girl and we infer that she is sad that he cannot recognize her efforts. (B) and (D) are close—there is a touch of anger here but it is not the overriding tone of the passage. (A) is inappropriate.

EXPLANATORY ANSWERS TO THE ISEE PRACTICE TEST 2

Passage 9

33. The correct answer is (A). The loss of his son creates an empty space in the father's heart. (B) is the closest of the other answers—but a vessel is not always empty. (C) and (D) are inappropriate.

34. The correct answer is (D). We can infer that she will continue to show the determination she showed in this passage. (A) is a possible response that is not supported by the tone or details of the passage. (B) and (C) refer to details in the passage but we would be wrong to assume they have such large importance.

35. The correct answer is (A). We must infer by the father's pleasure at his daughter's prize that there must be some warmth between them. There is nothing in the passage to suggest (B), (C), or (D).

36. The correct answer is (C). The "slow moving stream" is England's pace of living. (B) is its opposite and (A) and (D) are inappropriate.

37. The correct answer is (A). You can see that most of the sentences start with an "If . . ." clause and end with a "they do . . ." clause with the opposite information. (C) is incorrect but you should look up the words. (B) is true about the entire paragraph but not individual sentences. (D) is inappropriate.

38. The correct answer is (A). This refers to the high level of craftsmanship exhibited by the makers. (D) is closest since "industry" also has the meaning of an individual who works hard (but who is not necessarily "ingenious"). (B) and (C) are both inappropriate.

39. The correct answer is (D). This is discussed clearly in the last paragraph. Even though the passage concentrates on England, other parts of Europe are referred to. (B) is a statement of the opposite and (C) is incorrect.

40. The correct answer is (D). This is suggested in the last paragraph. (C) is contradicted in the passages, as are (A) and (B).

MATHEMATICS ACHIEVEMENT

1. The correct answer is (D).

   Factor out each of the given possibilities.

   The factors of 20 are $2 \times 2 \times 5$.

   The factors of 45 are $3 \times 3 \times 5$.

   The factors of 65 are 5×13.

   The factors of 90 are $2 \times 3 \times 3 \times 5$.

   Since $6 = 2 \times 3$, 90 has factors of 6 and 5.

2. The correct answer is (A). Translate the sentence into a mathematical equation, then solve.

   $$x - 6 = \frac{2}{3}x$$

   $$x - \frac{2}{3}x = 6$$

   $$\frac{1}{3}x = 6$$

   $$x = 6\left(\frac{3}{1}\right) = 18$$

3. The correct answer is (C). To subtract algebraic expressions, change the signs of the subtrahend and use the rules for addition.

   $(3a^3 - 6) - (2a^2 + 1) = (3a^3 - 6) + (-2a^2 - 1) = 3a^3 - 2a^2 - 7$

4. The correct answer is (B).

   $$\text{score} = \frac{\# \text{ correct}}{\# \text{ questions}}; \quad 88\% = \frac{88}{100} = .88$$

   $$.88 = \frac{n}{25}$$

   $$n = .88 \times 25 = 22$$

5. The correct answer is (C). The perimeter of a square is $4s$. With side length = 5, the perimeter is $4(5) = 20$.

   The perimeter of a rectangle is $2L + 2W$. With length = 6 and width = 5, the perimeter is $2(6) + 2(5) = 12 + 10 = 22$.

   The difference between the perimeters is $22 - 20 = 2$.

6. The correct answer is (B). Four students make up one-fifth of a class. Translating this into a mathematical equation, you get $\frac{1}{5}c = 4$.

   $$c = 4\left(\frac{5}{1}\right) = 20$$

7. The correct answer is (B).

   35% of $N = 70$. Divide the known part of the fractional equivalent of the percent.

   $$35\% = \frac{35}{100}$$

   $$70 \div \frac{35}{100}$$

   $$70 \times \frac{100}{35} \quad \text{invert divisor and multiply}$$

   $$= 2 \times 100 = 200$$

8. The correct answer is (C).

   $$A = \frac{1}{2}bh$$

   $$h = \sqrt{10^2 - 5^2} = \sqrt{100 - 25}$$
   $$= \sqrt{75} = 5\sqrt{3}$$

   $$\frac{1}{2}(10)(5\sqrt{3}) = 25\sqrt{3}$$

ISEE PRACTICE TEST 2

9. The correct answer is (A).

   Let x = number of hours to complete a job (father)

   $\dfrac{1}{x}$ rate of work (father)

   Let $2x$ = number of hours to complete a job (son)

   $\dfrac{1}{2x}$ rate of work (son)

   (rate of work) × (time of work) = part of job done

   $\dfrac{1}{x}(6) + \dfrac{1}{2x}(6) = 1$ job (completed)

   Multiply by $2x$: $2x\left(\dfrac{6}{x} + \dfrac{6}{2x} = 1\right)$

   $\dfrac{12x}{x} + \dfrac{12x}{2x} = 2x$

   Reduce: $12 + 6 = 2x$

   $18 = 2x$

   $2x = 18$

   Divide by 2: $x = 9$ (hours for father to complete the job alone)

   $2x = 18$ (hours for son to complete job alone)

10. The correct answer is (B). This is a problem in division.

$$12.6 \overline{)189.0} \quad \begin{array}{r} 15. \\ \hline \end{array}$$

$$\begin{array}{r} 126 \\ \hline 630 \\ 630 \\ \hline \end{array}$$

EXPLANATORY ANSWERS TO THE ISEE PRACTICE TEST 2

11. **The correct answer is (A).**

    Let d represent David's age now and $d + 5$ represent David's age 5 years from now.

    Let p represent Paul's age now and $p + 5$ represent Paul's age 5 years from now.

    Set up mathematical equations for the problem.

    $d = p + 5$
    $d + 5 = 2p$

    Substitute the value of d in the first equation into the second equation to find p.

    $(p + 5) + 5 = 2p$
    $p + 10 = 2p$
    $p = 10$

    Therefore, $d = 10 + 5 = 15$.

12. **The correct answer is (C).**

    $3x - 9 = 45$
    $3x = 54$
    $x = 18$
    $18 \div 9 = 2$

13. **The correct answer is (A).**

    Rearrange the fractions to make it easier to solve by combining fractions with like denominators.

    $$\frac{1}{2} - \frac{1}{2} + \frac{2}{3} - \frac{1}{3} - \frac{1}{3} + \frac{3}{4} - \frac{1}{4}$$

    The first five fractions cancel each other out, leaving

    $$\frac{3}{4} - \frac{1}{4} = \frac{2}{4} = \frac{1}{2}$$

14. The correct answer is (D).

    Round $19.95 to $20.00 and find 60% of 20.

    $$60\% = \frac{60}{100} = 0.6$$

    $$0.6 \times 20 = 12$$

15. The correct answer is (A). Add like monomials and add coefficients.

    $$\begin{array}{r} 2b + 5 \\ 4b - 4 \\ +3b - 6 \\ \hline 9b - 5 \end{array}$$

16. The correct answer is (B). In a parallelogram, opposite angles are equal; therefore, $B = D$, $D = 75°$.

17. The correct answer is (B). Set up a ratio for this problem and solve.

    l represents the number of laser discs purchased with d dollars $\left(\frac{l}{d}\right)$.

    10 laser discs can be purchased for x dollars $\left(\frac{10}{x}\right)$. So,

    $$\frac{l}{d} = \frac{10}{x}$$

    $lx = 10d$ (using cross-multiplication)

    $$\frac{10d}{l} = x$$

18. **The correct answer is (B).**

    Here, we must find the base. $B = \dfrac{P}{R} = \dfrac{124}{.08} = 1{,}550$

19. **The correct answer is (A).**

    To determine if a number is divisible by 9, the sum of the digits in that number will equal 9. The sum of the digits in 42,042 is $4 + 2 + 0 + 4 + 2 = 12$. By adding 6 to this number, the sum of the digits will equal $18 = 1 + 8 = 9$ and therefore be divisible by 9.

20. **The correct answer is (D).**

    Solving inequalities is very similar to solving equations.

    $$5x + 7 - 7 \geq x - 1 - 7$$
    $$5x - x \geq x - 8 - x$$
    $$\dfrac{4x}{4} \geq \dfrac{-8}{4}$$
    $$x \geq -2$$

21. **The correct answer is (C).**

    Find two factors of 28, one of which is a perfect square. Then reduce the perfect square and multiply.

    $$\dfrac{1}{2}\sqrt{4}\sqrt{7} = \dfrac{1}{2}\sqrt{2 \times 2}\sqrt{7} = \dfrac{1}{2}(2)\sqrt{7} = 1\sqrt{7} = \sqrt{7}$$

22. **The correct answer is (B).** A circle has a radius of 10 units. The area of the curve is $\dfrac{1}{4}$ that of the entire circle.

    $$A = \pi r^2$$

    $$A \text{ of } \dfrac{1}{4} \text{ circle} = \dfrac{1}{4}\pi(10)^2 = \dfrac{1}{4}\pi(100) = 25\pi$$

23. The correct answer is (C). To score an average of 90 on 4 exams, the total of the 4 exams added together must be $90 \times 4 = 360$. On her first 3 exams, Randi has scored a total of $85 + 81 + 95 = 261$. $360 - 261 = 99$. Therefore, she needs 99 points on her last exam.

24. The correct answer is (A).

$$3x - 6 = 10x - 11$$
$$3x = 10x - 5$$
$$-7x = -5$$
$$x = \frac{-5}{-7} = \frac{5}{7}$$

25. The correct answer is (A). If $x < y$ and $y < z$, then $x < z$. If one number is less than the second number, and the second number is less than the third number, then the first number is less than the third number.

26. The correct answer is (B).

If $g(x) = 2x^2 - 4x + 5$, then $g(3) = 2(3)^2 - 4(3) + 5 = 18 - 12 + 5 = 11$

27. The correct answer is (C).

Use the formula

$$A = \frac{1}{2}bh$$

$$75 = \frac{1}{2}(25)h$$

$$\frac{75}{12.5} = \frac{12.5h}{12.5}$$

$$6 \text{ inches} = h$$

28. The correct answer is (B).

To convert a decimal to a percent, multiply the decimal by 100.

$.09 \times 100 = 9.00 = 9\%$

EXPLANATORY ANSWERS TO THE ISEE PRACTICE TEST 2

29. The correct answer is (D).

Begin by determining the slope of $3x - 6y = 12$ by writing it in slope-intercept form.

$$3x - 6y = 12$$
$$6y = 3x - 12$$
$$y = \frac{1}{2}x - 2$$

Thus, the slope of the equation is $\frac{1}{2}$. The line we are looking for must also have that slope because parallel lines have the same slopes.

Using the point-slope form, the line is:

$$m(x - x_1) = (y - y_1), \text{ or}$$
$$\frac{1}{2}(x - 2) = (y - 3)$$
$$(x - 2) = 2(y - 3)$$
$$x - 2 = 2y - 6$$
$$x - 2y = -4$$

30. The correct answer is (B).

Let $x =$ the height of the tree. The product of the means equals the product of the extremes.

(objects) $\dfrac{6 \text{ ft.}}{x \text{ ft.}} = \dfrac{8 \text{ ft.}}{20 \text{ ft.}}$ (shadows)

$8x = (6)(20) = 120$

Divide by 8: $x = 15$ ft.

31. The correct answer is (B). To find the average of several numbers, find the sum and divide by the number of items.

$$\frac{2 + x}{2} = 7$$
$$2 + x = 14$$
$$x = 12$$

ISEE PRACTICE TEST 2

32. The correct answer is (A).

First calculate roots, then subtract.

$$\sqrt{16} = 4$$
$$\sqrt[3]{27} = 3$$
$$4 - 3 = 1$$

33. The correct answer is (B).

A prime number is a number that is divisible by itself and by 1. Hence, $64 = 8 \times 8 = 2 \times 2 \times 2 \times 2 \times 2 \times 2 \rightarrow 2$ is a prime number.

34. The correct answer is (D).

First find the area of the square.
$$A = s^2$$
$$= 4^2 = 16 \text{ sq. cm.}$$

Then, using the formula,
$$A = \pi r^2$$
$$16 \approx (3.14)r^2$$
$$5.10 \approx r^2$$
$$\sqrt{5.10} \approx r$$
$$2.3 \text{ cm.} \approx r$$

35. The correct answer is (D).

The perimeter of the square $= 4s$.

$$P = 4s = 4(2x + 2) = 8x + 8$$

The perimeter of the equilateral triangle is $3s$.

$$P = 3s = 3(4x) = 12x$$
$$8x + 8 = 12x$$
$$8 = 4x$$
$$2 = x$$

36. The correct answer is (C).

Find two factors of 250, one of which is a perfect square.

$$\sqrt{250} = \sqrt{25 \times 10}$$
$$= \sqrt{25}\sqrt{10} \quad \text{Reduce perfect square}$$
$$\sqrt{25} = 5$$
$$= 5\sqrt{10}$$

EXPLANATORY ANSWERS TO THE ISEE PRACTICE TEST 2

37. The correct answer is (D).

This problem can be solved very easily using a proportion.

$$\frac{4 \text{ inches}}{15 \text{ miles}} = \frac{5 \text{ inches}}{x \text{ miles}}$$

After cross-multiplication, this proportion becomes

$4x = 75$

$x = 18\frac{3}{4}$

38. The correct answer is (C).

Convert all measurements to the same units, such as inches. 3 feet is 36 inches.

We now have the ratio 5 inches to 36 inches, expressed as $\frac{5}{36}$.

39. The correct answer is (A).

$y = -5x + 4$
$y = -5(1) + 4$
$y = -5 + 4 = -1$

40. The correct answer is (B). When dividing terms, subtract the exponents. You can see this by expanding:

Remember x^5 is $x \times x \times x \times x \times x$ and x^7 is $x \times x \times x \times x \times x \times x \times x$. Then divide.

This is the basis for the rules of exponents.

$$\frac{4 \times x \times x \times x \times x \times x}{3 \times x \times x \times x \times x \times x \times x \times x} = \frac{4}{3x^2}$$

41. The correct answer is (B). To express a percent as a decimal, divide by 100. To express a decimal as a percent, multiply by 100. Literally, percent ("per cent") means "per hundred".

$.0825 \times 100 = 8.25$

42. The correct answer is (D).

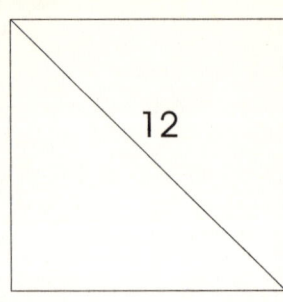

If the diagonal of a square is 12, then (by the Pythagorean theorem), the sides of the square must be $\dfrac{12}{\sqrt{2}} = \dfrac{12\sqrt{2}}{2} = 6\sqrt{2}$. Square this to get the area of 72.

43. The correct answer is (C). Convert all fractions to decimal equivalents:

$\dfrac{3}{5} = .6$ $\dfrac{4}{5} = .8$

$\dfrac{5}{6} = .8333$ $\dfrac{17}{20} = .85$

$\dfrac{7}{10} = .7$ $\dfrac{13}{15} = .8666$

$\dfrac{7}{10}$ is the only fraction between $\dfrac{3}{5}$ and $\dfrac{4}{5}$.

44. The correct answer is (A). Point D is vertically aligned with A's x-coordinate, 1, and horizontally aligned with C's y-coordinate, 4.

45. The correct answer is (B).

Using the formula for circumference, $C = \pi d$

$= (3.14)(9)$

$= 28.26$ inches ≈ 28 inches

NOTES

NOTES

NOTES

NOTES

Peterson's unplugged

- graduate programs
- distance learning
- adult education
- executive training
- colleges and universities
- private secondary schools
- internships and careers
- study-abroad programs
- financial aid/scholarships
- summer programs

Peterson's quality on every page!

For more than three decades, we've offered a complete selection of books to guide you in all of your educational endeavors. You can find our vast collection of titles at your local bookstore or online at **petersons.com**.

High school student headed for college?

Busy professional interested in distance learning?

Parent searching for the perfect private school or summer camp?

Human resource manager looking for executive education programs?

AOL Keyword: Petersons
Phone: 800-338-3282

Virtually anything is possible @ petersons.com

graduate programs
distance learning
adult education
executive training
colleges and universities
private secondary schools
internships and careers
study-abroad programs
financial aid/scholarships
summer programs

Peterson's quality with every click!

Whether you're a high school student headed for college or a busy professional interested in distance learning, you'll find all of the tools you need literally right at your fingertips!

Petersons.com is your ultimate online adviser, connecting you with "virtually any" educational or career need.

Count on us to show you how to:

Apply to more than 1,200 colleges online

Finance the education of your dreams

Find a summer camp for your child

Make important career choices

Earn a degree online

Search executive education programs

Visit us today at petersons.com
AOL Keyword: Petersons

Peterson's
Thomson Learning™